The Courts

and American

Education

Law

Frontiers of Education

Series Editor: Philip G. Altbach

Other titles in the series:

The Courts

and American

Education

Law

Tyll van Geel

PROMETHEUS BOOKS

Buffalo, New York

Published 1987 by Prometheus Books
700 East Amherst Street, Buffalo, New York 14215

Copyright © 1987 by Tyll van Geel

All Rights Reserved

Library of Congress Cataloging-in-Publication Data

van Geel, Tyll.
    The courts and American education law.

    (Frontiers of education)
    Bibliography: p.
    Includes index.
    1. Educational law and legislation—United States.
2. United States. Supreme Court. I. Title.
II. Series.
KF4119.V33   1987   344.73'07   86-25293
ISBN 0-87975-384-6   347.3047

Printed in the United States of America

For Alix and Tap with
much love

Preface

American educational law has undergone a dramatic transformation. Until approximately the middle of the 1950s educational law largely consisted of state rules, principles, and doctrines directed toward resolving conflicts over such matters as the authority of the state and local school boards, the interpretation of the state's compulsory education law, teacher certification and dismissal, the negligent supervision of pupils, and inadequate maintenance of school facilities. Federal statutes and federal constitutional doctrine played a comparatively minor role in resolving conflicts. Conflicts that today form the daily grist for the courts either did not arise or were settled outside the courtroom through the political process. The most significant exception was arguably the Supreme Court's decisions of the 1920s in which the Court declared that private schools could not constitutionally be eliminated by the states, and that the states could impose only "reasonable" regulations upon those schools.

Today, however, educational law consists not only of state statutes and cases, but also of an ever-growing body of federal statutes and federal judicial opinions dealing with the interpretation of those statutes and the U.S. Constitution. Indeed, the most dramatic and educationally and politically significant growth in educational law has been in the areas touched upon by the federal statutes and U.S. Constitution. Desegregation; the education of the handicapped; aid to private religious schools; prayers in the public schools; the searching and disciplining of pupils; teacher and student rights of freedom of speech; and prohibitions against discrimination in employment on the basis of race, gender, handicap, religion, and age are but some of the areas that have emerged as topics of federal concern in the later half of the twentieth century.

The process of change is not over. Having enacted a largely liberal educational and social agenda through legislation and judicial opinions, we are now in the midst of a strong movement, most visibly on display in the Supreme Court's opinions, toward enacting a more conservative vision of education and the society. Thus, we can anticipate movement away from, for example, the resistance the Court has shown toward letting financial assistance flow to private schools and allowing prayers to enter the public schools. Whatever the case may

7

be, it seems certain that developments in federal statutory and constitutional law will continue to hold an important place in the formation of American education law. This is not to downplay important developments in state statutory and constitutional law, e.g., the successful state constitutional challenges brought in a number of states to their systems for financing education, and the passage of state laws authorizing and regulating collective bargaining.

A quick glance at the table of contents will reveal what this book seeks to do. It offers a summary, analysis, and commentary upon this body of new educational law at the federal and state levels with somewhat less emphasis upon the conflicts that shaped the older body of educational law, e.g., conflicts over the authority of the local school board. That is, while these topics are not omitted, they are not given the detailed treatment that one might have found in older treatises on educational law.

This book also offers a new approach to organizing the field of educational law. Areas of educational law that in the past have not been grouped together are brought together in new ways. To take one example, the concern with negligence in the supervision of pupils and negligence in the maintenance of school facilities has traditionally been treated under a separate chapter heading, "Torts," whereas the issues of corporal punishment and procedural due process have been dealt with as issues relating to "student discipline." The topic of searching students and their lockers may have been treated under another heading such as "Privacy." In this book these areas of concern are brought together under one chapter on the grounds that they are related to the more general problem of providing students with a safe and orderly school. However, each section of the chapters has been provided with its own section number to facilitate the making of cross-references and to facilitate the finding of topics in which one may have a special interest.

This book also adopts a new approach to the sequence in which themes and topics are taken up. It begins with issues surrounding private education and private schooling. Those primarily interested in the law as it bears on public schooling could safely skip this chapter, but it is placed as the lead chapter for a number of reasons. First, private schooling was the first form of formal schooling provided to students in the United States. Second, the American system of education comprises both private and public schools: a fact of great political and doctrinal importance. The very existence of private schooling means that public schools cannot and do not enjoy a monopoly over formal educational efforts. This is important to assure the continuance of a plural society; it operates as a safety valve for those unhappy with the public institutions. Additionally, the very fact that private schools exist means those concerned with operating the public schools can proceed with programs many parents may dislike on the assumption that if parental dissatisfication is sufficiently great, those unhappy parents can exercise their option to exit the public schools and turn to private educational programs. In short, while private education serves only approximately 10 percent of the total school-age population, private education itself has an ideological and political significance far beyond the scope of its operations. In a metaphorical sense private education and private schools comprise the other half of formal schooling efforts in America.

The subsequent chapters turn to public educational institutions. These chapters begin with an examination of recent changes in the governing system of education, changes that involve both increased centralization of the governing system and the opening of the governing system to new participants. Chapters 3 and 4 take up the general topic of student access to the public schools—access that might be blocked by rules based on such considerations as the handicap of the student or his or her race. Chapters 5 through 8 take up issues affecting the internal operation of the school. In chapter 9 we turn to the new law of teacher rights. Note, however, that the teacher's right to freedom of speech is also taken up in other chapters, i.e., chapters 2 and 6.

This volume is intended to serve a number of purposes and audiences. It can be used as either the primary or supplementary text in courses in educational law offered in schools of education and law schools. The organization of the book into topics with their own section number, the extensive footnotes, the detailed table of contents and index, and the table of cases make it useful as a reference work for lawyers, school officials, parents, and students. In addition, it can be used as a supplement to courses in American educational history or to complement courses in educational philosophy.

The writing of a book such as this one builds on the work of many scholars. In the field of educational law one must point to the work of David L. Kirp and Mark G. Yudof as seminal in bringing a new approach to our understanding of the field. Lawrence Tribe's treatise, *American Constitutional Law,* showed that the old ways of writing a book on constitutional law need not be slavishly followed. Thanks must go to the people at Apple Computer, Inc. and the makers of Microsoft Word who have taken away much of the inconvenience associated with the writing of a book of this length and with so many footnotes. I would also like to acknowledge the assistance of my Fall, 1985 class in educational law in the Graduate School of Education and Human Development at the University of Rochester, who worked with and responded to an earlier draft of the book. Finally, I would like to give my profound thanks to Katharine Weinrich van Geel and Gretchen Hughes who provided enormous help in editing the manuscript and in preparing the table of cases.

Contents

9.   THE NEW LAW OF TEACHER RIGHTS   363

10.   AFTERWORD: THE REHNQUIST COURT   447

1

Private Education and Private Schooling

1.1. INTRODUCTION

Understanding the relationship between law and private education is fundamental to an understanding of both American education law and the American Creed.[1] The crucial nature of this body of law is seen in the fact that it addresses one of the most fundamental of social and political issues, namely, the legal relationship between, on the one hand, the family, parents, children and religion, and, on the other hand, the state. As will be revealed, American law's response to this question is incomplete and ambiguous, but like a geological outcropping, this ambiguity is itself determined by a deeper layer of values that itself is inchoate and changeable. Thus, along with attempting to provide an accurate description of the law in this area, this chapter will seek to uncover that crucial subterranean structure. These important subterranean values, we shall see later, have a significant influence on the law governing the public schools themselves.

1.2. CHILD-PARENT-STATE

The judiciary's resolution of the various disputes that have arisen over the years between the government and the family has rested on several basic assumptions. It is a central and abiding characteristic of American thought to posit the existence of fundamental individual rights and liberties that people simply have as people. These rights and liberties preexist the law and are not rooted in or derived from positive law—whether that law be the Constitution, the common law, or federal and state statutes. Though what should be included on that list of fundamental rights and liberties may be a matter of some dispute—are property rights and freedom of contract to be included?—few would contest the inclusion of a right of parents to retain possession of their biological children (absent proof of neglect) and to retain primary control of their upbringing.[2] This is not to say these rights are absolute and may not be constrained and regulated by government. But each time government does so regulate them, the judiciary approaches the question of the legitimacy of the

15

effort from a perspective that sees the state as standing in opposition to civil society. The state is taken to be something separate from the family and the church, and legislation regulating family and church is interpreted as a form of external intervention. Because the family and church are viewed as "natural" entities separate from government, legislation affecting these entities must be assessed to determine its legitimacy. It is here the U.S. Constitution becomes relevant in establishing the guidelines for settling which state interventions are legitimate and which illegitimate. In sum, one theoretically useful way to understand much of American constitutional law is to see it as one step in a four-step "legislative" process. First, under this conception there exists a state of nature in which people enjoy equally as people certain natural rights and liberties. Second, these people collectively adopt a constitution that recognizes the existence of these natural rights and liberties and provides for the establishment of a government to legislate on particular prob lems. The government having been established, the third step is the actual adoption by the legislature of specific pieces of legislation that may affect those natural rights and liberties. The fourth step is the resolution, in the face of challenges, of the question of the legitimacy of that legislation in light of the constitution.[3]

There are a number of reasons for recognizing a right in parents to control the upbringing of their children. First, parents, unlike other available agents, can and are more likely to serve the best interests and rights of their children—an important point if it is to be assumed that the interests of children ought to be protected as best they can.[4] Second, to an important extent the rights of parents over their children are an extension of the parents' own negative rights not to be interfered with in the living out of their own preferred life-style.[5] Third, private educational efforts can serve as a counterforce or countervoice to the potentially overweening influence of government on the formation of public opinion, and holding government in check remains a fundamental proposition in American political thought.[6] Fourth, in the face of considerable uncertainty about what the "truth" is in matters relating to aesthetics and ethical, political, religious, and even scientific discourse, there is considerable value to maintaining multiple centers of education.[7] Fifth, arguably, the social diversity made more possible by recognizing this parental right is itself desirable.[8] Last, assuring scope for a variety of educational programs permits experimentation in education and the continuation of the search for more effective methods of instruction.[9]

Given this background, it is not surprising that we shall find that state regulation of parental efforts to shape the education of their children raises controversial and politically significant constitutional issues.

Though American thought has paid considerable attention to the natural right of parents to be free from state control, considerably less attention has been paid to the natural rights of children vis-à-vis their parents.[10] One theory holds that children have no such natural rights except perhaps the right not to be truly physically abused. (It is only recently that philosophers have begun to question this tradition and to suggest that children do have certain moral rights in relationship to their parents, namely, the right to an education and the right to an "open future," a right not to have their basic occupational options foreclosed by a narrow educational program.)[11] Beyond this, the legal status of children vis-à-vis their parents is affected by the fact that by its own terms the U.S. Constitution is directly applicable and regulative only of what government does, and not of what one private individual does to another.[12] As a consequence, children have neither a strong moral and political tradition nor a constitutional base from which to argue (presumably through a so-called child advocate or guardian) that the law either fails to check and impose restraints on what their parents may do to them or fails in imposing sufficient positive duties on their parents to provide them with certain things. Stating this somewhat differently, neither the traditional version of the doctrine of natural rights nor the U.S. Constitution has much to say regarding the negative rights of children to be free from (1) parental vetos of the choices the child makes and (2) parental intrusions into the child's interests, for instance, mental and physical integrity. Similarly, the natural rights tradition and the U.S. Constitution have little to say regarding a child's affirmative or positive rights to an education vis-à-vis the parents.

However, having little to say does not mean having nothing to say. The Supreme Court has said that states may not expressly authorize a parental veto over the mature minor's decision to have an abortion.[13] In reaching this conclusion the Court implicitly recognized a limitation on the parent's natural right to control the upbringing of their child and indirectly created a negative constitutional right on the part of the minor in relation to the parent. Beyond this, however, parents continue to enjoy under state law, presumably as a matter of natural and constitutional right, considerable power to control the choices of their children. For example, parents have the right to select the religion in which their child will be brought up, to feed and clothe their child in their preferred style, to veto their child's decision to get married, to prevent their child's enlistment in the armed services, to keep the child's wages, and to physically punish the child.[14] Though children seem not to have any natural or constitutional rights that check or counterbalance parental rights on these matters, state law has created a number of important negative rights on the part of children, e.g., a right not to be physically abused.[15] These laws have not been challenged as a violation of the parent's right; but, presumably, if they were challenged, the courts would dismiss the challenge on the ground that the state interest in protecting the well-being of the child clearly overrides any parental interest in abusing the child. Finally, we might look at the positive rights children may have vis-à-vis their parents. In this regard, states have imposed a number of affirmative duties on parents, e.g., a duty to provide the child with an education and adequate medical care.[16] (The constitutional issues regarding state control over parental educational efforts will be taken up below in §§1.3 through 1.9) What we do not find in the judicial opinions is any direct creation of an affirmative constitutional right of children, for example, to an education to be supplied by their parents. The practical value of such a right would, of course, only arise in the unusual circumstance of a state that, under the influence of libertarianism, refused either to compel parents to educate their children, or, if it did compel some degree of formal education, failed to care about the adequacy of the parental educational effort.[17]

While constitutional law bearing on the child-parent relationship is meager, the body of constitutional law bearing on the relationship between the child and the government is vast, complex, and subtle. It is here where we engage the traditional issues of constitutional law—free speech, due process, equal protection—and the courts' efforts to strike that delicate balance between individual rights and governmental interests. Since much of this book is devoted to exploring the judicial handiwork in this area, nothing more will be said at the moment about the Constitution's structuring of this relationship.

In sum, the courts and, accordingly, the Constitution have had a lot to say about state law affecting both parents as parents and children as students in the public schools. For the reasons explored earlier, constitutional doctrine has had little to say directly regarding the rights of children vis-à-vis their parents. From the standpoint of the child, there is, thus, an important asymmetry in the law that is most clearly highlighted in connection with the question of the child's interest in autonomy and freedom from stultifying inculcation.[18] Though a plausible case can be made that the Constitution protects the child against state efforts to indoctrinate,[19] there is little in the Constitution itself or in judicial opinions upon which to make the case that the child must also constitutionally (as opposed to morally) be protected from parental efforts to indoctrinate and inculcate.

1.3. COMPULSORY EDUCATION LAWS

State efforts to regulate parents began early in the history of the United States. The colony of Massachusetts in 1642 passed the first compulsory education law—a statute that required all parents and masters to provide an education both in a trade and in the elements of reading to all children under their care.[20] Massachusetts was also the site for the first general compulsory attendance law passed in 1852.[21] This statute required persons having children between the ages of eight and fourteen under their control to send the children to school for twelve weeks annually, six weeks of which had to be consecutive. Today all states have a compulsory attendance law in place.[22]

The modern compulsory education law is a complex statutory scheme that may cover such matters as: (1) the ages between which children must attend some form of education; (2) a specification of the form of education that may satisfy the compulsory education law, e.g., public school, private school, home instruction, tutoring—although many state laws do not specifically state whether home instruction will satisfy the compulsory education law;[23] (3) the age of pupils the public schools must serve; (4) the length of the school year and school day and the minimum amount of attendance required (figures that may vary for public schools, private schools, and home instruction); (5) a list of the bases for granting exemptions from these requirements (e.g., exemptions may be granted to pupils who are employed, who are involved in work-study programs, who are suspended from school, or who live great distances from the public schools); (6) provision for the appointment of attendance officers; (7) the provision of criminal and noncriminal judicial proceedings for dealing with parents and children who violate the law; and (8) a specification of the penalties for parents (typically, a fine and jail sentence) and the child (e.g., declaring the child to be a truant) who violate their duties under the law.

Though serious and plausible constitutional questions may be raised about particular details of a state's compulsory education policy (e.g., a challenge based on differential treatment of compulsory attendance in public and private schools), the courts have left no room to doubt that they will read the Constitution as permitting states to impose legal duties on parent and child alike to see to it that the child attends some minimum amount of formal schooling.[24] As one court wrote,

> If it is within the police power of the state to regulate wages, to legislate respecting housing conditions in crowded cities, to prohibit dark rooms in tenement houses, to compel landlords to place windows in their tenements which will enable their tenants to enjoy the sunshine, it is within the police power of the state to compel every resident of New Jersey so to educate his children that the light of American ideals will permeate the life of our future citizens.[25]

The question of the state's intervention into the family via a compulsory education law becomes considerably more complex if what a particular set of parents argue is that they seek merely to be excused from compliance with the law because enforcement of the law against them interferes with their right to exercise freely their religion as protected by the first amendment.[26] Resolving this demand requires the court to consider whether the free exercise of religion is a preferred right, whether the state's interests are nevertheless strong enough to warrant infringement of that right, and whether protection of that right may itself violate the other religion clause of the first amendment, the establishment clause.[27]

The Supreme Court took on this nettlesome challenge in *Wisconsin v. Yoder*, a case in which three Amish parents were charged, tried, and convicted of violating the state's compulsory education law after they had declined to send their children, ages fourteen and fifteen, to public school, or to any private school or any other recognized exception to the compulsory attendance laws, after the children had completed the eighth grade.[28] (Under state law attendance at school was required until age sixteen.) The parents refused to send their children to the public high school because they did not want their children exposed to an education program that emphasized intellectual and scientific accomplishments, promoted worldly success, and encouraged the students' integration with contemporary society and politics. Instead the children were to be encapsulated within the Amish community, where they were to be provided with an education suited for life in that community. Under the education program of the Amish, Amish children learned by example and "by doing" the basic skills needed to perform their future roles as Amish farmer and housewife in a farming-based community that rejected all the technological advances of the twentieth century. Simultaneously, the children were expected to acquire the Amish attitudes favoring manual labor, self-reliance, and the belief that salvation requires living in a church community separate and apart from the world.

The parents, who had defended themselves in the trial court on the ground that enforcement of the compulsory attendance law violated their right to the free exercise of their religion, made a successful appeal on this same ground to the Wisconsin Supreme Court, and the U.S. Supreme Court affirmed.

In reaching this conclusion, the Court adopted a loose framework for analysis that involved first assigning the burden of proof to the Amish parents; and then, if they satisfied their burden, switching the burden to the state. Thus the Court began by saying that for the Amish even to get the Court to consider their free exercise claim, they must establish that (1) theirs is a religious, as opposed to a merely philosophical, claim; (2) their religion and their religious claim is sincerely held and advanced; and (3) enforcement of the compulsory education law against them would have a serious impact on the free exercise of their religious beliefs.[29] If the plaintiffs were able to establish these three points, the Court said, the burden of proof switches to the state to establish that uniform enforcement of its policy is necessary, is the least restrictive means, to the achievement of a compelling state interest.

The Court had little difficulty concluding that the Amish claim was a religious claim[30] sincerely held.[31] The Court also concluded that enforcement of the state's compulsory education law would significantly impact upon the Amish interest in the free exercise of their religion. The Court concluded that enforcement of the law could result in great psychological harm to the Amish children (by forced exposure to the modern and worldly influences in the modern school), could have interfered with the integration of the Amish children into the Amish community by interfering with the religious development of the Amish child, and ultimately could have resulted in the destruction of the Old Order Amish community in the United States. Two more years of formal schooling would have meant that the state would have "in large measure influence[d], if not determine[d], the religious future of the child."[32]

At the same time, the Court concluded that the state's interests would not have been furthered by refusing to grant the exemption or, conversely, harmed by granting the exemption. Two more years of formal schooling would have done little for a child destined to live out his or her life in a farm-based and non-modern community: the educational needs of these children were clearly different from most other children.[33] (Even if an Amish child were ultimately to leave the community, nothing in the record suggested to the Court that the informal Amish training in reliability, self-reliance, dedication to work, and practical agriculture would fail to find a ready market.)[34] Compelling attendance beyond the eighth grade would have brought few gains in terms of the Amish fulfilling their obligations as citizens.[35]

The limitations of this opinion are important to note. First, it is unlikely that even Amish parents could successfully argue that they had a first amendment right to exempt their children from the first eight years of formal schooling. Second, the careful way in which the Court tied its opinion to the Amish and their proven successful way of life strongly suggests that non-Amish but religiously motivated parents would have a hard time succeeding in obtaining an exemption from the last two years of a compulsory education law.[36] Third, the Court made clear that parents who sought an exemption for nonreligious reasons would not be successful.[37] Last, the majority refused to resolve a crucial and fundamental question raised by Justice Douglas: What should be done if a child desires to attend public high school in conflict with the wishes of his Amish parents?[38]

1.4. THE OPTION OF PRIVATE SCHOOLING

In the aftermath of World War I and a period of massive immigration to the United States, large numbers of people, especially rural Protestants, were seized with a hatred of anybody deemed racially inferior and/or foreign. The stage was set for severe conflict between the state and those parents who chose to comply with the state's compulsory attendance laws by sending their children to private schools. In Oregon this nativistic reaction was spearheaded by the Ku Klux Klan and the Oregon Scottish Rite Masons who together mounted a successful campaign in 1922 to get the state legislature to adopt a statute that required all parents, as of September, 1926, to send their children to the public schools exclusively. Private schools, it was believed, perpetuated a subversive and foreign culture. As one Klansman noted, "Somehow these mongrel hordes must be Americanized; failing that, deportation is the only remedy."[39]

The statute was challenged by a parochial school and military academy, and the Supreme Court declared it to be an unconstitutional infringement of the rights both of the schools and the parents who chose to send their children to private schools.[40] Though the opinion was decided at a time when property rights and related business interests were among the preferred values given special protection by the Court—a preference these interests no longer enjoy under the Constitution[41]—the resulting opinion continues to be endorsed by the Court for reasons having to do with protecting the parents' right to seek out the kind of education they prefer for their children.[42] Beyond protecting the parents' "natural" right to control the upbringing of their child, *Pierce v. Society of Sisters* may also be understood as a case that protects private schooling as a way of limiting the capacity of the government to indoctrinate the young; providing those who disagree with the curriculum of the publicly operated schools an option, an alternative educational program, drastically reduces government's ability to create a captive audience.[43] Whatever understanding one might have of the parental rights at stake, the *Pierce* decision clearly seems to reject the view that government has sufficiently strong interests in seeing that all children are inculcated with the same governmentally prescribed values and viewpoints.[44]

In sum, the Court in *Pierce* had four options from which to choose:[45] (1) affirmation of the legitimacy of a governmental monopoly of all formal schooling; (2) the option it chose of permitting parents to comply with compulsory attendance laws by sending (at their own expense) their children to private schools (which could be subject to "reasonable" state regulations);[46] (3) adopting a doctrine of "neutrality" under which the government would be required to give financial support to the parents' choice of the preferred education for their children;[47] and (4) abolishing compulsory attendance as a way of eliminating state coercion of parents. The choice of the second option established a basic pattern for American education that has remained virtually unchanged to this date.

1.5. HOME INSTRUCTION—A CONSTITUTIONAL RIGHT?

State policy toward home instruction has varied from those states that do not permit their compulsory education laws to be satisfied by instruction in the home, to those that explicitly allow home instruction that complies with certain regulations, and to yet others whose laws do not explicitly address the question, but that, by arguable implication, permit home instruction if it's "equivalent" or "comparable" to the instruction provided in the schools.[48]

The litigation over state regulation of home instruction has involved issues of both statutory and constitutional interpretation, but it is only the constitutional cases that will be reviewed here. The Supreme Court itself has not addressed the question whether states may prohibit all home instruction even if the instruction is comparable or equivalent to that offered in the public schools. But, a number of state courts have addressed the question and with virtual uniformity say that home instruction may be prohibited. A New Mexico court said the prohibition was rationally related to the state purpose of assuring that children were brought into contact with people in addition to the parents so that the children might be exposed "to at least one set of attitudes, values, morals, lifestyles and intellectual abilities."[49] A North Carolina court said that "the State has no means by which to insure that children who are at home are receiving an education."[50] A federal circuit court wrote that the parent "has not demonstrated that home instruction will prepare his children to be self-sufficient participants in our modern society or enable them to participate intelligently in our political system."[51] Even parents claiming that their religious beliefs require that they teach their children at home have systematically lost in court.[52] It is only in two unreported lower court opinions and dicta that we find judicial support for a parental constitutional right to educate a child at home.[53] Whether these lower courts are correct in their judgment that the U.S. Constitution does not protect a parent's right to instruct the child at home is open to question.[54] Given the preferred constitutional status of family autonomy and parental rights, at a minimum one would expect the courts today to question whether a total abolition of home instruction is necessary, is the least restrictive means, for the state to advance its legitimate interest in protecting children from negligent and incompetent parents.[55] When the parental interest is combined with a free exercise claim, the current majority on the Supreme Court would agree that an even more skeptical approach should be taken by the judiciary to the state's claims on behalf of a total prohibition of home instruction.[56]

1.6. THE REGULATION OF PRIVATE NONRELIGIOUS SCHOOLING

Working deliberately and carefully, the Supreme Court in *Pierce v. Society of Sisters* struck a delicate balance between the state and private education by interpreting the Constitution to protect the continued existence of private schooling, yet making it clear that the Court would not stand in the way of reasonable state regulations of private educational efforts.[57] "Public concernment" with private education has manifested itself in a variety of methods of state regulation touching on such matters as, for example, the length of the school year; the curriculum; the language of instruction; the testing of pupils; the selection of teachers; and health, safety, discrimination in admissions and employment, and zoning regulations.[58]

Before turning to specific examples of state regulation, it is important to recognize that, whatever it is that states do by way of regulating private education, the regulatory scheme must not be so comprehensive, intrusive, and detailed as to eliminate the possibility of private schools offering a program of instruction that is indistinguishable in important respects from the public school program.[59] The Court even said in one case that "parents have a First Amendment right to send their children to educational institutions that promote the belief that racial segregation is desirable, and that the children have an equal right to attend such institutions."[60] This clearly indicates that private schools may do things that public schools may not.[61]

Nevertheless, an important degree of regulation is constitutionally permissible. Private schools may be required to offer a program of instruction "equivalent" if not identical to that offered in the public schools.[62] (The claim that requiring private education to be "comparable" to that offered in the public schools was unconstitutionally vague has been rejected.)[63] If nothing else, this means that states may require that private schools offer certain courses or topics.[64] (Whether the doctrine of "institutional" academic freedom and/or the doctrine against compelled speech serve to limit the state's power has not been tested.)[65] Whether states may go further and attempt to prescribe the particular ideological viewpoint or values that are to be imparted by these courses is, however, extremely doubtful, except to the extent government may prohibit the actual preparation of students for imminent lawless action.[66] Any regulatory scheme involving prior approval of the program of a private school potentially raises an issue of prior restraint of free speech; and any scheme of prior restraint of free speech comes to the judiciary with a heavy presumption against its constitutional validity.[67]

May states seek to exclude "subversives" from teaching in private schools? A considerable body of judicial opinions suggests that such an effort would be an unconstitutional invasion of the teachers' first amendment rights of freedom of political association and speech.[68] A state effort to exclude from the private schools teachers with a nontraditional sex life would also probably find constitutional disfavor as an improper invasion of the teachers' right of privacy.[69] A state requirement that private school teachers in nonreligious schools be state certified would, with little doubt, be upheld.[70] In fact, the Supreme Court's general unwillingness to interfere with "economic" regulations would mean that state laws requiring private schools to maintain attendance and academic records would be upheld (assuming that they adequately protected the privacy rights of the pupils).[71] And, barring such problems as finding that the required tests are racially discriminatory, there is little doubt the courts would uphold a requirement that private school students take and achieve a certain score on a prescribed standardized test.[72]

Regulatory schemes that involve the licensing or approval of private schools *arguably* must assure adequate notice and an impartial pretermination hearing for schools that are threatened with a loss of license or approval.[73] It may even be the case that a hearing must be granted in connection with the initial request for a license or state approval. Licensing and prior state approval is a form of prior restraint of private educational efforts with entailed risks for free speech. As a consequence, licensing and approval ought to take place under a system of procedural safeguards that will minimize the risk of censorship, or the denial of licenses and approvals simply because of disagreement with the values and viewpoints of the educational program up for approval.[74]

1.7. THE CONSTITUTION AND PRIVATE RELIGIOUS SCHOOLS

State regulation of private religious or church-affiliated schools can raise the same issues discussed above in §1.6, but, in addition, can implicate either the free exercise clause and/or the establishment clause of the first amendment.[75] We turn first to the free exercise cases. These opinions—that involved claimants relying on *Wisconsin v. Yoder*[76] to seek free exercise exemptions from such state requirements as that all teachers of the young be state certified or that the program of instruction be approved by the state—almost uniformly uphold the state's position and deny the grant of the exemption.[77.] An examination of these opinions reveals a pattern of resistance to the religious claimants. Thus we find: (1) an adoption of a narrow interpretation of the *Yoder* opinion. That is, roughly speaking, the courts in these cases have concluded that *Yoder* only permits the grant of an exemption from state regulations when it appears that the children before the court are similar to the Amish in the sense that they are destined to live in a community in which the kind of educational program the state seeks to prescribe is a virtual irrelevancy. Since most children are not being prepared for a life similar to that of the Amish, the educational needs of these children are viewed as being the same as those children in the public schools; and the exemption is denied. (2) The impact of state's regulations on religious freedom is characterized as trivial, and (3) the state's claim that its regulations serve a compelling state purpose is accepted. A number of these courts also placed on the parents the burden of persuasion to prove, for example, that their preferred educational program was not harmful. But having so placed the burden of proof, the courts also ignored test data establishing that the parents' program of instruction was working and assumed, on the contrary, without evidence, that these programs of instruction were harmful to pupils.[78] (It should be noted that not all the lower courts have been hostile to free exercise claims.)[79]

Faced with the potential of free exercise challenges and wishing to avoid political confrontations with religious organizations, states may wish to solve both problems by exempting church-sponsored educational facilities from virtually all state regulation. Movement down this road, however, invites other political difficulties (when the nonreligious educational facilities complain of the advantages provided the church-sponsored facilities) and yet other constitutional difficulties when the exemption is unnecessarily broad and sweeping. If the state exempts church-affiliated facilities from regulations, e.g., minimum space per child requirements, that cannot be shown clearly to raise free exercise violations, then the state becomes so accommodating that it flirts with a violation of the establishment clause.[80]

State requirements may be so intrusive as to raise not merely a free exercise claim but also an establishment clause issue.[81] The Supreme Court has developed a three-part test to determine whether a law contravenes the establishment clause of the first amendment. "[A] statute must have a secular legislative purpose, must have a principal or primary effect that neither advances nor inhibits religion, and must not foster an excessive governmental entanglement with religion."[82] Using these tests, the courts have rejected arguments that certification, curricular, licensing, and reporting requirements involved excessive governmental entanglement with religion.[83] Minimum wage requirements have also been extended to lay teachers, bus drivers, and day-care employees in church-affiliated schools.[84]

1.8. PROHIBITING DISCRIMINATION BY PRIVATE SCHOOLS

Though in most respects private schools must constitutionally be allowed to set sail on their own course, does that mean they are also constitutionally protected against governmental efforts to prohibit discrimination in admissions (and other student-related matters), and employment on the basis of race, gender, religion, handicap, age, and national origin? The federal government, as well as state governments, assuming there were no constitutional obstacles, have extended a variety of antidiscrimination provisions to private education.[85] Active governmental pursuit to eliminate private discrimination set the stage for a historical confrontation between the state and its antidiscrimination policy, and private schools claiming that these efforts infringed their rights of privacy, freedom of association, and the free exercise of religion.[86]

We begin our analysis of the Supreme Court's handling of these problems by turning first to the question of whether such regulations infringe "freedom of intimate association." The Court's approach to this issue was recently clarified in a case involving a conflict between the State of Minnesota and the United States Jaycees over the enforcement of a state antidiscrimination law that state officials interpreted as requiring the Jaycees to admit women as regular voting members.[87] The Court began its analysis of this issue by establishing a continuum of types of associations deserving different degrees of constitutional protection. At one end of the continuum were certain kinds of highly personal relationships (and here they cited prior opinions dealing with the private schools and private education,[88] and the family),[89] deserving special protection because (1) they are a fundamental element of personal liberty; (2) they are crucial in transmitting shared ideals and beliefs; (3) they act as critical buffers between the individual and the state; and (4) they provide individuals with much of their emotional enrichment as part of a community of thoughts, experiences, and beliefs. At the other end were those associations that lacked the qualities of smallness, a high degree of selectivity, and seclusion from others. Thus, the Court noted, "the Constitution undoubtedly imposes constraints on the State's power to control the selection of one's fellow employees."[90] Thus, in determining the limits of state authority, a first step is to locate where on the continuum from the most intimate to the most attenuated of personal attachments the particular organization involved in a case falls. Relevant factors in making the assessment included size, purpose, policies, selectivity, and congeniality. Applyng this approach the Court concluded that the Jaycees lacked "distinctive characteristics that might afford constitutional protection to the decision of its members to exclude women."[91]

The analysis of the Court in *United States Jaycees* seems on its face and in its result inconsistent with an earlier decision of the Court in *Runyon v. McCrary*.[92] In that case the Court upheld against constitutional challenge the use of a federal law that prohibited discrimination in the making and enforcement of private contracts to bar a private school from excluding qualified children solely on the basis of race.[93] The Court denied that enforcement of the law infringed any parental right recognized in *Meyer, Pierce,* or *Yoder* (the private school could still operate and parents could still choose to send their children to those schools), and the parental choices regarding a child's education were simply not beyond reasonable state control. Thus, the Court in *Runyon* did not give the same degree of protection to "freedom of intimate association" that it did in *United States Jaycees;* nor did it seem to agree, as it did in the later case, that private schools clearly fell into the category of associations that deserved strong protection. Nevertheless, given the Court's continuous support of efforts to deal with racial discrimination, and the special role schools may play in ending racial prejudice, it is unlikely that, even after *United States Jaycees,* the Court would decide *Runyon* differently. This point is underscored by the fact that the schools in *Runyon* advertised in the telephone directory "yellow pages" and through mass mailings, which suggests that in *Runyon* the interest in freedom of intimate association had been partially waived.

State regulation of the discriminatory practices of private organizations may arguably infringe their right of freedom of expressive association. This issue was raised in *United States Jaycees,* but the Court concluded there was no infringement because admitting women imposed no restrictions on the organization's ability to exclude individuals with ideologies different from those of the existing members; furthermore, there was no evidence to indicate women members would take a different view on the issues to which the Jaycees addressed themselves.[94]

On this point *Runyon* and *United States Jaycees* are similar. The Court assumed in *Runyon* that parents had a first amendment right to send their children to schools that taught that segregation is desirable. It did not follow, said the Court, that it was permissible to engage in the practice of excluding racial minorities from the school. In effect, the Court found no infringement of the freedom of expressive association in *Runyon* because of the enforcement of §1981 to bar discrimination in admissions.

The *Runyon* Court explicitly declined to comment on the applicability of its decision to sectarian private schools, a context in which government's regulatory efforts would raise free exercise of religion and establishment clause issues. But in *Bob Jones University v. United States,* the Court faced a challenge from two religious schools that the denial of their tax-exempt status because of their racial policies infringed their free exercise rights.[95] The Court concluded that the governmental interest in prohibiting discrimination outweighed whatever burden the denial of the tax benefits placed on the exercise of religious beliefs.

Lower courts, faced with a series of free exercise challenges to the enforcement of §1981, have upheld the application of those laws to private, religious elementary schools on the grounds that their policies of racial discrimination were not in fact based on religious belief.[96] But the federal courts have split on the question of the constitutionality of subjecting private religious schools to employment discrimination laws. The Fifth Circuit has upheld the applicability of Title VII's prohibition against employment discrimination on the basis of sex and race to private religious colleges and seminaries.[97] This antidiscrimination requirement, said the court, did not create excessive church-state entanglement, did not burden the school religious exercises, and was justified as serving a compelling state interest. The court specifically noted that enforcement of the law in this case would not result in an ongoing interference with the college's religious practices.

The Sixth Circuit reached a different conclusion in a case in which a Christian school challenged on the basis of the free exercise and establishment clauses the applicability of a state statute prohibiting discrimination in employment on the basis of race, color, religion, sex, and national origin in a case, charging the school with discrimination on the basis of sex.[98] The court agreed with the school that its decision in February not to rehire Linda Hoskinson, who was pregnant, for the next school year was based on a religious belief that mothers should be at home with their children.[99] They also agreed with the school that use of the antidiscrimination law to bar such a policy would impose a heavy burden on the free exercise of religion.[100] At the same time, the court acknowledged that the state's interests in ending employment discrimination was substantial and compelling.[101] Nevertheless, the court concluded that the application of the law in this case, and extension of jurisdiction of the state's civil rights commission over the school, violated the free exercise clause because the state's interests did not "justify such a broad and onerous limitation."[102]

Accommodation of the religious beliefs in this case would not significantly interfere with the state's fulfillment of its goal of eradicating discrimination in employment. The state would still be able to regulate all employment practices of nonreligious institutions and would be able to regulate the employment practices of religious institutions except where religious belief is implicated. Further, it is clear that less burdensome alternatives such as the denial of tax exemptions as in the *Bob Jones University* case or denial of the use of public school bus transportation are available to help the state accomplish its goal while reducing interference with the exercise of religion.[103]

The court also concluded that enforcement of the civil rights statute and extension of the jurisdiction of the state's civil rights commission would transgress the establishment clause because it would create excessive entanglement between religion and the state.[104] The activity the state sought to regulate—employment—necessarily involved the state in regulating the "ideological resources of the school."[105] Every claim that the religious reasons given for a discharge were pretextual would involve the state commission in evaluating "the subjective sectarian decision to determine if it was made or if the real reason for dismissal was some form of prohibited discrimination."[106] Furthermore, as long as the school was in existence, noted the court, the civil rights commission would exert jurisdiction over employment disputes creating "a continuous relationship, rather than a one-time state-church encounter."[107]

The unwillingness of some courts to regulate private religious institutions was also reflected in *Maguire v. Marquette University*.[108] A female job applicant who was Catholic claimed that Marquette, a Jesuit university, discriminated against her on the basis of gender in refusing to consider her application for a position in the theology department. The court dismissed the claim on the grounds that to involve itself in the hiring policy of the theology department would violate the school's free exercise rights and create impermissible entanglement between government and religion. Because the first amendment prohibited the court from involving itself in the hiring decision, the court felt constrained to interpret Title VII in a way that would not bring it into conflict with the first amendment. Thus it held that Title VII grant of an exemption to religious schools to discriminate in hiring on the basis of *religion* should be read broadly to permit the theology department broad latitude when it makes a decision not to hire a female applicant of the same religion as the institution.[109] That is, the court seemed to say that the theology department may discriminate on the basis of gender. It is questionable whether this is a sound decision given the Supreme Court's refusal to permit racial discrimination in the name of religion. The decision is also vulnerable as regards a narrower point, namely, the court made no finding that the school's religion itself required that only males teach theology; thus insofar as the decision rests on the free exercise clause it may be in error for this reason. Furthermore, assuming Marquette does not claim that its religious beliefs require that only men teach theology, judicial oversight of a theology department to determine if it discriminated on the basis of *gender* would entail no greater entanglement than occurs between government and non religious schools. (See, §9.9.) It is not clear why religious institutions that do not claim a religious basis for discriminating in terms of gender should be free to discriminate in this way. Enquiry into whether it improperly discriminated on the basis of gender would not entail an examination of this institution's religious beliefs or the sincerity of those beliefs. In other words, contrary to the position of the court in *Ohio Civil Rights Commission v. Dayton Christian Schools*, examination of the employment decision in the *Marquette* case would not truly involve review and control of the "ideological resources" of the school.

1.9. REGULATION OF HOME INSTRUCTION

As discussed in §1.5, most courts that have considered the issue have ruled that parents do not have a constitutional right to engage in home instruction of their children. If states may prohibit home instruction altogether it would seem to follow that those states that do permit home instruction may regulate those instructional activities; and parental claims to be wholly free of such regulations have been rejected by the courts.[110]

But, in addition to claiming a right to be free from all regulations, parents have also challenged requirements (1) that home instructors be state certified; (2) that home instruction programs obtain prior approval from the state; and (3) that it is the parent who has the burden of proving that the home instruction meets state requirements. The certification requirements have survived both equal protection attacks (e.g., home instructors were required to be certified, but instructors in private schools were not) and free exercise claims for an exemption.[111] The equal protection challenges were turned aside because the courts, applying a deferential standard of review, found there was a rational basis for treating home instruction differently from instruction in schools. Assessing the quality of instruction in homes is more difficult than in schools; schools would have a system for supervising teachers; and schools would be under competitive pressure to do a good job. Finding a basis for distinguishing home instruction from private schools, one court also rejected an equal protection challenge brought against a statute that required prior review of home instruction programs but not of private school programs.[112]

It is not uncommon for state law to impose on parents the burden of establishing that their program of home instruction complies with state law requirements.[113] This allocation of the burden of persuasion has been constitutionally challenged in several cases. In *Scoma v. Chicago Board of Education*,[114] the court ruled that the presumption of state officials that parents who educate their children at home are in violation of state law is not a denial of equal protection, even though the same presumption is not operative as regards parents who send their children to private schools. The court adopted the same line of reasoning used by the courts discussed above to justify the teacher certification requirements imposed on home instruction.[115]

The most frequently raised constitutional challenge is that the statute permitting parents to satisfy the compulsory education law requirements by sending children to a "private school" is unconstitutionally vague because it fails to define the phrase "private school." The issue is usually raised as a defense by parents who have been convicted of violating their state's compulsory education law by instructing their children at home, a place the state claims is not a "private school." A majority of the courts have concluded that such statutes are sufficiently clear to convey to parents their statutory obligations.[116] Similarly, parents have had little success in claiming that state requirements that the private program of instruction be "substantially equivalent" to that in the public school is unconstitutionally vague.[117]

1.10. AID TO PRIVATE SCHOOLS: THEORY

Though the regulation of parents and their private schools has from time to time raised difficult free exercise and establishment clause issues that have forced the courts to reach decisions on theoretically delicate and politically controversial issues, even more politically divisive and complex problems have been raised by regular legislative efforts to try to provide some form of financial assistance to the many, and mostly religious, private schools of the nation.[118] The line-drawing the court has been forced to engage in to navigate between the Scylla of the establishment clause and the Charybdis of the free exercise clause has led to distinctions about what is and is not permissible aid that appear, at best, to be capricious.

We may begin to try to understand the Court's work in this area by outlining three first amendment theories. The first, the strict separation theory, according to Leo Pfeffer, rests on the assumption that separation guarantees freedom and freedom requires separation.[119] An important additional assumption is that aid to religion can fragment the body politic and that mutual abstinence between church and state serves the interest of social peace.[120] The strongest version of the theory would prohibit not just *unequal* direct and indirect governmental assistance to religions, but such aid to *all* religions.[121] Taken to its logical conclusion, this theory would lead to the end of a wide variety of traditional practices, e.g., the exemption of church-owned property from taxation, the imprinting on currency of the phrase "In God We Trust," the appointment of legislative chaplains, the provision for chaplains and churches in the armed forces, and the permission for temporary use of public buildings by religious groups. In the hands of a true zealot, perhaps even the elimination of police and fire protection for church facilities might be required.

A second theory, the governmental neutrality theory, as Justice Harlan observed, has a coat of many colors.[122] Under the resolute neutrality theory of Professor Philip B. Kurland, the two religion clauses of the first amendment are to be read "as a single precept that government cannot utilize religion as a standard for action or inaction because these clauses prohibit classification in terms of religion either to confer a benefit or to impose a burden."[123] An advantage of this theory is that it avoids a key difficulty of the strict separation theory, namely, the indeterminate nature of the first theory because of the difficulties in specifying what constitutes "aid."[124] But Professor Kurland's theory would permit substantial amounts of direct aid to flow to church-affiliated schools, under a program intended to aid all private schools, since such a program would not employ any religious classifications and could rest on a legitimate secular basis. This theory would, on the other hand, prohibit exemptions for church-affiliated schools from state regulations, since the exemption would require the use of a religious classification. The Kurland doctrine is clearly hard on individual religious dissenters seeking exemptions based on the free exercise clause.

In response to these kinds of difficulties with the equal protection version of neutrality, Professor Wilbur Katz has suggested that in order to be truly neutral the government is in some instances obliged to give aid to religion in order to avoid restricting the enjoyment of religious liberty.[125] Seeing liberty as the ultimate value served by both religion clauses of the first amendment, Professor Katz argues that in situations such as the isolated army base, the provision for facilities to worship may be necessary to avoid the restriction of religion; and the grant of exemptions to the military draft to conscientious objectors merely serves to maintain neutrality and see to it that government does not operate with hostility to religion.

The third of the theories, the accommodation theory, in one version is the same as the neutrality theory of Professor Katz, but the accommodationists usually mean more. Here the stress is on a pragmatic weighing and balancing of the competing interests and the acceptance of the very sorts of long-standing traditional practices the strict separationist theory would bring to an end. Mild and trivial infringements of the establishment clause are to be tolerated, even though special and significant aid for religion would not be acceptable. The most extreme version of the accommodationist theory is dramatically reactionary. Under this version the first amendment would be read to apply only to the federal government, not to the states; and the establishment clause would be narrowly interpreted to restrict only the formal establishment of an official state religion and church.[126]

1.11. AID TO PRIVATE SCHOOLS: 1947–1968

In 1947, in the midst of a contentious debate within Congress over the provision of federal aid to education and the question of the constitutionality of aid to private religious schools, the Supreme Court issued its decision in *Everson v. Board of Education*.[127] In a narrow five-to-four decision, the Court concluded that the establishment clause had not been violated by the reimbursement to parents of money expended for bus transportation of their children on regular public buses, even though part of the payments subsidized the sending of children to Catholic parochial schools.[128] Justice Black's majority opinion embraced the strict separationist theory, citing Jefferson's "wall of separation" metaphor, and announced the no-aid principle: government "[n]either can pass laws which aid one religion, aid all religions, or prefer one religion over another." Then two pages later Justice Black concluded that this program was constitutional since it did not aid religion, but merely was a general program to help parents get their children safely to school; this program had to be viewed as no different than police and fire protection, which if cut off would evidence governmental hostility to religion. Justice Jackson, in dissent, commented on the sudden turnabout in the opinion: "The case which irresistibly comes to mind as the most fitting precedent is that of Julia who, according to Byron's reports, 'whispering "I will ne'er consent"'—consented."[129]

The majority opinion was important in a number of respects, including its demonstration of the difficulty of deciding what constitutes aid. While Justice Black thought the bus program was a form of public welfare, Justice Rutledge said the case was not comparable to furnishing police and fire protection.[130] The opinion had only the appearance of providing a basis for predicting the judicial reaction to future state legislation. Despite the stress of no-aid and the observation of Justice Black that the state had approached the "verge" of its constitutional power, the opinion seemed to invite a broad expansion of state assistance to private schools in the name of assuring child safety.[131] The immediate political effect of the decision was to encourage Catholics to demand nothing less from Congress in the way of aid than what the Court seemed to approve, and to increase Protestant resistance to Catholic demands for a share in any federal financial assistance to education.[132]

Almost a year to the day after *Everson* the Supreme Court weighed in with a strong eight-to-one majority opinion written by Justice Black in *McCollum v. Board of Education,* striking down a policy that enabled the interfaith Champaign Council on Religious Education to offer classes in religious instruction to public school children on public school premises.[133] The classes were taught by members of the clergy at no expense to the schools, and were attended for thirty to forty-five minutes a week by pupils whose parents signed a written authorization. Students who did not attend these classes were not released from school but were required to go elsewhere in the building to pursue their secular studies. Attendance at both the secular and religious classes was strictly enforced.

Reiterating his wall of separation theory from the *Everson* case, Justice Black, in a short opinion, concluded that the wall had been breached:

> Here not only are the State's tax-supported public school buildings used for the dissemination of religious doctrines. The State also affords sectarian groups an invaluable aid in that it helps to provide pupils for their religious classes through use of the State's compulsory public school machinery. This is not separation of Church and State.[134]

In short, government could not "utilize its public school system to aid any or all religious faiths or sects in the dissemination of their doctrines and ideals."[135]

Justice Reed, who had joined Black in *Everson,* was now the sole dissenter. Deploying an accommodationist theory of the establishment clause, Reed stressed the long history of church-state involvement as regards such matters as the hiring of chaplains for each house of Congress and the armed services. "This is an instance where, for me, the history of past practices is determinative of the meaning of a constitutional clause, not a decorous introduction to the study of its text."[136] Stressing a tradition of similar school-religion involvements, the no-cost feature of the program, the fact that public school buildings have been opened to other community activities, and that to not permit this kind of program could frustrate the free exercise of religion in rural communities where there might not be nearby religious facilities to which the students can easily go for instruction, Justice Reed concluded that the cooperation between the school and a nonsectarian body should be permitted.[137]

In the four years that intervened between *McCollum* and the next establishment clause opinion, a significant change occurred in the political climate. The second "red scare" of American history overtook the country with its aversion to "godless Communism."[138] Itself being accused of having assisted communism in *McCollum*, the Court now ruled six-to-three in *Zorach v. Clauson* in favor of a released-time program in which students were allowed to leave the public schools during the day to go for religious instruction elsewhere where attendance was taken and the results reported back to the public school.[139] Those not released stayed in the classrooms. Justice Douglas, claiming that he was following the decision in *McCollum*, which embraced the separation principle of *Everson*, said: "The First Amendment, however, does not say that in every and all respects there shall be a separation of Church and State. Rather it studiously defines the manner, the specific ways, in which there shall be no concert or union or dependency one on the other. That is the common sense of the matter."[140] "The problem," he said, "like many problems in constitutional law, is one of degree."[141] Thus, following an essentially accommodationist line of analysis, Justice Douglas said government need not be hostile to religion, and that this program merely involved the schools accommodating their schedule to a program of *outside* religious instruction. "We are a religious people whose institutions presuppose a Supreme Being. . . . When the state encourages religious instruction or cooperates with religious authorities by adjusting the schedule of public events to sectarian needs, it follows the best of our traditions."[142]

Justice Jackson, along with the other dissenters, could see no meaningful distinction between this case and *McCollum*: "The distinction attempted between that case and this is trivial, almost to the point of cynicism, magnifying its nonessential details and disparaging the compulsion which was the underlying reason for its invalidity. . . . Today's judgment will be more interesting to students of psychology and of the judicial process than to students of constitutional law."[143] Professor Tribe, however, argues that the two opinions can be reconciled. Though in *McCollum* it was not even arguable that the free exercise clause required the use of the state's tax-supported building, it was arguable that the free exercise clause compelled the release of children.[144]

The Court thus stepped away from the politically uncomfortable no-aid principle of *Everson-McCollum* without repudiating it and simultaneously adopted a more accommodationist position.[145] As for the future, the Court could choose between a tough no-aid standard as announced, but not used, in *Everson,* or use *Everson* to allow an expansion of aid in the name of protecting the child, as well as adopting the "common sense" standard of *Zorach* that allowed encouragement of religious instruction but not the financing of religious groups. In 1962 and 1963 under the leadership of a new chief justice, Earl Warren, the Court chose the tougher line in striking down the practices of opening the school day with either a governmentally composed nondenominational prayer or readings from the Bible and the saying of the Lord's Prayer.[146] These decisions will be discussed at greater length later.[147] Suffice it to say here that the Court established in these cases two tests for resolving establishment clause cases: "[T]o withstand the strictures of the Establishment Clause there must be *a secular legislative purpose* and *a primary effect that neither advances nor inhibits religion. "*[148] It was with the "purpose" and "primary effect" tests that the Court approached the next aid-to-private-school case.

New York State provided the opportunity for the Court to reassess its position on aid to private schools when it passed a statute requiring local public school districts to *loan* textbooks in secular subjects, free of charge, to all private school students in grades seven through twelve. The books to be loaned were either books already approved for use in the public schools or those that were requested for use by the students, required for use as a text in the private school, and were approved by the local school board.[149] In the majority opinion, Justice White—who was joined by Chief Justice Warren and Justices Brennan, Harlan, Stewart, and Marshall—quickly concluded that because this program was so similar to the program in *Everson,* both the purpose and primary effects tests were satisfied. Only secular, not religious, books were to be loaned. There was no evidence in the record to indicate, contrary to the dissenting argument of Justice Douglas, that public school officials would be unable to determine whether the requested books were secular or religious. Justice White also stressed that private religious schools offered both a religious and a secular educational program, and that in the meager record before the Court there was no evidence that "secular and religious training are so intertwined that secular textbooks furnished to students by the public are in fact instrumental in teaching religion"—another point disputed by Justice Douglas.[150]

The author of the majority opinion in *Everson,* Justice Black, was now in dissent. This case was wholly different, Black argued, from *Everson,* where children were provided assistance similar to giving them police protection on the way to school. Books, he insisted, "are the most essential tool of education" and their provision "directly assists the teaching and propagation of sectarian religious viewpoints."[151]

The *Allen* decision was the last aid-to-private-school case to be decided by the Warren Court, and it seemed, once again, to open the way to the infusion of state money into religious schools. If it were true that the secular part of the school program could be separated from the religious part, and it were possible that the aid could be targeted to the secular benefit of the children, it seemed that almost any form of aid could be justified, e.g., the salaries of lay teachers in secular subjects. The decision also seemed to provide a constitutional base for the requirement, included as part of Title I of the Elementary and Secondary Education Act of 1965, that public schools receiving federal funds to educate the educationally deprived had to make similar compensatory education services available to disadvantaged *children* in private schools.[152]

1.12. AID TO PRIVATE SCHOOLS: THE BURGER COURT

In 1969 newly elected President Richard Nixon, who had campaigned against the liberal Warren Court and who had promised to appoint justices who were constitutional "strict constructionists," made the first of his four appointments to the Court, Chief Justice Warren Burger.[153] With those appointments the balance on the Court changed so that the Court no longer was predictably liberal on most issues. The first indication of the new Court's approach to establishment clause cases came in *Walz v. Tax Commission* in which the Court ruled in a seven-to-one decision that the inclusion of real property used solely for religious worship in a broad property-tax exemption category did not violate the establishment clause.[154] Applying the purpose and primary effect tests, the majority had no difficulty concluding that the long-standing practice, rooted in the eighteenth century and sustained by a long line of precedent, of granting property-tax exemptions for organizations that did charitable, educational, and other good works had a legitimate secular purpose and did not have the primary effect of advancing religion—after all, the practice had not in fact led to "an established religion or church." The lessons of history were worth more than logic. The Court added a new test to the other two for use in establishment clause cases—the excessive entanglement test that was based in the idea that governmental evaluation, control, and surveillance of religious institutions can lead to "direct confrontations and conflicts" between church and state.[155] But eliminating the tax exemption "would tend to expand the involvement of government by giving rise to tax valuation of church property, tax liens, tax foreclosures, and the direct confrontations and conflicts that follow in the train of those legal processes."[156] The thrust of the sole dissenting opinion by Justice Douglas (the author of the majority opinion in *Zorach*) was that exemptions were indistinguishable from grants and subsidies of public funds.[157] The majority responded saying that an exemption is not sponsorship because government does not transfer its money to the churches but merely abstains from demanding that the church support the state; besides, it entailed less church-state involvement.[158]

Thus, it appeared as of 1970 that the Court was continuing its move away from the tough no-aid language of *Everson* and moving toward the more accommodating stance of *Allen*. Even so, it was still unclear how the Court would respond to direct governmental assistance of the *private school* itself as opposed to aid channeled through children and parents. This issue finally reached the Court, after twenty years of controversy, in *Lemon v. Kurtzman*,[159] *Robinson v. DiCenso*,[160] and *Tilton v. Richardson*.[161]

In *Lemon* the Court examined a Pennsylvania statute that authorized the state to "purchase" from private schools, without any admixture of religious teaching, purely secular educational services, i.e., mathematics, modern foreign languages, physical sciences, and physical education. The schools were to be reimbursed for their costs with regard to teachers' salaries, textbooks, and instructional materials in the "purchased" courses. The Rhode Island statutes in *DiCenso* provided for direct salary supplements (of up to 15 percent of their salaries) to private school teachers of secular subjects who used textbooks approved for use in the public schools and who agreed not to teach any classes in religion. The Supreme Court struck both statutes down. (The *Tilton* decision will be discussed later.)

Writing for the majority in *Lemon* and *DiCenso*, Chief Justice Burger said that consideration of the cases must begin with the three criteria developed over the years: the purpose, primary effect, and entanglement tests. He then readily agreed that the purpose of the laws was to "enhance the quality of secular education" and not to advance religion.[162] He set aside consideration of the primary effect test because the Court concluded that the statutes failed under a modified version of the entanglement test. Under the first branch of the newly defined test, an aid program would fail if it produced excessive *administrative* entanglement between church and state. Here the need for excessive entanglement was unavoidable. First, because these were religious schools under the control of religious figures, and employing for the most part lay Catholic teachers, the *potential* for an impermissible fostering of religion in the secular classes was present, thereby necessitating "comprehensive, discriminating, and continuing state surveillance" in order to be certain that the state's restrictions that subsidized teachers not teach religion were obeyed.[163] Second, "the government's post-audit power to inspect and evaluate a church-related school's financial records and to determine which expenditures are religious and which are secular creates an intimate and continuing relationship between church and state."[164] Under the second branch of the newly defined entanglement test, an aid program would fail if it could lead to excessive *political* entanglement. Political entanglement involved the fostering of political divisions along religious lines, and these two programs, the Court concluded, did just that. The need for continuing annual appropriations "and the likelihood of larger and larger demands as costs and populations grow" created the possibility that political fragmentation and divisiveness along religious lines would be intensified—an evil "against which the

First Amendment was intended to protect."[165]

It is useful at this point to compare the *Lemon/DiCenso* opinion with the Court's opinion in *Tilton* in order to highlight the nature of the Burger Court's approach at this historical moment in these aid-to-private-school cases. The statute under review in *Tilton* was a federal statute authorizing federal grants and loans to institutions of higher education for the construction of academic facilities that could not be used for religious worship or as part of a school or department of divinity until twenty years after construction. After twenty years, Congress had determined, the federal government would have secured a secular benefit equal to or exceeding the value of the grant. In his plurality opinion upholding the program in part, the Chief Justice again quickly concluded that the purpose of the law was secular.[166] He also judged that the "principal or primary effect" of the aid program was not to advance religion.[167] He refused to concede that religion so permeated education in the institutions involved in *Tilton* that the aid would unavoidably advance religion, and he refused to base his decision on a "composite profile" of the "typical sectarian" institution of higher education. In higher education cases, the primary effect test would have to be used only case by case.[168] Chief Justice Burger, however, for purposes of applying the entanglement test, was willing to generalize about higher educational institutions. He concluded that in most such schools, including the ones involved in the case, religious indoctrination is not a substantial purpose of the colleges; the students are older and less impressionable; these colleges have a high degree of academic freedom; and college courses by nature of their own internal disciplines offer less opportunity for sectarian influences.[169] It thus followed, according to Chief Justice Burger, that in this case the need for administrative surveillance and the potential for divisive religious political fragmentation were less for the same reasons.[170]

The decisions in *Lemon/DiCenso* and *Tilton* raised a number of questions: (1) Were the New York textbook case and the bus transportation case still good law, or would this Court reach a different conclusion on those forms of aid if they were to come up for review again? If the *Allen* decision remained good law, could other items (e.g., audio visual equipment) be loaned to private school students? (2) If property-tax exemptions were constitutional, would a tax credit or tax deduction for parents sending their children to private church-affiliated schools be accepted as constitutional? Could these arrangements be justified on the child-benefit theory of *Everson-Allen* and survive the entanglement test as the property-tax exemption did in *Walz?* Might even a tuition grant be constitutional? (3) Though the salaries of teachers employed by private church-affiliated schools could not be subsidized, could publicly employed and supervised teachers provide services in these schools on the basis that they were less likely to attempt religious instruction; hence, less supervision would be needed and the entanglement test could be satisfied? (4) Would financial assistance to church-affiliated higher education institutions, almost regardless of the form of assistance, continue to be treated differently? (5) Did the eight justices who joined in the majority opinion in *Lemon/DiCenso* really interpret the tests used in that opinion the same way, or did the opinion paper over differences that would show up in other cases—especially in one involving tuition tax deductions or credits?[171]

As the Court has addressed these and other related issues in the years since *Lemon/DiCenso* and *Tilton,* what we see emerging is a dramatic split among the justices. Generally speaking, today we find Justices Brennan, Marshall, and Stevens voting to strike down all aid programs; they continue, however, to respect the textbook and bus transportation opinions. We also consistently found Chief Justice Burger, and Justices Rehnquist and White on the other side. Justice O'Connor gives every indication she will, with an occasional departure, vote with this group on this issue.[172] (Justice Stewart, whom O'Connor replaced, adopted a middle position, validating some forms of aid but not others.)[173] Justices Powell[174] and Blackmun have shifted from case to case between the accommodationist camp of Chief Justice Burger and the strict separationist camp of Justice Brennan.

Thus, where do matters now stand regarding the constitutionality of various forms of aid? The following provides a brief summary and commentary on the variety of forms of aid to have come up for review in recent years.

Books, Materials, and Equipment

Despite the requirements of the entanglement test—a test some members of the Court want to abandon[175]—the kind of textbook loan program upheld in *Allen* continues to be supported by a majority of the Court.[176] But neither the loaning of instructional materials and equipment to the private schools themselves or directly to their students has been upheld.[177] Those justices who favor upholding the loan of textbooks, but vote against the loan of materials (maps) and equipment (e.g., tape recorders), justify their position by arguing that books can be examined for ideological content, but equipment cannot. They have also expressed an unwillingness to overrule *Allen* because of the doctrine of *stare decisis.* They reject *Allen's* assumption that religion does not permeate the private school.[178] Most recently, they have said that the loan of books is a form of aid that confers an indirect, remote, or incidental benefit upon the religious institution.[179]

Transportation

The result in *Everson* continues to be embraced, but a majority struck down the subsidization of transportation for field trips. The majority stressed that the main recipient of the aid was the school and that it was the school that controlled the frequency, timing, and destination of trips that could be used for religious purposes.[180] The strict separationist camp also continues to accept the result in *Everson* on the theory that this is a form of aid that provides only an indirect, remote, or incidental benefit to religious institutions.[181]

Reimbursement for Testing and Other Expenses

With even Chief Justice Burger and Justices Rehnquist and White agreeing, the Court struck down a New York statute authorizing direct money grants for the maintenance and repair of private school facilities, including possibly even the school chapel.[182] With only Justice White dissenting, the Court also held unconstitutional another New York law that provided private schools with a single per-pupil allotment to cover the expense of maintaining pupil enrollment and health records, the recording of personnel qualifications and characteristics, and the preparation and submission to the state of various other reports as mandated by the state.[183] Among the mandated services for which the state provided reimbursement were administering, grading, compiling, and reporting of tests and examinations that were both state prepared and teacher prepared in subjects required to be taught under state law. Because the Court was concerned that teacher-prepared examinations would be drafted with an eye to the religious inculcation of pupils, aid that could be used for these tests was struck down.

In two subsequent cases, the Court upheld the supplying of state-prepared standardized tests and scoring services and cash reimbursement for costs associated with carrying out state testing and reporting requirements in connection with tests prepared by the state, but scored by private school personnel.[184] Justice White in the 1980 majority decision indicated that he was not prepared to presuppose bad faith on the part of the private school teachers scoring the tests that could lead to the need for supervision and thus excessive entanglement. His opinion also strongly suggested that the majority was not willing to embrace the view that religion always permeates every aspect of church-affiliated schools, or that aid inevitably helps religion. The dissenters stressed that direct aid unavoidably runs the risk of furthering the religious mission of the school. They particularly stressed that subsidization of attendance taking helped the school assure attendance at religious instruction. Entanglement problems were also present because the state had to assure that the administration and scoring of the tests were not done so as to violate the first amendment.

Provision of Remedial, Therapeutic, and Diagnostic Services

In 1975 the Court struck down the provision by public employees of remedial and accelerated instructional services, guidance, counseling and testing, and speech and hearing services to nonpublic school students on the premises of the private schools.[185] The Court said that because the services were provided in the religious atmosphere of the nonpublic school, there was a need for continuing surveillance to make sure the restrictions against religious instruction were maintained; but this need for surveillance in turn created excessive entanglement between church and state—hence the aid program was unconstitutional for this reason.

Two years later the Court upheld the provision of speech, hearing, and psychological services offered in a neutral place off the nonpublic school grounds (e.g., a mobile unit parked next to the nonpublic school). In that same opinion the Court upheld the provision of diagnostic speech, hearing, and psychological services provided in the nonpublic school. Because the diagnostician had only limited contact with pupils, the possibilities for violation of the restrictions against inculcation were less; hence, the need for supervision was less. These services, said the Court, were like nursing, dental, and optometric services that were not challenged.[186]

Remedial and enrichment courses offered in the private schools during the regular school day as supplements to the required core curriculum were struck down in 1985.[187] (The courses, offered by public employees, covered math, reading, art, music, and physical education.) Justices Brennan, Marshall, Blackmun, Powell, and Stevens said the program was unconstitutional because the primary effect was to advance religion. First, the public school employees might subtly or overtly conform their instruction to the environment in which they teach—and this reinforcement of the religious message of the school might go undetected. The symbolism of public school teachers in the private school suggested a union of church and state, or at least state endorsement and encouragement of religious beliefs. This was a program not of indirect, incidental aid to religious schools, but of direct and substantial aid, just like a direct cash grant. Chief Justice Burger and Justices O'Connor, White, and Rehnquist dissented.

Programs for the Educationally Disadvantaged

In 1985 the strict separationist group, joined by Justice Powell, struck down the provision of federally funded (Title I, now called Chapter One) remedial services for the educationally disadvantaged through programs operated in the religious school itself.[188] Again, the weapon used was the entanglement test: since the programs were operated in the religious school, constant surveillance would be necessary to check for the "subtle or overt presence of religious matter in Title I classes." Furthermore, the operation of the programs would require extensive administrative cooperation that could lead to conflicts between the public personnel offering the program and religious school officials. Justice Powell also stressed the danger of "political divisiveness" in this case and recognized that the interaction of the primary effect test (which forced the need for supervision) and the entanglement test created a dilemma—governments extending aid to religious schools must walk a narrow line between the two tests. He noted that the state must be *certain* that subsidized teachers do not inculcate religion. Justice O'Connor, along with Chief Justice Burger and Justices White and Rehnquist, dissented. In her opinion she attacked the majority's use of the entanglement test. She noted that in the nineteen-year history of the program there was never a single incident in which a Title I instructor subtly or overtly attempted to indoctrinate pupils in religion at public expense. She doubted the public employees who provide these programs would be influenced by the sectarian nature of the schools where they taught. Just as she thought the risk of inculcation by public employees was exaggerated, she also felt the degree of supervision required to manage the risk was overstated by the majority. The supervision involved here was no greater than that which any public school teacher receives in the public schools, where there was also a risk of inculcation. She also stressed that this program has not in fact created political divisiveness.

Community Education

Nineteen eighty-five saw the strict separationists on the Court prevail in striking down a community education program for children and adults that involved providing, in the private schools at the close of the regular school day, courses in arts and crafts, home economics, Spanish, gymnastics, yearbook production, drama, newspaper, humanities, chess, model building, and nature appreciation.[189] The same programs were offered in the public schools, but those courses taught in facilities "leased" for a nominal sum from the private schools were taught by instructors employed full time by the same nonpublic school. The rooms had to be free of religious symbols; and, when in use, a sign had to be in place saying it was a "public school classroom." The majority struck it down because the instructors in this program might engage in subtle or overt religious indoctrination. They also found that the program would have the primary effect of advancing religion in another way—the program carried a symbolic endorsement and encouragement of the religious beliefs taught at some other time of the day in the same classes. This program was indistinguishable in their view from a direct cash subsidy to the religious school. Justice O'Connor concurred because the instructors in the program were overwhelmingly full-time employees of the parochial schools. Chief Justice Burger and Justices White and Rehnquist dissented.

Tuition Reimbursement

Found unconstitutional was a New York tuition reimbursement program that provided parents in low-income brackets with unrestricted grants of fifty to one hundred dollars per child (but not more than 50 percent of tuition actually paid). The plan, concluded the majority, had the primary effect of advancing religion by providing an incentive and improving the opportunity of parents to send their children to church-affiliated schools.[190] Dissenting Chief Justice Burger said aid to individuals stands on an entirely different footing than direct aid to religious institutions; and he, as well as Justices Rehnquist and White, saw this program as no different from those upheld in *Allen* and *Everson.*

Tax Deductions for Tuition Expenses

Parents who had children attending private school, and who did not receive a tuition reimbursement under the New York law discussed above, using a complex formula could subtract from their adjusted gross income a specified amount to help compensate for their tuition costs. The majority concluded that this plan had the same impermissible primary effect as the reimbursement plan. The majority also rejected the claim that this plan was like the tax exemption upheld in *Walz:* there was a long history supporting those exemptions. This plan would increase rather than reduce governmental involvement with religion, and here the reductions flowed primarily to children attending sectarian schools. Last, the majority noted there would be annual pressure to enlarge the tax relief involved in the law, thus threatening continuing religious strife over aid to religion.[191] Chief Justice Burger and Justices Rehnquist and White argued that this plan of *indirect* aid to private schools was similar to the programs upheld in *Allen, Everson,* and *Walz.* To them it was just a matter of the state being neutral in providing the tax break to people who were paying public school taxes but not using those schools. Justice White especially stressed the importance of the private school system and the financial difficulties it faced.

Ten years after the New York case the Supreme Court reviewed and *upheld* a Minnesota law that permitted public and private school parents to deduct from their state taxes expenses incurred for tuition, textbooks, and transportation.[192] Justice Rehnquist, now writing for the majority, stressed that this was a program available to both public and private school parents; the program provided an attenuated financial benefit to private schools because it was channeled through the individual parents; and the degree of entanglement involved here in determining if costs of certain textbooks could be deducted was no more than in the New York textbook case. The dissenters could find no difference between the law here and the New York tax deduction scheme. For them the establishment clause forbade both direct and indirect aid.

Financial Assistance for Education

A unanimous Court has held that the establishment clause is not violated by providing financial assistance for educational and vocational training to a blind individual who chooses to use the money to attend a Christian college to study to become a pastor.[193] The Court found that the general aid program had a secular purpose and that any aid provided that ultimately flowed to religious institutions did so only as a result of the independent and private choices of the aid recipient. The Court noted that only a small proportion of the aid under this program did end up supporting sectarian education. There was no *state* action sponsoring or subsidizing religion.

Aid to Higher Education

Two years after the decision in *Tilton,* the Court once again upheld a program of financial assistance to higher education institutions. Stressing that religion did not permeate the schools involved in the case, the Court could find no constitutional fault with a program to assist construction of buildings (not to be used for sectarian instruction or worship) by issuance of revenue bonds.[194] Three years later the Court faced a more difficult case. The facts in *Roemer v. Board of Public Works of Maryland* were that the state provided private institutions (except those awarding primarily theological degrees) with a direct annual subsidy that could not be used for any sectarian purpose.[195] The record showed that the five church-affiliated schools that received funds had mandatory religion courses, had some classes that were begun with prayer, employed some instructors who wore religious garb to class, and that the great majority of the students were Roman Catholic. Nevertheless, the Court concluded that religion did not permeate these institutions and they were no more pervasively sectarian than those schools involved in *Tilton.* Having reached this conclusion, it was easy for the Court to conclude that the program survived both the primary effect test and the administrative branch of the entanglement test. Despite the fact this aid involved annual general appropriations for private schools, the Court said, this case was more like *Tilton* than like *Lemon.* The danger of political divisiveness was also slight. This problem was reduced because more than two-thirds of the aided schools were not religious, in sharp contrast to the situation in *Nyquist* where 95 percent of the aided schools were Roman Catholic parochial schools. The substantial autonomy of these schools from the Catholic hierarchy also lessened the chance that controversy surrounding the aid program would involve the Catholic church itself.

1.13. THE BURGER COURT IN PERSPECTIVE

Patterns are difficult to discern in this set of often seemingly contradictory opinions, but some tendencies are discernible. Regarding aid to private schools, a stable minority of accommodationists has emerged consisting of Chief Justice Burger, Justices Rehnquist, White, and frequently, Justice O'Connor. (See chapter 10, which discusses the retirement of Chief Justice Burger, the appointment of Justice Rehnquist as chief justice, and the appointment of Antonin Scalia to the Court.) This group of justices rejects the argument that any program that in some manner aids religiously affiliated institutions violates the establishment clause.[196] Even in regard to elementary and secondary schools, they have backed away from the assumption that religion permeates these institutions and that the religious and secular aspects of the program cannot be dealt with separately.[197] Thus, in their hands both the primary effect and the administrative entanglement tests have lost their bite. The justices are keenly aware of the society, and are sympathetic with state efforts to save the private schools from financial extinction.[198] This group has come to embrace the view of Justice Powell, originally expressed in *Wolman,* that today "The risk of significant religious or denominational control over our political processes—or even of deep political division along religious lines—is remote."[199] Thus, these justices are increasingly uncomfortable with the political branch of the entanglement test.[200] This group has validated both direct forms of aid (cash grants to private schools) and more indirect forms of aid.[201] The strong tendency of two of these justices to validate aid to private schools is reflected in their continuing opposition to the decision in *Lemon/ DiCenso.*[202] And the somewhat ad hoc nature of the group's approach to deciding establishment clause cases is reflected in the following quotation from the majority opinion in *Regan:* "What is certain is that our decisions have tended to avoid categorical imperatives and absolutist approaches at either end of the range of possible outcomes. This course sacrifices clarity and predictability for flexibility, but this promises to be the case until the continuing interaction between the courts and the States . . . produces a single, more encompassing construction of the Establishment Clause."[203]

There also has emerged a stable minority of separationists consisting of Justices Brennan, Marshall, and Stevens. This group continues to stress the pervasive sectarian nature of elementary-secondary schools as well as the institutions of higher education.[204] These justices continue to use the primary effect and administrative entanglement tests with considerable bite. Indeed, in their hands these two tests create a considerable dilemma for states, a Catch-22: the more a state tries to assure its aid program will not have the primary effect of advancing religion (i.e., by limiting the aid to secular purposes and supervising to assure compliance with the limit), the more likely the state will trip over the entanglement test. These justices also continue to stress the dangers of political fragmentation and divisiveness along religious lines.[205] The strength of the separationist beliefs of these justices is reflected in the expressed desire of Justices Marshall and Stevens to overrule the New York textbook case, *Allen.*[206]

Thus, two members of the accommodationist branch of the Court have expressed a desire to expand possibilities of aid flowing to private schools by overruling *Lemon,* while two others have urged the contraction of those opportunities by urging the overruling of *Allen.* The divisions on the Court are deep and irreconcilable.

Justices Powell and Blackmun have been crucial swing votes in many of these cases. They joined with the strict separationists in the view that religion permeates the religious school and that it is incumbent upon the states to be *certain* that publicly subsidized teachers who provide secular programs in the private schools do not inculcate religion.[207] Thus they voted with the separationists to strike down programs that involve the provision of instructional services in the private schools and the loan of instructional materials and equipment to nonpublic school students.[208] They also voted to allow diagnostic financial difficulties faced by private schools, appreciate the contributions of private schools to education and services to be provided in the private school and supported the provision of remedial and therapeutic services at a neutral site off the premises of the nonpublic school.[209] Having voted together in 1977, they split in 1980 over the question of reimbursing private schools for administering and grading state-prepared tests, with Powell voting to uphold and Blackmun voting with the separationists.[210] They disagreed on the provision of a tax deduction for school expenses, with Powell voting with the accommodationists and Blackmun voting with the separationists.[211]

Thus confusion and division abound in these cases, yet there is one point on which the Court has reached unanimity—the impermissibility of states loaning textbooks to students attending private, racially segregated schools.[212] Chief Justice Burger, distinguishing textbooks from other forms of state aid (e.g., electricity, water, police and fire protection) on the grounds these were "necessities of life," and with regard to which the state had an operating monopoly, said the provision of textbooks had the impermissible effect and tendency to "facilitate, reinforce, and support private discrimination."[213] Continuing, Chief Justice Burger wrote, "We need not assume that the State's textbook aid to private schools has been motivated by other than a sincere interest in the educational welfare of all Mississippi children. . . . [But] the Equal Protection Clause would be a sterile promise if state involvement in possible private activity could be shielded altogether from constitutional scrutiny simply because its ultimate end was not discrimination but some higher goal."[214] The majority opinion distinguished Allen on the grounds that "the transcendent value of free religious exercise in our constitutional scheme leaves room for 'play in the joints' to the extent of cautiously delineated secular government assistance to religious schools," whereas the Constitution "places no value on discrimination as it does on the values inherent in the Free Exercise Clause."[215] Whatever may be said about the Burger Court, whether one examines the Court's strong protection of the free exercise of religion or its willingness to accommodate governmental assistance to religion, it is hard to deny the preferred status of religion in its pantheon of values, and its strong antipathy toward discrimination, especially racial discrimination—an antagonism that has led the Court to rank its efforts to end discrimination as even more important than its efforts in support of religion. While the precise nature of the Court's racial policies will be explored in later chapters, at least this much can be said: It would appear that the Court almost unanimously agrees that the dangers to community arising from racial discrimination are more serious than the dangers to community that may arise from the practice of religion.

NOTES

1. Samuel P. Huntington claims the existence of an American creed and a predominant role for it in explaining American politics in *American Politics: The Promise of Disharmony* (Cambridge, Mass.: The Belknap Press of Harvard University Press, 1981).

2. The Supreme Court seems to have embraced the view that parents enjoy a natural right to control the upbringing of their children in Pierce v. Society of Sisters, 268 U.S. 510 (1925).

3. One version of such a contractual model of law is vividly outlined by James M. Buchanan in *The Limits of Liberty: Between Anarchy and Leviathan* (Chicago: University of Chicago Press, 1975). One might also profitably look at John Rawls, *A Theory of Justice* (Cambridge, Mass.: Harvard University Press, 1971).

4. Amy Gutman, "Children, Paternalism, and Education," *Philosophy and Public Affairs* 9 (1980): 338; John Coons and Stephen Sugarman, *Education by Choice: The Case for Family Control* (Berkeley, Calif.: University of California Press, 1978); Schoeman, "Rights of Children, Rights of Parents, and the Moral Basis of the Family," *Ethics* 91 (1980): 6; Robert Mnoonkin, "Child Custody Adjudication: Judicial Functions in the Face of Indeterminancy," *Law and Contemporary Problems* 39 (1975): 226.

5. Gutman, *supra*, note 4.

6. Mark G. Yudof, "When Governments Speak: Toward a Theory of Government Expression and the First Amendment," *Texas Law Review* 57 (1979): 863.

7. Frederick Schauer, *Free Speech: A Philosophical Enquiry* (Cambridge: Cambridge University Press, 1982).

8. The Supreme Court in Wisconsin v. Yoder, 406 U.S. 205, 226 (1972) praised the Amish community on the grounds that "Even their idiosyncratic separateness exemplifies the diversity we profess to admire and encourage." The Court also said in an earlier case that the state cannot "standardize its children" by forcing them to attend public schools. Pierce v. Society of Sisters, 268 U.S. 510, 535 (1925).

9. For a discussion of the importance of private education in contributing to the changes in the theory and methods of education, see Lawrence A. Cremin, *The Transformation of the School: Progressivism in American Education 1876-1957* (New York: Alfred A. Knopf, Inc., 1961).

10. *But see*, Tyll van Geel, "The Constitution and the Child's Right to Freedom from Political Indoctrination," in *Children's Intellectual Rights*, ed. David Moshman (San Francisco: Jossey-Bass, 1986). Other chapters in this monograph are also of interest.

11. Frederick A. Olafson, "Rights and Duties in Education," in *Educational Judgements*, ed. James F. Doyle (London: Routledge & Kegal Paul, 1973), 173-95; Joel Feinberg, "The Child's Right to an Open Future," in *Whose Child?* ed. William Aiken and Hugh LaFollette (Totowa, N.J.: Littlefield, Adams & Co., 1980), 124-53; Gutman, *supra*, note 4.

12. The first amendment to the Constitution says, for example, *"Congress* shall make no law respecting an establishment of religion, or prohibiting the free exercise thereof; or abridging the freedom of speech, or of the press." As Professor Tribe puts it, "Nearly all of the Constitution's self-executing, and thus judicially enforceable, guarantees of individual rights shield individuals only from government action. Accordingly, when litigants claim the protection of such guarantees, courts must first determine whether it is indeed governmental action—state or federal—that litigants are challenging." Lawrence Tribe, *American Constitutional Law* (Mineola, N.Y.: The Foundation Press, 1978), at 1147.

Over the years the Supreme Court has adopted a set of tests for determining if state action is present, i.e., the tests determine whether an arguably private actor such as a private educational institution is subject to the Constitution. Roughly speaking, the greater the extent of governmental involvement with a private actor, the more likely it is that the Court will find state action present. Blum v. Yaretsky, 457 U.S. 991 (1982); Lugar v. Edmondson Oil Co., 457 U.S. 922 (1982); Burton v. Wilmington Parking Authority, 365 U.S. 715 (1961). However, mere state authorization of a private actor's actions does not constitute state action. Jackson v. Metropolitan Edison Co., 419 U.S. 345 (1974). Significant state encouragement of a private actor's actions can, however, mean the extension of the Constitution to these activities. Blum v. Yaretsky, 457 U.S. 991 (1982); Reitman v. Mulkey, 387 U.S. 369 (1967). If the private actor is carrying out a function that traditionally and exclusively has been a public function, then the Court will also extend the reach of the Constitution. Blum v. Yaretsky, 457 U.S. 991 (1982); Marsh v. Alabama, 326 U.S. 501 (1946). These are difficult tests to satisfy; thus the mere fact that private institutions may be regulated by government and/or receive governmental assistance does not mean that the actions of the school officials are categorizable as "state action."

Since it is unlikely that any of these tests would be satisfied in the case of parental decisions regarding their children, or for that matter as regards the decisions of officials of private schools, parents and private school officials may adopt policies that if they were adopted by public schools would be limited by the Constitution. For example, private schools need not, unless they voluntarily agree to do so as a matter of the contractual arrangement with the student, follow the procedural due process requirements imposed upon public schools by the fourteenth amendment. *See, e.g.,* Bright v. Isenbarger, 314 F. Supp. 1382 (N.D. Ind. 1970), *aff'd,* 445 F.2d 412 (7th Cir. 1971); Blackburn v. Fisk University, 443 F.2d 121 (6th Cir., 1971). *See also,* §§ 8.6, 9.17, and 9.18.

13. Bellotti v. Baird, 443 U.S. 622 (1979). Under the guidelines outlined by the Court, every minor must be given the opportunity to go directly to a court without first consulting or notifying her parents regarding the decision of whether or not to have an abortion. If the court is persuaded she is mature, the court must authorize the abortion. If the court is not persuaded she is mature, the court could deny the abortion request of the immature minor who had not consulted her parents; or the court could defer the decision until there is parental consultation, in which the court may participate. It would also seem to follow from this case that parents do not have the right to impose an abortion on the mature minor. In re Smith, 16 Md. App. 209, 295 A.2d 238 (1972). Left undecided by these cases is the question of what other options the parent has under state law and the U.S. Constitution for dealing with a child who refuses to follow the parent's wishes regarding reproductive choice. For example, it is not clear whether it would be constitutionally permissible for the state to declare the child to be "in need of supervision" at the behest of a parent if the child persists in getting pregnant and seeking an abortion, or if the child insists on having her baby and refuses the abortion.

14. For a discussion of these matters see Alan Sussman and Martin Guggenheim, *The Rights of Parents* (New York: Avon Books, 1980), 9, 12, 13, 48, 56.

15. Id., 71.

16. Id., chaps. 2 and 3.

17. North Carolina has deregulated its private schools. Cynthia Wittmer West, "The State and Sectarian Education: Regulation and Deregulation," *Duke Law Journal* (1980): 766.

18. For a further discussion of this issue see van Geel, "The Constitution and the Child's Right to Freedom from Political Indoctrination," *supra,* note 10.

19. For the case that the Constitution limits state efforts to indoctrinate children see Tyll van Geel, "The Search for Constitutional Limits on Governmental Authority to Inculcate Youth," *Texas Law Review* 62 (1983): 197. *See also* §5.8.

20. William F. Aikman and Lawrence Kotin, *Legal Foundations of Compulsory School Attendance* (Port Washington, N.Y.: Kennikat Press, 1980), 11.

21. Id., 25.

22. For an overview of these laws see Patricia Lines, *Compulsory Education Laws* (Education Commission of the States, March, 1985). For an interpretive history of the passage of the laws see David Tyack, "Ways of Seeing: An Essay on the History of Compulsory Schooling," *Harvard Educational Review* 46 (1976): 355.

23. For a review of the legislation see James W. Tobak and Perry A. Zirkel, "Home Instruc-

tion: An Analysis of the Statutes and Case Law," *University of Dayton Law Review* 8 (1982): 1.

24. Stephens v. Bongart, 15 N. J. Misc. 80, 189 A. 131 (Juv. & Dom. Rel. Ct. 1937); Marsh v. Earle, 24 F. Supp. 385 (D.C. Penn. 1938); State v. Hoyt, 84 N. H. 38, 146 A. 170 (1929).

25. Stephens v. Bongart, Ibid., at 132.

26. The first amendment reads in part that "Congress shall make no law respecting an establishment of religion, or prohibiting the free exercise thereof." United States Constitution, Amendment 1. Though the language of the first amendment refers only to "Congress," the Supreme Court has concluded that the fourteenth amendment extends the reach of the free exercise clause to actions taken by the states, thereby "nationalizing," "absorbing," or "incor- porating" this aspect of the Bill of Rights (the first ten amendments). Cantwell v. Connecticut, 310 U.S. 296 (1940).

27. The two religion clauses of the first amendment are in tension with each other. Judicial protection of the free exercise of religion may be carried to the point that religion is being favored and "established" in violation of the establishment clause. For example, if the judiciary were to excuse church members from paying their income tax on the ground that the tax interfered with their free exercise of their religious beliefs, this would clearly go a long way toward benefitting religion. *Cf.,* U.S. v. Lee, 455 U.S. 252 (1982) (refusing to grant an Amish employer an exemption, claimed in the name of the free exercise of religion, from the requirement to pay social security taxes). On the other hand, excessive judicial zeal, in the name of the establishment clause, in preventing government from assisting religion could easily involve severe restrictions on the free exercise of religion. For example, if the judiciary were to say that police and fire protection were not to be made available to churches, the difficulties in maintaining churches would be greatly heightened. Commentators have suggested different ways in which to reconcile the two clauses. Tribe, *American Constitutional Law, supra.,* note 12, at 822; Wilbur Katz, *Religion and Ameri- can Constitutions* (Evanston, Ill.: Northwestern University Press, 1964); Philip B. Kurland, *Religion and the Law* (Chicago: Aldine Publishing Co., 1962).

28. 406 U.S. 205 (1972).

29. Ibid., at 215-19.

The initial three-point burden on the claimants involves a set of complex issues. Listed below are relevant court opinions and selected other materials for exploring the problems in this area. *The definition of religion and determining what is a religious claim:* United States v. Ballard, 322 U.S. 78 (1944); Fowler v. Rhode Island, 345 U.S. 67 (1953); Torcaso v. Watkins, 367 U.S. 488 (1961); Thomas v. Rev. Bd., Ind., Emply. Sec. Div., 450 U.S. 707 (1981); *cf.,* United States v. Seegar, 380 U.S. 163 (1975); Welsh v. United States, 398 U.S. 333 (1970). Kent Greenwalt, "Religion as a Concept in Constitutional Law," *California Law Review* 72 (1984): 753; George C. Freeman III, "The Misguided Search for the Constitutional Definition of 'Religion,'" *George- town Law Journal* 71 (1983): 1519; Jesse H. Choper, "Defining 'Religion' in the First Amend- ment," *University of Illinois Law Review* (1982): 579; Tribe, *American Constitutional Law, supra,* note 12, at 826-33. *The problem of sincerity:* Braunfeld wn, 36 U.S. 599, 609 (1961); United States v. Ballard, 322 U.S. 78, 92 (1944); Greenwalt, "Religion as a Concept in Constitu- tional Law," at 778-84. *The problem of impact:* Tribe, *American Constitutional Law, supra,* note 12, at 863-64.

30. The Court, without defining the term "religion," concluded that the Amish claims for an exemption were religiously based. "That the Old Order Amish daily life and way of life stem from their faith is shown by the fact that it is in response to their literal interpretation of the Biblical injunction from the Epistle of Paul to the Romans, 'be not conformed to this world. . . .' This command is fundamental to the Amish faith." *Id.,* at 216.

31. Wisconsin stipulated to the sincerity of the Amish parent's religious beliefs, and the Court gave no explicit attention to the question of the kind and amount of evidence sufficient to establish the sincerity of the claim. *Id.,* at 205, 209.

32. Id., 212, 218-19, 232.

33. There was evidence that the kind of informal education the parents were prepared to give their children was the ideal method of preparation for the Amish way of life. *Id.*, at 223, 224.

34. Id., at 224. The majority did not address the question that would have been raised had the state proceeded to enforce the compulsory education law against the parents on the theory that the Amish parents were preventing their children from attending high school contrary to the children's express wish to do so. The majority said this was not an issue in the case since the state had not premised its enforcement of the law on the theory that the Amish children wanted to attend high school but were prevented from doing so by the parents. *Id.*, at 231.

35. "The independence and successful social functioning of the Amish Community for a period approaching almost three centuries and more than 200 years in this country are strong evidence that there is at best a speculative gain, in terms of meeting the duties of citizenship, from an additional one or two years of compulsory formal education." *Id.*, at 226-27.

36. In §§1.7-1.9 we shall explore the implications of this opinion for exemptions that non-Amish parents have sought.

37. The Court emphasized that "A way of life, however virtuous and admirable, may not be interposed as a barrier to reasonable state regulation of education if it's based on purely secular considerations; to have the protection of the Religion Clauses, the claims must be rooted in religious belief," 406 U.S. at 15. Later, the Court wrote, "It cannot be overemphasized that we are not dealing with a way of life and mode of education by a group claiming to have recently discovered some 'progressive' or more enlightened process for rearing children." *Id.*, at 235, 233.

38. Justice Burger, writing for the majority, said this issue had not been raised in the case because the state had never tried the case on the theory that the parents were preventing their children from attending public school against their wishes. He went on to note that recognition of such a state claim would "call into question traditional concepts of parental control over the religious upbringing and education of their minor children" and that "intrusion by the State into family decisions in the area of religious training would give rise to grave questions of religious freedom comparable to those raised here." *Id.*, at 231-32.

39. David Tyack, "The Perils of Pluralism: The Background of the *Pierce* Case," *American Historical Review* 74 (1968): 74, 79.

40. Pierce v. Society of Sisters, 268 U.S. 510 (1925). The opinion in *Pierce* is significant in that the Court permitted the schools to assert not only their own constitutional right, but also the substantive due process rights of the parents and children as third parties. Normally, litigants are only allowed to assert their own constitutional rights, not those of a third party. In this case, however, the third parties' (parents and children) enjoyment of their rights depended on the school's freedom from injury, i.e., being shut down. Letting the school assert the rights of the parents and children served to protect those rights that might not otherwise have been protected. If the parents and children had to go to court in their own names, by the time the case was resolved they might merely have won a right to attend an empty building. Tribe, *American Constitutional Law, supra,* note 12, at 107-8. In the remainder of this chapter no sharp distinction will be drawn between the rights of private schools and the rights of their clients.

41. West Coast Hotel Co. v. Parrish, 300 U.S. 379 (1937); Nebbia v. New York, 291 U.S. 502 (1934).

42. Norwood v. Harrison, 413 U.S. 455, 461 (1973). Chief Justice Burger has written, citing both *Pierce* and *Wisconsin v. Yoder,* that "constitutional interpretation has consistently recognized that the parents' claim to authority in their own household to direct the rearing of their children is basic in the structure of our society." H. L. v. Matheson, 450 U.S. 398, 410 (1981) (upholding a Utah law requiring physicians to notify, if possible, the parents or guardian of any minor upon whom an abortion is to be performed). For an exploration of alternative readings of the *Pierce* opinion see Stephen Arons, "The Separation of School and State: *Pierce* Reconsidered," *Harvard Educational Review* 46 (1976): 76.

43. Yudof, "When Governments Speak," *supra,* note 6 at 888-91.

44. Joseph Tussman comes perilously close to advocating total state control of all formal education in *Government and the Mind* (New York: Oxford University Press, 1977). For a critical examination of various state interests in inculcating the young see Tyll van Geel, "The Search for Constitutional Limits on Governmental Authority to Inculcate Youth," *supra*, note 19.

45. *Compare*, Mark G. Yudof, David L. Kirp, Tyll van Geel, and Betsy Levin, *Educational Policy and the Law*, second edition (Berkeley, Calif.: McCutchan Publishing Corporation, 1982), 13-18.

46. §§ 1.6-1.9 will discuss the question of constitutional limits on state regulation of private schooling.

47. Professor Arons argues that *Pierce* should be understood as a first amendment case protecting the rights of parents and children to be free from governmental coercion of individual consciousness, and that freedom from such coercion must be achieved by assuring that all parents, not just the rich, have the practical possibility of seeking out the kind of education they prefer. Thus, government must be neutral and support alternative education programs by, for example, paying equally for any family's school choice. Arons does not examine the question whether there are moral or legal limits on the parents' efforts to inculcate their children.

48. Tobak and Zirkel, "Home Instruction: An Analysis of the Statutes and Case Law," *supra*, note 23, at 11. Tobak and Zirkel count fourteen states that explicitly deny home instruction as an option. Fifteen states explicitly allow home instruction as an acceptable alternative to attendance at the public schools. In twenty-one states there is at most an implied exception permitting home instruction. Since the publication of this article, a number of states—i.e., Arkansas, Kentucky, New Mexico, Tennessee, Virginia, Washington, Wyoming—have changed their laws to expressly permit home instruction subject to regulations such as requiring students instructed at home to be tested annually.

49. State v. Eddington, 99 N.M. 715, 663 P.2d 374, 378 (N.M. App. 1983), *cert. denied*, 104 S. Ct. 354 (1983). New Mexico today permits home instruction. *See also* In Interest of Sawyer, 672 P. 2d 1093 (Kan. 1983).

50. Delconte v. North Carolina, 308 S.E.2d 898, 904 (N.C. 1983), *reversed on other grounds*, 329 S.E. 2d 637 (N.C. 1985).

51. Duro v. District Attorney, 712 F.2d 96, 99 (4th Cir. 1983), *cert. denied*, 104 S. Ct. 998 (1984).

52. Burrow v. State, 669 S.W. 2d 441 (Ark. 1984). *See also* State v. Morrow, 343 N.W. 2d 903 (Neb. 1984).

53. State v. Novel, Nos. S791-00114A & S791-0115A (Mich. Dist. Ct., Allegan County, Jan. 9, 1980); Perchemlides v. Frizzle, No. 16641 (Mass. Super. Ct., Hampshire County, Nov. 13, 1978).

54. *See* Tyll van Geel, "The Constitution and State Regulation of Religious and Nonreligious Private Education," in *The Church, the State and the Schools*, ed. C. B. Vergon (Ann Arbor, Mich.: The University of Michigan School of Education, 1986), chap. 7; Devins, "A Constitutional Right to Home Instruction?" *Washington University Law Quarterly* 435 (1982):62.

55. Permitting home instruction but requiring parents to comply with certain reasonable regulations is an obvious, less extreme alternative. The regulation of private schooling will be taken up in §1.7.

56. The Court has written: "[W]hen the interests of parenthood are combined with a free exercise claim of the nature revealed in this record, more than merely a 'reasonable relation to some purpose within the competency of the State' is required to sustain the validity of the State's requirement under the First Amendment." Wisconsin v. Yoder, 406 U.S. 205, 233 (1972). It is an interesting question whether parents motivated by purely secular concerns should get less judicial and constitutional protection than parents who combine their interests of parenthood with a religious motivation.

57. 268 U.S. 510 (1925). The Court specifically noted that its opinion did not deal with the

power of the state "reasonably to regulate" all schools; to inspect and supervise and examine them, their teachers, and pupils; to require that teachers be of good moral character and patriotic; to require that courses essential to good citizenship be taught; to require that nothing be taught which is "manifestly inimical to the public welfare." *Id.*, at p. 534.

58. For an overview of state regulation of private schooling see Lines, *Compulsory Education Laws, supra,* note 22, at Tables 6 and 6, 33-46. (This review of state legislation does not take up health, safety, and zoning regulations.) Ms. Lines notes that only a few jurisdictions require the licensing of private schools—American Samoa, the District of Columbia, Hawaii, Nevada, and Puerto Rico. Maryland, Pennsylvania, and Wyoming also license all but church schools. Some of these states, as well as Idaho, Kansas, Michigan, and Tennessee, require accreditation. All schools except church-affiliated schools must be accredited in Nebraska (if parents object to accreditation) and North Carolina. Other forms of approval are required in Alaska, Delaware, Maine, Massachusetts, New Hampshire, North Dakota, Ohio, Pennsylvania, Rhode Island, South Dakota, the Virgin Islands, Washington, and Wyoming. Though exempting church schools, Alabama and New Jersey also require approval. The primary method for enforcing these regulations is to prosecute parents under the compulsory education laws for sending their children to unapproved, unaccredited, or unlicensed schools. Id., at 30. Yet other states regulate private schools by requiring that they provide instruction equivalent or comparable to that offered in the public schools, with the primary mechanism of enforcement again being prosecution of the parents. With increasing frequency states are also requiring privately educated students to be subjected to standardized testing.

Nonconstitutional litigation over the interpretation of these statutes has most frequently involved the regulation of home instruction. See notes 62-65, supra.

59. In Farrington v. Tokushige, 273 U.S. 284 (1927) the Supreme Court struck down under the due process clause of the fourteenth amendment a regulatory scheme that prohibited students from (1) attending these schools until after they had completed the second grade in the public schools, and (2) attending them for more than one hour each day, after the public schools had closed, and then for not more than six hours a week. To further guarantee that these schools, largely attended by Japanese children, could not foster disloyalty, complete control of the curriculum was given over to the state's department of education.

60. Runyon v. McCrary, 427 U.S. 160, 176 (1976) (upholding the use of 42 U.S.C. § 1981 to prohibit private schools from denying admission to qualified children solely on the basis of race).

61. It is unlikely the courts would permit public schools to teach the desirability of racial segregation. *Cf.,* Lowen v. Turnipseed, 488 F. Supp. 1138 (N.D. Miss. 1980); Smith v. St. Tammany Parish Sch. Bd., 316 F. Supp. 1174 (E.D. La. 1970), *aff'd,* 448 F. 2d 414 (5th Cir. 1971).

62. In dictum in Wisconsin v. Yoder, 406 U.S. 205, 213 (1972) the Court said parents had a right to provide "an equivalent education in a privately operated system."

63. Sheridan Road Baptist Church v. Dept. of Educ., 132 Mich. 1, 348 N.W. 2d 263 (Mich. App. 1984). *See also* Bangor Baptist Church v. State of Maine Dept. of Educ. and Cultural Services, 549 F. Supp. 1208 (1982) ("equivalent instruction" not vague). Burrow v. State of Arkansas, 282 Ark. 479, 669 S.W. 2d 441 (Ark. 1984). Parents were successful in claiming a Georgia statute was vague because it failed to define the term "private school." Roemhild v. State, 251 Ga. 569, 308 S.E. 2d 154 (Ga. 1983).

Closely related to this problem is the problem of delegating authority to officials without the laying down of clear parameters within which this authority must be exercised. In an old New York case a statute that granted wide-ranging authority to the State Commissioner of Education to set standards for private schools was struck down as an unconstitutional delegation of authority because it granted "unlimited, unrestrained, undefined power" to issue regulations and deny licenses. Packer Collegiate Institute v. The University of State of New York, 298 N.Y. 184, 81 N. E. 2d 80 (1948). Without standards to guide the discretion of the commissioner, inconsistent and arbitrary decisions could be reached; and, by calling for a greater legislative specification of the commissioner's authority, the court sought to assure licenses would be granted and denied on the basis of considered policy, not administrative whim.

64. The Court has said private schools may be required to offer instruction in English. Meyer v. Nebraska, 262 U.S. 390, 402 (1923). The Court also has said that states may require that courses "essential to good citizenship" be taught. Pierce v. Society of Sisters, 268 U.S. 510, 534 (1925). *See also* West Virginia Bd. of Educ. v. Barnette, 319 U.S. 624, 631 (1943).

65. (1) Institutional academic freedom: Griswold v. Connecticut, 381 U.S. 479, 482-83 (1965); Regents of the University of California v. Bakke, 438 U.S. 265, 312 (1978); Finkin, "On 'Institutional' Academic Freedom," *Texas Law Review* 61 (1983):817; (2) Compelled Speech: Wooley v. Maynard, 430 U.S. 705 (1977); Abood v. Detroit Bd. of Educ., 431 U.S. 209 (1977); Miami Herald Publishing Co. v. Tornillo, 418 U.S. 241 (1974).

66. The Court has said parents have a first amendment right to send their children to schools that advocate racial segregation. Runyon v. McCrary, 427 U.S. 160, 176 (1976). But the Court has also said that the prohibition of programs preparing people for imminent lawless action is permissible. Yates v. United States, 354 U.S. 298 (1957). It seems clear that the Court's dictum in Pierce v. Society of Sisters, 268 U.S. 510, 534 (1925) that states may prohibit teaching that is "manifestly inimical to the public welfare" is not a proposition the Court would adopt today. Unfortunately, Justice Blackmun has quoted that dictum with approval as regards the control of the curriculum by public school boards of education. Board of Education v. Pico, 457 U.S. 853, 880 (1982) (Blackmun, J., concurring).

Kansas, Maine, and Nebraska require their private schools to instruct in patriotism to develop a love of country; and Texas's compulsory education law permits attendance only at private schools where good citizenship is taught. Michigan private schools must select textbooks that recognize the achievements and accomplishments of ethnic and racial groups. Kan. Stat. Ann. §21.033 (1975 Supp.); Me. Rev. Stat. Ann. tit. 20 §1222 (1965); Neb. Rev. Stat. §79-213 (1971); Texas Educ. Code Ann. §21.033 (1975 Supp.); Mich. Stat. Ann. §15-3365 (1) (1975).

67. New York Times Co. v. United States, 403 U.S. 713 (1971); Nebraska Press Ass'n v. Stuart, 427 U.S. 539 (1976).

Even if the regulatory scheme did not rely on a prior approval mechanism, any effort to regulate the content of the instruction in private schools would raise grave free speech issues. Board of Education v. Pico, 457 U.S. 853 (1982) (removal of books from public school library because of school board disagreement with content of books may violate free speech rights of students); West Virginia State Bd. of Educ. v. Barnette, 319 U.S. 624 (1943) (requiring students to salute in a flag ceremony violates their right of freedom of speech). In Runyon v. McCrary, 427 U.S. 160 (1976), the Court in dictum indicated it would be constitutionally impermissible for government to prohibit a private school from teaching racism.

Any state attempt to regulate the content of the educational program of private schools would presumably only survive judicial review if the state could prove that the need to control was "necessary to achieve a compelling state interest." This is the test widely assumed to be the appropriate test when government seeks to regulate the content of a speech activity. Tribe, *American Constitutional Law, supra,* note 12, at 576 et. seq.

68. Baird v. State Bar of Arizona, 401 U.S. 1 (1971); In re Stolar, 401 U.S. 23 (1971); United States v. Robel, 389 U.S. 258 (1967); Keyishian v. Bd. of Regents, 385 U.S. 589 (1967); Elfbrandt v. United States, 384 U.S. 11 (1966). According to these cases, for example, it is only the knowing membership in an organization advocating the overthrow of the government by force or violence and a specific intent to further the organization's illegal goals that can be made the basis for criminal or other sanctions.

69. *Cf.,* Stanley v. Georgia, 394 U.S. 557 (1969) (reversing a conviction for knowing "possession of obscene matter").

70. *Cf.,* Williamson v. Lee Optical Co., 348 U.S. 483 (1955); Ohralik v. State Bar Ass'n, 436

U.S. 447, 460 (1978) (state has special responsibility to maintain standards in the licensed professions); Lupert v. California State Bar, 761 F. 2d 1325 (9th Cir. 1985).

71. *Cf.*, Whalen v. Roe, 429 U.S. 589 (1977).

72. *See* §7.6. Tyll van Geel, "What Is Reasonable Regulation of Home Instruction?" in *School Law Update 1987* (Topeka, Kan.: NOLPE, Forthcoming).

73. Whether a pretermination hearing would be required depends importantly on whether the courts would deem the license to operate the school to be a sufficiently important "property" interest to warrant protection against an erroneous termination by provision of the safeguards of a pretermination hearing. The court would also consider the risk that the termination decision could be erroneous and the burden a pretermination hearing would impose on the state. *Cf.*, Cleveland Bd. of Educ. v. Loudermill, 470 U.S.—(1985) (holding that tenured public employees are entitled to a pretermination hearing); Dixon v. Love, 431 U.S. 105 (1977) (driver's licenses may be suspended without a prior hearing); Barry v. Barchi, 443 U.S. 55 (1979) (horse-trainer license may be suspended without prior hearing); Mackey v. Montrym, 443 U.S. 1 (1979) (driver's license may be suspended for refusal to take breath analysis test), *Cf.*, Bell v. Burson, 402 U.S. 535 (1971).

74. Freedman v. Maryland, 380 U.S. 51 (1965) (holding that a noncriminal process that requires the prior submission of a film to a licensing board avoids constitutional infirmity only if it takes place under certain procedural safeguards).

75. The first amendment states in part that "Congress shall make no law respecting an establishment of religion, or prohibiting the free exercise thereof." United States Constitution, Amendment 1.

76. 406 U.S. 205 (1972). For an analysis of the opinion in this case see, §1.3.

77. Fellowship Baptist Church v. Benton, 620 F. Supp. 308 (S.D. Iowa, 1985) (reporting requirements, teacher certification requirements); State v. Patzer, 382 N.W. 2d 631 (N.D. 1986); Johnson v. Charles City Comm. Sch. Bd. of Educ., 368 N.W. 2d 74 (Iowa, 1985) (refusal to grant exemption under statute permitting exemptions in certain cases); Attorney General v. Bailey, 386 Mass. 367, 436 N.E. 2d 139 (Mass. 1982) (state reporting requirements); New Jersey State Bd. of Higher Educ. v. Shelton College, 90 N.J. 470, 448 A. 2d 988 (N.J. 1982) (state licensing requirements); State v. Rivinius, 328 N.W. 2d 220 (1982) (teachers not certified); State v. Faith Baptist Church, 107 Neb. 802, 301 N.W. 2d 571 (1981), *appeal dismissed for want of a substantial federal question,* 454 U.S. 803 (1981) (failure to get approval and failure of teachers to be certified); State v. Shaver, 294 N.W. 2d 883 (Sup. Ct. N.D. 1980) (teachers not certified); Sheridan Road Baptist Church v. Department of Education, 132 Mich. 1, 348 N.W. 2d 263 (Mich. App. 1984) (teachers not certified).

78. *See, e.g.*, State v. Riddle, 285 S.E. 2d 359 (Sup. Ct. Apps., W. Va. 1981). In that case the evidence showed that the Riddle children, who were being instructed at home, scored higher or above average on standardized tests. The Court in fact said at one point that the "Riddles did an excellent job—possibly better than the public schools could do." *Id.*, at 361. But then at the conclusion of the opinion, the Court, after denying the Riddle's claim, said that noncompliance with state laws "leads ineluctably to a hideous result." To exempt parents from state law would mean they could keep "their children in medieval ignorance, quarter them in Dickensian squalor." *Id.*, at 366-67.

79. In State v. Whisner, 47 Ohio St. 2d 181, 351 N.E. 2d 750 (1976), relying on Wisconsin v. Yoder, the Ohio Supreme Court agreed to grant an exemption to a complex and extensive system of state regulation that the court said had the effect of obliterating the philosophy of the school and imposing that of the state. *Id.*, at 770. The court also agreed that these regulations infringed the parent's traditional right to control the upbringing of his child. "The expert testimony received in this regard unequivocally demonstrates the absolute suffocation of independent thought and educational policy, and the effective retardation of religious philosophy engendered by application of these 'minimum standards' to non-public educational institutions." *Id.*, at 768-70. *See also*

State ex. rel. Nagel v. Olin, 64 Ohio St. 2d 341, 415 N.E. 2d 279 (1980) (granting an Amish parent an exemption to the same regulations discussed in *Whisner* that the state had not yet amended). *See* Kentucky State Board v. Rudasill, 589 S.W. 2d 877 (Ky. 1979), *cert. denied,* 100 S. Ct. 2158 (1980) (striking down under the Kentucky State Constitution a number of state requirements governing the curriculum including that textbooks be approved by the state).

80. Forest Hills Early Learning Center, Inc. v. Lukhard, 728 F.2d 230 (4th Cir. 1984); Arkansas Day Care Ass'n, Inc. v. Clinton, 577 F. Sup. 388 (1983). *See also* State Fire Marshall v. Lee, 101 Mich. App. 829, 300 N.W.2d 748 (Mich. Ct. App. 1981) (upholding, in part, safety regulations in the face of a constitutional challenge). Zoning regulations have traditionally been upheld. *See, e.g.,* Congregation Beth Yitzchok v. Town of Ramapo, 593 F. Supp. 655 (S.D. N.Y. 1984) (denial of preliminary injunction to stop enforcement of town code that was used to prohibit opening of a Jewish school for children ages three to five in a house purchased for a parsonage and synagogue).

Professor Tribe suggests that voluntary accommodation of religion should be held to be permissible if it's "arguably compelled" by the free exercise clause. Tribe, *American Constitutional Law, supra,* note 12, at 822. The court in *Lukhard* imposed a tougher standard on the state: the state was required to show that as a matter of law the regulations from which the church-sponsored facilities were exempted violated their free exercise rights. Forest Hills Early Learning Center, Inc. v. Lukhard at 242.

81. The federal district court in Catholic High School Ass'n of Archdiocese v. Culvert, 573 F. Supp. 1550 (S.D. N.Y., 1983) held that extension of jurisdiction of the state labor board over labor relations in private religious schools creates a threat of excessive church-state entanglement in violation of the establishment clause. But the Second Circuit Court of Appeals reversed, 753 F.2d 1161 (2d Cir. 1985). In contrast to the lower court, the circuit court concluded that extending labor board jurisdiction did not cause excessive entanglement of church and state because the board's supervision of the collective-bargaining process was neither comprehensive nor continuing, and that requiring the school to bargain in good faith did not involve the government compelling the parties to agree on specific terms. The Supreme Court avoided deciding this issue when it interpreted the National Labor Relations Act as not giving the National Labor Relations Board jurisdiction over private schools. N.L.R.B. v. Catholic Bishop of Chicago, 440 U.S. 490 (1979). *See also* Universidad Central de Bayamon v. N.L.R.B., 778 F.2d 906 (1st Cir. 1985).

82. Wolman v. Charles City Comm. Sch. Bd. of Educ., 368 N.W.2d 74, 84 (1977) (citations omitted).

83. Sheridan Rd. Baptist Church, 132 Mich. 1, 348 N.W.2d 263 (Mich. App. 1984); New Jersey State Bd. of Higher Educ. v. Shelton College, 90 N.J. 470, 448 A.2d 988 (1982); Attorney General v. Bailey, 386 Mass. 367, 436 N.E.2d 139 (1982).

84. Donovan v. Shenandoah Baptist Church, 573 F. Supp. 320 (W.D. Va. 1983); Marshall v. First Baptist Church, 23 BNA Wage and Hour Cases 386 (D.C.S.C. 1977). *See also* Archbishop of the Roman Catholic Apostolic Archdiocese of San Juan v. Guardiola, 628 F. Supp. 1173 (D. Puerto Rico, 1985) (enforcement of minimum wage law as to a church's lay employees).

85. Title VII, 42 U.S. §2000e-2a (1982) (prohibiting discrimination in employment on the basis of race, gender, national origin, and religion). Title VII, however, expressly permits discrimination in hiring on the basis of religion by certain schools: "It shall not be unlawful employment practice for a school, college, university, or other educational institution or institution of learning to hire and employ employees of a particular religion if such school, college, university, or other educational institution or institution of learning is, in whole or in substantial part, owned, supported, controlled, or managed by a particular religion, or by a particular religious corporation, association, or society." 42 U.S.C. 2000e-2(e)(2) (1982).

See also Civil Rights Act of 1964, Title IX, 42 U.S.C. §2000c,d (1982) (prohibiting discrimination on the basis of race in federally assisted programs); Title IX, 20 U.S.C. §1681 (1982) (prohibiting discrimination on the basis of gender in federally assisted programs); Rehabilitation Act of 1973 (§504), 29 U.S.C. §794 (1982) (prohibiting discrimination on the basis of handicap in federally assisted programs); Age Discrimination in Employment Act of 1967, as amended 1978, 29 U.S.C. §621 (1982) (prohibiting discrimination in employment on the basis of age for people between the ages of 40 and 70); Equal Pay Act of 1963, 29 U.S.C. 206(d)(1982) (prohibiting discrimination in pay on the basis of sex or jobs that require equal skill, effort, responsibility, and that are performed under similar working conditions).

86. It is theoretically important to note that, though the Supreme Court has unequivocally stated that purposeful racial discrimination by government is unconstitutional (Brown v. Bd. of Educ., 347 U.S. 483 (1954)), it has never said that government has an affirmative constitutional duty to prohibit racial discrimination by private employers and others, though forceful arguments interpreting the Constitution in this way have been made. C.L. Black, "Foreword: 'State Action,' Equal Protection and California's Proposition 14," Harvard Law Review 81 (1967): 69. The Court has taken steps to prohibit government from encouraging private, i.e., nongovernmental, discrimination. Reitman v. Mulkey, 387 U.S. 369 (1967).

87. Roberts v. United States Jaycees, 104 U.S. 3244 (1984).

88. Wisconsin v. Yoder, 406 U.S. 205 (1972); Pierce v. Society of Sisters, 268 U.S. 510 (1925); Meyer v. Nebraska, 262 U.S. 390 (1923).

89. See, e.g., Zablocki v. Redhail, 434 U.S. 374 (1978); Moore v. City of East Cleveland, 431 U.S. 494 (1977) (plurality opinion).

90. Roberts v. United States Jaycees, at 473.

91. Id., at 474. The Court noted that the Jaycees were neither small nor selective, and much of the central activity of the organization involved the participation of strangers.

92. 427 U.S. 160 (1976).

93. 427 U.S. 160 (1976). The statute involved in 42 U.S.C. §1981 says, in part, that all persons shall have the same right to make and enforce contracts as is enjoyed by white citizens.

94. The Court also concluded that the state had a strong interest in eliminating barriers to the economic, social, and political advancement of women. Assuring women access to the kinds of services, training, and other benefits provided by the Jaycees was instrumental to that end. Id., at 476-78.

95. 461 U.S. 574, (1983). Bob Jones University prohibited interracial dating and marriage as well as the advocacy of interracial marriage. Goldsboro Christian Schools discriminated on the basis of race in admissions.

See also EEOC v. Mississippi College, 626 F.2d 477 (5th Cir. 1980), cert. denied, 453 U.S. 912 (1981); and EEOC v. Southwestern Baptist Theological Seminary, 651 F.2d 277 (5th Cir. 1981), cert. denied, 456 U.S. 905 (1982), both denying exemptions to Title VII.

96. Fiedler v. Marumsco Christian Sch., 631 F.2d 114 (4th Cir., 1980) (suit brought under §1981 by two students expelled from private religious school for interracial dating; Brown v. Dade Christian Schools, Inc., 556 F.2d 310 (5th Cir. 1977) (en banc), cert. denied, 434 U.S. 1063 (1978) (plurality opinion declined to reach issue of constitutionality of application of §1981 because of substantial evidence the policy of segregation was not the exercise of religion).

97. E.E.O.C. v. Mississippi College, 626 F.2d 477 (5th Cir. 1980). See also E.E.O.C. v. Southwestern Baptist Theological Seminary, 651 F.2d 277 (5th Cir. 1981); E.E.O.C. v. Fremont Christian Sch., 609 F. Supp. 344 (N.D. Cal. 1984).

It is important to note that religious educational institutions are, among others, specifically exempted from Title VII with respect to the employment of individuals of a particular religion in order to perform work connected with the carrying on by the institution of its activities. 42 U.S.C. §2000e-2(e)(2) (1982). This exemption has been construed to permit religious schools to discriminate on the basis of religion with respect to employees who are carrying out the religious work of the employer. E.E.O.C. v. Mississippi College. See also Maguire v. Marquette University, 627 F. Supp. 1499 (E.D. Wis. 1986), aff'd, 781 F.2d 1362 (9th Cir. 1986).

98. Dayton Christian Schools v. Ohio Civil Rights Com'n, 766 F.2d 932 (6th Cir. 1985), *rev'd on other grounds sub nom.*, Ohio Civil Rights Commission v. Dayton Christian Schools, 106 S. Ct. 2718(1986). The plaintiff in the case claimed that the policy requiring mothers to be home with their preschool children was discriminatory on the basis of gender. She was also not rehired because she consulted an attorney, a failure to follow the school's "Biblical Chain-of-Command."

99. In reaching this conclusion the court relied on the testimony of school officials. *Id.*, at 936-40. The court also concluded that the theory of the "Biblical Chain-of-Command" was also a religiously based doctrine.

100. State interference with the employment policy of the school affected its ability to provide students with the appropriate role-models. "[T]he congregations and parents are faced essentially with either supporting a school staffed by faculty who flout basic tenets of their religion or abandoning their support of Christian education altogether. The burden on the parent's exercise of religion is particularly onerous in light of the heightened parental interest in their children's education." *Id.*, at 952.

101. Id., at 953-54.

102. Id., at 954.

103. Id., at 955.

104. Id., at 960. In a footnote the court expressed its disagreement with the conclusion of the Second Circuit that the first amendment did not prohibit New York State's labor relations board from exercising jurisdiction over labor relations in private religious schools. Catholic High Sch. Ass'n of New York v. Culvert, 753 F.2d 1161 (2d Cir. 1985).

105. Id., at 958.

106. Id., at 960.

107. Id., at 958.

108. 627 F. Supp. 1499 (E.D. Wis. 1986).

109. Id., at 1506.

110. Scoma v. Chicago Bd. of Educ., 391 F.Supp. 452 (N.D. Ill. 1974); In Matter of Franz, 55 A.D.2d 424, 390 N.Y.S.2d 940 (A.D. 1977).

111. Hanson v. Cushman, 490 F. Supp. 109 (W.D. Mich. 1980); People v. Turner, 121 Cal. App. 2d Supp. 861, 263 P.2d 685 (1985), *appeal dismissed*, 347 U.S. 972 (1954). In Jernigan v. State, 412 So.2d 1242 (Ala. Crim. App.), *cert. denied*, No. 81-481 (Ala. 1982), the court concluded the certification requirement did not infringe their religious values and that the program of instruction was not an adequate substitute for the public school program in preparing the children for life in modern society.

112. State v. Bowman, 653 P.2d 254 (Or. 1982). *See also* State v. Riddle, 285 S.E.2d 359 (Sup. Ct. Apps. W. Va, 1981) (free exercise challenge rejected); State v. McDonough, 468 A.2d 977 (Me. 1983).

113. *See, e.g.*, State v. Moorehead, 368 N.W.2d 60 (Iowa 1981) (interpreting a state statute as imposing on the parents the burden of producing sufficient evidence that their program of instruction is "equivalent instruction by a certified teacher" in order to qualify for the exemption to the compulsory education law); People v. Levisen, 404 Ill. 574, 90 N.E.2d 213 (Ill. 1950) (imposing on parents the burden of proof that a plan of home instruction qualifies as a private school); *In re* Falk, 110 Misc. 2d 104, 441 N.Y.S.2d 785 (Fam. Ct. 1981). *But see* State v. Davis, 598 S.W.2d 189 (Mo. Ct. App. 1981) (imposing the burden on the state to establish that parents did not provide their children with a program of instruction substantially equivalent to that in the public schools); Sheppard v. State, 306 P.2d 346 (Okla. Crim. App. 1957); Wright v. State, 21 Okla. Crim 430, 209 P. 179 (1922) (both imposing the burden on the state to prove beyond a reasonable doubt that the children were not receiving an equivalent education).

In New Jersey the burden of proof is divided between parent and state. The state has the initial burden of alleging a violation of the compulsory attendance law. The burden then shifts to the parents to introduce evidence that their program meets the statutory requirements. The ultimate burden of persuasion rests with the state to establish that the parents are not in compliance. State v. Vaughn, 44 N.J. 142, 207 A.2d 537 (1965); State v. Massa, 95 N.J. Super. 382, 231 A.2d 252 (Morris Ct. 1967).

114. 391 F. Supp. 452, 462 (N.D. Ill. 1974).

115. The court also justified the shift in the burden of proof against a due process challenge on the grounds that home instruction was an exception to the basic statutory requirement, and that the burden of proof may permissibly shift when a law sets forth an exception that is not part of a crime, but operates to prevent an act otherwise included from being a crime. 391 F. Supp. at 462.

116. State v. Buchner, 472 So.2d 1228 (Fla. App. 2 Dist. 1985); Burrow v. State, 669 S.W.2d 441 (Ark. 1984); State v. White, 325 N.W.2d 76 (Wis. 1982); State v. Bowman, 653 P.2d 254 (Or. 1982); contra., State v. Popanz, 112 Wis. 2d 166, 332 N.W.2d 750 (Wis. 1983); Roemhild v. State, 308 S.E.2d 154 (Ga. 1983).

117. Mazanec v. North Judson-San Pierre Sch. Corp., 763 F.2d 845 (7th Cir. 1985) (the term "equivalent" is not vague); Braintree Baptist Temple v. Holbrook Pub. Schools, 616 F. Supp. 81 (D.C. Mass. 1984) (a requirement that the private school program equals in "thoroughness and efficiency" that in public schools is not vague); State v. Moorehead, 308 N.W.2d 60 (Iowa 1981) ("equivalent instruction" not vague); contra., Ellis v. O'Hara, 612 F. Supp. 379 (D.C. Mo. 1985) ("substantially equivalent" unconstitutionally vague); State v. Newstrom, 371 N.W.2d 525 (Minn. 1985) (the requirement that pupils be taught by teachers "whose qualifications are essentially equivalent to the minimum standards for public school teachers of the same grades or subjects" is vague).

118. The political aspects of the effort to aid private religious schools is taken up in such works as these: Richard Morgan, The Politics of Religious Conflict: Church and State in America (New York: Pegasus, 1968); Frank J. Munger and Richard F. Fenno, Jr., National Politics and Federal Aid to Education (Syracuse: Syracuse University Press, 1962); Sidney W. Tiedt, The Role of the Federal Government in Education (New York: Oxford University Press, 1966); Gilbert Elliott Smith, The Limits of Reform: Politics and Federal Aid to Education (New York: Garland, 1982).

119. Leo Pfeffer, "The Case for Separation," in Religion in America, ed. John Cogley (New York: Meridian Books, Inc., 1958), 52, 60. Leo Pfeffer is perhaps the foremost exponent of the separationist theory. His other works include God, Caesar, and the Constitution (Boston: Beacon Press, 1975); Church, State and Freedom, rev. ed. (Boston: Beacon Press, 1967); and Religion, State and the Burger Court (Buffalo, N.Y.: Prometheus Books, 1984).

It was Thomas Jefferson who first said that the religion clauses of the first amendment were intended to "erect a wall of separation between church and state," a phrase that has become so well known that many erroneously believe it appears in the first amendment itself. The phrase appears in a letter of Jefferson's refusing a request of a Baptist association for a day to be established for fasting and prayer in thanksgiving for the nation's welfare. See Saul Padover, The Complete Jefferson (New York: Duell, Sloan and Pearce, Inc., 1943), 518-19.

James Madison's views are perhaps best captured in a letter written after the adoption of the first amendment. "The tendency to a usurpation on one side or the other, or to a corrupting coalition or alliance between them, will be best guarded agst. by an entire abstinence of the Govt. from interference in any way whatever, beyond the necessity of preserving public order & protecting each sect agst. trespasses on its legal rights by others." Everson v. Board of Education, 330 U.S. 1, 40, n.28 (1947) (Rutledge, J., dissenting). Equally as important is Madison's "Memorial and Remonstrance Against Religious Assessments" of 1785, reprinted as an appendix to Justice Rutledge's dissenting opinion.

There has been a considerable body of scholarship attempting to interpret these and other writings of the period with no clear resolution of the issues. Donald A. Gianella, "Religious

Liberty, Nonestablishment, and Doctrinal Development—Part II. The Nonestablishment Principle," *Harvard Law Review* 81 (1968): 13, 516.

120. Tribe, *American Constitutional Law, supra,* note 12, at 819.

121. A less extreme version stresses that only direct aid is to be prohibited. Paul G. Kauper, *Religion and the Constitution* (Baton Rouge, La.: Louisiana State University Press, 1964), 62-63.

122. Bd. of Educ. v. Allen, 392 U.S. 236, 249 (1968) (Harlan, J., concurring).

123. Philip B. Kurland, *Religion and the Law* (Chicago: Aldine Publishing Co., 1962), 18.

124. Tribe, *American Constitutional Law,* 820, 821.

125. Wilbur G. Katz, *Religion and American Constitutions* (Evanston, Ill: Northwestern University Press, 1964), 13, 21, 22.

126. The first amendment by its own terms says "*Congress* shall make no law respecting an establishment of religion, or prohibiting the free exercise thereof." (emphasis added). It is argued that the original intention of this amendment was to restrict only Congress and to leave the states free of the restrictions imposed in the amendment; thus, the Court's decisions to extend the free exercise and establishment clauses to the states in 1940 and 1947 were wrong. Cantwell v. Conn., 310 U.S. 296 (1940); Everson v. Bd. of Educ. of Ewing Township, 330 U.S. 1 (1947). Under this same view even Congress would be permitted to aid *all* religions *equally* so long as it did not evidence a preference for one religion. Robert L. Cord, *Separation of Church and State* (New York: Lambeth Press, 1982). For a different view of that history see Everson v. Board of Education, 330 U.S. 1, 28 (1947) (Rutledge, J., dissenting).

The question of the framers' intent has been extensively explored by many commentators without definitive results. Justice Brennan has concluded that "too literal [a] quest for the advice of the Founding Fathers" is often futile. Abington Sch. Dist. v. Schemmp, 374 U.S. 203, 237 (1963) (Brennan J., concurring). Professor Tribe has written, "The historical record is ambiguous, and many of today's problems were of course never envisioned by any of the Framers. Under these circumstances one can only examine human values and historical purposes underlying the religion clauses to decide what doctrinal framework might best realize those values and purposes today." Tribe, *American Constitutional Law, supra,* note 12, at 816.

127. 330 U.S. 1 (1947). For a brief summary of those debates, see Diane Ravitch, *The Troubled Crusade: American Education 1945-1980* (New York: Basic Books, Inc., 1983), chap. 1, and the materials cited in note 112, *supra.*

128. Ewing Township acted pursuant to a state law that permitted provision of transportation to children attending public schools and any private schools except those operated for profit. Under the township's policy reimbursement only went to public school parents and parents sending their children to Catholic schools. The majority opinion avoided dealing with the dissenters' argument that the policy of the township used a religious test to determine who were the beneficiaries. 330 U.S., at 25 (Jackson, J., dissenting). Justice Black writing for the majority merely said there was no evidence there were children who would have gone to a school other than the public and Catholic schools. 330 U.S., at 4, n.2.

129. 330 U.S., at 19 (Jackson, J., dissenting). Jackson's observation is most aptly directed to the following passage from Justice Black's opinion: "The First Amendment has erected a wall between church and state. That wall must be kept high and impregnable. We could not approve of the slightest breach. New Jersey has not breached it here." 330 U.S., at 18.

130. The furnishing of fire and police protection "are matters of common right, part of the general need for safety. . . . The First Amendment does not exclude religious property or activities from protection against disorder or ordinary accidental incidents of community life. It forbids support, not protection from interference or destruction." 330 U.S., at 60-61, n.56 (Rutledge, J., dissenting).

131. Justice Black's verge comment appears at 330 U.S., at 16. The possibility of an expansive reading of the case is commented on by Pfeffer. Leo Pfeffer, *God, Caesar, and the Constitution, supra,* note 119 at 269. Justice Rutledge is reported to have been concerned about this, according to the notes of Justice Murphy on the conference among the justices on the case. Rutledge is

quoted by Murphy to have said: "First it has been books, now buses, next churches and teachers. Every religious institution in [the] country will be reaching into [the] hopper for help if you sustain this. We ought to stop this thing at [the] threshold of [the] public school." Quoted in Henry J. Abraham, *Freedom and the Court: Civil Rights and Liberties in the United States*, 4th ed. (New York: Oxford University Press, 1982), 263.

132. Ravitch, *The Troubled Crusade, supra*, note 127, at 29-32.

133. 333 U.S. 203 (1948).

134. 333 U.S., at 212.

135. 333 U.S., at 211.

136. 333 U.S., at 256 (Reed, J., dissenting).

137. 333 U.S., at 238, 252, 255.

138. For one review of this period see David Caute, *The Great Fear: The Anti-Communist Purge Under Truman and Eisenhower* (New York: Simon and Schuster, 1978).

139. 343 U.S. 306 (1952). Justice Black took note of the extensive commentary on the *McCollum* opinion in his *Zorach* dissent. "Probably few opinions from this Court in recent years have attracted more attention or stirred wider debate." 343 U.S., at 317 (Black, J., dissenting).

140. 343 U.S., at 312.

141. 343 U.S., at 314.

142. 343 U.S., at 313-14.

143. 343 U.S., at 325 (Jackson, J., dissenting). The dissenters stressed that the use of the compulsory education law to get attendants, who might not have been enthusiastic about attending religious instruction, was use of the machinery of the state both in *McCollum* and *Zorach* in aid of religion.

144. Tribe, *American Constitutional Law, supra*, note 12, at 824.

145. Robert B. McCloskey, *The Modern Supreme Court* (Cambridge, Mass.: Harvard University Press, 1972), 96.

146. Engel v. Vitale, 370 U.S. 421 (1962); Abington Sch. Dist. v. Schempp, 374 U.S. 203 (1963).

147. *See* infra, chap. 5.

148. Abington Sch. Dist. v. Schempp, 374 U.S. 203, 222 (1963) (emphasis added).

149. Board of Education v. Allen, 392 U.S. 236 (1968).

150. 392 U.S., at 248 and 262 (Douglas, J., dissenting).

151. 392 U.S., at 252-53 (Black, J., dissenting).

152. 20 U.S.C. §241a et. seq. Effective October 1, 1982 Title I was superseded by chapter 1 of the Education Consolidation and Improvement Act of 1981, 20 U.S.C. §3801 et. seq. that incorporated by reference many sections of Title I and includes almost identical provisions concerning the participation of nonpublic school students. In Wheeler v. Barrera, 417 U.S. 402 (1974), the Court sidestepped the issue of whether this Title I requirement was constitutional; but in Aguilar v. Felton, 105 S. Ct. 3232 (1985), the Supreme Court concluded that the provision of such aid to educationally deprived students in private religious schools was unconstitutional. The case will be discussed at greater length at the conclusion of this section.

153. Nixon's appointees included Warren E. Burger, Harry A. Blackmun, Lewis F. Powell, Jr., and William H. Rehnquist. They replaced Earl Warren, John Marshall Harlan, Abe Fortas, and Hugo Black. Nixon was upset with the Warren Court for its decisions in a number of areas, most notably the rights of the criminally accused and busing. James F. Simon, *In His Own Image* (New York: David Mckay Company, Inc., 1973).

154. 397 U.S. 664 (1970).

155. 397 U.S., at 674.

156. Id.

157. Id., at 709.

158. Id., at 675.

159. 403 U.S. 602 (1971).

160. 403 U.S. 602 (1971) (decided with *Lemon* in one opinion).

161. 403 U.S. 672 (1971).

162. 602 U.S., at 613.

163. Id., at 619, Professor Gianella comments, "It is clear that a state cannot insure the constitutionality of an aid program by omitting all administrative controls designed to exclude religion." Donald A. Gianella, "Lemon and Tilton: The Bitter and the Sweet of Church-State Entanglement," in *1971 Supreme Court Review,* ed. Philip B. Kurland (Chicago: University of Chicago Press, 1972), 147, 164.

164. Id., at 621-22.

165. Id., at 622-23.

166. 403 U.S. 672, 679. The twenty-year provision was struck down. If the building were converted to a chapel after the twenty-year limitation were over, Justice Burger reasoned, the grant would have had the effect of advancing religion—the structure must be assumed to have value after twenty-years. *Id.,* at 683.

167. Id., at 679, 681-82.

168. Id., at 681-82.

169. Id., at 686.

170. Justice Burger also argued that in *Lemon* and *DiCenso* teachers were subsidized; and, since teachers are not necessarily religiously neutral, greater surveillance would be needed to assure that there would be no subsidization of religious instruction. *Id.,* at 687-88. This is a silly argument since subsidizing buildings where religious instruction might take place also would be a subsidization of such instruction.

He argued that this one-time, single-purpose grant meant there would not be the annual audits that were involved in *Lemon/DiCenso. Id.,* at 688. This argument also overlooks the problem that surveillance may be needed to see how the buildings are in fact used.

171. Richard E. Morgan, "The Establishment Clause and Sectarian Schools: A Final Installment?" in *Church and State: The Supreme Court and the First Amendment,* ed. Philip B. Kurland, (Chicago: University of Chicago Press, 1975), 232.

172. Justice O'Connor replaced the retiring Justice Stewart, who seemed to take a position midway between the separationists and the accommodationists on the Court. *See, e.g.,* Wolman v. Walter, 433 U.S. 229 (1977). As we shall see, Justice O'Connor is not completely in Justice Burger's camp. *See,* infra, discussion of Grand Rapids Sch. Dist. v. Ball, 105 S. Ct. 3216 (1985). In September, 1986, Antonin Scalia joined the Court to take the seat held by retired Chief Justice Burger. See *infra,* chap. 10.

173. Stewart voted with Blackmun in Wolman v. Walter, 433 U.S. 229 (1977), which affirmed the constitutionality of the loan of textbooks and the provision of certain services, but struck down the loan of instructional materials and equipment and the subsidization of transportation for field trips. Blackmun and Stewart parted company in Committee for Public Education v. Regan, 444 U.S. 646 (1980), in which Stewart's vote was crucial in making up a five-man majority upholding direct grants to private schools to pay for the costs of administering and scoring tests and keeping attendance records. (Stewart retired in July, 1981.) Blackmun dissented, along with Justices Marshall, Brennan, and Stevens, from the decision upholding Minnesota's tuition tax-deduction system. Mueller v. Allen, 103 S. Ct. 3062 (1983). Justice Stewart's replacement, Justice O'Connor, voted with the majority in *Mueller.*

174. Justice Powell seems to have shifted his position on tuition tax credits and deductions. In 1973 he wrote the majority opinion in Committee for Public Education v. Nyquist, 413 U.S. 756 (1973), striking down New York State's system of tax deductions for parents sending their children to private schools. In 1983 he voted with the majority to uphold Minnesota's tax deduction system that varied in some respects from New York's. Mueller v. Allen, 463 U.S. 388 (1983).

175. Justice O'Connor has been especially vocal in her criticism of the entanglement test. Aguilar v. Felton, 87 L. Ed.2d 290, 305 (1985) (O'Connor, J., dissenting).

176. Wolman v. Walter, 433 U.S. 229 (1977); Meek v. Pittenger, 421 U.S. 349 (1975).

177. Wolman v. Walter, 433 U.S. 229 (1977); Meek v. Pittenger, 421 U.S. 349 (1975).

178. Wolman v. Walter, 433 U.S. 229, 251., n. 18 (1977).

179. Grand Rapids Sch. Dist. v. Ball, 105 S. Ct. 3216 (1985).

180. Id. Chief Justice Burger, and Justices Rehnquist, Powell, and White dissented in separate opinions.

181. Grand Rapids Sch. Dist. v. Ball, 105 S. Ct. 3216 (1985).

182. Committee for Public Education v. Nyquist, 413 U.S. 756 (1973). The Court found that the statute failed the primary effect test.

183. Levitt v. Committee for Public Education, 413 U.S. 472 (1973).

184. Wolman v. Walter, 433 U.S. 229 (1977); Committee for Public Education and Rel. Lib. v. Regan, 444 U.S. 646 (1980).

185. Meek v. Pittenger, 421 U.S. 349 (1975).

186. Wolman v. Walter, 433 U.S. 229 (1977). Justice Brennan was the sole dissenter on the issue of the provision of therapeutic and diagnostic services.

187. Grand Rapids Sch. Dist. v. Ball, 105 S. Ct. 3216 (1985).

188. Aguilar v. Felton, 105 S. Ct. 3232 (1985).

189. Grand Rapids Sch. Dist. v. Ball, 105 S. Ct. 3216 (1985).

190. Committee for Public Education v. Nyquist, 413 U.S. 756 (1973). See also Sloan v. Lemon, 413 U.S. 825 (1973) (striking down a similar tuition reimbursement plan in Pennsylvania).

191. Id.

192. Mueller v. Allen, 103 S. Ct. 3062 (1983).

193. Witters v. Washington Department Services for the Blind, 106 S. Ct. 748 (1986).

194. Hunt v. McNair, 413 U.S. 734 (1973).

195. 426 U.S. 736 (1976).

196. Mueller v. Allen, 463 U.S. 388 (1983). See also Lynch v. Donnelly, 104 S. Ct. 1355 (1984) (upholding the city of Pawtucket's paying for a Nativity scene as part of its annual Christmas display); Marsh v. Chambers, 463 U.S. 783 (1983) (upholding state legislature's practice of opening each legislative day with a prayer by a chaplain paid by the state).

197. Committee for Public Education v. Regan, 444 U.S. 646, 661 (1980).

198. Mueller v. Allen, 463 U.S. 388 (1983).

199. Wolman v. Walter, 433 U.S. 229, 263 (1977) (Powell, J., concurring in the judgment in part and dissenting in part); and quoted with approval in the majority opinion in Mueller v. Allen, 463 U.S. 388, 400 (1983).

200. Justice O'Connor has in fact called for the elimination of the political divisiveness test as an independent test of constitutionality. Lynch v. Donnelly, 465 U.S. 668, 689 (1984) (O'Connor, J., concurring).

201. Committee for Public Education v. Regan, 444 U.S. 646 (1980); Roemer v. Maryland Public Works Bd., 426 U.S. 736 (1976); Mueller v. Allen, 463 U.S. 388 (1983).

202. Roemer v. Maryland Public Works Bd., 426 U.S. 736, 768 (1976) (White, J., with whom Justice Rehnquist joins, concurring in judgment).

203. Committee for Public Education v. Regan, 444 U.S. 646, 662 (1980).

204. Committee for Public Education v. Regan, 444 U.S. 646, 662, 671 (1980) (Blackmun, J., with whom Brennan, J., and Marshall, J., join, dissenting; Stevens, J., dissenting); Roemer v. Maryland Public Works Bd., 426 U.S. 736, 770, 775 (1976) (Brennan, J., with whom Marshall, J., joins, dissenting; Stevens, J., dissenting).

205. Lynch v. Donnelly, 465 S. Ct. 681 669 (1984) (Brennan, J., with whom Marshall, J., Blackmun, J., and Stevens, J., join, dissenting).

206. Wolman v. Walter, 433 U.S. 229, 257, 265 (1977) (Marshall, J., dissenting; Stevens, J.,

dissenting). Justice Stevens would also overrule *Everson,* the bus transportation case.

207. Aguilar v. Felton, 105 S. Ct. 3232, 3239 (1985) (Powell, J., concurring).

208. Id., Wolman v. Walter, 433 S. Ct. 229 (1977).

209. Wolman v. Walter, 433 U.S. 229 (1977).

210. Committee for Public Educ. v. Regan, 444 U.S. 646 (1980). The majority, whom Powell joined, stressed that if assistance in carrying out these state-mandated tests could be provided "in-kind" by the state hiring people to do the grading for the private school, it could also do so by providing payments in cash to do the work. Blackmun, however, stressed in his dissenting opinion that this was a direct cash payment to the schools and ran the risk of advancing religion.

211. Mueller v. Allen, 463 U.S. 388 (1983).

212. Norwood v. Harrison, 413 U.S. 455 (1973) (Douglas, J., and Brennan, J., concurred in the result).

213. Id., at 465, 466.

214. Id., at 466-67. In a later case the Court took the position that the equal protection clause could only be violated by state action that had the *purpose* to discriminate, thus leaving the status of the Norwood decision somewhat in doubt. Washington v. Davis, 426 U.S. 334 (1976).

215. Id., at 469-70.

2

Change in the System of Governance of the Public Schools

2.1. INTRODUCTION

A discussion of the governing system of public education can proceed down either of two tracks: one can describe and analyze the institutions, participants, processes, and dynamics of that system; or one can discuss the legal framework of the system and those legal developments that have been both a cause and an effect of the actual operation of the system.[1] Though this chapter will concentrate on assessing the legal framework and associated doctrines and principles, it is useful to keep in mind that the system in practice has dramatically changed over the years. These changes have taken a variety of forms, including the expansion of state control of local school districts, the expansion of federal influence and control over both states and local districts, significant changes in the governing structures of big-city school districts, the rise of teacher unionism and collective bargaining, and the increase of minority involvement in the politics and governance of local school districts.[2] Accompanying these changes has been a lively debate over their effects. Has or has not federal involvement in education improved the learning achievement of minority students? Has the expansion of federal power meant the loss of state and local power, or is this not a zero-sum game, i.e., has federal expansion also expanded state and local influences on education? What form ought federal involvement in education to take? Is collective bargaining by public school teachers inconsistent with democratic control of education, and/or does it distort the normal political process to the advantage of the teachers?

At the same time as the system in operation has changed, certain aspects of the legal framework itself also changed, and it is these changes that will be explored here. The analysis begins with an assessment of the legal authority of the state because the state is, in constitutional theory, the one unit of government that enjoys inherent and plenary power over education.[3] The state's legal authority will be assessed with special reference to the control of the local school district. With the central place of the states and their control of local school districts in mind, the chapter turns to an assessment of the legal place of the federal government and the evolution of legal doctrine that has accompanied the increase in federal influence over state and local educational efforts. The last four sections of the chapter turn to reforms that are specifically directed to changing the decision-making processes of the local school district.

Two themes stand out in these legal developments. The judiciary has not stood in the way of increased federal and state control of education, but has instead recognized the constitutional permissibility of involvement, especially federal, in education. Simultaneously, as legal doctrine has served to allow increased centralization of the educational system, it has also served the interests of those seeking to expand the range of participants in local education decision-making. Thus, legal doctrine, by permitting an expanded role for the federal and state government and by expanding the number of participants in decision-making at the local level, has made possible the emergence of a new, more complex, and intricate decision-making process in education.[4]

2.2. THE STATE LEGISLATURE: CONTROL OF STATE AND LOCAL EDUCATIONAL AGENCIES

Though the federal government is in theory a government of delegated, enumerated, and limited powers, state governmental authority is inherent, not enumerated but plenary, and limited only by such external checks as the civil rights and liberties protected by the U.S. and state constitutions. States derive their authority from the tenth amendment to the Constitution that reads as follows: "The powers not delegated to the United States by the Constitution, nor prohibited by it to the States, are reserved to the States respectively, or to the people." State power over education is part of the states' sovereign police powers that repose in and are exercised by the state legislature.[5] Abundant judicial opinions support the proposition that it is the state legislature that enjoys the preeminent authority to control public elementary, secondary, and higher education in the state by setting up a system of public educational institutions and arranging for its financing and regulation.[6] It is important to stress that while the federal Constitution assumes state authority over education, it does not impose an affirmative obligation on the states to establish a public school system; however, the people of all states, except Connecticut have, through the states' own constitutions, imposed just such a duty.[7]

State legislatures have chosen to exercise their authority by setting up organizational structures of public education that fall into three patterns. The most unique is the single statewide system in Hawaii; seventeen other states have a two-tiered state-local system; and the rest have a three-layered system consisting of state agencies, intermediate units, and local districts.[8] The degree to which unfettered authority is delegated to local school districts varies across the states. A variegated pattern exists ranging from the not fully centralized to the not fully decentralized.[9] These differences will be described in greater detail later.

The extent of legislature authority over education is reflected in the fact that in most states the authority of the state boards of education (both those concerned with higher education and those concerned with elementary-secondary education), the chief state school officer, and the department of education depends on what authority has been delegated to them by the legislature.[10] The authority of these state agencies is perhaps best summarized by Remmlein:

> In any phase of school management wherein the state board of education has been given powers of operation, the rules and regulations of the state board have the force and effect of law. However, being a creature of the legislature in most states, the state board has only the powers delegated to it or implied in the delegated powers. In the states where the state board is created by constitutional provision, its constitutional powers are very general, and in specific instances it depends upon the legislature for its authority to act. In either case, if the state board acts outside its delegated or implied power, the rule or regulation is void. There is, however, a presumption of authority, and until challenged in court, all rules and regulations of the board are presumed to be valid and have effectiveness as enforceable as a statute enacted by the legislature.[11]

A central issue that emerges from this is the question of to what extent may the legislature delegate authority to the state board and chief state school officer. The rule here is easy to state but more difficult to apply: the legislature may not constitutionally delegate "legislative power" to other agencies but may delegate administrative power to "fill in the details."[12] In theory, the way to settle whether a claim of unconstitutional delegation of authority is justified is to determine if a grant of authority is accompanied by sufficient standards for the guidance of the agency's discretion: the absence of standards to guide the exercise of discretion is suggestive of the fact that legislative power to make basic policy choices has been improperly delegated.[13] While this doctrine has been used from time to time to strike down legislation, it is today viewed as a "flexible doctrine" that in fact has little bite. Courts seem to have recognized the necessity for the legislature to delegate important discretion to other agencies of government, the impracticality and meaninglessness of demanding an extensive list of standards in areas that require expertise, and that legislatures cannot answer all policy questions in advance.[14] Thus, today, state boards and chief state school officers have authority to regulate a variety of matters including: teacher certification, minimum educational standards, the course of study, textbook selection (in some states), the behavior of school board members, the dismissal of teachers and the disciplining of students (chief state school officers in some states), the promotion of racial integration, and consolidation and reorganization of school districts.[15]

Even though the delegation doctrine no longer provides a promising legal route to attack the state boards of education and chief state school officers, the exercise of state authority has been subject to numerous other constitutional and nonconstitutional challenges. In *Miller v. Board of Education*[16] the Supreme Court of Kansas upheld the authority of the state board of education to issue regulations even without specific legislative authorization to do so. Said the court, the Kansas constitutional provision granting the state board authority to exercise general supervision of the public schools was self-executing, and failure of the legislature to adopt enabling legislation did not deprive it of authority. Nor could the legislature adopt legislation that was in derogation of that provision. (Other chapters in the book will go into the many challenges raised by students and teachers based on individual constitutional rights.)

The standard nonconstitutional challenge is the claim that the state board exceeded its legislatively delegated authority, hence its action is *ultra vires*. The resolution of these challenges depends on a careful interpretation of the statutory language pursuant to which the state agencies or officer claims to be acting. For example, in *Bailey v. Truby*[17] a local board of education challenged the authority of the state board to issue a rule that required students to maintain a 2.0 or "C" grade-point average in order to participate in extracurricular activities. The local board argued that state statutes had given it the exclusive authority to regulate extra-curricular activities. The court disagreed, finding that the legislature had given the local boards authority subject to the general supervisory authority of the state board. The court went on to say that even if the legislature had sought to place exclusive authority in the local boards, such a grant of authority would fail to the extent it interfered with the state board's constitutionally granted authority to supervise the schools of the state.

To take another example, the State Board of Education in California sought to revoke the teacher certificate of Marc Morrison on the grounds he had engaged in immoral and unprofessional conduct after it came to light he had engaged in a homosexual relationship for a one-week period.[18] The Supreme Court of California reversed, stressing that it was dangerous to allow the terms "immoral and unprofessional conduct" to be broadly interpreted since perfectly innocent behavior, e.g., signing a petition, could be deemed "unprofessional" in the eyes of some people. The state board of education should not be allowed to prevent someone from teaching in California schools merely because the board disapproves of that person's private behavior. The diploma to teach may only be removed if a teacher's behavior is "clearly related to his effectiveness in his job," and indicates he is unfit to teach. The legislature, said the court, could not have meant to compel disciplinary measures against teachers if their conduct did not affect students or fellow teachers. Based on this interpretation of the statute the court concluded that Morrison's single week-long homosexual relationship was insufficent to establish that his presence in the schools presented a significant danger of harm to students or fellow teachers.

In another case the state commissioner and board attempted to establish state policies on student responsibilities, corporal punishment, procedural requirements for suspensions, free speech, hair and dress codes, and searches of student lockers.[19] The lower court struck the policies down, saying the state board and commissioner had only those powers enumerated in the statutes, and that power over these subjects was not on the list. The state board was not "a super school board."[20] On appeal the Supreme Court of Pennsylvania reversed the decision.[21] The court concluded the regulations were properly issued pursant to the state board's "legislative rule-making power." The court also acknowledged that the legislature had delegated substantial authority over student discipline to local schools boards, but the court noted that,

> It does not follow . . . that this grant of power to local boards precludes any action by the State Board in the area. The two grants of authority may be read as complementary rather than as mutually exclusive. . . . By and large, the State Board's regulations here in question establish broad guidelines within which discipline is to be carried out; the local boards retain discretion under the School Code to determine the nature of the discipline to be administered and the conditions under which it will be imposed. We leave for another day any question that might be posed by irreconcilable state and local regulations.[22]

In addition to considering claims that a state agency acted beyond its statutory authority, the courts will also review the claim that the agency abused its lawful authority. Success in court on this ground is difficult to achieve because courts generally take the position that administrative action will not be overturned unless it is clear the agency acted arbitrarily.[23]

Turning now from the state agencies to local boards of education, we find here a parallel set of concerns. Like the state agencies, local boards of education are creatures and instrumentalities of the state legislature and have no inherent authority, but only that which has been delegated. It follows that local boards may exercise only those powers that are expressly conferred or are clearly or necessarily implied.[24] Thus, local boards have no authority to contract, to buy and sell property, to tax or to incur debts unless delegated such authority by the state legislature.[25] The authority of the district to shape its educational program, discipline pupils, and hire and fire teachers is also subject to state statutory control. Again, as with the state agencies, the scope of the board's power depends upon a careful interpretation of the statutes imposing on local districts mandatory duties and general, permissive authorizations on local districts.[26] Neither may boards exercise authority in areas that have been preempted by state authority.[27] That authority that the local board of education has may only be exercised according to the formal procedures specified by the legislature, and courts have generally agreed that local boards may not delegate their discretionary authority, only ministerial duties, to subcommittees of the board or the professional staff.[28] Although the board may agree with the teachers' union to submit a wide range of matters to arbitration, e.g., the determination of teacher salaries, it may not commit to arbitration other issues that the courts have deemed to be too essential to the board's role as governing body of the school district, e.g., the decision whether or not to grant a teacher tenure.[29] Even if a school board may have been delegated the authority to regulate a particular activity, the regulation may still be challenged as an abuse of that discretion.[30]

With this we come to the end of our brief review of state legislative authority to control education. It is against this background that we can best understand the recent developments in educational law and policy that have transformed the public education institutional arrangements. The first of these changes to be taken up is the sudden policy change in many states involving significant state legislative efforts to reform public education. An *Education Week* national survey found that: almost all states have acted to raise high-school graduation requirements and institute student-assessment tests; nearly a quarter of the states have established career-ladder or merit pay plans for teachers; twenty-eight states have revised teacher certification standards; in twenty-nine states prospective teachers must pass minimum-competency tests; thirteen states have lengthened the school day or year; and other states have mandated districts to develop policies on homework, attendance, and discipline.[31] This enormous amount of activity has all taken place without the necessity of a change in legal doctrine because state legislatures have plenary authority over education; and because they may delegate significant, broad policy-making authority to state boards and chief state school officers, these changes have occurred with few doubting that the legal authority existed to make the changes.[32] This increase in the exercise of state authority over public education has further moved the public school system away from one marked by extreme fragmentation and significant decentralization of authority, i.e., a system that largely consisted of a collection of districts of varying size, each characterized by its own values, common interests, and educational policies that were shared within the district but that were distinct from other communities.

2.3. DOCTRINAL CHANGE AND THE EXPANSION OF THE FEDERAL ROLE

Federal involvement in education has a long history dating back to the Northwest Ordinance of 1787 (a law requiring states in the old Northwest Territory to set aside a plot of land in each township and to use the proceeds from the rental of that land for common schools); the Morrill Act of 1862 (providing aid to scientific, engineering, and agricultural programs in colleges); and the Smith-Hughes Vocational Education Act of 1917 (giving categorical aid to public secondary schools for vocational education programs). Despite this long history, many commentators agree that the federal role in education under went a significant change, discontinuous with the past, in mid-twentieth century.[33] Federal judicial involvement with the schools suddenly became a feature of national life with the Supreme Court's decision in *Brown v. Board of Education* striking down the purposeful segregation of the races.[34] The proportion of revenue receipts of local school districts derived from federal aid tripled, starting in the 1960s, shifting from 2.9 percent in 1950 to 9.8 percent in 1978-79.[35] Congress passed a variety of pieces of legislation that had enormous implications for the operation of the public schools.[36]

This shift in the federal government's role in education was built upon several important doctrinal changes that proceeded it, and was accompanied by several other legal changes that simultaneously occurred. It is these doctrinal changes upon which this section of the chapter will concentrate. To assist in the appreciation of the significance of these changes, it would be useful at the outset to sketch a model of the federal-state relationship that is dramatically opposed to the model a majority on the Supreme Court has in fact embraced.

At the heart of this model is the notion that states as states have a right to sovereignty within the constitutional scheme that acts as an external check on the authority of the federal government, whether that authority is exercised by Congress pursuant to the interstate commerce clause, the general welfare clause, or the thirteenth, fourteenth, and fifteenth amendments.[37] (It is useful at this point to draw a distinction between internal and external limits on congressional authority. Internal limits are limits inherent in the grant of the power itself. External limits are limits on congressional power that derive from the constitutional structure, or from specific constraints on governmental authority contained in other parts of the Constitution such as the Bill of Rights.) The notion of state sovereignty as an external check on congressional power is analogous to an individual's invocation of a right guaranteed in the Bill of Rights.[38] Thus, under this view congressional power to enforce the thirteenth, fourteenth, and fifteenth amendments, all adopted between 1865 and 1870, "sharply altered the balance of power between the Federal and State Governments," but it should not be read to affect drastically "the original understanding at Philadelphia."[39] Neither may congressional authority under the commerce clause be exercised in such a way that it affects state functions that are essential to the separate and independent existence of the states.[40] In this model congressional preemption of a field, thereby ousting state authority, is not to be lightly inferred.[41] This model also takes a cautious if not hostile approach toward the doctrine that the fourteenth amendment fully incorporates the Bill of Rights and thereby makes the first ten amendments directly applicable to the states.[42] The eleventh amendment's limit on the jurisdiction of the federal courts to entertain suits against states is to be broadly and vigorously enforced.[43]

With this model in mind we turn to an historical analysis of eight different aspects of the federal-state relationship. The unmistakable message of this history is that, as the scope of the national government has expanded, legal doctrines which might have served to check and constrain the national government have been set aside in favor of doctrines which legitimate the national government's control of state policy in general and educational policy in particular.

The Supremacy Clause and Federal Preemption of State Law

Article 6, section 2 states that "This Constitution, and the Laws of the United States which shall be made in Pursuance thereof . . . shall be the supreme Law of the Land." In *Gibbons v. Ogden,* Chief Justice Marshall wrote that in regard "to such acts of the State Legislatures as do not transcend their powers, but . . . interfere with, or are contrary to the law of Congress, made in pursuance of the constitution, . . . [i]n every such case, the act of Congress . . . is supreme; and the law of the State, though enacted in the exercise of powers not controverted, must yield to it."[44] Whether federal law "preempts" state action is at bottom one of statutory interpretation—of the legislative purpose of Congress. Thus, the Court has said that the question of preemption turns on "whether under the circumstances, . . . [the state] law stands as an obstacle to the accomplishment and execution of the full purposes and objectives of Congress."[45] In a later case Justice Douglas elaborated on the doctrine in this area:

> The question in each case is what the purpose of Congress was . . . [This] may be evidenced in several ways. The scheme of federal regulation may be so pervasive as to make reasonable the inference that Congress left no room for the state to supplement it. Or the Act of Congress may touch a field in which the federal interest is so dominant that the federal system will be assumed to preclude enforcement of state laws on the same subject . . . Or the state policy may produce a result inconsistent with the objective of the federal statute.[46]

The intricacies of doctrine in this area need not be further explored here.[47] Suffice it to say that unless it is clear federal law was intended to oust the state totally from the field, it is permissible for state law to be "more royal than the king," to provide individuals with more protection than federal constitutional or statutory law provides.[48] Thus, not all "conflict" between federal and state law necessarily leads to a striking down of the state law; but when state law does in fact frustrate federal purposes state law must yield. This was made clear in *Lawrence County v. Lead-Deadwood School District,* a case involving the Payment in Lieu of Taxes Act under which the federal government is required to compensate local governments for the loss of tax revenues resulting from the tax-immune status of federal lands located in their jurisdictions, and for the cost of providing services related to these lands.[49] While the federal law said that each unit of general local government receiving money under the act "may" use the monies for "any" governmental purpose, a state law required local governments to distribute this money in the same way it distributed general tax revenues. The county, which received the federal money in this case, typically allocated 60 percent of its general tax revenues to its school districts, and the state law here would have required that the federal money be distributed in the same way—but the county refused. On a vote of seven to two the Court ruled that it was Congress's intention to preclude the kind of state-imposed limitation on the use of federal funds involved in the case. In regard to the argument of the school district and state that concerns of federalism should prohibit Congress from intruding into the state's efforts to provide fiscal guidance to its subdivision, the majority answered that Congress was merely dictating the use of federal funds, not state funds. Justice Rehnquist dissented on the grounds that it was "settled doctrine" in this court "that counties were totally subordinate to the States which created them, and that against this background it was not plausible to read Congress's intent to be one of usurping state control of its own instrumentalities."[50]

Incorporation of the Bill of Rights

The expansion of federal influence over education has been dramatically advanced by the Supreme Court's willingness to extend the protections of, for example, the first and fourth amendments to the states and to public education.[51] The importance of the incorporation of these provisions into the fourteenth amendment is manifest throughout this book whenever, for example, the free speech rights of students and teachers are considered. (This is not to say that state constitutions do not also protect the free speech rights of students and teachers, but historically, protection of these rights has been sought by invoking the U.S. Constitution.)[52]

Congressional Enforcement of the Thirteenth, Fourteenth, and Fifteenth Amendments

It is not only the judicially developed incorporation doctrine that has expanded the body of federal law applicable to states and localities. By their own terms the thirteenth, fourteenth, and fifteenth amendments grant to Congress authority to enforce their terms by appropriate legislation.[53] Congress's powers to affect education pursuant to these amendments is broad and sweeping because the Court has pushed aside various arguments that would have limited that power. Acting under the fourteenth amendment, the Court has said Congress may override the limits of the eleventh amendment.[54] In upholding the constitutionality of the Voting Rights Act of 1965,[55] the Court rejected the argument that "Congress may do no more than to forbid violation of the Fifteenth Amendment in general terms—that the task of fashioning specific remedies or of applying them to particular localities must necessarily be left entirely to the courts."[56] The Court has even made it clear that Congress may under these amendments make illegal that which the Court itself has said is not a constitutional violation. Thus, the Court has upheld congressional elimination of English literacy tests as a requirement for eligibility to vote, even though those same tests were earlier declared by the Court to be constitutionally permissible.[57] What Congress may not do is adopt measures that "restrict, abrogate, or dilute" the guarantees of the fourteenth amendment.[58] The importance of these rulings for education will be highlighted in a later section of this chapter.

The Commerce Clause and State Sovereignty

The Court has served as handmaiden for the expansion of congressional power under the commerce clause in two ways. First, the Court has given a broad and generous interpretation to Congress's authority under the commerce clause, thereby permitting Congress to regulate a wide range of activities—including various forms of discrimination.[59] Second, the Court has permitted the extension of these regulatory activities to the states and their subdivisions, despite claims that such regulation interfered with state sovereignty.[60] Thus, today Congress may, for example, directly prohibit discrimination in employment by colleges enrolling out-of-state students without having to bother making those restrictions a condition for the receipt of federal funds.

Conditional Grants of Financial Aid

By far and away Congress's most powerful tool for shaping the priorities of state and local educational agencies has been the conditional grant of financial assistance.[61] Again, the Supreme Court has legitimized the expansion of congressional power by refusing to impose significant limits on congressional spending power. Existing doctrine determines the constitutionality of conditions on national grants case by case by examining to see if the expenditure is reasonably related to a legitimate national end, and that the state was induced, not coerced, into accepting the conditions.[62] The practical effect of this test has been to lift all internal limits on congressional spending power. With the Court's unwillingness to use the principle of state sovereignty as an external check on congressional power,[63] the way has been left open for continued congressional determination of local and state educational priorities through the use of the conditional grant. Because the Court views conditional grants to be in the nature of a contract, it has stressed that the legitimacy of the "contract" between the federal government and the state rests on whether the state voluntarily and knowingly accepted the conditions attached to the federal grant.[64] There could, of course, added the Court, be no knowing acceptance if a state is unaware of the conditions or is unable to ascertain what is expected of it; hence Congress is required to act with a clear voice so that states that accept federal grants are cognizant of the implications of their acceptance of the grant. That Congress's conditions may conflict with beliefs and practices of the recipient that normally would be protected by the first amendment is of little constitutional significance—Congress is free to attach reasonable and unambiguous conditions to federal assistance that educational institutions are not obligated to accept.[65] Many of these regulations are directed toward various forms of discrimination (see §§5.9, 7.3, 7.4, 9.9 et. seq.) and in this way affect the curriculum of the public schools. Direct federal control of the curriculum is a sensitive issue, hence Congress has passed a statute that specifically states that no provision of any program shall be construed to authorize any department to exercise any direction, supervision, or control over the curriculum, program of instruction, selection of library resources, textbooks, other instructional materials, or over the personnel of any educational institution.[66]

A number of interesting issues have arisen in connection with the administration of the federal grant system. An issue of central importance is the question of to what extent should the courts defer to the federal administration's interpretation of the statute imposing conditions on the receipt of federal funds. The Supreme Court has taken the position that it will exercise great deference to the interpretations of statutes suggested by the agency charged with administering the statutes.[67] The Court also brushed aside constitutional objections to an authorization to the secretary of education to recover from states federal funds that have been used in ways that violate the conditions attached to the grant.[68] The Court has strengthened the hand of federal administrators in other ways. Under the Title I program neither the fact that the state was in "substantial" compliance nor that it acted without bad faith in administering the federal funds absolves it of liability if the funds were in fact misused.[69] Ambiguities in the contract between federal and state government, said the Court, should not invariably be resolved against the federal government.[70] Finally, the Court said states may be held liable under regulations in effect at the time the grants were made even if those regulations were later declared by Congress to be a misinterpretation of the basic statute.[71]

Avoiding the Limits of the Eleventh Amendment

The U.S. Constitution and federal statutes applicable to the states provide a basis for suits against the states. The eleventh amendment to the Constitution stands as a potential barrier to such suits brought in the federal courts. (The question of whether states could bar suits against themselves brought in state courts—suits that claim a state violation of federal statutory or constitutional law is another question not taken up here. Nor do we here discuss the doctrine of state "sovereign immunity" to bar suits in state courts based on claimed violations of state law.) The eleventh amendment provides:

The judicial power of the United States shall not be construed to extend to any suit in law or equity, commenced or prosecuted against one of the United States by Citizens of another State, or by Citizens or Subjects of any Foreign State.

The significance of the eleventh amendment is underscored by the Court's interpretation that this amendment immunizes an unconsenting state from suits in federal courts brought even by its own citizens.[72] In other words, the eleventh amendment recognizes the principle of sovereign immunity so that a state may not be sued in federal court by its own citizens to redress a claimed violation of the citizen's federal constitutional or statutory rights by the state.[73] Accordingly, a teacher or student could not sue the state itself either to obtain an injunction prohibiting the state from violating his or her U.S. constitutional or statutory rights in the future,[74] or to seek damages from the state for a violation of those rights.[75]

The actual practical significance of this body of doctrine is significantly undercut by a number of important "exceptions." Suits by the U.S. government itself to enforce the U.S. Constitution or federal statutes against the states are not barred by the eleventh amendment.[76] Hence, for example, suits to end racial segregation brought by the Attorney General of the United States can proceed despite the eleventh amendment. Nor does the eleventh amendment serve to bar the federal courts from hearing appeals from state court opinions in which the state is a party in a suit charging a violation of federal constitutional or statutory law.[77]

The limits of the eleventh amendment are also overcome if Congress, acting pursuant to the enforcement provision of the fourteenth amendment (this section empowers Congress to enforce the provisions of the fourteenth amendment by legislation), intends to overrule and abrogate the eleventh amendment in regard to the enforcement of that particular statute. For Congress to abrogate the states' eleventh amendment immunity from suit in federal court, it must make its intention to do so "unmistakably clear in the language of the statute."[78] The eleventh amendment protections may also be voluntarily waived by a state.[79] An important question in this connection is whether a state waives eleventh amendment immunity by accepting federal funds. The Court has held that the mere acceptance of federal financial assistance does not establish that a state has consented to suit in federal court over violations of that grant-in-aid program and its associated regulations.[80] For the receipt of federal funds to have this effect, Congress itself must manifest a clear intention to condition participation in the program on a state's consent to waive its immunity.[81] Applying this test the Court concluded that §504 of the Rehabilitation Act of 1973 (the act prohibits discrimination on the basis of handicap in federally assisted programs) did not carry such a clear condition, hence acceptance of federal funds did not subject the state to suit under §504 in the case of a suit seeking retroactive monetary relief.[82]

The gaps in the eleventh amendment shield are made even wider by the long-standing doctrine that, while the state itself may not be sued in federal court, suits against individual state officials will be heard. In other words, the Court has adopted the fiction that such suits are not suits against the state itself.[83] State officials may even be required to pay monetary damages so long as the damages are payable by the officer himself or herself and not out of the state treasury. Yet a federal court, consistent with the eleventh amendment, may enjoin a state officer "to conform their future conduct to the requirements of federal law even though such an injunction may have an ancillary effect on the state treasury."[84] Thus, the courts may order state officials to undertake a range of compensatory education programs to restore victims of racial segregation in the schools to the position they would have occupied in the absence of discrimination.[85]

In regard to the field of education, perhaps the most important step the Court has taken to avoid the implications of the eleventh amendment is its holding that the amendment does not bar suits directed to political subdivisions of the state, such as the local school district.[86] These units may be sued directly, even for money damages—without resort to the fiction that the suit is directed only to individual local school officials. In determining whether a particular unit, such as a school district, is a mere "arm of the state" and covered by the eleventh amendment, or a political subdivision and not covered by the eleventh amendment, the Court looks to the extent to which the unit exercises corporate powers, can enter into contracts, can sue and be sued under state law, can issue bonds, and buy and sell property. Thus, while school districts typically have sufficient autonomy to be viewed as "political subdivisions," state universities may lack such independence and be viewed as state agencies protected by the eleventh amendment.[87]

In sum, though the eleventh amendment could operate as an enormous obstacle to federal judicial control of education in the states, the federal courts have limited the scope of the amendment in a number of ways so as to limit the practical effect of the amendment.

Expanding the Availability of §1983

Section 1983 says in part that every person who, under color of state law, deprives another person of rights protected by the Constitution and laws shall be liable for monetary damages or other equitable remedies.[88] This act was intended to promote a "vast transformation from concepts of federalism that had prevailed in the late 18th century."[89] By opening the federal courts to suits alleging constitutional violations Congress greatly expanded the power of these courts. This point is underscored when one realizes that almost all constitutional litigation discussed in this book arose in federal courts because §1983 made this forum available.

Having said this, some important details about the new law need to be discussed. The Supreme Court has said that the eleventh amendment bars use of §1983 against the states themselves—Congress did not intend to override the sovereign immunity of the states with the passage of this act.[90] But individual state and local officials may be sued under §1983,[91] as well as the political subdivisions of the state, such as the local school board.[92] The Court has also held that persons acting "under color of" state law could be sued under §1983 although their acts were not authorized by the state and may even have been forbidden by the state.[93] Even acts of negligence that result in a deprivation of federal constitutional or statutory rights may be actionable if the negligence results from systematic inadequacies in procedure or supervision that contribute to the deprivation.[94]

An important distinction must be made between suits against state and local officials and suits against a political subdivision, such as a local school board. State and local officials may defend themselves against §1983 suits for monetary damages (the defense is not available as injunctive relief) by establishing that he or she neither knew nor reasonably should have known that the action taken would violate the federal constitutional or statutory rights of the plaintiff.[95] This judicially created limitation of §1983 liability known as "qualified good-faith immunity" is not available as a defense by such political entities as the school board.[96] Furthermore, the Court has said that cities, counties, and school boards would only be liable for monetary damages or injunctive relief if "the action that is alleged to be unconstitutional implements or executes" official governmental policy.[97]

It is not necessary to exhaust whatever state judicial or administrative remedies might be available, before bringing a §1983 action,[98] but state court adjudications—which in fact have been brought—of constitutional issues preclude subsequent §1983 actions.[99] A plaintiff may be barred from bringing a federal suit under §1983 if he or she could have raised those claims in a prior state court suit and if state law required the plaintiff to bring all claims arising out of the same incident.[100] Injunctive relief may not be obtained under §1983 unless that plaintiff can show that he or she faces a threat of more harm in the future.[101] Section 1983 is not available as a remedy if another federal statute was intended by Congress to be the sole avenue of redress.[102] Finally, the Supreme Court has held that state statutes of limitations dealing with personal injury actions are to govern whether a §1983 action is barred as not timely.[103]

Interpreting Federal Statutes as Authorizing Individual Suits

Sometimes federal statutes prohibiting, for example, discrimination on the basis of race or gender in federally assisted programs are not clear whether the only method of enforcement is by action of a federal agency, or whether the statutes may be enforced by individual suits, private rights of action, or injunctive and even monetary relief. Clearly, the more willing the courts are to permit these statutes to be used by individuals, the greater the potential impact of these laws on state and local educational policies. Significantly, the Supreme Court has said that the mere fact that Congress has failed specifically to authorize for private litigants a cause of action to support their statutory rights is not inconsistent with an intent on its part to have such a remedy available. Hence, the Court has determined statute by statute whether inferring such a private right of action is consistent with the statutory scheme.[104] Thus, the courts have concluded that private causes of action are available pursuant to laws passed pursuant to its power under the spending clause to place conditions on the grant of federal funds—Title VI,[105] Title IX,[106] and §504.[107] Whether and under what circumstances damage remedies are available is a separate issue that will be taken up at appropriate places throughout the book.

In sum, the unmistakable thrust of legal doctrine has been to expand the reach of the Constitution and federal statutory law to states, localities, and state and local officials. Though there are important barriers that preclude this body of law from having its full impact—limits because of the eleventh amendment and other doctrines surrounding §1983—the change in the legal relationship of federal-state-local entities is unmistakable. The model of this relationship sketched out at the beginning is not the operative model. Current doctrine does give some recognition to the notion of state sovereignty, but in reality this doctrine serves as only a rather puny check on the power of Congress and the federal courts to reach out and control the educational policy of the states and localities in significant respects.

2.4. REFORMING THE POLITICAL PROCESS

The federal government's use of its authority is reflected on virtually every page of this book. We turn here to one specific example—judicial and congressional efforts to reform the political processes of local school districts. Animated by various notions of equity that at times seem contradictory, these reform efforts have been directed toward reapportionment, voting qualifications, and racial discrimination in the establishment and operation of electoral systems.

One of the Supreme Court's more revolutionary steps to assure equality of participation in the political process was the adoption of the proposition that equal numbers of voters should elect equal numbers of representatives to governing bodies, whether it be Congress, state legislatures, or school boards.[108] Thus, over the years the courts have struck down various non-at-large school board election systems (i.e., systems in which board members are elected to the board from election districts) on the grounds that election districts were malapportioned.[109] The idea is that when heavily and lightly populated districts elect one board member, then the votes of the electorate in the heavily populated district have been diluted, i.e., count for less than the votes in the less populous districts. The political vision that has undergirded the attack on malapportionment has been one that stresses the equality of the individual as opposed to a pluralist vision that sees malapportionment as one permissible device for protecting the interests of identifiable groups in the political process. Thus, the movement toward reapportionment refuses to group voters according to their interests for purposes of representation, and refuses to afford arguably "coherent" minority groups greater representation than their numbers deserve as a way of assuring their interests are given some protection against a potentially tyrannous majority.

In the field of education malapportionment has not been the most significant issue facing the courts and Congress. The problem most frequently confronted has been that of the at-large election system under which a majority of the voters in the district can elect all the members of the local board, and, as a consequence, an outvoted racial minority may be without any representation. Successful challenges to the at-large system under the Constitution must establish that the at-large system of voting was either originally adopted, or subsequently maintained, with the purpose of discriminating against the minority population.[110] To establish an intent to discriminate in the adoption of the at-large system, courts are permitted to consider the "Zimmer" factors: (1) the number of minority candidates elected to office; (2) the proportion of the population that is black or other minorities compared to the proportion of blacks or other minorities who are registered to vote; (3) the responsiveness of elected officials to minority interests; (4) the openness of the political process to minority candidates; (5) the history of efforts to discriminate against minority voters and candidates; (6) the extent of voter polarization along racial lines; and (7) the rationale offered for the adoption of the at-large election system.[111] Thus, an important contradiction emerges. Though the Court has repeatedly asserted that groups do not have a constitutional right to proportional representation,[112] evidence that a racial minority has not had proportional representation is relevant in proving discriminatory intent.

In addition to the fourteenth amendment, challenges to electoral systems based on a charge of racial discrimination may be brought pursuant to: (1) §5 of the Voting Rights Act;[113] and (2) §2 of the Voting Rights Act, as amended in 1982.[114] Sixteen states are subject to the provisions of §5 that require that districting plans be precleared by either the United States Attorney General or the Federal District Court for the District of Columbia.[115] To be approved redistricting plans must not have the "purpose or effect of denying or abridging the right to vote" of blacks and other minorities.

The amended §2 of the Voting Rights Act prohibits any voting law or practice "imposed or applied by any State or political subdivision in a manner which *results* in a denial or abridgement of the right of any citizen of the

United States to vote on account of race or color." The statute also expressly states that nothing in the "section establishes a right to have members of a protected class elected in numbers equal to their proportion in the population." At the same time, the statute states a violation

> is established if, based on the totality of the circumstances, it is shown that the political processes leading to nomination or election in the State or political subdivisions are not equally open to participation by [minorities] in that its members have less opportunity than other members of the electorate to participate in the political process and to elect representatives of their choice. *The extent to which members of a protected class have been elected to office . . . is one circumstance which may be considered.*

Thus, the Zimmer factors enumerated above remain relevant, not as evidence of an intent to discriminate, but as objective evidence of the adverse effect of the at-large election system on minority voters. In addition, the legislative history of the act indicates a range of other background factors may be taken into account.[116]

If it is established that an at-large system violates either the fourteenth amendment or the Voting Rights Act, the remedy is adoption of an election system in which board candidates run for office from electoral districts. The design of these districts is a tricky matter. The effort to draw election-district boundary lines may run afoul of two contradictory criticisms. On the one hand, the effort to create "safe" minority districts, i.e., districts in which the size of the minority population is such that it virtually assures the election of a minority candidate, may be challenged on the grounds the districts have been "packed."[117] That is, it may be argued that minority votes have been diluted by being excessively concentrated in one or two election districts, thereby depriving minority voters of the opportunity to influence elections in other districts. On the other hand, an effort to avoid "packing" can lead to the charge that minority votes have been diluted by being fragmented among a large number of districts: in none of these districts do the minority voters have sufficient numbers to affect the election outcome.[118] (The flip side of the minority fragmentation coin is the claim that the districts have been drawn in order to create "safe" white districts—an effort that would be viewed suspiciously as a form of impermissible racial discrimination.[119] Obviously, to avoid the "packing" and "cracking" pitfalls requires careful planning made more difficult by the absence of any clearly articulated principle of what is fair. Is the goal to maximize black political influence? In this connection, it is important to note the Supreme Court has upheld a districting scheme that created a "safe" minority district but in the process fragmented a Hasidic Jewish community.[120]

Finally, note should be taken of federal efforts to eliminate a variety of voting eligibility requirements. For example, the Supreme Court struck down requirements that had the effect of prohibiting an unmarried, childless man living rent free with his parents from voting in school district elections.[121] The Court appreciated the state's efforts to permit only those who had a primary interest in the school district to vote, but said that even a childless, propertyless single male who paid no property taxes might have a direct interest in how the schools were run. Congress has added its weight to the opening of the political process by prohibiting making the passing of an English literacy test a qualification for voting.[122]

The body of law and doctrine reviewed in this section embraces an important and profound inconsistency. On the one hand, the malapportionment cases rest on a notion of equality that stresses the right of the *individual* to equal treatment, a right to vote and to have that vote count equally with other voters. On the other hand, the attacks on the at-large election district and the Voting Rights Act tend to embrace a notion of the right of *groups* to be represented and effectively heard in the political process. While the courts reject the notion that any group has a right to have elected representation, the courts seriously question the legality of a system pursuant to which a racial minority group does not gain representation. In addition, while these materials stress the right of the individual to vote, this same body of law reacts with some degree of hostility if black and white voters tend to vote in "blocks" for black and white candidates, respectively. Perhaps the best description of the present situation is that constitutional doctrine today rests, first, on an individualistic principle of equity, but that it has, perhaps for political reasons, also accommodated itself to electoral realities and carved out an exception to the individualistic principle in order to provide special protection for racial minorities. Doctrine is, thus, not elegant and coherent, but it is at least a politically workable compromise.

2.5. THE TEACHER AS CITIZEN: THE RIGHT TO CRITICIZE

The modern judicial effort to assure equal access to the process of collective decision-making has extended to the public school teacher. Today, someone who joins the teaching staff of a public school does not, and may not be required to, as a condition of employment, forgo his or her rights as a citizen to participate in the political life of the school district.[123] Nevertheless, the teacher's rights to engage in the politics of running the district are not of unlimited scope and of absolute weight. The precise extent of the teacher's rights thus need to be examined. We here take up the right of the teacher publicly to criticize the school board and his or her superiors and co-workers. In §2.6 we turn to the right of the teacher to become involved in the election politics of the district and the right of the teacher to take a seat on the school board himself. Other related first amendment rights of teachers—for example, the right to engage in nonschool related politics, and to join "subversive" organizations—will be taken up in chapter 6.

A teacher who complains that he or she was dismissed because of his or her criticism of the school board or other school officials must first persuade the court that the speech activity he or she engaged in was a constitutionally protected speech activity.[124] The principles for determining if the speech activity is constitutionally protected are complex and will be the primary focus of this portion of the chapter. If successful in demonstrating the activity is constitutionally protected, the plaintiff must then show that his or her engagement in this activity was a substantial motivating factor in the decision or action taken against him or her—whether it be dismissal, demotion, or reprimand. If the plaintiff is successful in meeting this burden, the burden of persuasion switches to the employer to establish that the "same decision" to dismiss, demote, etc., would have been taken even in the absence of the protected conduct.[125]

The question we now turn to is the question of how one determines if the speech activity was constitutionally protected. The doctrines that have emerged primarily from two Supreme Court cases can perhaps best be organized in terms of a "decision-tree."[126] The basic outline of the decision-tree will first be sketched and then its elements commented upon in greater detail. A first and central issue is whether the speech activity—e.g., a letter to an editor, a speech, participation in a demonstration—dealt with "a matter of public concern." If a court concludes the speech activity did not involve a matter of public concern, the precise degree of protection the courts will provide for the speech activity is not clear.[127] However, if the court concludes the speech activity did deal with a matter of public concern, then the court must determine whether the statements made were truthful or contained errors.[128] If the materials contain errors, the statement will not be protected if this false statement were made knowing it was false or in reckless disregard of whether or not it was true.[129] The Court has not decided whether a speech that was knowingly or recklessly false, but that had no harmful effects, might as a result be protected by the first amendment.[130] (It should also be noted that a false statement may bring into question the fitness of the teacher to perform his or her duties and, thus, be evidence of the teacher's general incompetence, its own distinct ground for dismissal.)[131] If, however, the statement is truthful, or in error, but not made knowing it was false or in reckless disregard of the truth, it will be deemed "protected speech" only if on balance the court decides the speech ought to be protected. Thus, whether or not this speech that has been determined to be a matter of public concern is considered to be "protected speech" depends on the court's balancing the interest of the teacher to speak out on a matter of public concern, with the board's interest in the effective and efficient fulfillment of its responsibilities to the public.

Two aspects of this decision-tree have received the greatest judicial attention: the issue of whether or not a particular speech activity is a matter of public concern, and the balancing of the interests of teacher and school district in regard to truthful statements that are matters of public concern to determine if the speech is "protected speech." The Court has said that whether an employee's speech, as a matter of law, is to be deemed a matter of public concern must be determined by the content, the form, and the context of the given statement.[132] To understand this "formula" it is necessary to realize that the Court is attempting to delimit the scope of the first amendment because it does not want to interpret the first amendment as requiring public offices "to be run as a round-table for employee complaints over internal office affairs."[133] Thus, taking the factors listed in the formula together, the Court seeks to draw a line between (1) those expressions that are merely the personal grievances of individual employees regarding the details of their conditions of employment and with regard to which it can be said the public is only indirectly and remotely interested; and (2) those larger issues that directly bear on the nature and quality of the public service, on the question of whether the agency is discharging its responsibilities. Applying this approach in *Connick v. Myers*, the Court said an assistant district attorney's questionnaire, distributed to fellow staff members, could not be deemed as dealing with a matter of public concern insofar as it solicited views on the office's transfer policy, office morale, the need for a grievance committee, and the level of confidence in supervisors. The Court acknowledged that discipline and morale in the district attorney's office were related to the agency's efficient performance of its duties. But in this case the context of the distribution of the questionnaire was in the face of an unwanted transfer, and the purpose of the questionnaire, said the Court, was not to evaluate the performance of the office but to gather ammunition for continuing the controversy with the employee's superiors. The Court also acknowledged that, in different circumstances, the subject matter of the questionnaire could have been a topic communicated to the public and of general interest.[134] Thus, it appears that the telling factors in this case, which kept this communication out of the category of "a matter of public concern," were not the content of the speech so much as the motivation behind it, as evidenced in part by the audience to which the speech was directed.

A different combination of factors can lead to a different conclusion. Thus, the Court agreed that one of the questions in the same questionnaire—a question dealing with whether other assistant district attorneys felt pressure to work in political campaigns of candidates supported by the office—was to be viewed as a matter of public concern. The Court based its conclusion on the facts that the Court itself had said official pressure to work for political candidates was a violation of an employee's first amendment rights, and the legislative branch of government itself had adopted a policy that government service should depend on merit and not political service.[135] The Court was probably also influenced by the fact that the topic of political pressure was not itself an issue in Myer's own personal employment dispute; hence the raising of the issue appeared not to be motivated by a personal interest. Thus, when a topic has been the subject of attention from the courts and legislature of the land and it is not raised for the purpose of achieving immediate personal gain, it can fall into the "public concern" category. A topic can be a matter of public concern even if other topics raised by an employee are not, and even if the topic is raised against a background of the employee pursuing a personal grievance with his or her employer. We see these points underscored in other cases in which the Court agreed that a school employee's complaints to her superior over the district's racial policies were a matter of public concern.[136] Presumably, under the approach adopted in *Connick*, a letter one teacher wrote attacking the school district's handling of a bond issue and its allocation of funds between the academic and athletic programs would continue to be viewed as touching on matters of public concern, as the Court held in *Pickering v. Board of Education*.[137] The fact that the bond issue was itself part of an ongoing public debate in the district between the teachers' organization and the superintendent would underscore the fact of public concern.

In a useful interpretation of *Connick*, one court suggested that the line between speech that is and is not a matter of public concern be drawn in the following way:

> We should ask whether the employee's grievances are not more properly channeled to well-defined forums such as review committees or arbitrators; whether the employee would have reason to make mention of his grievances but for his employment status; how significant is the subject of the employee's speech to the general public; and whether the subject of the employee's speech has become a public issue of attention from the press, politicians, public interest groups or the public at large?[138]

Since the decision in *Pickering*, and especially the decision in *Connick*, in which the Court outlined its approach to determining whether a communication is a matter of public concern, the lower courts have provided further guidance on the question whether a speech activity is a matter of public concern. Thus, we find that the courts have concluded that the following topics are of public concern: public comments on matters relating more generally to the curriculum and school program;[139] comments touching on the safety and physical well-being of the students;[140] public comments on matters in dispute between the board and the teachers' union;[141] and comments on publc corruption.[142] One lower court has interpreted *Connick* not to require that every word of a communication be about a matter of public concern.[143] It also seems clear that the courts will not permit teachers to turn their personal grievances into "matters of public concern" by simply asserting that the complaints they raise are a matter of the public interest or the welfare of the children.[144] The teacher's unilateral claim that he or she is raising a question of broader interest than his or her personal interest is insufficient to garner first amendment protection.[145]

We now turn away from the question whether a particular expression is, as a matter of law, a "matter of public concern." Assuming the court agrees that the expression is a "matter of public concern," as noted above, the burden switches to the employer to justify its dismissal of the employee, and the court must then balance the employee's interests and the employer's interests. (Recall that even if the teacher's speech was a matter of public concern, it may not be "protected speech" because the board might nevertheless be justified in dismissing the teacher. Only "protected speech" is an impermissible basis for discharge or other sanction. In other words, "protected speech" is a subcategory of speech that is a "matter of public concern.") In *Connick* the Court said that the "state's burden in justifying a particular discharge varies depending on the nature of the employee's expression."[146] This suggests the need for a further two-pronged inquiry into the teacher's speech: (1) to what extent has the teacher mixed personal matters with issues of public concern? and (2) how serious or fundamental are the issues of public concern raised by the teacher? Presumably, the more clearly focused the teacher's speech is on a matter of public concern, and the more serious that issue, the greater the first amendment protection, i.e., the weightier must be the state's interests to warrant dismissal. Each case thus involves a "particularized balancing" of the competing interests. Summarizing the decisions in *Pickering* and *Connick*, one court has said the factors to be weighed include:

> (1) the need for harmony in the office or work place; (2) whether the government's responsibilities require a close working relationship to exist between the plaintiff and co-workers when the speech in question caused or could cause the relationship to deteriorate; (3) the time, manner, and place of the speech; (4) the context in which the dispute arose; (5) the degree of public interest in the speech; and (6) whether the speech impeded the employee's ability to perform his or her duties.[147]

The court should also have noted that the Supreme Court said in *Pickering* that some positions may involve such a need for confidentiality that public statements might furnish a permissible ground for dismissal.[148] The Court has also stressed that an employer does not have to allow events to unfold "to the extent that the disruption of the office and the destruction of working relationships is manifest before taking action."[149] It is only after balancing these factors that a court will decide whether or not the teacher's speech was not merely a "matter of public concern" but falls into that narrower category of "protected speech."

Using this approach the Court in *Connick* assessed whether the one question that was a matter of public concern on the questionnaire fell into the category of "protected speech."[150] The Court contended that, though the distribution of the questionnaire did not impede Myers's ability to perform her job, the distribution of the questionnaire during office hours and in the office (as opposed to distribution in nonwork areas on the employee's own time) did threaten the functioning of the office and the authority of the employer to run the office. Given the limited matters of public concern involved in the questionnaire, the employer did not have to "tolerate action which [it] reasonably believed would disrupt the office, undermine [its] authority, and destroy close working relationships."[151] Myers's speech was not "protected speech," hence the Court did not have to in this case continue to the next step of determining whether the dismissal was motivated by a desire to suppress "protected speech."

The Court reached a different conclusion in *Pickering*. There, the Court found that Pickering's letter discussing the handling of the bond issue threatened neither discipline in the work place, nor harmony among co-workers. Importantly for future cases, the Court also noted that the employment relationship between the board, and to a lesser extent the superintendent, did not involve the kind of close working relationship for which it could be claimed that personal loyalty and confidence are necessary for the proper operation of the district.

When we turn to the opinions of the lower courts, we find that they have been willing to protect teachers even though their speech may have influenced their working relationships with co-workers. The significant fact in several of these cases seems to have been the courts' assessment that there was a strong public interest in knowing what the teacher had to say that outweighed the school's interest in harmony.[152] The courts have also been willing to protect teachers despite proof that their speech activities caused difficulties between them and their immediate supervisors, the criticism was internal, and the tone harsh.[153] Criticism of one's superiors does not lose first amendment protection because it is privately, as opposed to publicly, expressed to the superior.[154] It is also worth noting that a properly filed grievance may be a basis for disciplinary action.[155] A teacher's vigorous advocacy as union spokesperson gets strong protection from the courts.[156] When the teacher's activities constitute unremitting personal criticism of his or her superiors, then the resulting disharmony tends to result in a decision in favor of the school district.[157] Open public ridicule or attacks on the integrity of one's superior also tend not to garner much judicial protection.[158] As might be expected in light of the fact that teachers do not work in a close personal relationship with the board or superintendent, public criticism of the board and/or superintendent on matters of public concern is frequently protected.[159] In one case the court concluded that the teacher's article, with a number of errors concerning the superintendent's position on a number of important issues, adversely affected the superintendent's working relationship with the teachers in the school district.[160] Thus, it was at least permissible for the superintendent to take the relatively mild step—mild in terms of its effect on the teacher's free speech rights—of placing in the teacher's personnel file a letter in rebuttal to the article.[161] It also seems clear that the more vituperative and insulting the language used, the more profane and excessive the expression of opinion, the less protection will the teacher receive.[162] It is arguable that school boards can require teachers to pursue their concerns first through a "narrowly drawn" grievance procedure;[163] but it also seems clear that the school boards may not seek to stifle open criticism by requiring genuine matters of public concern to be pursued exclusively through channels.[164]

In sum, we can see that teachers have been afforded reasonably strong protection, to date, to speak out on matters of public concern. There is a strong possibility that the Court's recent decision in *Connick* will have the effect of lowering the degree of protection afforded by the lower federal courts. The Supreme Court's caution in defining what constitutes a matter of public concern, and especially its balancing of the employee's and employer's interests, suggests a narrowing of the scope of the first amendment protections. Perhaps the most significant point in this regard is the Court's statement that it is not necessary for the employer "to allow events to unfold to the extent that disruption of the office and the destruction of working relationships is manifest before taking action." It thus appears that employers may act on the mere apprehension of trouble. Further underscoring the possible conservative tone in the Court's opinion is its failure to address the question whether the employer must establish the possibility of disruption, or whether the employee must establish the unlikelihood of disruption. Nor is it clear from the opinion what sort of evidence will suffice to indicate the possibility of disruption. In *Connick* itself there was little evidence of actual disruption. In fact, the federal district court had concluded that the questionnaire had no adverse effect on Myers's relationship with her superiors.[165] We, thus, may witness a movement on the part of the Supreme Court toward greater deference to the judgment of the employer that the employee's speech has the potential for being disruptive. Indeed, it is striking that the employer is permitted to act to sanction the employee even before the employer has itself suffered any adverse consequences.

2.6. TEACHER AS CITIZEN: INVOLVEMENT IN SCHOOL POLITICS

The Supreme Court in *Branti v. Finkel* and *Elrod v. Burns,* made it clear that public employees may not be dismissed *solely on the grounds* of the employee's political affiliation. In each case the central question is whether the employer "can demonstrate that party affiliation is an appropriate requirement for the effective performance of the public office involved."[166] Based on these principles, a lower court ruled that the refusal to hire teachers for summer employment because they supported the losing opponents of the current school board was impermissible.[167] In another case the court upheld the dismissal of the director of vocational education because he was personally close to a member of the board who had been defeated in his bid for reelection. The court found that the teacher was associated with the old board member out of personal friendship, and not to further a particular program, policy, or objective, and the first amendment did not protect mere personal affinity not related to the expression of beliefs or ideas.[168]

Political affiliation can also involve public criticism of the school board, and the question then becomes whether an employee affiliated with the opposition who is openly critical of the board and who is dismissed by the board is to be protected by *Connick-Pickering* or *Branti-Elrod*. It makes a difference because the analysis of the legality of the board's action is different depending on which line of cases is deemed applicable. The lower courts have split on how these two lines of cases affect each other. The Fifth Circuit has taken the position that *Connick* blended the *Pickering* and *Branti-Elrod* cases into a single approach.[169] Under this approach the Fifth Circuit places patronage and expression cases on a single spectrum. At one extreme are the cases involving non-policy-making employees who are discharged solely because of political affiliation—in these cases the employee clearly prevails. At the other extreme are those cases in which the employer prevails because of the disruptive nature of the employee's speech activity. In the middle are those cases in which the balancing approach of *Connick-Pickering* does not produce an automatic result.

The Fourth Circuit's approach is different. Rather than seeing all public employee cases as falling on a balancing spectrum, the Fourth Circuit adopted a two-step analysis of these cases.[170] Under this approach the court must first ask whether the dismissal was motivated by party affiliation alone or an overt speech activity. If the employer is motivated solely by party affiliation, then the *Branti-Elrod* test applies. But if the dismissal is based on the employee's speech activity, then the *Connick-Pickering* approach is to be used.

We now broaden the inquiry to ask whether states or school boards may prohibit teachers from becoming actively involved in the election campaigns of board members, whether those elections are partisan or nonpartisan elections. More precisely, may teachers be prohibited from endorsing candidates for the board, circulating petitions for board candidates, soliciting or receiving contributions for board candidates, wearing campaign buttons, distributing campaign literature in school facilities, and making campaign contributions to board candidates? Despite the significant infringement on free speech rights, the courts have upheld such limitations whether applied to partisan or nonpartisan elections.[171] These restrictions are seen as serving important interests. First, they help to assure that employment and advancement in the public service are made to depend on merit and not political performance. Second, the restrictions help to assure that public confidence in the service remains high—that the public service is not perceived as operating on the basis of political influence and connections. Third, the restrictions help prevent the creation of powerful political machines. Fourth, they protect the employees' right to be free of employer pressure in their political decisions and affiliations.

Finally, as might be expected, teachers have been prohibited from serving as members of the school board that governs the school district in which the teacher is employed.

The courts appear to have reasoned that an insuperable conflict of interest exists between an employee school teacher and the employer board of education, and that such conflict of interest leads to an incompatibility which cannot be bridged by any effort on the part of a member-schoolteacher to avoid voting or taking part in matters involving conflict, the court apparently taking the position that the voters are entitled to school board members who are free to vote on all matters and that the mere possibility of conflict is sufficient to create an incompatibility between the two positions.[172]

2.7. COLLECTIVE BARGAINING

Some would argue that the most significant change in decision-making in education since the 1960s has been the rise of collective bargaining and the development of legal protections for the union movement.[173] Relying on the right of freedom of association as protected by the first and fourteenth amendments, the courts extended to public employees a right to form and join unions, while simultaneously holding that employers were not constitutionally required to bargain collectively with these public employee unions.[174] Legislatures in over thirty states have today adopted legislation protecting the right of teachers to join unions, and authorizing and requiring the boards to engage in collective bargaining.[175] In the absence of legislation authorizing school boards to engage in collective bargaining, the courts are split on the legality, thus the enforceability, of the collective bargaining agreements.[176]

Private educational institutions are not covered by state collective-bargaining laws directed to public employees. These institutions may be covered by state collective-bargaining laws written for the private sector as well as by the federal National Labor Relations Act.[177] In a controversial decision the Supreme Court said that the act's exclusion of "supervisors and managerial employees" from the benefits of collective bargaining applied to the full-time faculty of Yeshiva University.[178] The Court concluded that the managerial exclusion applied to the faculty of the university because the faculty exercised authority that the Court said was unquestionably managerial, i.e., they decided what courses to offer, when they would be scheduled, and to whom they would be taught; determined teaching methods, grading policies, and matriculation standards; and decided what students would be admitted, retained, and graduated.[179]

Despite the many legal developments favoring collective bargaining, public-sector collective bargaining remains controversial. Is bargaining consistent with the managerial prerogatives of the school board and its role as the sole, democratically elected governing body of the district? Is the right to join a union and bargain collectively just a natural extension of everybody's civil right not to work for a particular employer except on terms voluntarily agreed to? Does collective bargaining give teachers and other public employees too great a political advantage? Is the recognition of bargaining rights a necessary corrective to protect public employees who otherwise would be at a political disadvantage vis-a-vis taxpayer and other groups intent on holding down taxes? These and other underlying issues continue to bedevil the development of the law in this area, as we shall see. It should be underscored that not all the issues that arise in collective bargaining are addressed here.[180]

The Scope of Collective Bargaining and Arbitrability

Crucial to the allocation of political power between board and union is determining which topics will be subject to negotiation and arbitration.[181] In specifying the subjects of bargaining most states have adopted vague statutory language that merely requires the employer to bargain over "wages, hours, and other terms and conditions of employment."[182] Other states have developed lists of bargaining subjects.[183] Some public-sector bargaining laws contain a "management rights clause" that limits the scope of bargaining by excluding certain subjects thought to be at the heart of management prerogatives and the mission of the schools."[184]

Faced with these general and often vague statutes, public employment boards and courts have had to decide case by case whether a particular demand placed on the bargaining table is a proper subject of negotiations. To aid in these decisions the boards and courts have developed a tripartite categorization scheme under which subjects are labeled as mandatory, permissible, or prohibited subjects of negotiation.[185] The crucial question remains: how broadly or narrowly should the statute be interpreted, i.e., should the statute be understood to define the category of mandatory subjects broadly or narrowly? Should the category of prohibited subjects be broadly or narrowly defined?

The courts in various states have approached and answered these questions differently:

Alaska: "[A] matter is more susceptible to bargaining the more it deals with the economic interests of employees and the less it concerns professional goals and methods."[186]

Iowa: "We apply a two-step analysis in considering whether a proposal is within the scope of mandatory bargaining under §20.9. The proposal must come within the meaning of one of the subjects listed as mandatory in §20.9. . . . Second, there must be no legal prohibition against bargaining on the particular topic. . . . [I]n the cases, we found legislative intent to adopt a restrictive approach to interpreting the subjects listed in §20.9."[187]

Michigan: "Any matter which has a material or significant impact upon wages, hours, or other conditions of employment or which settles an aspect of the relationship between employer and employee is a mandatory subject, except for management decisions which are fundamental to the basic direction of the corporate enterprise or which impinge only indirectly upon employment security."[188]

Massachusetts: "[T]he analysis to be utilized is essentially the same in all instances: whether the ingredient of public policy in the issue subject to dispute is so comparatively heavy that collective bargaining, and even voluntary arbitration, on the subject is, as a matter of law, to be denied effect."[189]

Minnesota: This state adopts the impact test with a twist. Impact on terms and conditions of employment does not make a subject a mandatory subject "if the decision and its implementation are so inextricably interwoven that requiring the public employer to meet and negotiate the method of carrying out its decision would require the employer to negotiate the basic policy decision. . . . If, however, the inherent managerial policy decision is severable from its implementation, the effect on implementation on the terms and conditions of employment is negotiable to the extent that negotation is not likely to hamper the employer's direction of its functions and objectives."[190]

New York: The Court of Appeals in New York has said that absent an express prohibition, it is to be presumed the local board has the authority to bargain with a union, i.e., the subject is a mandatory subject of negotiation. However, public policy "whether derived from, and whether explicit or implicit in statute or decisional law, or in neither, may also restrict the freedom to arbitrate."[191]

Wisconsin: This state has adopted the rule that at matter is a mandatory subject of negotiation if it is primarily related to wages, hours, and conditions of employment, but not if it is primarily related to educational policy and school management operation, or to the formulation or management of public policy.[192]

Applying such approaches as these, the courts have arrived at different conclusions about whether a particular item is a mandatory subject of negotiation.[193] Despite these differences some patterns or trends are discernible. Courts are in general agreement that such topics as the design of the curriculum, the criteria for promotion and the grant of tenure, and the size of the staff are not mandatory subjects of negotiation but are matters of policy committed to the discretion of the school board.[194] On the other hand, besides wages and other obviously traditional subjects of negotiations, the courts have agreed that such matters as the procedures used, not the criteria, in evaluating or laying off of teachers are mandatory subjects.[195] Last, even states like New York that have favored a broad definition of the scope of bargaining have in recent years become more protective of school board prerogatives.[196] Lying behind these conclusions are changing visions of the proper relationship between school boards and the representative of their employees.[197]

The Right to Strike

For a number of reasons that have been subjected to extensive criticism, a majority of states prohibit strikes by public employees.[198] No court has held that public employees have a constitutional right to strike, but a number of courts have held there is no improper discrimination when private-sector employees are permitted to strike but public-sector employees are not.[199] Even though a strike might be illegal, one court held that a police officer could not be dismissed for making public comments that resorting to a "sick-in" or "blue flu" would be a more effective way of pressing the union's demands.[200] The court could find no evidence in this case that the statements actually adversely affected the police department's efficiency or the ability of the officer effectively to carry out his job.

Protecting the Incumbent Union

Though public-sector unions have been denied the right to strike, constitutional doctrine has accommodated efforts to secure the place of the incumbent in important ways, thereby enhancing its position as the incumbent bargaining representative vis-à-vis a challenging union and, accordingly, its position vis-à-vis the employer school board. In *Abood v. Detroit Board of Education* the Court held that an "agency shop" agreement requiring a teacher who is a member of the bargaining unit, but not a member of the union, to help finance the union's collective bargaining activities did not violate his first amendment right to freedom of association and nonassociation.[201] The agency shop was a fair way to distribute the costs of negotiating and administering the agreement—activities the union was required to undertake on behalf of all members of the bargaining unit, even nonunion members. The Court also held that use of such fees "for political and ideological purposes unrelated to collective bargaining" would violate the first amendment rights of employees who objected to these expenditures.[202]

In *Perry Education Association v. Perry Local Educators' Association,*[203] the Court protected the incumbent union further by holding that the free-speech rights of the rival union were not violated when it was not given the same access to the interschool mail system as was the incumbent union. The restriction was reasonable, said the Court, because it allowed the exclusive bargaining agent to perform its duties better, and because it helped to assure labor peace. In *Minnesota State Board for Community College v. Knight,* the Court upheld a statute that prevented participation by nonunion faculty members in statutorily mandated "meet and confer" sessions between faculty and administration, at which views were exchanged on policy questions outside the scope of mandatory bargaining.[204] The majority said that faculty involvement in academic governance was not a constitutionally based right. In an earlier case the balance was struck differently between the exclusive union representation and the individual right of public employees to participate in public decisionmaking. In *City of Madison Joint School District No. 8 v. Wisconsin Employment Relations Commission,*[205] the Court protected the right of teachers to speak out at public school board meetings on important issues even if those issues were currently the subject of bargaining between the board and the teachers' exclusive representative. In *Smith v. Arkansas Highway Employees, Local 1315,*[206] the Court upheld the constitutionality of a policy not to consider a grievance initiated by an employee unless the employee bypassed the union's grievance procedure and submitted his complaint directly to the designated employer representative. The Court protected the right of the employee to speak freely and petition openly without fear of retaliation and rejected the view that the first amendment imposed an obligation on government "to listen, to respond or, in this context, to recognize the association and bargain with it."

In sum, through its more recent decisions in *Connick, Perry,* and *Knight* the Burger Court has backed away from protecting the free speech rights of the individual employee and tended to favor the employer and incumbent union. The current tendency in the Court is to favor efficiency and controlled administration over individual rights and the open conflict that may accompany protection of those rights.

The First Amendment and Unions

The free speech clause of the first amendment is implicated by union activities in a variety of ways. First, union representatives may seek to gain access to school property in order to try to gain convenient access to the faculty to persuade them to seek union representation in the first place. School rules limiting the access of union representatives were tested in *Texas State Teachers Association v. Garland Independent School District.*[207] School rules permitted union organizers to meet or recruit teachers on school premises before 8:00 A.M. or after 3:45 P.M. and distribute literature on school premises (parking lots, hallways, and placement on teachers' desks) during non-school hours. The Fifth Circuit rejected the claims that these rules violated the free speech rights of the union representatives. Because the school property itself was not a traditional public forum (like the streets and parks) and had not been designated a public forum by the school district, the union representatives did not have a constitutional right of access to the schools.[208] Since the school property was not a public forum, rules regarding its use need only be rationally related to a legitimate state end, and these rules met that test.[209]

The Fifth Circuit went on to consider the constitutionality of school rules prohibiting the teachers themselves from promoting the unionization of the faculty during non-class time. So long as such speech activities did not materially and substantially disrupt the school, said the court, they must be permitted.[210] Similarly, the teachers could not be precluded from using the school mail system and billboards for the same purposes.

Once a union has been selected, a range of other speech activities can implicate the first amendment. As already discussed, the Supreme Court has held that the free speech rights of a minority union are not infringed when the incumbent union is given exclusive access to the school mail system.[211]

Despite the fact the advocacy of the objectives of an incumbent union may at times be annoying, engender rancorous feelings, and create an atmosphere of hostility and ill will, the lower courts have strongly protected public employees against retaliation and efforts to suppress union activities.[212] Even union picketing outside the private business offices of school-district board members has been permitted.[213] Despite these decisions two points remain unclear. First, what matters in a dispute between union and school board are matters of public concern and their public discussion by teachers invoke the protection of *Pickering* and *Connick*?[214] Second, under *Pickering* and *Connick* exactly how disruptive may teachers be in pressing union-related issues of public concern?[215] For further discussion of *Pickering* and *Connick,* see §2.5.

2.8. GOVERNMENT IN THE SUNSHINE; FREEDOM OF INFORMATION

Statutes controlling the formal procedures school boards must follow in taking official action have long been part of educational law.[216] While these requirements served, to an extent, to assure that school boards would be accountable to the public, in the late 1960s a reform movement began that ultimately swept all fifty states. Thus, today every state has passed some version of what have come to be called "sunshine laws," which, more than heretofore, seek to open to the public the deliberative and voting processes of public bodies.[217] Though these laws vary in important details, they typically require that "meetings" of the board at which either deliberations take place or formal action is taken be open to the public. This general rule is then qualified by lists of specific exceptions for executive sessions dealing with such matters as labor negotiations, personnel management where sensitive private matters may be taken up, and the purchase of real property.[218]

A variety of legal issues have arisen regarding the interpretation of these acts. A threshold question is what sorts of agencies and committees are covered by the acts. The interesting questions here have not been whether boards of education are required to comply with these acts—they are—but whether subcommittess of the board and other such "agencies" are covered. The answer generally seems to be that subcommittees of the board are not covered by these laws; hence, they may meet in executive session.[219]

Even assuming the board of education is subject to the requirements of the open meeting law, the question arises whether every gathering of the members of the board—excluding those meetings specifically exempted from the act—is subject to the provisions of the law. In other words, the question has arisen, what constitutes a "meeting" of the board within the meaning of the law? In Minnesota the state's supreme court held that gatherings of the members of the school board at which information was presented by an administrator touching on such questions such as long-range planning, enrollment decline, the goals of the board, staff reassignments and reductions, management design, and extracurricular activities were "meetings" within the meaning of the statute and had to be open to the public. [220] When the meeting, however, is informal, is not deliberative and not likely to lead to a consensus, and/or a quorum is not present, then the courts are not inclined to conclude that a "meeting" has occurred.[221] One court even ruled that a prearranged telephone conference in which all members of the board participated was not a "meeting."[222] Other courts have ruled that meetings to evaluate the paper credentials of candidates for the position of superintendent and to evaluate the performance of the superintendent did not fall within any of the exceptions to the open meeting requirement, despite the fact that the discussions might prove to be embarrassing for the individuals being evaluated [223] In Florida the courts interpreted that state's sunshine law to permit the board to meet privately with its negotiators—not to permit such strategy sessions would give the employees, said the court, too great an advantage and damage the public interest.[224]

It is common for the open meeting laws to provide explicitly for exceptions to the basic requirements of the law; hence the issue arises whether a particular meeting may be held in executive session because it falls within none of the exceptions. The issue more frequently raised is whether a particular meeting on a personnel matter is exempted from the law. These cases have been variously decided depending on the wording of the statute and the facts of the case.[225]

The validity of action taken in violation of the law is handled differently from state to state, with not all states holding that the action is voidable.[226]

Brief mention should be made of state freedom-of-information acts. Today every state except Mississippi has some sort of freedom-of-information law determining access to state and local records.[227] These acts vary in how liberally they define the concept of a "public record" and vary in their exemptions to the basic disclosure requirements. Of particular importance to education is the fact that one-third of these laws contain exemptions for interagency or intra-agency memoranda.[228] A majority of the state laws provide for an exemption based on considerations of privacy.[229] Washington State's law, for example, exempts personal information relating to students and employees.[230]

Last, a New York court overturned a school board's restriction on the recording of school board meetings with hand-held tape recorders. The court said the prohibition was inconsistent with assuring the public is fully informed.[231]

2.9. THE AMERICAN CREED AND THE GOVERNING STRUCTURE

A belief in a limited central government was at one point a hallmark of the American Creed,[232] but we have seen that constitutional doctrine today no longer serves the purpose of limiting the role of the federal government. Pursuant to this expanded authority the Congress and federal courts have done much to further change the governing system of the country. State legislatures, starting in the 1960s, have themselves passed major pieces of legislation that have transformed the decision-making processes of local school districts. At bottom four values seem to have been served by these changes: centralization, equality in political participation, equalization of the rights of public employees so they have roughly the same rights to bargain collectively as employees in private industry, and openness in government. In short, we have seen in this century a revolution in the governing system of education, a revolution that bespeaks of a change in the American creed. But it is ironic that as the processes of government have been opened to a wider range of people at the local level, two developments have made access to local decision-making less meaningful: the more vigorous use of federal and state authority to control education, and the growth of the teacher union movement. Educational decision-making has become more centralized, legalized, and unionized. It has also become more open to the ordinary citizen, but it would appear that the value of this openness to the citizen has been diminished.

NOTES

1. Whether law is a cause of political practices or merely reflects political realities is a difficult question. For one exploration of this problem see Saltzman, "Bargaining Laws as a Cause and Consequence of Growth of Teacher Unionism," *Industrial and Labor Relations Review* 38 (1985):

2. Tyll van Geel, *Authority to Control the School Program* (Lexington, Mass.: D.C. Heath and Company, 1976); Diane Ravitch, *Troubled Crusade: American Education 1945-1980* (New York: Basic Books, Inc., 1983); David K. Cohen, "Policy and Organization: The Impact of State and Federal Educational Policy on School Governance," *Harvard Educational Review* 52 (1982): 474; Joseph M. Cronin, *The Control of Urban Schools* (New York: Free Press, 1973); "Affirmative Action and Electoral Reform," *Yale Law Journal* 90 (1981):1811; Anthony M. Cresswell and Michael J. Murphy, *Unions, and Collective Bargaining* (Berkeley, Calif: McCutchan Publishing Corp., 1980); Susan Moore Johnson, *Teacher Unions in Schools* (Philadelphia: Temple University Press, 1984).

3. The Tenth Amendment to the United States Constitution places the states in this pivotal position: "The powers not delegated to the United States by the Constitution, nor prohibited by it to the States, are reserved to the States respectively, or to the people." Article I to the Constitution does not expressly delegate to the Congress any authority over education; thus by implication this power is reserved to the state. The federal government in legal theory is a government of limited enumerated powers, not a government of inherent authority. In other words, "an act of Congress is invalid unless it is affirmatively authorized under the Constitution. State actions, in contrast, are valid as a matter of federal constitutional law unless prohibited, explicitly or implicitly, by the Constitution." Lawrence Tribe, *American Constitutional Law* (Mineola, N.Y.: The Foundation Press, 1978), 225.

4. Cohen, "Policy and Organization: The Impact of State and Federal Education Policy on School Governance," *supra* note 2; van Geel, *Authority to Control the School Program, supra* note 2.

5. The police power is the inherent authority of the state to legislate in order to protect the peace, good order, health, morals, and general welfare of the society. Railroad Co. v. Husen, 95 U.S. 465 (1877).

6. This proposition, as well as many others to be discussed in this chapter, may be considered "black letter law": so well settled as to be virtually beyond dispute. For more detailed review of some of the points taken up in this section see the following works: Leroy J. Peterson, Richard A. Rossmiller, and Marlin M. Volz, *The Law and Public School Operation,* 2d ed. (New York: Harper & Row, Publishers, Inc., 1978); William D. Valente, *Law in the Schools (Columbus, Ohio: Charles E. Merrill Publishing Company, 1980); Kern Alexander and M. David Alexander, American Public School Law,* 2d ed. (St. Paul, Minn.: West Publishing Company, 1985); E. Edmund Reutter, Jr., and Robert R. Hamilton, *The Law of Public Education,* 3d ed. (Mineola, N.Y.: The Foundation Press, Inc., 1985); Edward C. Bolmeier, *The School in the Legal Structure,* 2d ed. (Cincinnati, Ohio: The W. H. Anderson Company, 1973); William A. Kaplan, *The Law of Higher Education* (San Francisco: Jossey-Bass Publishers, 1978).

7. Bolmeier, *The School in the Legal Structure, supra,* note 6, at 88.

8. Valente, *Law in the Schools, supra,* note 6, at 35-36. Typically at the state level one finds a state board of regents or board of education with general supervisory and policy-making functions; a chief state school officer filled by election in twenty-one states; and a state department of education—the administrative staff of the board and chief state school officer. The intermediate units may either be organized in terms of county boundaries or be simply complex multi-district units that do not coincide with county lines. These units typically provide special educational services and other administrative services for the local districts. The local school districts, which in some, notably southern, states coincide with county boundaries, are the basic operating educational unit in the states.

9. van Geel, *Authority to Control the School Program, supra,* note 2, at 73.

10. Peterson, et. al, *The Law and Public School Operation, supra,* note 6, at 11, 13, 38. In some states the state board's authority is in part directly derived from the state constitution, thus legislative efforts to regulate the authority of the board and state superintendent can raise a constitutional issue. Bd. of Elementary and Secondary Educ. v. Nix, 347 So.2d 147 (La. 1977). In addition, a legislative effort to regulate the curriculum of the public schools was challenged in Louisiana on the grounds it infringed the constitutional powers of the state board of education that, under the state's constitution, was created to "supervise and control the public elementary and secondary schools . . . as provided by law." The court rejected the challenge and concluded that the authority of the state board was subject to the direction of the state legislature. Aguillard v. Treen, 440 So.2d 704 (La. 1983).

The Oregon Supreme Court concluded that the establishment in the state constitution of the position of state superintendent did not limit the legislature in creating a state board of education with its own authority to issue rules and regulations. State Bd. of Educ. v. Fasold, 445 P.2d 489 (Ore. 1968).

Similarly, state legislative efforts to regulate state boards of higher education that derive their authority from the state constitution can raise the constitutional issue of whether the legislature is improperly interfering with the governance of the state university system. University of Oklahoma v. Baker, 638 P.2d 464 (Okla. 1981); Bd. of Regents University of Nevada System v. Oakley, 97 Nev. 605, 637 P.2d 1199 (Nev. 1981). *See also* Harold W. Horowitz, "The Autonomy of the University of California Under the State Constitution," *UCLA Law Review* 25 (1977): 23.

11. Madlaine K. Remmlein, *School Law* (New York: McGraw-Hill Book Co., 1950), 3.

12. Obviously, to delegate "legislative power" to appointed officials not directly responsible to the public would undermine democratic control. John Locke wrote in 1690 that "the legislature cannot transfer the power of making laws to any other hands; for it being but a delegated power from the people, they who have it cannot pass it over to others." John Locke, *The Second Treatise of Civil Government* (New York: The Bobbs-Merrill Co., Inc., 1952), 81.

13. State v. Kinnear, 70 Wash.2d 482, 423 P.2d 937 (1967) (en banc).

14. Matter of Bd. of Educ. of City of Trenton, 176 N.J. Super, 553, 424 A.2d 435 (Superior Ct., A.D., N.J., 1980), *aff'd.* 86 N.J. 327, 431 A. 2d 808 (Sup. Ct. N.J. 1981); Kenneth Culp Davis, *Discretionary Justice* (Urbana, Ill.: University of Illinois Press, 1969), 27ff; Peterson, et. al,

The Law and Public School Operation, supra, note 6, at 9; Alexander and Alexander, *American Public School Law, supra,* note 6, at 88-90; Valente, *Law in the Schools, supra,* note 6, at 23-29.

15. *See, e.g.,* State of Kansas v. Bd. of Educ., 215 Kan. 551, 527 P.2d 952 (1974) (upholding delegation of power to the state school board to reorganize school districts by transferring territory between districts).

16. 212 Kan. 482, 511 P.2d 705 (1973).

17. 321 S.E.2d 302 (1984).

18. Morrison v. State Bd. of Education, 1 Cal.3d 214, 461 P.2d 375, 82 Cal. Rptr. 175 (Cal. 1969). A California appeals court has held that there is no need for an unfitness finding where dismissal for unprofessional conduct relates to classroom conduct. Powers v. Bakersfield City Sch. Dist., 157 Cal. App.3d 560, 205 Cal. Rptr. 185, 194 (Cal. App. 5 Dist. 1984).

A number of cases have adopted the Morrison approach with varying results. *See, e.g,* Bd. of Educ. of Long Beach Unified Sch. Dist. of Los Angeles Cty. v. Jack M., 566 P.2d 602 (Cal. 1977) (teacher who was once observed masturbating in a public toilet stall by a deputy sheriff and who invited the officer to engage in a homosexual act was not unfit to teach); Pettit v. State Bd. of Educ., 10 Cal.3d 29, 109 Cal. Rptr. 665, 513 P.2d 889 (Cal. 1973) (teacher who in a private home, but in the presence of twenty other people, engaged in multiple acts of sexual intercourse and oral copulation with men not her husband, was unfit to teach).

19. Girard Sch. Dist. v. Pittenger, 370 A.2d 420 (Commwealth Ct. 1977).

20. For a review of other cases see Reutter and Hamilton, *The Law of Public Education, supra,* note 6, at chap. 3.

21. Girard Sch. Dist. v. Pittenger, 392 A.2d 261 (Pa. 1978).

22. Id., at 265. *Cf.,* District Township v. City of Dubuque, 7 Iowa 7 ((Clarke), 262 1858) (interpreting a provision of the Iowa constitution stating that education "shall be under the management of a board of education").

23. van Geel, *Authority to Control the School Program, supra,* note 2, at 113-15; Alexander and Alexander, *American Public School Law, supra,* note 6, at 93-94.

24. Kiddie Korner Day Schools Inc. v. Charlotte-Mecklenburg Bd. of Educ., 285 S.E.2d 110 (N.C. App. 1981) (upholding authority of board to offer an after school day-care program at a fee of fifteen dollars per day); Bartnett v. Durant Comm. Sch. Dist., 249 N.W.2d 626 (1977) (upholding authority of board to pay tuition expenses of teachers); Bettendorf Ed. Ass'n v. Bettendorf Comm. Sch. Dist., 262 N.W.2d 550 (1978); Burton v. Pasadena City Bd. of Educ., 71 Cal. App. 3d 52, 139 Cal. Rptr. 383 (1977) (board could not condition access of child to a school on agreement of parents to allow use of corporal punishment); Independent Sch. Dist. No. 8 of Seiling v. Swanson, 553 P.2d 496 (1976) (holding school board did not have the statutory authority to impose a student hair code). Parsippany-Troy Hills Educ. Ass'n v. Bd. of Educ., 188 N.J. Super. 161, 457 A.2d 15 (N.J. Super. A.D. 1983), *cert. denied,* 94 N.J. 527 (N.J. 1983); Peterson, et. al., *The Law and Public School Operation, supra,* note 6, at 38.

25. Peterson, et. al., *The Law and Public School Operation, supra,* note 6, at 132, 133, 149, 151, 180.

26. In Clark v. Jefferson County Bd. of Educ., 410 So.2d 23 (Ala. 1982) the court concluded a county board of education had implied authority to establish a day-care center; Welling v. Bd. of Educ. for Livonia Sch. Dist., 382 Mich. 620, 171 N.W.2d 545 (1969) (upholding authority of district to order half-days session); Peterson, et. al., *The Law and Public School Operation, supra,* note 6, at generally; Alexander and Alexander, *American Public School Law, supra,* note 6, at chaps. 7, 17, 18. In Independent Sch. Dist. No. 8 of Seiling v. Swanson, 553 P.2d 496 (Okla. 1976) the Oklahoma Supreme Court concluded that because regulating a student's hair style affected the private lives of students outside of school, such a rule was like a rule regulating a student's out-of-school activities—a power the district did not have; hence it concluded that the school board had not been delegated the authority to impose hair-style codes.

27. Columbia Cty. Adm. Sch. Dist. No. 5 Joint v. Prichard, 585 P.2d 701, 36 Or. App. 643 (Or. App. 1978) (prohibiting a local board from establishing additional qualifications for membership on the local board as this was a field preempted by state legislation).

28. Peterson, et. al., *The Law and Public School Operation, supra*, note 6, at 41, 46; Dalanes v. Bd. of Educ., 120 Ill. App. 3d 505, 75 Ill. Dec. 823, 457 N.E.2d 1382 (Ill. App. 2nd Dist. 1983).

29. Bd. of Educ. of Carroll Cty. v. Carroll Cty. Educ. Ass'n Inc., 53 Md.A. 355, 452 A.2d 1316 (Mo. App. 1982).

30. *See, e.g.*, Johnson v. Joint Sch. Dist. No. 60, Bingham Cty., 95 Idaho 317, 508 P.2d 547 (1973) (striking down a portion of the school's dress code that prohibited female students from wearing slacks, pantsuits, or culottes to school).

31. Anne Bridgman, "States Launching Barrage of Initiatives, Survey Finds," *Education Week* 4 (1985): 1, 31.

32. Some challenges have been raised but notably not on the grounds that the legislature, and/or state board and chief state school officer lacked authority to impose the reform. Rather the challenges have had other bases such as that the policy violated a constitutional right or was inconsistent with a federal statute, and therefore unlawful as a violation of the supremacy clause of the U.S. Constitution. Bd. of Educ. v. Ambach, 107 Misc. 2d 830, 436 N.Y.S.2d 564 (N.Y. Sup. Ct. 1981) (unsuccessful challenge to the commissioner's denial of award of high school diploma to two handicapped students due to their failure to pass state competency tests); Debra P. v. Turlington, 474 F. Supp. 244 (M.D. Fla. 1979), *aff'd in part and vacated in part and remanded*, 644 F.2d 397 (5th Cir. 1981), *on remand*, 564 F. Supp. 177 (M.D. Fla. 1983), *aff'd*, 730 F.2d 1405 (11th Cir. 1984) (upholding in part and denying in part challenges to Florida's competency testing program).

33. Ravitch, *The Troubled Crusade: American Education 1945-1980, supra*, note 2; Marvin Lazerson disputes the claim of Kaestle and Smith that the modern role of the federal government in education is continuous with general trends in American history. Kaestle and Smith, "The Federal Role in Elementary and Secondary Education, 1940-1980"; Marvin Lazerson, "Responses," *Harvard Educational Review* 52 (1982): 409.

34. 347 U.S. 483 (1954).

35. Carl F. Kaestle and Marshal S. Smith, "The Federal Role in Elementary and Secondary Education, 1940-1980," *Harvard Educational Review* 52 (1982): 384, 401. By far and away the most significant of the new form of federal assistance was that provided through Title I of the Elementary and Secondary Education Act of 1965 that provided aid for educational deprived citizens. Title I was formally found at 20 U.S.C. 241 a et. seq. (1976), now to be found as Chapter I of the Education Consolidation and Improvement Act of 1981, 20 U.S.C. §3801 et. seq. (1982).

36. Civil Rights Act of 1964, Title IV, 42 U.S.C. §2000(d) (1982) (prohibiting discrimination of the basis of race in federally assisted programs); Civil Rights Act of 1964, Title VII, 42 U.S.C. §2000e-2a (1982) (prohibiting discrimination in employment on the basis of race, gender, national origin, and religion); Education Amendments of 1972, Title IX, 20 U.S.C. §1681 (1976) (prohibiting discrimination on the basis of gender in federally assisted programs); Equal Pay Act of 1963, 29 U.S.C. §206(d) (1982) (prohibiting discrimination in pay on the basis of sex for jobs that require equal skill, effort, responsibility, and that are performed under similar working conditions); Age Discrimination in Employment Act of 1967, as amended 1978, 29 U.S.C.§621 (1982) (prohibiting discrimination in employment on the basis of age as regards people between the ages of forty and seventy; Rehabilitation Act of 1973, §504, 29 U.S.C. §794 (1982) (prohibiting discrimination on the basis of handicap in federally assisted programs); Equal Educational Opportunities Act of 1974, 20 U.S.C. §1701 (1976) (prohibiting discrimination on the basis of race, color, sex, or national origin by failing to take action to overcome language barriers that impede equal participation in educational programs).

37. Article 1, §8 gives Congress the authority to "regulate Commerce . . . among the several States." In addition to this enumerated power, Article 1, §8 also empowers Congress to "make all Laws which shall be necessary and proper for carrying into Execution" the specific powers of §8 and all other powers vested by the Constitution. The "necessary and proper" clause explicitly recognizes that Congress has powers that may be implied from the explicit powers. Article 1, §8 also provides that "Congress shall have Power . . . to pay the Debts and provide for the common

Defense and general Welfare of the United States." This authority to spend money with conditions attached provides Congress with a powerful regulatory tool. The thirteenth, fourteenth, and fifteenth amendment, by their own terms give to Congress power to enforce the articles by appropriate legislation.

This paragraph closely follows the analysis by Jeff Powell in his article "The Complete Jeffersonian: Justice Rehnquist and Federalism," *Yale Law Journal* 91 (1982): 1317.

38. Fry v. United States, 421 U.S. 542, 552-53 (1975) (Rehnquist, J., dissenting).

39. Trimble v. Gordon, 430 U.S. 762, 778 (1977).

40. National League of Cities v. Usery, 426 U.S. 833, 845 (1976) (majority opinion by Rehnquist, J.). This decision has been overruled in Garcia v. San Antonio Metro. Transit Authority, 105 S.Ct. 1005 (1985).

41. Ray v. Atlantic Richfield Co., 435 U.S. 151, 180-87 (1978) (Marshal, J., concurring in part and dissenting in part). Justice Rehnquist joined in this opinion of Marshall.

42. Nevada v. Hall, 440 U.S. 410, 441 n. 6 (1979) (Rehnquist, J., dissenting).

43. The amendment states, "The Judicial power of the United States shall not be construed to extend to any suit in law or equity, commenced or prosecuted against one of the United States by Citizens of another State, or by Citizens or Subjects of any Foreign State." U.S. Const. Amendment 11.

44. 22 U.S. (9 Wheat.) 1, 209 (1824).

45. Hines v. Davidowitz, 312 U.S. 52 (1941) (holding that a state law requiring the registration of aliens was preempted by a federal law on the same subject).

46. Rice v. Santa Fe Elevator Corp., 331 U.S. 218 (1947).

47. For a further analysis of developments in this area see Tribe, *American Constitutional Law, supra*, note 3, at 376-401.

48. Compare San Antonio Indep. Sch. Dist. v. Rodriguez, 411 U.S. 1 (1973) (holding Texas's system for financing schools did not violate the equal protection clause of the U.S. Constitution), with Serrano v. Priest, 5 Cal.3d 584, 487 P.2d 1241, 96 Cal. Rptr. 601 (1971) (holding California's system for financing schools did violate the equal protection clause of the California Constitution).

49. 105 S.Ct. 695 (1985). State courts are also sensitive to the preemption issue. In the Matter of "A" Family, 184 Mont. 145, 602 P.2d 157 (1979) (recognizing federal law preempted a state regulation on the handicapped).

50. In Shepard v. Godwin, 280 F. Supp. 869 (D.C. Eastern Vir., 1968) the district court held that a state formula for state assistance to local districts that deducted from the share otherwise allocable to the district a sum equal to a substantial percentage of any federal "impact" funds receivable by the district contravened the supremacy clause. (Today such a deduction has been specifically authorized by Congress in an amendment to the Impact Aid Act in 1974. 20 U.S.C. §240 (d) (2) (A) (1982)). In Wheeler v. Barrera, 417 U.S. 402 (1974) the Supreme Court concluded that Title I evinced a clear intention that state constitutional spending proscriptions were not to be preempted as a condition to accepting federal funds.

51. *See, e.g.,* Fiske v. Kansas, 274 U.S. 380 (1927); Near v. Minnesota, 283 U.S. 697 (1931); DeJonge v. Oregon, 299 U.S. 353 (1937); Hague v. CIO, 307 U.S. 496 (1939); Cantwell v. Connecticut, 310 U.S. 296 (1940); Everson v. Bd. of Education, 330 U.S. 1 (1947); Wolf v. Colorado, 338 U.S. 25 (1949). Other provisions of the Bill of Rights have also been made applicable to the states but are of less relevance to education, e.g., the fifth and sixth amendments deal with the rights of the criminally accused. The Court has specifically said that the eighth amendment's prohibitions against cruel and unusual punishments is not applicable to school disciplinary procedures. Ingraham v. Wright, 430 U.S. 651 (1977).

52. *See* Project Report, "Toward an Activist Role for State Bills of Rights," *Harvard Civil Rights-Civil Liberties Law Review* 8(1973): 271.

53. The thirteenth amendment prohibits slavery and involuntary servitude; the fourteenth amendment prohibits, among other things, any state from depriving "any person of life, liberty,

or property, without due process of law," as well as denying them "the equal protection of the laws." The fifteenth amendment protects the right of citizens to vote and prohibits the denial or abridgement of the right to vote "on account of race, color, or previous condition of servitude."

54. Fitzpatrick v. Bitzer, 427 U.S. 445 (1976) (upholding the enforcement of Title VII—which prohibits discrimination in employment on the basis of race, gender, national origin, and religion—against the states). The eleventh amendment will be taken up in greater detail later.

55. 42 U.S.C. §§1971, 1973-1973bb-1 (1976) (further amended by the Voting Rights Act Amendments of 1982, 42 U.S.C.A. §§1973, 1973b, 1973aa-1a, 6 (West. Supp. 1983). The act is aimed at eliminating racial discrimination that affects the right to vote.

56. South Carolina Katzenbach, 383 U.S.301, 327 (1966).

57. Katzenbach v. Morgan, 384 U.S. 641 (1966) (upholding §4(e) of the Voting Rights Act of 1965); Lassiter v. Northampton Cty. Bd. of Elections, 360 U.S. 45 (1959) (upholding an English literacy requirement as constitutionally permissible).

58. Katzenbach v. Morgan, at 651 n. 10.

59. Katzenbach v. McClung, 379 U.S. 294 (1964).

60. Garcia v. San Antonio Metropolitan Transit Authority, 105 S.Ct. 1005 (1985). The Court in this decision reversed course and overruled National League of Cities v. Usery, 426 U.S. 833 (1976).

61. Spending on education is based on the power of Congress to lay and collect taxes for the general welfare. U.S. Constitution, Article 1, Section 8. The regulations that have accompanied federal assistance to local districts have come in two forms: (1) those attached to a particular grant of money, e.g., the conditions that accompany federal assistance for aid to handicapped children under the Education for All Handicapped Children Act, 20 U.S.C.§§1401-61 (1982); and (2) those regulations that are not attached to a particular grant of money, but that are enforced by a threat of the cutoff of all federal financial assistance, e.g., Title IX of the 1972 Education Amendments, 20 U.S.C. §§1681-86 (1982), which prohibits discrimination on the basis of gender.

For a review of the grant system see: Mark Suben, "Federal Grants and the Tenth Amendment: 'Things as They Are' and Fiscal Federalism," *Fordham Law Review* 50 (1981): 130; Lewis B. Kaden, "Politics, Money, and State Sovereignty: The Judicial Role," *Columbia Law Review* 79 (1979): 847.

62. This is the interpretation of Stewart Machine Co. v. Davis, 301 U.S. 548 (1937) offered by a lower court in Vermont v. Brinegar, 379 F. Supp. 606, 616 (D. Vt. 1974), as quoted in "Taking Federalism Seriously: Limiting State Acceptance of National Grants," *Yale Law Journal* 90 (1981): 1694, 1697.

63. Garcia v. San Antonio Metropolitan Transit Authority, 105 S. Ct. 1005 (1985); Bell v. New Jersey and Pennsylvania, 461 U.S. 773 (1983).

64. Pennhurst State School and Hospital v. Halderman, 451 U.S. 1 (1981); Bennett v. Kentucky Dept. of Educ., 84 L.Ed.2d 590 (1985).

65. Grove City College v. Bell, 104 S. Ct. 1211 (1984) (holding, among other things, that the prohibition against sex discrimination attached to the right to continue to receive federal funds did not violate the first amendment rights of Grove City College since it could terminate its participation in the student financial aid program at any time). The Court in *Grove City College* also held that federal prohibitions against sex discrimination are applicable to colleges, even if they refuse all forms of direct federal assistance, if they admit students who themselves participate in a federal financial assistance program. The Court said that receipt of federal assistance by some of Grove City's students did not make the prohibition against sex discriminatin applicable to the entire institution, but only to the "program" that can be deemed to have received federal assistance—in this case the college's student financial aid program.

66. 20 U.S.C. § 1232a (1982).

67. Irving Indep. Sch. Dist. v. Tatro, 104 S.Ct. 3371 (1984); Lau v. Nichols, 414 U.S. 563 (1974).

68. Bell v. New Jersey and Pennsylvania, 461 U.S. 773 (1983) (rejecting the view that state sovereignty is violated when states are ordered to repay misused federal assistance).

69. Bennett v. Kentucky Dept. of Educ., 105 S.Ct. 1544 (1985).

70. Id. The Court found it necessary in this case to adopt the government's suggestion that the secretary of education would rely on any reasonable interpretation of the Title I requirements to determine that state expenditures violated grant conditions. The Court also did not decide if a state may be held liable where its interpretation of an ambiguous requirement is more reasonable than the government's interpretation advanced after the grants were made.

71. Bennett v. New Jersey, 105 S.Ct. 1544 (1985).

72. Hans v. Louisiana, 134 U.S. 1 (1890). At least that is how the Court today interprets the result in *Hans*. Atascadero State Hospital v. Scanlon, 87 L.Ed.2d 171, 177 (1985).

73. Atascadero State Hospital v. Scanlon, 87 L.Ed.2d 171 (1985); Pennhurst State Sch. & Hospital v. Halderman, 465 U.S. 89 (1984).

74. Alabama v. Pugh, 438 U.S. 781 (1978).

75. Edelman v. Jordan, 415 U.S. 651 (1974).

76. Employees v. Department of Pub. Health & Welfare, 411 U.S. 279 (1973).

77. *See, e.g.*, Thomas v. Review Bd., Ind. Empl. Sec. Div., 450 U.S. 707 (1981).

78. Atascadero State Hospital v. Scanlon, 87 L. Ed.2d 171, 179 (1985). In this case the Court found that Congress had not so clearly indicated that it intended to abrogate the states' eleventh amendment protections when it adopted §504 of the Rehabilitation Act of 1973, 29 U.S.C. §794 (1982), which prohibits discrimination on the basis of handicap in programs receiving federal funds.

Lower federal courts have concluded, however, that Congress did intend to subject the states to suit in federal court under the Education for All Handicapped Children Act, 20 U.S.C. §1401 (1982). David D. v. Dartmouth Sch. Comm., 775 F.2d 411 (1st Cir. 1985); Parks v. Pavkovic, 753 F.2d 1397 (7th Cir. 1985); Crawford v. Pittman, 708 F.2d 1028 (5th Cir. 1983).

79. Id. at 179. The state must express this waiver in unequivocal language to permit itself to be sued in federal courts.

80. Florida Dept. of Health v. Florida Nursing Home Ass'n, 450 U.S. 147, 150 (1981).

81. Atascadero State Hospital v. Scanlon, 87 L.Ed.2d 171, 183 (1985).

82. Id.

83. Ex Parte Young, 209 U.S. 123 (1908). In other words, action of a state official that violates the Constitution is not deemed to be an act of the state itself—it is simply an illegal act by the official who attempts to use the name of the state. In the cases discussed in chapter 1 involving attacks on state aid to private church-affiliated schools, the plaintiffs typically name a state official, such as the chief state school officer, as the defendant. Lemon v. Kurtzman, Superintendent of Public Instruction of Pennsylvania, 403 U.S. 602 (1971). Thus, the concept of what is "state action" is narrowly defined for purposes of enforcing the eleventh amendment. If the Court had not drawn this fictional distinction between the state itself and state officers, the eleventh amendment might have served as a bar to the enforcement of the thirteenth, fourteenth, and fifteenth amendments against the states. Judicial efforts to deal with state-sponsored racial discrimination, for example, could have been blocked.

Note that the use of the fiction that the unconstitutional acts of state officials are not "state action" is abandoned by the Court for purposes of enforcement of the fourteenth and other amendments. Home Tel. & Tel. Co. v. City of Los Angeles, 227 U.S. 278 (1913). Thus, such unconstitutional acts are deemed to be a form of state action and subject to the limits of the fourteenth amendment and other amendments.

84. Quern v. Jordan, 440 U.S. 332, 337 (1979).

85. Milliken v. Bradley, 433 U.S. 267 (1977). In *Milliken* the Court approved the ordering of compensatory or remedial education programs for children subjected to past acts of de jure segregation. The remedial efforts approved also include magnet schools, in-service training for teachers, the institution of testing programs free of racial bias, and career guidance programs. Despite the eleventh amendment, the Court approved a requirement that the state pay half the costs of the program because that amendment is not violated when a state payment is ordered as

a necessary consequence of compliance with a substantive federal question in the future. Here segregation victims would continue to experience bad effects until such "future time as the remedial programs help dissipate the continuing effects of past misconduct." The remedy, though in part "compensatory," also operated prospectively by bringing about the delayed benefits of a unitary school system. Id., 289-90.

86. Mt. Healthy City Sch. Dist. v. Doyle, 429 U.S. 274 (1977).

87. See, e.g., Harden v. Adams, 760 F.2d 1158 (11th Cir. 1985) (concluding, inter alia, that Troy State University was protected by the eleventh amendment).

88. 42 U.S.C. §1983 (1982). The Supreme Court has interpreted §1983 to allow the award of compensatory and punitive damages but not damages for the "abstract value" of a right protected by the Constitution. Memphis Community Sch. Dist. v. Strachura, 91 L.Ed.2d 249 (1986); Carey v. Piphus, 435 U.S. 247 (1978).

89. Mitchum v. Foster, 407 U.S. 225, 242 (1972). The law was adopted in 1871 in order to expand the jurisdiction of the federal courts as part of the effort to protect the civil liberties and civil rights of the newly freed slaves following the Civil War and the passage of the thirteenth, fourteenth, and fifteenth amendments. "Developments in the Law—Section 1983 and Federalism," Harvard Law Review 90 (1977): 1133, 1141 et seq.

90. Quern v. Jordan, 440 U.S. 332, 341 (1979).

91. The fictional doctrine that state officials may be sued despite the eleventh amendment does not apply when the state official is accused of violating state, rather than federal, law. Pennhurst State Sch. and Hospital v. Halderman, 104 S. Ct. 900, 919 (1984).

92. Monell v. Department of Social Services, 436 U.S. 658 (1978); Quern v. Jordan, 440 U.S. 332 (1979). A §1983 action may also be brought in state courts. Martinez v. California, 444 U.S. 277 (1980).

93. Monroe v. Pape, 365 U.S. 167 (1961).

94. Parratt v. Taylor, 451 U.S. 527 (1981).

95. In Wood v. Strickland, 420 U.S. 308 (1975) the Court said a school official would enjoy qualified immunity (no absolute immunity) from suit unless it were shown that the official "knew or reasonably should have known that the action he took within his sphere of official responsibility would violate the constitutional rights of the [plantiff], or if he took the action with the malicious intention to cause a deprivation of constitutional rights or other injury" (emphasis added). In a later case the Court said the qualified "good faith" immunity was an affirmative defense that must be pleaded by the official. Gomez v. Toledo, 446 U.S. 635 (1980). In 1982 the Court overruled the subjective element of the good-faith defense (see the italicized language in Wood). The Court held that "government officials performing discretionary functions, generally are shielded from liability for civil damages insofar as their conduct does not violate clearly established statutory or constitutional rights of which a reasonable person should have known." Harlow v. Fitzgerald, 457 U.S. 800, 818 (1982).

96. Owen v. City of Independence, 445 U.S. 622 (1980).

97. Monell v. Department of Social Servs., 436 U.S. 658, 690 (1978). Thus a frequent issue in suits in which the political subdivision is charged with violating federal law is whether the officials involved in the incident were acting pursuant to official policy. Sometimes the question is phrased in terms of whether the actions involved are part of a pattern or practice of illegal behavior. See, e.g., Doe v. Thomas, 604 F. Supp. 1508 (N.D. Ill. 1985). It is also said there must be a nexus between the illegal act and policy and procedure. City of Oklahoma City v. Tuttle, 105 S.Ct. 2427 (1985).

98. Patsy v. Board of Regents of State of Florida, 457 U.S. 496 (1982); Monroe v. Pape, 365 U.S. 167, 183 (1961).

99. Allen v. McCurry, 499 U.S. 90 (1980).

100. Migra v. Warren Cty. Sch. Dist. Bd. of Educ., 104 S.Ct. 892 (1984). See also Tompkins v. Gargiul, 104 S. Ct. 1263 (1984) (mem.); Gargiul v. Tompkins, 739 F.2d 34 (2d Cir. 1984) (on remand). Other important jurisdictional limits are discussed in two other cases. Pennhurst State

School and Hospital v. Halderman, 104 S.Ct. 900 (1984) (discussing limits on pendent jurisdiction); Younger v. Harris, 401 U.S. 31 (1971) (placing limits on the bringing of federal anticipatory challenges designed to abort pending or threatened state court proceedings).

101. City of Los Angeles v. Lyons, 461 U.S. 95 (1983).

102. Smith v. Robinson, 104 S. Ct. 3457, 3469 (1984).

103. Wilson v. Garcia, 85 L.Ed.2d 254 (1985).

104. In Cort v. Ash, 422 U.S. 66 (1975) the Court listed the factors to be considered in determining whether a private remedy is implicit in a statute not expressly providing such a remedy.

105. Alexander v. Choate, 105 S.Ct. 712 (1985); Guardian Ass'n v. Civil Service Commission, 463 U.S. 582 (1983).

106. Cannon v. University of Chicago, 441 U.S. 677 (1979).

107. Miener v. State of Missouri, 673 F.2d 969 (8th Cir. 1982); Marvin H. v. Austin Indep. Sch. Dist., 714 F.2d 1348 (5th Cir. 1983). *See* Smith v. Robinson, 104 S. Ct. 3457 (1984) (holding that a handicapped child could not circumvent the procedural requirements of the Education of All Handicapped Children Act, 94-142, by resort to the antidiscrimination provisions of §504, and that §504 could not be relied upon to obtain damages and attorney fees not available under 94-142.)

108. Hadley v. Junior College District, 397 U.S. 50 (1970); Avery v. Midland County, 390 U.S. 474 (1968); Reynolds v. Sims, 377 U.S. 533 (1964). The one person-one vote, one vote-one value doctrine rests on a theory of democracy that stresses the need to protect the individual right to vote, as opposed to a theory that suggests that minority interests (economic, racial, or ethnic) may be protected against "majority tyranny" by assuring them of greater representation in the legislative body than their numbers warrant. Thus, under the latter theory a small ethnic community may be assured one representative on a school board to assure its interests are protected in an election system in which representatives run from districts and not at large; whereas other districts with larger populations may also get only one representative. The Supreme Court rejects this arrangement on the grounds it dilutes the vote of the individual voters in the election districts with the larger populations.

The one person-one vote, one vote-one value doctrine does not apply when members of the governing board are appointed from various districts that comprise the school district. Sailors v. Board of Education, 387 U.S. 105 (1967).

109. Barnes v. Bd. of Directors Mt. Anthony Union High Sch. Dist., 418 F. Supp. 845 (D.C. Vt. 1976); Oliver v. Bd. of Educ. of City of New York, 306 F. Supp. 1286 (S.D. N.Y. 1969); *cf.,* Cook v. Luckett, 735 F.2d 912 (5th Cir. 1984).

110. Rogers v. Lodge, 458 U.S. 613 (1982); Mobile v. Bolden, 446 U.S. 55 (1980); Brown v. Bd. of Sch. Comm. of Mobile Cty., Ala., 706 F.2d 1103 (11th Cir. 1983), *aff'd,* 104 S. Ct. 520 (1983); NAACP by Campbell v. Gadsden Cty. Sch. Bd., 691 F.2d 978 (1982); McMillan v. Escambia Cty., Fla., 688 F. 2d 960 (5th Cir. 1982).

111. Rodgers v. Lodge, 458 U.S. 613 (1982); White v. Register, 412 U.S. 755 (1973); Zimmer v. McKeithen, 485 F.2d 1297 (5th Cir. 1973) (en banc), *aff'd on other grounds sub nom.,* East Carroll Parish Sch. Bd. v. Marshall, 424 U.S. 636 (1976) (per curiam). *Cf.,* City of Mobile v. Bolden, 446 U.S. 55 (1980) in which the Court specifically stated that the Zimmer criteria were insufficient to establish discriminatory intent. In *Rogers* the Court may have accepted the view that meeting the Zimmer criteria was sufficient to prove discriminatory intent.

112. Whitcomb v. Chavis, 403 U.S. 124 (1971).

113. 42 U.S.C. §1971 (1982).

114. 42 U.S.C. §1973(c) (1982).

115. The states covered are: Alabama, Alaska, Arizona, California, Florida, Georgia, Louisiana, Michigan, Mississippi, New Hampshire, New York, North Carolina, South Carolina, South Dakota, Texas, and Virginia. 50 Fed. Reg. 19122 (1985) (to be codified at 28 C.F.R. §51).

116. A Senate report lists seven factors: (1) extent of history of official discrimination; (2) extent to which voting is racially polarized; (3) extent to which unusually large election districts

majority vote requirements, or anti-single shot provision (or similar practices) are used; (4) denial of access to a candidate slating process; (5) discrimination in such areas as education, employment, and health that hinder opportunity to participate in the political process; (6) overt or subtle racial campaign appeals; and (7) extent of minority electoral success. S. Rep. No. 417, 97th Cong., 2nd Sess, *reprinted in* 1982 U.S. Code Cong. and Ad. News 205.

In Thornburg v. Gingles, 92 L.Ed.2d 25 (1986) a sharply divided Court examined the questions of: (1) the general legal principles relevant to the claim that §2 has been violated through the use of a multimember district; (2) the standard to be used to determine if there is a legally significant racial bloc voting in a multimember district; (3) the type of evidence relevant for establishing the existence of racial bloc voting; (4) and the legal significance of the fact that in the past some black candidates may have had electoral success. The degree of division on the Court is reflected in the fact that one majority of five justices agreed, for example, to the answer to questions 1 and 2, but a different group of five constituted the majority on the answer to question 3. In any event, this decision(s) is the latest and most important word from the Court on the interpretation and application of §2, and the use of the seven factors listed in the Senate report.

For discussions of the Voting Rights Act see generally volume 33, no. 1 (1985), of the *U.C.L.A. Law Review;* Barnes, "Vote Dilution, Discriminatory Results, and Proportional Representation: What is the Appropriate Remedy for a Violation of Section 2 of the Voting Rights Act, *U.C.L.A. Law Review* 32 (1985):1203; McKenzie and Krauss, "Section 2 of the Voting Rights Act: An Analysis of the 1982 Amendment," *Harvard Civil Rights-Civil Liberties Law Review* 19 (1984): 155, 163ff.

117. The effort to create "safe" districts is itself permissible. United Jewish Organizations v. Carey, 430 U.S. 144 (1977). But *cf.*, Peters v. Moses, 613 F. Supp 1328 (W.D. Vir. 1985) (striking the reservation of two seats on an appointed school board for minority citizens). *Also see* Mayor v. Educational Equality League, 415 U.S. 605 (1974) (dismissal of claim that Mayor's predominantly white appointments to a school board nominating panel were racially biased).

For a challenge that the creation of the safe district resulted in "packing," see Latino Pol. Action Comm. v. City of Boston, 609 F. Supp. 739, 746 (D.C. Mass. 1985), *aff'd,* 784 F.2d 409 (1st Cir. 1986). *See also* Wright v. Rockefeller, 376 U.S. 52 (1964); Panior v. Iberville Parish Sch. Bd, 536 F.2d 101 (5th Cir. 1976).

118. Id.

119. See Gomillon v. Lightfoot, 364 U.S. 339 (1960).

120. United Jewish Organizations v. Carey, 430 U.S. 144 (1977).

121. Kramer v. Union Free Sch. Dist. No. 15, 395 U.S. 621 (1969). The Court has also struck down state efforts granting only property-tax payers the right to vote in various bond elections. Phoenix v. Kolodziejski, 399 U.S. 204 (1970); Cipriano v. City of Houma, 395 U.S. 701 (1969). Year-long durational residency requirements have also been struck down. Dunn v. Blumstein, 405 U.S. 330 (1972).

122. Voting Rights Act of 1965, 42 U.S.C. §1973(b)(e)(1)(1976). The authority of Congress to impose this prohibition on the states was upheld in Katzenbach v. Morgan, 384 U.S. 641 (1966).

123. Pickering v. Bd. of Educ., 391 U.S. 563 (1968). Thus, today the Court rejects the positions expressed so pithily by Justice Holmes who, when sitting on the Supreme Judicial Court of Massachusetts, said: "A policeman may have a constitutional right to talk politics, but he does not have a constitutional right to be a policeman." McAuliffe v. Mayor of New Bedford, 155 Mass. 216, 220, 29 N.E. 517, 517 (1892).

124. Mt. Healthy City Sch. Dist. Bd. of Educ. v. Doyle, 429 U.S. 274 (1977).

125. Id., at 287. *Compare* Goss v. San Jacinto Jr. College, 588 F.2d 96 (5th Cir. 1979); Zoll v. Eastern Allamakee Community Sch. Dist., 588 F.2d 246 (8th Cir. 1978).

126. Connick v. Myers, 461 U.S. 138 (1983); Pickering v. Bd. of Educ., 391 U.S. 563 (1968). *See also* Givhan v. Western Line Consolidated Sch. Dist., 439 U.S. 410 (1976) (holding that the fact that a teacher's criticism of the school board's policies on racial issues is privately expressed to the principal does not remove it from protection of Pickering).

127. The Court has written that speech that is not a matter of public concern is not "totally beyond the protection of the first amendment." Connick v. Myers, 461 U.S., at 147. Thus, the Court suggested that false criticism of the employer on grounds not of public concern is entitled to the same protection in a libel action that is accorded to the same statement made by a person on the street. Id. "We only hold that when a public employee speaks not as a citizen upon matters of public concern, but instead as an employee on matters only of personal interest, absent the most unusual circumstances, a federal court is not the appropriate forum in which to review the wisdom of a personnel decision taken by a public agency allegedly in reaction to the employee's behavior." *Id.*

It is not clear from this passage whether the Court is suggesting that teachers should not even enjoy the protections usually afforded by the lower courts for teacher speech activities not related to matters of public concern, e.g., the teacher may not be dismissed unless the speech activity causes material and substantial disruption of the school. See infra, §6.4. In this connection consider Rowland v. Mad River Loc. Sch. Dist., Montgomery Cty., 730 F.2d 444 (6th Cir. 1984), *cert. denied,* 105 S.Ct. 1373 (1985), in which the Court upheld the dismissal of a teacher who had informed a school secretary and several other teachers that she was bisexual. The Court said that these statements were not a matter of public concern and were not protected speech. In a dissent from the denial of certiorari, Justice Brennan argued that Majorie Rowland's comments on her bisexuality ineluctably involved her in a debate that was a matter of public concern. He also added that even if her speech did not touch on a matter of public concern, her speech deserved constitutional protection. The case, he said, poses the "open question whether nondisruptive speech even can constitutionally serve as a basis for termination under the First Amendment." *Id.,* at 1376.

128. In Pickering v. Bd. of Educ., 391 U.S. 563 (1968) the teacher's letter to a local newspaper attacked the school board's handling of a local bond issue and its allocation of financial resources between the school's educational and athletic program, and charged the superintendent with attempting to prevent teachers from opposing the proposed bond issue. The letter contained a number of errors, such as the amount of money the district expended on athletics: Pickering overstated the amount.

129. The Court concluded in Pickering that the erroneous statements by the teacher were neither made knowingly nor in reckless disregard of the truth. *Compare* Gregory v. Durham Cty. Bd. of Educ., 591 F. Supp. 145, 153 (M.D. N.C. 1984) (article with errors was based on information taken from newsletter of a teachers' organization, but was not published in reckless disregard of the truth).

It would seem to be clear that expressions of "opinion" cannot be adjudged as to whether they were knowingly or recklessly false. Wichert v. Walter, 606 F. Supp. 1516, 1525 (D, N.J. 1985).

130. Pickering v. Bd. of Educ., 391 U.S. 563, 574 n. 6 (1968).

131. *See* Megill v. Bd. of Regents, 607 F.2d 114 (1st Cir. 1976); Rosado v. Garcia Santiago, 562 F.2d 114 (1st Cir. 1977). *See also* Lindsey v. Bd. of Regents, 541 F.2d 1073, 1085 (5th Cir. 1976).

132. Connick v. Myers, 461 U.S. 138, 147-8 (1983).

133. Id., at 149.

134. Id., at 148 n. 8.

135. Id., at 149.

136. Givhan v. Western Line Consolidated Sch. Dist., 439 U.S. 410 (1979). In *Connick* the Court stressed that *Connick v. Myers* was factually distinguishable from the Givhan case because Mrs. Givhan spoke on a matter of general concern not tied to a personal employment dispute.

137. Pickering v. Bd. of Educ., 391 U.S. 563 (1968), *aff'd,* 781 F.2d 1508 (11th Cir. 1986). Note that the Eleventh Circuit Court's opinion specifically rejects the view that the degree of attention paid to the subject of the employee's speech is relevant in determining whether the speech is a matter of public concern.

138. Ferrara v. Mills, 596 F. Supp. 1069 (S.D. Fla. 1984).

139. Cox v. Dardanelle Pub. Sch. Dist., 790 F. 2d 688 (8th Cir. 1986) (criticism of decision to abandon ability grouping of students and the principal's administrative style in dealing with teachers). Johnson v. Lincoln Univ. of Com., 776 F. 2d 443 (3d Cir. 1985) (comments on grade inflation and admission standards); Wells v. Hico Independent Sch. Dist., 736 F.2d 243 (5th Cir. 1984) critical comments by teacher at school board meeting on the board's handling of a reading program); McGee v. South Pemiscot Sch. Dist. R-V, 712 F.2d 339 (8th Cir. 1983) (critical comments on the elimination of junior-high track, a topic that had been a campaign issue during the school board elections); Zoll v. Eastern Allamakee, Community Sch. Dist., 588 F.2d 246 (8th Cir. 1978) (complaint that athletics were stressed over academics, and that the quality of the elementary school was in jeopardy); Bernasconi v. Tempe Elementary Sch. Dist. No. 3, 548 F.2d 857 (9th Cir. 1977) (advising parents that their children were being placed in classes of the mentally retarded because they were being tested in English rather than in their native tongue); Eckerd v. Indian River Sch. Dist., 475 F. Supp. 1350 (D. Del. 1979) (scheduling of the band, grading policies, involvement of band members in musical activities). *Contra*, Clark v. Holmes, 474 F.2d 928 (7th Cir. 1972), *cert. denied*, 411 U.S. 972 (1973) (course content and student counseling not matters of public concern); Jones v. Kneller, 482 F. Supp. 204 (E.D. N.Y. 1979), *aff'd mem.*, 633 F.2d 204 (2d Cir.), *cert. denied*, 449 U.S. 920 (1980) (bickering among faculty over teaching methods not protected speech).

140. Bowman v. Pulaski Cty. Special Sch. Dist., 723 F.2d 640 (8th Cir. 1983) (public comments on the excessive use of corporal punishment by a coach); Swilley v. Alexander, 629 F.2d 1018 (5th Cir. 1980) (public disclosure of incident in which a school principal required children to go outdoors for tornado drills during lightning storms, and sent small children home unattended without notifying parents; Lusk v. Estes, 361 F. Supp 653 (N.D. Tex. 1973) (public comments on robberies and assults being committed in the teacher's school).

141. Hinkle v. Christensen, 733 F.2d 74 (8th Cir. 1984); Reichert v. Draud, 701 F.2d 1168 (6th Cir. 1983); Hickman v. Valley Local Sch. Dist. Bd. of Educ., 619 F.2d 606 (6th Cir. 1980); Wichert v. Walter, 606 F. Supp. 1516 (D. N.J. 1985); Knapp v. Whitaker, 577 F. Supp. 1265 (C.D. Ill. 1983), *modified*, 757 F.2d 827 (4th Cir. 1985).

142. Gobla v. Crestwood Sch. Dist., 609 F. Supp. 972 (M.D. Pa., 1985).

143. Anderson v. Central Point Sch. Dist., 746 F.2d 505 (9th Cir. 1984). This is consistent with the decision in *Connick* in which the Supreme Court agreed that part of Myer's communication was a matter of public concern despite its being part of a larger message that did not fall into this category.

144. *See* Day v. South Park Indep. Sch. Dist., 768 F.2d 696 (5th Cir. 1985) (complaint about teaching evaluation not a matter of public concern); Renfroe v. Kirkpatrick, 722 F.2d 714 (11th Cir. 1984) (grievance based on teacher's unwillingess to share job with another teacher). It was only after the grievance had been pressed to the board itself that the teacher raised the issue of the welfare of the students. In Callaway v. Hafeman, 628 F. Supp. 1478 (W.D. Wis. 1986) a court held that a complaint to school officials about sexual harassment were not a matter of public concern. *Compare* Johnson v. Butler, 433 F. Supp. 531 (W.D. Va. 1977) (complaint by teacher regarding her status as a "floating" teacher did raise a matter of public concern).

145. The courts continue to refuse to recognize personal employment disputes as matters of public concern. Renfroe v. Kirkpatrick, 722 F.2d 714 (8th Cir. 1984) (job sharing); Ferrara v. Mills, 596 F. Supp. 1069 (S.D. Fla. 1984) (teacher's course assignments and course selection by students); Gregory v. Durham Cty. Bd. of Educ., 591 F. Supp. 145 (M.D. N.C. 1984) (scheduling of mandatory training program, inter alia).

146. Connick v. Myers, 461 U.S. 138, 150 (1983). Elsewhere in the opinion the Court also stressed in regard to Connick's questionnaire, "We caution that a stronger showing may be necessary if the employee's speech more substantially involved matters of public concern." Id., at 152. It may be remembered the Court had concluded that only one question out of the fourteen questions on the questionnaire dealt with a matter of public concern. That particular question, however, raised a matter of especially grave importance.

147. Bowman v. Pulaski Cty. Special Sch. Dist., 723 F.2d 640, 644 (8th Cir. 1983).

148. Pickering v. Bd. of Educ., 391 U.S. 563, 570 n. 3 (1968).

149. Connick v. Myers, 461 U.S. 138, 152 (1983).

150. Recall that though the Court concluded most of the questions on the questionnaire did not deal with a matter of public concern, one question did.

151. Id., at 154.

152. Trotman v. Bd. of Trustees of Lincoln Univ., 635 F.2d 216, 225 (3d Cir. 1980) (speech not deprived of protection merely because it is strident); McGill v. Bd. of Educ. of Pekin Elementary Sch. Dist., 602 F.2d 774 (7th Cir. 1979) (despite evidence teacher was a source of friction and lack of cooperation among teachers, her right to criticize the school and advocate collective bargaining is protected); Bernasconi v. Tempe Elementary Sch. Dist. No. 3, 548 F.2d 857 (9th Cir.), *cert. denied*, 434 U.S. 825 (1977) (public criticism of how non-English-speaking students were tested and assigned to classes for the mentally retarded upset other teachers); Lusk v. Estes, 361 F. Supp. 653 (N.D. Tex. 1973). *See also* Johnson v. Lincoln Univ. of Com., 776 F.2d 443, 454 (3d Cir. 1985) ("some evidence of disruption" caused by plantiff's speech is not controlling). *Compare* Wagle v. Murray, 546 F.2d 1329 (9th Cir. 1976), *vacated on other grounds*, 431 U.S. 935 (1977), *opinion on remand*, 560 F. 2d 401 (9th Cir. 1977), *cert. denied*, 434 U.S. 1014 (1978); Stolberg v. Board of Trustees, 474 F.2d 485 (2d Cir. 1973). Phillips v. Puryear, 403 F. Supp. 80 (W.D. Va. 1975).

153. Cox v. Dardanelle Pub. Sch. Dist., 790 F.2d 668 (8th Cir. 1986) (teacher-principal relationship is not so personal and intimate that teachers must be precluded from filing responsible grievances); Hickman v. Valley Local Sch. Dist. Bd. of Educ, 619 F.2d 606 (6th Cir. 1980) (teacher's active pursuit of union issues protected); Bowman v. Pulaski Cty. Special Sch. Dist., 723 F.2d 640 (8th Cir. 1983) (assistant coaches' public comments about excessive use of corporal punishment by the head coach under whose direction and control they were); Hillis v. Stephen F. Austin State University, 665 F.2d 547 (5th Cir.), *cert. denied*, 457 U.S. 1106 (1982) (professor's criticism at a meeting with his department chair of the chair's directive protected speech).

154. Givhan v. Western Line Consolidated Sch. Dist., 439 U.S. 410 (1979); Eckerd v. Indian River Sch. Dist., 475 F. Supp. 1350 (D. Del. 1979) (teacher's criticisms privately voiced to principal did cause considerable strain in the relationship but the teacher's interests outweighed the school's interests).

155. Roberts v. Van Buren Public Schools, 773 F.2d 949 (8th Cir. 1985) (concluding that grievances filed by two teachers were not protected under the first amendment).

156. Hinkle v. Christensen, 733 F.2d 74 (8th Cir. 1984); Professional Ass'n of College Educators v. El Paso Cty. Comm. College Dist., 730 F.2d 258 (5th Cir. 1984); Columbus Educ. Ass'n v. Columbus City Sch. Dist., 623 F.2d 1155 (6th Cir. 1980); Roberts v. Lake Central Sch. Corp., 317 F. Supp. 63 (N.D. Ind. 1970).

157. Derrickson v. Bd. of Educ. of the City of St. Louis, 738 F.2d 351 (8th Cir. 1984); Cotten v. Bd. of Regents, 395 F. Supp. 388 (S.D. Ga. 1974), *aff'd*, 515 F.2d 1098 (5th Cir. 1975).

158. Barbre v. Garland Indep. Sch. Dist., 474 F. Supp. 687 (N.D. Tex. 1979); Jones v. Battles, 315 F. Supp. 601 (D. Conn. 1979).

159. Wells v. Hico Indep. Sch. Dist., 736 F.2d 243 (5th Cir. 1984); McGee v. South Pemiscot Sch. Dist. R-V, 712 F.2d 339 (8th Cir. 1983); Zoll v. Eastern Allamakee Comm. Sch. Dist., 588 F.2d 246 (8th Cir. 1978); Gieringer v. Center Sch. Dist. No. 58, 477 F.2d 1164 (8th Cir. 1973).

160. Gregory v. Durham Cty. Bd. of Educ., 591 F. Supp. 145 (M.D. N.C. 1984).

161. A letter of reprimand was judged by another court not to constitute a restriction on the teacher's right to speak. Aebisher v. Ryan, 622 F.2d 651 (2d Cir. 1980). Another court did view a letter of reprimand as an infringement on the teacher's free speech rights. Columbus Ed. Ass'n v. Columbus City Sch. Dist., 623 F.2d 1155 (6th Cir. 1980).

162. Maybe v. Reagan, 537 F.2d 1036, 1050 (9th Cir. 1976) (discussions will not always be models of decorum). Even strident and abrasive comments have been protected. Jorden v. Cagel, 474 F. Supp. 1198 (N.D. Mass. 1979), *aff'd mem.*, 620 F.2d 298 (5th Cir. 1980); Puentes v. Bd. of

Educ., 24 N.Y.2d 996, 250 N.E.2d 232, 302 N.Y.S.2d 824 (1969). Profane, vituperative, and insulting speech not conducive to rational discussion has not enjoyed protection. *See, e.g.,* Meehan v. Macy, 392 F.2d 822, 835 (D.C. Cir. 1968), *modified,* 425 F.2d 469, *aff'd with modifications en banc,* 425 F.2d 472 (1969); Duke v. North Texas State University, 469 F.2d 829 (5th Cir. 1972), *cert. denied,* 412 U.S. 932 (1973).

163. Pickering v. Bd. of Educ., 391 U.S. 563, 572 n.4 (1968) (dictum).

164. Brockell v. Norton, 732 F.2d 664 (8th Cir. 1984); Knapp v. Whitaker, 577 F. Supp. 1265 (C.D. Ill. 1983), *modified,* 757 F.2d 827 (4th Cir. 1985); Lusk v. Estes, 361 F. Supp. 653 (N.D. Tex. 1973).

165. Myers v. Connick, 507 F. Supp. 752, 759 (E.D. La. 1981).

166. Branti v. Finkel, 445 U.S. 507, 518 (1980); Elrod v. Burns, 427 U.S. 347 (1976).

167. Solis v. Rio Grande City Independent Sch., 734 F.2d 243 (5th Cir. 1984). *But see* Avery v. Jennings, 604 F. Supp. 1356 (S.D. Ohio 1985) (holding that *Branti* and *Elrod* do not apply to a refusal to hire).

168. Burris v. Willis Indep. Sch. Dist., 537 F. Supp. 801 (S.D. Tex. 1982), *modified,* 713 F.2d 1087 (5th Cir. 1983).

169. McBee v. Jim Hogg County, 730 F.2d 1009 (5th Cir. 1984) (en banc).

170. Jones v. Dodson, 727 F.2d 1329 (4th Cir. 1984). The Eighth Circuit has also adopted this approach. Horton v. Taylor, 767 F.2d 471 (8th Cir. 1985).

171. The central cases in this area deal with federal employees. U.S. Civil Service Commission v. Letter Carriers, 413 U.S. 548 (1973); Broadrick v. Oklahoma, 413 U.S. 601 (1973). The principles of these cases have been extended to local public employees. Wachsman v. City of Dallas, 704 F.2d 160 (5th Cir. 1983); Magill v. Lynch, 560 F.2d 22 (1st Cir. 1977), *cert. denied,* 434 U.S. 1063 (1978); Morial v. Judiciary Commission, 565 F.2d 295 (5th Cir. 1977) *(en banc),* *cert. denied,* 435 U.S. 1013 (1978).

172. Annotation: "Right of Schoolteacher to Serve as Member of School Board in School District Where Employed," 70 A.L.R. 3d 1188 (1976), 1189. In Wright v. State Com. on Ethics, 389 So.2d 662 (Fla. App. 1980) the court ruled that a teacher who took an unpaid leave of absence could serve on the school board.

173. For two reviews of these developments see Anthony M. Cresswell and Michael J. Murphy, *Teachers, Unions, and Collective Bargaining* (Berkeley, Calif.: McCutchan Publishing Corporation, 1980); and Bruce S. Cooper, *Collective Bargaining, Strikes, and Financial Costs in Public Education: A Comparative Review* (Eugene, Oreg.: ERIC Clearinghouse on Educational Management, 1982).

174. McLauglin v. Tilendis, 398 F.2d 287 (7th Cir. 1968) (protecting the right to join a union). Smith v. Arkansas State Highway Employees, Local 1315, 441 U.S. 463, 465 (1979) ("[T]he First Amendment does not impose any affirmative obligation on the government to listen, to respond or, in this context, to recognize the association and bargain with it.") The courts have also upheld restrictions prohibiting supervisors from joint unions with rank-and-file employees on the grounds that such a restriction was narrowly drawn to protect efficiency. Elk Grove Firefighters Local No. 2340 v. Willis, 400 F. Supp. 1097 (N.D. Ill. 1975), *aff'd mem.,* 539 F.2d 714 (7th Cir. 1976).

175. "Developments in the Law—Public Employment," *Harvard Law Review* 97 (1984): 1611, 1679. The specifics of these laws differ. Most laws require the public employer to bargain in good faith about terms and conditions of employment. In other states employees are only entitled to "meet and confer" with the public employer. *Id.,* at 1680.

176. Chicago Div. Ill. Educ. Ass'n v. Bd. of Educ., 222 N.E.2d 243 (Ill. 1966) (implied power to bargain); Commonwealth v. Cty. Bd. of Arlington Cty. 232 S.E.2d 30 (Va. 1977) (no implied power). The courts have also split on the question whether collective bargaining in the absence of express authorization is an improper delegation of board authority. Nichols v. Bolding, 277 So. 2d 868 (Ala. 1973) reviews the cases on this point.

177. 29 U.S.C. §151 et. seq. (1982).

178. National Labor Relations Board v. Yeshiva University, 444 U.S. 672 (1980).

179. Id., at 686-90.

180. For example, criteria for formation of a bargaining unit, election procedures for electing a bargaining representative, and mediation.

181. For a more detailed discussion of the issues behind deciding the scope of negotiations, see Tyll van Geel, *Authority to Control the School Program* (Lexington, Mass.: D.C. Heath & Co., 1976), 124-29. For a review of cases in this area see Annotation: "Negotiable Issues in Public Employment," 84 A.L.R.3d 242 (1978).

182. New York Civil Service Law §200 et. seq (McKinney's 1983).

183. Iowa Public Employment Relations Act, Chapter 20 §20.9 (1978).

184. Minnesota Public Employment Labor Relations, Minn. Stat. Chap. 179a §179A.03. 19, §179A.07 (Supp. 1985).

185. Mandatory topics are those topics that must be bargained over if one side insists on bargaining on this topic. Refusal to bargain on these topics violates the statutory duty to bargain. "Permissible" topics are those topics that employer or union need not bargain over if they choose not to. Neither party may invoke impasse resolution procedures to resolve a dispute over these topics. Prohibited subjects are of two sorts: (1) those topics the board may not as a matter of law negotiate over, i.e., the board must retain unilateral control of this topic; and (2) those topics that are controlled by existing law that may not be contravened by the agreement. Contractual terms related to these topics are unenforceable. Some states like New Jersey have divided the subjects of negotiation into only two categories: mandatory and nonnegotiable matters. Ridgefield Park Ed. Ass'n v. Ridgefield Park Bd. of Ed., 78 N.J. 144, 393 A.2d 278 (1978) (holding that teacher transfers are nonnegotiable and the board cannot bargain to limit its discretion on this topic). New York recognizes all three categories.

186. Kenai Peninsula Borough Sch. Dist. v. Kenai Peninsula Educ. Ass'n., 572 P.2d 416, 422 (Sup. Ct. Alaska, 1977).

187. Charles City Educ. Ass'n v. Public Employment Relations Board, 291 N.W. 2d 663, 666-67 (Sup. Ct. Iowa, 1980).

188. West Ottawa Educ. Ass'n v. West Ottawa Pub. Sch. Bd. of Educ., 337 N.W.2d 533, 540 (Mich. App. 1983). This "impact" test was at one time used by Kansas National Educ. Ass'n of Shawnee Mission v. Bd. of Educ., 212 Kan. 741, 512 P.2d 426, 435 (Sup. Ct. Kansas, 1973) ("The key . . . is how direct the impact of an issue is on the well-being of the individual teacher, as opposed to its effect on the operation of the school system as a whole"). New Jersey also uses an impact test coupled with two further requirements: the subject must not be preempted by statute or regulation, and the agreement must not interfere with the determination of public policy. Teaneck Bd. of Educ. v. Teaneck Teachers Ass'n., 94 N.J. 9, 462 A.2d 137 (N.J. 1983).

189. Sch. Comm. of Boston v. Boston Teachers Union, Local 66, 389 N.E.2d 970, 973 (Sup. Jud. Ct., Mass., 1979).

190. University Educ. Ass'n v. Regents of U. of Minn., 353 N.W.2d 534, 539 (Sup. Ct. Minn., 1984).

191. Susquehanna Val. Cent. Sch. Dist. v. Susquehanna Teachers Ass'n, 37 N.Y.2d 614, 616-17, 376 N.Y.S.2d 427, 339 N.E.2d 132, 133 (N.Y. 1975).

192. West Bend Educ. Ass'n v. Wis. Emply. Relations Comm., 121 Wis.2d 1, 357 N.W.2d 534 (Wis. 1984). Other states have adopted a similar test. San Mateo City Sch. Dist. v. Public Employment Relations Bd., 33 Cal.3d 850, 663 P.2d 523, 191 Cal. Rptr. 800, (Cal. 1983); Metro. Technical Community College Educ. Ass'n v. Metro. Technical Community College Area, 203 Neb. 832, 281 N.W.2d 201 (Neb. 1979).

193. The courts have split as to whether class size is a mandatory subject of negotiations. San Mateo City Sch. Dist. v. Public Employment Relations Bd., 33 Cal. 3d 850, 663 P.2d 523, 191 Cal. Rptr. 500 (Cal. 1983) (en banc) (it is); West Irondequoit Teachers Ass'n v. Helsby, 42 A.D.2d 808, 346 N.Y.S.2d 418 (1973), aff'd, 35 N.Y.2d 46, 315 N.E.2d 775, 358 N.Y.S.2d 720 (1974) (it is not, but the impact of a change in class size on working conditions is a mandatory subject). It is

interesting to note that both California and New York tend to favor a broad notion of what is a mandatory subject of negotiations.

194. University Educ. Ass'n. v. Regents of University of Minnesota, 353 N.W.2d 534 (Minn. 1984) (faculty promotion criteria); Teaneck Bd. of Educ. v. Teaneck Teachers Ass'n., 94 N.J. 9, 462 A.2d 137 (N.J. 1983) (hiring decision); West Ottawa Educ. Ass'n. v. West Ottawa Pub. Sch. Bd. of Educ., 337 N.W.2d 533 (Mich. App. 1983) (elimination of a course); Metro Tech. Com. Col. Ed. Ass'n. v. Metro Tech. Com. Col. Area, 203 Neb. 832, 281 N.W.2d 201 (Neb. 1979) (instructor contact-hours management prerogative); Kenai Peninsula Borough Sch. Dist. v. Kenai Peninsula Educ. Ass'n., 572 P.2d 416 (Alaska, 1977) (choice of instructional materials).

195. City of Beloit v. Wis. Employment Rel. Comm., 73 Wis.2d 43, 242 N.W.2d 231 (Wis. 1976).

196. *Compare* Bd. of Educ. of Union Free Sch. Dist. No. 3 of Town of Huntington v. Associated Teachers, 30 N.Y.2d 122, 282 N.E.2d 109, 331 N.Y.S.2d 17 (N.Y., 1972) (holding all issues are mandatory unless explicitly exempted by statute from bargaining), with Susquehanna Valley Cent. Sch. Dist. v. Susquehanna Valley Teachers Ass'n, 37 N.Y.2d 614, 339 N.E.2d 132, 376 N.Y.S.2d 427 (N.Y., 1975) (recognizing that public policy, whether explicit or implicit in statute, decisional law, or in neither, may also restrict scope of bargaining and arbitrability).

197. Courts also go beyond a simple consideration of the legislative history of the act they are called upon to interpret to consider the general literature debating the proper allocation of power between school board and union. *See, e.g.,* Sch. Comm. of Boston v. Boston Teachers Union Local 66, 389 N.E.2d 970, 974 (Sup. Jud. Ct., Mass., Suffolk, 1979), citing Harry Wellington and Ralph Winter, "The Limits of Collective Bargaining in Public Employment," *Yale Law Journal* 78 (1969): 1107; and van Geel, *Authority to Control the School Program, supra* note 181.

198. "Developments in the Law—Public Employment," *supra* note 175, at 1703. Eight states by statute permit the right to strike—Hawaii, Minnesota, Montana, Oregon, Pennsylvania, Vermont, and Wisconsin. Id. The right to strike has been denied because of the fear of the damages brought on by an interruption in essential services and because it is thought allowing employees to strike would improperly enhance the power of public-sector employees. Harry H. Wellington and Ralph K. Winter, *The Unions and The Cities* (Washington, D.C.: Brookings Institution, 1971). For a summary of the criticisms of this argument, see "Developments in the Law—Public Employment," 1712 et seq.; Kurt L. Hanslowe and John L. Acierno, "The Law and Theory of Strikes by Government Employees," *Cornell Law Review* 67 (1982):1021.

199. *See, e.g,* United Federation of Postal Clerks v. Bount, 325 F. Supp. 879 (D.D.C. 1971), *aff'd,* 404 U.S. 802 (1971).

200. Tygrett v. Barry, 627 F.2d 1279 (D.C. Cir. 1980).

201. 431 U.S. 209 (1977).

202. Id., at 232, 234. *Abood* left somewhat unclear what union activities could be financed by fees from objecting workers. In Ellis v. Railway Clerks, 104 S.Ct. 1883 (1984) the Court clarified this point saying that compelled fees could be used on conventions, social activities, and publications to the extent the substance of the publication was not political and could be charged to the dissenting employee. The *Ellis* decision also made clear that pure rebate schemes—under which the union refunded to objecting employees the pro rata portion of the agency fee expended impermissibly—were constitutionally not allowable. Objecting members had to be given the opportunity to obtain an advance reduction, or the money had to be placed in an interest-bearing escrow account. For decisions examining *Ellis* and its implications for public employment see Hudson v. Chicago Teachers' Union, 743 F.2d 1187 (7th Cir. 1984); Cumero v. Public Employment Relations Bd., 213 Cal. Rptr. 326 (Cal. App. 1 Dist. 1985).

203. 460 U.S. 37 (1983). The outcome of the case would have been different if the Court had concluded that the mail system was a "public forum," or that the restriction was an effort to suppress expression merely because public officials opposed the speaker's (the excluded union's) viewpoint.

204. 104 S. Ct. 1058 (1984).

205. 429 U.S. 167 (1976).

206. 441 U.S. 463 (1979).

207. 777 F.2d 1046 (5th Cir. 1985).

208. Id., at 1051-52. *See also* Professional Ass'n. of College Educators v. El Paso Cty. Comm. College Dist., 730 F.2d 258 (5th Cir. 1984), *cert. denied*, 105 S.Ct. 248 (1984).

209. The court also upheld denial of access to the school mail facilities. 777 F.2d at 1052.

210. Id., at 1055.

211. Perry Educ. Ass'n. v. Perry Local Educators' Ass'n., 460 U.S. 37 (1983).

212. *See, e.g.,* Hickman v. Valley Bd. of Educ., 619 F.2d 606 (6th Cir. 1980); Columbus Educ. Ass'n. v. Columbus City Sch. Dist., 623 F.2d 1155 (6th Cir. 1980). *Compare* Pietrunti v. Bd. of Educ., 128 N.J. Super. 149, 319 A.2d 262, *cert. denied*, 419 U.S. 1057 (1974) (upholding dismissal of president of local union who used "insulting and vituperative language" in a personal attack on the superintendent at a faculty orientation meeting.)

In Lake Park Educ. Ass'n. v. Bd. of Educ. of Lake Park, 526 F. Supp. 710 (N.D. Ill. 1981) the district took a series of steps to frustrate the union. The union was to be charged commercial rates for using school facilities for meetings. Teachers were threatened with an increase in their teacher loads. Unfavorable comments on unions and union members were made. No union members were appointed to newly created positions. These activities, the court concluded, violated the first amendment rights of the teachers.

213. Pittsburg Unified Sch. Dist. v. California Sch. Employees Ass'n., 213 Cal. Rptr. 34 (Cal. App. 1 Dist. 1985).

214. The Court in *Connick* stressed that not every employment relations issue was a matter of public concern. On the other hand, it is clear that some of these issues are matters of public concern. City of Madison Joint Sch. Dist. No. 8 v. Wisconsin Employment Relations Commission, 429 U.S. 167 (1976).

215. One court has suggested the test is whether the teacher's activities "materially and substantially disrupt" the operations of the school. Hastings v. Bonner, 578 F.2d 136 (5th Cir. 1978).

216. For a review of these requirements touching on such matters as notice, time and place of meetings, quorum and voting requirements, and executive sessions, the following may be consulted. Leroy J. Peterson, Richard A. Rossmiller, and Marlin M. Volz, *The Law and Public School Operation* (New York: Harper & Row Publishers, Inc., 1978), chap. 2.

217. Richard J. Bindeglass, "New Jersey's Open Public Meeting Act: Has Five Years Brought 'Sunshine' Over the Garden State?" *Rutgers Law Journal* 12 (1981): 561.

218. Douglas Q. Wickham, "Let the Sun Shine In! Open-Meeting Legislation Can Be Our Key to Closed Doors in State and Local Government," *Northwestern University Law Review* 68 (1973): 480; Kern Alexander and M. David Alexander, *American Public School Law*, 2d ed. (St. Paul, Minn.: West Publishing Company, 1985), 124-25.

219. Daily Gazette Co. v. North Colonie Bd. of Educ., 67 A.D. 2d 803, 412 N.Y.S.2d 494 (1979); Washington Sch. Dist. No. 6 v. Superior Court of Maricopa Cty., 541 P.2d 1137 (Ariz. 1975); Selkowe v. Bean, 109 N.H. 247, 249 A.2d 35 (1969).

220. St. Cloud Newspapers Inc. v. District 742, Com. Schools, 332 N.W.2d 1 (Minn. 1983). *See also* Reeves v. Orleans Parish Sch. Bd., 281 So.2d 719 (La. 1973).

221. *See, e.g.,* Nabhani v. Coglianese, 552 F. Supp. 657 (N.D. Ill., 1982); Tri-Village Publishers v. St. Johnsville Bd., 110 A.D.2d 932, 487 N.Y.S.2d 181 (1985); Judge v. Pocius, 28 Pa. Comwlth. 139, 367 A.2d 788 (1977); Moberg v. Independent Sch. Dist., 336 N.W.2d 510 (Minn. 1983).

222. Roanoke City Sch. Bd. v. Times-World Corp., 226 Va. 185, 307 S.E.2d 256 (1983).

223. Brown v. East Baton Rouge Parish Sch. Bd., 405 So. 2d 1148 (Ct. App. of La. First Circuit, 1981); Ridenour v. Bd. of Educ. of City of Dearborn Sch. Dist., 111 Mich. App. 798, 314 N.W. 2d (Ct. of Apps. Mich. 1981).

224. Bassett v. Braddock, 262 So.2d 425 (Fla. 1972). *Contra*, Littleton Educ. Ass'n. v. Arapahoe Cty. Sch. Dist., 553 P.2d 793 (Colo. 1976) (en banc).

225. Annot., 38 A.L.R.3d 1070 (1971), Supp. 86ff (Aug. 1985).

226. Id.

227. Burton A. Braverman and W. R. Heppler, "A Practical Review of Open Records Laws," *George Washington Law Review* 49 (1981); 720, 722.

228. Id., at 743-44. *See also* Annot., 26 A.L. R.4 640 (1984).

229. Id., at 745.

230. Id.

231. Mitchell v. Bd. of Educ. of Garden City U. F. Sch. Dist., 493 N.Y.S.2d 826 (App. Div. 1985).

232. Samuel P. Huntingon, *American Politics: The Promise of Disharmony* (Cambridge, Mass.: The Belknap Press of Harvard University Press, 1981), 37.

3

Access to Public Schooling

3.1. INTRODUCTION: THE EQUAL PROTECTION CLAUSE

Today, education is perhaps the most important function of state and local governments. Compulsory school attendance laws and the great expenditures for education both demonstrate our recognition of the importance of education to our democratic society. It is required in the performance of our most basic public responsibilities, even service in the armed forces. It is the very foundation of good citizenship. Today it is a principal instrument in awakening the child to cultural values, in preparing him to adjust normally to his environment. In these days it is doubtful that any child may reasonably be expected to succeed in life if he is denied the opportunity of an education. *Such an opportunity, where the state has undertaken to provide it, is a right which must be made available to all on equal terms.*[1]

The last sentence from one of the Supreme Court's most frequently quoted passages contains two important points. First, access to education only becomes a "right" if the state has voluntarily undertaken to provide it, i.e., access to education is not itself a federal constitutional right.[2] Second, the Court said that if a state does provide education, it must be provided to all on an equal basis. This chapter will address several issues related to the second point: the exclusion of certain types of pupils from the public schools, the charging of tuition and other fees that has the effect of excluding certain students from the schools, and a failure to provide transportation services that has the effect of "excluding" some students from attendance. The chapter concludes with a discussion of the notion of a constitutional right to an education. The question of the "functionally excluded" child is taken up in chapter 7.[3]

Before proceeding with an examination of specific issues, it should prove to be of use to provide a brief introduction to the equal protection clause of the fourteenth amendment. We begin with the observation that governmental policies unavoidably do not treat everyone the same. Policy-making almost inherently entails the adoption of a criterion, say criterion A, in terms of which people are compared; people who differ in terms of the criterion are then treated differently. Thus, government may compare or measure people in terms of gender, race, wealth, physical fitness, criminal guilt, etc., and prescribe, for example, that only those with a certain ability to see will be eligible for a driver's license.[4] As might be expected, people adversely affected by these governmental policies may raise the constitutional claim that the difference in treatment in this instance violates the fourteenth amendment's equal protection clause that states that no state shall deprive any person of the equal protection of the laws. When this claim is raised, the plantiff argues that criterion A ought not be used to distribute benefits and/or burdens, i.e., the plaintiff claims a right not to be subjected to a policy that treats people differently on the basis of criterion A. Stated more directly, the plaintiff claims that the government's policy without sufficient warrant infringes his or her right to be free from the kind of harm they suffer because of the use of criterion A.[5]

The courts approach the resolution of these cases by using what is called a "standard of review" or test. Three different standards of review have been developed by the Supreme Court for use in different types of equal protection cases.[6] These three tests share a common generic structure: (1) each test requires the court to identify the goal(s) or purpose(s) the government is seeking to advance by its differential treatment of people; (2) each test requires the court to examine the legitimacy and importance of that purpose or goal; and (3) each test requires the court to examine the question of how the means chosen by government (the choice of criterion A) serves to advance the purpose. The three tests differ in their operation according to all three points.

The so-called "rational basis test" operates in a manner favorable to government's policy. The test states that the criterion must be rationally related to a legitimate governmental purpose.[7] As this test is used, government's policy is presumed to be constitutional; accordingly the plaintiff carries the burden of persuading the court either that purpose J is illegitimate, or that criterion A is not rationally related to that purpose.[8] First, in determining the purpose of government's policy, courts using the rational basis typically are willing to speculate about the purpose of the policy even in the absence of solid evidence on the question.[9] Second, the court will determine whether this purpose is "legitimate." This is a minimal test in that very few purposes are found to be illegitimate. If the court were to conclude that the policy's purpose(s) were illegitimate, the policy would be struck down. Assuming the purpose has been deemed to be legitimate, the court examines the third issue: does the use of criterion A advance or serve the realization of purpose J? In carrying out this analysis the court is also favorably disposed toward the legislature. As long as there is some conceivable and plausible reason for using criterion A, even if that criterion is not the best that could be used, the court will sustain its use, hence, the law. In other words, even if the use of criterion A does harm the plaintiff, the court will uphold its use, and in upholding its use the court also concludes that the plaintiff does not have a right to avoid the harm inflicted by the use of criterion A.

The second test is the so-called "middle level" test that states that a policy will be upheld if the criterion is "substantially" related to the achievement of a "legitimate and important" governmental purpose. When this test is used, it is *government* that must establish that the purpose of its policy is not merely legitimate, but also "important" and that the criterion, for example, criterion B, is an accurate, not a crude, way of identifying those people who should be treated differently from others in order to advance the government's purposes.[10] In other words, unless government can come up with a more convincing case for the use of criterion B, the court will conclude that the plaintiff has a right not to suffer the harm that accompanies the use of the criterion.

The third standard of review is called the strict-scrutiny test. It places on government the task of persuading the court that the adoption of criterion C was "necessary" in order to achieve a purpose that is not just "legitimate," but is also "compelling." This is a tough test and, when used, it is unlikely that a court would conclude that the policy under attack is constitutional.[11]

The selection of the appropriate test for a case is itself the subject of a complex, often ambiguous, vague, and inconclusive body of doctrine. Roughly speaking, the middle-level test is used when the criterion (criterion B) speaks in terms of gender, i.e., when males and females are treated differently.[12] If the criterion speaks in terms of race (criterion C), then the strict-scrutiny test is used.[13] If the policy touches on what the courts have termed a "fundamental interest," then strict scrutiny is also used.[14] If the criterion involves the use of neither gender nor race, and the policy does not affect a fundamental interest, then by default the rational-basis test is to be used. In sum, criteria like criteria B and C comes to the court with a strike against them since it is presumed that the plaintiff has a right not to have to suffer the injuries typically associated with the use of such criteria, e.g., the imposition of a stigma. Similarly, policies that affect a "fundamental" interest come to court with a presumption that the plaintiff has a right not to have those sorts of interests harmed by government.

Thus, although equal protection analysis talks in terms of differences in treatment between groups of people and in terms of inequalities and discrimination, it may also be understood as a body of doctrine dealing with the rights of people not to be subjected to certain kinds of harms.

3.2. STATE CONSTITUTIONS AND THE EXCLUSION OF STUDENTS: SHARED TIME

For a variety of reasons states have not always opened the doors of public schools to all children. The exclusionary practice that has gained the greatest notoriety has been, of course, the barring from public schools those children deemed not to be educable, e.g., the mentally handicapped.[15] There exist a number of other bases for at least temporarily excluding students from the schools: age,[16] health,[17] suspension and expulsion for misbehavior and/or truancy,[18] and residency requirements.[19] An important question that arises from time to time is whether these exclusions can be squared with state constitutional provisions that typically provide that the legislature is required to establish and maintain a system of common schools for *all* the children of the state.[20]

Despite the seemingly absolute language of the state constitutions, state courts have refused to sustain challenges to the exclusion of children. In a Wisconsin case the state supreme court described Merritt Beattie, a 13-year-old boy, as follows:

Merritt has been a crippled and defective child since his birth, being afflicted with a form of paralysis which affects his whole physical and nervous make-up. He has not the normal use and control of his voice, hands, feet and body. By reason of said paralysis his vocal cords are afflicted. He is slow and hesitating in speech, and has a peculiar high rasping, and disturbing tone of voice, accompanied with uncontrollable facial contortions, making it difficult for him to make himself understood. He also has an uncontrollable flow of saliva, which drools from his mouth onto his clothing and books, causing him to present an unclean appearance. He has a nervous and excitable nature.[21]

Merritt attended public school from the first to the fifth grade when the board at the beginning of the school year in 1917 refused to admit him. It was claimed by the board that Merritt's "physical condition and ailment produces a depressing and nauseating effect upon the teachers and school children; that by reason of his physical condition he takes up an undue portion of the teacher's time and attention, distracts the attention of other pupils, and interferes generally with the discipline and progress of the school."[22] The Wisconsin Supreme Court ruled against the claim that the exclusion of Merritt violated Article 10, §3 of the state constitution, which read as follows:

The Legislature shall provide by law for the establishment of district schools, which shall be as nearly uniform as practicable; and such schools shall be free and without charge for tuition to all children between the ages of four and twenty years; and no sectarian instruction shall be allowed therein.

The court based its conclusion in part on the premise that, "The right of a child of school age to attend the public schools of this state cannot be insisted upon when its presence therein is harmful to the best interests of the school." Furthermore, the court noted, it would not interfere with a school board's conclusion, unless the board's action was unreasonable, that a student's presence was detrimental to the best interests of the school. Here there was no evidence that the board acted with bad faith or ill will.

The dissent objected on several grounds. First, Justice Eschweiller said there was no evidence that the boy's presence did have a harmful influence on other children. Second, he argued the majority erroneously accepted the assumption that the claimant had the burden of proof to establish that the school board was arbitrary and unreasonable. In the case of the claimed denial of a constitutional right, the burden should have been on the school board to show its action was reasonable.

In another case the Supreme Court of Illinois used a different approach to deny the claim that the state constitution required the state to compensate the parents of a handicapped child for the maintenance costs of institutionalizing their son.[23] Article 8, §1 of the state constitution provided: "The general assembly shall provide a thorough and efficient system of free schools, whereby all children of this state may receive a good common school education." The court said this provision was inapplicable to the case because the term "common school education" implied "the capacity, as well as the right, to receive common training," but in this case it was admitted the boy had been adjudicated incompetent and was "mentally deficient or feeble minded."

Age-based policies of exclusion have also not been successfully challenged.[24] In a Montana case the parents of Debra P. Ronish sought a court order to have their daughter admitted to first grade when the school district denied her admission because her sixth birthday fell three days after the age cut-off date of the board.[25] (To be admitted to the first grade, children had to reach the age of six by November 15; Debra's sixth birthday fell on November 18.) The parents argued that the state constitution, which provided that the public schools "shall be open to all children . . . between the age of six and twenty-one years," required that a student must be admitted to public school at any time upon reaching their sixth birthday. The court said this claim raised the question of what the term "all" meant. Did it literally mean that all six-year-olds had to be admitted to the public schools? "No," said the court. The term "all" had to be considered in connection with the other requirement that the state provide a "thorough" system of education. It would make no educational sense, argued the court, to require the admission of students reaching the age of six in March, only several months before the school year ended. Thus, a reasonable interpretation of the constitution merely required that the child be allowed to enter the first grade sometime during his or her seventh year after reaching the sixth birthday. "This would be accomplished by admitting children who become six after a 'cut-off' date at the commencement of the next school year. Thus the child whose birthday falls after the 'cut-off' date would be admitted the following September in the ordinary course of schooling while he is still six years old."[26] The Wisconsin Supreme Court also ruled that the state constitutional provision stating that schools established by the legislature "shall be free and without charge for tuition to all children between the ages of 4 and 20 years" did not impose on the state a duty to provide schools for four-year-olds; thus there was no constitutional violation in a district's denial of admission to kindergarten to a child who failed to attain the age of five before December 1.[27] The constitutional provision simply meant that if a program of education is provided, it must be provided free of charge to those between the ages of four and twenty. The court also denied the parents' claim that the district's refusal to admit their precocious four-year-old, in the face of the fact other districts have admitted such children to the schools, was a violation of the state constitutional requirement that the schools be as uniform as practicable. The opportunity to apply for early admission was uniform across the state, but the decision whether or not to admit, said the court, was a matter committed to the discretion of the local school district.

The constitutionality of requiring children to be vaccinated as a condition for admission to public schools has frequently been raised. Again the courts have uniformly upheld this requirement against a range of constitutional arguments, including the claim that the vaccination requirement violated the parents' and child's rights to the free exercise of religion.[28]

We turn now to a somewhat different problem—shared time. The Michigan Supreme Court has held that Michigan law requires public schools to admit private school students to nonessential, elective courses such as band, art, domestic science, and advanced courses in math and science.[29] Once such courses are offered to public school students, they must be made available to private school students. While requiring that these nonessential courses be made available does not violate the establishment clause of the first amendment, said the court, requiring the districts to open the regular school program to private school students would make it possible for a nonpublic school to offer a complete program while conducting only a small percentage of the classes at the nonpublic school. This more far-reaching arrangement might constitute impermissible assistance to the religious schools. (For additional discussion of aid to private religious schools see §§1.10-1.12.)

3.3. EXCLUSION AS A DENIAL OF EQUAL PROTECTION OF THE LAWS

With the retirement of Chief Justice Warren in 1969, the "Warren Court" came to an end, but it left a legacy of aggressive use of the equal protection clause of the fourteenth amendment to end a variety of forms of unequal treatment in governmental programs, including education.[30] In the years since 1969, the equal protection clause has continued to prove to be the most effective avenue for obtaining judicial reform of education, especially for tackling state policies excluding students from the public schools. Educationally and politically the most significant use of the equal protection clause came in two lower federal court cases addressing the exclusion from public schooling of students labeled as mentally retarded, emotionally disturbed, physically handicapped, hyperactive, and having behavioral problems. In *Mills v. Board of Education,*[31] the federal district court in the District of Columbia ruled that insufficient funds was not a sufficient reason wholly to deny these "exceptional" children access to public education. If funds were not available to fund every needed and desirable educational program, then those funds that were available had to be used in such a way that no child was "entirely excluded from publicly supported education consistent with his needs and ability to benefit therefrom."[32] The second case was settled with a consent decree in which the state of Pennsylvania agreed to end the exclusion of the mentally retarded children from the state's public schools and to provide them with a free program of education and training appropriate to each child's capabilities.[33] In short, these courts made clear that the exclusion of "exceptional" children on the grounds they were "noneducable" or were expensive to educate, could not withstand constitutional scrutiny. All children could and were to be educated; public schools had the responsibility to provide training even in such basic skills as eating and self-care.

These landmark decisions, similar litigation in other states,[34] and lobbying by the handicapped led to the passage by Congress of the Rehabilitation Act of 1973, a general civil rights act that prohibits discrimination in any federally funded or assisted program or activity against otherwise qualified handicapped persons solely by reason of his or her handicap.[35] A practical effect of this law is to prohibit the exclusion of handicapped children from public education services. The law also serves, for example, to preclude the exclusion of mentally retarded children from regular classes because they are carriers of serum hepatitis.[36] Two years later, to help meet the rising demand for special educational services, Congress passed the Education for All Handicapped Children Act,[37] a law authorizing federal grants for special education programs. Receipt of these funds was conditioned upon accepting an important number of regulatory requirements, most important for these purposes, a promise to make available to all handicapped children a free, appropriate education consisting of special education[38] and related services[39] designed to meet their unique needs.[40] Following the passage of these two laws, state legislatures have revised their laws to bring them into conformity with federal law.[41] In sum, today the exclusion of the handicapped from publicly supported educational services is no longer legally permissible. The question as to what kinds of services the handicapped are entitled at public expense is an issue taken up in chapter 7.

Note that professional schools, if not also other higher education programs, may establish criteria for admission—criteria deemed necessary to assure the student will benefit from the program, and to assure his or her safe participation in the program—that may have the effect of excluding certain handicapped applicants.[42] It remains true, however, that mere possession of a handicap is not a permissible ground for denial of admission, that is, if the individual is able to meet the requirements of the program despite his or her handicap, admission cannot be denied solely because of the handicapping condition. The Court even went on to say that the occasion may arise when a refusal to modify a program to accommodate the needs of the handicapped may be unreasonable and discriminatory.

We now turn to another issue, the exclusion from free public schooling of children not legally admitted to the United States. In a close five-to-four decision (discussed again in §3.6), the Supreme Court ruled that the equal protection clause's protections extended even to those illegally in the United States,[43] and that the state's reasons for excluding children who were illegal aliens from as personally and socially an important public service as education were constitutionally insufficient.[44] Adopting a fairly strict form of review the majority concluded, first, that although the federal government did not approve of the presence of these children within the state, contrary to the state's argument, there was no federal policy to withhold from these children, present in this country through no fault of their own, access to basic education. Second, the mere fact these children were undocumented was an insufficient reason, given the potential effect on these children and society, to deny them an education. Third, this method of protecting the state against an influx of illegal aliens is flawed—even assuming illegal aliens have a negative impact on the state's economy; their reason for coming was to get employment, and denial of a free education was likely to be ludicrously ineffective to stem the tide. Fourth, the record did not support the claim that educational resources were so limited that these children needed to be excluded, or that their exclusion would otherwise improve the ability of the state to offer a high-quality educational program. Finally, the Court rejected the claim that these children could be singled out because their illegal status made it less likely than other children that they would remain in the state and put their education to productive social or political uses within the state. The state had no assurance that any child would remain in the state, and besides, the record indicated that many of these children would remain indefinitely. "It is difficult to understand precisely what the State hopes to achieve by promoting the creation and perpetuation of a subclass of illiterates within our boundaries, surely adding to the problems and costs of unemployment, welfare, and crime. It is thus clear that whatever savings might be achieved by denying these children an education, they are wholly insubstantial in light of the costs involved to these children, the State, and the Nation."[45]

The success of claimants in these and other cases[46] has not heralded a judicial willingness to eliminate all state efforts to limit access to the schools. In *Martinez v. Bynum*[47] Roberto Morales, a U.S. citizen by birth who lived in Mexico with his Mexican parents, moved to Texas without his parents to live with his sister for the primary purpose of attending school in Texas. He was denied tuition-free admission pursuant to a Texas statute that barred tuition-free admission to a minor who lives apart from a "parent, guardian, or other person having lawful control of him under an order of a court" if his presence in the school district is "for primary purpose of attending the public free schools."

In upholding the statute, the Court said that a bona fide residence requirement furthered the substantial state interest in assuring that services provided for residents were enjoyed only by residents, and that this statute did establish a bona fide residence requirement. In fact, the majority argued the state had been generous insofar as under the law a child who came to Texas for health reasons and had no intention of staying—one of the requirements, according to the majority, for establishing residency—could be admitted to the schools. It was only the child who (1) lived apart from his or her parents; (2) came to the district for the primary purpose of making use of the schools; and (3) who then intended to leave after completion of his or her education who could not be admitted tuition free. Justice Marshall dissented, arguing that the majority had used the wrong definition of a bona fide residence requirement (he disagreed that an intent to remain indefinitely was part of the usual definition of residency); that states could not impose a residency requirement that included a test of an intent to stay indefinitely; and that students who came to a district to use the schools could meet the usual residency requirement. He also argued that excluding those whose motive was to use the schools while admitting other children tuition-free who were residing in the state *for any other reason* and who made clear they were not intending to remain in the state could not be justified as serving a state interest in preserving resources for residents and avoiding fluctuating student populations. (In other cases the Court has struck down "durational" residency requirements, e.g., a requirement that one be a resident for a year before being eligible for social services, and a state law that created an irrebuttable presumption of nonresidency for state university students whose legal addresses were in another state before they applied for admission.[48]

The Eighth Circuit struck down the exclusion of children who did not have a parent or legal guardian living in the school district.[49] Applying the relatively strict standard of review used by the Supreme Court in *Plyler v. Doe,* the court concluded that the requirement that a child's parent or legal guardian had to reside in the district for the child to be eligible for admission to the schools violated the equal protection clause. The court rejected the three arguments the district offered in support of the policy. The need to prevent undesirable fluctuations in enrollment could be handled by means other than the policy of excluding this class of pupil. The purpose of preserving the use of the scarce school resources for the children of those who supported education with their taxes was, under Supreme Court precedent, an illegitimate purpose. The need for the school district to have an adult with whom school officials may effectively and authoritatively deal with in matters of punishment, educational progress, and medical needs was satisfied by dealing with those relatives with whom the child resided.

A minimum age requirement of six was unsuccessfully constitutionally attacked. In that case a father argued his precocious son was entitled to entry to the first grade and that denial of admission on the basis of age violated the equal protection clause of the fourteenth amendment and created an unwarranted conclusive presumption a child was not ready for the first grade.[50] The court rejected both claims with the same response: the line drawn reasonably approximated the results that would have been achieved if a child-by-child determination of readiness were made; hence, the age line was a reasonably accurate and practical method for determining readiness, a method that cost less to administer than would a policy of case-by-case determination.

3.4. TUITION AND OTHER FEES

Faced with tight finances, school districts have from time to time attempted to relieve the problem by charging their pupils a variety of fees. Unchecked, these fees could have the effect of excluding the poor from obtaining a public education, or, at the very least, reducing the quality of the education they might obtain if they were able to pay the required fee for textbooks or equipment. The most typical constitutional challenge to these fees argues that the charging of a fee violates the state's constitutional provision imposing on the legislature a duty to establish a system of *free* common schools.[51] The response of the judiciary to these challenges has been mixed. For the most part, if the fee can be characterized as a tuition, matriculation, or registration fee, a majority of the courts have concluded that the fee violates the state constitution.[52] Some courts have drawn a distinction between elements that are necessary or fundamental to an educational program (for which fees may not be charged) and those other elements, such as extracurricular activities, for which fees may be charged.[53] If the fee is specifically for the purchase or rental of books or the purchase of supplies, the courts have split.[54] North Carolina exemplifies the distinction. That state's highest court concluded the state's constitution prohibited the charge of tuition (public funds must be used for providing the physical plant and personnel salaries), but that other reasonable fees (what is reasonable is to be determined on a case-by-case basis) for supplementary supplies and materials were permissible.[55] The school district conceded that to penalize or deny enrollment to students who would not pay the fee because of economic hardship would be unconstitutional, but they defended the procedure used when students sought a waiver of the fees. The court concluded the system was unconstitutional. Under the district's system students were not notified in advance of the possibility of obtaining a waiver, and a student unable to pay the fee had first to be identified by the teacher (probably by the student's nonpayment of the fee) and then referred to the principal. The court said this system was unconstitutional because it forced a student to run the risk of being stigmatized on the basis of his or her economic status; students who might qualify for the waiver might instead elect to forgo the educational opportunities to avoid the stigma. The court concluded that for the waiver system to be constitutional, the district had to give adequate and timely notice of the waiver policy to students and to establish a system whereby students could confidentially apply for its benefits.[56]

The problem of the denial to the indigent of adequate educational opportunities because of the inability to pay a textbook fee was addressed in a different way, and with a different result, by the Second Circuit Court of Appeals.[57] After the voters of the district failed to approve a proposed real-estate tax to finance school operations, the board concluded that although it had authority to continue to tax the district for certain expenditures, it lacked statutory authority to raise money for textbooks. It thus imposed a textbook fee with the consequence that indigent children who could not pay the fee attended class without textbooks. Several issues were raised in the case, but the most important claim was that the fee was unconstitutional because it conditioned access to education, a fundamental right, on the basis of payment of a fee, i.e., the district had engaged in wealth-based discrimination. The majority rejected the argument, because "all similarly situated students are being treated alike" insofar as all students were being charged the same fee. The *district* did not treat people differently. "[T]hose who can afford textbooks will also no doubt receive a better eduation than those who cannot but that is because they had the financial means to supplement that which the State provides and not because the State has provided them with more than has been provided plaintiffs." The dissent argued that the state had discriminated on the basis of wealth when it chose to offer a curriculum keyed to textbooks and only the nonindigent could make use of that method of instruction.

3.5. DISTANCE FROM SCHOOL AS A BARRIER TO ACCESS

The sheer distance to the nearest public school or the difficulty of the terrain that needs to be traversed to get to a public school can serve as an effective barrier to public schooling. In recognition of this problem thirteen states exempt from the compulsory education requirement children who reside far from the nearest school or available public transportation.[58] Exempting pupils from the compulsory education law does not, however, solve another problem. A failure of the state to establish a school near a community may violate the state's constitutional requirement that the legislature establish a system of public schools open to all children. This challenge was raised in an Alaska case by plaintiffs who sought to have the state open a secondary school in their own community in the way other communities had their own secondary school.[59] For some pupils the state schools available to the plaintiffs were free boarding schools to which the state would transport the pupils. The state's supreme court ruled that the state's constitution permitted this arrangement. In another case, a court ruled that Hutterite children and parents were not discriminated against on the basis or race, color, sex, or national origin, nor were they being forced to violate their religious beliefs when the school district refused to establish a school at their colony, rather than requiring the Hutterite children to be bused to a school in a nearby town.[60]

Though challenges to a district's transportation policy are typically litigated in terms of state statutory requirements, in one case an interesting constitutional problem was raised when poor parents challenged the district's policy of providing students bus transportation to school either for the morning kindergarten session or from the afternoon session.[61] Relying on both the due process and equal protection clauses, the court concluded that one-way busing service was a form of unconstitutional discrimination against poor children. By resting its decision on the due process clause as well as the equal protection clause, the court seemed to suggest that school districts have an affirmative constitutional duty to provide children with transportation because not to provide it "constitutes an impermissible barrier to access of such children of low income to enjoyment of the right to secure educational opportunity, otherwise available to students not arbitrarily and adversely affected by such system."[62] In other words, if the school district had provided no transportation services, the failure to provide such a program would deny the poor access to the schools and would itself be a constitutional violation.[63] The Third Circuit Court of Appeals reversed the district court holding that the one-way busing policy did not affect a fundamental interest, thus only the rational basis test should apply, and under that test the board's policy was constitutionally permissible.[64] Whether the district court's opinion was consistent with Supreme Court precedent in existence at the time of the decision[65] is an interesting but perhaps moot question, given the Court's more recent concern that children not be wholly excluded from the public schools.[66] Equally as interesting is whether the Third Circuit's opinion is consistent with Supreme Court precedent. In support of the Third Circuit, one could argue that the most recent Supreme Court decision dealt with a policy of deliberate exclusion by the state, not merely a state's failure to take steps to make up for the impoverished condition of the children that made it impossible for them to take advantage of an opportunity afforded by the state.

In another constitutional case the plaintiff successfully claimed that the district had violated equal protection requirements by failing to provide children who live on a steep, curving gravel road transportation to school.[67] The court did not accept the district's argument that it would have to purchase a smaller bus at great expense in order to service this route.

The failure of a district to provide adequate transportation is typically litigated as a question of whether the school district has complied with the state statutory requirements imposed on the local school district to provide transportation. The issues involved in these cases have included such questions as whether the pupil lived the requisite minimum distance from the school in order to be eligible for the service the district was required to provide to eligible pupils; whether the pupil was eligible because the student faced the sort of hazards in getting to school from which the statute sought to protect the students; whether it was reasonable for the district to require the pupil to go to a pick-up point some distance from the student's home; and whether it was reasonable, under the discretionary authority granted by the state, for the school district to impose residence a certain minimum distance from the school as a requirement for eligibility for transportation.[68] In one important case, the Supreme Court of California held it was arbitrary and capricious to refuse to provide transportation to pupils in a remote area even though the extra cost to the district per pupil in 1966 would have been $375 per pupil (less some state assistance if the pupils attended the district's schools).[69] The court stressed that the absolute denial of an education to these pupils made the district's cost-based arguments unpersuasive.

3.6. IS THERE A CONSTITUTIONAL RIGHT TO AN EDUCATION?

The United States Constitution does not use the word "education," much less expressly recognize a right to an education.[70] Even the majority in *Plyler v. Doe* stated flatly that "Public education is not a 'right' granted to individuals by the Constitution."[71] Though *equal* deprivation of *all* students of state support or provision of education would be constitutionally acceptable, the equal protection clause remains as a potentially important barrier to the *uequal* denial of educational opportunities to *some* children. But the stronger this form of protection, the more the Court may be understood as indirectly and implicitly supporting the notion of a right to an education.[72] How much protection the equal protection clause provides, as interpreted by the Burger Court, remains a matter of some uncertainty, however.

The Burger Court has used at least two different "tests" for determining the constitutionality of state legislation challenged under the equal protection clause. In *San Antonio Ind. Sch. Dist. v. Rodriguez*[73] the Court upheld Texas's system for financing public schools, despite the fact that the system resulted in great differences in the amount of money spent per pupil among districts within the state, by using the "rational basis test"—a test that requires the *plaintiffs* to establish that a state policy is either irrational or serves an illegitimate purpose.[74] This test, which favors the state, was chosen for use in this case in preference to a more stringent test that favors the plaintiffs because, in part, the Court said education was not a fundamental interest either expressly or implicitly protected by the Constitution.[75] Only if a state policy adversely affects such a fundamental interest or discriminates on the basis of a criterion such as race would the Court use the more stringent "strict scrutiny" test that imposes on *government* the burden of persuading the judiciary that its policy is "necessary to achieve a compelling state interest." The majority noted, however, that the tougher test might be called into play if plaintiffs show they were absolutely deprived of an education or were at least being deprived of a minimally adequate education—a showing that had not been made in this case, despite the inequalities in the amount of money spent per pupil among the districts. (The Court never offered its definition of a minimally adequate program.)[75] In this connection the majority opinion said a more compelling case of judicial intervention would be made if public education were made available by the state only to those able to pay a tuition fee that had the effect of absolutely depriving a clearly defined class of poor people from receiving an education. It is important to stress that the Court's minimum-protection doctrine as adopted by the Burger Court left plaintiffs with little real protection. This is made clear by the majority's cursory treatment of the evidence presented in the case that the education program in districts spending lower amounts of money per pupil was not adequate. "No proof was offered at the trial persuasively discrediting or refuting the State's assertion [that it offered all students an adequate program]." By not responding to the evidence of the plaintiffs with more care, the majority left the impression it will rarely disbelieve a state's claim that its program meets minimum standards of adequacy.[77]

Nine years later in *Plyler v. Doe*[78] the Court issued an opinion that, in one sense, is consistent with the decision in *Rodriguez,* despite the use of a stricter test.[79] Unlike the situation in *Rodriguez,* here a group of children were wholly excluded from the public schools. Thus, *Plyler* may be seen as an application of the *Rodriguez* notion that strong judicial protection against inequalities in educational policy would be forthcoming if the case involved something like the absolute deprivation of educational opportunities.

There is, however, language in *Plyler* that suggests that a majority of the Court may be willing to consider education per se as a fundamental interest, and that even inequalities short of total deprivation would evoke close judicial examination.[80] At least the ground has been laid in this opinion for a majority of the Court to move in the future in the direction of a stronger assault on inequalities in the provision of education, a more careful examination of the charge that a particular program is not minimally adequate.

Let's now look at a case of de jure discrimination. If the Court were to move in the direction implied by the opinion in *Plyler,* a number of explicit criteria for excluding children from the schools could be seriously questioned, e.g., the minimum age requirement. Using a test like the strict-scrutiny test, it could be argued that states must justify their exclusion from an age-appropriate public school program, for example, of three-year-old children. When strict scrutiny is used, the desire of the state to save money is not an acceptable justification, as we have seen in the decisions dealing with the exclusion of the handicapped.

Even certain forms of de facto wealth discrimination might be handled differently now that we have *Plyler* rather than only *Rodriguez* as a guide. Following *Rodriguez* it was conceivable the Court might conclude that a textbook fee was constitutional because the program of instruction was still minimally adequate for the indigent who did not have textbooks. (Recall the majority in *Rodriguez* seemed willing to accept considerable differences in the quality of programs offered children.) After *Plyler*'s language stressing the importance of education, it seems less likely the Court would accept the view that a textbook-based instructional program could be minimally adequate for students without textbooks. The strict-scrutiny test would thus be applied with the probable result that the fee would be struck down.

Though the direction of the Burger Court is somewhat unclear, it seems unlikely that the *Plyler* decision marked a departure from the decision in *Rodriguez*. *Plyler* involved the special case of "innocent" children being absolutely deprived of an education through no fault of their own because they were placed in an illegal status by their parents. This point is underscored by Justice Powell, who wrote the majority opinion in *Rodriguez,* in a concurring opinion in *Plyler* in which he underscored the "unique character of the case before us," and the fact that this case was different from *Rodriguez* because there "no group of children was singled out by the State and then penalized because of their parents' status."[81] Furthermore, while Justice Stevens has joined the Court since *Rodriguez* and voted with the majority in *Plyler,* Justice White, who dissented in *Rodriguez* (thereby taking a "liberal" position), now dissents in *Plyler* (taking a so-called "conservative" position). In sum, a majority of the Court seem today to continue to embrace the approach in *Rodriguez.*[82]

NOTES

1. Brown v. Board of Education, 347 U.S. 483, 493 (1954) (emphasis added).

2. The question of whether education is a federal constitutional right is, in one sense, easily answered—there is no explicit recognition of the right in the U.S. Constitution. It may be argued, however, that Supreme Court precedent, issued after the opinion from which the quotation was taken, has recognized an implicit U.S. constitutional right to an education. This question will be taken up later in §3.6.

3. As commonly used, the "functionally excluded" child is the non-English-speaking child who is formally admitted to the school but is provided a program of instruction conducted entirely in English. It is said that this child is excluded from the school as effectively as if he or she had not been admitted to the classrooms in the first place. To date, the concept of functional exclusion has not been used in the law to apply to any child who is, by reason of other factors in his or her background, not prepared to take advantage of the educational program formally made available.

4. When government expressly treats people differently in terms of, say, gender, this is called de jure discrimination. Government also unavoidably engages in de facto discrimination. For example, government may establish a criterion for comparing and sorting people for a job that speaks in terms of characteristic X (e.g., the ability to lift 150 pounds), but that, as an accidental and unintended by-product, has the effect of sorting out people in terms of characteristic Y (e.g.,

gender.) We then say that criterion X is "gender neutral" but has a discriminatory impact on, say, women as a group. That is, it is said women are disproportionately affected by criterion X and disproportionately excluded from the job, i.e., whereas 50 percent of the men pass the requirement, only 10 percent of the women do.

5. *See* Peter Westen, "The Empty Idea of Equality," *Harvard Law Review* 95 (1982): 537, 567; Peter Westen, "To Lure the Tarantula from Its Hole: A Response," *Columbia Law Review* 83 (1983): 1186.

6. It has been argued that the Court has not in fact adopted three distinct tests, but instead adhered to a single sliding-scale test. Under this conception of the Court's handiwork, the Court shifts the level of scrutiny of a state or local policy according to the degree of presence of certain factors. Thus, the more fundamental the interest affected by the policy, and the more the group affected is in need of special judicial protection, the more vigorous will be the judicial review. San Antonio Indep. Sch. Dist. v. Rodriguez, 411 U.S. 1 (1973) (Marshall, J., dissenting).

7. Hooper v. Bernalillo Cty. Assessor, 105 S. Ct. 2862, 2866 (1985).

8. For example, suppose a school board said that only teachers who live in the school district, criterion A, will be considered for promotion to administrative positions. The purpose of the policy is, arguably, to assure that only people who are dedicated to the school district and its populace will be placed in administrative positions. The plaintiff must establish that this purpose is illegitimate (a task at which the plaintiff is not likely to succeed), or that criterion A does not serve the purpose. How might it not serve the purpose? Clearly, some teachers who live in the district may not be truly dedicated to the district, whereas others who live outside might be. But a court using the rational-basis test is likely to conclude that the use of criterion A is not irrational, i.e., there may be on average a difference between teachers living in the district and those outside it in terms of dedication to the district. Hence, the use of criterion A is permissible—there is no right not to be subjected to criterion A in this instance.

9. U.S. Railroad Retirement Bd. v. Fritz, 449 U.S. 166 (1980).

10. If one returns to the example in note 8, we can see the effect of this test. The government would have to persuade the court that obtaining administrators dedicated to the district is not merely a legitimate objective, but also an important objective. Arguably the board would be successful in doing this. In addition, the board would have to persuade the court that the criterion of where a teacher lived was not an excessively sloppy or crude way of measuring the degree of dedication of teachers. Because where a person lives is not a precise measure of dedication to his or her job, the board would have a harder time persuading the court of the appropriateness of criterion A under the middle-level test.

11. Sticking with the same example, we can see that it is unlikely that a court would be persuaded that securing dedicated administrators is a "compelling" purpose, as that term is understood. Protecting the lives and safety of people, and protecting the national interest are "compelling" purposes. It is also clear that criterion A was not "necessary" for the school district to achieve its purpose. There are other less crude measures for determining who would be a dedicated administrator.

12. *See, e.g.,* Mississippi University for Women v. Hogan, 458 U.S. 718 (1982).

13. *See, e.g.,* Bolling v. Sharpe, 347 U.S. 497 (1954); Brown v. Bd. of Educ., 347 U.S. 483 (1954). A criterion that speaks in terms of race is a species of what the courts have called a "suspect criterion," but there is no clear definition of what constitutes a suspect criterion. It may involve an unalterable trait. It may involve a trait that distinguishes its possessor from the majority. It may be a trait that has only been used for the purpose or effect of stigmatizing those with it. It may be a trait that is rarely relevant to any legitimate governmental objectives. Gerald Gunther, *Constitutional Law,* 11th ed. (Mineola, N.Y.: The Foundation Press, 1985), 643.

14. Plyler v. Doe, 457 U.S. 202 (1982). The absolute denial of access to public schooling has been viewed as a policy that affects a fundamental interest. Again, the definition of the generic concept of a fundamental interest has not been adequately articulated by the courts. Thus while

the Supreme Court has recognized that the right to interstate travel is a fundamental interest, the right to intrastate travel has not been so recognized. Shapiro v. Thompson, 394 U.S. 832 (1969) (interstate travel); McCarthy v. Philadelphia Service Comm'n, 424 U.S. 645 (1976). For one effort on the part of the Court to grapple, with the concept of a fundamental interest, see Bowers v. Hardwick, 106 S. Ct. 2841 (1986) (holding that homosexuals do not have a fundamental right to engage in consensual sodomy, even in the privacy of the home).

15. It is common for state compulsory-education laws to exempt the handicapped from compliance. William F. Aikman and Lawrence Kotin, *Legal Implications of Compulsory Education,* (Port Washington, N.Y.: Kennikat Press, 1980), 171 et seq.

16. In some states such as Nebraska and New Jersey, the state constitution itself imposes on the legislature a duty to provide a system of common schools for persons between certain ages, e.g., five and twenty-one. Edward C. Bolmeier, *The School in the Legal Structure,* 2d ed. (Cincinnati: W. H. Anderson Company, 1973), 93-94. In other states age limitations are wholly a matter of statutory law. Id., at p. 225. *See also* Leroy J. Peterson, Richard A. Rossmiller, Martin M. Volz, *The Law and Public School Operation,* 2d ed. (New York: Harper & Row Publishers, Inc., 1978), 195.

17. It is common for states and local boards of education to require that pupils be vaccinated and meet other health pre-admission requirements in order to protect the other pupils in the school. Rossmiller, et al, *The Law and Public School Operation, supra* note 16, at 290-94.

18. Unless state law specifically requires the provision of educational services to students suspended from school, authority to suspend or expel pupils allows the schools to relieve themselves of the duty to provide public education to persons of compulsory-education age. Aikman and Kotin, *Legal Implications of Compulsory Education, supra* note 15, at 178.

19. Entitlement to attend schools in a particular district without payment of tuition depends on whether the child has properly established residency in the district. Rossmiller et. al., *The Law and Public School Operations, supra* note 16, at 302. The Supreme Court has said "residence" entails both physical presence and an intention to remain. Martinez v. Bynum, 103 S. Ct. 1838 (1983).

20. The New York constitution is typical. Article 9, §1 states: "The legislatures shall provide for the maintenance and support of a system of free common schools, wherein all the children of this state may be educated." Excerpts from state constitutions are reprinted in Bolmeier, *The School in the Legal Structure, supra* note 16, at 89 et seq. Three constitutions explicitly recognize a right to an education—North Carolina, Wyoming, and Puerto Rico. The constitution of Alabama expressly denies citizens any right to an education. Aikman and Kotin, *Legal Implications of Compulsory Education, supra* note 15, at 200-201. One commenator has grouped state constitutional provisions into four groups that differ in the extent to which they require the state to provide an educational program of a certain quality. Gershon M. Ratner, "A New Legal Duty for Urban Public Schools: Effective Education in Basic Skills," *Texas Law Review* 63 (1985): 777, 815.

21. State v. Bd. of Educ. of City of Antigo, 169 Wis. 231, 172 N.W. 153, 154 (Wis. 1919).

22. Id.

23. Dept. of Public Welfare v. Haas, 15 Ill. 2d 204, 154 N.E. 2d 265 (Ill. 1958).

24. Nonconstitutional challenges to age-based exclusion decisions have been successful. In Fogel v. Goulding, 51 Misc. 2d 641, 273 N.Y.S. 2d 554 (N.Y. Sup. Ct. 1966) the court ruled it was arbitrary and capricious for the school to deny access to first grade because a child was not six when the child had completed kindergarten in an unregistered kindergarten.

25. State of Montana v. Sch. Dist. No. 1 of Fergus Cty., 136 Mt. 453, 348 P. 2d 797 (Mont. 1960). *Accord,* Detch v. Bd. of Educ. of the Cty. of Greenbrier, 117 S.E. 2d. 138 (Sup. Ct. App. 1960); Simonson v. Sch. Dist. No. 14, 127 Colo. 575, 258 P. 2d 1128 (1953).

26. Id., at 102. The Wisconsin Supreme Court struck down a district's policy of requiring a child to be five years of age prior to September 1 in order to be admitted to kindergarten. Under state statutes age admission for first grade was six by December 1. The court found that only by

adopting the same cut-off date would age admission to kindergarten and first grade be integrated, and the state constitution required district schools to be as nearly uniform as practicable. Pacyana v. Bd. of Educ. Joint Sch. Dist. No. 1, 57 Wis. 2d 562, 204 N.W. 2d 671, 672-3 (Wis. 1973). *See also* Zweifel v. Joint Dist. No. 1, Belleville, 76 Wis. 2d 648, 251 N.W. 2d 822 (Wis. 1977).

27. Zweifel v. Joint Dist. No. 1, Belleville, 76 Wis. 2d 648, 251 N.W. 2d 822 (Wis. 1977).

28. Rossmiller et al., *The Law and Public School Operation, supra* note 16, at 292-93. In Hanzel v. Arter, 625 F. Supp. 1259 (S.D. Ohio 1985) a court rejected the claim that the right of privacy encompassed the decision of a parent not to have his or her child vaccinated.

State attempts to accommodate parents who may object to vaccinations on religious grounds by granting these parents and their children an exemption have been struck down in a number of cases. Avard v. Dupuis, 376 F. Supp. 479 (D.N.H. 1974); Brown v. Stone, 378 So. 2d 218 (Miss. 1979), *cert. denied,* 449 U.S. 887 (1980); Dali v. Bd. of Educ., 358 Mass. 753, 267 N.E. 2d 219 (Mass. 1971). *Cf.,* Kleid v. Bd. of Educ., of Fulton Kentucky Indep. Sch. Dist., 406 F. Supp. 902 (W. D. Ky. 1976) (upholding against establishment clause challenge a state law that expresssly exempted from inoculation members of nationally recognized churches).

29. Snyder v. Charlotte Pub. Sch. Dist., 365 N.W. 2d 151 (Mich. 1984).

30. The most notable example is, of course, the decision in Brown v. Bd. of Educ., 347 U.S. 483 (1954) (striking down the purposeful segregation of pupils on the basis of race). In decisions leading up to the decision in *Brown,* the Supreme Court ruled that denying admission to institutions of higher education on the basis of race violates the equal protection clause. Sweatt v. Painter, 339 U.S. 629 (1950); Missouri ex rel. Gaines v. Canada, 305 U.S. 337 (1938).

31. 348 F. Supp. 866 (D.D.C. 1972).

32. The court's judgment and decree required that each school-age child be provided with a publicly supported education suited to his needs regardless of the child's mental, physical, or emotional disability. If the child is not admitted to a regular public school program, an alternative program suited to the child's needs must be provided. The school board was also required to develop a comprehensive plan that provided for the identification, notification, assessment, and placement of all exceptional children. This plan had to include materials on the curriculum, educational objectives, teacher qualifications, and ancillary as well as compensatory education services.

33. Pennsylvania Ass'n for Retarded Children (PARC) v. Commonwealth, 334 F. Supp. 1257 (E.D. Pa. 1971), 343 F. Supp. 279 (E.D. Pa. 1972). The court stressed that placement in a regular public school class was preferable to placement in a special class, and that placement in a special public school class was preferable to any other type of placement in another type of program of education and training.

34. *See, e.g.,* In the Interest of G. H., 218 N.W. 2d 441 (N.D. 1974); McMillian v. Bd. of Educ. of N.Y., 430 F. 2d 1145 (2d Cir. 1970).

35. 29 U.S.C. §794 (1982).

36. New York State Ass'n for Retarded Children, Inc. v. Carey, 612 F. 2d 644 (2d Cir. 1979). The school board was unable to demonstrate that the presence of these children created anything more than a remote health hazard to other children.

37. 20 U.S.C. §§1400-1461 (1982).

38. The act defined "special education" as "specially designed instruction, at no cost to parents or guardians, to meet the unique needs of a handicapped child, including classroom instruction, instruction in physical education, home instruction, and instruction in hospitals and institutions."

39. The act defines "related services" as "transportation, and such developmental, corrective, and other supportive services (including speech pathology and audiology, psychological services, physical and occupational therapy, recreation, and medical and counseling services, except that such medical services shall be for the diagnostic and evaluation purposes only) as may be required to assist a handicapped child to benefit from special education, and includes the early identification and assessment of handicapping conditions in children."

40. For a review of the legislative history of the statute see Lauren A. Larson, "Beyond Conventional Education: A Definition of Education Under the Education for all Handicapped Children Act of 1975," *Law and Contemporary Problems* 48 (1985): 63, 67-71.

41. "Note: State Response to the Education for All Handicapped Children Act of 1975," *Law and Contemporary Problems* 48 (1985): 275.

42. Southeastern Community College v. Davis, 442 U.S. 397 (1979) (concluding that exclusion of an applicant with a serious hearing disability from a clinical nursing program did not violate the Rehabilitation Act of 1973). The regulations enforcing the Rehabilitation Act of 1973, 29 U.S.C. §701 (1982), specially state that post-secondary institutions may not limit the number of handicapped persons who are admitted, or use any "test or criterion for admission that has a disproportionate, adverse effect on handicapped persons" unless the test has been validated as an accurate predictor of success in the education program and alternative tests of criteria that have a less disproportionate effect are not shown to exist by the Assistant Secretary for Civil Rights of the Department of Education. 34 C.F.R. §104.42 (1985). The regulations also impose limitations on pre-admission inquiries as to whether a candidate is handicapped unless the institution is taking remedial steps to correct the effects of past discrimination. 34 C.F.R. §§104.42(b)(4) and 104.42(c) (1985).

The regulations also spell out the kinds of accommodations that post-secondary institutions may have to make. Academic requirements that are shown to be essential to the program need not be modified. Modifications may include changes in the length of time permitted for completion of the program, adjustments in course requirements, changes in how examinations are given, and the provision of auxiliary aids for students with impaired sensory, manual, or speaking skills. 34. C.F.R. §104.44 (1985). The handicapped are also to be assured an equal opportunity to participate in physical education and athletics, must be provided housing convenient and comparable to the nonhandicapped, provide financial assistance and employment opportunities on a nondiscriminatory basis. 34 C.F.R. §§104.45, 104.46, 104.47 (1985).

43. Plyler v. Doe, 467 U.S. 202 (1982). The Court's review of the terms of the amendment (the amendment prohibits the denial of equal protection of the laws to "any person within [the state's] jurisdiction"), its own precedent, and the purpose and history of the fourteenth amendment led it to conclude that it should provide protection for all people within a state. "The Equal Protection Clause was intended to do nothing less than the abolition of all caste-based and invidious class-based legislation. That objective is fundamentally at odds with the power the State asserts here to classify persons subject to its laws as nonetheless excepted from its protection." *Id.*, at 202.

44. Id., at 221, 224-230.

45. Id., at 230. The dissenters disagreed with the standard of review adopted by the majority. They approached the case by asking whether the state's policy bore a rational relationship to a legitimate state purpose. Using that standard the dissenters concluded that "it simply is not 'irrational' for a state to conclude that it does not have the same responsibility to provide benefits for persons whose very presence in the state and this country is illegal as it does to provide for persons lawfully present." *Id.*, at 250 (Burger, C. J., dissenting). The Chief Justice also agreed that barring these children from public education could serve to deter unlawful immigration. *Id.*, at 249 n. 10 (Burger, C. J., dissenting). In sum, he said if he were a legislator, he would not vote to deny illegal alien children public schooling; however, this was a matter of public policy for a legislature to decide, not the Court. *Id.*, at 252-53.

46. Knight v. Bd. of Educ. of City of N.Y., 48 F.R.D. 108 (E.D. N.Y. 1969) (striking down the expulsion of 670 students with bad attendance records in order to relieve overcrowded conditions).

47. 103 S. Ct. 1838 (1983).

48. Memorial Hospital v. Maricopa Cty., 415 U.S. 250 (1974) (striking down a statute requiring a year's residence as a condition for an indigent's receiving non-emergency free hospi-

talization or medical care); Vlandis v. Kline, 412 U.S. 441 (1973) (striking down the state's residency requirement for obtaining lower state tuition).

49. Horton v. Marshall Public Schools, 769 F. 2d 1323 (8th Cir. 1985). The students involved in the case lived with relatives not their parents or guardians, and their parents lived out of state.

50. Hammond v. Marx, 406 F. Supp. 853 (D. Me., N.D. 1975).

51. State constitutions in about half the states require the establishment of a system of free public schools. "The Constitutional Mandate for Free Schools," *Wisconsin Law Review* (1971): 971, 973.

52. *See, e.g.*, Concerned Parents v. Caruthersville Sch. Dist., 548 S.W. 2d 554 (Mo. 1977) (en banc) (striking down a registration fee for courses in which academic credit is given). This opinion also reviews a number of other state court opinions dealing with a similar issue. The Supreme Court of New Mexico drew a distinction between fees for elective and nonelective courses, holding that reasonable fees for the former were permissible under the wording of that state's constitution. The state constitution called for a system of free public schools "sufficient for the education . . . of all children." Norton v. Bd. of Educ. of Sch. Dist. No. 16, 89 N.M. 470, 553 P. 2d 1277 (N.M. 1976). For a review of cases in this area, see Annot., 41 A.L.R. 3d 752 (1972).

53. Kelly v. East Jackson Public Schools, 372 N.W. 2d 638 (Mich. App. 1985); Paulson v. Minidoka Cty. Sch. Dist. No. 331, 93 Idaho 469, 463 P. 2d 935 (1970); Bond v. Ann Arbor Sch. Dist., 383 Mich. 693, 178 N.W. 2d 484 (1970).

54. The opinion in Cardiff v. Bismark Pub. Sch. Dist., 263 N.W. 2d 105 (1978) reviews many of these decisions and reaches the conclusion that in North Dakota the charging of fees for textbooks, at least in the elementary grades, violates the state's constitution.

55. Sneed v. Greensboro City Bd. of Educ., 299 N.C. 609, 264 S.E. 2d 106 (N.C. 1980). Following this line of analysis, an Illinois court upheld charging a supervisory fee of five dollars to students who resided 0.7 miles or less from their school and ate their lunches in school. The court reasoned that providing students a secure place to eat lunch could not be considered an educational service for which a fee could not be charged. Ambroiggio v. Bd. of Educ., 101 Ill. App. 3d 187, 56 Ill. Dec. 622, 427 N.E. 2d 1027 (Ill App. 1981).

56. The court rested its conclusion on two constitutional bases: by imposing the stigma and discouraging students from taking their educational opportunities they were denied their right of equal access; and the failure to provide notice violated their right to procedural due process of law.

57. Johnson v. New York State Educ. Dept., 449 F. 2d 871 (2d Cir. 1971).

58. Aikman and Kotin, *Legal Implications of Compulsory Education, supra* note 15, at 179. The states are Alabama, Alaska, Florida, Louisiana, Michigan, Montana, Nevada, Oregon, Pennsylvania, Tennessee, Utah, Virginia, and West Virginia. Puerto Rico also grants such an exemption. The terms and conditions of the exemption vary somewhat from jurisdiction to jurisdiction.

59. Hootch v. Alaska State-Operated School System, 536 P. 2d 793 (Alas. 1975).

60. Deerfield Hutterian Ass'n v. Ipswich Bd. of Educ., 468 F. Supp. 1219 (D. S.D. 1979).

61. Shaffer v. Bd. of Sch. Directors of the Albert Gallatin Area Sch. Dist., 522 F. Supp. 1138 (W.D. Pa. 1981).

62. Id., at 1142.

63. *Cf.,* Rose v. Nashua Bd. of Educ., 506 F. Supp. 1366 (D. N.H. 1981) in which the court concluded that state law created a protectable property interest in school transportation. Nevertheless, the court concluded that the district was permitted in this case to summarily suspend certain bus routes without affording a prior hearing. The school district's compelling interest in the safety of the bus operator and student riders and in the prevention of vandalism justified the suspension pending a post-termination hearing.

64. Shaffer v. Bd. of Sch. Directors, 687 F. 2d. 718 (3d. Cir. 1982).

65. San Antonio Independent Sch. Dist. v. Rodriguez, 411 U.S. 1 (1973). For a fuller discussion of these cases, see §§ 3.6, 7.2.

66. *Cf.*, Plyler v. Doe, 457 U.S. 202 (1982). For a fuller discussion of this case, see §§ 3.3, 3.6.

67. Shewsbury v. Bd. of Educ., Wyo. Cty., 265 S.E. 2d 767 (W. Va. 1980).

68. For a review of many of these cases see Annot., 52 A.L.R. 3d 1036 (1973). Sigmon v. Bd. of Educ. for Cty. of Roane, 324 S.E. 2d 352 (1984) (holding that it was an abuse of discretion not to consider reorganization of bus routes so that all children could be served).

69. Manjares v. Newton, 64 Cal. 2d 365, 49 Cal. Rptr. 805, 411 P. 2d 901 (Cal. 1966).

70. A constitutional right to an education would protect children against the circumstance in which a state decided wholly to withdraw from the support of education, leaving the provision and financing of education entirely to parents and the private market. Any child, rich or poor, could use the right to claim in court that the state's withdrawal from the field of education violated his or her constitutional right. Courts would be within their rights to order the legislature to provide support once again for a minimally adequate educational program for all children. (The notion of a minimally adequate program can be defined in many different ways.) Thus no child would have to run the risk of being absolutely deprived of a minimally adequate education because of the economic circumstances of his or her parents. For a further discussion and elaboration of these matters and an assessment of one argument in support of the idea that a right to an education is a constitutional right see Tyll van Geel, "Does the Constitution Establish a Right to an Education?" *School Review* 82 (1974): 293.

71. 457 U.S. 202, 221 (1982).

72. For example, the greater the range of expressly stated criteria establishing access to public educational services, e.g., the minimum age requirement, struck down in the name of equal protection of the laws, the more the Court can be understood as moving toward embracing a right to an education. Similarly, the more the Court strikes down neutral criteria that draw no expressly stated distinctions among children but have a discriminatory effect on some, e.g., textbook fees, the more it may be understood as embracing a right to an education.

73. 411 U.S. 1 (1973).

74. The Court found that the inequalities in the amount of money spent per pupil among districts did not make' unconstitutional a system of finance designed to enhance the local control of education.

75. If this tougher test had been used, it is likely the Court would have concluded, as did Justice Marshall in dissent, that the state could not justify adversely affecting the education of students in this way in the name of enhancing local control of education, when other systems of finance could have preserved local control without so adversely impinging on the fundamental interest of education.

76. A minimally adequate education could be defined in terms of a minimum level of inputs, i.e., to be minimally adequate the program must be supported with a minimum level of dollars, or supplied with a minimum quality of teacher, etc. A minimally adequate program may also be defined in terms of outputs. Thus, the minimally adequate program would be one that assured, for example, that on average children achieved a minimum level of competency, or that each child achieved this minimum level of competence. If this kind of output standard were used, the schools would be forced to spend more money on some than on others, since more money might be required to bring some children up to the minimum standards than for others.

77. *Cf.*, Johnpoll v. Elias, 513 F. Supp. 430 (E.D. N.Y. 1980), in which a parent claimed that placement of his emotionally and physically handicapped son in a particular high school would prevent him from obtaining an education as guaranteed by the fourteenth amendment. The parent argued that placement in another school would better serve the educational needs of his son. The court responded by saying, "With all due respect to the plaintiff's parental concern, this court cannot be used as a vehicle to review fundamental administrative decisions such as student placement." Id., at 432.

78. 457 U.S. 202 (1982).

79. The law excluding illegal-alien children from the public schools could only be accepted as constitutional if the state could establish that it "furthered some substantial goal of the State."

80. The majority spoke of education as important to maintaining our basic institutions, as essential for the transmitting of values on which the society rests, as providing the basic tools by which individuals might lead economically productive lives. "In sum, education has a fundamental role in maintaining the fabric of our society." *Id.,* at 221.

81. Id., at 236, 239 n. 3 (Powell, J., concurring).

82. The majority consists of Burger, White, Powell, Rehnquist, and O'Connor, all of whom dissent in *Plyler,* except Powell, whose position was explained in the text. The liberal minority consists of Brennan, Marshall, Blackmun, and Stevens—those who, with Powell, comprised the majority in *Plyler.*

4

Assailing Segregation on the Basis of Race and Gender

4.1. INTRODUCTION

In 1896 in *Plessy v. Ferguson* the Supreme Court concluded there was no constitutional obstacle to a Louisiana statute requiring railway companies to provide "equal but separate accommodations" for black and white passengers.[1] The *Plessy* standard, which came to be known in an interesting transposition of the statutory phrase as the "separate but equal" doctrine, was subsequently extended to public schooling in ways that indicated it was an orthodoxy that needed little analysis.[2] The educational reality for students living under the *Plessy* standard was that educational facilities and services were separate but unequal, a point the National Association for the Advancement of Colored People (NAACP) raised in a series of cases that sought equalization (not an end to separation) of educational facilities and programs in higher education.[3] In these cases the Court, while avoiding reaching the broad issue of whether *Plessy* should be overturned, began to undercut the doctrine through its recognition that the interaction among students was an essential part of learning and that, at least in some circumstances, the separation of the races made the provision of an equal education impossible.[4] Four years after the last of these higher education cases, the Court, again at the behest of the NAACP, extended this reasoning to elementary and secondary education. That decision, *Brown v. Board of Education* (*Brown I*), is arguably the most important decision the Supreme Court has issued in this century.[5] As a result, not only did the doctrine of "separate but equal" lose its constitutional imprimatur, but the door was also opened to a long and winding path leading to affirmative efforts to advance the educational opportunities of racial minorities.

This chapter will outline legal developments in this area as they bear primarily on the question of racial segregation of pupils among school buildings. The so-called second-generation problems, e.g., segregation within schools, racial bias in testing, discrimination in employment, will be taken up at other points in later chapters. The emphasis here is on the right of minority students to be free of one form of racial discrimination—segregation based on race. Dealt with later will be other negative entitlements, as well as more affirmative claims such as a claim to a right to a minimally adequate education. In §4.8 we turn to segregation on the basis of gender.

4.2. BROWN 1 AND 2 AND THE AFTERMATH

Four separate cases arising in Kansas, South Carolina, Virginia, and Delaware were consolidated for decision in *Brown 1;* and they had one basic fact in common: explicitly, by state law or local district policy, black and white students were assigned to separate schools.[6] A unanimous Supreme Court in a brief opinion concluded that segregation in public schools deprived black students of the equal protection of the laws.[7]

> To separate [children] from others of similar age and qualifications solely because of their race generates a feeling of inferiority as to their status in the community that may affect their hearts and minds in a way unlikely ever to be undone. The effect of this separation on their educational opportunities was well stated by a finding in the Kansas case by a court which nevertheless felt compelled to rule against the Negro plaintiffs:
>
> > "Segregation of white and colored children in the public schools has a detrimental effect upon the colored children. The impact is greater when it has the sanction of law; for the policy of separating the races is usually interpreted as denoting the inferiority of the Negro group. A sense of inferiority affects the motivation of a child to learn. Segregation with the sanction of law, therefore, has a tendency to retard the educational and mental development of Negro children and to deprive them of some of the benefits they would receive in a racial[ly] integrated school system."
>
> Whatever may have been the extent of psychological knowledge at the time of *Plessy v. Ferguson,* this finding is amply supported by modern authority. [Footnote 11 omitted.] Any language in *Plessy v. Ferguson* contrary to this finding is rejected.
>
> We conclude that in the field of public education the doctrine of "separate but equal" has no place. Separate educational facilities are inherently unequal.

In the famous footnote 11 the Court cited, among other things, the research of Professor Kenneth B. Clark on the attitudes of black and white children, and two opinion surveys asking researchers their beliefs about the effects of segregation on black children.[8]

Though *Brown 1* itself did not use the strict-scrutiny test,[9] the companion decision in *Bolling v. Sharpe*[10] did. It seems fair to say that racial segregation produced by the express use of a racial criterion triggers the use of the strict-scrutiny test, thus imposing on government the burden of justifying its policy by demonstrating that the segregation is "necessary to achieve a compelling state interest." The psychological and sociological evidence adduced in *Brown 1* thus may be seen as the Court's way of saying that not merely did government fail in meeting its burden of proof, there is reason to believe that the government's purposes are illegitimate—they are in fact harmful and intended to harm. These students have been denied the right not to be harmed in this way solely on the basis of their race.

We can look at the Court's use of the strict-scrutiny test in a somewhat different way. If the law or policy expressly treats people differently on the basis of race, courts will treat this as a "suspect" classification and require the decision-maker to rebut the suspicion that this classification was chosen either out of racial animus or because of stereotypic views of the disadvantaged group. As Professor Ely puts it: "Naturally you suspect *(le mot just)* that the law's motivation was that most naturally suggested by its terms, namely a desire to disadvantage blacks. But you know that is not *necessarily* the case, and so you listen. What would it take to allay your suspicion?"[11] It is at this point that a test is imposed on government: to allay the court's fears, government must prove that it used a racial classification because it was necessary (there was no other more direct means) to achieve a goal of very great importance, a compelling state interest.[12] If the government fails to meet this test, the court's suspicions will not have been allayed, and the official action will be struck down as most probably having been improperly motivated. Consider Professor Brest's example of the school principal who argues that it was for aesthetic reasons that he seated black and white students on different sides of the stage at a graduation ceremony. No other classification criterion, race in this case, would achieve the same aesthetic effect; but the purpose is so "trivial" that the aesthetic argument can be seen as pretextual and the real purpose as something else.[13]

While it was clear from *Brown 1* that at least the explicit, purposeful segregation of the races in public schooling was no longer constitutionally allowable, other fundamental questions were not answered. What was now to be expected of districts that had engaged in de jure segregation? Would the Court also prohibit de facto segregation as it had prohibited de jure segregation in public schooling?[14] In situations in which segregation exists, but the government has not expressly acknowledged that it has used race to assign pupils to schools, what proof will suffice to prove that the consideration of the race of the pupils was a cause of the decision?[15] How is the term "segregation" to be defined, whether one speaks of de jure or de facto segregation?[16] If the segregation in a district is both de jure and de facto, how is it to be determined, how much of the segregation is to be characterized as de jure, and how much de facto? Would the principles of *Brown 1* be extended to other areas beyond education?[17]

At bottom, the answer to these questions turned on several more ultimate questions. What values did the Court take to underlay the fourteenth amendment? Did the Court understand the fourteenth to simply create a right not to be purposefully treated disadvantageously on the basis of race? Or did the Court rest *Brown 1* on the more powerful notion that the fourteenth was concerned not just with preventing purposeful harm, but also with preventing de facto injuries, i.e., policies that have the unintended effect of maintaining or exacerbating the unequal economic, social, and political status of racial minorities. Might the court have embraced the notion that the fourteenth amendment permitted, or even required, that government take affirmative steps to equalize the social and economic status of blacks as a group? With what sort of harm(s) was *Brown 1* concerned: (1) interference with the freedom of association of racial minority students; (2) academic performance; (3) the ultimate status and income of minority students; (3) the racial attitudes of black and white students; (4) the stigma and insult to dignity that any reasonable, objective person would agree segregation inflicts; and/ or (5) psychological damage?

Brown 1 does not provide an unequivocal answer to these questions, and even today, after much litigation, the Court's answers are incomplete and unclear, and commentators disagree on what the answers should be.[18] Thus, as we shall see, there is much in the body of law developed subsequently to Brown 1 that must necessarily remain indeterminate.

In any event, a year after *Brown 1,* the Court issued an opinion (*Brown 2*) dealing with the problem left open in *Brown 1*—the question of the appropriate relief to be ordered.[19] The forging of the remedial order in *Brown 2* was significantly influenced by fear of a violent reaction. The opinion thus noted the variety of local problems involved in implementing the mandate of *Brown 1* and made clear to the federal district courts that, when they did fashion remedies, those remedies must be practical and encompass both public and private needs. Though a "prompt and reasonable start toward full compliance" was to be made, the Court acknowledged that a transition period would be needed prior to the implementation of racially nondiscriminatory school systems. Steps were to be taken "with all deliberate speed," with good-faith compliance occurring "at the earliest practicable date."

The ordering of relief by the district courts was made difficult by massive resistance that took the form of school closings, cleverly worded pupil placement laws, and certain types of voucher schemes that perpetuated segregation. Disorder and even violence accompanied efforts to end segregation.[20] Federal district judges, operating under enormous personal pressure, responded in various ways: some judges engaged in transparent maneuvers of delay, others complied with *Brown 1* by ordering token steps toward desegregation, and yet others took courageous steps to fulfill the promise of *Brown 1.*[21] When these opinions were appealed, the primary response of the Supreme Court was to refuse to review. There were two notable exceptions, however, to the Court's virtual abandonment of the field of battle. In *Cooper v. Aaron*[22] the Court held that violence, especially violence stimulated by a state governor, would not excuse implementation of a federal district court's desegregation order. In *Griffin v. County Board of Education*[23] the Court declared unconstitutional the Virginia statutes that suspended the compulsory education law in the state, permitted counties to close their public schools instead of integrating them, and authorized public financial support for the nominally private segregated schools that began operating after the public schools had closed. In other cases the court prohibited the use of minority-to-majority transfer provisions in desegregation plans, because such a device permitted white students to flee predominantly black schools.[24] The Court also required that desegregation plans include plans for faculty integration.[25]

4.3. CONGRESS AND THE SUPREME COURT STEP IN

Ten years after *Brown 1*, in seven of the eleven southern states only 2.4 percent of black students attended desegregated schools. With a Supreme Court that refused to take aggressive action and a Congress and two presidents who were at best reluctant to help the Court, there was little incentive to change a long-standing way of life. In 1964, President Johnson, riding a wave of public sympathy and support in the aftermath of the assassination of President Kennedy in November 1963, engineered the passage of the Civil Rights Act of 1964[26] that in part forbade discrimination based on race in any program receiving federal funds. The passage and aggressive enforcement of this law against recalcitrant southern shool districts seemed to have spurred the Supreme Court to more aggressive action.[27] (For many years after the enactment of Title VI it was unclear whether or not the statute forbade only purposeful discrimination or prohibited policies that had an unintended discriminatory impact.[28] Today, a majority of the Court seems to accept the view that Title VI by itself reaches only instances of intentional discrimination, but that administrative regulations that incorporate a disparate impact approach are valid; hence disparate impact may be redressed through agency regulations designed to implement the purpose of Title VI.[29] Today students may also seek redress under the more recently adopted Equal Educational Opportunity Act.[30])

The last major school decision of the 1960s and the last major school decision of the Warren Court set the Supreme Court on the course of actively pursuing racial integration. The case arose in New Kent County, Virginia, where the district adopted a "freedom-of-choice" plan in order to remain eligible for federal financial aid after a desegregation suit had been filed. Although there was no residential segregation in the county, because children could attend the school of their choice, the schools remained as segregated after the plan as before. *Green v. New Kent County Board of Education*[31] unanimously held that the district remained unconstitutionally segregated. School boards that had operated dual school systems had a duty not merely to stop segregating, but to affirmatively and immediately come forward with a plan to desegregate that realistically promised to convert to a system without "white" schools and "Negro" schools, one with "just schools." The clear implication was that former dual systems had to produce racially integrated schools and the use of race as a criterion had in effect become mandatory in judicially required desegregation plans.

Justice Rehnquist has since charged that *Green* was a "drastic extension of *Brown*,"[32] but it may be offered in response (1) that the duty to integrate is a way of making certain the old policy has in fact been discarded; (2) that integration is an appropriate remedy to eliminate the effects of a past illegal practice; and (3) that it is foolish to suppose that choices under the freedom-of-choice plan were in fact "free" and not conditioned by a long history of segregation, if not contemporaneous threats.[33] Professor Brest has observed that Justice Rehnquist's charge was wholly off the mark. Though *Green* only required the board to undo the present effects of past de jure segregation, the Court's standard for judging the adequacy of the desegregation plan—the plan must produce "just schools"—tended to blur the distinction between eliminating the effects of de jure and de facto discrimination.[34] *Green* thus raised the question left unanswered in *Brown 1*: would the Court also formally declare de facto segregation unconstitutional? The decision in *Green* also left unanswered what a desegregated school building should look like: must the building contain a certain proportion of black to white pupils? What should that proportion be? On what basis should the proportions be determined? Were the proportions to be decided on the basis of educational considerations? If so, if there were insufficient black or white pupils in this district to provide the best educational mix, would that mean students from other districts were to be involved in the desegregation plan? Or were the proportions simply to be dictated by the racial makeup of the district as a whole?

The retirement of Chief Justice Warren in 1969 meant the answers to these questions would have to be left to the new Burger Court. The Burger Court's first major school opinion in *Swann v. Charlotte-Mecklenburg Board of Education*[35] also left unanswered the issue of de facto segregation. The opinion touched on three questions: (1) what evidence might be relevant in establishing a practice of covert de jure segregation? (2) what evidence will suffice to establish that school board decisions caused or contributed to the present state of segregation? and (3) what techniques may federal district courts use to eliminate the dual school system and bring about integration now? To answer the first question, the Court provided a catalog of factors that were to be used as indicia of de jure segregation: the racial composition of the teachers and staff, the quality of buildings and equipment, the organization of sports activities, the closing of schools about to become racially mixed, and the building of new buildings in white areas farthest from the black population. On the second question the Court stated that it was willing to assume, absent contrary evidence brought forward by school officials, that in a district that had long stopped practicing de jure segregation, a continued pattern of segregation in the face of new student-assignment policies was the result of illegal activity. The court indulged in this presumption of continuing effects even though it was seventeen years after *Brown 1* and many intervening factors could have produced the present pattern. The Court acknowledged that at some point the link between past segregative policies and present segregation would become severed and that it would not be possible to attribute present segregation to past illegal actions, i.e., the present segregation would be deemed de jure segregation. But the Court never clarified the point at which the link would be considered to be severed; clearly, the longer the Court allowed the presumption to run, the more de facto segregation would be labeled a product of de jure segregation. In regard to the third question, the Court upheld the power of district courts to require school boards to alter attendance zones and to transport pupils throughout the district in order to reach the goal of achieving a racial mix in each school that approximated the racial composition of the school population as a whole.[36]

Justice Powell in a concurring opinion in a later case noted:

[i]n imposing on metropolitan southern school districts an affirmative duty, entailing large-scale transportation of pupils to alleviate conditions which in large part did *not* result from historic, state-imposed *de jure* segregation. Rather, the familiar root cause of segregated schools in *all* the biracial metropolitan areas of our country is essentially the same: one of segregated residential and migratory patterns, the impact of which on the racial composition of the schools was often perpetuated and rarely ameliorated by action of public school authorities. This is a national, not a southern, phenomenon. And it is largely unrelated to whether a particular State had or did not have segregative school laws.[37]

In 1973 the Court continued its assault on segregation in the south when it ruled that the loan of textbooks to students attending private schools that discriminated on the basis of race was unconstitutional.[38]

4.4. THE COURT TURNS NORTH

What has been termed "northern school segregation" does not involve a pattern in which all school buildings of a district are either 100 percent black or 100 percent white, but rather buildings that reflect a variety of racial proportions: many of the buildings are nearly all of one race, a few may be racially balanced, and others may merely be disproportionately of one race or the other. The very existence of the mixed pattern suggests that a variety of forces have been at work in determining which schools children attend, including decisions by school officials, housing officials, real estate agents, banks, and families. Furthermore, the de jure segregation that does exist is not the product of statutory mandate, but the result of a series of covertly race-dependent decisions taken by the school board over a period of years regarding such matters as the closing of schools, the building of new schools, the use of mobile classrooms to relieve overcrowding by avoiding sending pupils outside their home areas, the manipulation of attendance zones, and the use of optional or noncontiguous attendance zones permitting students to leave neighborhood schools to go to schools where they are in a majority.[39] Thus, while the pursuit of a neighborhood school policy in a district with no prior history of de jure segregation is permissible even though it may perpetuate de facto segregation (the mere existence of de facto segregation does not create an obligation to alleviate or rectify the segregation),[40] the manipulation of that neighborhood school policy can provide the basis for inferring a purpose to discriminate.[41] In this case the underlying purpose to segregate is disguised; proving the probability of its existence requires reliance on circumstantial evidence, and the drawing of inferences and the estimate of probabilities. We shall turn to the problem of proving a purpose to segregate by indirect evidence in a moment.

Meanwhile, it should be noted that almost all the attention in these cases has been on the activities of the local school board in segregating the schools; thus school boards were not held responsible for dismantling the segregative effects of discrimination in housing by other governmental agencies.[42] In *United States v. Yonkers*[43] a federal district court took an unusual step. It concluded that, while the school board itself had engaged in some unlawful discriminatory acts, the real cause and responsibility for the segregation of the schools lay with the city, mayor, and the public housing authority. It was these parties, concluded the court, that had, in response to the desire of white residents to keep public housing out of their neighborhoods, systematically located almost all public housing facilities in the area of the city most heavily populated by blacks. It was the combination of the school district's neighborhood school policy in conjunction with a public housing authority that contained black residents in one part of the city that led to the segregation of the schools.[44] The court noted that if a single agency had controlled both housing and school policies, no one would dispute that the resulting segregation in the schools would be actionable. Continuing, the court added, "It is inconceivable that state action may be factionalized such that two state agencies could be permitted to collectively engage in precisely the same conduct, yet avoid legal accountability for the identical result."[45]

These points aside, what is it that a plaintiff must establish to convince a court that the district has unconstitutionally segregated its pupils when the district, unlike the situation in *Brown I*, has not openly and expressly segregated its student body? Three major points, each of which will be taken up in turn, need to be established. First, the plaintiff must show that the district is in fact "segregated," i.e., that despite the fact that not all schools are made up entirely of pupils from one race, the pupils are segregated. Second, that the board's pupil-assignment policies were motivated by an improper purpose to segregate.

Third, that these improperly motivated policies were a major cause of the pattern of segregation found in the district.

First, how do we know a "segregated" system (whether it be de facto or de jure segregation) when we see one, in the face of the fact that student populations of most of the school buildings in the typical "northern" district are not 100 percent of one race? (A related question is: when has a school district that has implemented a desegregation plan become "unitary," as opposed to a "dual," system?) Neither the Supreme Court nor the lower federal courts have offered a clear answer to this question(s). One approach is to examine the racial composition of each school's student body; the racial composition of the school's faculty and staff; the community's and school administration's perceptions or attitudes toward the schools; and the physical characteristics of the schools.[46] An obviously crucial factor in this list is the racial composition of the student body in each school. In this connection, it should be stressed that the Supreme Court would accept a school as "integrated," and not segregated, if it were 100 percent of one race and the student population of the district as a whole were also 100 percent of that same race. Similarly, if the school population were 90 percent minority and 10 percent nonminority, a building that reflected that same ratio would probably be deemed to be integrated.[47] Beyond this we know very little. The courts have been unwilling to provide a definitive statement regarding when the racial composition of a school leads to the conclusion that it is segregated. "Suffice it to say that substantial separation of the races amounts to 'segregation' of the races."[48] Clearly, what is "substantial" separation must be determined in light of the possibilities for integration in that school district. Thus, the obvious starting point for assessing the degree of separation is the racial makeup of that district.[49] In the context of determining whether the desegregation plan had produced an integrated education program, another court was more precise when it stated that an integrated education could occur when an individual school building was not more than 70-75 percent of one race.[50]

Second, how can it be established that the board's actions were taken with an intent to segregate? In *Keyes v. Denver School District No. 1* for the first time the Court dealt with a claim that a district that was never segregated by statute was nevertheless segregated by race-dependent school board decisions in constructing schools, the use of mobile classrooms, the use of optional attendance zones, and the gerrymandering of student attendance zones.[51] The district court concluded that the school board had engaged in deliberate racial segregation of a number of schools in the Park Hill section of the school district. It refused, however, to order desegregation for the segregated core city area because the plaintiffs had to prove de jure segregation in each part of the city for which they sought relief. This they had not done. In dealing with the case on appeal, the Supreme Court again finessed the de jure/de facto issue. First appearances would seem to suggest that the Court clearly resolved the ambiguity when it wrote that plaintiffs in school desegregation cases must "prove not only that segregated schooling exists but also that it was brought about or maintained by intentional state action."[52] The majority opinion then went on to find the district court had made two errors. First, the district court had failed to recognize that board actions that promoted segregation in one substantial part of a school district would have the reciprocal effect of keeping other nearby schools predominantly white. Thus, proof of purposeful segregation in a substantial part of a district created a rebuttable presumption that those same actions caused segregation in the entire district.[53] Second, the district court failed to use the principle "that a finding of intentionally segregative school board actions in a meaningful portion of a school system . . . creates a presumption that other segregated schooling within the system is not adventitious. It establishes in other words, a prima facie case of unlawful segregative design on the part of school authorities, and shifts to those authorities the burden of proving that other segregated schools within the system are not also the result of intentionally segregative actions."[54]

The practical effect of these presumptions was to blur the distinction between the de jure/de facto segregation that the Court had erected earlier. A well-prepared case proving de jure segregation in a substantial portion (how substantial?) of a district could easily lead to an order for systemwide desegregation, whether or not in fact the remaining segregation was de jure or de facto.

Starting in 1974 the Court sharply backed away from its strong pro-integration thrust by laying down strict rules concerning when interdistrict busing could be a permissible remedy in school desegregation suits.[55] Later, in 1977 in *Dayton I*[56] the Court required the lower courts to determine, on a school-by-school basis, the relative contributions to school segregation of school board actions and of independent causes, such as demographic changes, to school segregation. At a minimum the Court seemed to be drastically limiting, if not overruling, the two *Keyes* presumptions and at the same time limiting the opportunities to go after de facto segregation. That opportunity was further restricted in the Court's decision in *Washington v. Davis*.[57]

The decision in *Davis* is best seen against the backdrop of lower federal court activity. Without clear guidance from the Supreme Court on whether de facto segregation was unconstitutional or how de jure segregation was to be proven, the lower federal courts took a variety of positions. At the heart of the dispute among these courts was the use of the principle that people may be presumed to have intended the natural and foreseeable consequences of their acts. Several courts took the position that a discriminatory purpose (de jure segregation) could be established if racial segregation was the reasonably foreseeable consequence of the school board's decisions;[58] others said only a rebuttable presumption of an intent to discriminate is raised by proof of the existence of a reasonably foreseeable segregative effect.[59]

Davis, a noneducation case, held that "[t]he central purpose of the Equal Protection Clause of the Fourteenth Amendment is the prevention of official conduct discriminating on the basis of race." Official action is not unconstitutional "solely because it has a racially disproportionate impact"; plaintiffs must show in addition a "racially discriminatory purpose."[60] As for proving the likelihood of a discriminatory purpose, the Court said that "an invidious discriminatory purpose may be inferred from the totality of the relevant facts." The Court went on to note that discriminatory impact is not irrelevant in establishing a discriminatory purpose, but standing alone cannot establish that the decision was racially dependent. Thus, having drastically limited the use of the foreseeability test, the Court remanded a number of lower court decisions for reconsideration to determine if they reached their conclusions through improper reliance on that test.[61]

In decisions since *Davis,* the Court has reaffirmed the view that the fourteenth amendment only proscribes purposeful, not de facto, racial discrimination and that proof of a discriminatory purpose as a cause of the decision is a necessary condition for establishing a constitutional violation. It also elaborated on the proof that is necessary to establish the probability of the existence of discriminatory purpose.[62] Whether the Court should have interpreted the fourteenth as embodying a discriminatory purpose requirement, whether it should have so drastically cut back on the use of the foreseeability test, and whether it should have extended the fourteenth to cover de facto segregation as well are matters under continuing debate.[63] In any event, the lower courts continue to use the foreseeability test aggressively;[64] and the Supreme Court continues to affirm decisions that make such aggressive use of the test.[65] In this and other ways, the Court continues to assault de facto segregation.[66]

It should be noted at this point that all the plaintiff need establish is that a purpose to segregate was "a" motivating force in the board's decision.[67] Once the plaintiff has made out a prima facie case that the board had been in part improperly motivated, the burden switches to the board to establish that the "same decision" would have been made even if the improper motive had not been present.[68]

Let us now summarize and analyze what has been said regarding the use of indirect evidence to establish that the district was motivated in part by a purpose to discriminate. The plaintiff must produce enough evidence (make out a prima facie case) that an official action seemingly neutral on its face might have in fact been caused by an improper motive. It is here the use of evidence of a discriminatory impact becomes relevant, with the proviso that it may not be the sole basis for raising the suspicion. Once the prima facie case has been made out, the district must be given the opportunity to show that the "same decision" would have been reached even if the improper motive had not affected its choices. One way the district can accomplish this would be to argue that its policies were necessary to achieve a compelling state purpose.[69] The plaintiff may then seek to establish that the improper motive was a necessary factor in producing the decisions of the board, i.e., that those decisions cannot be explained except by reliance on an improper motive by the board.

In sum, the Court articulates the question whether there is a probability of an improper motive at work in decision-making as an empirical question, a matter of determining the likely cause of a decision. The method of proof and analysis usually involves making a comparative evaluation, i.e., are the racial effects of the policy outweighed by the legitimate purposes the government claims it was serving?[70] The more severe the adverse impacts (in the Court's assessment), the less plausible (the Court assumes) is it that official action was taken for legitimate reasons; the less important (in the Court's assessment) are the claimed legitimate purposes, the less likely (the Court assumes) these purposes were the determinant of the decision and vice versa. A normative assessment is being used to arrive at a purported empirical judgment about a probable existence of a factor that affected a particular decision.[71] A finding of a likelihood of improper motivation may, thus, be restated in the following way. In our view, says the Court, the racial effects of the legislation so outweigh the advantages that we do not believe a school board would have, because they should not have, made this value choice if they weren't influenced by some form of racial bias. Unprejudiced boards do not make this kind of decision.

In addition to establishing that the district is "segregated" and that the board's decisions were motivated by an improper motive, the plaintiff must also convince the Court that these improperly motivated decisions caused the present pattern of segregation. There are three major problems. First, if the plaintiff has established that the board took improperly motivated decisions twenty or thirty years ago, it may be the case that the present state of segregation is more the product of intervening population changes than a result of the board's decisions. Second, the board's decisions may have occurred simultaneously with major demographic changes, and it may be unclear whether it was the board's decisions or the demographic changes that were the major cause of the present state of segregation. Third, proof may only be available to establish purposeful segregation with regard to part of the district, yet the pattern of segregation may be district-wide. In regard to the first problem, the Court's approach has been to create a presumption that, absent evidence to the country, purposeful efforts to segregate, even efforts taken twenty or thirty years ago, are the cause of the present pattern of segregation regardless of any major demographic changes that may have occurred in the interval.[72] The Court also said that at some point the link between past segregative policies and present segregation would become severed. This caveat provides the school board the opportunity to establish it should no longer be held accountable for today's segregation, i.e., that today's segregation is de facto.[73]

As for the second problem, the courts have been reluctant to accept proof, in the form of statistical analysis, that seeks to establish that demographic change is the better explanation for the present pattern of segregation than segregative acts. The courts have taken the position that, even if the particular decisions by a school board or housing authority had a limited segregative effect in quantitative terms, these decisions send out a message that this area of the city is the "black" area, this the "white" area. The result of these "messages," the courts believe, is that the affected school(s) are stigmatized as "black" schools, with the further consequence that people make housing and schooling choices accordingly.[74]

The Supreme Court has dealt with the third problem by erecting another presumption, namely, that school board actions that promote segregation in one part of the school district are to be presumed to have the reciprocal effect of keeping other schools in the district segregated as well.[75] The Court noted that unless the school board could demonstrate that a natural boundary, for example, a river, created a natural barrier that restricted the spill-over effects of the segregative acts in a substantial part of the district, it may be presumed that the entire district became segregated because of the board's improper actions. A major highway, said the Court, could not generally be considered to be such an effective barrier.[76]

The judiciary's willingness to use sweeping presumptions and its reluctance to accept social-science evidence tending to explain segregation as produced by demographic changes is yet another way the courts have blurred the distinction between de jure and de facto segregation. It is understandable why the courts have adopted this broad-brush approach. Separating the demographic influences from the effects of policy is an extremely difficult, if not impossible, task. If the plaintiffs were given the task of having to precisely sort out the effects of policy from the effects of demographic change, the effort to use the courts to end racial segregation would have been brought to a stand-still.

4.5. REMEDIES FOR UNLAWFUL SEGREGATION REVISITED

As already noted, school districts found liable for segregation may be and have been ordered to move beyond merely stopping the practice of segregating. Courts have ordered districts to undertake affirmative efforts to integrate through the extensive shuffling of pupils throughout the system. Because the effects of unlawful segregation include more than the mere separation of pupils on the basis of race, "[m]atters other than pupil assignment must on occasion be addressed by federal courts to eliminate the effects of prior segregation."[77] With this principle in mind, the Court has approved a package of remedies that include a remedial reading program, in-service training for teachers, magnet schools, racially nonbiased testing procedures, and counseling and career guidance programs to facilitate integration.[78] Special remedial problems have occurred in those school districts where desegregation has created a mixing of white and Mexican-American pupils. To make integration go more smoothly, one district court ordered extensive bilingual-bicultural educational programs, special education programs, extracurricular activities, personnel policy modifications, and community involvement.[79] Another district court imposed a plan that "require[d] an overhaul of the system's entire approach to the education of minorities; its proposals extend[ed] to matters of educational philosophy, governance, instructional scope and sequence, curriculum, student evaluation, staffing, noninstructional service and community involvement."[80] On appeal, however, the Tenth Circuit Court of Appeals reversed, saying the plan exceeded the remedial powers of the district court because the plan did not meet the limitation that only proven constitutional violations be remedied.[81] As occurred in Boston, the federal judge may even take over the operation of a school to assure the fulfillment of the desegregation plan.[82]

Despite the seemingly enormous powers of the federal district courts to fashion remedies, they must operate within a certain set of limitations imposed by the Supreme Court. Generally speaking, the scope of the remedy is limited by the nature and extent of the constitutional violation.[83] Hence, for example, federal district courts may not require the implementaiton of interdistrict integration plans unless there has been a proven interdistrict violation, e.g., the suburbs were directly involved in producing the segregation in the city.[84] Since the courts must acknowledge the interests of state and local authorities in managing their own affairs, they will be reluctant to order a full-scale consolidation of districts if a more minor boundary adjustment will accomplish the task of remedying the interdistrict wrong.[85]

As noted earlier, the ride on the bus may not be so long as to damage the health of the student or interfere with the educational process.[86] Thus when the district is large, and the population pattern is such that considerable cross-district busing may be required to mix the races, the courts are expected to proceed slowly in the imposition of plans requiring extensive busing.[87] The courts have also said that the burden of being bused may not be discriminatorily placed upon a particular group, i.e., black children.[88] Courts have not consistently adhered to this admonition.[89] It might be noted that school districts are constitutionally free to integrate voluntarily, and the Court has blocked efforts by the Washington State legislature to try to end Seattle's voluntary integration plan directed at de facto segregation.[90]

The possibility of white flight precipitated by desegregation remains a difficult issue in the formulation of a remedy. One thing is clear: fear of white flight is not an excuse for avoiding desegregation.[91] Beyond adopting this stand, the courts have reacted differently to this issue. One court said that to propose integration plans that take white flight into account is to let community racial attitudes control the formulation of the plan in the same way that such attitudes led to the original constitutional violation.[92] Yet other courts have stressed that white flight might be considered in choosing among plans, since not to do so defeats the purpose of attempting to achieve maximum exposure of the races to each other.[93] It is also the case that a board need not "ignore the probability of white flight in attempting to formulate a *voluntary* plan which would improve the racial balance in schools without at the same time losing the support and acceptance of the public. . . . [T]here is a valid distinction between using the defense of white flight as a smokescreen to avoid integration and realistically considering and dealing with the practical problems involved in making voluntary efforts to achieve integration."[94]

The issue of racial quotas has come up in various ways. The Supreme Court has said that quotes for the racial mixture in each school building are a permissible starting point in the fashioning of a desegregation remedy,[95] but a court may not rigidly require a particular racial balance.[96] The issue of the quota becomes even more controversial when the remedy involves an upper limit to the number of minority students that will be permitted to attend, for example, a magnet school. Even this kind of quota has been upheld as necessary to promote integration.[97] Hiring quotas have been imposed as a remedy in school desegregation cases.[98]

The leaving in place of some one-race schools is yet another sore point. On this score the Supreme Court has said plans that leave racially imbalanced schools in existence are not per se impermissible, but that the district bears the burden of justifying the continued existence of these schools.[99] Yet the closing of formally disproportionately black schools can be controversial within the black community and must be done in a way that is not discriminatory.[100]

Racial integration plans must also involve the integration of the faculty. It may also be the case that integration of the faculty may result in the laying-off of faculty members and administrators. Retrenchment of this sort must be carried out according to objective and reasonable nondiscriminatory standards.[101]

Another issue has been the question of who pays for these expensive desegregation remedies. The courts have reached out beyond the school board itself to obtain substantial financial contributions from municipalities,[102] states,[103] and even the federal government.[104]

At some point the remedy phase of the case must come to an end, and the federal district court must relinquish jurisdiction. That point is reached once a satisfactory desegregation plan has been fully implemented and the segregation attributable to the district's wrongdoing has been eliminated and the district has become a unitary district. Even if the school buildings resegregate at this point, because of demographic changes, the district need not once again affirmatively mix the races unless it is once again established that the recurring segregation was the product of an intent to segregate.[105] The difficulty here is that the Supreme Court has never fully defined the notion of a unitary system, nor specified precisely when a desegregation case should be closed. The result has been continued dispute in the courts on this question.[106]

Once a district has been judicially declared to be a unitary system, changes in its pupil-assignment policy may only be successfully challenged by establishing that the new policy was itself adopted as a form of purposeful discrimination.[107] That is, action that has a segregative effect by districts that have not been declared to be "fully unitary" may be successfully challenged without proof of discriminatory intent.[108] The nonunitary district has an affirmative obligation to adopt only policies that eliminate the consequences of their prior unconstitutional conduct.[109] The fully unitary district can adopt new pupil-assignment plans that take into account the problem of white flight.[110]

To conclude this section, several brief observations are in order. First, the frequent debates over integration remedies, including busing, turn on the consideration of a number of underlying factors, e.g., the value of an integrated education for black and white students; the educational benefits of the neighborhood school; and the theory of judicial remedies (is the remedy to be designed to impose retribution, to compensate the victims, and/or to deter?) If the purpose is to compensate for past injuries, exactly what injuries have black students incurred, i.e., what is the harm imposed by de jure segregation? Other issues include the proper role of the courts vis-à-vis other branches of government; the value of local control of education (an issue that arises when courts consider interdistrict remedial plans); the financial costs of the plans; the likelihood of the plan stimulating white flight; and the fairness of the plan when racial employment quotas are involved.[111] (See also §9.13.)

Second, it is misleading to view the remedy phase of the case as involving the substitution of the federal judge for the local school board; frequently the remedy finally imposed is the product of a complex bargaining process among a variety of participants—school board, superintendent, teachers, parent organizations, community organizations, the local chapter of the NAACP, and the mayor—with the judge or his or her representative acting as mediator and, perhaps ultimately, as arbitrator.[112]

4.6. TITLES IV AND VI OF THE CIVIL RIGHTS ACT OF 1964

In the preceding sections we concentrated on challenges pursuant to the fourteenth amendment to racial segregation in the schools brought by individuals affected by that segregation. In addition, Congress has authorized the federal government to go after segregation in the schools. Title IV authorizes the Attorney General of the United States, upon receiving a complaint, to file a civil action under the fourteenth amendment for such relief as may be appropriate.[113] The attorney general may also seek to enforce Title VI.[114] (Title VI[115] provides that no person shall be denied, on account of race, color, or national origin, participation in or the benefits of any program receiving federal financial assistance. A program that does discriminate may lose its federal assistance.) In addition, both an individual parent or student may seek enforcement of Title VI,[116] and the Department of Education may seek enforcement of Title VI by administrative action. The department requires that elementary and secondary schools' applicants and recipients for federal assistance provide assurances of their compliance with Title VI and with the desegregation plans that the department may demand of them. The department may investigate actual compliance on its own initiative or upon complaint. If a violation is found, the department notifies the recipient and seeks voluntary compliance. If voluntary compliance is not forthcoming, the department may either pursue administrative fund-termination proceedings or may refer the case to the Department of Justice with a recommendation for appropriate action.[117] It is important to note that the Court has concluded that proof of discriminatory intent is not required to establish a violation of Title VI.[118]

As noted earlier, the adoption of Title VI in 1964 marked a significant turning point in the federal effort to eliminate de jure segregation in the South.[119] Though the Johnson administration vigorously pursued a policy of racial integration, President Nixon campaigned and was elected on a promise to reduce the amount of "forced busing." Among the steps taken by the Nixon administration was to seek from the courts a delay in the implementation of desegregation plans—a delay approved by the Fifth Circuit, but reversed by the Supreme Court.[120] In addition, enforcement efforts by the federal government itself were slowed, promoting several court suits that ordered the administration to continue enforcement of the law.[121] Congress stepped into the game by adopting a series of statutory amendments limiting the power of the then-Department of Health, Education, and Welfare (HEW, now the Department of Education) from using its power and money to require "directly or indirectly" student transportation beyond the school closest to their home. A constitutional challenge to these amendments was rejected by the court of appeals for the District of Columbia.[122] The court stressed that these amendments did no more than to take HEW out of the busing business, while not restricting its authority to terminate funds with respect to other desegregation remedies. The Department of Health, Education, and Welfare could still negotiate with districts to get them to adopt busing programs voluntarily, and HEW still could refer the case to the Department of Justice with recommendations for legal action. Thus, as interpreted, the amendment did not dilute or abrogate the constitutional guarantee of equal protection; nor was there proof the amendments were adopted with an impermissible motive.

4.7. PREFERENTIAL TREATMENT ON THE BASIS OF RACE

It was clear from *Brown I* and its progeny that the purposeful discrimination (in the form of racial segregation) on the basis of race was unconstitutional, and it was clear from *Swann* and employment discrimination cases that race could, indeed must, be used in the design of remedies for proven instances of past discrimination. Without stretching history too far, drafters of the fourteenth amendment could be at least understood as not opposed to interpreting the fourteenth amendment to prohibit racial segregation and as permitting the use of race to remedy a proven case of a constitutional violation.[123] But could the fourteenth amendment be interpreted, consistent with the original understanding, to permit the use of a racial criterion to allocate a scarce resource so as to provide a benefit to a racial minority when not in response to a proven specific instance of past unconstitutional discrimination? Could precedent be interpreted as permitting affirmative-action programs? What did the theory of judicial review demand: strict scrutiny only to protect harm to discrete, insular, politically powerless minorities; or was strict scrutiny also permitted on behalf of a member of the white majority? What did the principles of social justice demand and/or permit? Was it moral for government to seek to equalize the social and economic status of "groups" at the expense of arguably innocent individuals? These issues reached the Supreme Court in the case of *Regents of the University of California v. Bakke.*[124]

In order to increase its minority enrollment, the publicly-operated Davis Medical School modified its admissions policy by reserving sixteen of the one hundred available spaces in each entering class for educationally and/or economically disadvantaged applicants who were either black, Mexican-American, Asian, or American Indian. Minority candidates could apply for admission by either seeking one of the eighty-four seats not part of the special admissions program or by seeking one of the sixteen set-aside seats. The special admissions program operated with a separate committee. Students seeking admissson by this route had to meet lower admission criteria regarding both undergraduate grades and scores on the Medical College Admission Test. The inevitable result was that minority candidates with grade and test scores lower than some rejected white applicants were admitted to Davis. Allan Bakke was one of those white students who would have been admitted but for the special admissions program.[125] Bakke sued claiming that the preferential admissions program violated the fourteenth amendment's prohibition against discrimination on the basis of race.

The Court was severely divided on the central issue of whether a racial criterion may be used in the competitive admissions process of publicly operated professional schools, and if so, whether the particular use of race by Davis was proper. Five justices agreed for different reasons that Bakke had been improperly excluded from the school. Four of these justices relied on their interpretation of Title VI of the Civil Rights Act of 1964 to reach this conclusion.[126] Justice Powell, whose opinion will be examined, based his conclusion on the fourteenth amendment. A different combination of five justices agreed on the general principle that race could be taken into consideration in admitting of students. Four of these five concluded that Davis's use of race was permissible.[127] Justice Powell disagreed that Davis's use of race was permissible, but did agree that race could be taken into consideration in another way. As a consequence of these shifting majorities, those wno thought Bakke should have been admitted to medical school were happy because his admission was ordered; but those who wanted to continue the use of preferential admissions programs also won a victory of sorts.

We shall briefly analyze Justice Powell's crucial opinion, and the opinion of Justice Brennan, which was joined by Justices White, Marshall, and Blackmun.[128] The Davis admissions program involved the explicit use of race, thereby seeming to suggest that, as discussed earlier, it would be the school that would have to justify its program as necessary to achieve a compelling state interest.[129] Justice Brennan, however, took the position that a racial classification used for "benign" purposes need not be subjected to the severe standard of review that is used when a racial criterion is suspected to have been used to discriminate in a way that stigmatizes. Moreover, no fundamental right was involved in the case, and whites as a class did not need the special protection of the judiciary against a biased political process that the stricter standard of review provided. Nevertheless, Justice Brennan observed, because there was a significant risk that a racial classification ostensibly being used for benign purposes could be misused, it was appropriate to use a test that was "searching," i.e., the racial classification has to serve an "important and articulated" purpose and it must be "substantialy related" to achieving that purpose. In addition, the official action would have to fall if it stigmatized any group. Justice Brennan concluded that Davis's program easily passed these two sets of requirements. Its purpose of remedying the effects of past societal discrimination was important, and the quota system was necessary to achieving it. No other practical means to the ends were available that would work in the foreseeable future. Nor was there any evidence that Bakke was stamped as inferior or that the Davis program intentionally or unintentionally stigmatized any minority group.

Justice Brennan supported his position by his interpretation of the original intent of the framers of the fourteenth amendment and precedent. He stressed that active judicial review should be exercised on behalf of minority groups that have suffered a history of discrimination and are less able to protect themselves through the normal political process. Bakke did not fall into that group. In addition, Justice Brennan's opinion implicitly embraced a notion of social justice that stressed that social and economic equality is not merely to be sought among "individuals," but that government may also pursue a policy of assuring social and economic equality among "groups." Precedent, he said, showed that race could be used to remedy wrongs, that those wrongs need not just be proven instances of a constitutional violation, and that the general problem of societal discrimination against blacks could also be addressed through affirmative action programs.

Justice Powell disagreed with everything in the Brennan opinion: Brennan's interpretation of the intent of the framers of the fourteenth amendment, his interpretation of precedent, his underlying theory of judicial review, and his moral vision. For Powell, whenever a racial criterion was used it had to be reviewed with the strictest of tests. His reading of the fourteenth amendment and precedent led him to conclude that the amendment was not designed to protect only racial minorities. He rejected the notion that only certain groups were to receive the strong protection of the strict-scrutiny test. If this theory were to be adopted, he argued, great difficulties would arise in deciding which groups in society were to get the special protection of the strict-scrutiny test. Powell's moral vision was one that stressed the importance of equality among individuals. In his view policies that stressed equality among "groups" were pernicious in that they harmed innocent victims, such as Bakke. Moreover, there were serious problems of justice and aroused racial antagonisms connected with the idea of a preference for groups. Thus, applying the stricter test, Justice Powell concluded that the Davis program was unconstitutional. First, no branch of government constitutionally could adopt as a goal the remedying of the effects of "societal discrimination." Government could seek to remedy specified constitutional or statutory violations, but only if a legislature, court, or proper administrative tribunal (not a university) made the findings of which minorities were deserving of a preference because they were injured by a proven wrong. Second, there was no evidence this program was needed or would promote the goal of improving the delivery of health care services to minority communities. Third, though the goal of increasing the diversity of the student body was a compelling purpose (it served to promote the Constitution's concern with free-dom of speech by fostering a robust exchange of ideas), the quota here did not adequately serve that purpose. The program focused solely on racial and ethnic diversity and would hinder the attainment of genuine diversity. Justice Powell went on to say that race may be used in an admissions process designed to achieve diversity in the student body if it is only a "plus." A process that did not set target quotas, but used race as only one factor among many in comparing candidates would be permissible. So long as a minority applicant's "plus" could in theory be outweighed by another applicant's different individual attributes, race could be considered.[130]

The deep split in the Court in *Bakke* left uncertain the Court's future han-dling of racial preferences. Subsequent cases have not cleared up the uncertainty. In *Fullilove v. Klutznick*[131] a badly split Court upheld a requirement in a congressional spending program that 10 percent of the funds be set aside to procure services or supplies from minority-owned and controlled business. The plurality opinion of Chief Justice Burger, who was joined by Justices White and Powell, upheld the program without making a choice between the approaches of Justices Powell and Brennan in *Bakke*. In a concurring opinion Justice Powell could be interpreted as adopting a test different from what he used in *Bakke*.[132] Justices Marshall, Brennan, and Blackmun, using the same approach they adopted in *Bakke,* voted to uphold the program. Justices Stewart and White dissented, arguing the fourteenth amendment was "color-blind." Justice Stevens dissented, saying this program could not survive review under the strict-scrutiny test used by Justice Powell in *Bakke*. Turning to another case, the Court has permitted a race-conscious vote redistricting that aided minority voters but unintentionally diluted the voting strength of the Hasidic Jewish community.[133] The Court's approach to constitutional challenges to affirmative action in employment will be taken up in §9.13. In that section the Court's most recent word on the proper approach to afirmative action will be discussed.

4.8. GENDER SEGREGATION

The issue of segregation on the basis of gender has been a less divisive and politically significant issue in education. The issue that has arisen with the greatest frequency has been the question of the right of a female student to access to an all-male athletic team, a question to be dealt with in §5.9. The most significant Supreme Court pronouncement on gender segregation in education came in *Mississippi University for Women v. Hogan*.[134] In a five-to-four decision the Court sustained a male's equal protection challenge to the state's policy of excluding men from the Mississippi University For Women School of Nursing (MUW). Hogan, a registered nurse, sought admission to MUW's baccalaureate program but was told he could only audit courses and would have to attend one of the state's coeducational nursing schools, located elsewhere in the state, in order to obtain credits toward a degree. The majority opinion, written by Justice O'Connor, applied the middle-level test (see §3.1) and rejected the state's claim that the single-sex admission policy of this school could be justified as "benign" and as a form of compensation for past discrimination against women. Justice O'Connor agreed in "limited circumstances a gender-based classification favoring one sex can be justified if it intentionally and directly assists members of the sex that is disproportionately burdened"; yet such a "benign" justification required "searching analysis." This sort of compensatory purpose can only be established, continued Justice O'Connor, if members of the gender benefited by the discriminatory policy actually suffered a disadvantage related to the discrimination. In this case the state had made no showing that women had lacked opportunities to obtain training in nursing when the school opened, or that today women are deprived of such opportunities. In fact, MUW's policies perpetuated the stereotype that nursing was exclusively women's work. Furthermore, the record did not support the claim that excluding men from the school was necessary to reach any of the educational goals of MUW. The fact that men were permitted to audit MUW classes clearly showed that the women in MUW were not adversely affected by the presence of men. Finally, Justice O'Connor rejected an argument based on Title IX of the Education Amendments of 1972.[135] Title IX exempted from coverage undergraduate institutions if they "traditionally and continually from [their] establishment [have] had a policy of admitting only one sex." Mississippi argued that this exemption was a valid limitation on the equal protection clause—a limitation Congress could impose pursuant to its authority under §5 of the amendment to adopt legislation enforcing the amendment. Justice O'Connor doubted that with the passage of Title IX Congress intended to exempt colleges from constitutional obligations. Even if Congress did intend to exempt single-sex colleges from the limits of the fourteenth amendment, she said that under §5 of the amendment Congress was "limited to adopting measures to enforce the guarantees of the Amendment; §5 grants Congress no power to restrict, abrogate, or dilute those guarantees."

NOTES

1. 163 U.S. 537 (1896). In a famous dissent Justice Harlan asserted "Our Constitution is color-blind, and neither knows nor tolerates classes among citizens."

2. Gong Lum v. Rice, 275 U.S. 78, 85-26 (1927).

3. For an account of the NAACP's litigation strategy leading up to and including the cases consolidated under the name Brown v. Bd. of Educ., 347 U.S. 483 (1954) see Richard Klugar, *Simple Justice* (New York: Knopf, 1975).

4. McLaurin v. Oklahoma State Regents, 339 U.S. 637 (1950); Sweatt v. Painter, 339 U.S. 629 (1950); Missouri ex. rel. Gaines v. Canada, 305 U.S. 337 (1938).

5. 347 U.S. 483 (1954).

6. In a separate opinion issued the same day as *Brown 1*, the Court dealt with segregation in the District of Columbia. Bolling v. Sharpe, 347 U.S. 497 (1954). The Court reached the same conclusion as it did in *Brown 1*, but based on the fifth amendment, not the fourteenth as in Brown 1. The District of Columbia is not a state, thus the fourteenth, which by its own terms is directed to the states, is not applicable to the district.

7. 347 U.S. 483, 494-95 (1954).

8. The Court's citing of social-science evidence raised a considerable controversy regarding its use of this evidence in this case and regarding the proper use of social-science evidence generally in constitutional litigation. Did the Court really rely on this evidence in *Brown 1?* Did the evidence support the point for which it was used? What was the quality of this evidence? Should the Court have cited any body of social-science evidence in this case, or for that matter should it use such evidence in any constitutional law case? The literature on this debate is too extensive to cite fully, but one might begin with: Edmund Cahn, "Jurisprudence," *New York University Law Review* 30 (1955): 150; Charles Black, "The Lawfulness of the Segregation Decisions," *Yale Law Journal* 69 (1960): 421; Kenneth B. Clark, "The Social Scientists, the Brown Decision, and Contemporary Confusion," in *Argument,* ed. L. Friedman (New York: Chelsea House Publishers, 1969); *Education, Social Science and the Judicial Process,* ed. R. C. Rist and R. J. Anson (New York: Teachers College Press, 1977).

9. For a discussion of these and the other equal protection tests see, §3.1.

10. 347 U.S. 497 (1954).

11. John Hart Ely, "The Centrality and Limits of Motivation Analysis," *San Diego Law Review* 15 (1978): 1155, 1158.

12. This is a standard test used on cases in which an overt racial classification is used. Korematsu v. United States, 323 U.S. 214 (1944).

13. Paul Brest, *Processes of Constitutional Decision-Making* (Boston: Little Brown and Company, 1975), 489. The example is repeated in the second edition: Paul Brest and Sanford Levinson, *Processes of Constitutional Decision Making: Cases and Materials,* 2d ed. (Boston: Little Brown and Company, 1983), 448.

14. A decision based or dependent upon a certain characteristic of people is a de jure classification, e.g., assigning pupils to different schools based on their race. If a district assigns pupils based on a different characteristic, e.g., to schools closest to their homes, this decision is a de jure decision on the basis of residence. Now, because the district is residentially segregated, that de jure decision will have the de facto effect of having an impact in terms of a second characteristic, race. The ensuing racial segregation is de facto, the product of a decision not dependent on the racial characteristics of the pupils. It is an "adventitious" impact, or perhaps even a racially disproportionate impact. Brest and Levinson, *Processes of Constitutional Decision-Making, supra* note 13, at 469-70.

15. This is the problem raised by so-called "northern" school segregation, a topic taken up later in §4.4

16. Is a building that is 90 percent black and 10 percent white in a district with a pupil population that is 90 percent black and 10 percent white "segregated"? Is a building that is 60 percent black and 40 percent white in a district with a school population that is 60 percent white and 40 percent black "segregated"? Obviously this problem did not arise in *Brown I* where the schools were 100 percent white and 100 percent black. The issue is a problem in "northern" school districts.

17. The answer to this last question came quickly—yes. A series of decisions following *Brown I* struck down segregation in other public facilities. *See, e.g.,* Holmes v. City of Atlanta 350 U.S. 879 (1955) (golf courses).

18. The range of material on this question is too extensive for a complete listing. Some samples include: J. Morris Clark, "Legislative Motivation and Fundamental Rights in Constitutional Law," *San Diego Law Review* 15 (1978): 953; Kenneth Karst, "The Supreme Court 1976 Term—Forward: Equal Citizenship Under the Fourteenth Amendment," *Harvard Law Review* 91 (1977): 1; Peter M. Shane, "School Desegregation and the Fair Governance of Schools," *University of Pennsylvania Law Review* 132 (1984): 1041; Mark G. Yudof, "Equal Educational Opportunity and the Courts," *Texas Law Review* 51 (1973): 411.

19. Brown v. Board of Education, 349 U.S. 294 (1955) (*Brown 2*).

20. Several histories of this period have been written. *See, e.g.,* J. Harvie Wilkinson III, *From Brown to Bakke: The Supreme Court and School Integration: 1954-1978* (Oxford: Oxford University Press, 1979); Raymond Wolters, *The Burden of Brown: Thirty Years of School Desegregation* (Knoxville: The University of Tennessee Press, 1984).

21. J. W. Peltason, *58 Lonely Men: Southern Federal Judges and School Desegregation* (Urbana: University of Illinois Press, 1971).

22. 358 U.S. 1 (1958).

23. 377 U.S. 218 (1964).

24. *E.g.,* Goss v. Bd. of Educ., 373 U.S. 683 (1963).

25. *E.g.,* Bradley v. Sch. Bd., 383 U.S. 103 (1965).

26. Title VI, 42 U.S.C. §2000(d) (1982). For a further discussion of Title VI, see §4.6.

27. For two accounts of the efforts to enforce Title VI of the Civil Rights Act of 1964 see Gary Orfield, *The Reconstruction of Southern Education* (New York: Wiley-Interscience, 1969); Frederick Wirt, *Politics of Southern Equality* (Chicago: Aldine Publishing Co., 1971); for a more general account of the Johnson administration and education see Diane Ravitch, *The Troubled Crusade: American Education 1945-1980* (New York: Basic Books, Inc., 1983).

28. In Lau v. Nichols, 414 U.S. 563 (1974) a majority of the Court seemed to embrace the view that Title VI reached policies with a discriminatory impact; but then in Regents of Univ. of California v. Bakke, 438 U.S. 265 (1978) a majority of the Court seemed to say that Title VI only reched purposeful discrimination.

29. Alexander v. Choate, 105 S. Ct. 712, 717 (1985), interpreting a prior decision in Guardians Ass'n. v. Civil Service Commission, 463 U.S. 582 (1983).

30. 20 U.S.C. §1703(d) (1983). The Equal Educational Opportunity Act provides that "No State shall deny equal educational opportunity to an individual on account of his or her race, color, sex, or national origin."

31. 391 U.S. 430 (1968).

32. 430 U.S. 651, 662 (1977).

33. Mark G. Yudof, David L. Kirp, Tyll van Geel, and Betsy Levin, *Educational Policy and the Law*, 2d ed. (Berkeley, Calif.: McCutchan Publishing Corporation, 1982), 440-41.

34. Paul Brest, "Race Discrimination," in *The Burger Court*, ed. Vincent Blasi (New Haven, Conn.: Yale University Press, 1983), 115.

35. 402 U.S. 1 (1971).

36. The Court noted that an objection to busing of pupils would have validity when the time or distance of the trip was such as to risk the health or impinge on the educational process. *Id.*, at 30-31.

37. Keyes v. Denver Sch. Dist. No. 1, 413 U.S. 189, 223 (1973) (Powell, J., dissenting).

38. Norwood v. Harrison, 413 U.S. 455 (1973).

39. *See, e.g.*, Columbus Bd. of Educ. v. Penick, 443 U.S. 449, 461-62 (1979); Arthur v. Nyquist, 573 F.2d 134, 145 n.21 (2d Cir.), *cert. denied*, 439 U.S. 860 (1978).

40. Diaz v. San Jose Unified Sch. Dist., 733 F.2d 660, 664 (9th Cir. 1984) *(en banc), cert. denied*, 105 S. Ct. 2140 (1985); Alexander v. Youngstown Bd. of Educ., 675 F.2d 787 (6th Cir. 1982).

41. One court has also said that mere proof of a consistent neighborhood school policy is not enough to prove absence of segregative intent. Diaz v. San Jose Unified Sch. Dist., 612 F.2d 411, 416 (9th Cir. 1979). In a later opinion in that same case, the ninth circuit elaborated by noting that a district can be consistent in following a neighborhood school policy and yet act with segregative intent in the construction of buildings. Rejecting decisions that do not threaten the neighborhood school policy but that could be integrative is suggestive of an intent to segregate. Diaz v. San Jose Unified Sch. Dist., 733 F.2d 660, 665 (9th Cir. 1984) *(en banc), cert. denied*, 105 S. Ct. 2140 (1985).

42. Bell v. Bd. of Educ., Akron Pub. Schools, 683 F.2d 963 (6th Cir. 1982).

43. 624 F. Supp. 1276 (S.D. N.Y. 1985). *See also* Arthur v. Nyquist, 415 F. Supp. 904 (W.D. N.Y. 1976), *aff'd in part*, 573 F.2d 134 (2d Cir.), *cert. denied sub nom.*, Manch v. Arthur, 439 U.S. 860 (1978).

44. In this case the mayor appointed the members of the school board, and the board itself was fiscally dependent upon the city for its budget. This close interconnection between the school board and city administration may mean that holdings in the case will not be generalized to other locations where the public housing authorities have engaged in the purposeful segregation of their facilities.

45. 624 F. Supp. at 1534. In a subsequent order the district court ordered the closing of eight schools, changes in attendance zones, the operation of magnet schools, the adoption of a voluntary transfer program, staff reassignments, changes in the special education program, the adoption of a human relations program, and changes in the public housing program. United States v. Yonkers Bd. of Educ., 635 F. Supp. 1538 (S.D.N.Y. 1986).

46. Keyes v. Sch. Dist. No. 1, 413 U.S. 189, 196 (1973). For an example of one court's examination of these range of factors see United States v. Yonkers Bd. of Educ., 624 F. Supp. 1276 (S.D. N.Y. 1985).

47. In other words, for purposes of determining whether a building is integrated one looks to the population of that school district alone, not to what the ratios could be if other school districts were involved in an integration plan. Milliken v. Bradley, 418 U.S. 717 (1974).

48. Arthur v. Nyquist, 415 F. Supp. 904, 912 n. 9 (W.D. N.Y. 1976), *aff'd in part*, 573 F.2d 134 (2d Cir.), *cert. denied sub nom.*, Manch v. Arthur, 439 U.S. 860 (1978).

49. *See* Hart v. Community Bd. of Educ., N.Y. Sch. Dist. No. 21, 512 F.2d 37 (2d Cir. 1975).

50. Tasby v. Wright, 520 F. Supp. 683, 711-712 (N.D. Texas 1981). The district's school population as whole was 42 percent minority.

51. 413 U.S. 189 (1973).

52. Id., at 198.

53. The board could rebut this inference by demonstrating that a natural boundary, for example, a river, created a natural barrier that restricted the spill-over effects. The Court pointedly noted, however, that "a major highway is generally not such an effective buffer between adjoining areas." *Id.*, at 205.

54. Id., at 208.

55. Milliken v. Bradley, 418 U.S. 717 (1974). This case will be discussed at greater length in §4.5. It is arguable that the Court was backing down in the face of rising public opposition to school busing—an opposition first fueled by President Nixon in his campaigns for the presidency in 1968 and 1972. For a review of these developments see Ravitch, *The Troubled Crusade*, *supra* note 27.

56. Dayton Bd. of Educ. v. Brinkman, 433 U.S. 406 (1976).

57. 426 U.S. 229 (1976).

58. *See, e.g.*, United States v. Texas Educ. Agency, 532 F.2d 380, 389-92 (5th Cir.), *vacated and remanded per curiam sub nom.*, Austin Indep. Sch. Dist. v. United States, 429 U.S. 990 (1976).

59. *See, e.g.*, Oliver v. Michigan State Board of Educ., 508 F.2d 178, 182 (6th Cir. 1974), *cert. denied*, 421 U.S. 963 (1975). *Cf.*, Armstrong v. Brennan, 539 F.2d 625 (7th Cir. 1976).

60. 426 U.S. 229, 239-242 (1976).

61. *See, e.g.*, Austin v. Ind. Sch. Dist. v. United States, 429 U.S. 990 (1977) (mem.), *remanding*, United States v. Texas Educ. Agency, 532 F.2d 380 (5th Cir. 1977).

62. Personnel Administrator of Mass. v. Feeney, 442 U.S. 256 (1979); Arlington Heights v. Metropolitan Housing Corp., 429 U.S. 252 (1977); Mt. Healthy City Sch. Dist. Bd. of Educ. v. Doyle, 429 U.S. 274 (1977).

63. Justices Marshall and Stevens emphasize the continued use of the foreseeability test. Washington v. Davis, 426 U.S. 229, 253 (1976) (Stevens, J., concurring); Personnel Administrator of Mass. v. Feeney, 442 U.S. 256, (1979) (Marshall, J., dissenting). Professor Karst calls Washington v. Davis "as ill an wind as any experienced by our constitutional law in recent memory." Kenneth L. Karst, "The Costs of Motive-Centered Inquiry," *San Diego Law Review* 15 (1978): 1163. Professor Karst takes the position that the fourteenth amendment requires government to "treat each individual as a person, one who is worthy of respect, one who 'belongs.'" Kenneth L. Karst, "The Supreme Court 1976 Term—Forward: Equal Citizenship Under the Fourteenth Amendment," *Harvard Law Review* 91 (1966): 1, 6. Thus in his view even demeaning impact per se is unlawful. Others have stressed that if the existence of a disproportionate impact alone were sufficient to strike a law down, the legislatures would be unable to act whenever it was foreseeable that a decision might have a greater-than-average adverse effect on a protected group. Bruce E. Rosenblum, "Discriminatory Purpose and Disproportionate Impact: An Assessment after *Feeney*," *Columbia Law Review* 79 (1979): 1376, 1384.

64. A federal district court summarized the use of the test in the following way. (1) An inference of intent is appropriate where a foreseeably segregative decision is made despite the existence of less segregative alternatives; (2) The lack of persuasive evidence of credible explanation for foreseeably segregative conduct may also justify an inference of improper motive; (3) A consistent pattern of foreseeably segregative decisions is also probative of an improper motive. United States v. Yonkers Bd. of Educ., 625 F. Supp. 1276, 1379-1380 (S.D. N.Y. 1985). A particularly tricky problem is the use of the neighborhood school system. See supra, text at notes 37 and 38 above.

65. In two opinions the Court reaffirmed its view that the foreseeability test could not be used by itself to establish a prima facie case of purposeful racial discrimination. There is reason to believe that by affirming the Sixth Circuit in *Columbus* and *Dayton 2*, the Court was as a practical matter affirming the use of the foreseeability test, without more, to prove intent. The district court in Columbus, despite disclaimers, seems to have used the foreseeability test alone to establish intent. Justice Rehnquist, dissenting in *Columbus*, suggested the Court's affirmance was an implicit affirmation of the use of the foreseeability test, but he did not make a final opinion on this question because the district court and the Court majority both resolutely maintained they were using foreseeable effects as but one of several kinds of proof of intent. Columbus Bd. of Educ. v. Penick, 443 U.S. 449 (1979); Penick v. Columbus Bd. of Educ., 429 F. Supp. 229, 241-43 (S.D. Ohio 1977), *rev'd on other grounds*, 583 F.2d 787 (6th Cir. 1978), *aff'd*, 443 U.S. 449 (1979).

66. In Columbus Bd. of Educ. v. Penick, 443 U.S. 449 (1979) the Sixth Circuit upheld the imposition of a systemwide desegregation remedy in Columbus, Ohio, because (1) the Columbus schools were "openly and intentionally" segregated on the basis of race in 1954, and (2) after *Brown 1*, the Columbus school board "never actively set out to dismantle this dual system." The segregation of 1954 was deemed to have continuing and present systemwide impact because *Brown 2* was said to have imposed on Columbus (even though it was not a party to the litigation in *Brown 1* and *2*) a constitutional duty to desegregate that Columbus never fulfilled. The racial imbalance of 1979 was thus to be treated as the vestige of a policy of de jure segregation that had been abandoned twenty-five years earlier. The Supreme Court embraced this theory. As expressed in the accompanying opinion in *Dayton 2*, "[T]he measure of the post-*Brown 1* conduct of a school board under an unsatisfied duty to liquidate a dual system" is "the effectiveness, not the purpose, of the actions in decreasing or increasing the segregation caused by the dual system." Thus any school board that practiced de jure segregation that ended in 1954-55 in any substantial part of the district (see the discussion of *Keyes* above) might be presumed to have segregated throughout the whole district, and would from that point forward have been under an *affirmative duty* to integrate. Any post-1955 decisions that failed to affirmatively seek to integrate would be deemed as perpetuating a condition of unlawful segregation. It is clear that under this approach boards could be held liable for segregation that could not have been the product alone of intentional acts of discrimination by the school board. Dayton Bd. of Educ. v. Brinkman, 443 U.S. 526 (1979). Professor Shane argues that this was true in both *Dayton 2* and *Columbus*. Peter M. Shane, "School Desegregation Remedies and the Fair Governance of Schools," *supra* note 18, at 1073-74.

67. Arlington Heights v. Metropolitan Housing Corp., 429 U.S. 252 (1977).

68. *Cf.*, United States v. Yonkers, 624 F. Supp. 1276, 1375-6 (S.D. N.Y. 1985).

69. Larry G. Simon, "Racially Prejudiced Governmental Actions: A Motivation Theory of a Constitutional Ban Against Racial Decisions," *San Diego Law Review* 15 (1978): 1041, 1109. Professor Simon argues that impact alone should be enough to establish a prima facie case triggering the requirement of a response from the government.

70. One perhaps misleading way of stating the inquiry is to ask the question whether a rational and nonbiased decision-maker would have made this same decision given its adverse effects.

71. Professor Clark has claimed that "[O]ne can acknowledge a kind of balancing in this context and can also acknowledge looking for evidence of probable legislative prejudice is different from balancing the good and bad effects of the law." J. Morris Clark, "Legislative Motivation and Fundamental Rights in Constitutional Law," *San Diego Law Review* 15 (1978): 953, 981.

72. Dayton Bd. of Educ. v. Brinkman, 443 U.S. 526 (1979) (Dayton II); Columbus Bd. of Educ. v. Penick, 443 U.S. 449 (1979); Swann v. Charlotte-Mecklenburg Bd. of Educ., 402 U.S. 1 (1971).

73. Keyes v. Sch. Dist. No. 1, Denver, 413 U.S. 189, 213-14 (1973); Swann v. Charlotte-Mecklenburg Bd. of Educ., 402 U.S. 1, 31-32 (1971). The Denver school board unsuccessfully attempted to establish that today's segregation was not the product of its past illegal activities. Keyes v. Sch. Dist. No. 1, Denver, 521 F.2d 465, 472 (10th Cir. 1975), *cert. denied*, 423 U.S. 1066 (1976).

74. Keyes v. Sch. Dist. No. 1, Denver, 413 U.S. 189, 203 (1973); United States v. Yonkers Bd. of Educ., 624 F. Supp. 1276, 1367, 1395 (1985).

75. Keyes v. Sch. Dist. No. 1, Denver, 413 U.S. 189, 201-02 (1973).

76. Id., at 203, 205.

77. Milliken v. Bradley, 433 U.S. 267, 283 (1977); United States v. State of Mississippi, 622 F. Supp. 622 (S.D. Miss. 1985).

78. Id.

79. United States Texas Educ. Agency, 342 F. Supp. 24, 28-38 (E.D. Tex. 1971), *rev'd on other grounds*, 495 F. 2d 848 (5th Cir. 1972).

80. Keyes v. Sch. Dist. No. 1, Denver, 368 F. Supp. 207 (1973), *rev'd*, 521 F. 2d 465, 480-81 (10th Cir. 1975), *cert. denied*, 423 U.S. 1066 (1976).

81. Id., at 481-82.

82. Robert Dentler and M. Scott, *Schools on Trial: An Inside Account of the Boston Desegregation Case* (Cambridge, Mass.: Abt Associates, 1981), 178. This account of the litigation and political infighting over the implementation of the judicial decree is one of the best case studies of its kind.

83. Id., at 16.

84. Milliken v. Bradley, 418 U.S. 717 (1974). *See also* Little Rock Sch. Dist. v. Pulaski Cty. Special Sch. Dist. No. 1, 778 F.2d 404 (8th Cir. 1985); United States v. Bd. of Sch. Com'rs, 637 F.2d 1101 (7th Cir. 1980), *cert. denied*, 101 S. Ct. 114, 115 (1980); Evans v. Buchanan, 393 F. Supp. 428 (D.Del. 1975), *aff'd sub nom.*, Buchanan v. Evans, 423 U.S. 963 (1975). *Cf.*, Lee v. Lee Cty. Bd. of Educ., 639 F.2d 1243 (5th Cir. 1981). When school district boundary lines are drawn to create segregated school districts, the courts will simply order a consolidation of the school districts. Hoots v. Comw. of Pennsylvania, 672 F.2d 1107 (3d Cir. 1982).

85. Milliken v. Bradley, 433 U.S. 267, 280-81 (1977); Little Rock Sch. Dist. v. Pulaski Cty. Special Sch. Dist. No. 1, 778 F.2d 404 (8th Cir. 1985).

86. Swann v. Charlotte-Mecklenburg Bd. of Educ., 402 U.S. 1, 30-31 (1971).

87. *See* Tasby v. Wright, 520 F. Supp. 683, 732-33, 736, 739, 744 (N.D. Texas 1981) (rejecting busing as a remedy when many routes would require an hour or more of busing one way, and it appeared would disrupt some naturally integrated schools, would not be needed in connection with other schools that would in time become naturally integrated, and would disrupt educational programs.)

88. *E.g.*, NAACP v. Lansing Bd. of Educ., 559 F.2d 1042, 1052 (6th Cir.), *cert. denied*, 434 U.S. 997 (1977).

89. *E.g.*, Fitzpatrick v. Bd. of Educ. of City of Enid, 578 F.2d 858 (10th Cir. 1978).

90. Washington v. Seattle Sch. Dist. No. 1, 458 U.S. 457 (1982). In Crawford v. Los Angeles Bd. of Educ., 458 U.S. 527 (1982) the Court rejected a constitutional attack on a California constitutional amendment designed to curb the powers of the state courts to order busing so that state courts had no more authority under the fourteenth amendment than federal district courts.

91. United States v. Scotland Neck Bd. of Educ., 407 U.S. 484, 485, 491 (1972).

92. Morgan v. Kerrigan, 530 F.2d 401, 421 (1st Cir.), *cert. denied sub. nom.*, White v. Morgan, 426 U.S. 935 (1976).

93. United States v. State of Mississippi, 622 F. Supp. 622 (S.D. Miss. 1985).

94. Higgins v. Bd. of Educ. of City of Grand Rapids, 508 F.2d 779, 794 (6th Cir. 1974) (emphasis in original). *See also* Riddick by Riddick v. Sch. Bd. of Norfolk, 784 F.2d 521 (4th Cir. 1986).

95. Swann v. Charlotte-Mecklenburg Bd. of Educ., 402 U.S. 1 (1971); Kelly v. Metropolitan Cty. Bd. of Educ. of Nashville, 687 F.2d 814 (6th Cir. 1982), *cert. denied*, 459 U.S. 1183 (1983).

96. Pasadena City Bd. of Educ. v. Spangler, 427 U.S. 424, 436-38 (1976).

97. Johnson v. Chicago Bd. of Ed., 604 F.2d 504 (7th Cir. 1979), *remanded*, 449 U.S. 915 (1981), 457 U.S. 52 (1982). *Cf.*, Parent Association of Andrew Jackson High Sch. v. Ambach, 738 F.2d 574 (2d Cir. 1984).

98. Morgan v. Kerrigan, 388 F. Supp. 581 (D. Mass. 1975), *aff'd.*, 530 F.2d 401 (1st Cir.), *cert. denied*, 426 U.S. 935 (1976). *Cf.*, Oliver v. Kalamazoo Bd. of Educ., 706 F.2d 757 (6th Cir. 1983).

99. Swann v. Charlotte-Mecklenburg Bd. of Educ., 402 U.S. 1 (1971); United States v. DeSoto Parish Sch. Bd., 574 F.2d 804 (5th Cir. 1978); Stout v. Jefferson Cty. Bd. of Educ., 537 F.2d 800 (5th Cir. 1976); Carr v. Montgomery Cty. Bd. of Educ., 377 F. Supp. 1123 (M.D. Ala. 1974), *aff'd.*, 511 F.2d 1374 (5th Cir.), *cert. denied*, 423 U.S. 986 (1975).

100. Wharton v. Abbeville Sch. Dist. No. 1, 608 F. Supp. 70 (D.S.C. 1984) (closing of predominantly black school was not discriminatory.

101. Singleton v. Jackson Municipal Separate Sch. Dist., 419 F. F.2d 1211 (5th Cir. 1970) (en banc), *rev'd and remanded on other grounds*, 396 U.S. 1032 (1970) *on remand*, 425 F.2d 1211 (5th Cir. 1970).

102. Arthur v. Nyquist, 547 F. Supp. 468 (W.D. N.Y. 1982); Arthur v. Nyquist, 618 F. Supp. 804 (D.C. N.Y. 1985).

103. Little Rock Sch. Dist. v. Pulaski Cty. Special Sch., 778 F.2d 404 (8th Cir. 1985); Liddle v. State of Missouri, 731 F.2d 1294 (8th Cir. 1984); Kelley v. Metropolitan Cty. Bd. of Educ. of Nashville, 615 F. Supp. 1139 (D.C. Tenn. 1985).

104. United States v. Bd. of Educ. of City of Chicago, 621 F. Supp. 1296 (D.C. Ill. 1985) (enforcement of consent decree).

105. Pasadena City Bd. of Educ. v. Spangler, 427 U.S. 424 (1976). Once a school district has been declared to be a unitary district and the courts relinquish jurisdiction, the local school might even be able to move toward a neighborhood school policy and segregate schools so long as the adoption of this policy is not proven, by the plaintiff challenging the change in policy, to have been motivated by an intent to segregate. Spangler v. Pasadena, 611 F.2d 1239, 1245 (9th Cir. 1979).

106. Vaughns v. Bd. of Educ. of Prince George's Cty., 758 F.2d 983 (4th Cir. 1985); Keyes v. Sch. Dist. No. 1, Denver, Colo., 609 F. Supp. 1491 (D.C. Colo. 1985); Whittenberg v. Sch. Dist. of Greenville Cty., 607 F. Supp. 289 (D.C. S.C. 1985); In determining whether a former dual school system has become a unitary system, a court must review six aspects of a school district: faculty, staff, transportation practices, extracurricular activities, facilities, and pupil assignment. Green v. New Kent Cty. Sch. Bd., 391 U.S. 430, 435 (1968).

107. In other words, once a former dual school system has been declared to have become a unitary system, the slate is wiped clean and the burden of proof switches back to the plaintiff to establish that school board policies have been adopted with an intent to segregate. Riddick by Riddick v. Sch. Bd. of City of Norfolk, 784 F. 2d 521 (4th Cir. 1986).

108. Pitts v. Freeman, 755 F. 2d 1423, 1427 (11th Cir. 1985).

109. Id., at 1426.

110. Riddick by Riddick v. Sch. Bd. of City of Norfolk, 784 F.2d 521 (4th Cir. 1986).

111. The literature debating remedies for segregation is too extensive to completely cite. The following are samples from the debate: Shane, "School Desegregation Remedies and the Fair Governance of Schools" *supra*, note 18; W. Hawely, et. al., *Strategies for Effective Desegregation* (Lexington, Mass.: Lexington Books, 1983); Lino A. Graglia, *Disaster by Decree* (Ithaca, N.Y.: Cornell University Press, 1976); Wolters, *The Burden of Brown supra*, note 20; Gary Orfield, *Must We Bus?* (Washington, D.C.: Brookings Institute, 1978); Stephen B. Kanner, "From Denver to Dayton: The Development of a Theory of Equal Protection Remedies," *Northwestern University Law Review* 72 (1977): 382.

112. David L. Kirp, *Just Schools* (Berkeley, Calif.: University of California Press, 1982); David L. Kirp, "Legalism and Politics in School Desegregation," *Wisconsin Law Review* (1981): 924. *See* San Francisco NAACP v. San Francisco Unified Sch. Dist., 576 F. Supp. 34 (N.D. Cal. 1983).

113. 42 U.S.C. §2000(c)-d (1982). Besides receiving the complaint the attorney general must

also determine that the signers of the complaint are unable to initiate and maintain appropriate legal proceedings.

114. Brown v. Califano, 627 F.2d 1221, 1232 n. 67 (D.C. Cir. 1980).

115. 42 U.S.C. §2000d-1 (1982).

116. Guardians Ass'n v. Civil Service Commission, 463 U.S. 582 (1983).

117. 45 C.F.R. §80.8 (1985).

118. Guardians Ass'n v. Civil Service Commission, 463 U.S. 582 (1983). The court seemed to adopt this position in Lau v. Nichols, 414 U.S. 563 (1974), but then a majority of the Court in Regents of the University of California v. Bakke, 438 U.S. 265 (1978) could be understood as having adopted the position that Title VI prohibits only purposeful discrimination on the basis of race. The Court settled the problem in *Guardians* and also held that in cases merely alleging discriminatory impact, the grantee must be given the opportunity to demonstrate some "business necessity" for the practices that have the discriminatory impact. The Court also concluded that even if the plaintiff should win the case, the plaintiff is only eligible for prospective declaratory and injunctive relief. That is, additional relief in the form of money damages is not available in a case where no intentional discrimination has been proved.

119. See §4.3, and materials in note 22.

120. Alexander v. Holmes Cty. Bd. of Educ., 396 U.S. 19 (1969) (per curiam).

121. Adams v. Richardson, 480 F.2d 1159 (D.C. Cir. 1973); Adams v. Califano, 430 F. Supp. 118 (D.D.C. 1977); Brown v. Weinberger, 417 F. Supp. 1215 (D.D.C. 1976); Adams v. Weinberger, 391 F. Supp. 269 (D.D.C. 1975). Only recently, the federal courts have had to order the federal government to comply with a consent decree the administration itself had agreed to. United States v. Bd. of Educ. of City of Chicago, 621 F. Supp. 1296 (D.C. Ill. 1985).

122. Brown v. Califano, 627 F.2d 1221 (D.C. Cir. 1980).

123. Alexander Bickel, "The Original Understanding and the Segregation Decision," *Harvard Law Review* 69 (1955): 1.

124. 438 U.S. 265 (1978). *Cf.,* Defunis v. Odegaard, 416 U.S. 312 (1974); Uzzell v. Friday, 592 F. Supp. 1502 (M.D. N.C. 1984).

125. The school conceded that it could not prove Bakke would not have been admitted absent the preferential admissions program. Id., at 280.

126. Chief Justice Burger, Justices Stevens, Stewart, and Rehnquist agreed that Title VI prohibited the use of a racial criteria for any purpose, benign or not. Id.

127. Justices Brennan, White, Marshall, and Blackmun.

128. Numerous articles have been written on the opinions in this case. One might sample the nine articles in the *Harvard Civil Rights-Civil Liberties Law Review* 14, no. 1 (1979).

129. *See supra,* text accompanying note 13 in chapter 3.

130. Justice Brennan could see no constitutional difference between the kind of admissions program approved by Justice Powell and the Davis program.

131. 448 U.S. 448 (1980). Other commentators have agreed with Justice Brennan. Paul Brest, "Race Discrimination," *supra* note 34, at 127.

132. Justice Powell said the thirteenth and fourteenth amendments confer on Congress the authority to select "reasonable remedies" to repair the effects of discrimination.

133. United Jewish Organization of Williamsburg v. Carey, 430 U.S. 144 (1977).

134. 458 U.S. 718 (1982). *See also* Vorchheimer v. Sch. Dist. of Philadelpia, 532 F.2d 880 (3d Cir. 1976), *aff'd by an equally divided Court,* 430 U.S. 703 (1977) (upholding the operation by the Philadelphia school district of a system of coeducational high schools along with two single-sex, academically oriented high schools for male and female students).

135. 20 U.S.C. §1681 (1982) (prohibiting discrimination on the basis of gender in programs receiving federal assistance).

5

Legal Limits on Socialization

5.1. INTRODUCTION

To some, the constitutional right of parents to send their children to private schools (see §1.4) raises a profound social and political problem. Extensive use of the right appears to diminish the chance that a commonly shared "American Creed" will be fostered, and in a society as diverse as the American society a shared creed, it is believed, is necessary to the maintenance of our stable democratic government and the minimization of social conflict.[1] Thus, to resist the tendency of this society to move toward chaos, public schooling must have a unique function that goes beyond the transmission of knowledge and the teaching of skills in reading and mathematics. The public schools should inculcate or instill those attitudes, dispositions, values, and beliefs that make up the "American Creed."

Others take a different position. For them, the effort to have the public schools inculcate an American Creed has the potential of becoming a self-serving effort to impose on the young, in violation of the young's interest in autonomy and self-determination, the particular views of those who happen to be in power.[2] Still others view the problem in less black-and-white terms: they see the challenge as one of maintaining continuity, fostering knowledge, retaining the values of the past "while accommodating change, criticism, growth, and individual autonomy."[3] That is, for these commentators the question is inevitably one of balance. We thus have at least a three-sided debate.

We find here the same tensions among child, family, and state that were raised in chapter 1. While in that chapter the tensions were manifested in state efforts to impose a compulsory education requirement and to regulate private educational efforts, here they arise in the context of public schooling. Accordingly, in this chapter we review the judiciary's response to the question of what limits, if any, do the first and fourteenth amendment impose on the public schools in shaping and imposing the educational program. Specific questions such as the following will be taken up: To what extent and in what ways has the judiciary permitted religious materials to be introduced in the school program?

May school boards remove books from the school library because they disagree with their contents? What may schools do to foster traditional notions of what it means to be female or male?

From another perspective the materials of this chapter relate to issues taken up in chapters 1 and 2, and to be taken up in chapters 7 and 8. Rights that impose limits on the authority of the school board to control the school program also serve to allocate authority. The more the first amendment is read to limit the authority of the school board, the more authority is effectively allocated to parents, for example, to control the religious upbringing of their child, a matter touched on in chapter 1. Similarly, the rights of teachers also affect the authority of the school board to control the school program. We dealt with one aspect of those rights in chapter 2. In chapter 6 we turn to, among other things, the question of the academic freedom of teachers: clearly, the more strongly the individual teacher is protected in making his or her own unique curricular decisions, the more limited the authority of the school board and state to shape a uniform program intended to socialize students in a common set of values. Similarly, the more the rights of students to exercise a right of free speech within the schools is recognized—a topic taken up in chapter 6—the more the school is opened to a set of alternative ideas that can serve as a check or countervoice to the perspectives officially promoted by the school board.

Then this brings us to another debate. What is the better method for the judiciary to use to protect the right of a student to freedom of conscience and thought: the direct imposition of constitutional limits on the school board in shaping the school program (e.g., the imposition of a requirement that the board not discriminate against ideas in shaping the school program); or the recognition of such individual rights as the right of a teacher to academic freedom and the free speech rights of students?[4] To date, the Supreme Court has adopted both techniques.

5.2. RELIGION AND THE SCHOOLS: AN INTRODUCTION

From the beginning of the public school movement, the question of the proper place of religion in the schools has been under continual debate. For some the answer has been straightforward: the first amendment means that, except for objective instruction about different religions, religion has no proper place in the schools.[5] For others the answer has been in the finding of a compromise that would satisfy the various Christian denominations, if not the atheists. Under one such compromise the public schools could instruct pupils in those common values and ideals on which the Protestant sects agreed, but that instruction in those values that were based on Christianity would not be taught in a religious context. It would be left to the family, church, and Sabbath school to instruct in specific doctrine. Another version of the compromise allowed for readings from the King James Bible—a text shared by Protestant denominations.[6] As Leo Pfeffer describes it, the *modus vivendi* arrived at in the 1840s was simply the "Bible yes, sectarianism no."[7] More recently Episcopal Bishop James A. Pike noted the existence of three possible governmental policies toward religion: "at one extreme, the establishment of a particular church; at the other extreme, the secularization of public life, a policy he warned had been chosen by Soviet Russia. The third policy he called the middle way, the American experiment, the 'public recognition,' to quote his language, 'by solemn declaration and by prayer—of God and his Providence.'"[8] It is this third way that Justice Rehnquist has embraced. As he interprets the establishment clause it serves primarily to prohibit the designation of any church as the national church, and the asserting by government of one religious denomination or sect over others. It does not require government to be neutral between religion and irreligion.[9]

None of these positions has met with universal acclaim. While those who have argued for total segregation say this is essential to promote liberty, those opposed to such separation say their liberty to pray is infringed when prayer is excluded from the public schools.[10] As for the other compromises, Catholics and others have objected to its Protestant taint. Even when the compromise took the form of the introduction of a seemingly wholly nondenominational prayer—"Almighty God, we acknowledge our dependence upon Thee, and we beg Thy blessings upon us, our parents, our teachers and our Country"—Jews and some Protestants were opposed, while Catholics were in strong support.[11] Although Justice Rehnquist holds the view that government must be neutral between religion and irreligion, a majority of the Supreme Court itself has over the years adhered to the view that government may not pass laws that aid one religion, aid all religions, prefer one religion over another, or that fail to be neutral between believers and nonbelievers.[12]

5.3. CONSTITUTIONAL LIMITS ON RELIGION IN THE SCHOOLS

The Supreme Court's response to the introduction of religion into the regular school day of the public schools by school officials has been to say "no" in all cases except one.[13] Struck down have been such practices as these: the making available on a voluntary basis religious classes in the school building during regular school hours;[14] the opening of the school day with a ceremony, in which students were not compelled to participate, that involved the saying of a non-denominational prayer composed by the state;[15] the opening of the school day with a voluntary ceremony in which passages from the Bible were read and/or the Lord's Prayer was used;[16] the posting on school walls of copies of the Ten Commandments purchased with privately donated funds;[17] and the passage of a law that authorized at the commencement of the school day a one-minute period of silence "for meditation or voluntary prayer."[18] Only a released-time program that allowed those students who wanted to leave school during regular school hours for one hour a week to receive religious instruction off school grounds in nearby religious facilities was upheld.[19] In an important footnote the Court wrote:

> There is of course nothing in the decision reached here that is inconsistent with the fact that school children and others are officially encouraged to express love for our country by reciting historical documents such as the Declaration of Independence which contain references to the Deity or by singing officially espoused anthems which include the composer's professions of faith in a Supreme Being, or with the fact that there are many manifestations in our public life of belief in God. Such patriotic or ceremonial occasions bear no true resemblance to the unquestioned religious exercise that the State of New York has sponsored in this instance.[20]

In another case the Court stressed that "Nothing we have said here indicates that such a study of the Bible or religion, when presented objectively as part of a secular program of education, may not be effected consistently with the First Amendment.[21]

One can cull from these opinions a set of reasons or arguments in support of the Court's resistance to permitting religion to enter the regular school day. First, the Court has rejected the historical interpretation of the establishment clause that it merely prohibits governmental preference of one religion over another; according to the Court, government may not pass laws that either prefer one religion to another or aid all religions.[22] Second, the union of church and state destroys government and degrades religion (by opening the door to persecution of religious dissenters by government, by encouraging violent struggles over the control of government because those who control government control religion, and by stimulating armed resistance to the persecuting government).[23] Third, even though participation in such ceremonies may be voluntary, "When the power, prestige and financial support of government is placed behind a particular religious belief, the indirect coercive pressure upon religious minorities to conform to the prevailing official approved religion is plain."[24] Fourth, the claim that religious exercises may serve to combat communism and juvenile delinquency or promote moral values in contradiction to the materialistic trend of the times is not sufficient to save these religious practices.[25] Fifth, the brevity of the ceremonies also provided no defense. "The breach of neutrality that is today a trickling stream may all too soon become a raging torrent, and in the words of Madison, 'it is proper to take alarm at the first experiment on our liberties.'"[26] Sixth, the Court insisted that keeping religion out of the schools did not indicate hostility to religion or prayer. "It is neither sacrilegious nor antireligious to say that each separate government in this country should stay out of the business of writing or sanctioning official prayers and leave that purely religious function to the people themselves and to those the people choose to look to for religious guidance."[27] Seventh, the Court rejected the claim that the exclusion of religious exercises from school meant that a "religion of secularism" would be established. Clearly, said the Court, a "religion of secularism" could not be established by government affirmatively opposing or showing hostility to religion; but excluding religious ceremonies did not have this effect.[28] Last, in the Court's most recent opinion, it placed the issue of religion in the schools in a larger context.

> Just as the right to speak and the right to refrain from speaking are complementary components of a broader concept of individual freedom of mind, so also the individual's freedom to choose his own creed is the counterpart of his right to refrain from accepting the creed established by the majority. At one time it was thought that this right merely proscribed the preference of one Christian sect over another, but would not require equal respect for the conscience of the infidel, the atheist, or the adherent of a non-Christian faith such as Mohammedism or Judaism. But when the underlying principle has been examined in the crucible of litigation, the Court has unambiguously concluded that the individual freedom of conscience protected by the First Amendment embraces the right to select any religious faith or none at all. This conclusion derives support not only from the interest in respecting the individual's freedom of conscience, but also from conviction that religious beliefs worthy of respect are the product of free and voluntary choice by the faithful, and from recognition of the fact that the political interest in forestalling intolerance extends beyond intolerance among Christian sects—or even intolerance among "religions"—to encompass intolerance of the disbeliever and the uncertain.[29]

Before we turn to some general issues under current debate, it is important to note that while in fact the Court seems to have embraced the "wall of separation" metaphor in the school cases, there are indications that we may, in the not too distant future, see the Court adopt a more accommodating view. Justice Rehnquist has openly called for rejection of the "wall of separation" metaphor, and said he sees no constitutional difficulty in the schools' endorsing prayer.[30] Justices Burger and White have argued that a statute that calls for a period of silence for "meditation or prayer" at the start of the school day does not endorse religion but accommodates the private, voluntary religious choices of those who wish to pray.[31] A fourth justice, Justice O'Connor, has said a law that permits prayer, meditation, and reflection without endorsing one alternative would be constitutional.[32] Underscoring the move toward the greater accommodation, recognition, and/or acknowledgement of religion is the Court's decision in *Lynch v. Donnelly* in which the Court upheld the Pawtucket, Rhode Island, erection of a Christmas display comprised of figures and decorations including a creche.[33]

At the heart of the debate between the current majority of the Court and what may be an emerging majority is the question of what the drafters of the establishment clause intended to prohibit. As noted earlier, as Justice Rehnquist interprets the history of the establishment clause, it was intended primarily to prohibit the designation of any church as the national church, and the asserting of a preference of one religious denomination or sect over others. Others view the history of the clause as inconclusive regarding its application in the public school context because there were no public schools at the time of the adoption of the amendment; thus, deciding what the framers would have intended regarding prayers and other forms of religious instruction and devotional exercises in public schools remains speculation. But one might ask, even if the original intent behind the first amendment could not be understood to encompass a prohibition on prayer in public schools, should that mean the modern-day court is precluded from extending the Constitution in this way? The fact remains that the intent of the framers cannot conclusively be established to be in favor of prayers in public schools; thus, it would seem the modern court is free to make up its own mind. The real question is whether the Court has made the correct choice to exclude devotional exercises from the public schools.

Second, does the prohibition of a school-endorsed moment of prayer infringe on the freedom of those who want to pray? Is it correct that "a compulsory state educational system so structures a child's life that if religious exercises are held to be an impermissible activity in schools, religion is placed at an artificial and state-created disadvantage"?[34] Is it not an adequate answer that any student may at any time bow his or her head and silently pray in school or seek out a church, temple, or other religious center before school has begun or after it has closed? (See §5.4.) Why is free exercise only protected by a school-directed prayer during school hours?

A third and related problem has to do with the response to be made to those who believe that moral values and theology are one and that a school that teaches the idea that moral values may or do have a nontheistic basis is not being neutral but hostile to religion.[35] Might it be answered that so long as the school does not affirmatively attack that view, it is not hostile to religion?[36] (For a further discussion of this issue see §5.5 below.)

Four, how is the term "religion" as used in the establishment clause to be interpreted?[37] This is a difficult legal-political question. Since there is no universally agreed-upon definition of the term "religion," the Court is largely free to define the term as it thinks best. The narrower the definition, the more the public schools may be used to include and/or promote viewpoints and perspectives at least closely affiliated with what some would say are religious views, e.g., scientific creationism or transcendental meditation, without violating the Constitution.[38] Under a broad definition of religion, much of what the public schools teach might be open to challenge. For example, when the Court excludes religious exercises from the school program, has it by default embraced a religion—the religion of secularism—the Court's protestations to the contrary not withstanding?[39] For example, a federal district court judge ordered forty-four textbooks removed from the Alabama public schools because he said they unconstitutionally promoted the religion of "secular humanism." (See chapter 10.)

We turn now from these more general problems in constitutional interpretation to some more specific problems. First, is a required daily moment of silence a permissible way to accommodate religion in the public schools while remaining within constitutional bounds? The lower courts have split on the question of whether a moment of silence for meditation may be set aside at the start of the school day;[40] and two justices whom one would not expect to agree with each other have gone on record endorsing the constitutionality of the requirement.[41] Since a moment of silence can serve a secular purpose, is not inherently religious, does not require participants to compromise their beliefs, and can be implemented in a way that does not overtly promote religion, it would seem in theory such laws would have a reasonable chance of surviving judicial review by the Supreme Court.[42] However, a legislative history that indicates the law was passed to promote religion and/or implementation of the law that conveys the message that the school wants the students to use the moment for prayer would clearly jeopardize its chances of survival. "[A]n important concern of the effects test is whether the symbolic union of church and state . . . is sufficiently likely to be perceived by adherents of the controlling denominations as an endorsement, and by the nonadherents as a disapproval, or their individual religious choices."[43]

Second, officially sponsored devotional sessions aside, what other religiously related activities might be allowed in the schools? To answer this question we have to turn to a brief review of a sample of lower court opinions. One lower court upheld the offering of a Christmas program that involved the temporary display of religious symbols and the singing of religious hymns so long as the purpose of the program was not to advance religion.[44] The lower courts have also struck down the use of student volunteers to open the day with a prayer;[45] struck down the singing of a religious anthem at a pep rally;[46] prohibited the distribution of free Bibles in school by the Gideon Society to students who wanted them.[47] In *Breen v. Runkel* a federal district court rejected the claim of teachers that their right to the free exercise of religion permitted them to pray in the classrooms, read from the Bible, and tell stories that had a biblical basis.[48]

Although a majority of courts has said that schools may open the graduation and/or baccalaureate ceremonies with a prayer, the issue remains a close one.[49] Despite what the courts upholding the practice have said, is it accurate to say that opening the ceremony with a prayer is not intended to serve a religious purpose? Though a religious ceremony may be used in a dramatic production for secular purposes, the use of the invocation in this context is different. How can the primary effect of the prayer not be to promote religion? The claim that the effect of this one-time prayer is less than when each of 180 days of the school year is opened with a prayer—a practice that is, of course, prohibited—is subject to serious question. Government's invoking of religion at this salient moment of high attention and emotion may very well carry more weight than the repetitive saying of a routine prayer in a routine way. The very fact that government thinks it important to include religion on an occasion of such moment in the lives of the students, their families, and the school carries the message that the state believes religion should play a significant part in responding to, dealing with, and interpreting significant transitions and occasions. Thus, we learn from the use of prayers at these occasions that the school district believes that life's great moments are religious moments, or at least moments when religion should be called upon. That students may be in charge of the graduation ceremony and may be the ones who decide to have a prayer should make no difference in this case. The school's official graduation ceremony, after all, is not an extracurricular function but an officially sponsored school ceremony that the school itself established to recognize and honor its graduating students. The prayer cannot be said without the explicit message that it comes with the school's endorsement. The fact that attendance at the ceremony is voluntary cannot work to save the practice. The voluntariness of the prayers that opened the school day did not prevent that practice from being declared unconstitutional. Few would doubt that a state-run religious ceremony would be unconstitutional even if attendance were voluntary. Finally, if prayers may be used to end the school experience, may they not also be used to open the school year and at other significant occasions in the life of the school? There appears to be no principled basis for distinguishing between the graduation and baccalaureate ceremonies and other significant dates in the school year.

Prayers aside, what did the Supreme Court mean in *Schempp* when it said that the objective study of the Bible or religion as part of a secular program was permissible? Does the objective study of religion require an examination of the atrocities that have been undertaken in the name of religion?[50] When does the study of the Bible move from being objective teaching about the Bible, as might be accomplished in a history or literature course, to the teaching of religion?[51] This much is certain: the courts have consistently declared unconstitutional programs of bible instruction in which the hiring and supervision of teachers and the selection of materials was controlled by a private religious group. Supervision and control of the course must be under the exclusive direction of the school district. Neither may teachers be hired with a view to their religious beliefs, nor may religious tenets be advanced in these courses. Requiring the course to be offered on an elective basis has been another judicial demand. It is somewhat unclear why this must be a feature of a constitutionally acceptable program, if the course is taught in an objective manner. Perhaps the answer lies in the fact that only the Bible is the subject of the course. Such a course may carry the implicit message that those religions based on the Bible garner more official endorsement than nonbiblically based religions. Before accepting this argument one needs to consider the implications of accepting the principle that whenever a course carries an implicit message it is subject to first amendment restrictions. (See, §5.6). It would seem that those who believe a biology course that includes a unit on evolutionary theory may be a required course cannot at the same time claim that a course undertaking the objective study of the Bible may only be offered as an elective.

Statutes requiring the teaching of "scientific creationism" or "creation science" have been struck down on the grounds that "scientific creationism" is religion, not science, and that such statutes had as their purpose the advancement of religion.[52]

5.4. STUDENT-INITIATED RELIGIOUS ACTIVITIES IN SCHOOL

Though public schools may not officially initiate and sponsor religious activities in the schools, at least during the regular school day, is the Constitution violated if schools merely give permission to students to conduct religious activities on their own initiative on school grounds, either during the school day or before or after the school day?

We might profitably approach this question by first taking note of those cases in which the school district rented its facilities to an outside religious group for use for its own for religious purposes (see, §6.11). As long as this rental arrangement was part of a broader policy to make the school's facilities available to community groups for a fee, the courts have agreed that the lease had neither the purpose nor effect of promoting religion. So long as the district does not attempt to regulate the religious program, except to impose the usual rules to protect the facilities from damage, excessive entanglement between church and state would be avoided.[53] (For purposes of convenient reference this problem will be termed the "Lease Case.") We should also take into account the decision in *McCollum* in which the Supreme Court struck down as a violation of the establishment clause a released-time program that involved ending public school classes an hour early a day a week to permit students who wished to do so to take religious instruction from religious instructors in the public school's classrooms.[54] Attendance was taken in these classes, and those students not attending went to other classrooms for continuation of their nonreligious studies.

Against this background consider, first, the arrangement under which school officials permit a "student volunteer" to lead those students who wish to participate in a "voluntary" prayer. Clearly this situation is a far cry from the leasing arrangement noted above, but it shares some important similarities with *McCollum*. Even though all the participants may be volunteers, these "volunteers" are in a different situation from the participants in the Lease Case. Furthermore, official school involvement is so deep that few courts would doubt that this is a school-initiated, sponsored, and endorsed religious activity that has the purpose and primary effect of advancing religion.[55] Contrast our voluntary prayer case with a school attempt to, for example, prohibit a student from privately praying at his or her desk before an examination. Such a rule would most certainly violate that student's right to the free exercise of religion. As in the Lease Case, this student is making use of school facilities in a personal way for his personal use, in the same way those facilities are made available to other students to, for example, discuss politics among themselves. One would also be hard pressed to say that the school's failure to prevent the student from praying had the purpose and primary effect of promoting religion.[56] Even if one accepts the "impressionable youth" doctrine,[57] it is difficult to believe that the individual silent prayer of a student would be construed by other students as school support and endorsement of religion.

We turn now to several more ambiguous cases. Consider the case of assemblies controlled and directed by a student council, assemblies that the school administration accommodates by adjusting the class schedule, and that are opened with a prayer. Even though attending the assembly is not required, lower courts have struck down these arrangements. One court noted that a religious activity in the institutionally coercive setting of schools populated by impressionable students would unavoidably give the impression of state support of religion.[58] It was also noted that when students must choose between attending a major school function and listening to a prayer chosen by a select group of students, "It is difficult to conceive how this choice would not coerce a student wishing to be part of the social mainstream and, thus, advance one group's religious beliefs." The court also rejected the claim that prohibiting the prayer violated some students' right of free exercise of religion: the establishment clause violation simply took precedence in this case. Besides, those students who wanted to worship were free to do so before or after school. This case is closer to *McCollum* than it is to the Lease Case. Unlike the Lease Case, the student council is an official organ of the school, subject to the ultimate direction and control of school officials.

The desire of student-initiated religious clubs to use school facilities raises a problem closer to the Lease Case. In *Widmar v. Vincent*[59] the Supreme Court ruled that it was an unconstitutional violation of the students' right of free speech for the University of Missouri to deny permission to a student religious group to use university facilities for meetings in which there were prayers, hymns, Bible commentary, and discussions of religious views and experiences. The university sought to justify exclusion of this club, but not other nonreligious clubs, by arguing that denial of access was justified by its interest in maintaining strict separation of church and state. The Court noted the university's interest in the separation of church and state might be a sufficient reason for exclusion if permitting the students to use the facilities would violate the establishment clause.[60] But, concluded the Court, permitting this club to use the facilities would not transgress the establishment clause: neither the purpose, the primary effect, nor the entanglement test would be violated. Having opened its facilities to other student groups, opening these facilities equally to all groups would serve only the purposes of advancing the exchange of ideas and avoiding the entanglement of religion that occurs when the university seeks to exclude religious activities from campus. Finally, the Court noted, opening the facilities equally to all groups would not confer the imprimatur of state approval on religion. University students are young adults, less impressionable than younger students, and "are able to appreciate that the University's policy is one of neutrality toward religion."[61]

The *Widmar* opinion suggests that the Court would agree that it is constitutionally permissible for elementary and secondary schools to deny student-initiated religious clubs use of their facilities; in fact, the opinion also suggests that school districts that permit their facilities to be used by such clubs violate the establishment clause. Those federal circuit courts of appeal that have ruled on the question have reached that conclusion.[62] Of these cases the opinion in *Bender* is particularly interesting. In that case the school district excluded a student-initiated club (Petros) from participation in the school's "activity period"—a thirty-minute time slot, provided on Tuesday and Thursday mornings after attendance was taken—during which time student clubs could meet under supervision of a faculty advisor. The Third Circuit concluded that this activity period was a "limited public forum"; consequently, the refusal to recognize Petros because of the content of the club's activities was a denial of the members' first amendment rights to equal nondiscriminatory access to the forum. (For a discussion of the concept of a "public forum see §§6.4 and 6.8.) Unlike the Supreme Court in *Widmar*, this court also concluded that to let Petros meet would violate the establishment clause. The court found the primary effect and entanglement tests would be violated. (See §§1.11 and 1.12.) The younger and more impressionable students of the high school would almost necessarily get the impression that the school was endorsing religion if the club were to meet with a school-appointed monitor in school facilities. Furthermore, the court believed that the school-appointed monitor could and probably would get entangled in religious disputes that might spring up among the club members. The Third Circuit also noted that the educational mission of a high school was more circumscribed than that of a university, in that it consisted of a structured program designed "[to inculcate] fundamental values necessary to the maintenance of a democratic political system." Thus, the court found it unlikely that school authorities would create a "truly open forum" of "unregulated dialogue." In sum, the court stressed that the activities in which Petros intended to engage would be conducted during school hours, on school premises, and under official school supervision. Having reached these conclusions, the court had to resolve the conflict between the students' free speech rights and the establishment clause. In the context of this case the court concluded that the establishment clause concerns took precedence. The court said that denial to these students of access to the activity period would not seriously impair the group's interests since it could meet off school premises and at other times than during school hours; whereas granting the students access would create unavoidable and unremediable establishment clause problems. (On appeal to the Supreme Court the Third

Circuit Court of Appeals' opinion was vacated and remanded on the grounds that the circuit court lacked jurisdiction since the appeal from the district court opinion had been filed by only one member of the school board and he lacked standing to appeal a decision—he could not step into the shoes of the board and invoke its right to appeal.)[63]

In light of the Lease Case, was *Bender* correctly decided? Could it not be argued that the facts in *Bender* were sufficiently like the Lease Case that it should have been decided the same way? While there are similarities between the two cases, there are a number of important differences: Petros was to meet during the school day after attendance had been taken; the meetings would take place during a time when all other, arguably impressionable students were in the school; Petros would not be paying rent for the facilities; and public school personnel on the public payroll would be used to supervise Petros. In other words, *Bender* may be said to share more in common with *McCollum* than it does with the Lease Case.

School districts within the jurisdiction of courts that have ruled in a manner similar to *Bender* face a difficult legal dilemma: should they comply with the recently adopted Equal Access Act (EAA)?[64] Briefly, EAA makes it unlawful for schools that receive federal financial assistance and that have created a "limited open forum" to deny equal access or fair opportunity to, or discriminate against, any "student-initiated" noncurriculum-related groups on the basis of the religious, political, or philosophical content of their speech.[65] The congressional sponsors of the act assumed the constitutionality of the law was secured by *Widmar*. As we have seen, the lower courts have refused to extend the holding of *Widmar* into the elementary- and high-school context.

The implementation of EAA can be accomplished in a way that avoids the difficulties of *Bender*. The limited open forum need not be instituted during school hours when the entire "impressionable" student body is present. The clubs could also be required to contribute to the costs of providing adult supervision. Implementation of EAA in this way moves us away from *McCollum* toward the Lease Case, away from unconstitutionality and toward constitutionality.

5.5. EXCLUSION OF NONRELIGIOUS MATERIALS FOR RELIGIOUS REASONS

The attempt to shape the school program to accommodate the religious sensibilities of some have taken two additional forms: (1) state-initiated steps to exclude courses or materials because of religiously based objections, and (2) constitutional challenges to ostensibly nonreligious courses or materials on the grounds they violate the establishment clause.

In *Epperson v. Arkansas*[66] the Court struck down an Arkansas statute, the product of a fundamentalist religious fervor of the 1920s, making it unlawful for a public school teacher to teach or to use a textbook that taught the "theory or doctrine that mankind ascended or descended from a lower order of animals." This law violated the establishment clause, said the Court, because it "selects from the body of knowledge a particular segment which it proscribes for the sole reason that it is deemed to conflict with a particular religious doctrine; that is with a particular interpretation of the Book of Genesis by a particular religious group." Continuing, the Court said, "The State's undoubted right to prescribe the curriculum for its public schools does not carry with it the right to prohibit, on pain of criminal penalty, the teaching of a scientific theory or doctrine where that prohibition is based upon reasons that violate the First Amendment."

Several observations on the *Epperson* opinion are in order. First, the opinion is consistent with the view that even if the state believed that the theory of evolution was a "religious" doctrine and its teaching violated the establishment clause, it could not be excluded, at least under the circumstances of this case. The Court will not let states manipulate the definition of religion so as to provide an excuse to eliminate certain topics from the school curriculum.[67] Second, the Court will not let states accommodate the religious sensibilities of religious groups, even in the name of the free exercise of religion, by excluding offending topics from the school curriculum.

Whether *Epperson* was correctly decided remains a serious question. One might ask why the motivation for removing the study of evolution from the schools is constitutionally relevant. The answer seems to be that by acting for these reasons, a legislature adds its imprimatur to those religious views and may in turn "stigmatize"—if that is the right word—the theory of evolution and those who value it as a scientific theory. Does the opinion preclude a state from even excluding the entire subject of biology if the reasons are to accommodate the religious sensibilities of one group? Perhaps, but Justice Stewart in concurring argued that it was one thing for the state to decide a subject would not be included in the curriculum and quite another to "make it a criminal offense for a public school teacher so much as to mention the very existence of an entire system of respected human thought." Thus perhaps the case is best understood as standing for the notion that while teachers may not insist on teaching biology in a literature class, they must be free from religiously based efforts to prevent them from fine-tuning their biology classes by introducing, if they so wish, a "system of respected human thought." Protection of the teacher's discretion to this extent might be justified on the ground that "The greater the ability of the school system [or state] to control what goes on in every classroom, the greater the danger of its promulgating a uniform message to its captive listeners."[68]

Further insight into *Epperson* may be gained by looking at its use by the lower courts. In *Pratt v. Independent School District*,[69] the school board removed from use in the classroom a film version of Shirley Jackson's short story "The Lottery." Objections had been lodged against the film by parents on the grounds that it led students to question their family loyalties, values, traditions, and religious beliefs, and because it portrayed a vengeful rather than a loving God. Contrary to the recommendation of its own Committee for Challenged Materials, the board voted to stop the use of the film at the junior and senior high school levels. When this action was challenged in court, the board stated that it had removed the film because of its "undue emphasis on violence and bloodshed," which had the effect of "distorting the short story and overshadowing" its themes. The federal district court concluded, however, that the film had been excluded because of its ideological content and its feared impact on the students' religious and moral values. On appeal the Eighth Circuit relied heavily on *Epperson* in holding the evidence warranted finding the board had acted because it agreed with those citizens who found the film's "ideological and religious themes to be offensive." Expert witnesses had testified they found the film had no adverse effects on students' attitudes toward family or religious values. The film contained a single brief scene of violence, and the board previously had shown no concern about violence in curriculum materials. In these circumstances, the court held, the removal had the effect of sending the message that the ideas of the films were unacceptable and not to be discussed. At stake was "the right to receive information and to be exposed to controversial ideas," and if these films could be "banned by those opposed to their ideological theme, then a precedent is set for the removal of any such work." (*Cf.*, §5.8.)

In *Daniels v. Waters*[70] the court was confronted with a more sophisticated effort to exclude materials from the schools. The statute included these provisions: (1) books that taught evolution were prohibited if they did not contain a disclaimer that evolution was a theory and was not represented to be scientific fact, and if they did not place an equal emphasis upon other theories including the Genesis account in the Bible; (2) the Bible was declared not to be a textbook and did not have to carry the same disclaimer; and (3) also prohibited was the teaching of occult or satanical beliefs regarding human origins. Relying on *Epperson*, the court concluded that the unevenhanded treatment of the theory of evolution and the Book of Genesis gave the Bible an impermissible preferential position. The court concluded further that enforcement of the provision excluding the teaching of occult or satanical beliefs would involve impermissibly entangling the state in "the most difficult or hotly disputed of theological arguments."[71] In a more recent decision creationists did secure a ruling in California that evolution could not be presented as fact in the public schools and that the textbooks must be screened to determine if they met this requirement.[72]

We turn to suits brought to obtain from a court an order to exclude ostensibly nonreligious materials from the school curriculum. In *Wright v. Houston Independent School District*,[73] the plaintiffs claimed that the uncritical teaching of the theory of evolution, ignoring the biblical account of human creation, established the religion of secularism. The district court disagreed.

In the case at bar, the offending material is peripheral to the matter of religion. Science and religion necessarily deal with many of the same questions, and they may frequently provide conflicting answers. But, as the Supreme Court wrote twenty years ago, it is not the business of government to suppress real or imagined attacks upon a particular religious doctrine. . . . Teachers of science in the public schools should not be expected to avoid the discussion of every scientific issue on which some religion claims expertise.[74]

The court thus refused to order the schools to balance the curriculum by requiring equal time for different theories of human creation. In light of the multiple views on human origins, the court said, the proposed solution of the plaintiffs would be more onerous than the problem they purported to alleviate. But it might be asked, "What is so 'onerous' about the plaintiff's proposal?"[75] Then one should recall that the effort on the part of Arkansas to require that public schools provide balanced treatment of evolution and scientific creationism was struck down because the court concluded scientific creationism was a religious doctrine and teaching it would violate the establishment clause.[76]

Efforts to remove sex education courses wholly from the public schools have failed. These courses, say the courts, do not establish a religion but are neutral presentations of health-related materials that further legitimate educational objectives without evincing antagonism toward religion or supporting nonreligion.[77] In fact, as *Epperson* suggests, it would violate the establishment clause if schools were to stop such instruction in order to conform to the religious objections of some parents.[78]

In sum, the lower courts appear to have interpreted the Supreme Court's statement in *Schempp,* namely, that "the State may not establish a 'religion of secularism' in the sense of affirmatively opposing or showing hostility to religion,"[79] to mean that a religion of secularism is only established if the curriculum shows hostility to religion. "But why is such hostility required when religion is established if the Bible is read without comment?"[80] Perhaps the answer lies in the threat that public schooling might become constitutionally impossible if the establishment clause were implicated every time ostensibly nonreligious materials were said to have indirect, secondary, or diffuse religious effects.[81] Hence, just as Christmas programs are tolerated because they are not seen as directly advancing theistic religion,[82] so the teaching of evolution and sex education may be understood not to promote a religion of secularism directly. (See chapter 10.)

5.6. EXEMPTING STUDENTS WHO OBJECT FOR RELIGIOUS REASONS

The controversies reviewed in §§5.3-5.5 have involved claims that the strictures of the establishment clause were breached by such activities as the school's sponsoring devotional exercises, permitting students to engage in religious activities on school grounds, or using ostensibly nonreligious materials. We now turn to a different argument: This course, textbook, or method of instruction is so at odds with the religious beliefs of the students that it has the potential of undermining their faith or interfering with their religiously based way of life, if the students are forced to be exposed to it by the threat of suffering a penalty for nonattendance or failure to learn the material. Furthermore, since the state does not have a compelling state interest, for example, to require a student to learn the theory of evolution, continued coercion violates the student's right to free exercise of religion, and the student must be excused from attending the course.[83]

The lower courts have reached different conclusions on whether the exemption is constitutionally required. Exemptions were granted to some students excusing them from sex education instruction, coeducational physical-education classes, and officers' training programs.[84] However, another court refused to exempt a student from officers' training.[85] Different courts have refused to excuse students from classrooms in which audio-visual equipment was used or exempt Jewish students who wished to wear a yarmulke from a rule forbidding basketball players from wearing hats or other headwear.[86] But in *Church of God v. Amarillo Independent School District* a federal district court said the free exercise clause required the school to allow more than only two days excused absences for religious holidays.[87] The outcome of these cases have turned on such questions as whether the requirement does indeed conflict with a religious tenet, whether the exemption would disrupt the school program, whether the exemption would affect the student's academic progress, and whether the exemption might pose a safety hazard.

A recent case in which parents sought to have their children excused from using the "Holt Basic Readers" is worthy of more extensive comment.[88] The plaintiffs, who rejected any concept of a world community, believed that Jesus Christ was the only means to salvation; hence, they rejected the view that "all religions are merely different roads to God." Based on these views, they objected to "the underlying philosophy of the readers, taken as a whole, which is geared to making the school children better participants in the world community. The books are aimed at fostering a broad tolerance for all of man's diversity, in his races, religions and cultures. They intentionally expose readers to a variety of religious beliefs, without attempting to suggest that one is better than another." To illustrate their interpretation of the texts, plaintiffs selected materials from the readers. They pointed to the poem based on an Hindu fable of six blind men who each feel a different portion of an elephant and reach different conclusions about what the whole animal must be like on the basis of their own limited experience. The court agreed that the obvious conclusion of the poem was that "each religion described God from its own limited vantage point, based on incomplete revelation, and that all are only partly right and partly wrong." The plaintiffs also pointed to a passage from *The Diary of Anne Frank* that was included in the readers. In this passage Anne says to Peter van Daan that she wished he had a religion, but Peter says "No thanks! Not me!" and interrupts and walks away when Anne tries to persuade him. The court agreed that this passage also supported the plaintiffs' contention that the textbooks as a whole "tend to instill in the readers a tolerance for man's diversity."

What the district court failed to mention in its opinion was that the plaintiffs had also introduced an essay written by a senior vice president of the publisher that commented that "school reading programs involve more than simply the teaching of reading skills but also the shaping of student values."[89] The essay went on to contrast the value of the old books and those of the new Holt books. The former books "'emphasized a Judeo-Christian value system in a most direct way,' while the latter emphasized the need for students 'to have a sense of themselves as participants in a national and world community; to understand and to be mindful of the richness of our diversity.'" The plaintiffs argued that these statements showed that Holt rejected the traditional Judeo-Christian values in favor of contrary values. The plaintiffs further supported this claim by showing that the books discussed, without disapproval, Chinese, Islamic, and Buddhist philosophy. The students were so opposed to these readers that they refused on religious grounds to read the Holt series or to attend classes in which the series was used—a refusal that twice led to their suspension from school for periods of three and ten days. The rigorous enforcement of the requirement that they not be permitted to use an alternative reader, an option that in the course of the controversy had at one time been made available to the plaintiffs, led to many of the students withdrawing from the public schools and enrolling in private Christian schools.[90]

Nevertheless, the federal district court concluded that nothing in the books could be considered "a violation of the plaintiff's constitutional rights." The first amendment, said the court, "does not guarantee that nothing offensive to any religion will be taught in the schools."[91]

> What is guaranteed is that the state schools will be neutral on the subject, neither advocating a particular religious belief or expressing hostility to any or all religions. From what this Court has read, it would appear that the Holt Basic Readings carefully adopt this constitutionally mandated neutrality. Moreover, they are well calculated to equip today's children to face our increasingly complex and diverse society with sophistication and tolerance.[92]

The federal district court thus dismissed the case without trial. The plaintiffs appealed and the Sixth Circuit reversed and remanded the case for trial.[93] The Sixth Circuit said a trial was needed on several issues of contested fact: (1) the sincerity of the belief of the plaintiffs; (2) the question of whether the Holt books offended their beliefs; and (3) the issue of whether excusing these students from using the Holt books would frustrate the state's interest in teaching reading.

The federal district court opinion, issued following the trial, characterized the case before it as follows:

This action juxtaposes two of our most essential constitutional liberties—the right of free exercise of religion and the right to be free from a religion established by the state. Moreover, it implicates an important state interest in the education of our children. The education of our citizens is essential to prepare them for effective and intelligent participation in our political system and is essential to the preservation of our freedom and independence.[94]

With little difficulty the court went on to conclude that the plaintiffs had met their burden of proof, i.e., it was clear that (1) their's was a religious claim, (2) that it was sincerely held, and that (3) the readers and the school board's policy that the plaintiffs must use Holt readers or face exclusion from the public schools had an impact on the plaintiffs' right to the free exercise of their religion.[95] The court then turned to the question of whether the school board could justify its policy of uniform use of the Holt reading series as the least restrictive means of achieving some compelling state interest. At this point the federal district court's opinion took a subtle but crucial tack. The court said that it "must decide whether the state can achieve literacy and good citizenship for all students without forcing them to read the Holt series."[96] The outcome of the case now rested on how the court defined the terms "literacy and good citizenship." The definition the court *implicitly* adopted was the most narrow, i.e., the compelling interest of the school was merely to teach students the technical skill of recognizing written words (literacy) and the duty to obey the law (good citizenship). Given this implicit understanding of the state's interests, the court had no difficulty in concluding that these interests could be served by alternative sets of reading materials.[97] The court also concluded that the plaintiffs could be accommodated without materially and substantially disrupting the educational process. The court noted that at one point in the conflict these plaintiffs had in fact been provided with an alternative reading series for a period of weeks without any detriment. (The court ultimately ordered that the plaintiffs be permitted to opt out of the school's reading program by withdrawing to a study hall or library during the reading period and that parents then would be obligated by the state's compulsory education law to provide their children with their own reading program. The children, noted the court, could then be tested with the standardized achievement tests used by the state.[98]) Finally, the court concluded that it was unlikely that a decision in favor of the plaintiffs would open the floodgates to a barrage of similar requests and that chaos would result in the schools of Tennessee. But the court's reasons for this conclusion seem off the mark. First, the court noted that this kind of free exercise claim had never been raised before.[99] (Hardly a convincing argument that there will not now be a spate of such requests in the future given the outcome of this case.) Second, the court said that "although there are a variety of sects in and around Hawkins County, the area is relatively homogeneous from a religious standpoint."[100] (It is hard to see how the area can both have a variety of sects and homogeneity.

Whatever the case, the situation seems ripe for many more requests for exemptions to surface.) Then, in a statement that may make even less sense given what it just said about the religious background of the county, the court said, "Accommodating the beliefs of the small group of students involved in this case probably would not wreak havoc in the school system by initiating a barrage of requests for alternative materials."[101] But, while the court's reason for granting the plaintiffs' request was administratively feasible are weak, the court may nevertheless be correct. The remedy the court in fact ordered in this case would appear to be one that would be easily administered with regard to many hundreds, even thousands, of pupils.

As indicated, crucial to the court's decision was its definition of the state's goals. Clearly, if the state's goals are as narrowly defined as the court implicitly defined them, then alternative methods of instruction would be appropriate to the realization of those goals. But if the state's goals were defined differently, then it is far from clear that the state's interests could be achieved by simply letting the parents substitute their religiously-oriented reading texts for the more cosmopolitan and catholic texts of the public schools. For example, if the state's goals are understood to include a broad introduction to alternative cultures and lifestyles, to different religions, and to include the necessity of encouraging children to approach alternative religions and lifestyles with respect and tolerance, then the grant of the exemption might be seen as frustrating the state's interests. But now we encounter two additional issues. Is the state's goal in cultivating tolerance and respect for alternative viewpoints a "compelling" state interest? On the one hand, it could be argued that tolerance and mutual respect are essential civic virtues in a pluralistic democracy. On the other hand, one could claim that the state has no legitimate interest in attempting to undermine the parents' effort to get their children to accept parental religious views. But even assuming the state interest is compelling (as discussed in §§1.4-1.7), parents have a constitutional right to send their children to private schools, which must be left free to an important extent to provide their own religiously-based educational program. If parents may totally substitute private religious schools for public schools, may they not be allowed to substitute private instruction for selected portions of the public school curriculum? The answer to that question would seem to hinge on the administrative feasibility of such an arrangement—an arrangement that approaches a "shared time" arrangement long advocated by various religious groups. (see, §3.2.)

5.7. OVERVIEW—RELIGION IN THE SCHOOLS

American courts have walked a thin line in dealing with religion in the public schools. The courts have used the establishment clause as a sword to stop the deeply religious from introducing overtly religious activities in the public schools, such as devotional prayer sessions or the teaching of scientific creationism.[102] At the same time the courts have been unwilling to let the deeply religious use of that same clause as a sword to reshape the public school curriculum for themselves *and other noncomplaining parents and their children.*[103] With the notable exception of the *Mozert* decisions, the courts have not been generous in granting the deeply religious exemptions from courses and materials they find offensive. Thus, theistic (and presumably atheistic) materials are excluded (unless the object of "objective study") while nontheistic materials (even if arguably religious under a broad definition of religion) may remain in the program, may not be excluded to accommodate those with religious objections (especially theistic religious objections), and to an important extent may be required reading even for those with objections rooted in theistic beliefs. (The major exception to this proposition is the decision of a federal district court judge ordering the removal from Alabama public schools of 44 textbooks on the grounds that, because they omit references to religious influences in American history, they establish the religion of "secular humanism. [See, chapter 10.]) Hence, theistic beliefs may not directly shape the public school program, whereas other beliefs, which under a broad definition of religion can be viewed as religious, may. The American notion of neutrality means that public schools may not directly promote theistic beliefs or ovetly attack them: theistic beliefs are to be left alone. Nontheistic beliefs may, however, be promoted and attacked. (More about this later in §5.8.) Furthermore, courses and materials that might indirectly promote theistic beliefs, e.g., Christmas celebrations and courses in the Bible, will probably get a closer scrutiny in the courts than materials that might indirectly undermine theistic beliefs, e.g., promotion of tolerance and the scientific theory of knowledge, with its implied opposition to authority and revelation. Perhaps the balance that has been struck can be summarized as nontheism yes, overt theism and atheism, no. (See chapter 10.)

5.8. POLITICAL SOCIALIZATION

Though the Supreme Court has actively worked to keep theistic principles from shaping the public school program, its role in *directly* constraining efforts at political socialization has been much more modest. (The judiciary's *indirect* influence on the efforts of public schools to socialize students politically has been more extensive.)[104] In fact, only two Supreme Court opinions directly address political socialization in the schools: one dealing with the right of students to abstain from participating in a flag-salute ceremony,[105] and the other dealing with the authority of the school board to remove books from the school library.[106] These opinions are of interest not only because of what they tell us are the limits on governmental efforts to inculcate children in community values, but also because of the many issues left unresolved—issues touching on the proper relationship between government's claimed interest in inculcating students and the students' interest in freedom of conscience, belief, thought, and speech.[107] Specifically, the issues not settled include the following: What right(s), if any, do students have that may serve to limit the authority of the state and school boards to inculcate the youth in community values? What are the interests of the state in inculcating the youth, and what evidence supports the state's claim for the efficacy and necessity of these efforts? To the extent students have rights to be protected, what method(s) is (are) the most effective and appropriate for the judiciary to use—direct limits on state authority or indirect methods? Is there room for compromise here? For example, perhaps the state should be relatively free to inculcate a certain limited set of values, e.g., values related to maintaining democracy. Or do logic and other considerations suggest the state should be either left virtually free of constraints or heavily constrained by direct limitations? Is governmental inculcation of youth consistent with the notion that in a democracy it is public opinion that should control government, not government public opinion?

The necessary starting point for understanding the Supreme Court's position on the limits the Constitution imposes on governmental efforts to inculcate youth must begin with an attempt to understand the Supreme Court's position with regard to recognizing the student's interest in freedom of belief, conscience, and thought. The Court's clearest declaration of such an interest has come in the context of the establishment clause case, *Wallace v. Jaffree,*[108] where the Court identified "the individual's freedom of conscience" and "freedom of mind" as central to *all* the clauses of the first amendment. Because this declaration of the student's interests came in the context of an establishment clause case, however, we can't be sure a majority of the court would recognize such a right as protecting students against nonreligious socialization. Indeed the history of the Court's activity in this area is, to this point, ambiguous. In *Meyer v. Nebraska*[109] and *Pierce v. Society of Sisters,*[110] while protecting the rights of parents and children to attend private schools that were subject to only reasonable state regulations, the Court stressed the continuing power of the state to control the curriculum of the public schools and to make certain that "studies plainly essential to good citizenship . . . be taught, and that nothing be taught which is manifestly inimical to the public welfare."[111]

Having opened the door to extensive socialization of pupils who continued to attend the public schools, the Court took an important step in closing the door part way in *West Virginia State Board of Education v. Barnette.*[112] The case arose when students who were Jehovah's Witnesses brought suit to restrain enforcement of laws and regulations that required all students on pain of expulsion to participate in a flag-salute ceremony in which the Pledge of Allegiance was said. Though they based their opposition to the ceremony on the grounds that it was inconsistent with their religious beliefs, the Supreme Court decided the case not as a free exercise of religion case, but as a first-amendment free speech (or freedom not to speak) case. While permitting the state to continue to offer a flag-salute ceremony (compare this result to the prayer cases in which no prayer ceremony was allowed to continue), the Court required that it be offered on a voluntary basis. An extensive quotation from the Court best captures the reasons for its conclusion:

> The Fourteenth Amendment, as now applied to the States, protects the citizen against the State itself and all of its creatures—Boards of Education not excepted. These have, of course, important, delicate, and highly discretionary functions, but none that they may not perform within the limits of the Bill of Rights. That they are educating the young for citizenship is reason for scrupulous protection of constitutional freedoms of the individual, if we are not to strangle the free mind at its source and teach youth to discount important principles of our government as mere platitudes.[113]

> Struggles to coerce conformity of sentiment in support of some end though essential to their time and country have been waged by many good as well as by evil men. Nationalism is a relatively recent phenomenon but at other times and places the ends have been racial or territorial security, support of a dynasty or regime, and particular plans for saving souls. As first and moderate methods to attain unity have failed, those bent on its accomplishment must resort to an ever-increasing severity. As governmental pressure toward unity becomes greater, so strife becomes more bitter as to whose unity it shall be. Probably no deeper division of our people could proceed from any provocation than from finding it necessary to choose what doctrine and whose program public educational facilities shall compel youth to unite in embracing.[114]

> If there is any fixed star in our constitutional constellation, it is that no official, high or petty, can prescribe what shall be orthodox or force citizens to confess by word or act their faith therein. If there are any circumstances which permit an exception, they do not now occur to us.

> We think the action of the local authorities in compelling the flag salute and pledge transcends constitutional limitations on their power and invades the sphere of intellect and spirit which it is the purpose of the First Amendment to our Constitution to reserve from all official control.[115]

Although these passages strongly advance the idea of constitutional protection of the student's interest in freedom of belief, more so than in *Meyer* and *Pierce,* other passages in *Barnette* signal a retreat from full protection.

> [T]he State may "require teaching by instruction and study of all in our history and in the structure and organization of our government, including the guarantees of civil liberty, which tend to inspire patriotism and love of country." Here, however, we are dealing with a compulsion of students to declare a belief. They are not merely made acquainted with the flag salute so that they may be informed as to what it is or even what it means. The issue here is whether this slow and easily neglected route to aroused loyalties constitutionally may be short-cut by substituting a compulsory salute or slogan.[116]

National unity as an end which officials may foster by persuasion and example is not in question.[117]

These passages suggest that states and school boards may seek to inculcate officially approved beliefs so long as the method of doing so is not analogous to requiring the uttering of a pledge, salute, or slogan. In short, *Barnette* leaves us with an important ambiguity: Did the students win in this case, (1) because any effort by public schools (whether through coercion or persuasion) to produce "uniformity of sentiment" is impermissible as an infringement of the right of freedom of mind; (2) because this method of trying to produce "uniformity of sentiment" was improperly coercive; (3) because students have a right not to participate in political demonstrations, even a right of nonassociation;[118] or simply (4) because students have a right not to be made to say things, spread an ideological message, with which they may disagree and make it seem as if they agree with that message?[119]

The first and second interpretations of *Barnette* especially have important implications for the public school curriculum. The first interpretation would obviously mean public schools would not constitutionally be allowed intentionally to seek to promote or foster community values—at a minimum schools would be required to present students with a range of alternative positions and then let the students arrive at their own conclusions. Even the second interpretation could have far-reaching consequences. It may be unconstitutional for a course to use examinations with questions that expect the students to answer "true" to the statement that the United States provides more equality of opportunity than any other country, or that the free enterprise system is the system that best promotes prosperity and liberty.[120]

Since *Barnette,* the one point that seems to have emerged with clarity is that the first interpretation is, at least today, not embraced by any member of the Supreme Court. Every member of the Court has embraced the view that the public schools are vitally important for "inculcating fundamental values necessary for the maintenance of a democratic political system."[121] Those values that may be inculcated appear to include not just traditional political values, but also traditional social and moral values. The point on which the Court is deeply fragmented, however, is the proper accommodation between the school's authority to inculcate and the right of the students to freedom of mind and conscience. The differences of opinion among the justices on this point are reflected in *Pico.*

The story behind *Pico* begins when three school board members attended a conference in September, 1975, sponsored by a politically conservative organization, at which they were given a list of books and excerpts from the books that were deemed to be objectionable and not proper reading material for students. The board later determined that their own libraries contained ten of the books and that one of the listed books was used in a twelfth-grade literature course. In February, 1976, the board unofficially directed that the listed books be removed from the libraries. Considerable publicity was given to this directive and the board defended its action in a press release in which it characterized the books as "anti-American, anti-Christian, anti-Semitic, and just plain filthy." The press release also went on to proclaim that "It is our duty, or moral obligation, to protect the children in our schools from this moral danger as surely as from physical and medical dangers." Following the objection of the superintendent to the procedures followed by the board, the board appointed a book review committee, consisting of parents and members of the school staff, to recommend whether the books were to be retained. The committee's report, which recommended that some but not all of the books be retained, was rejected by the board that decided that only one book should be returned to the shelves without restrictions. No reasons were given by the board for rejection of the recommendations of the committee. Plaintiffs brought suit, charging the board had ordered the removal of the books because particular passages in the books offended their social, political, and moral tastes and not because the books as a whole lacked educational value.

For a fragmented *plurality*, Justice Brennan announced the judgment of the Court, sending the case back to the lower court for a trial to determine the purposes of the board in removing the books.[122] (The trial was never held as the board ultimately agreed to place all the books back on the shelves without restriction.) Justice Brennan based this order on the rule that if the removal of books from a school library is motivated by an intent to suppress or deny access to ideas, the removal is impermissible. He may also have hinted that removal of a book would be permissible if prompted by the "pervasive vulgarity" of a book, by its "educational unsuitability," its "bad taste," "irrelevance," or "inappropriateness" for the student's age and grade level. In suggesting a distinction between permissible and impermissible motives, Justice Brennan did not elaborate on how the courts were to ascertain the difference between an intent to suppress ideas and an intent to remove books because they were, for instance, educationally unsuitable. These rules were an outgrowth of Justice Brennan's attempt to accommodate the board's authority to inculcate community values and a student's right to receive ideas—a right that Justice Brennan recognized as a necessary predicate for the recipient's meaningful exercise of his own right of free speech. This accommodation, Justice Brennan stressed, was being struck here only insofar as the school library was concerned, not the classroom.[123] Thus, Justice Brennan apparently would not apply the rules noted above to school board decisions regarding materials in the classroom.

Because a majority of five did not agree on the reasons for sending the case back to trial, we today have no agreed-upon constitutional doctrine specifying what limits, if any, school boards must work within when removing books from their libraries, much less in regard to what limits must guide their selection of books for purchase for the library and their control of the classroom curriculum.

Justice Brennan's opinion is subject to a number of attacks from different perspectives. The conservative perspective, perhaps best reflected by *Pico* dissenters, takes the position that since school boards have the authority to inculcate youth in community values, they must be left free from judicial censors to make decisions concerning the appropriateness of the books in the library and curriculum.[124] If a right of students to receive ideas were to be recognized, it would be the students who would affirmatively control the content of the school program.

Justice Blackmun offers a different kind of criticism. He agrees with Justice Brennan that the central problem is accommodating, on the one hand, the school board's authority to inculcate and, on the other hand, the first amendment. However, he rejects the notion of a right to receive ideas and stresses that the principle—which he would apply to both the library and the classroom—is that the first amendment prohibits discrimination between ideas. "[T]he State may not act to deny access to an idea simply because state officials disapprove of that idea for partisan or political reasons."[125] He also suggests that he would allow the removal of books if they merely contained "offensive language," or because the ideas advanced were "manifestly inimical to the public welfare."

An elaboration and variation of the Blackmun approach has been offered by one commentator. Under this approach the accommodation between the state interest and the first amendment interests of the students is struck by recognizing that both interests "are aspects of the same social interest in approximating an ideal of communal self-government."[126] Government thus may inculcate insofar as that effort is directed toward promoting the "community's continued capacity to govern itself through critical and independent intellectual inquiry, public debate, and participation in elections." However, the inculcation effort goes too far if it is done "for the purpose of influencing the outcomes of future public debates." The author recognizes that drawing the distinction between proper and improper inculcation would be extremely difficult at best, and thus suggests that the best way to advance the ideal of self-government is not through direct limits on the school boards, but by direct methods such as protecting the free-speech rights of students and teachers to bring alternative ideas into the school. In this way the boards are left free to indoctrinate, but students will be exposed to diverse ideas that will encourage critical and independent thought. In addition the author embraces Justice Blackmun's no-discrimination principle with a twist—the board may discriminate against ideas if it serves to advance the ideal of preparing students for their roles as citizens in a system of self-government.

Finally, all the justices, including Justices Brennan and Blackmun, have been criticized for undervaluing the importance to a democracy that government not attempt to control the beliefs of the young and overstating, without any solid evidence, the necessity for governmental efforts to inculcate the young.[127] Justice Brennan undervalues the student's interest in freedom of belief by seemingly exempting the board's control of the classroom from the limitation of the first amendment. Justice Blackmun also undervalues this student interest by suggesting boards may remove books that contain ideas he says are "manifestly inimical to the public welfare." All the justices overvalue the governmental interest in inculcation. A better approach would be to recognize the student's strong interest in freedom of mind and conscience—an interest that is also an aspect of the social interest in democracy—and to impose upon boards a requirement that the classroom be a marketplace of ideas. This ideal is itself best attained if schools were required to follow a "principle of fairness": "(1) When a school provides instruction on matters of a political or moral nature, it must adequately and objectively cover the issues explicitly and implicitly touched upon by the materials; (2) The coverage must be fair in that it accurately and objectively reflects the opposing view on the issues; and (3) The instruction must devote reasonable attention to the major opposing views."[128]

An alternative to the principle of fairness that also would serve to protect the students' interest in freedom of belief would be the principle embraced by several lower courts, namely, that whatever it is the board does in controlling the curriculum, it may not "impose a pall of orthodoxy" upon the students, faculty, and the school.[129]

We turn now to a number of other cases. All the justices agreed that school boards are not powerless with regard to screening materials for vulgarity. There were, however, important differences among the justices regarding the scope of the board's power. While Justice Brennan suggested that only the "pervasively vulgar" book was subject to board control, Justice Blackmun would permit the board to remove books with "offensive" language. It appears that both justices have staked out a position that rests on an educationally unsound basis. Justice Blackmun's approach too easily opens the door to attacks upon a broad range of literature, including Shakespeare and Joyce, and Justice Brennan's position may be overly protective of books that many would consider inappropriate for high school students, e.g., D. H. Lawrence's *Lady Chatterley's Lover.*

Books may be challenged not only because of their vulgarity, but also on the grounds that they adversely reflect a particular race. This enormously complex question[130] has arisen for discussion in only one case. In *Lowen v. Turnispeed*[131] a state textbook-rating committee, appointed by the governor and the state superintendent of education of Mississippi, approved a book entitled *Your Mississippi* for purchase and use in the public schools, but refused to rate another book, *Mississippi: Conflict and Change,* even though the committee had the authority to approve up to five texts. The authors and publishers of the rejected book, together with parents, students, and local officials, charged that the single book approved for use deprecated black Mississippians and championed white supremacy. They charged the rating committee acted for racial reasons. The district court agreed the rating process had been racially motivated. For ten years the rating committee had given its approval to the single text. The court noted the whole state system for approving books was part of a legislative scheme to assure that controversial materials would be eliminated from the school curricula. The committee itself had split along racial lines, with five white members refusing to even rate the rejected book while the two black members supported its adoption. Two of the white members of the committee had said the rejected book was "too racially oriented," and another argued that it "did not present a true picture of the history of Mississippi." The fact that the rejected book had received favorable reviews also contributed to the court's finding of racial bias. The court avoided the more controversial and legally complex route of barring the use of *Your Mississippi* by ordering that both books were to be eligible for consideration for use by local school districts.

Another claim that may be raised in book selection and removal cases is that those doing the selection violated procedural due-process requirements. This claim was also raised in the *Lowen* case, and the court concluded that the procedure for rating books was unconstitutional because Mississippi law did not provide for review of the rating committee's decision "without giving those adversely affected by it a voice in the matter."[132] This is an unusual decision since government is not normally required to hold a hearing in deciding to award a contract.

Courts have imposed other procedural due-process requirements on school boards. One court said books could only be removed from a library in light of preestablished, nonvague standards.[133] Another court concluded that the due process clause was violated when a board failed to follow its own procedures for the removal of books from use in the schools.[134]

Attention should be drawn to the fact that book-selection decisions may be challenged on the basis of state statutes that, for example, prohibit the use of materials that reflect adversely on persons because of their race, sex, color, creed, national origin, or ancestry.[135]

The efforts of school officials to control the school program have extended beyond the classroom and library to the school's auditorium and school newspaper. The authority of school officials to extend control to these areas is importantly conditioned by whether or not the activity in question is "extra-curricular" or an extension of and part of the school's own program. Extracurricular activities are not, according to the courts, subject to the same degree of control as the classroom because these activities are the student's own, and control directly implicates the student's right to freedom of speech. We can see the distinction in two cases in which school officials ordered the canceling of stage productions. (The newspaper cases are discussed in §6.8.) In *Seyfried v. Walton* the decision of school officials to cancel production of the musical *Pippin* was upheld because the production was an integral part of the school's educational program.[136] The decision to cancel was viewed as if the board had simply decided not to purchase a particular book. In *Bowman v. Bethel-Tate Board of Education*, the decision to cancel the entertainment planned by third graders for the final PTA (Parent-Teachers Association) meeting of the year was struck down.[137] The board in this case disagreed with the ideas contained in the play chosen for production—*Sorcerer*—and the court, relying on *Pico* and *Tinker*,[138] concluded that the board could not simply halt production of an extracurricular activity because of disagreement with the content of the play. The court maintained that the production in this case was an extracurricular activity because participation was completely voluntary, no letter grade was given, and no sanction imposed for nonparticipants.

5.9. SOCIALIZATION INTO TRADITIONAL GENDER ROLES

For most of their history the public schools have been intimately involved in defining and reinforcing the traditional gender roles. While female students were required to take courses in home economics, their male colleagues were required to take courses in wood and metal working. While male students were offered a full range of athletic opportunities, the women, who were presumed to be either too fragile or insufficiently interested, were offered a more modest range of opportunities.[139] Today most such practices are violations of either or both the equal protection clause of the fourteenth amendment and Title IX of the Education Amendments of 1972 Act (usually simply called Title IX).[140] In addition, sixteen states have now included an equal rights amendment—a prohibition against discrimination on the basis of sex—in their constitutions.[141] Students may also be protected by state civil-rights laws.[142]

We may begin the examination of the impact of these new legal developments by turning first to the regular school program. With limited exceptions, the regulations implementing Title IX prohibit excluding a girl or boy from a class because of sex or offering separate courses for girls and boys.[143] School counselors may not steer girls and boys into courses thought to be appropriate for their gender or provide job counseling that rests on stereotypic notions of what work is suitable for the two genders. In physical education schools may group students by physical ability and separate girls and boys for participation in contact sports such as football, basketball, and wrestling. Sex education courses may be taught to separate groups of boys and girls, and choruses selected on the basis of vocal range may be predominantly of one sex. Even textbooks that may depict women in traditional female roles are not forbidden by Title IX regulations, because the regulations specifically exempt textbooks from coverage of Title IX.[144]

We turn now to the extracurricular athletic program. The regulations permit schools to sponsor separate teams when team selection is based on competitive skill or the activity is a contact sport. Hence, if the school has only one team in a noncontact sport, girls must be allowed to try out for it. A number of courts have recognized a constitutional right on the part of girls to try out for all-male teams in noncontact sports, especially when a girls' team is not available.[145] When a girls' team is available, however, some courts have upheld the "separate but equal" principle in the face of requests by females to be permitted to try out for a place on the boys' team.[146] The constitutionality of these later decisions, as well as of the Title IX regulations that embrace the same principle, is subject to serious question.[147]

Shifting to contact sports, a surprising number of courts, but not all, have said girls may try out for a place on a boys' athletic team in a contact sport.[148] However, Justice Stevens, acting on a request to lift the stay of an opinion pending appeal, said that, in language that could apply to contact and non-contact sports alike, he would not find a rule excluding girls from boys' teams unconstitutional.[149] Continuing, he said, "It seems to me that there can be little question about the validity of the classification in most of its normal applications. Without a gender-based classification in competitive contact sports, there would be substantial risk that boys would dominate the girls' programs and deny them an equal opportunity to compete in interscholastic events."[150] What Justice Stevens failed to consider was whether a rule permitting girls to try out for the boys' team, but denying boys the opportunity to try out for girls' teams, might be the constitutionally required rule. This rule, even more than Justice Steven's preferred approach, would protect the girls' athletic opportunities. Justice Stevens's approach makes especially little sense when a girl is prohibited from trying out for a boys' team in a noncontact sport and there is no girls' team available.

In several states, judges have concluded that their state's equal rights amendment prohibited restrictions on girls' participation on boys' teams, even in contact sports.[151]

The courts have reached different conclusions regarding the permissibility of a policy of requiring girls to play basketball under a set of rules different from those used by the boys.[152] The correctness of those decisions upholding the practice is subject to serious doubt. There would appear to be no legitimate and/or important goal to be achieved by such a policy. There is no basis for believing that women are physically incapable of playing basketball under the same rules as men.

Boys have achieved mixed results when they have sought from the courts an order to enable them to try out for a girls' team.[153] When the boys lose these cases, the prevailing theory has held that excluding boys is a permissible means to assure equal athletic competition for girls.

We turn now to the broader question of the operation of an entire athletic program. Title IX regulations mandate "equal athletic opportunities" for both sexes and suggest a variety of indicia for determining whether a school's athletic program has met this mandate.[154] Though the indicia include such matters as the comparability of facilities and the availability of athletic scholarships, the regulations do not require that equal amounts of money be spent on men and women's athletics. It is not clear how the courts would rule on a constitutional challenge to the failure of a school to spend equal amounts of money per student on the male and female athletic programs.

A number of other prohibitions in the regulations enforcing Title IX should be made note of here. The regulations specifically prohibit subjecting boys and girls to different rules of behavior and of appearance. Of particular importance to colleges and universities is the prohibiton against subjecting women and men to different parietal rules. Whether different parietal rules for males and females would be struck down by the current Supreme Court under the equal protection clause is not certain.[155]

As important as Title IX has been for changing school policies, especially in the field of athletics, that era may be coming to a close. In *Grove City College v. Bell* the Supreme Court held that Title IX applies only to the specific program within a school district, college, or university receiving federal financial assistance.[156] Hence, even though the chemistry department may be the recipient of federal assistance, the athletic program may not be subject to the requirements of Title IX if it receives no direct federal assistance. The full implications of this opinion are underscored by the facts. The case arose when Grove City College insisted it was not a recipient of federal financial assistance, hence subject to Title IX, merely because students attending the school themselves received federal financial assistance. The Supreme Court disagreed, holding Title IX did apply, but that only Grove City College's financial assistance program would be deemed to be the "program" receiving federal financial assistance. Thus, the Court rejected the claim that aid to students generally, or aid to one part of the college, provided benefits throughout the college, thereby making the whole college a beneficiary. The Court said "it would be difficult, if not impossible to determine which programs or activities derive such indirect benefits," hence only the program directly affected by the indirect aid was subject to Title IX. As for the future, the Department of Education may only demand in a situation like Grove City College an assurance of compliance from the financial aid program, and individual suits under Title IX against, for example, the athletic department, may be dismissed without a hearing on the merits. Unless Congress amends Title IX so as to make it applicable to an entire institution if one portion of the institution receives financial assistance, the usefulness of Title IX as a tool for extensive reform may have come to an end.

The legal developments reviewed in this section were intended to change the school's role in defining and reinforcing traditional gender roles. Today the public schools may no longer seek to enforce those traditional roles through rules and polices that exclude students from courses or limit their athletic opportunities. Furthermore, it appears that most of these new requirements would not merely be viewed by the Supreme Court as constitutionally permissible, but would in fact be deemed to be constitutionally required. If this is true, we must ask whether this conclusion is consistent with the view held by all the justices that the public schools may establish and apply their curriculum in such a way as to transmit community values.[157] It would seem that if the inculcation of community values is the primary function of public schools, and if those community values include acceptance of traditional gender roles, schools should have the discretion to adopt those means most suitable for encouraging socialization into those roles. Requirements that male students take shop and female students take home economics would seem to be but a logical part of the school program. We, in short, may be confronted with an inconsistency.

Perhaps a court that embraced both the principle that public schools may transmit community values and the rule that public schools may not assign male and female students to different classes would seek refuge in the following distinction. Those community values that may be the focus of the curriculum are only those that have to do with the maintenance of the political community, i.e., the values of patriotism, the duty to obey the law, tolerance. Those values that are arguably more private and not directly related to the maintenance of the polity may not be the basis for the imposition of rules and requirements that limit the liberty of students to seek their own preferred life-style.

Undoubtedly those who strongly believe in traditional gender roles would respond that these roles are essential for the maintenance of the family, and that the survival of the traditional family is of fundamental importance for maintenance of the social fabric and the polity. This is a powerful argument, but it has at least one central weakness, namely, it is far from clear that continued viability of the family depends upon males and females adhering to traditional gender roles. Thus, a school policy that embraces the need to limit the freedom of students to seek their own life-styles rests on a set of questionable assumptions.

Of course, one can seek in another way to reconcile the seeming inconsistency between the principle of indoctrination of community values and the rule of no gender discrimination. The assumption that the public schools may properly seek to transmit community values may itself be weakened or lifted. Resolving the inconsistency in this way may appear to be a radical move, but it does have its supporters.[158]

5.10. PREGNANCY, MARRIAGE, AND GROOMING

School boards have been given general authority by state legislatures to issue rules and regulations controlling the behavior of their pupils and have used this authority to issue rules governing student behavior in order to serve two general purposes: (1) in order to educate pupils and (2) to protect other students or the physical plant from harm—physical danger, disease, and even moral harm.[159] In chapter 8 we shall examine these rules, again emphasizing the second function these rules are intended to serve. Here the emphasis is upon those rules insofar as they are intended to serve the purpose of educating or socializing pupils.

As has been repeatedly noted throughout this chapter many see as a primary function of the public schools the enculturation of pupils in community values. As we have also seen, the logical extension of this principle can produce many controversial policies. Perhaps no policies have been more controversial during the past several years than those designed to send the message that the primary function of schooling is to learn English, math, science, etc. Thus, the Texas "no pass, no play" statute was widely attacked and challenged in court as a denial of equal protection and substantive due process.[160] The Supreme Court of Texas, reversing a lower court's judgment that the law was unconstitutional, concluded that the rule would provide an incentive to students to maintain a minimum level of performance in their classes, and that the rule was "rationally related to the legitimate state interest in providing a quality education to Texas' public school students."

Over the years schools have also attempted to encourage students to concentrate upon their studies by establishing policies that penalized teenage marriage. The modern trend in the decisions is to bar school boards from excluding from school students who marry.[161] Excluding married students from participation in extracurricular activities has met a more favorable reception in the courts.[162] Those decisions that uphold the exclusion of married students, even from extracurricular activities, are subject to serious question, given the United States Supreme Court's view that marriage is a "fundamental right" and restrictions on the right to marry may only be imposed if necessary to achieve a compelling state interest.[163] Given this approach, it is unlikely the Supreme Court would accept as justifications for excluding married students arguments such as the following: the rules are needed to make the married student concentrate on his or her studies; they are needed to discourage teenage marriage; the rules are needed to get the married teenager to spend time with his or her family; and that they are needed to protect the school against moral and disciplinary problems married students may create in school.[164] In any event, Title IX regulations prohibit rules concerning marriage that treat students differently on the basis of gender. As noted earlier, the usefulness of Title IX for attacking these problems has been sharply curtailed by the Court's decision in *Grove City College*.[165]

Rules excluding pregnant students from school were also once a prominent feature of school codes. Constitutional challenges to the exclusion of unwed mothers from the regular school program have generally been successful.[166] In addition, Title IX regulations prohibit the exclusion of pregnant students or students who have had an abortion.[167] Special schools or educational programs may be offered pregnant students, but their participation must be wholly voluntary. The pregnant student must also be allowed to take a leave of absence for as long as her physician deems medically necessary.

As for grooming rules, an issue that came into prominence in the 1960s during the period of student rebellion against the mores of conventional society,[168] the response of the judiciary has been decidedly mixed, with the federal circuit courts badly split over whether hairstyle rules are an impermissible invasion of the student's interest in liberty.[169] It should be noted that most of these cases were decided prior to the Supreme Court's decision in *Kelly v.*

Johnson[170] in which the Court upheld a hair-length regulation of a police department. The Court assumed for purposes of argument that the claimant did have a liberty interest in matters of personal appearance but went on to conclude that the regulation could be found unconstitutional if it were not rationally related to a legitimate purpose. Using this test, the Court concluded the regulation was rationally related to the legitimate purposes of building *esprit des corps* and making police officers readily recognizable to members of the public. The Court's adoption of the rational-basis test suggests that it would have no difficulty in upholding student hair-code rules on the grounds that these rules were rationally related to, for example, the purpose of minimizing distractions. If these rules draw sharp distinctions between male and female students, e.g., requiring male students to sport a "buzz" or "crewcut," it is less clear what the Court would do since such a rule could be simply reviewed under the lenient rational-basis test, or the tougher middle-level test used in gender discrimination cases.[171] Clearly, the more strongly the Court embraces the view that public schools may enculturate students in community values, the less likely a constitutional challenge to the rules would be successful. Note, however, that Title IX regulations prohibit discrimination in the application of rules of appearance.

Students seeking to challenge school hair codes do have available several other avenues of attack. Assuming Title IX applies to the program the student is in, Title IX's prohibition against discrimination in the application of rules of appearance may be useful.[172] The statutory authority of the district to issue a hair code may also be challenged.[173]

We turn now to dress codes. Judicial view as to the constitutionality of these regulations has also diverged.[174] Title IX regulations prohibit different dress-code rules for male and female students. However, it is far from clear whether the equal protection or due process clauses would be interpreted by the Supreme Court to limit school board authority to control student dress. Chances are that, as to nondiscriminatory rules, only the rational-basis standard of review would be used by the Court to decide these challenges. Under that standard it would not be difficult for the Court to defer to the school's judgment that these codes are needed to serve the school's purposes of enculturating the students in standards of good grooming and to minimize distractions and disruption.[175] However, if the rules are discriminatory, e.g., they prohibit female students from wearing pants, then the rules may be examined pursuant to the middle-level test. Because it is difficult to conceive of a purpose those rules would serve that today's Court would agree was "important," application of that test would most likely result in a decision against the rule. Again, the more strongly the justices believe school officials may enculturate students in community values, the more likely it is such a no-pant rulewould be upheld.

NOTES

1. For a critical examination of the evidence in support of this position see Tyll van Geel, "The Search for Constitutional Limits on Governmental Authority to Inculcate Youth," *Texas Law Review* 62 (1983): 197.

2. Id.; Stephen Arons and Charles Lawrence III, "The Manipulation of Consciousness: A First Amendment Critique of Schooling," *Harvard Civil Rights, Civil Liberties Law Review* 15 (1980): 309.

3. Mark G. Yudof, David L. Kirp, Tyll van Geel, and Betsy Levin, *Educational Policy and the Law*, 2d ed. (Berkeley, Calif.: McCutchan Publishing Corporation, 1982), 123.

4. Cf., Tyll van Geel, "The Search for Constitutional Limits on Governmental Authority to Inculcate Youth," *supra* note 1, and Mark G. Yudof, "When Governments Speak: Toward A Theory of Government Expression and the First Amendment," *Texas Law Review* 57 (1979): 863.

5. Leo Pfeffer, "The Case for Separation," in *Religion in America*, ed. John Cogley (New York: Meridian Books, 1958), 52.

6. Lawrence Cremin, *The American Common School* (New York: Teachers College Press, 1951), 66-70.

7. Leo Pfeffer, *God, Caesar, and the Constitution* (Boston: Beacon Press, 1975), 171.

8. Wilber G. Katz, *Religion and American Constitutions* (Evanston, Ill.: Northwestern University Press, 1964), 35-36.

9. Wallace v. Jaffree, 105 S. Ct. 2479, 2520 (Rehnquist, J., dissenting).

10. Compare the following statements of Leo Pfeffer and Justice Stewart. First Pfeffer: "The fathers of the First Amendment were convinced that the free exercise of religion and the separation of church and state were two ways of saying the same thing: the separation guaranteed freedom and freedom required separation." Pfeffer, "The Case for Separation," *supra* note 5, at 60. Next Justice Stewart dissenting in Abington Sch. Dist. v. Schempp, 374 U.S. 203, 312 (1963)—a case that prohibited opening the school day with readings from the Bible and the saying of the Lord's Prayer: "[T]here is involved in these cases a substantial free exercise claim on the part of those who affirmatively desire to have their children's school day open with the reading of passages from the Bible."

11. Pfeffer, *God, Caesar, and the Constitution, supra* note 7, at 199. The use of this prayer to open the school day was struck down in Engel v. Vitale, 370 U.S. 421 (1962).

12. Everson v. Bd. of Educ., 330 U.S. 1 (1947).

13. The Court's negative response has come both when it used the language of the strict separation theory (McCollum v. Bd. of Educ., 333 U.S. 203 (1948) and the theory of neutrality (Abington Sch. Dist. v. Schempp, 374 U.S. 203 (1963).

The introduction of religion into the public schools implicates the establishment clause of the first amendment. In determining whether or not the practice is permissible the Court uses the same three tests discussed in chapter 1, i.e., the purpose, primary effect, and excessive entanglement tests . See, *supra* text accompanying notes 148 and 155 in chapter 1. In the cases discussed in this chapter the efforts to introduce religion into the schools were struck down either because the school's purpose was to advance religion, or because the primary effect of the practice was to promote religion.

14. McCollum v. Bd. of Educ., 333 U.S. 203 (1948).

15. Engel v. Vitale, 370 U.S. 421 (1962).

16. Abington Sch. Dist. v. Schempp, 374 U.S. 203 (1963).

17. Stone v. Graham, 449 U.S. 39 (1980).

18. Wallace v. Jaffree, 105 S. Ct. 2479 (1985). The Court concluded that the law had been adopted with the purpose to promote religion. The inclusion of the phrase "or voluntary prayer" was a crucial fact affecting the Court's decision. *See also* Karen B. v. Treen, 653 F.2d 897 (5th

Cir. 1981), *aff'd mem.*, 455 U.S. 913 (1982) (affirming the Fifth Circuit's striking down of a voluntary prayer law).

19. Zorach v. Clauson, 343 U.S. 306 (1952). Under the released-time program those not released stayed in school for instruction or study hall, whereas those released upon their parents' request were required to report to their religious centers where attendance was taken and reported back to the public schools. In dissent, Justices Black and Jackson argued that the compulsory education law was being used to help religious sects to get pupils. The majority viewed the released-time program as simply a permissible accommodation of the public school schedule to a program of outside religious instruction. In Lanner v. Wimmer, 662 F.2d 1349 (10th Cir. 1981) a relased-time program involving the release of students everyday, struck down was the practice of granting state credit depending on whether or not the program was "mainly denominational" in content.

20. Engel v. Vitale, 370 U.S. 421, 435 n 21 (1962).

21. Abington Sch. Dist. v. Schempp, 374 U.S. 203, 225 (1963).

22. Id., at 216 (1963). Today, former Chief Justice Burger and Justices White and Rehnquist take the position that the accommodation of religion in an evenhanded way without discrimination among sects is permitted by the first amendment. Wallace v. Jaffree, 105 S.Ct. 2479 (1985) (Burger, C. J.; White, J.; and Rehnquist, J., dissenting).

23. Engle v. Vitale, 370 U.S. 421, 431 (1962).

24. Id.

25. In Abington Sch. Dist. v. Schempp, 374 U.S. 203, 222 (1963) the Court approached the case in terms of a two-part test: If the purpose or primary effect of an enactment is the advancement or inhibition of religion it is not permissible. Using this test the Court concluded in *Schempp* that even if the purpose was not strictly religious, the method was; and this suggested the motive really was religious. Note that the prayer ruled on in the Engle case was adopted as a way of combating communism and juvenile delinquency. Philip B. Kurland, "The Regent's Prayer Case: 'Full of Sound and Fury, Signifying . . .'" in *Church and State—The Supreme Court and the First Amendment*, ed. Philip B. Kurland (Chicago: University of Chicago Press, 1975), 4.

26. Abington Sch. Dist. v. Schempp, 374 U.S. 203, 225 (1963).

27. Engel v. Vitale, 370 U.S. 421, 435 (1962); McCollum v. Bd. of Educ., 333 U.S. 203, 211 (1948).

28. Abington Sch. Dist. v. Schempp, 374 U.S. 203, 225 (1963).

29. Wallace v. Jaffree, 105 S.Ct. 2479, 2488-2489 (1965).

30. Id. at 2479 (Rehnquist, J., dissenting).

31. Id., (Burger, C. J., and White, J., dissenting).

32. Id., (O'Connor, J., concurring).

33. 104 S.Ct. 1355 (1984).

34. Abington Sch. Dist. v. Schempp, 374 U.S. 203, 313 (1963) (Stewart, J., dissenting). Justice Burger argues that it is hostility toward religion to oppose a moment-of-silence statute that includes a reference to prayer. Wallace v. Jaffree, 105 S. Ct. 2479, 2505 (1985) (Burger, J., dissenting).

35. Ernest J. Brown, "Quis Custodiet Ipsos Custodes?—The School Prayer Cases," in *Church and State—The Supreme Court and the First Amendment*, ed. Philip B. Kurland (Chicago: University of Chicago Press, 1975), 45-46.

36. Consider the following principle: "Nothing that the public school says or does shall have as its purpose, or as an avoidable feature or effect of its manner of achieving its purpose, the manifesting of approval or disapproval of any citizen's religion or irreligion." Nicholas Woltersoff, "Neutrality and Impartiality," in *Religion and Public Education*, ed. Theodore R. Sizer, (Boston: Houghton Mifflin Company, 1967), 16.

37. Over the years the Court in various contexts has offered a variety of definitions of the term "religion." George C. Freeman III, "The Misguided Search for the Constitutional Definition of Religion," *Georgetown Law Journal* 71 (1983): 1519. The Court has never defined the term for

purposes of resolving questions even similar to those raised by challenges to the public school curriculum.

38. *See* §5.5. In McLean v. Arkansas Bd. of Educ., 529 F. Supp. 1255 (E.D. Ark., W.D. 1982) the court held that scientific creationism was not science but a religious perspective on the origins of the world and life, and the statutory requirement that it be taught in the schools violated the establishment clause. In Aguillard v. Edwards, 765 F.2d 1251 (5th Cir. 1985) the Fifth Circuit held that a law requiring the teaching of creation science whenever evolution was taught violated the establishment clause because it had as its purpose the promotion of religion.

In Malnak v. Yogi, 592 F.2d 192 (3rd Cir. 1979) the court also excluded the teaching of transcendental meditation on the grounds it was a religion. Judge Adam's concurring opinion contains a lengthy and interesting discussion of the problem of defining the term.

39. A sufficiently broad definition of religion could turn the establishment clause into a basis for arguing that the public school system unavoidably violates the Constitution and must be closed down. Since it is unlikely courts would want to reach such a conclusion, their definition of religion is likely to be designed to avoid this consequence.

40. *Striking down period of silence:* Walter v. West Virginia Bd. of Educ., 610 F. Supp. 1169 (D.C. W. Va. 1985); May v. Cooperman, 572 F. Supp. 1561 (D. N.J. 1983); Duffy v. Las Cruces Public Schools, 557 F. Supp. 1083 (1983); Beck v. McElrath, 548 F. Supp. 1161 (1982), *vacated and remanded*, 718 F.2d 1098 (6th Cir. 1983); *Upholding moment of silence:* Gaines v. Anderson, 421 F. Supp. 337 (D. Mass. 1976).

41. Wallace v. Jaffree, 105 S.Ct. 2479, 2498-99 50 (1985) (O'Connor, J., concurring); Abington Sch. Dist. v. Schempp, 374 U.S. 281 &n. 57 (1963) (Brennan, J., concurring).

42. A reading of the various opinions in *Wallace v. Jaffree* clearly suggests a majority of the Court (Justices Powell, O'Connor, White, Rehnquist, and Chief Justice Burger) would support a properly drafted moment-of-silence statute.

43. Grand Rapids Sch. Dist. v. Ball, 105 S.Ct. 3216 (1985).

44. Florey v. Sioux Falls Sch. Dist. 49-5, 464 F. Supp. 911 (D. S.D. 1979), *aff'd.*, 619 F.2d 1311 (8th Cir. 1980), *cert. denied*, 449 U.S. 987 (1980). The Eighth Circuit was convinced that the historical and cultural significance of Christmas warranted permitting a prudent and objective observance of the holiday.

45. Karen B. v. Treen, 653 F.2d 897 (5th Cir. 1981), *aff'd.* 455 U.S. 913 (1982).

46. Doe v. Aldine Ind. Sch. Dist., 563 F. Supp. 883 (S.D. Tex. 1982).

47. Meltzer v. Bd. of Pub. Instruction of Orange Cty., Fla., 548 F.2d 559 (5th Cir. 1977), *aff'd and reversed in part*, 577 F.2d 311 (5th Cir., 1978) (*en banc*).

48. 614 F. Supp. 355 (D.C. Mich. 1985). The court also rejected the claim that these activities were not "state action" subject to the limitations of the establishment clause of the first amendment.

49. *Upholding the practice:* Stein v. Plainwell Community Schools, 610 F. Supp. 43 (D.C. Mich. 1985); Doe v. Aldine Indep. Sch. Dist., 563 F. Supp. 883 (S.D. Tex. 1982); Grossberg v. Deusevio, 380 F. Supp. 285 (E. D. Va. 1974) (graduation); Wood v. Mount Lebanon Sch. Dist., 342 F. Supp. 1293 (W.D. Pa. 1972) (graduation); Goodwin v. Cross Cty. Sch. Dist., 394 F. Supp. 417 (E.D. Ark. 1973); Chamberlain v. Dade Cty. Bd. of Pub. Instruction, 160 So.2d 97 (Fla. 1964), *rev'd in part and dismissed in part*, 377 U.S. 402 (1964) (baccalaureate exercise). *Holding the practice unconstitutional:* Graham v. Central Community Sch. Dist., 608 F. Supp. 531 (D. Iowa, 1985); Bennett v. Livermore, no. H-01312-6 (Cal. App. 1983).

50. Frederick A. Olafson, "Teaching *About* Religion: Some Reservations," in *Religion and Public Education*, ed. Sizer, *supra* note 35, at 84.

51. Hall v. Bd. of Sch. Comm. of Conecuh Cty., 656 F. 2d 999 (5th Cir. Unit B 1981), *modified*, 707 F.2d 464 (11th Cir. 1983); Crockett v. Sorenson, 568 F. Supp. 1422 (W.D. Vir. 1983); Wiley v. Franklin, 474 F. Supp. 525 (E.D. Tenn. 1979).

52. Aguillard v. Edwards, 765 F.2d 1251 (5th Cir. 1985); McLean v. Arkansas Bd. of Educ., 529 F. Supp. 1255 (E.D. Ark., W.D. 1982).

53. Leasing facilities to church groups that discriminate on the basis of race, however, creates a difficult dilemma. Failure to prohibit the leasee from discriminating on the basis of race may be viewed as "state action" promoting racial discrimination: Burton v. Wilmington Parking Authority, 365 U.S. 715 (1961). Yet to regulate raises the question of excessive entanglement between church and state. Lemon v. Kurtzman, 403 U.S. 602 (1971).

54. 333 U.S. 203 (1948).

55. Karen B. v. Treen, 653 F.2d 897 (5th Cir. Unit A 1981), *aff'd*, 455 U.S. 913 (1982).

56. Professor Tribe would say that school policies "'arguably compelled' by the free exercise clause are not forbidden by the establishment clause." Lawrence Tribe, *American Constitutional Law* (Mineola, N.Y.: Foundation Press, 1978), 822.

57. In Widmar v. Vincent, 454 U.S. 263 (1981) the Supreme Court noted that high school students are different from college students in terms of maturity and impressionability; thus they would be less able to appreciate that a neutral policy treating all groups alike was not state support and endorsement of the religious groups that incidentally might benefit from the policy. The view that high school students are especially impressionable had been criticized by a number of commentators. Note "The Constitutional Dimensions of Student-Initiated Religious Activity in Public High Schools," *Yale Law Journal* 92 (1983): 499; G. Sidney Buchanan, "Accommodation of Religion in the Public Schools: A Plea for Careful Balancing of Competing Constitutional Values," *UCLA Law Review* 28 (1981): 1000.

58. Collins v. Chandler Unified Sch. Dist., 644 F.2d 759 (9th Cir. 1981), *cert. denied*, 454 U.S. 863 (1981). The court also concluded the entanglement test was violated (see chapter 1) because school officials had a duty to supervise the assembly. *See also* Goodwin v. Cross Cty. Sch. Dist. No. 7, 394 F. Supp. 417 (E.D. Ark. 1973).

59. 454 U.S. 263 (1981).

60. Since the Court concluded that accommodation would not violate the establishment clause, it did not have to reach the questions that would arise if the accommodation of free exercise and free speech rights did violate the establishment clause. *Id.*, at 273 n. 13.

61. Id., at 274 n. 14.

62. Bell v. Little Axe Ind. Sch. Dist. No. 70, 766 F.2d 1391 (10th Cir. 1985); Nartowicz v. Clayton Cty. Sch. Dist., 736 F.2d 646 (11th Cir. 1984); Bender v. Williamsport Area Sch. Dist., 741 F.2d 538 (3d Cir. 1984), *vacated and remanded on other grounds*, 106 S. Ct. 1326 (1986); Lubbock Civil Liberties Union v. Lubbock Ind. Sch. Dist., 669 F.2d 1038 (5th Cir. 1982), *cert. denied*, 103 S. Ct. 800 (1983); Brandon v. Bd. of Educ. of Guilderland Cent. Sch. Dist., 635 F.2d 971 (2d Cir. 1980, *cert. denied*, 454 U.S. 1154 (1981).

63. Bender v. Williamsport Area Sch. Dist., 106 S. Ct. 1326 (1986).

64. Title VIII of Public Law 98-377.

65. The act says a limited open forum exists when a school offers an opportunity for "non-curriculum related" (undefined term) student groups to meet on school premises during noninstructional (undefined) time. The term "student-initiated" is also not defined by the act.

66. 393 U.S. 97 (1968).

67. Fundamentalists do not agree that the theory of evolution is a scientific theory; even if some might concede it is a scientific theory, they stress it is only a theory for which there is no solid evidence.

68. Yudof, "When Governments Speak: Toward a Theory of Governmental Expression and the First Amendment," *supra* note 4, at 876.

69. 670 F.2d 771 (8th Cir. 1982).

70. 515 F.2d 485 (6th Cir. 1975).

71. *Cf.*, Mercer v. Michigan State Bd. of Educ., 379 F. Supp. 580 (E.D. Mich. 1974), aff'd, 419 U.S. 1081 (1974) (refusal to consider challenge to state law prohibiting the discussion of birth control in public schools).

72. Segraves v. California, No. 278978 (Cal. Super., 1981), as noted in Martha McCarthy, "Religion and Public Schools: Emerging Legal Standards and Unresolved Issues," *Harvard Educational Review* 55 (1985): 307.

73. 366 F. Supp. 1208 (S.D. Tex. 1972), *aff'd*, 486 F.2d 137 (5th Cir. 1973), *cert. denied*, 417 U.S. 969 (1974).

74. 366 F. Supp. at 1211.

75. Yudof, et al., *Educational Policy and the Law, supra* note 3, at 134.

76. McClean v. Arkansas Bd. of Educ., 529 F. Supp. 1255 (E.D. Arkansas, W.D. 1982).

77. *See, e.g.*, Smith v. Ricci, 89 N.J. 514, 446 A.2d 501 (N.J. 1982), *appeal dismissed sub nom.*, Smith v. Brandt, 459 U.S. 962 (1982); Citizens for Parental Rights v. San Mateo City Bd. of Educ., 51 Cal. App.3d 1, 124 Cal. Rptr. 68 (1975); Cornwell v. State Bd. of Educ., 314 F. Supp. 340 (D. Md. 1969), *aff'd*, 428 F.2d 471 (4th Cir. 1970), *cert. denied*, 400 U.S. 942 (1970).

78. Hopkins v. Hamden Bd. of Educ., 29 Conn. Sup. 397, 289 A.2d 914, 922 (Conn. C.P. 1971).

79. Abington Sch. Dist. v. Schempp, 374 U.S. 203, 225 (1963).

80. Yudof, et. al., *Educational Policy and the Law, supra* note 3, at 134.

81. *See* Grove v. Mead Sch. Dist. No. 354, 753 F.2d 1528 (9th Cir. 1985), *cert. denied*, 106 S.Ct. 85 (1985) (upholding the refusal of a district to remove from use the book *The Learning Tree* by Gordon Parks).

The notions of indirect, secondary, diffuse, and ancillary religious effects are discussed in "The Establishment Clause, Secondary Religious Effects, and Humanistic Education," *Yale Law Review* 91 (1982):1196. *Cf.*, Arons and Lawrence, "The Manipulation of Consciousness: A First Amendment Critique of Schooling," *supra* note 2, which argues the present structure of the education system massively violates the first amendment.

82. Florey v. Sioux Falls Sch. Dist. 49-5, 464 F. Supp. 911 (D.S.D. 1979), *aff'd*, 619 F.2d 1311 (8th Cir. 1980), *cert. denied*, 449 U.S. 987 (1980).

83. *See "Freedom of Religion and Science Instruction in Public Schools,"* Yale Law Journal 87 (1978): 515. Besides excusal, the remedy sought could be the exclusion of the offending course or materials from the school. As noted in §5.5 this solution raises problems under the establishment clause. Another solution might be to "neutralize" the curriculum by requiring that "equal time" be devoted to the opposing viewpoint of scientific creationism, but this solution also has been determined to violate the establishment clause because scientific creationism is religion, not science. McClean v. Arkansas Bd. of Educ., 529 F. Supp. 1255 (E.D. Ark. 1982). These claims to be exempted from certain school requirements rest upon the free exercise clause of the first amendment. As was discussed in §1.3, the plaintiff in these cases must first seek to establish that (1) theirs is a religious claim, as opposed to a merely philosophical claim; (2) their religion and their religious claim is sincerely held and advanced; and (3) enforcement of the school's requirement against them would have a serious impact on the free exercise of their religious beliefs. If the plaintiffs satisfy their burden of proof, then the burden switches to the state, and it must establish, if the exemption is not to be granted, that their policy serves a compelling state interest and that enforcement of this policy is the least restrictive means to the achievement of the policy. Wisconsin v. Yoder, 403 U.S. 205 (1972).

84. Valent v. New Jersey State Bd. of Educ., 114 N.J. 63, 274 A.2d 832 (N.J. Super. 1971) (sex education course); Moody v. Cronin, 484 F. Supp. 270 (C.D. Ill. 1979) (coeducational physical education classes in which students wore "immodest apparel"); Spence v. Bailey, 465 F.2d 797 (6th Cir. 1972) (exemption from ROTC).

85. Sapp v. Renfroe, 511 F.2d 172 (5th Cir. 1975).

86. Davis v. Page, 385 F. Supp. 395 (D. N.H. 1974) (No excusal from classes in which audio-visual equipment is used); Menora v. Ill. High School Ass'n, 683 F.2d 1030 (7th Cir. 1982) (*en banc*), *cert. denied*, 103 S. Ct. 801 (1983) (wearing of yarmulke barred). In *Menora* the Seventh Circuit Court of Appeals directed the district court to retain jurisdiction to give the plaintiffs the opportunity to propose a form of secure headcovering that would not fall off, yet complies with Jewish law.

87. 511 F. Supp. 613 (N.D. Tex. 1981). The students claimed a right to eight to ten days in excused absences.

88. Mozert v. Hawkins Cty. Public Schools, 582 F. Supp. 201 (E.D. Tenn. 1984), *rev'd.*, 765 F.2d 75 (6th Cir. 1985). That the plaintiffs were not arguing that the use of the books violated the establishment clause and must be simply dropped from the curriculum, but were arguing that the series was so offensive as to violate their own right in the free exercise of their religion is made clearer in the opinion of the court in this case. Mozert v. Hawkins Cty. Public Schools, 579 F. Supp. 1051 (E.D. Tenn. Northeastern Div. 1984).

89. 765 F.2d at 77.

90. Mozert v. Hawkins Cty. Pub. Schools, 647 Supp. 1194, 1196-97 (E.D. Tenn. 1986).

91. Quoting from Williams v. Bd. of Educ. of the Cty. of Kanawha, 388 F. Supp. 93, 96 (D. W.Va. 1975).

92. Mozert v. Hawkins Cty. Public Schools, at 203.

93. 765 F.2d 75 (6th Cir. 1985).

94. Mozert v. Hawkins Cty. Pub. Schools, 647 F. Supp. 1194, 1195 (E.D. Tenn. 1986).

95. Id., at 1197-1200. The parties to the case had stipulated that the plaintiffs' beliefs were religious and sincerely held. The parties also stipulated that the materials were offensive to the plaintiffs' beliefs. And the court concluded that the school's policy of forcing the plaintiffs to choose between public schooling with these readers and no public schooling had the effect of conditioning receipt of an important benefit upon engaging in conduct proscribed by the plaintiffs' religious beliefs.

96. Id., at 1201.

97. The court noted that Tennessee had approved several reading series for use in Tennessee schools, indicating "the expendability of any particular series." *Id.* The court also noted that Tennessee "has, *by allowing* children to attend private schools or to be taught at home, also acknowledged that its interests may be accomplished in other ways and may yield to the parental interest in a child's upbringing" (emphasis added). *Id.* It should be noted that Tennessee is constitutionally prohibited from barring students from attending private schools (*see* §1.4), and while lower courts have said prohibiting home instruction is constitutionally permissible, the Supreme Court has not yet decided the issue (*see* §1.5). Thus, Tennessee's policy regarding private instruction may not provide a convincing example of how Tennessee itself accepts the view that alternative methods of instruction to the Holt series can serve its interests.

98. Id., at 1203. The court noted that "no single, secular reading series on the state's approved list would be acceptable to the plaintiffs without modifications." *Id.* Thus, requiring the state to provide the plaintiffs with an alternative reading program in the public schools was not possible since any accommodation would have the effect of advancing a particular religion—a violation of the establishment clause.

99. Id., 1202.

100. Id.

101. Id.

102. It will be recalled that those seeking more religion in the schools have not lost every battle, e.g., courts have upheld prayers at baccalaureate exercises and the celebration of Christmas. *See* §5.3.

103. For example, the courts have refused to say the teaching of evolution violates the establishment clause. See text accompanying note 71, *supra*.

104. The courts directly constrain the public school efforts at socialization when they lay down specific prohibitions on, for example, the method of socialization. The courts indirectly affect the power of the schools to socialize when they protect the free speech rights of students and teachers in the public schools. By protecting those rights, the schools are opened to ideas and viewpoints that are different from those officially espoused through the school program. The voices of the students and teachers thus serve as a countervailing force to the voice of the school. Teachers and students are constitutionally given, in effect, public school resources, class time, dollars, equipment, the building itself to introduce their own viewpoints and opinions. The more these individual rights are protected, the greater will be the diversity of messages "broadcast" to

the students in the school; accordingly, the danger that the official school perspective will overwhelm the students will be reduced. Yudof, et al., *Educational Policy and the Law, supra* note 3, at 193-94. Judicial protection of the free speech rights of students and teachers will be taken up in chapters 7 and 8.

105. West Virginia State Bd. of Educ. v. Barnette, 319 U.S. 624 (1943).

106. Bd. of Educ. v. Pico, 457 U.S. 853 (1982).

107. These issues are too complex to explore fully here, and the growing body of literature touching on these issues too extensive to provide a complete listing. Some materials that might be consulted: Arons, "The Separation of School and State: *Pierce* Reconsidered," *Harvard Educational Review* 46 (1976): 76; Arons and Lawrence, "The Manipulation of Consciousness: A First Amendment Critique of Schooling" *supra* note 2; Steve Shiffrin, "Government Speech," *UCLA Law Review* 27 (1980): 565; Van Geel, "The Search for Constitutional Limits on Governmental Authority to Inculcate Youth" *supra,* note 2; Yudof, "When Governments Speak: Toward a Theory of Government Expression and the First Amendment" *supra,* note 4; "State Indoctrination and the Protection of Non-State Voices in the Schools: Justifying a Prohibition of School Library Censorship," *Stanford Law Review* 35 (1983): 497.

108. 105 S. Ct. 2479 (striking down an Alabama statute that authorized a period of silence for meditation or prayer).

109. 262 U.S. 390 (1923).

110. 268 U.S. 510 (1925).

111. Id., at 534.

112. 319 U.S. 624 (1943).

113. Id., at 637.

114. Id., at 640-41.

115. Id., at 642 (footnote omitted).

116. Id., 631 (footnotes and citation omitted) (quoting Minersville School Dist. v. Gobitis, 310 U.S. 586, 604 (1940) (Stone, J., dissenting).

117. Id., at 640.

118. *Cf.,* Abood v. Detroit Bd. of Educ., 431 U.S. 209 (1977).

119. *Cf.,* Wooley v. Maynard, 430 U.S. 705 (1977).

120. Tyll van Geel, *Authority to Control the School Program* (Lexington, Mass.: Lexington Books, 1976), 23.

121. The unanimity on this point is most clearly on display in the various opinions issued in Board of Education v. Pico, 457 U.S. 853 (1982). The Court has embraced this proposition also in Ambach v. Norwick, 441 U.S. 68 (1979) and Plyler v. Doe, 457 U.S. 202 (1982).

122. Justices Marshall and Stevens joined in Justice Brennan's opinion; Justice Blackmun joined except in the central section of Justice Brennan's opinion. Justice White agreed only with the decision to send the case back to trial, not with the reasons for doing so offered by either Justices Brennan and Blackmun in their opinions. White preferred to see the facts of the case more fully developed before he took a position on the constitutional issues at stake. Justices Burger, Powell, Rehnquist, and O'Connor all dissented, each writing their own opinions.

123. Justice Brennan stressed he was not addressing the authority of the power to control the curriculum in the classroom or even to decide what books to purchase for the library. His decision was limited to the question of authority to remove books from the library. The library was a place dedicated to self-education; the classroom was a place where the board's interest in inculcation could hold sway.

124. Justice Rehnquist concedes a board may exceed constitutional limitations if it removed all books written by Democrats or by black authors. *Id.,* at 907.

125. Id., at 878-79. He added in a footnote, "In effect, my view presents the obverse of the plurality's analysis: while the plurality focuses on the failure to provide information, I found crucial the State's decision to single out an idea for disapproval and then deny access to it." *Id.,* at 879 n. 2.

126. Walter Kamiat, "State Indoctrination and the Protection of Non-State Voices in Schools: Justifying a Prohibition of School Library Censorship," *Stanford Law Review* 35 (1983): 497, 501.

127. *See* van Geel, "The Search for Constitutional Limits on Governmental Authority to Inculcate Youth." This article provides an extensive review of a large body of social-science evidence that was used by the Court and others to support the view that the inculcation of the young is necessary to maintain a stable democratic government. The article concludes that this evidence fails to provide any substantial support for the proposition that a stable self-governing system of government depends upon governmental inculcation of the young.

128. Id., at 290 (footnotes omitted).

129. Zykan v. Warsaw Comm. Sch. Corp., 631 F.2d 1300, 1306 (7th Cir. 1980); Right to Read Defense Committee of Chelsea v. Sch. Committee, 454 F. Supp. 703, 714 (D. Mass. 1978). *See also* Cary v. Bd. of Educ., 598 F.2d 535 (10th Cir. 1979); Minarcini v. Strongsville City Sch. Dist., 541 F.2d 577 (6th Cir. 1976).

130. Should any materials containing a racial slur be considered as inflicting a constitutionally recognized harm? Should truthful materials that nevertheless damage the reputation of a racial group be subject to challenge? If materials paint a stereotype should they be subject to challenge? Yudof, *et al., Educational Policy and the Law, supra* note 3, at 165-66. Presumably a constitutional challenge would only be successful if it were proven the materials were selected with the purpose of inflicting a stigma. See chapter 4. A parallel set of concerns may be raised regarding the depiction of the males and females in school materials. Note that the regulations implementing Title IX, a statute that prohibits discrimination on the basis of gender in federally funded programs, 20 U.S.C. §1681 et seq. (1982), specifically states that regulations are not applicable to textbooks or curricular materials. 34 C.F.R. §106.42 (1985).

131. 488 F. Supp. 1138 (N.D. Miss. 1980).

132. Id., at 1153. "Since the publishers of the books were given an opportunity to present their positions to the committee, presumably the court had in mind the authors, students, faculty, and school districts across the state, and indeed they were the plantiffs." Yudof, *et al., Educational Policy and the Law, supra* note 3, at 164.

133. Scheck v. Baileyville Sch. Comm., 530 F. Supp. 679 (D. Me. 1982).

134. Salvail v. Nashua Bd. of Educ., 469 F. Supp. 1269 (D.N.H. 1979). *Contra,* Bicknell v. Vergennes Union H.S. Bd. of Directors. 638 F.2d 438 (2nd Cir. 1980).

135. *See, e.g.,* Cal. Educ. Code Ann. §51501 (1978 Special Pamphlet) as quoted in Yudof, *et al., Educational Policy and the Law, supra,* note 3, at 166-67.

136. 668 F.2d 214, 216 (3d Cir. 1981).

137. 610 F. Supp. 577 (D.C. Ohio 1985).

138. Tinker v. Des Moines Independent Community Sch. Dist., 393 U.S. 503 (1969) (discussed in §6.5).

139. The 1984 Summer Olympic Games held in Los Angeles were the first games in which a marathon competition for women was held.

140. 20 U.S.C. §1681 et seq. (1976). Title IX prohibits discrimination on the basis of gender in programs receiving federal assistance. The Supreme Court has said enforcement of Title IX may be accomplished by an individual private action brought in federal court. Cannon v. University of Chicago, 441 U.S. 677 (1979). Regulations implementting Title IX can be found at 34 C.F.R. §106 (1985).

141. Commonwealth v. Pennsylvania Interscholastic Athletic Ass'n, 18 Pa. Comwlth. 45, 334 A.2d 839 (1975) (applying the Pennsylvania Equal Rights Amendment to strike down exclusion of girls from boys' team); Attorney General v. Massachusetts Interscholastic Athletic Ass'n, Inc., 378 Mass. 342, 393 N.E.2d 284 (1979) (applying the Massachusetts Equal Rights Amendment: Alaska, California, Colorado, Connecticut, Hawaii, Illinois, Louisiana, Maryland, Massachusetts, Mississippi, Montana, New Hampshire, New Mexico, Pennsylvania, Texas, Utah, Virginia,

Washington, and Wyoming). Grace Belsches-Simmons, "Teenage Pregnancy and Schooling: Legal Considerations," *Education Law Reporter* 24 (1985): 5.

142. National Organization For Women W. Essex Ch. v. Little League Baseball, Inc., 127 N.J. Super 522, 318 A.2d 33 (1974) (holding that exclusion of girls from participation in Little League Baseball violates state law against discrimination). Alaska, Arizona, California, Louisiana, Maryland, New York, North Dakota, Oregon, and Texas have passed statutes similar to Title IX. *Id.,* at 8-9.

143. The regulations implementing Title IX appear at 45 C.F.R. Part 86.

144. This interpretation of Title IX is probably consistent with the intent of Congress. *Cf.,* Federal Non-Interference With Curriculum Statute, 20 U.S.C. §1232(a) (1976).

145. *See e.g.,* Brenden v. Ind. Sch. Dist., 477 F.2d 1292 (8th Cir. 1973); Bednar v. Nebraska Sch. Activities Ass'n, 531 F.2d 922 (8th Cir. 1976); Hoover v. Meiklejohn, 430 F. Supp. 164 (D. Colo. 1977). For a more complete listing of judicial opinions in this area see Virginia P. Croudace and Steven A. Desmarais, "Where the Boys Are: Can Separate Be Equal in School Sports?" *Southern California Law Review* 58 (1985): 1425.

146. Bucha v. Ill. H.S. Ass'n, 351 F. Supp. 69 (N.D. Ill. 1972).

147. Current Supreme Court doctrine holds that discrimination on the basis of gender is permissible only if it serves important governmental objectives and if the discrimination is substantially related to the achievement of those objectives. Mississippi University for Women v. Hogan, 458 U.S. 718 (1982); Craig v. Boren, 429 U.S. 190 (1976). It is far from clear that the exclusion of girls who have the skills to make it onto an all-male team is a form of discrimination that serves an important governmental objective. Excluding females from the boys' team in a noncontact sport in order to prevent either bodily or psychological harm would seem to rest on assumptions about females (and males) that are grounded in stereotypical conceptions of the two genders. Courts have rejected these sorts of arguments in support of the strict separation of the genders. Leffel v. Wisconsin Interscholastic Ass'n, 444 F. Supp. 1117 (E.D. Wis. 1978); National Organization for Women, W. Essex Ch. v. Little League Baseball, Inc., 127 N.J. Super. 522, 318 A.2d 33 (1974). And the Supreme Court has specifically said that gender classifications based on stereotype or traditional ways of thinking about women will not withstand judicial review. Mississippi University for Women v. Hogan, at 724-25; Rostker v. Goldberg, 453 U.S. 57, 74 (1981).

But it might also be argued that strict separation is needed, i.e., denying the superior female an opportunity to compete on the male team, is needed to assure that the girls' teams do not lose their best athletes to the boys' teams. But this argument presumes it is permissible to sacrifice the best interests of the exceptional female athlete to the interests of the other girls to have her on the team as a way of uplifting the general level of play and skill of the less talented girls. *Cf.,* Croudace and Desmarais, "Where the Boys Are: Can Separate Be Equal in School Sports?" *supra* note 143, at 1450, 1455-56.

148. Lantz v. Ambach, 620 F. Supp. 663 (D.C. N.Y. 1985); Force v. Pierce City R-VI Sch. Dist., 570 F. Supp. 1020 (W.D. Mo. 1983) in which the court ruled that Title IX (as opposed to the regulation implementing the act) did not require gender-segregated teams even in contact sports, and that constitutionally schools could not exclude girls from trying out for the boys' football team. In this case no girls' team was available, thus technically the court was not called upon to decide if a district could, under the United States Constitution, establish sex-segregated teams. *See also* Yellow Springs v. Ohio High Sch. Ath. Ass'n, 647 F.2d 651 (6th Cir. 1981); Leffel v. Wisconsin Interscholastic Athletic Ass'n, 444 F. Supp. 1117 (E.D. Wis. 1978); Hoover v. Meiklejohn, 430 F. Supp. 164 (D. Colo. 1977); Clinton v. Nagy, 411 F. Supp. 1396 (N.D. Ohio 1974). *But see* O'Connor v. Bd. of Educ. Dist. No. 23, 545 F. Supp. 376 (N.D. Ill. E.D. 1982) upholding the exclusion of a girl from a boys' basketball team at least when there is a girls' team available. *See also* Bucha v. Illinois High School Ass'n, 351 F. Supp. 69 (N.D. Ill. 1972); Ritacco v. Norwin Sch. Dist., 361 F. Supp. 930 (W.D. Pa. 1973).

149. O'Connor v. Bd. of Educ. of Sch. Dist. 23, 449 U.S. 1301 (1980).

150. Id., at 1307.

151. In Commonwealth v. Pennsylvania Interscholastic Athletic Ass'n, 334 A.2d 839 (Cmwlth Ct. 1975) the court so ruled even where a girls' team was available. Attorney General v. Massachusetts Interscholastic Athletic Ass'n, Inc., 378 Mass. 342, 393 N.E.2d 284 (1979); Darrin v. Gould, 85 Wash. 2d 859, 540 P.2d 882 (1975).

152. The rules in question establish a game called "half-court" basketball, or "six-on-six" or "three-on-three." The boys' game is known as "full-court" or "five-on-five." The girls' team has six players, while the boys' has five. Three girls play as forwards and are almost always on offense, while three girls play as guards and are almost always on defense. Players under the girls' rules may not cross the center line in the middle of the court. Only the forwards can score points. Under the boys' rules, all players play offense and defense and range the full length of the court. Cape v. Tennessee Sec. Sch. Athletic Ass'n, 563 F.2d 793 (6th Cir. 1977) (upholding the girls' rules); Jones v. Oklahoma Sec. Sch. Activities Ass'n, 453 F. Supp. 150 (W.D. Okla. 1977) (upholding the girls' rules); Dodson v. Arkansas Activities Ass'n, 468 F. Supp. 150 (W.D. Okla. 1977) (striking down separate girls' rules).

153. Gomes v. Rhode Island Interscholastic League, 469 F. Supp. 659 (D.R.I. 1979), *vacated as moot*, 604 F.2d 733 (1st Cir. 1979) (boy could try out for girls' volleyball team when no boys' team was available), Attorney Gen. v. Massachusetts Interscholastic Athletic Ass'n, 378 Mass. 342, 393 N.E. 2d 284 (1979). *Contra,* Clark v. Arizona Interscholastic Ass'n, 695 F.2d 1126 (9th Cir. 1982) *cert. denied,* 464 U.S. 818 (1983). Petrie v. Illinois H.S. Ass'n, 75 Ill. App.3d 980, 31 Ill. Dec. 653, 394
N.E.2d 855 (Ill. App. 1979).

154. 34 C.F.R. §106.41 (1985).

155. In Michael M. v. Superior Court, 450 U.S. 464 (1981) the Supreme Court upheld a California statutory rape law that punished the male but not the female participant in intercourse when the female was under 18 and not the male's wife. *See also* Mollere v. Southeastern Lousiana College, 304 F. Supp. 826 (E.D. La. 1969) (striking down a rule that required women to live on campus); Robinson v. Bd. of Regents, 475 F.2d 707 (6th Cir. 1973), *cert. denied,* 416 U.S. 982 (1973) (upholding earlier curfew for women students).

156. 465 U.S. 555 (1984).

157. Board of Education v. Pico, 457 U.S. 853 (1982).

158. Arons and Lawrence, "The Manipulation of Consciousness: A First Amendment Critique of Schooling," *supra,* note 2.

159. Stephen R. Goldstein, "The Scope and Sources of School Board Authority to Regulate Student Conduct and Status: A Nonconstitutional Analysis," *University of Pennsylvania Law Review* 117 (1969): 373. For a further discussion of the authority of school boards see, §2.

160. Spring Branch I.S.D. v. Stamos, 695 S.W.2d 556 (1985), *cert denied,* appeal denied 54 U.S.L.W. 3560 (February 25, 1986). The statute provided that a student, other than a mentally retarded student, must be suspended from extracurricular activities during the grading period following a grade-reporting period in which the student received a grade of lower than the equivalent of 70 on a scale of 100. The statute gave the principal the discretion to lift the suspension if the class involved was an advanced class. The suspension was not to apply to the summer or the first reporting period of the regular school term.

161. Anderson v. Canyon Indep. Sch. Dist., 412 S.W.2d 387 (Tex. Civ. App. 1967); Carrollton-Farmers Branch Indep. Sch. Dist. v. Knight, 418 S.W.2d 535 (Tex. Civ. App. 1967); Bd. of Educ. v. Bentley, 383 S.W.2d 677 (Ky. App. 1964). *Contra,* State ex rel. Thompson v. Marion Cty. Bd. of Educ., 202 Tenn. 29, 302 S.W. 2d 57 (1957).

162. *See* Board of Directors of Ind. Sch. Dist. of Waterloo v. Green, 147 N.W.2d 854 (1967) and cases cited therein; Estay v. LaFourche Parish Sch. Bd., 230 S.2d 443 (La. App. 1969), *Contra,* Hollon v. Mathis Indep. Sch. Dist., 358 F. Supp. 1269 (D.C. Texas 1973), *vacated on other grounds,* 491 F.2d 92 (5th Cir. 1974); Moran v. Sch. Dist., 350 F. Supp. 1180 (D.C. Mont. 1972); Davis v. Meek, 344 F. Supp. 298 (N.D. Ohio 1972); Holt v. Shelton, 341 F. Supp. 821 (M.D. Tenn. 1972); Indiana H.S. Athletic Ass'n. v. Raike, 329 N.E.2d 66 (Ct. Ap. 1975).

163. Bell v. Lone Oak Indep. Sch. Dist., 507 S.W.2d 636 (Tex. Civ. App. 1974), *set aside on other grounds*, 515 S.W.2d 252 (Tex. 1974). *See also* Zablocki v. Redhail, 434 U.S. 374 (1978).

164. Board of Directors of Ind. Sch. Dist. of Waterloo v. Green, 147 N.W.2d 854, 858-59 (1967).

165. *See supra*, text accompanying note 146.

166. Shull v. Columbus Municipal Separate Sch. Dist., 338 F. Supp. 1376 (D.C. Miss. 1972); Ordway v. Hargraves, 323 F. Supp. 1155 (D. Mass. 1971) (prohibiting exclusion); Perry v. Grenda Municipal Separate Sch. Dist., 300 F. Supp. 748 (D.C. Miss. 1969); *contra*, Houston v. Prosser, 361 F. Supp. 295 (N.D. Ga. 1973) (requiring student to attend night school permissible).

167. 45 C.F.R. § 8;6.40 (6) (1985).

168. For one good review of the student uprisings of this period see Godfrey Hodgson, *American in Our Time: From World War II to Nixon, What Happened and Why* (New York: Vintage Books, 1976).

169. The First, Second, Fourth, Seventh, and Eight Circuits have upheld student objections, whereas the Third, Fifth, Sixth, Ninth, Tenth, and Eleventh Circuits have not. *See, e.g.,* Davenport v. Randolph Cty. Bd. of Educ., 730 F.2d 1395 (11th Cir. 1984); Richards v. Thurston, 424 F.2d 1281 (1st Cir. 1970); Zeller v. Donegel Sch. Dist., 517 F.2d 600 (3d Cir. 1975). Yudof et al., *Educational Policy and the Law, supra* note 3, at 169.

170. 425 U.S. 238 (1976).

171. *See* Craig v. Boren, 429 U.S. 190 (1976).

172. 34 C.F.R. 106.31 (b) (4) (1985).

173. Indep. Sch. Dist. No. 8 of Seiling v. Swanson, 553 P.2d 496 (1976) (holding that school districts had not been delegated the statutory authority to adopt a hair code).

174. *See, e.g.,* Wallace v. Ford, 346 F. Supp. 156 (E.D. Ark. 1972) (upholding and striking down specific provisions of the school's dress code); Bannister v. Paradis, 316 F. Supp. 185 (D. N.H. 1970) (striking down a rule prohibiting students from wearing blue jeans); Dunkerson v. Russell, 502 S.W. 2d 64 (1973) (upholding school rule that forbade female students from wearing blue jeans); Johnson v. Joint Sch. Dist. No. 60, 95 Idaho 317, 508 P.2d 547 (1973) (striking as in excess of district's authority a school rule prohibiting female students from wearing slacks, pantsuits, or culottes).

175. The decision in Wallace v. Ford, 346 F. Supp. 156 (E.D. Ark. 1972) is interesting for the careful way in which the court examined the school dress code line by line, upholding some provisions and striking others down.

6

Free Speech Rights of Teachers and Students

6.1. INTRODUCTION

The principle of freedom of speech holds that the individual should be free from governmental threats, sanctions, or coercion directed toward prohibiting the individual from expressing him- or herself. The theory behind the principle is that freedom of speech is so valuable, for a variety of reasons, that even if speaking out causes some harm, government may still not impose regulations or sanctions unless it has a justification for doing so that is stronger than would be required if it were restricting another activity not involving freedom of speech. [1] Thus, prohibiting an optician from fitting or duplicating lenses without a prescription from an opthamologist or optometrist requires a weaker justification from government than prohibiting pharmacists from advertising drug prices.[2] Sometimes the burden imposed on government to justify restrictions on freedom of speech is put in these terms: for restrictions or sanctions based on the *viewpoint* of what the person said to be constitutionally permissible, government must prove that these restrictions were necessary to achieve a compelling state interest.[3] However the legal doctrines are phrased, the central idea is that freedom of speech is an especially valuable freedom that deserves especially strong protection by the courts against governmental restriction.

At first inspection, it seems a small step from acknowledging the right of citizens to freedom of speech, to acknowledging a right on the part of teachers and students to freedom of expression. Indeed, in one respect the passage is a comparatively easy one. As discussed in §2.5, the mere fact one has taken employment in a public school system does not mean one loses one's right as a citizen to speak, outside the classroom, on education issues of public concern. That one is also a teacher only means that the speech may have consequences that would not occur but for the fact one is employed by the school district; these consequences will be considered by the court in determining whether in particular instances the right to speak will or will not be fully protected. Matters get more complex when we seek to extend the basic citizen's right to freedom of expression to a student as a way of checking or restraining the authority of the

211

school board to control the ideological content of the school program. As discussed in §5.8, a right to express what one thinks does not necessarily entail a right not to be told what to think. Thus, to use the basic notion of a citizen's right to express his or her thoughts as a limit on the school board's authority to shape the content of the school program, one needs also to posit a right to self-determination in political beliefs, a right to freedom of belief as a necessary concomitant to the right of expression. But acknowledging a student's right to freedom of belief—a right to hear, as Justice Brennan put it—is deeply inconsistent with what some take to be the primary function of the public schools, namely, the inculcation or indoctrination of the young in the basic political values of the society. As we shall see shortly, adherence to the view that the public schools should, and may, engage in such inculcation poses a major problem for the easy extension of a right of freedom of expression to students and teachers inside the school itself.

Consider first the claim that teachers enjoy the protection of the first amendment's free-speech clause while on the job in the school and classroom. If one agrees that it is the proper function of the public schools to inculcate the young, one is hard pressed to justify a public school teacher's claim to academic freedom, a claim to a right to autonomously control the selection of materials and the message to be conveyed in the classroom.[4] Though freedom of inquiry and research and freedom of teaching may have a place within a university devoted to the advancement of knowledge and the discovery of truth, it is difficult to support these freedoms in the context of a public school devoted to the inculcation of the young. Academic freedom in the public school context would have the effect of frustrating the democratically elected school board's control of the message to be conveyed to the students, and could have the further effect of authorizing each teacher to engage in his or her program of inculcation behind the closed doors of the classroom.

Similar difficulties are encountered in the effort to extend the usual right of freedom of expression to the students in the school. If the right to freedom of expression is grounded in the value of discovering the truth, or at least in the value of eliminating error, but public school students are in school to receive the truth as propounded by the school board, the justification for the right is far from clear. Similarly, if one grounds freedom of speech on its importance for a system of self-government or on its felicitous effects upon self-realization, the need to extend the right to public school students who are to be molded by the school board is far from certain.

These difficulties in extending a right of freedom of expression to students and teachers are greatly eased if one moves away from—relaxes—the assumption that a primary function of the public schools is to inculcate the young.[5] That is, if we adopt a model of public schooling that stresses the importance of the school as a marketplace of ideas, a place for personal growth and development, the place for freedom of speech in the school is made more comfortable.

Even if we only express our fear that the unchecked authority of the school board to inculcate is dangerous, a function has been found for freedom of expression in the schools, i.e., to protect the voices of students and teachers as a countervailing force to the potentially overweening voice of the school board.[6]

Our willingness to embrace strong protection of the free speech rights of student and teacher is, thus, importantly shaped and conditioned by our conception of education and the appropriate function of the public schools. The diversity of opinions on these issues is clearly reflected in the judicial opinions to be discussed in this chapter. As a consequence the body of constitutional doctrine dealing with the free speech rights of students and teachers in the schools is not marked by the degree of cohesion that would occur if there were a consensus among the judiciary on the function of the public schools and the concept of education.

6.2. CONSTITUTIONAL CONSTRAINTS ON EXCLUDING PERSONS FROM TEACHING BECAUSE OF THEIR BELIEFS OR POLITICAL ACTIVITIES

To help to assure that the public schools serve the purpose of inculcating students in those fundamental values the state and school board think are necessary for the maintenance of democracy, it would be perfectly logical to require public school teachers to pass an ideological litmus test. When the argument first arose during the Red scare of the 1950s, the Supreme Court upheld a New York law disqualifying from the civil service and public school system any person who "advocates, advises or teaches" governmental overthrow by force or violence or who organizes or joins any group advocating such doctrine.[7] This law, said the Court in *Adler v. Board of Education,* did not infringe the right to free speech; it merely made a person choose between membership in the proscribed organization and employment in the school system. The state was free, said the Court, to "protect the school from pollution and thereby defend its own existence." The Court also noted:

> A teacher works in a sensitive area in a schoolroom. There he shapes the attitude of young minds towards the society in which they live. In this, the state has a vital concern. It must preserve the integrity of the schools. That the school authorities have the right and duty to screen officials, teachers, and employees as to their fitness to maintain the integrity of the schools as a part of ordered society, cannot be doubted.[8]

The dissenting Justice Douglas, joined by Justice Black, offered a different view of education.

> What happens under this law is typical of what happens in a police state. Teachers

are under constant surveillance; their pasts are combed for signs of disloyalty; their utterances are watched for clues to dangerous thoughts. A pall is cast over the classrooms. There can be no real academic freedom in that environment. Where suspicion fills the air and holds scholars in line for fear of their jobs, there can be no exercise of the free intellect. Supiness and dogmatism take the place of inquiry. A "party line"—as dangerous as the "party line" of the Communists— lays hold. It is the "party line" of the orthodox view, of the conventional thought, of the accepted approach. A problem can no longer be pursued with impunity to its edges. Fear stalks the classroom. The teacher is no longer a stimulant to adventurous thinking; she becomes instead a pipe line for safe and sound information. A deadening dogma takes the place of free inquiry. Instruction tends to become sterile; pursuit of knowledge is discouraged; discussion often leaves off where it should begin.[9]

In the years following this decision the political climate changed and the Supreme Court changed in its willingness to permit the ideological screening of teachers. In a series of decisions, the Court struck down on the grounds of vagueness various versions of the so-called "disclaimer oath," i.e., the oath that required the oath taker to swear that he or she was not or ever had been a member of the Communist Party or otherwise lent his or her aid, advice, counsel, support, or influence to it.[10] The Court also made clear that people could not be criminally convicted of advocating the violent overthrow of government unless the advocacy went beyond the preaching of a mere abstract doctrine, to become advocacy of an immediate duty to overthrow the government to a group of sufficient size, cohesiveness, and disposition to act as to justify the belief that action will occur. Mere membership in a party that advocated the violent overthrow of the government could not be made a criminal offense. It was only active membership in the organization coupled with the specific intent to accomplish the illegal aims of the organization that was punishable as a crime.[11]

Then in 1967 the Court overruled *Adler* in the case of *Keyishian v. Board of Regents* and struck down a series of laws that required that teachers, as well as others, sign a certificate declaring they were not Communists, or that if they had been Communists, they had communicated that fact to the President of the State University of New York.[12] Also struck down were laws that disqualified people from governmental employment for utterance of seditous words, for active *or inactive* membership in the Communist Party, or for advocating or teaching the doctrine of the forceful overthrow of government. The Court found these laws to be overbroad because they imposed sanctions for active and inactive membership unaccompanied by proof of a specific intent to further the unlawful goals of the organization, and because they prohibited even the abstract teaching of the doctrine of the violent overthrow of the government.[13] The new attitude of the Court is expressed in the following quotation from Justice Brennan's majority opinion:

Our Nation is deeply committed to safeguarding academic freedom, which is of transcendent value to all of us and not merely to the teachers concerned. That freedom is therefore a special concern of the First Amendment, which does not tolerate laws that cast a pall of orthodoxy over the classroom. . . . The classroom is peculiarly the "marketplace of ideas." The Nation's future depends upon leaders trained through wide exposure to that robust exchange of ideas which discovers truth "out of a multitude of tongues, [rather] than through any kind of authoritative selection." (footnote omitted)[14]

The Warren Court also protected the teacher's right of association in other ways—a right the Supreme Court has recognized as implicit in the first amendment, because associating with others is an important way for "amplifying" one's voice. By limiting the extent the state or school board could compel disclosure of a teacher's association ties, the Court protected teachers from harassment and retaliatory measures because of his or her political ties. Thus, in *Shelton v. Tucker* the Court ruled unconstitutional a law requiring teachers to file annually an affidavit listing every organization to which they belonged or contributed.[15] These particular disclosure requirements, said the Court, swept too broadly because of their demand for unlimited and indiscriminate disclosure. What is not clear is what sort of more limited disclosure requirements would be permissible.

Before turning to the Burger Court, it is important to stress that the decisions of the late 1950s and 1960s were premised upon a conception of the public schools as a "marketplace of ideas." It is this very premise that is not so much attacked as ignored by the Burger Court in favor of a very different conception of public schooling.

The Burger Court is a court less anxious to protect the individual teacher. This court has upheld the use of the so-called "affirmative-oath" that pledges the oathtaker to uphold the Constitution; the Court even upheld an oath that committed the oathtaker to oppose the overthrow of the government by force, violence, or by an illegal or unconstitutional method.[16] In a later case, two school teachers, who were legal aliens, challenged on equal protection grounds a New York statute that denied certification as a public school teacher to any person who was not a citizen of the United States, unless that person manifested an intention to apply for citizenship.[17] The Court rejected the claim that these teachers had been improperly discriminated against. Exclusion of aliens from teaching in public schools, said the Court, was rationally related to the legitimate interests of the schools, i.e., an alien teacher might not adequately teach civic virtues, the role of the citizen, and the appropriate attitudes toward government and the political process. Furthermore, the Court stressed, the teacher served as a role model and exemplar for students, and the state could take this in account in excluding people who did not wish to become U.S. citizens.

As for the first amendment-based claim that "restriction of an alien's freedom to teach in public schools is contrary to principles of diversity of thought and academic freedom embodied in the First Amendment," the Court's response was a curious mixture of misapprehension and intellectual acuity.[18] On the one hand, the Court misinterpreted the argument as a claim that these teachers' first amendment free-speech rights were harmed by exclusion. In response to this understanding of the claim, the Court simply said that "opportunity to teach in the public schools so long as they elect not to become citizens" is not protected by the first amendment. On the other hand, the Court correctly recognized the argument to mean that excluding these teachers infringed the free speech interests of *students* who have an interest in a program presenting a diversity of viewpoints. To this the Court answered that the "argument would bar any effort by the State to promote particular values and attitudes toward government." This comment is indicative of an insensitivity, or even indifference, to the interest of the student in freedom of mind and the autonomous development of belief.[19] It is a far cry from the Warren Court's interest in maintaining the classroom as the marketplace of ideas. Even the dissenters in *Ambach v. Norwick* did not pick up on this first amendment issue but merely argued that excluding illegal aliens was not a rational means to achieve such state purposes as having the schools serve as an "'assimilative force' by which diverse and conflicting elements in our society are brought together on a broad but common ground."

In other cases the Burger Court has been sensitive to the free speech rights of public employees. The Court has blocked newly elected public officials from discharging employees solely because of their political affiliation with an opposing political party.[20] The Court wrote:

> For at least a quarter-century, this Court has made clear that even though a person has no "right" to a valuable governmental benefit and even though the government may deny him the benefit for any number of reasons, there are some reasons upon which the government may not rely. It may not deny a benefit to a person on a basis that infringes his constitutionally protected interests—especially, his interest in freedom of speech. For if the government could deny a benefit to a person because of his constitutionally protected speech or associations, his exercise of those freedoms would in effect be penalized and inhibited. This would allow the government to "produce a result which [it] could not command directly." Such interference with constitutional rights is impermissible.[21]

Based on these principles a lower court ruled that the refusal to hire teachers for summer employment because they supported the losing opponents of the current school board was impermissible.[22] However, winning such suits is not easy since the burden falls on the challenging teacher to show, by a preponderance of the evidence, that the protected political activity was a motivating factor in the school board's action, and that "but for" this motivation the "same decision" to dismiss the teacher would not have been reached.[23] (This requirement will hereinafter be referred to as the Mt. Healthy doctrine or requirement.) Thus, to succeed plaintiffs must establish that they were not dismissed because of, for example, incompetency and inefficiency, as the board might claim.[24]

The lower courts have consistently protected teachers from dismissal because of their participation in political activities. For example, one court blocked the dismissal of a teacher who had participated in the civil rights movements' efforts to end segregation in the schools.[25] A federal district court struck down one Alabama statute that denied a pay raise to any teacher who failed to pledge that he had not participated in, "encouraged or condoned . . . any extracurricular demonstration which was not approved by the city, county, or state Board of Education."[26] This law, the court said, "constitutes a comprehensive interference with associational freedom which goes far beyond what might be justified in the protection of the state's legitimate interest." Two federal circuit courts protected the right of college faculty members to send an invitation to other faculty members to participate in a peace program on the Vietnam War, and to write a letter to a local paper defending the ACLU's (American Civil Liberties Union) position favoring the legalization of marijuana.[27] The Tenth Circuit concluded that an Oklahoma statute that permitted the firing of teachers for "public homosexual conduct"—which was defined as "advocating, soliciting, imposing, encouraging or promoting public or private homosexual activity in a manner that creates a substantial risk that such conduct will come to the attention of school children or school employees"—was unconstitutional.[28] The Tenth Circuit stressed that the first amendment did not permit someone to be punished for merely advocating illegal conduct at some future time, and that the statute could lead someone who objected to the social and political views of the teacher to conclude that the statements per se would adversely affect students and teachers. A teacher's first amendment right could only be restricted if the employer shows that restriction is necessary to prevent the disruption or insure effective performance of the employee. Hence, the statute was overbroad.

In an interesting nonschool case, the Eleventh Circuit Court of Appeals upheld the dismissal of a clerical employee in a sheriff's office because he was a publicly active regular recruiter for the Ku Klux Klan.[29] The court stressed that dismissal was appropriate in this case because the presence of the clerk in the sheriff's office severely strained relationships between the office and Jacksonville's black community, impeded progress made in nurturing trust between the black community and the sheriff, and caused strains within the sheriff's office staff. The plaintiff could not claim especially strong protection, said the court, because he was not merely a passive member of the Klan. Though the court stressed that the presence of a member of the Klan in a sheriff's office was a particularly sensitive issue, and the enforcement agencies were "qualitatively different" from other governmental agencies, it is not unlikely that a similar set of considerations would lead this court to uphold the dismissal from public school teaching of a publicly active member of the Klan, especially in a district that served a mixed racial population.

We now turn to prohibitions against engaging in political activities, such as running for office. The prevailing view appears to be that a flat prohibition against public employees' running for public office is not permissible.[30] However, other limitations may be allowable. Courts have split on a requirement that an employee running for political office take a leave of absence.[31] The courts have generally upheld prohibitions on running for offices that have budgetary or other authority over the position held by the employee.[32] Finally, the Supreme Court and lower federal courts have upheld limitations on the involvement of public employees in partisan political activities (e.g., involvement in political campaigns) in order to insulate public employees from political pressures and to ensure that the employees not only execute the laws impartially, but also appear to be doing so.[33]

6.3. ACADEMIC FREEDOM: THE RIGHT TO TEACH CONTRARY TO PREFERENCES OF SUPERIORS

To what extent, if at all, do publicly employed faculty members have a constitutionally protected right to teach what and how they want (using public resources such as money, facilities, class time, and equipment) without restraint from their superiors? Vast expansion of the notion of academic freedom could have the effect of wresting control of the school program from the democratically elected legislature and school board, with the further consequence that the kind of educational program desired by the public may be frustrated.[34] Severe contraction of the notion of academic freedom could have the effect of making publicly employed faculty members the conduits for only those perspectives, beliefs, values, and opinions that have been officially approved, thereby undermining the notion of the classroom as the marketplace of ideas. In other words, who constitutionally should control the content of the school program—teachers alone, state and school boards alone, or does the Constitution establish a form of joint control? As discussed in §6.1 the choice among the alternative possible arrangements for governing the schools is importantly conditioned and shaped by the position one takes on the role of the public school and the concept of education.

What choice has the judiciary made? The question is susceptible to at least two answers: (1) With a few exceptions, most courts continue today to accept a *limited* conception of academic freedom in the schools; or, (2) While the early academic freedom cases embraced a limited notion of the right of the teacher autonomously to select at least supplementary materials, the more recent cases have moved toward rejection of even this most modest version of academic freedom in the context of the public schools.

We shall explore these alternatives by first suggesting that the cases can most easily be explained as embracing a limited conception of academic freedom.

The courts have made clear that even if there is a principle of academic freedom, its scope does not include the following:[35] control over the selection of basic texts to be used in a course in elementary-secondary schools; selection of a method of instruction such as team teaching; authority to change the basic content of a course from, for example, consumer economics to politics; authority to require the school board to offer a particular symposium; authority to change a course, e.g., from a broad survey of twenty-five plays to a more concentrated examination of eleven plays; or discretion to introduce obscenity or near obscenity into the classrooms of elementary-secondary schools.[36] It may be recalled (see §5.8) that even the plurality opinion in *Board of Education, Island Trees School District v. Pico,* which imposed limits on the power of boards to remove books from the school library, was careful to say its decision was not to be understood as limiting the control of the school board of the curriculum in the classroom.[37]

Assuring the school board basic control of the school's curriculum is not necessarily inconsistent with a limited right of teachers to introduce supplementary materials into the classroom. Thus, a number of courts have recognized that teachers enjoy discretion in introducing extra or supplementary materials into the school program,[38] but it is a limited autonomy granted to teachers. Discipline may be imposed on the teacher for introducing materials with which the board disagrees if the board is able to demonstrate that a basic interest of the board was frustrated or was about to be frustrated by the teacher's behavior. Hence, the lower courts have said dismissal is permissible: if the teacher's activity was reasonably expected to cause material and substantial disruption; if what the teacher said, or brought into the class, was not relevant to the course and was shocking and disturbing for the students in the class; or if the materials introduced or statements made did not serve a serious educational purpose and/or were shocking and inappropriate.[39] (It should be recalled at this point that for a teacher to be successful in challenging his or her dismissal, the Mt. Healthy requirements must be satisfied.) *The interpretation and relative weight to be attached to these various guidelines remain a matter of considerable speculation.*

Using such general, even vague and ambiguous guidelines the lower courts have both protected and not protected teachers. For example, dismissals were upheld when teachers introduced into French, industrial arts, and language arts classes various articles, poems, and pictures dealing with the 1969 rock festival "Woodstock" and which talked about drugs, sex, and used vulgar language.[40] Another dismissal was upheld after a teacher in a biology class had spoken about his personal experiences with prostitutes in Japan, and after he used as much as a whole class session to criticize in strong language the superintendent, the school board, the school system, and to complain about teacher salaries.[41] In another case the court upheld the denial of tenure after the teacher had used his classroom as "his personal forum to promote union activities, to sanction polygamy, to attack marriage, to criticize other teachers, and to sway and influence the minds of young people without full and proper explanation of both sides of the issues."[42] A federal district court upheld the dismissal of a teacher who violated a school district rule against classroom discussion of "any aspect of the recent labor dispute" when he permitted his fifth-grade class to discuss the teachers' strike.[43] Teachers who proselytize in a class are also subject to dismissal.[44]

In contrast, other teachers were protected even though they discussed the word "fuck" in class; assigned a serious article that used the word "motherfucker"; assigned Kurt Vonnegut's book *Welcome to the Monkey House* that contained arguably vulgar material; wore a black armband in class to protest against the Vietnam War; used role playing to teach about Reconstruction; assigned in a civics class balanced materials, including his personal views and the views of others, on the Vietnam War and race relations; and showed films on human sexuality objected to by some parents.[45] In *Wilson v. Chancellor* a teacher sought an injunction to bar the school board from enforcing a board order banning "all political speakers" from the high school.[46] The board had adopted the order after it learned that Wilson had invited a Communist to his class to speak after a Democrat, Republican, and a member of the John Birch Society had spoken. The court struck the rule down on two grounds: (1) the blanket prohibition violated the teacher's academic freedom; and (2) the effect of the ban was improperly discriminatory. An Arkansas federal district court said a college faculty member had a right to inform the class of his Communist beliefs but stressed it was not acknowledging a right to proselytize.[47] Finally, a number of decisions have held that the due process clause of the fourteenth amendment prohibits punishment without prior notice that the challenged behavior was forbidden, e.g., that the book or article introduced into the class was not the kind of book or article that could be used.[48] If school officials do not establish limits on the operation of the school-sponsored newspaper in advance, the disciplining of advisors for writing otherwise constitutionally protected articles in the school paper, for example an article that did not cause material and substantial disruption, would clearly be a constitutional violation.[49]

One court upheld the teacher's right not to participate in the Pledge of Allegiance in light of the fact her nonparticipation did not cause material and substantial disruption of the school program because another teacher was also present in the classroom who did lead the students in the pledge.[50] The dismissal of another teacher was upheld when she said her religious beliefs made it impossible for her to teach subjects having to do with love of country, the flag, or other patriotic matters.[51]

Merely answering questions of students on scientific and religious matters has been determined by one court to be an impermissible basis for dismissing a teacher without warning.[52]

There thus exists an impressive body of cases that rest on the idea that a limited notion of academic freedom should be recognized in the schools, that the schools should to some limited extent be a marketplace of ideas. However, as suggested above, it is also possible to interpret this body of cases in a different way. One could argue that although the courts have at one time recognized a certain degree of constitutionally protected discretion in public school teachers to select materials, the more recent cases suggest that academic freedom has lost favor with the judiciary. We begin with the decision in *Pico* (see §5.8) in which, as noted, every member of the Court appears to have acknowledged that the school board enjoys virtually unlimited control of the content of the curriculum in the classroom as a necessary adjunct to the carrying out of its function of inculcating the young. As one court expressed it, the only limitations on the board are that it may not design a curriculum to favor a particular religion, to promote racial or partisan bias, or to exclude discussions of "an entire system of respected human thought."[53] It can be argued that the modern trend in the cases is to accept this conception of public schooling and to reject the notion that public school teachers have any autonomy in selecting either basic texts[54] or supplementary materials.[55] That this is the prevailing doctrine today is given some further support in a case dealing with a school-sponsored newspaper. It appears that if school officials promulgate constitutionally permissible rules and guidelines for the operation of the paper, disregard of those guidelines may be a basis for dismissal of the faculty-advisor for insubordination. In one case the dismissal of an advisor was upheld when the advisor refused to comply with the school policy requiring him to show controversial articles to the principal for prepublication review for accuracy.[56] (What are constitutionally permissible guidelines for the operation of a school newspaper is a matter that the courts have not examined. It is not clear, for example, whether school officials could establish a school newspaper but prohibit *in advance* the publication of any articles on, say, sex and drugs.)[57] Whatever the school officials may do, it can be argued that teachers may not be required to follow directives that would violate the constitutional rights of the student editors of the paper.[58]

We might, finally, consider the attempt by one public school teacher to get a court to agree that a school rule requiring him to wear a tie in class violated his right to academic freedom.[59] Richard Brimley argued that he refused to wear a tie because he wished to present himself as not tied to "establishment conformity," and he wanted to symbolically communicate his affiliation with the ideas of the generation to which his students belonged. He believed this kind of dress enabled him to have a better rapport with his students, thus enhancing his ability to teach. The court's response to this argument was twofold: the refusal to wear a tie was more "action" than "speech" protected by the first amendment, and the school board's interest in promoting respect for authority and traditional values, as well as discipline in the classroom, outweighed Brimley's interests.

Now that we have reviewed the two alternative interpretations of the academic freedom cases, we can ask which is the better interpretation. The second interpretation has the advantage of strongly upholding the tradition of the public schools as instruments of inculcation. It has the further advantage of not asking the courts to take on the job of "book reviewer" for the schools, a job the courts arguably are not well equipped to undertake.[60] Furthermore, the standards used by those courts that embrace the notion of a limited right to academic freedom are themselves vague, subject to a variety of interpretations; accordingly, this approach arguably lacks a principled basis for deciding what teachers may or may not do with their limited right to academic freedom. For these reasons the "no-right" approach is to be preferred.

The case for the "limited-right" approach is also strong. A limited constitutional right balances the state's interest in inculcating pupils with the student's interests in using the school as a marketplace of ideas. Under this approach the board retains its authority to control the basic curriculum, but at the same time the teacher is permitted, within limits, to bring to the students' attention alternative viewpoints and perspectives. This approach prohibits the board from simply requiring the teacher to read from a board-prepared script, a fact that increases the chances for greater spontaneity in the classroom; hence the chances for a lively and improved educational experience for the students. Though the standards used by the courts in determining whether the school board acted properly in disciplining a particular teacher do not establish a bright-line between appropriate and inappropriate materials, the standards are no less vague than most constitutional standards.[61] A majority of courts have to date embraced the notion of a limited right to academic freedom.

6.4. OTHER IN-SCHOOL SPEECH ACTIVITIES OF TEACHERS

As discussed in §2.5, when a teacher speaks with administrators and other teachers on matters of "public concern," a special set of considerations comes into play to determine if the teacher's speech is "protected speech." In one case the Supreme Court held that a teacher's vigorous expression of belief to the school principal that the district's employment policies were racially discriminatory was a matter of public concern and protected speech, even if the teacher's persistence on the point resulted in strains between him- or herself and the principal.[62]

We turn here to a different kind of in-school speech activity—speech that is not a "matter of public concern" in the sense that it is not specifically directed toward policies and practices of the school in which the teacher is employed. Although the Supreme Court has not itself addressed the question of the test to be used in appraising the constitutionality of school rules and sanctions directed to these speech activities, several lower courts have.[63] In *James v. Board of Education of Central District No. 1* Charles James challenged his dismissal because he refused to obey the school board's rule that he not engage in any political activities while in school. In this case James symbolized his opposition to the Vietnam War by wearing a black armband into the school.[64] In upholding James's constitutional right to wear the armband the court examined the school board's action in light of two tests. First, the court asked whether the wearing of the armband threatened to disrupt the classroom or school. Here the court concluded the board had made no showing whatsoever that the wearing of the armband posed any threat to the orderly operation of the school. Second, the court asked if James's armband threatened to impair the school board's legitimate interests in regulating the curriculum. It concluded it did not. James did not attempt to proselytize his students. The students did not take the armband as anything more than an expression of James's personal views. The wearing of the armband did not interfere with James's teaching. The students in this case were eleventh grade sixteen- or seventeen-year-olds, and "It would be foolhardy to shield our children from political debate and issues until the eve of their first venture into the voting booth." There was a greater danger that the school's action would impose that "pall of orthodoxy," condemned in *Keyishian*, "which chokes freedom of dissent." The court was also disturbed by the allegation that another teacher was permitted to display a pro-Vietnam War sign in his classroom. "The Board's actions under such circumstances would indicate that its regulation against political activity in the classroom may be no more than the fulcrum to censor only that expression with which it disagrees."

The approach of the *James* court reflects the approach other courts have taken when dealing with the right of teachers to assist students in the distribution of an underground newspaper, the right of teachers to distribute other forms of literature, and the right of teachers to engage in demonstrations on school property. Basically, these activities must be permitted unless the board can justify a restraint on the grounds that the activity poses a reasonably foreseeable threat to the orderly operation of the school.[65] Using a similar test the Fifth Circuit struck down a school rule that forbade teachers to carry on discussions relating to the Texas State Teachers Association[66] among themselves on school grounds during lunch hour or other nonclass time. The district simply failed to establish that such conversations would result in "'material and substantial interference with the activities or discipline of the school.'" For the same reason the court struck down the school's rule that barred teachers from using the internal mail system to communicate with each other about the employee organization.[67]

Given this standard it is not surprising that teachers have not been protected by the courts when they have engaged in demonstrations that did or threatened to disrupt the school by, for example, disrupting classes or posing a threat of violence.[68] One court also upheld the dismissal of two community college faculty members who voiced disagreement with the school's change in its tenure system by refusing to particpate in two mandatory activities: a scheduled faculty workshop and commencement.[69] This conduct, said the court, "went beyond pure speech into the realm of breach of the express obligations of their employment." And few would doubt the authority of the school to dismiss a teacher who addressed his black students as "dumb niggers" and who, in another incident, said to a black student, "I wish you would swing at me because then I would have to defent [sic] myself and I would just love to make a black grease spot out of him [sic] on the floor."[70]

The Sixth Circuit has reached a surprising and potentially far-reaching decision in *Rowland v. Mad River Local School District, Montgomery County, Ohio*.[71] The court upheld the dismissal of a teacher who had merely told a secretary, an assistant principal, and several teachers who were her friends that she was bisexual and had a female lover. The court held that since her comments were not a matter of public concern the first amendment offered her no protection. The clear implication of the decision was that, at a minimum, there are certain categories of *privately communicated and nondisruptive* speech (e.g., speech touching on personal sexual matters) that receive no protection in the school context—a principle wholly at odds with the approach of every court reviewed above. Read most broadly, the Sixth Circuit might even have embraced the view that teachers enjoy no first amendment rights in the public school building except with regard to one category of speech, speech touching on matters of public concern. The implications of this decision are disturbing. (The case also raises the question whether someone may be dismissed from a teaching position merely because of his or her sexual preference. See §9.6.)

Those decisions that do protect teachers' nondisruptive speech activities suggest that, in a sense, as to them the school is a "public forum." Before proceeding we should at this point introduce the concept of the public forum. A "traditional public forum" is a place that by long tradition has been open and available for assembly and debate, places such as parks and streets. In these traditional public forums government may not prohibit all communicative activity.[72] Any viewpoint- or content-based exclusions are only justified if necessary to serve a compelling state interest and the prohibition is narrowly drawn to achieve that end.[73] Speech activities in a public forum may be limited by time, place, and manner regulations that are content-neutral, narrowly tailored to serve a significant governmental interest, and leave open ample alternative channels of communication. A second category of public forum (the voluntary public forum) consists of public property that by tradition has not been open to expressive activity but that the government has voluntarily opened. So long as the property remains open to the public government must follow the same standards applicable in a traditional public forum. A third category of property is that which neither by tradition nor designation has become a public forum. In addition to time, place, and manner regulations, government may limit the use of this property to its intended purposes, whether it be communication or something else. Regulation of speech in this location is permitted so long as the regulations are "reasonable" and not an effort to suppress merely because of disagreement with the speaker's *viewpoint*. In brief, some courts seem to have taken the position that *as to teachers* the school grounds are a "traditional public forum," i.e., the school is a place where the speech activities of teachers may not be excluded merely to avoid expense or inconvenience, may not be excluded either on the basis of the viewpoint expressed or on the basis of the content (i.e., whether the speech deals with politics or union affairs).

While the public schools may be a public forum for teachers in regard to their nondisruptive informal conversations, it also seems clear the schools are not public forums for organized teacher activities. In *May v. Evansville-Vanderburgh School Corporation*[74] the court declared that since the school was not a public forum there was no violation of teachers' first amendment rights to deny them the use of school facilities prior to the start of the school day to conduct voluntary meetings for prayer, religious devotions, and religious speech. The Court also concluded that the board's policy was justified as an effort to avoid infringement of the religious establishment clause of the first amendment. (See also §§5.4 and 6.11.) Similarly, another court held that strict controls on the access of union organizers to school facilities were permissible because the school was not a public forum.[75] But the court also held that the teachers' own informal discussions among themselves over the union's organizing efforts could not be restrained by the school district.

The need of school officials to maintain order has led the courts to agree that schools may set time and place limits on free speech activities by teachers.[76] On the one hand, teachers do not have an absolute right to use all parts of the school building for expressive purposes; on the other hand, teachers may not be prohibited from distributing literature in all areas of the school at all times if there is no disruption.[77] (The right of teacher organizations to gain access to teachers' mailboxes is discussed in §2.7.) Any rules requiring that the materials to be distributed must have prior approval of school officials must be precise so as to avoid giving school officials unbridled discretion to determine what may or may not be distributed.[78] More generally, school rules governing the free speech activities of teachers must not be overbroad or vague.[79]

6.5. LIMITS ON ADVOCACY BY STUDENTS

A variety of arguments point to the conclusion that students should not enjoy a right of freedom of speech in the schools. First, it can be argued that students are too immature to be afforded such a right. Second, as discussed in §6.1, the imperative of extending students a right of freedom of speech depends importantly on one's conception of the basis of the right of free speech, and, clearly, some theoretical justifications of the right do not point us toward recognition of such a right on behalf of students, especially elementary and secondary school students.[80] Next, many advocates of the school as instruments of inculcation will be uncomfortable with justifying the free speech rights of students as necessary to maintain the school as a marketplace of ideas. As Justice Holmes said, persecution for the expression of opinions is perfectly logical "[i]f you have no doubt of your premises or your power and want a certain result with all your heart."[81] Fourth, it can also be argued that the need to maintain calm and civility in the schools, the need to maintain a peaceful sanctuary where learning can take place, marks the schools as a singularly inappropriate place for permitting the turmoil and clamor of the marketplace, even the marketplace of ideas. It might also be added that since the school is not a traditional public forum,[82] school officials have the option of severely limiting expressive activity in the school facilities.

The Supreme Court, however, in *Tinker v. Des Moines Independent Community School District,* a case that predates the Court's more recent concern with schools as places of inculcation, took a different approach to the free speech rights of students.[83] (Whether the Court will, in light of its more recent conception of the public schools as a place for inculcating values, retreat from this decision remains to be seen.) In *Tinker* the Court agreed that students were to be protected, within certain limits discussed below, in their efforts to communicate with each other and the faculty. The schools, said the Court, should be marketplaces of ideas, not "enclaves of totalitarianism," and that students "may not be regarded as closed-circuit recipients of only that which the State chooses to communicate." Finally, by implication, the Court was understood to say that students' school facilities, such as hallways and the open spaces on school grounds, are a traditional public forum.[84] As we shall see, these areas are nevertheless subject to regulation by the school.[85]

Having concluded that students could enjoy the protections of the free speech clause, the Court had next to decide what kind of student conduct is to be deemed to be "speech" protected by the first amendment. Though the Court concluded in *Tinker* that the wearing of a black armband—once again in protest against the Vietnam War—was the type of symbolic act that was "akin to pure speech," it provided no definition of when conduct is to be deemed "speech" for purposes of the first amendment.

The third issue the Court confronted in *Tinker* was, assuming that the free speech clause of the first amendment does apply to the case, when may school districts act to abridge the exercise of that right. On this issue the Court concluded that students are immune from discipline unless school officials establish that there were facts that reasonably led them to forecast substantial disruption of or material inference with school activities, or unless school officials prove that the activity did in fact materially and substantially disrupt the school.[86] The Court also stressed that "undifferentiated fear or apprehension of a disturbance" is not enough to warrant disciplinary action; school officials must be able to show that their actions were "caused by something more than a mere desire to avoid the discomfort and unpleasantness that always accompany an unpopular viewpoint." Finally, the Court noted that free speech rights of students could be curtailed if the speech activity involved the "invasion of the rights of others."

The last issue for the Court was the question whether in this case school officials met their burden of proof under the material and substantial disruption standard. On this question the Court concluded that the suspension of the Tinker children for wearing the armband was not justified because there was insufficient proof that their actions were going to or did cause material and substantial disruption. The Court reached this conclusion in the face of the facts that (1) friends of a student killed in Vietnam were in the school; (2) other students talked to the Tinker children about wearing the armband; (3) two or three boys made unfriendly remarks to John Tinker; (4) one student made smart remarks to John for ten minutes while other students watched, and a football player told these students to leave John alone; and (5) John never felt physically threatened in these encounters.[87]

The decision in *Tinker* established the basic framework for deciding student free speech issues. We turn now to the elaborations by the lower courts of the principles laid down in *Tinker*. As to the question of what sorts of student activities may be termed "speech" for purposes of the first amendment, the lower courts have concluded that wearing of a beret, buttons, and badges are all forms of speech, and that the free speech clause protects the right of a male homosexual high-school student to bring a male escort to a senior prom.[88] On the other hand, the courts have rejected claims that one's hair style is a form of speech, and that social dancing is a speech activity.[89] (That an activity does not obtain the protection of the free speech clause of the first amendment does not necessarily mean it may be prohibited since the activity may enjoy protection of another amendment, or even the free exercise clause of the first amendment.) These activities simply do not have sufficient communicative content to entitle them to the protection of the first amendment. Another court concluded that the social functions (including dances) of a gay student organization could be classified as efforts to organize the gay community on campus and to educate the public and conveyed an ideological message, hence were protected by the first amendment.[90]

It is in connection with the application of the material and substantial disruption standard that we see the greatest divergence of opinion among the lower courts. In one case a lower court upheld the application of a rule banning the wearing of all buttons to a student wearing a button soliciting participation in a demonstration against the Vietnam War despite the fact there was no proof that this particular button might be the cause of disruption in the school.[91] The rule itself had been adopted because black and white students had been wearing racially inflammatory messages in a school with a student population 70 percent black and 30 percent white. In another case a court concluded the school had been materially and substantially disrupted when twenty-nine black students silently stood up and walked out of a school pep rally (at which attendance was optional) in order to protest to the playing of "Dixie."[92] The school program was not interrupted, but the protest did take place against a background of black opposition to the use of the song and the canceling of one assembly because of student unrest. The results in the case can perhaps best be justified on the grounds that school officials needed to discipline the protesting black students as a kind of show of authority to keep the lid on a difficult situation, even though the particular action of the black students was itself not disruptive. The difficulty with this analysis is that there was no evidence that the failure to discipline the protesting students would have invited later disruption of the school. This decision might be compared with the decision in *Boyd v. Board of Directors of McGehee School District*[93] in which a black student, one of twenty-five black football players who walked out of a pep rally and refused to participate in the football game scheduled for that night, was protected from being suspended from participation on the football team for the remainder of the season. The court simply concluded that the protest occurred "without any substantial intrusion of the work and discipline of the school."

Strong protection of free speech was also afforded by the Ninth Circuit in *Fraser v. Bethel School District No. 403,* a case in which Mathew Fraser nominated another student for a school office with a nominating speech that relied on considerable sexual innuendo.[94] The audience of students reacted with hooting and yelling, and three students were seen simulating sexual acts. One of three arguments made to support discipline of Fraser was that his speech caused material and substantial disruption.[95] The court rejected this claim saying that while the reaction of the audience was boisterous, it was "hardly disruptive of the educational process." Neither did the sexually suggestive movements of three students "rise to the level of a material interference with the educational process." In reversing the decision of the Ninth Circuit, five members of the Supreme Court placed no reliance on the disruptive impact of the case but instead stressed that authority of school officials to prohibit what Chief Justice Burger called "vulgar," "indecent," and "offensive" speech in the public schools.[96] (This aspect of the case will be discussed more fully in §6.7.) But the majority opinion (written by Chief Justice Burger and joined in by Justices White, Powell, Rehnquist, and O'Connor) took note of what might be viewed as a form of "disruption," namely, the possible disturbing psychological impact of the speech on the less mature members of the audience "many of whom were only 14 years old and on the threshold of awareness of human sexuality. Some students were reportedly bewildered by the speech and the reaction of the mimicry it provoked."[97] Chief Justice Burger also characterized the speech as "glorifying male sexuality, and in its verbal content, the speech was acutely insulting to teenage girl students."[98]

Compare this Supreme Court decision with the problem in *Trachtman v. Anker* in which staff members of the student newspaper sought permission from school officials to conduct a survey, the results of which were to be published in the newspaper, that involved distributing to eleventh and twelfth grade students a questionnaire asking about their sexual attitudes, preferences, knowledge, experience, and covering such topics as premarital sex, contraception, homosexuality, masturbation, and the extent of the students' sexual experience.[99] The questionnaire was to have been accompanied by a cover letter explaining the survey, stressing the importance of honest and open answers, but advising students that they need not answer any of the questions, and if they felt uncomfortable they ought not to push themselves. School officials denied permission to distribute the questionnaire, and the Second Circuit Court of Appeals upheld their decision agreeing with the school officials and their expert psychological witnesses that there was a probability that it would result in psychological harm to some students. Thus, the court extended the meaning of the material and substantial disruption test to include more than physical disruption of the school. The court also hinted that this activity deserved less than the usual first amendment protection because these students were not engaged in advocacy but were using other students as research subjects in order to gather information.[100] The court suggested that the school's action was here permissible because they did not seek to prevent the disruption of the questionnaire off school grounds.[101]

This opinion has been subjected to a strong and telling criticism.[102] First, nothing in *Tinker* indicated the Supreme Court meant to protect students from psychological harm, that this was the kind of disruption that school officials use as a basis for suppressing free speech. Second, the questionnaire did not invade the privacy rights of other students since filling it out was completely voluntary. Third, even if school officials may protect the health and welfare of their students—their psychological well-being—the evidence in the case was insufficient to establish possible harm to the students. Fourth, there was an alternative and less restrictive way to protect the students, i.e., allowing distribution of the questionnaire and then offering individual and group discussion sessions to students who wished to discuss it.

Despite the inherent difficulties in applying the material and disruption standard, some points are well established. In-school demonstrations that in fact disrupt class schedules, disrupt administrative services, involve loud noise, or interfere with scheduled activities do involve material and substantial disruption and open the students to discipline.[103] Judges have proven to be sympathetic toward school officials trying to administer racially, ethnically, and politically tense schools and have upheld the banning of provocative buttons and other symbols in these circumstances.[104] At least when it comes to demonstrations and the wearing of provocative buttons, the courts have been reluctant to second-guess the forecast of school administrators that the speech activity could lead to substantial disruption.[105] It might be noted in this connection that the courts have been permitting the disciplining of the "speaker" even though the actual source of the violence or disruption is other students who disagree with the speaker's message. It is the heckler who in effect holds a veto over the right of other students to speak; but it may be asked whether doctrine that permits a "heckler's veto" is adequately protective of the right of free speech. Should not, at a minimum, school officials be first required to make reasonable efforts to protect the speaker, and only if these efforts fail be permitted to take steps to curtail the speech activity?[106]

Perhaps because newspapers traditionally have been recognized as a protected mode of speech, the courts have been more willing to protect students against discipline for distributing their own publications (the so-called underground newspaper) on school grounds. In particular, courts have assured students of the right to distribute materials that are openly critical of named school officials and school policies, encourage students to object to those policies, and/or to discuss controversial topics on politics or, say, contraception.[107] (The question of the use of offensive language will be taken up in §6.7.) It seems clear that school officials may not forecast disruption merely on the basis that a publication contains comments critical of school personnel and policies. But in one case the suspension of university students for distributing a publication that by strong implication urged the student body to take disruptive actions was upheld.[108] The court accepted the argument of the school officials that they could reasonably forecast the document would lead to disruption of the school.

The Fourth Circuit Court of Appeals reached in *Williams v. Spencer* what might be considered a controversial decision.[109] The court concluded that school officials could suppress an underground newspaper that carried an advertisement for a "head shop"—a store that specializes in the sale of drug paraphernalia—featuring a waterpipe used to smoke marijuana and hashish. School officials argued, and the court agreed, they had the authority to suppress materials that "encouraged" actions that endangered the "health and safety of students." The opinion may be criticized insofar as it rests on a principle that is exceptionally vague—the court accepted the principle that the school may prohibit material that "encourages actions which endanger the health and safety" of students. There is also a danger that such a principle may be used to prohibit the publication of a wide range of materials merely because they "encourage" activities school officials consider to be unhealthy or unsafe. Might not the rule be used to suppress materials discussing contraception and abortions? Could colleges and universities relying on such a rule ban publications with articles or advertisements for cigarettes, beer, and wine? The court might have based its decision on a sounder footing if it had stressed that it was only authorizing the suppression of an *advertisement* that, as a form of "commercial speech," receives less protection from governmental regulation than pure political speech.[110] Even using the more permissive standards of the commercial speech cases, an interesting question arises whether educational institutions may ban advertisements for contraception and abortion clinics.[111]

Efforts by school officials to discipline students for the distribution of publications off school grounds on sidewalks and streets near the school have been stopped by at least two courts.[112] In neither case, however, was there proof that the publications in question had produced disruption in the school itself; hence it remains unclear whether school officials could discipline pupils for free speech activities off school grounds that have ramifications for school order and discipline. If the courts ever recognize such authority in school officials, however, it is likely to be highly circumscribed and limited to the situation in which the free speech activity has a rather direct and immediate impact upon the school. Otherwise, as one court said, "It is not difficult to imagine the lengths to which school authorities could take the power they have exercised in the case before us. If they possessed this power, it would be within their discretion to suspend a student who purchases an issue of *National Lampoon* . . . at a neighborhood newsstand and lends it to a friend. And, it is conceivable that school officials could consign a student to a segregated study hall because he and a classmate watched an X-rated film on his living room cable television."[113]

We now turn from *Tinker's* material and substantial disruption standard to its concern with speech that invades "the right of others." The Eighth Circuit Court of Appeals has interpreted this phrase to mean that school officials are justified in limiting student speech only when the speech activity "could result in tort liability for the school."[114] Applying that standard, the court said the school principal was not justified in requiring the faculty advisor for the school newspaper to delete two pages of one issue of the paper on the grounds that two articles on divorce and pregnancy could expose the school to suits for invasions of privacy. The court concluded that the anonymity of parents and students were sufficiently protected in the articles that no successful tort action could have been maintained against the school.[115]

The Eighth Circuit's interpretation of *Tinker* appears to be overly restrictive. Limiting the discretion of school officials to act only in that situation in which the *school* itself might be vulnerable to tort liability does not comport with the language the Supreme Court used in *Tinker*. The Supreme Court said school officials may act when the "rights of others" have been invaded, and that phrase would seem to include any situation in which the speech activity creates a tortious harm, e.g., invades privacy or defames reputation, even if the school itself is not subject to liability. School officials are, after all, permitted to prevent fights—batteries—even if they themselves might not be liable for the battery.

6.6. SCHOOL REGULATIONS: THE PRIOR REVIEW OF PUBLICATIONS BEFORE DISTRIBUTION

In *Jacobs v. Board of School Commissioners* the court examined a number of school rules governing the distribution of written materials on the school grounds.[116] One rule that prohibited the distribution of any literature that was not written by a student, teacher, or school employee was struck down: "[W]e think that authorship by a non-school person of the material distributed is not germane to any of the constitutional standards which must be met before conduct which is also expression can be prohibited." Another rule prohibiting the distribution of anonymous publications was also struck down. "School authorities could not reasonably forecast that the distribution of any type of anonymous literature would substantially disrupt or materially interfere with school activities or discipline." Other rules prohibited students from selling literature in school, and these also were struck down because the court was not convinced that good order could not be maintained without this prohibition.[117] In this connection it is worth noting other courts have split on the question of bans on the solicitation of money by students for political causes.[118]

In addition, the school in *Jacob* prohibited the distribution of any literature while classes were being conducted. In reviewing this rule the court acknowledged, as have a number of other lower courts, that schools may establish reasonable time, place, and manner regulations governing the distribution of literature.[119] Such rules are typically justified as appropriate means to allocate space to competing uses, to assure safe use of facilities, and generally to ensure a speech activity does not unnecessarily interfere with other legitimate activities.[120] The particular rule in the *Jacobs* case was found wanting because the court said the rule was too broad and not sufficiently narrowly drawn to protect the school's legitimate interest in prohibiting disruption. It could not be forecast that distribution of literature any time classes were in session would materially disrupt or interfere with school activities and discipline. In another case, however, another rule prohibiting all student demonstrations inside any school building was upheld because it served the purposes of preserving property, limiting the chances for vandalism, and protecting the normal operations of the school and safety.[121] The court stressed that the rule did not deny the right of students to engage in protest activities, it only limited the places where those activities could occur. This is in keeping with the Supreme Court's requirement that a valid time, place, and manner restriction must permit the existence of alternative forums for the expression of protected speech.[122]

Whatever rules districts do establish to regulate speech activities, they must avoid the vice of vagueness. (A rule is constitutionally vague if persons "of common intelligence must necessarily guess at its meaning and differ as to its application.")[123] Vague rules that regulate speech conduct have generally met with judicial hostility because such rules tend to "chill" the exercise of free speech rights; that is, vague rules tend to encourage unnecessary self-censorship. Thus, courts confronted with school rules regulating the conduct of speech have generally been quick to strike down rules employing general and undefined terms.[124] The *Jacobs* court struck down as both vague and overbroad (the rule seemed to prohibit speech activities that were constitutionally permissible) a rule that prohibited the distribution of literature that was likely to "produce a significant disruption of the normal educational processes . . . or injury to others."[125] The court rhetorically asked whether decorum in the lunchroom is a "normal educational process." Is a strident discussion among students "disruption?" Does injury to others mean only physical harm, or does it include hurt feelings? That the rule used language taken almost verbatim from *Tinker* did not matter; regulations themselves had to be more specific.[126] Another court reached the contrary conclusion regarding a regulation that also tracked the language of *Tinker*.[127]

We turn now to those cases that have dealt with school rules requiring that students submit whatever materials they wish to distribute on school grounds to a school official for prior approval and clearance. *Tinker* itself invited the establishment of these systems of prior review when it said school officials could prohibit a speech activity if there was evidence that might reasonably lead school authorities to forecast substantial disruption. Though the Seventh Circuit Court of Appeals has concluded that *Tinker* should not be read as permitting a system of licensing designed to prevent the exercise of first amendment rights, the Second, Fourth, and Fifth Circuits have said a properly designed system of prior review would be constitutionally acceptable.[128] Since there is a heavy presumption against systems of prior review, it is the board that has the burden or proving that its system meets certain important requirements.[129] Those requirements include: (1) The establishment of nonvague standards by which it will be determined whether the materials may or may not be distributed; (2) a nonvague specification as to in what circumstances students must seek prior approval; (3) a definite indication as to whom the material may be submitted for review; (4) the establishment of a brief time period during which the reviewing official must act; (5) an indication of the effect if the reviewing official fails to act within the required time period; and (6) a way to obtain a prompt review of an adverse decision by the reviewing official.[130]

6.7. CATEGORIES OF SPEECH WITH REDUCED OR NO FIRST AMENDMENT PROTECTION

The materials of §6.5 explored the meaning and application of the material and substantial disruption test—a test to be used when school officials regulate those speech activities of students that fall within the ambit of the free speech clause of the first amendment. But traditional first amendment doctrine recognizes certain categories of speech that fall outside the protection of the first amendment: obscenity, libel, and fighting words.[131] (What is obscene for minors includes a broader range of materials than that which is deemed to be obscene for adults.)[132] Speech that falls into any of these categories may be suppressed regardless of whether there is proof at hand that the communication, for example, poses a clear and imminent danger of lawless action.[133] In addition, the Court has recognized other categories of speech to which it provides a degree of protection less than that provided to speech that has traditionally been considered to be the special concern of the first amendment, namely, political speech. These other categories include commercial speech and offensive speech, neither of which has to date been clearly defined by the Court.[134]

It follows that, within the context of schools, student communications that are obscene, libelous, or constitute "fighting words" may be suppressed even if the "material and substantial disruption" test is not satisfied. We turn first to the suppression of "fighting words." The Supreme Court has written that fighting words (words that when said face-to-face are likely to cause the average addressee to fight), like obscenity and libel, by their very utterance tend to inflict an injury and are not an essential part of the exposition of ideas; hence, words that fall into these categories are of slight social value.[135] Consequently, a student who said of a teacher "He's a prick" in a voice loud enough for the teacher to hear was not protected from disciplinary action.[136]

Though the power of school officials to constrain the distribution of materials they deem libelous has not been fully litigated, lower courts have commented that this would be a legitimate basis for suppression.[137] Similarly, there are strong indications the lower courts would agree that materials deemed obscene as to minors (let alone adults) could be suppressed.[138] In fact, in one case—*Papish v. Board of Curators of the University of Missouri* (1971)—the federal district court concluded that a student newspaper that contained a political cartoon on the front page depicting a policeman raping the Statue of Liberty and Goddess of Justice, and an article using the word "motherfucker" was obscenity as to students on the University of Missouri campus; thus the dismissal of the student distributing the paper was proper.[139] The Supreme Court ultimately reversed the lower court decision saying the materials were not legal obscenity as to adults, and that "the mere dissemination of ideas—no matter how offensive to good taste—on a *state university campus* may not be shut off in the name alone of 'conventions of decency.'"[140]

It is an interesting and important question whether a student who distributed that same paper in a public high school would be protected from disciplinary action. By way of background to an exploration of this and related issues, brief mention should be made of several Supreme Court opinions. First, recall the multiple opinions in *Board of Education v. Pico,* all of which agreed that school boards have the authority to exclude from the schools materials that were at least pervasively vulgar.[141] The Court has also upheld the efforts of the Federal Communications Commission to question the decision by a radio station to broadcast, during normal daytime operating hours, materials that contain "patently offensive words dealing with sex and excretion."[142] In reaching this conclusion the Court placed great stress on the fact radio broadcasts are uniquely accessible to children. Finally, and most relevant for the *Papish* example, the Court has upheld a statute that limited the distribution to minors by bookstores and motion pictures of materials, not legally obscene for adults, that even depicted nudity ("the showing of the human male or female genitals, pubic area or buttocks with less than a fully opaque covering, or the showing of the female breast with less than a fully opaque covering of any portion thereof below the top of the nipple") as well as sexual conduct.[143] On the other hand, the Court has said in *Cohen v. California* (1971) that the state may not criminally convict someone for publicly displaying or using the word "fuck" even in a public place where children may be present. [144] (In this case a man was convicted for wearing into a courthouse a jacket bearing the words "Fuck the Draft.") The state has no right to "cleanse public debate to the point where it is grammatically palatable to the most squeamish among us." To permit the state such power runs the danger that government will seize upon "the censorship of particular words as a convenient guise for banning the expression of unpopular views." Furthermore, said the Court, the Constitution is concerned not only with protecting the cognitive dimension of speech but also those words chosen for their emotive force.

We now can safely conclude that a student distributing the *Papish* paper in a high school would not be immune from disciplinary action. But what of students who distribute publications that contain frequent uses of such expletives as "fuck" and other words relating to sexual intercourse and bodily functions, and quips such as "Oral sex may cause tooth decay"? The lower courts have with some exceptions prohibited districts from disciplining students merely because of the use of offensive words.[145] One case is particularly interesting because the facts were so similar to those in *Cohen,* but in the school case the student who wore a button with the same slogan was denied protection from suspension.[146] The court placed stress on the fact that the students in the school were a "captive audience" and day after day, upon seeing him, whether or not they read the button again, they would be reminded of his vulgar message.

These conclusions are strongly underscored by the Supreme Court's decision in *Bethel School District No. 403 v. Fraser.*[147] In that case Mathew Fraser nominated at a student assembly (students were not required to attend the assembly but instead could report to study hall) another student for student office with a speech that Chief Justice Burger described as containing an "elaborate, graphic, and explicit sexual metaphor."[148] Fraser was disciplined for giving the speech by being suspended for two days and being removed from the list of candidates for graduation speaker. Fraser went to court alleging that his free speech rights had been violated and the federal district court and Ninth Circuit Court of Appeals agreed, but the Supreme Court reversed. In reaching the conclusion that school officials had acted constitutionally, the Court began by distinguishing this case from *Tinker v. Des Moines Independent Community School District,*[149] on the grounds that the black armbands worn by the Tinker children communicated a political message, whereas this nominating speech communicated a sexual message.[150] Chief Justice Burger moved on to state a major premise of his opinion, namely, that one central function of the public schools is to prepare students for citizenship and that "inculcating" students in fundamental values was part of that task. Among the most important fundamental values students are to be inculcated in are "habits and manners of civility," i.e., the taking "into account consideration of the sensibilities of others."[151] The values necessary to the maintenance of a democratic political system, the Chief Justice argued, "disfavor the use of terms of debate highly offensive or highly threatening to others."[152] Even the most heated political discourse in a democratic society requires consideration for the personal sensibilities of other participants and audiences."[153] He went on to note that the House of Representatives and the U.S. Senate had rules setting bounds on the types of arguments that could be used in debate, e.g., rules prohibiting "impertinent" speech.[154] He further stressed that the latitude afforded adults to use offensive speech, citing to *Cohen,* need not be extended to children.[155] At this point, the Chief Justice added yet another important premise to his argument, namely, that the public school may teach by example "the shared values of a civilized social order," that the state may "determine that the essential lessons of civil, mature conduct cannot be conveyed in a school that tolerates lewd, indecent, or offensive speech and conduct such as that indulged in by this confused boy."[156] Then, changing direction again, the Chief Justice argued that school officials were permitted to act in this case to protect immature students from being damaged by exposure to sexually explicit, indecent, and lewd speech.[157] After discussing precedents he said supported this line of argument, the Chief Justice concluded this theme of this opinion by saying, "A high school assembly or classroom is no place for a sexually explicit monologue directed towards an unsuspecting audience of teenage students."[158]

The Chief Justice's opinion is flawed in a number of respects. First, he refused to acknowledge that Fraser's speech was a "political" speech: it was after all a nominating speech delivered at an assembly solely devoted to student electoral politics. As political speech it deserved the same level of protection provided the black armbands of the *Tinker* case. Hence, greater leeway should have been afforded Fraser in choosing how to express his opinion. Second, the Chief Justice assumes, once again, that public schools may engage in the "inculcation" of pupils, a proposition that itself is subject to serious question. (See §5.8.) Third, the Chief Justice confuses two forms of civility in pubic speech: he equates the use of a sexual metaphor with personal ad hominem attacks on those others with whom one is debating. The rules of debate of the House and Senate to which he refers deal only with personal attacks on other House and Senate members, with attacks on the House or Senate itself. A strong case could be made that such forms of debate do undermine the possibility of debate; the use of "vulgar" language or "sexual innuendo" may be shocking or offensive to some but is not itself a direct assault on the institution of debate. In fact, Chief Justice cites no House or Senate rules that deal with the use of sexual innuendo. Fourth, the Chief Justice says that children need not be extended the same latitude as adults. The first thing to note about this line of argument is that it contradicts the Chief Justice's early argument that adults may be controlled in the use of "vulgar" language in political debate. He now seems to say that *even if* adults may use the language of sex, children may not. He offers no expressly stated argument in support of this conclusion. We must infer that his argument at this point is the same argument he makes somewhat later, namely, that public schools may teach students the "shared values of civilized order," may instruct pupils that "mature conduct" does not involve the use of the sexual metaphor. But even this argument lacks any support. Indeed, the implications of this line of argument reach far into the school curriculum—it suggests that the plays of Shakespeare may and *should* be removed from the school curriculum because of their use of the sexual metaphor and innuendo. The fact that Shakespeare is so central to Western culture, furthermore, is an important piece of evidence to contradict the Chief Justice's conception of the values of our civilized order. Fifth, the Chief Justice's claim that this speech damaged immature students is only supported by his notation that, "Some students were reported as bewildered by the speech and the mimicry it provoked."[159] Even assuming these "reports" are an accurate description of the actual internal response of some students and not just a report of the observer's subjective impression, bewilderment hardly counts as psychological damage. Bewilderment suggests a lack of comprehension, hence the likelihood of damage seems slight. Furthermore, even if in time these students came to an appreciation of the sexual metaphor used in the speech, it is hard to believe that even the youngest students in the audience, the fourteen year olds, would develop sexually related psychological difficulties from exposure to what amounts to an elaborate joke. Anybody familiar with Johnny Carson will recognize that his jokes are often equally as explicit, yet no one has suggested that Mr. Carson should not be permitted to broadcast into our very homes where children even younger than fourteen may tune in his show. Sixth, the Chief Justice takes no note of the fact that the student assembly was a "public forum," and control of the content of speeches in such a form are subject to a variety of important restraints.[160]

A different and difficult issue would be raised by rules governing the use of the publicly available bulletin boards prohibiting the posting of materials that were offensive because they were said to stigmatize or degrade women and/or racial minorities. That a majority of the Court may be willing to entertain the possibility that school officials constitutionally may control the dissemination of such materials is hinted at in the majority opinion in the *Bethel* case discussed in the previous paragraphs. There, Chief Justice Burger made the observation that the speech of Fraser, for which he could be disciplined, "glorified male sexuality" and "was acutely insulting to teenage girl students."[161] Suppression of such materials could be viewed as suppression of materials merely because of disagreement with the viewpoint expressed. On the other hand, those materials might be classified as "offensive" materials, as a form of "group libel," and as materials posing a clear and present danger of inciting violence towards women and/or minorities. Two lower courts have rejected such arguments in a case dealing with a city ordinance directed toward making, inter alia, individuals liable for civil damages for selling materials that involve the graphic, sexually explicit subordination of women, whether in words or pictures.[162]

6.8. PUBLIC FORUMS: THE SCHOOL-SPONSORED STUDENT NEWSPAPER, STUDENT ASSEMBLIES, BULLETIN BOARDS

It is common for educational institutions to establish various forums for communication among students, e.g., the student newspaper, assemblies, bulletin boards. Even the common rooms in school dormitories might be viewed as such forums. A number of questions arise in regard to the establishment and operation of these forums. Are the courts likely to view these as a traditional public forum?[163] By definition the answer must be "no." Indeed, one court has, at least by implication, agreed that a school newspaper need not be operated as a public forum—that it can be established as an integral part of journalism class and be subjected to more constraints than if it were operated as a public forum.[164] Accordingly, public schools have the option of establishing, for example, the school newspaper as a voluntary forum or operating it as a category-three forum. Next, how is it determined if a particular newspaper, bulletin board, assembly, or common room has been voluntarily established by an educational institution as a category-two forum? If it is determined that the newspaper or bulletin board is a voluntary forum, do the same standards apply to it as apply to voluntary forums generally?[165] If the answer is that something like the school newspaper or bulletin board is not a voluntary public forum, what regulations of the forum would be considered "reasonable"?[166] We shall take each of the questions up in turn.

First, how is it determined if, for example, a newspaper has been established as a voluntary public forum, or as merely an integral part of the curriculum? There is no litmus-paper test to answer this question. The answer apparently turns on whether the school intended to designate the paper as a public forum.[167] Indicia that will point to a paper being but an extension of the curriculum include the following: production of the paper by the journalism class, i.e., it is not an extracurricular activity; awarding of academic credit for work on the paper; official policy statements explaining the status of the paper; the teacher working on the paper takes the job as part of regular teaching duties and not as an extracurricular activity; and the extent of control formally exercised over the paper by the teacher and other school personnel.[168] The Third Circuit has agreed that university dormitories are not voluntary public forums and that the university is not required to operate them as such.[169] However, the mere fact that a school paper may operate under a policy that potentially controversial articles must be submitted to the principal for prior review does not mean that the paper will not be viewed by the courts as a voluntary public forum. Thus, in *Gambino v. Fairfax County School Board* students succeeded in obtaining an injunction forbidding the school from barring publication of an article entitled "Sexually Active Students Fail to Use Contraception."[170] Having created the paper as a public forum, school officials could not now on an ad hoc basis exclude articles they deemed objectionable.

If the newspaper or other forum has been established as a voluntary forum, what standards must guide the school's regulation of the forum? Restrictions based solely on disagreement with the viewpoint expressed by students are not permitted. For example, a student editor arranged for the school paper to be published with a blank space where the editorial he wanted to print would have been but for the censorship of the university president based on a college rule prohibiting editorials critical of the governor or legislature.[171] The court barred the suspension of the editor, saying the university could not force the student as a condition of attending the school to forfeit his constitutional right of academic and/or political expression. At a minimum this court said that whatever other restrictions a school may impose upon the school newspaper, it may not impose restrictions as to the viewpoint expressed in the paper.

More generally, if the paper does operate as a student-run extracurricular activity, the courts have sided with students against school officials who have suspended editors, censored articles, prevented the distribution of the paper, or undercut the financial support of the paper in response to individual articles to which the officials objected.[172] Even a student yearbook has been viewed as a voluntary public forum; thus the school could not refuse to print a quotation a student had chosen for inclusion next to her picture in the yearbook.[173] Thus, the prevailing doctrine is, as regards at least most papers that have been established as public forums, "that school sponsored student newspapers should be viewed as independent *student* publications with school adminstration restraints on their content viewed as outside governmental censorship, rather than as school publications with school authorities exercising control of the newspaper as its publisher."[174]

Nevertheless, the "material and substantial disruption" test is still applicable to the student newspaper run as a public forum, just as it applies to the underground paper.[175] (Avoiding material and substantial disruption of the school may be seen as a compelling state interest.) Thus, one court upheld the authority of a school principal to prevent distribution of an issue of the school paper because he believed its content would create substantial disruption in the school.[176] The paper contained an angry letter to the editor from the lacrosse team, an equally angry response from the editors, and another letter critical of the performance of a student government officer that contained several libelous statements. In another case, the court rejected the claims of school officials that articles that discussed teacher attitudes toward homosexual teachers, that used the word "damn," that discussed the school district's past history of racial segregation, and that were critical of the student body president were disruptive of the school.[177] And, as noted above, even in regard to voluntary public forums, the school may impose valid time, place, and manner regulations.

If the school paper is a public forum, that would suggest that the student editors, as well as school officials themselves, must be constrained in refusing to publish materials from other students solely because they disagree with the viewpoint expressed. The opinion in the one case that seems to have litigated this proposition agrees. In *Zucker v. Panitz* the court enjoined the principal from barring the publication of an advertisement expressing opposition to the Vietnam War because the paper was operated as a public forum and had to remain open to the free expression of ideas.[178]

Assuming the school paper, bulletin board, assembly, or dormitory is not a voluntary public forum, in addition to time, place, manner regulations, the school presumably may preserve the forum for its intended purposes and impose reasonable regulations that are not directed to the suppression of expression merely because of opposition to the viewpoint of the speaker. In *Bethel School District No. 403 v. Fraser,* Mathew Fraser nominated another student for office with a nominating speech filled with sexual innuendo.[179] (The assembly was deemed not to be a voluntary public forum since it had been called for the limited purpose of hearing only nominating speeches.) The Supreme Court agreed with school officials that Fraser could be disciplined because his speech was both disruptive and inappropriate for the audience. (For a more extensive discussion of this case see §6.7.)

One further point also seems to be clear. Even when the school newspaper is operated as a voluntary public forum, student free speech rights are not violated by a policy requiring that the paper be submitted to a school official, such as the principal, for prior review so long as the standards used by the school official in deciding whether the paper may or may not be published meets with constitutional requirements, i.e., the *Tinker* standard.[180]

6.9. PUBLIC FORUMS: BARRING ACCESS TO STUDENT CLUBS; A RIGHT NOT TO ASSOCIATE

The Supreme Court has written that, "Through its policy of accommodating their meetings, the University has created a forum generally open for use by student groups. Having done so, the University has assumed an obligation to justify its discriminations and exclusions under applicable constitutional norms. [In a footnote at this point the Court wrote that it "has recognized that the campus of a public university at least for its students, possesses many of the characteristics of a public forum."] The Constitution forbids a State to enforce certain exclusions from a forum generally open to the public, even if it was not required to create the forum in the first place."[181]

What are those constitutional principles pursuant to which the university may justify denial of use of its facilities? First, the standards may vary depending on whether the denial is to a purely social group or a group that has gathered to advocate a particular viewpoint. If the group excluded was formed for purposes of engaging in a speech-related activity, its first amendment rights would be directly implicated, and the exclusion would have to meet first amendment requirements. If the exclusion affects a purely social organization, the governing principles are likely to be those of the fourteenth-amendment equal protection clause and/or relevant antidiscrimination statutes.

Assuming the excluded group is engaged in activities cognizable under the first amendment, the exclusion will be treated as a restriction of the rights of freedom of speech and the related right of freedom of association: "If an organization is to remain a viable entity in a campus community in which new students enter on a regular basis, it must possess the means of communicating with these students. Moreover, the organization's ability to participate in the intellectual give and take of campus debate, and to pursue its stated purposes, is limited by denial of access to the customary media for communicating with the administration, faculty members, and other students."[182]

Denial to a group of the use of school facilities based solely on the viewpoint expressed by the group may only be done if necessary to serve a compelling state interest.[183] Exclusion of a group, even a group espousing radical political ideas, may not be based simply upon disagreement with those ideas.[184] The Court has even held that a university that has opened its facilities to other student groups may not exclude a religious group on the grounds that granting the group recognition would represent an establishment of religion.[185] Nor is mere affiliation of the student group with a national organization known for its disruptive practices enough, per se, to justify exclusion.[186] However, if the university can establish with substantial evidence that the group would constitute a disruptive force on campus, or if the group refuses to agree to reasonable campus rules, it may be excluded.[187] What remains unclear is whether, per se, a group's advocacy of violent disruption would constitute sufficient evidence that it would be a disruptive influence if the group has also, albeit hypocritically, agreed to obey campus rules barring disruption. It should also be noted that the reasonable campus rules groups may be asked to abide by must themselves be constitutional and not, in effect, require groups to forfeit their right of free speech in order to gain access to campus facilities.

Based on these principles homosexual organizations have successfully challenged the denial of recognition.[188] Universities have failed to convince the courts that they may exclude gay organizations on the grounds that homosexual conduct is illegal, and that the university could exclude a group that was likely to promote and encourage an illegal activity. First, as one court noted, the law does not make it a crime to *be* homosexual.[189] Second, these organizations do not in fact advocate homosexual conduct, and, in any event, advocacy of illegal conduct may only be proscribed if the advocate is inciting to imminent illegal conduct.[190] Mere undifferentiated fear or apprehension of illegal conduct is not enough to justify a violation of first amendment rights. In the absence of proof that the mere presence of a gay organization on campus will encourage homosexual conduct, exclusion is not permitted. Indeed, if homosexual organizations could be excluded for the reasons argued for by universities, a case could be made for the banning of the traditional fraternity on the grounds that these organizations promote and encourage sexual harassment and violence towards women.

High school students successfully attacked a school board policy forbidding recognition of student organizations that advocated controversial ideas or addressed only one side of an issue.[191] As for state statutes and school policies that exclude secret fraternities, sororities, and clubs from high school facilities, several court decisions predating the constitutional decisions noted above have upheld these policies.[192] These exclusions may still be constitutional, at least as far as the first amendment is concerned, if the organizations are purely social and arguably are not protected by the first amendment. In any event, it is likely the courts would tolerate extensive regulations of these organizations to assure they did not, for example, discriminate on the basis of gender or race, even if those regulations have some effect on the speech activities of the organization.[193] The same conclusion is applicable to college and university organizations.

While student groups enjoy considerable constitutional protection in gaining access for themselves to school facilities, the problem changes if the groups seek to use school facilities for themselves and nonstudents. (See §6.11 for discussion of a similar problem addressed from a slightly different perspective.) In *Student Coalition for Peace v. Lower Marion School District Board of Education* a student organization sought permission to use an athletic field for a Peace Fair that would be open to the public and would involve speakers on peace and nuclear disarmament, the distribution of literature, and forms of entertainment.[194] The school district denied permission, and the students sought an injunction claiming that denial violated their first amendment rights and the federal Equal Access Act, discussed in chapter 5.[195] The Third Circuit held that the field was neither a traditional public forum, nor had it become a public forum by designation even though the school had from time to time let nonstudent groups use the field. In determining whether the school district had designated the athletic field a public forum, the court used an approach developed by the Supreme Court in *Cornelius v. NAACP Legal Defense Fund.*[196] According to *Cornelius,* courts must look to the policy and practice of government to ascertain whether it intended to designate a place as a public forum. The Third Circuit concluded that the students had not met their burden of showing that permission to use the field had been granted as a matter of course in the past; hence neither the policy nor practice of the district manifested an intent to designate the field as a public forum. Because the field was not a public forum, control of access could be based on the subject matter of the speaker so long as the distinctions were reasonable in light of the purposes served by the property and were viewpoint neutral.[197] Here the Third Circuit found the restriction reasonable. The desire to avoid a potentially disruptive political controversy and to maintain the appearance of neutrality was sufficient justification to exclude the fair from the field. The other activities that had in the past been permitted on the field simply posed less of a threat than the Peace Fair. As to the Equal Access Act, the Third Circuit held that the Act could be interpreted to protect student groups wishing to invite nonstudents to the school if the school's "limited open forum" (a concept defined in the act, see §5.4, and different from the first amendment concept of a public forum discussed earlier in the Third Circuit's opinion) encompassed participation by nonstudents in student events, as long as those nonstudents did not "direct, conduct, control, or regularly attend" such activities.[198] The court remanded the case for determination as to whether the school district had maintained a limited open forum after the Equal Access Act had become law.

We turn now to a somewhat different problem: the objections of students to being required to pay a mandatory student activities fee that supports campus newspapers, speakers, and other programs advocating positions with which the students disagree. Students have argued that forced support of these activities violates their right not to associate, their right not to be forced "to speak."[199] In rejecting these claims the courts have stressed that the required support of campus newspapers is permissible, even though the editorial stance of the paper may conflict with the beliefs of the plaintiff, when the papers are operated as public forums in which a variety of viewpoints are expressed.[200] And in *Galda v. Rutgers* a federal district court rejected such a claim as regards a student-run corporation engaged in research, lobbying, and advocacy for social change.[201] For the claim to have been upheld, the plaintiffs would have had to establish that the organization functioned "essentially as a political action group with only an incidental educational component."[202] In this case Rutgers did succeed in providing sufficient evidence to demonstrate that the corporation significantly enhanced the educational opportunities of the students at the university. Specifically, the organization provided students with an opportunity to learn advocacy and to learn about the workings of the political and governmental processes, and helped students to learn the values of citizenship and to develop the tools needed to participate effectively in a democracy. The fact that students who objected to paying the mandatory fee could obtain a refund was found to be legally irrelevant. Since the university had established that the organization had substantial educational value, the court concluded, Rutgers could have made the fee mandatory, rather than refundable, and could have pursued and collected the fee from students who failed to pay it.[203] In another case, the Supreme Court of Washington held that the university could not mandate that students be members of a student organization, but that a mandatory service and activities fee could be required for use by the student organization so long as the organization does not become the vehicle for the promotion of one particular political, social, economic, or religious viewpoint.[204]

6.10. PUBLIC FORUMS: EXCLUDING OUTSIDE
SPEAKERS FROM THE SCHOOL

The Supreme Court has never held "that a campus must make all of its facilities
equally available to students and non-students alike, or that a university must
grant free access to all of its grounds or buildings."[205] But when schools have
created a forum for outside speakers, frequently under the control of a student
organization, the courts have held that school officials may not veto a chosen
speaker solely because of disagreement with the speaker's views.[206] (For additional discussion of the concept of a public forum see §6.8.) A rule barring
speakers who "advocate the violent overthrow of the government," candidates
for public offices, and barring those "whose presence will constitute a clear and
present danger of inciting riot" has also been struck down.[207] In reaching this
decision the court said, among other things, that a speaker advocating the
violent overthrow of the government could be barred if the advocacy were the
kind that prepared a group for imminent action, and there was a reasonable
apprehension of imminent danger to the essential functions and purposes of the
school.

The fear of disruption was also sufficient justification for the board's cancellation of a school program on tolerance. In that case David Solmitz, a high
school teacher, planned an all-day "Symposium on Tolerance" as a response to
the drowning of a Bangor homosexual by three Bangor high school students.[208]
The superintendent refused to permit a homosexual to appear on the program,
but a compromise was reached permitting Dale McCormick, a lesbian, to appear. When word of the symposium was publicized, the board received fifty or
more telephone calls critical of McCormick's presence on the program. Some
parents threatened to keep their children from school; others said they would
attend the symposium to monitor it; and a few phone calls warned the board to
expect bomb threats and sabotaging of the school furnace if the program were
held. In the face of these threats the board voted to cancel the program. Solmitz,
Sonja Roach, a student, and McCormick filed suit claiming the cancellation of
the program violated their rights of free speech. The court, in rejecting Solmitz's
claim, said the protections of academic freedom do not "permit a teacher to
insist upon a given curriculum for the whole school where he teaches." The
court also rejected the claim that the board had acted out of impermissible
motives, saying, "We decline to take the novel step of declaring that a permissible decision of elected officials is infected with the invidious motives of their
constituents." (It should be noted that this is hardly a novel step.)[209] As to the
student's claim, the court again stressed that students have no right to demand a
curriculum of their own choice, and that the program was cancelled in order to
preserve the safety and security of the school district. The court also rejected the
claim of McCormick to speak on the grounds that the school had not become a
public forum, even a voluntary public forum. The fact that over the years

teachers had invited speakers to their classrooms did not make the school itself a public forum. Outside speakers do not have an independent right to address the students in the schools. In any event, the cancellation was of the entire program and was not suppression of a particular viewpoint.

6.11. SCHOOL PROPERTY: USE BY OUTSIDERS

Because school districts hold school property as trustees for the state and not as owners, state statutes, along with constitutional limitations, play an important role in shaping the policies school districts may or may not adopt regarding the use of their facilities by outside groups.[210] In other words, a starting point for determining whether the school district must or may permit its facilities to be used for social functions (dances), concerts, athletic events, other forms of entertainment, political meetings, lectures, commercial purposes, or religious purposes is the state statutes. In determining whether school officials have the statutory authority to make their buildings available for a specific use in cases in which the statutes are not explicit, a central concern of the courts is whether the particular use in question will interfere with the proper maintenance of the school building, and whether the activity will interfere with the conduct of the school.[211] Nor may school officials impose conditions on the use of the property that are inconsistent with state law.[212]

Statutory issues aside, the constitutional questions surrounding the use of public facilities touch upon matters of freedom of speech and the establishment of religion. We turn first to the question whether people from without the school have a right of access to school facilities. In other words, are some of the buildings and grounds of an educational institution a traditional public forum from which the public may not be excluded? The answer is "no," i.e., the facilities of public educational institutions need not be opened for public use.[213] Only if an area of a college, for example, has been opened for public use might an institution be prevented from excluding a particular free speech activity.[214] (Recall, though an area may not be a public forum as to the outside public, it may be a public forum as to the students and faculty.) The public sidewalks near a public school, however, remain a public forum. Nevertheless, because of their proximity to the school, restrictions may be imposed upon demonstrations to prevent them from disturbing the peace and good order of the school.[215]

The question has also arisen whether private educational institutions may invoke the state's trespass laws to evict outsiders who seek to enter school grounds to distribute literature. In *State v. Schmid* the New Jersey Supreme Court held that Princeton University could not use the law against trespass to bar entry to a U.S. Labor Party activitist.[216] The court approached the decision by noting that it had to balance the university's interests in protecting its private property against Schmid's interests in freedom of expression as protected by the state constitution's affirmative protection of freedom of expression.[217] In striking that balance the court noted that Princeton had institutionally committed itself to freedom of expression, and that the university had generally extended an invitation to the public to come to the university for a variety of purposes. In addition, the court acknowledged that Princeton should be allowed considerable autonomy in making sure the outside expressive activity did not interfere with the university's educational goals. In this case Princeton's decision to exclude Schmid was based on a policy that lacked any standards to guide the decision-makers in deciding whether a particular activity would or would not be compatible with the school's educational commitments. The court concluded that regulations devoid of reasonable standards designed to protect both the interests of the university and the individual exercise of freedom of expression would not be invoked to prohibit a noninjurious and reasonable exercise of that freedom.

In an appeal to the Supreme Court Princeton argued that it was protected under the first amendment of the U.S. Constitution by the doctrine of "academic freedom."[218] As an institution, Princeton argued, the university was protected by the doctrine of academic freedom in the choices it made as to which beliefs and viewpoints to which it would expose students. The Supreme Court never responded to this controversial interpretation of its precedent because it dismissed the case as moot after Princeton amended its guidelines for public access to the university. The sweeping implications of the doctrine of institutional academic freedom for the authority of the state to regulate private education suggests that only the narrowest interpretation of this novel doctrine is likely to gain favor in the courts.

We turn now from the uninvited guest to the guidelines public institutions must follow when renting their facilities to outside groups. The clear message that emerges from the cases is that, once having decided to rent facilities to outside groups, the institution may not refuse to rent to a particular group solely on the grounds of disagreement with the political viewpoint of that group. Thus, school boards have been barred from refusing to rent their facilities to a chapter of the American Nazi Party,[219] the American Civil Liberties Union,[220] and to an organization that wanted to present a lecture by Angela Davis, a member of the Communist Party.[221] It might even follow that a refusal to rent to a religious organization that wanted to use the facilities for religious purposes would be impermissible.[222] (We shall return to this question below.) Furthermore, educational institutions may require of prospective renters assurances that the property will not be put to illegal uses; but they cannot require an oath that the lessee does not believe in the violent overthrow of the government.[223] A refusal to rent facilities to an organization that wished to hold a dance did not, however, violate the first amendment because social dancing was not "speech" within the meaning of the first amendment.[224]

A different problem is presented when the outside organization claims a right of access to areas of the school with regard to which the students exercise some control and with regard to which the students have extended an invitation. This problem was confronted in *American Future Systems, Inc. v. Pennsylvania State University,* a case in which a retailer of household goods sought to use the common areas and individual dormitory rooms to hold group sales demonstrations.[225] The Third Circuit sustained the university's position that the common rooms could only be used for demonstrations and not for sales, and that the individual dorm rooms could not be used for group sales demonstrations. The court held that dormitories were not public forums for first amendment purposes and that the university had sufficiently strong interests at stake to warrant the restrictions on "commercial speech"—interests in maintaining the dormitory as a place where students may reside and study without disruption. The most difficult issues in the case related to the question of whether the university's interests could have been served as well by more limited restrictions; if so, the more excessive restrictions could not survive.[226] The Third Circuit interpreted this test to not require the university to adopt the "least restrictive means," but merely an "acceptable" means. Using this very lenient interpretation of the test, the Third Circuit upheld the university's regulations. The court noted that the restrictions did not prevent commercial information from reaching the students. An individual student could still invite a commercial vendor to conduct a one-on-one demonstration and sale in that student's room. In addition, the telephone, mail system, student newspaper, and college radio station were all available to American Future Systems. Furthermore, the university indicated it would permit use of other university facilities, e.g., the Nittany Lion Inn, for group sales and demonstrations.

If one agrees that the university's obligation is merely to adopt "acceptable" regulations, then the Third Circuit's opinion seems unimpeachable. However, if the Third Circuit misinterpreted Supreme Court precedent, and the university's obligation was to use only the least restrictive means for achieving its "substantial interests," then the Third Circuit's decision is most certainly in error.[227] As the court itself acknowledged, "we might be able to imagine alternative regulations that accomplish Penn State's objectives while interfering less with the student's and [American Future System's] rights to communicate."[228] For example, noise restrictions and limits on the size of the group attending the demonstration could by themselves satisfy the realization of the university's goals. Furthermore, the distinction the university drew between the demonstration and the sale of goods as regards the use of the common rooms makes little sense in terms of the university's espoused goal of maintaining the quiet and peace of the dorm.[229] One suspects that the university's regulations were intended to serve additional purposes not articulated by the university, namely, protecting putatively gullible students from sophisticated salespersons.

We turn now to the topic of making public facilities available to religious organizations. As suggested above, the Supreme Court's decision in *Widmar v. Vincent* arguably can be interpreted to require an educational institution to make its facilities available to religious groups even for religious purposes if those facilities have been made available to other groups.[230] In *Widmar* the Court said that failure to extend the same invitation to religious groups was an infringement of the students' right of freedom of speech, and that the University could not justify this infringement by its interest in promoting the separation of church and state. If the establishment clause is not violated in these circumstances, it is difficult to see how it would be violated by an educational institution's policy of renting its facilities to religious groups on the same basis as it does to other groups. This interpretation of *Widmar* is consistent with those lower court opinions that in the past have upheld the rental of public facilities to religious groups for religious purposes.[231]

NOTES

1. Seen generally, Frederick Schauer, *Free Speech: A Philosophical Enquiry* (Cambridge: Cambridge University Press, 1982).

2. *Compare* Williamson v. Lee Optical Co., 348 U.S. 483 (1955) with Virginia Pharmacy Bd. v. Virginia Consumer Council, 425 U.S. 784 (1976) and Central Hudson Gas v. Public Service Comm'n, 447 U.S. 557 (1980).

3. Laurence Tribe, *American Constitutional Law* (Mineola, N.Y.: Foundation Press, 1978), 602. If freedom of speech were treated as an ordinary species of liberty, the person attacking the governmental sanction or regulation would have the burden of proof and would have to establish that the regulation was not reasonably related to a legitimate governmental purpose.

In recent years the Supreme Court has drawn a distinction between suppression of speech based, on the one hand, on the viewpoint expressed and, on the other hand, the subject matter and/or medium of expression. Permitting labor picketing but not picketing to express a political message regardless of the viewpoint is a form of subject matter suppression. Police Dept. v. Mosley, 408 U.S. 92 (1972); Carey v. Brown, 447 U.S. 455 (1980). Limiting the use of billboards is an example of a limit on the medium of expression regardless of the content or viewpoint expressed. Metromedia, Inc. v. San Diego, 453 U.S. 490 (1981). *See also* City Council v. Taxpayers for Vincent, 104 S. Ct. 2118 (1984); Clark v. Community for Creative Non-Violence, 104 S. Ct. 3065 (1984).

4. Stephen R. Goldstein, "The Asserted Constitutional Right of Public School Teachers to Determine What They Teach," *University of Pennsylvania Law Review* 124 (1976): 1293-1357.

5. Tyll van Geel, "The Search for Constitutional Limits on Governmental Authority to Inculcate Youth," *Texas Law Review* 62 (1983): 197-297.

6. Mark G. Yudof, "When Governments Speak: Toward a Theory of Government Expression and the First Amendment," *Texas Law Review* 57 (1979): 863-918.

7. Adler v. Bd. of Educ., 342 U.S. 485 (1952).

8. Id., at 493.

9. Id., at 510 (Douglas, J., dissenting).

10. Elfbrand v. Russell, 348 U.S. 11 (1966); Baggett v. Bullitt, 377 U.S. 360 (1964); Cramp v. Bd. of Pub. Inst., 368 U.S. 278 (1961).

11. Scales v. United States, 367 U.S. 203 (1961); Yates v. United States, 354 U.S. 298 (1957).

12. Keyishian v. Bd. of Regents, 385 U.S. 589 (1967).

13. The advocacy of illegal activities continues to be protected by the courts. In Tygrett v. Barry, 627 F.2d 1279 (D.C. Cir. 1980) the court prohibited a police department from terminating a probationary police officer for advocating resort to a "sick-in" or "blue-flu."

14. Id., at 603.

15. 364 U.S. 479 (1960). *Cf.*, Barenblatt v. United States, 360 U.S. 109 (1959). The question of whether teachers may invoke the fifth amendment's privilege against self-incrimination when questioned by a school official is not clear. In Beilan v. Board of Education, 357 U.S. 399 (1958) the Court upheld the dismissal of a teacher on the grounds of "incompetence"—a term defined by the state to mean the insubordinate refusal to answer questions of a superior—when he refused to answer questions on Communist associations. This case has probably been limited if not undermined by *Shelton* and a series of subsequent cases. *See, e.g.,* Lefkowitz v. Turley, 414 U.S. 70 (1973); Baird v. State Bar of Arizona, 401 U.S. 1 (1971).

16. Cole v. Richardson, 405 U.S. 676 (1972); Connell v. Higgenbotham, 403 U.S. 207 (1971).

17. Ambach v. Norwick, 441 U.S. 68 (1979).

18. Id., at 79 n. 10.

19. *See* chapter 5.

20. A public employee may be dismissed, however, if the "hiring authority can demonstrate that party affiliation is an appropriate requirement for the effective performance of the public office involved." Branti v. Finkel, 445 U.S. 507, 518 (1980). *See also* Elrod v. Burns, 427 U.S. 347 (1976).

21. Branti v. Finkel, 445 U.S., at 514-15 (citation omitted) (quoting Perry v. Sinderman, 408 U.S. 593, 597-98 [1972]).

22. Solis v. Rio Grande City Ind. Sch., 734 F.2d 243 (5th Cir. 1984).

23. Mt. Healthy City Bd. of Educ. v. Doyle, 429 U.S. 274 (1977).

24. Miller v. Bd. of Educ. of the Cty. of Lincoln, 450 F. Supp. 106 (S.D. W. Va. 1979). *See also* Burris v. Willis Indep. Sch. Dist., 537 F. Supp. 801 (S.D. Tex. 1982), *modified,* 713 F.2d 1087 (5th Cir. 1983) (director of vocational education not protected because association with old board members was based on friendship only, not in order to further a particular program, policy, or objective).

25. Johnson v. Branch, 364 F.2d 177 (4th Cir. 1966). In Franklin v. Atkins, 409 F. Supp. 439 (Colo. 1976); 562 F.2d 1188 (1977) the court upheld the denial of a faculty appointment at the University of Colorado to an outstanding young English scholar because there was clear and convincing evidence he had engaged in campus disruptions at another university, and that this was a reasonable basis to conclude he posed a threat of disruption at the University of Colorado.

26. Alabama Educ. Ass'n. v. Wallace, 362 F.Supp. 682 (M.D. Ala. 1973).

27. Stolberg v. Board of Trustees, 474 F.2d 485 (2d Cir. 1973); Wagle v. Murray, 546 F.2d 1329 (9th Cir. 1976), *vacated on other grounds,* 431 U.S. 935 (1977), *opinion on remand,* 560 F.2d 401 (9th Cir. 1977), *cert. denied,* 434 U.S. 1014 (1978).

28. National Gay Task Force v. Bd. of Educ. of City of Oklahoma City, 729 F.2d 1270 (10th Cir. 1984), *aff'd by an equally divided court,* 105 S. Ct. 1856 (1985).

29. McMullen v. Carson, 754 F.2d 936 (11th Cir. 1985). The clerk was dismissed after he had been interviewed about his recruitment activities on a locally televised news broadcast.

30. Hickman v. City of Dallas, 475 F. Supp. 137 (N.D. Tex. 1979); Minielly v. State, 342 Or. 490, 411 P.2d 69 (Ore. 1966) *(en banc). Contra,* Jones v. Board of Control, 131 So. 2d 713 (Fla. 1961).

31. Allen v. Bd. Educ. of Jefferson Cty., 584 S.W.2d 408 (Ky. App. 1979) (required leave unconstitutional when it was not determined if political activity would adversely affect performance of duties); *contra,* Bart v. Telford, 677 F.2d 622 (7th Cir. 1982).

32. Wilson v. Moore 346 F. Supp. 635 (W.D. Va. 1972) (upholding state constitutional provision that prohibited college athletic director from holding office as state legislator); Lay v. City of Kingsport, 454 F.2d 345 (6th Cir.) *cert. denied,* 409 U.S. 846 (1972) (permissible to bar assistant superintendent from holding office as alderman); Haskins v. State *ex. rel.* Harrington, 516 P.2d 1171 (Wyo. 1973) teacher may not be elected to board governing his or her own district).

33. U.S. Civil Service Commission v. Letter Carriers, 413 U.S. 548 (1973); Broadrick v. Oklahoma, 413 U.S. 601 (1973); Magill v. Lynch, 560 F.2d 22 (1st Cir. 1977). The Hatch Act that was upheld in *Letter Carriers* and *Broadrick* does not prohibit all political activities. Federal

employees are permitted to vote and contribute funds, express opinion on political subjects and candidates, display stickers and badges, and take part in nonpartisan elections. In Montgomery v. White, 320 F. Supp. 303 (E.D. Tex. 1969) the district court struck down a regulation prohibiting "all political activity except voting."

34. The question of academic freedom again picks up themes discussed in chapters 2 and 5, i.e., issues of who shall participate in the governance of schools, and limits on the effort of the state to inculcate pupils in officially approved beliefs and opinions.

35. *But see* Aguillard v. Edwards, 765 F.2d 1251, 1257 (5th Cir. 1985) in which the court said, "Academic freedom embodies the principle that individual instructors are at liberty to teach that which they deem to be appropriate in the exercise of their professional judgment. The principle of academic freedom abjures state interference with curriculum or theory as antithetical to the search for truth." This is an extraordinarily broad conception of academic freedom for the public schools. It is doubtful any other courts would accept this as the appropriate conception of academic freedom for the public schools. (The statement was made in rejecting the claim of the state that academic freedom was promoted by a state law requiring the teaching of "creation-science" if evolution were taught. The court said that the law was inconsistent with academic freedom as defined in the quotation. The court struck the law down on the grounds that it had as its purpose the advancement of religion.)

36. Parducci v. Rutland, 316 F. Supp. 352 (M.D. Ala. 1970) (suggesting in dictum that introduction of obscenity into the classroom may be prohibited); James v. Bd. of Educ., 461 F.2d 566 (2d Cir.), *cert. denied,* 409 U.S. 1042 (1972) (suggesting in dictum that indoctrination by a teacher may be prohibited); La Rocca v. Bd. of Educ., of Rye City Sch. Dist., 63 A.D.2d 1019, 406 N.Y.S.2d 348 (App. Div. 1979) (promoting religious beliefs prohibited); Cary v. Bd. of Educ., 598 F.2d 535 (10th Cir. 1978) (denying claim of teachers to a right to select textbooks for their courses); Minarcini v. Strongsville City Sch. Dist., 541 F.2d 577 (6th Cir. 1976) (deciding, inter alia, board control of textbook selection did not violate teachers' rights); Johnson v. Stuart, 702 F.2d 193 (9th Cir. 1983) (denying standing to teachers to challenge statutory criteria for selection of textbooks); Ahern v. Bd. of Educ., 327 F. Supp. 1391 (D. Neb. 1971), *aff'd,* 456 F.2d 399 (8th Cir. 1972) (teacher may not convert economics course to a course on politics); Hetrick v. Martin, 480 F.2d 705 (6th Cir. 1973), *cert. denied,* 414 U.S. 1075 (1973) (upholding dismissal for converting drama survey course into an intensive study of a more limited number of plays); Mc-Elearney v. University of Illinois, 612 F.2d 285, 288 (7th Cir. 1979) ("Academic freedom does not empower a profesor to dictate to the University what research will be done using the school's facilities or how many faculty positions will be devoted to a particular area."); Solmitz v. Maine Sch. Administrative Dist., 495 A.2d 812 (1985) (teacher lacks a right to require board to offer students a symposium on tolerance). *Cf.,* Dale v. Bd. of Educ., Lemmon Independent Sch. Dist., 316 N.W.2d 108 (1982) (upholding on statutory grounds dismissal of a teacher who devoted excessive time to creationism in his biology class).

37. 457 U.S. 853, 869 (1982).

38. *See, e.g.,* Keefe v. Geanakos, 418 F.2d 359 (1st Cir. 1969); Dean v. Timpson v. Independent Sch. Dist., 486 F. Supp. 302 (E.D. Tex. 1970); Parducci v. Rutland, 316 F. Supp. 352 (M.D. Ala. 1970). *Contra,* Fisher v. Fairbanks North Star Borough Sch. Dist., 704 P.2d 213 (Alaska, 1985).

39. *See, e.g.,* James v. Bd. of Educ., 461 F.2d 566 (2d Cir.), *cert. denied,* 409 U.S. 1042 (1972) (material and substantial disruption); Keefe v. Geanakos, 418 F.2d 359 (1st Cir. 1969) (shocking or inappropriate); Brubaker v. Bd. of Educ., Sch. Dist. 149, Cook Cty., Ill., 502 F.2d 973 (7th Cir.), *aff'd by an equally divided en banc. court,* 502 F.2d 1000, *cert. denied,* 421 U.S. 965 (1975) (irrelevancy and inappropriateness); Mailloux v. Kiley, 323 F. Supp. 1387 (D. Mass.), *aff'd on other grounds,* 448 F.2d 1242 (1st Cir. 1971) (serious educational purpose).

40. Brubaker v. Bd. of Educ., Sch. Dist. 149, Cook Cty. Ill., 502 F.2d 973 (7th Cir.), *aff'd by an equally divided en banc court,* 502 F.2d 1000, *cert. denied,* 421 U.S. 965 (1975).

41. Moore v. Sch. Bd., 364 F. Supp. 355 (N.D. Fla. 1973).

42. Knarr v. Bd. of Sch. Trustees, 317 F. Supp. 832, 836 (N.D. Ind. 1970), *aff'd*, 452 F. 2d 649 (7th Cir. 1971). *Compare* Petrie v. Forest Hills Sch. Dist. Bd. of Educ., 5 Ohio App. 3d 115, 449 N.E.2d 786 (Ohio Ct. App. 1983).

43. Nigosian v. Weiss, 343 F. Supp. 757 (E.D. Mich., 1971).

44. LaRocca v. Bd. of Educ., of Rye City Sch. Dist., 63 A.D.2d 1019, 406 N.Y.S.2d 348 (A.D. 1978).

45. Mailloux. v. Kiley, 323 F. Supp. 1387 (D. Mass.), *aff'd on other grounds*, 448 F.2d 1242 (1st Cir. 1971); Keefe v. Geanakos, 418 F.2d 359 (1st Cir. 1971); Parducci v. Rutland, 316 F.Supp. 352 (M.D. Ala. 1970); James v. Bd. of Educ., 461 F.2d 566 (2d Cir.), *cert. denied*, 409 U.S. 1042 (1972); Kingsville Ind. Sch. Dist. v. Cooper, 611 F.2d 1109 (5th Cir. 1980); Sterzing v. Fort Bend Ind. Sch. Dist., 376 F. Supp. 657 (S.D. Tex. 1972), *vacated on other grounds*, 496 F.2d 92 (5th Cir. 1974); Stachura v. Truszkowski, 763 F.2d 211 (6th Cir. 1985), *U.S. appeal pending.*

46. 418 F.Supp. 1358 (D. Oregon 1976).

47. Knarr v. Bd. of Sch. Trustees, 317 F. Supp. 352 (M.D. Ala. 1970), *aff'd*, 452 F.2d 649 (7th Cir. 1971).

48. *See, e.g.*, Mailloux v. Kiley, 448 F.2d 1242 (1st Cir. 1971), *aff'g*, 323 F. Supp. 1387 (D. Mass. 1971); Keefe v. Geanokos, 418 F.2d 359 (1st Cir. 1969); *see also* Webb v. Lake Mills Comm. Sch. Dist., 344 F. Supp. 791 (N.D. Iowa, C.D. 1972).

49. Endress v. Brookdale Community College, 144 N.J. Super. 109, 364 A.2d 1080 (1976).

50. Russo v. Central Sch. Dist. No. 1, 469 F.2d 623 (2d Cir. 1972), *cert. denied*, 411 U.S. 932 (1973).

51. Palmer v. Bd. of Educ. of City of Chicago, 603 F.2d 1271 (7th Cir. 1979), *cert. denied*, 444 U.S. 1026 (1980).

52. Moore v. Gaston County Bd. of Educ., 357 F. Supp. 1037 (W.D. N.C. 1973).

53. Fisher v. Fairbanks North Star Borough Sch. Dist., 704 P.2d 213, 217 (Alaska, 1985) (quoting from Epperson v. Arkansas, 393 U.S. 97, 116 [1968]).

54. Cary v. Bd. of Educ., 598 F.2d 535 (10th Cir. 1979); Minarcini v. Strongsville City Sch. Dist., 541 F.2d 577, 579-80 (6th Cir. 1976).

55. Fisher v. Fairbanks North Star Borough Sch. Dist., 704 P.2d 213 (Alaska, 1985).

56. Nicholson v. Bd. of Educ. Torrance Unified Sch. Dist., 682 F.2d 858 (9th Cir. 1982).

57. In other contexts the Supreme Court has wrestled with the question of what limits, if any, government may impose on the use of public facilities for free speech activities, once those facilities have been opened up to some speech activities. The following cases are relevant to this problem: Perry v. Ed. Ass'n v. Perry Local Educator's Ass'n, 460 U.S. 37 (1983); Southeastern Promotions, Ltd. v. Conrad, 420 U.S. 546 (1975); Lehman v. Shaker Heights, 418 U.S. 298 (1974).

58. David Rubin and Steven Greenhouse, *Rights of Teachers* (New York: Bantam Books, 1983), 130. The topic of the rights of student editors will be discussed in §6.8.

59. East Hartford Educ. Ass'n v. Bd. of Educ., 562 F.2d 838 (2d Cir. 1977).

60. *Cf.*, Parducci v. Rutland, 316 F.Supp. 352 (M.D. Ala. 1970) in which the court assessed the appropriateness of Kurt Vonnegut's story "Welcome to the Monkey House" for a junior English class.

61. One of the standards, namely, did the materials cause "material and substantial disruption" is the principle standard for determining the limits of the free speech rights of students. *See* §6.5.

62. Givhan v. Western Line Consolidated Sch. Dist., 439 U.S. 410 (1976). The Court did note that when a "government employee personally confronts his immediate superior, the employing agency's institutional efficiency may be threatened not only by the content of the employee's message, but also by the time, and place in which it is delivered." *Id.*, at 415 n.4.

63. In an opinion dissenting from the denial of certiorari Justice Brennan noted that the question remains open "whether nondisruptive speech ever can constitutionally serve as the basis

for termination under the First Amendment." Rowland v. Mad River Local Sch. Dist. Montgomery Cty., 105 S. Ct. 1373, 1376 (1985) (Brennan, J., dissenting).

64. 461 F.2d 566 (2d Cir.), *cert. denied*, 409 U.S. 1042 (1972).

65. Bertot v. Sch. Dist. No. 1, 522 F.2d 1171 (10th Cir. 1975) (assisting in distribution of underground newspaper protected); Los Angeles Teachers Union v. Los Angeles City Bd. of Educ., 71 C.2d 551, 78 Cal. Rptr. 723, 455 P.2d 827 (Cal. 1969) (en banc) (distribution to other teachers of petition dealing with financing of public education protected). *Cf.*, Rowland v. Mad River Local Sch. Dist., Montgomery Cty., Md., 615 F.2d 1362 (6th Cir. 1984), *cert denied*, 105 S. Ct. 1373 (1985).

66. Texas State Teachers Ass'n. v. Garland Indep. Sch. Dist., 777 F.2d 1046 (5th Cir. 1985).

67. The court, however, upheld the school policy of denying the Texas State Teachers Association itself from meeting or recruiting during school hours and from using school communication facilities for the distribution of information concerning the employee organization. The organization could, however, meet or recruit teachers on school premises before and after the school day, upon request to and approval of the principal. School policy also permitted the distribution of literature on school premises during nonschool hours. *Cf.*, Perry Educ. Ass'n. v. Perry Local Educators' Ass'n., 460 U.S. 37 (1983) (upholding policy of permitting the incumbent union to use the internal school mail system while denying access to the minority union). *See*, §2.5.

68. Rozman v. Elliott, 335 F. Supp. 1086 (D. Neb. 1971), *aff'd*, 467 F.2d 1145 (8th Cir. 1972); Trotman v. Bd. of Trustees of Lincoln University, 635 F.2d 216 (3rd Cir. 1980), *cert. denied*, 451 U.S. 896 (1981); Whitsel v. Southeast Local Sch. Dist., 484 F.2d 1222 (6th Cir. 1973).

69. Shaw v. Bd. of Trustees of Frederick Comm. College, 549 F.2d 929 (4th Cir. 1976).

70. Clarke v. Bd. of Educ. of Sch. Dist. of Omaha, 215 Neb. 250, 338 N.W.2d 272 (1983). The court agreed that the teacher's behavior was immoral conduct within the meaning of the teacher dismissal statute. If the teacher had defended himself on the grounds of freedom of speech, the court undoubtedly would have ruled that such speech is not protected speech. The teacher's racial epithet and invitation to a fight clearly fall into the unprotected category of "fighting words," i.e., words that are likely to cause the average addressee to fight. Chaplinsky v. New Hampshire, 315 U.S. 568 (1942).

71. 730 F.2d 444 (6th Cir. 1984), *cert. denied*, 105 S. Ct. 1373 (1985).

72. Perry v. Educ. Ass'n. v. Perry Local School Educators' Ass'n., 460 U.S. 37 (1983).

73. Id.; see note 3 for a discussion of content- and viewpoint-based suppression.

74. 615 F. Supp. 761 (D.C. Ind. 1985), *aff'd*, 787 F.2d 1105 (7th Cir. 1986).

75. Texas State Teachers Ass'n. v. Garland Indep. Sch. Dist., 777 F.2d 1046 (5th Cir. 1985). *See* supra note 67.

76. Piarowski v. Illinois Comm. College Dist. 515, 759 F.2d 625 (7th Cir. 1985) (no infringement of professor's freedom of speech to require that certain of his sexually explicit works of art be relocated from a gallery near a heavily trafficked mall to an alternative site); Close v. Lederle, 424 F.2d 988 (1st Cir. 1970) (university officials could order removal from heavily trafficked corridor of sexually graphic paintings by a faculty member).

77. Connecticut State Federation of Teachers v. Bd. of Educ. Members, 538 F.2d 471 (2d Cir. 1976); Friedman v. Union Free Sch. Dist., 314 F. Supp. 223 (E.D. N.Y. 1970). In May v. Evansville-Vanderburgh Sch. Corp., 787 F.2d 1105 (7th Cir. 1986) the court upheld the school's policy of denying teachers of religious groups use of school facilities for religious purposes prior to the start of the school day.

78. Hall v. Bd. of Sch. Commissioners of Mobile City, Ala., 681 F.2d 965 (5th Cir. 1982). Prior review rules applicable to teachers presumably must meet the same requirements as the rules applicable to students. *See* §6.6.

79. Adamian v. Jacobsen, 523 F.2d 929 (9th Cir. 1975) (striking down as overbroad and

vague a university rule that required faculty members "to be accurate, to exercise appropriate restraint, to show respect for the opinion of others . . .)"

80. For example, the theory that holds free expression is to be protected because of its importance for making the system of self-governance work does not provide support for protecting the rights of students in the public school context.

81. Abrams v. United States, 250 U.S. 616, 630 (1919) (Holmes, J., dissenting).

82. *See supra*, materials on public forums at note 72.

83. Tinker v. Des Moines Ind. Comm. Sch. Dist., 393 U.S. 503 (1969).

84. For a discussion of the concept of a public forum see materials at note 72, *supra*.

85. *See, e.g.*, Powe v. Miles, 407 F.2d 73 (2d cir. 1968); Goldberg v. Regents of U. of Cal., 248 Ca.2d 867, 57 Cal. Rptr. 463 (1967).

86. Tinker v. Des Moines Ind. Comm. Sch. Dist., 393 U.S. 503 (1969).

87. Mark G. Yudof, David L. Kirp, Tyll van Geel, and Betsy Levin, *Educational Policy and the Law*, 2d ed. (Berkeley, Calif.: McCutchan Publishing Corporation, 1982), 214-15.

88. Hernandez v. Sch. Dist. No. 1, Denver 315 F. Supp. 289 (D. Colo. 1970) (assuming a beret is a form of free speech in deciding the case); Guzick v. Drebus, 421 F.2d 594 (6th Cir. 1970), *cert. denied*, 401 U.S. 948 (1970); Fricke v. Lynch, 491 F. Supp. 381 (D.R.I. 1980) (right of male to bring male escort to dance).

89. Karr v. Schmidt, 460 F.2d 609 (5th Cir. 1972) (en banc), *cert. denied*, 409 U.S. 989 (1972); Jarman v. Williams, 753 F.2d 76 (8th Cir. 1985).

90. Gay Students Organization v. Bonner, 509 F.2d 652 (1st Cir. 1974).

91. Guzick v. Drebus, 431 F.2d 594 (6th Cir. 1979), *cert. denied*, 401 U.S. 948 (1970).

92. Tate v. Bd. of Educ. of Jonesboro, Ark., Spec. Sch. Dist., 453 F.2d 975 (8th Cir. 1972).

93. 612 F. Supp. 86 (D.C. Ark. 1985).

94. 755 F.2d 1356 (9th Cir. 1985), *rev'd*, 106 S. Ct. 3195 (1986). Mathew Fraser's speech spoke of the other student as a "man who is firm—he's firm in his pants. . . . If necessary, he'll take an issue and nail it to the wall. He doesn't attack things in spurts—he drives hard, pushing and pushing until finally—he succeeds. Jeff is a man who will go to the very end—even the climax, for each and every one of you. . . . [H]e'll never come between you and the best our high school can be."

95. The district also argued that Mathew could be disciplined because his speech was "indecent," and because school officials had the authority to regulate the speech of students who participate in assemblies. The court rejected both of these arguments. For a further discussion of these points see §§6.7 and 6.8.

96. Bethel Sch. Dist. No. 403, Fraser, 106 S.Ct. 3159 (1986). Justice Brennan, long noted for his vigorous defense of freedom of speech, concurred in the judgment of the Court stressing that school officials had authority to "restrict a high school student's use of disruptive language in a speech given to a high school assembly." *Id.*, at 3168.

97. Id., at 558-59.

98. Id., at 558.

99. Tachtman v. Anker, 563 F.2d 512 (2d Cir. 1977). *Cf.*, In Kuhlmeier v. Hazelwood Sch. Dist., 795 F.2d 1368 (8th Cir. 1986) the court concluded that there was no evidence upon which school officials could forecast that the publication in a school newspaper of articles on divorce and teenage pregnancy would cause disruption in the school, that the article would create the impression that the school officials endorsed the sexual norms of the students interviewed, or that the articles were inappropriate given the age and immaturity of some of the readers of the paper.

100. Id., at 516 n. 2.

101. Id., at 515 n. 3.

102. Comments—"Behind the Schoolhouse Gate: Sex and the Student Pollster," *New York University Law Review* 54 (1979): 161.

103. Gebert v. Hoffman, 336 F. Supp. 694 (E.D. Pa. 1972); Commonwealth v. Bohmer, 372 N.E.2d 1381 (Mass. 1978); Sword v. Fox, 446 F.2d 1091 (4th Cir. 1971), cert. denied, 404 U.S. 994 (1971) (upholding regulations that prohibit demonstrations in buildings but allow demonstrations elsewhere); McAlpine v. Reese, 309 F. Supp. 136 (E.D. Mich. 1970); Powe v. Miles, 407 F.2d 73 (2nd Cir. 1968); Goldberg v. Regents of U. of Cal., 248 Ca.2d 867, 57 Cal. Rptr. 463 (1967).

104. Melton v. Young, 465 F.2d 1332 (6th Cir. 1972); Hernandez v. Sch. Dist. No. 1, 315 F. Supp. 289 (D. Colo. 1970); Guzick v. Drebus, 431 F.2d 594 (6th cir. 1970), cert. denied, 401 U.S. 948 (1970); Hill v. Lewis, 323 F. Supp. 55 (E.D. N.C. 1971).

105. See, e.g., Karp v. Becken, 477 F.2d 171 (9th Cir. 1973) (signs brought on campus can be taken from students but students may not be suspended).

106. Cf., Feiner v. New York, 340 U.S. 315, 322 (1951) (Black, J., dissenting); Ferrell v. Dallas Indep. Sch. Dist., 392 F.2d 697, 706 (5th Cir. 1968) (Tuttle, J., dissenting), cert. denied, 393 U.S. 856 (1968).

107. Scoville v. Bd. of Educ. of Joliet Township, 425 F.2d 10 (7th Cir. 1970), cert. denied, 400 U.S. 826 (1970); Sullivan v. Houston Indep. Sch. Dist., 307 F. Supp. 1328 (S.D. Tex. 1969); Shanley v. Northeast Indep. Sch. Dist., Bexar Cty. Tex., 462 F.2d 960 (5th Cir. 1972).

108. Norton v. Discipline Committee of East Tenn. State Univ., 419 F.2d 195 (6th Cir. 1969).

109. 622 F.2d 1200 (4th Cir. 1980).

110. See Central Hudson Gas. v. Public Service Comm'n, 447 U.S. 557 (1980). For commercial speech to be protected by the first amendment, it must concern a lawful activity and not be misleading. If the commercial speech in question meets these tests, it may be regulated only if government's interest is substantial, and by regulations that directly advance the governmental interest served, and that are not more extensive than necessary to serve that interest.

111. Such a ban would implicate, first, the constitutional rights of minors to obtain contraception. Carey v. Population Services International, 431 U.S. 678 (1977). And the right of the mature minor to obtain an abortion. Bellotti v. Baird, 443 U.S. 622 (1979).

112. Thomas v. Bd. of Educ., Granville Cent. Sch. Dist., 607 F.2d 1043 (2d Cir. 1979); Shanley v. Northeastern Ind. Sch. Dist., Bexar Cty., Tex., 462 F.2d 960 (5th Cir. 1972).

113. Thomas v. Bd. of Educ., 607 F.2d at 1051.

114. Kuhlmeier v. Hazelwood Sch. Dist., 795 F.2d 1368, 1376 (8th Cir. 1986).

115. Id.

116. 490 F.2d 601 (7th Cir. 1973).

117. The court did suggest that commercial activities by nonschool persons on school grounds could be prohibited. Id., at 608. The court in Peterson v. Bd. of Educ., 370 F. Supp. 1208 (D. Neb. 1973) said that commercial sales could only be banned if the school could show they would be disruptive.

118. Katz. v. McAuley, 438 F.2d 1058 (2d Cir. 1971), cert. denied, 405 U.S. 933 (1972) (upholding the ban); contra, Cintron v. St. Bd. of Educ., 384 F. Supp. 674 (D. Puerto Rico 1974); New Left Ed. Project v. Bd. of Regents, 326 F. Supp. 158 (W.D. Tex. 1970), vacated, 404 U.S. 541 (1972), on remand, 472 F.2d 218 (5th Cir. 1973), cert. granted and vacated as moot. 414 U.S. 807 (1973). The question of the right of access of commercial companies to college dormitories has also been litigated. American Future Systems, Inc. v. Pennsylvania State Unversity, 618 F.2d 252 (3d Cir. 1980), 752 F.2d 854 (3d Cir. 1985). For a further discussion of these cases, see §6.11.

119. Time, place, manner regulations must be content-neutral, narrowly tailored to serve a significant governmental interest, and leave open ample alternative channels of communication. Heffron v. Int'l Soc. for Krishna Consc., 452 U.S. 640 (1981).

120. Cf., Heffron v. Int'l Soc. for Krishna Consc., 452 U.S. 640 (1981).

121. Sword v. Fox, 446 F.2d 1091 (4th Cir. 1971), cert. denied, 404 U.S. 994 (1971).

122. Heffron v. Int'l Soc. for Krishna Consc., 452 U.S. 640 (1981). See supra, note 117.

123. Connally v. General Construction Co., 269 U.S. 385, 391 (1926).

124. One federal court invalidated a school rule because the words "decency, taste, obscenity,

and libelous" were not defined. Liebner v. Sharbaugh, 429 F. Supp. 744 (E.D. Va. 1977). *See also* Nitzberg v. Park, 525 F.2d 378 (4th Cir. 1975); Shanley v. Northeast Indep. Sch. Dist., Bexar City, Tex., 462 F.2d 960 (5th Cir. 1972); Sullivan v. Houston Ind. Sch. Dist., 307 F. Supp. 1328 (S.D. Texas 1969).

125. Jacobs v. Bd. of Sch. Commissioners, 490 F.2d 601, 604 (7th Cir. 1973), *vacated as moot*, 420 U.S. 128 (1975). The court in Williams v. Spencer, 622 F.2d 1200 (4th Cir. 1980) rejected a challenge that a school rule prohibiting the distribution of materials "which encourages actions would endanger the health and safety of students" was unconstitutionally vague.

126. *Accord*, Nitzberg v. Parks, 525 F.2d 378, 383 (4th Cir. 1975).

127. Eisner v. Stamford Bd. of Educ., 440 F.2d 803 (2d Cir. 1971).

128. Fujishima v. Bd. of Educ., 460 F.2d 1355 (7th Cir. 1972); Eisner v. Stamford Bd. of Educ., 440 F.2d 1345 (2d Cir. 1971); Nitzberg v. Park, 525 F.2d 378 (4th Cir. 1975); Baughman v. Freienmuth, 478 F.2d 1345 (4th Cir. 1973); Quarterman v. Byrd, 453 F.2d 54 (4th Cir. 1971); Shanley v. Northeast Indep. Sch. Dist., Bexar Cty., Tex., 462 F.2d 960 (5th Cir. 1972).

129. Freedman v. Maryland, 380 U.S. 51 (1965); Eisner v. Stamford Bd. of Educ., 440 F.2d at 810.

130. *See* cases cited in note 90, *supra.*

131. Miller v. California, 413 U.S. 15 (1973) (obscenity); Chaplinsky v. New Hampshire, 315 U.S. 568 (1942) (fighting words); New York Times v. Sullivan, 376 U.S. 254 (1964) (libel). Materials depicting children in sexual conduct, even though not within definition of obscenity as defined in the *Miller* decision, may also be suppressible as falling outside the ambit of the first amendment. New York v. Ferber, 458 U.S. 747 (1982).

132. Ginsberg v. New York, 390 U.S. 629 (1968).

133. Tribe, *American Constitutional Law, supra* note 3, at 582, 602, 617, 638, 656. Content-based denials of access to places government has opened to expressive activities must be necessary to serve a compelling state interest. Widmar v. Vincent, 454 U.S. 263, 269-70 (1981).

134. Central Hudson Gas v. Public Serivce Comm'n, 447 U.S. 557 (1980) (commercial speech); FCC v. Pacifica Foundation, 438 U.S. 726 (1978) (offensive speech).

135. Chaplinsky v. New Hampshire, 315 U.S. 568 (1942).

136. Fenton v. Stear, 423 F. Supp. 767 (W.D. Pa. 1976). *Cf.*, McCall v. State, 354 So.2d 869 (Fla. 1978) (striking down as vague a law making it a crime to upbraid, abuse, or insult any member of the instruction staff on school property or in the presence of pupils at a school activity); Butts v. Dallas Indep. Sch. Dist., 436 F.2d 728 (5th Cir. 1971) (concluding that black armbands worn in protest to the Vietnam War were not per se akin to "fighting words").

137. Shanley v. Northeastern Indep. Sch. Dist., Bexar Cty., Tex., 462 F.2d 960 (5th Cir. 1972). *See also* Frasca v. Andrews, 463 F.Supp. 1043 (E.D. N.Y. 1979) (upholding suppression of an issue of the school newspaper because, among other things, it contained an article with arguably libelous statements about a student officer).

These courts have not commented, however, on the implications for student publications of various constitutionally based defenses that may be raised when public officials and public figures sue for defamation. *See, e.g.*, New York Times Co. v. Sullivan, 376 U.S. 254 (1964). Note also that the distinction between suppression because materials are libelous and because of disagreement with the viewpoint expressed may at times be hard to draw. Libel consists of "false" statements that damage the reputation of an individual. One may disagree with an expression of opinion but is it "false"? Consider the case of a school newspaper that says that the student council president is doing a poor job. May that paper be suppressed as libelous, or does the article simply state a matter of editorial opinion? Traditional libel law would provide the author of the article protection, first, perhaps because the student council president is a "public figure," and, second, because the author only expressed an opinion and not a statement that is false in the sense the claimed "fact" is refutable by empirical evidence.

138. Id., Baughman v. Freienmuth, 478 F.2d 1345, 1349 (4th Cir. 1973). Whether a particu-

lar publication is legally obscene for adults has been the subject of extensive litigation. *See, e.g.,* Miller v. California, 413 U.S. 15 (1973). To make matters more difficult the Supreme Court has said that materials not obscene for adults may be as to minors. Ginsberg v. New York, 390 U.S. 629 (1968).

139. Papish v. Bd. of Curators of University of Mo., 331 F. Supp. 1321 (W.D. Mo. 1971).

140. 410 U.S. 667, 670 (1973) (emphasis added).

141. 457 U.S. 853 (1982). *See* chapter 5.

142. FCC v. Pacifica Foundation, 438 U.S. 726 (1978).

143. Ginsberg v. New York, 390 U.S. 629 (1968).

144. 403 U.S. 15 (1971).

145. Jacobs v. Bd. of School Commissioners, 490 F.2d 601 (7th Cir. 1973), *vacated as moot,* 420 U.S. 128 (1975); Scoville v. Bd. of Education of Joliet Township, 425 F.2d 10 (7th Cir. 1970), *cert. denied,* 400 U.S. 826 (1970) ("Oral sex may cause tooth decay"); Vail v. Bd. of Educ. of Portsmouth, 354 F. Supp. 592 (D.N.H. 1973) *vacated,* 502 F.2d 1159 (1st Cir. 1973); Koppell v. Levine, 347 F. Supp. 456 (E.D. N.Y. 1972); *contra,* Baker v. Downey City Bd. of Educ., 307 F. Supp. 517 (C.D. Calif. 1969).

146. Hinze v. Superior Court of Marin Cty., 119 Ca.3d 1005, 174 Cal. Rptr. 403 (Cal. App. 1981).

147. 106 S.Ct. 3159 (1986).

148. Id., at 3162.

149. 393 U.S. 503 (1969).

150. Bethel Sch. Dist. No. 403 v. Fraser, 106 S.Ct., at 3163.

151. Id., at 3164.

152. Id., at 3165.

153. Id., at 3164.

154. Id.

155. Id., at 3164.

156. Id.

157. Id., at 3165.

158. Id., at 3166.

159. Id., 3165.

160. *See supra,* note 72 and, *infra,* §6.8.

161. Bethel Sch. Dist. No. 403 v. Fraser, 106 S.Ct., at 3165.

162. American Booksellers Ass'n v. Hudnut, 598 F. Supp. 1316 (S.D. Ind. 1984), *aff'd,* 771 F.2d 323 (7th Cir. 1985).

163. For a discussion of the different types of public forums, see materials at note 72, *supra.*

164. Kuhlmeier v. Hazelwood Sch. Dist., 795 F.2d 1368 (8th Cir. 1986) (striking down decision of principal to bar publication of two articles in a student-run school newspaper produced through a journalism class.) *See also* Seyfried v. Walton, 668 F.2d 214 (3rd Cir. 1981) (upholding decision of superintendent to cancel school dramatic production of *Pippin* because of sexual theme; the play was deemed simply to be an integral part of the school curriculum and under the control of the school). But a federal district court in Bayer v. Kinzler, 383 F. Supp. 1164 (E.D. N.Y. 1974) took the position that even if the school newspaper was part of the curriculum, that did not lessen the degree of protection provided student speech. The court argued that if a speech activity could be simply viewed as part of the curriculum, thereby denying it the protection of the first amendment, the paper could be seized merely because of disagreement with political articles in the paper. In this case the paper was seized by the principal because it contained a four-page supplement, comprising articles on contraception and abortion.

165. Recall that as to these forums for government to enforce viewpoint- or content-based exclusions, it must establish that the exclusion is necessary to achieve a compelling state purpose and is narrowly drawn to achieve that end. Government may also enforce time, place, and manner

regulations that are content-neutral, are narrowly tailored to serve a significant government interest, and leave open ample alternative channels of communication.

166. *See* note 3 for a discussion of viewpoint- and subject matter-based suppression. *See supra,* materials at note 72 for limits imposed on government in regulating category-three forums.

167. Cornelius v. NAACP Legal Defense Fund, 105 S.Ct. 3439, 3449 (1985). To determine the intent of the government, one must examine its policies and practices.

168. Nicholson v. Bd. of Educ., Torrence Unified School Dist., 682 F.2d 858, 863 (9th Cir. 1982). Despite the fact that a school newspaper was published by a journalism class under the supervision of a faculty advisor, and that the paper was submitted to the principal for review prior to publication, the Eighth Circuit concluded that the paper was a public forum. Kuhlmeier v. Hazelwood Sch. Dist., 795 F.2d 1368 (8th Cir. 1986). The court stressed that the faculty advisor exercised minimal editorial control, the students chose the staff members, determined the articles to be printed, and the various school policy statements supported the notion that the paper was to be a vehicle for the free expression of diverse viewpoints. The court also took note of the fact that since 1976 the paper had been publishing stories dealing with teenage dating, drug and alchohol use, desegregation, runaways, religions and cults. This last point was of significance because the two articles censored by the principal in this case involved divorce and student pregnancy, topics which seemed to have no greater potential for disruption and "harm" than those topics published earlier.

169. American Future Systems, Inc., v. Pa. State U., 752 F.2d 854 (3d Cir. 1985). In this case a commercial vendor of cookware and other household items, joined by a number of university students, challenged university regulations prohibiting student-initiated group sales demonstrations in dormitory rooms. The Third Circuit rejected the challenge.

170. 429 F. Supp. 731 (E.D. Vir.1977), *aff'd,* 564 F.2d 157 (4th Cir. 1977). The Eighth Circuit has stressed that if the school newspaper is a public forum, it is the *Tinker* standards which are to determine if school officials acted constitutionally in censoring articles to be published in the paper. Kuhlmeier v. Hazelwood Sch. Dist., 795 F.2d 1368 (8th Cir. 1986).

171. Dickey v. Alabama State Board of Educ., 273 F. Supp. 613 (M.D. Ala. 1967).

172. Stanley v. McGrath, 719 F.2d 279 (8th Cir. 1983); Bayer v. Kinzler, 383 F. Supp. 1164 (E.D. N.Y. 1974), *aff'd without op.* 515 F.2d 504 (2nd Cir. 1975); Joyner v. Whiting, 477 F.2d 456 (4th Cir. 1973); Reinke v. Cobb Cty. Sch. Dist., 484 F. Supp. 1252 (N.D. Ga. 1980); Frasca v. Andrews, 463 F. Supp. 1043 (E.D. N.Y. 1979); Trujillo v. Love, 322 F. Supp. 1266 (D. Colo. 1971); Antonelli v. Hammond, 308 F. Supp. 1329 (D. Mass. 1970).

173. Stanton v. Brunswick Sch. Dept., 577 F. Supp. 1560 (D. Me. 1984). The quotation the student had chosen from a *Time* magazine article stated, "The executioner will pull this lever four times. Each time 2000 volts will course through your body, making your eyeballs first bulge, then burst, and then broiling your brains. . . ."

174. *See* Panarella v. Birenbaum, 32 N.Y.2d 108, 296 N.E.2d 238, 343 N.Y.S.2d 333 (1973). Quoted in Yudof et al., *Educational Policy and the Law, supra* note 87, at 203.

175. Kuhlmeier v. Hazelwood Sch. Dist., 607 F. Supp. 1450, 1463 (E.D. Mo. 1985), *rev'd,* 795 F.2d 1368 (8th Cir. 1986) (dictum).

176. Frasca v. Andrews, 463 F. Supp. 1043 (E.D. N.Y. 1979).

177. Reineke v. Cobb Cty. Sch. Dist., 484 F. Supp. 1252 (N.D. Ga. 1980).

178. 299 F. Supp. 102 (S.D. N.Y. 1969). *Cf.,* In Mississippi Gay Alliance v. Goudelock, 536 F.2d 1073 (5th Cir. 1976) the Fifth Circuit held a student newspaper need not take advertising from an off-campus group. The court found there was no "state-action" because the newspaper operated independently of faculty and administrative control.

179. 106 S. Ct. 3159 (1986). The text of the speech can be found in footnote 94.

180. Kuhlmeier v. Hazelwood Sch. Dist., 795 F.2d 1308 (8th Cir. 1986); Nicholson v. Bd. of Educ. Torrance Unified Sch. Dist., 682 F.2d 858 (9th Cir. 1982). The court also concluded that termination of a faculty advisor for failing to comply with prior-review requirement was permissible.

181. Widmar v. Vincent, 454 U.S. 263, 267-68 (1981).

182. Healy v. James, 408 U.S. 169, 181 (1972).

183. Widmar v. Vincent, 454 U.S. 263, 270, (1981).

184. Healy v. James, 408 U.S. 169, 187, (1972).

185. Widmar v. Vincent, 454 U.S. at 277. For a further discussion of this issue see §5.4.

186. Healy v. James, 408 U.S. at 188-91.

187. Id., at 189, 193. Cf., Merkey v. Bd. of Regents of State of Florida, 344 F. Supp. 1296 (N.D. Fla. 1972) in which the court concluded there was substantial evidence that a student group posed a threat of disruption. Among other things, several of the members of the group had themselves been recently involved in disruptive activities and that the group advocated violent revolution.

188. Gay Liberation v. University of Missouri, 558 F.2d 848 (8th Cir. 1977), cert. denied, 434 U.S. 1080 (1978); Gay Alliance of Students v. Mathews, 544 F.2d 162 (4th Cir. 1976); Gay Students Organization of University of New Hampshire v. Bonner, 509 F.2d 652 (1st Cir. 1974); Cf., Bowers v. Hardwick, 106 S.Ct. 2841 (1986) (holding that there is no fundamental constitutional right on the part of homosexuals to engage in consensual sodomy).

189. Gay Students Services v. Texas A & M University, 737 F.2d 1317, 1328 (5th Cir. 1984).

190. Id.

191. Dixon v. Beresh, 361 F. Supp. 253 (E.D. Mich. 1973).

192. See, e.g., Bradford Board of Educ., 18 Ca. 19, 121 P. 929 (Cal. App. 1912).

193. See Roberts v. United States Jaycees, 468 U.S. 609 (1984). The regulations enforcing Title IX, 20 U.S.C. §1681 (1982) (prohibiting discrimination on the basis of gender in federally assisted programs) prohibit assistance to organizations that discriminate on the basis of sex. 45 C.F.R. §86.31(b)(7) (1985). See Iron Arrow Honor Society v. Schweiker, 652 F.2d 445 (5th Cir. 1981), vacated, 458 U.S. 1102 (1982).

194. 776 F.2d 431 (3rd Cir. 1985).

195. 20 U.S.C.A. §§4071 et seq. (Supp. 1985).

196. 105 S.Ct. 3439 (185).

197. Id., at 3451.

198. 776 F.2d at 442. The Equal Access Act states that a school does not violate the equal access requirement if the school "uniformly provides that . . . nonschool persons may not direct, conduct, control, or regularly attend activities of student groups." 20 U.S.C.A. §4071(c) (Supp. 1985).

The court also held that the Equal Access Act could be enforced by a private cause of action for an injunction.

199. Cf., Abood v. Detroit of Educ., 431 U.S. 209 (1977); Wooley v. Maynard, 430 U.S. 705 (1977); West Virginia State Bd. of Educ. v. Barnett, 319 U.S. 624 (1943).

200. Uzzell v. Friday, 547 F.2d 801 (4th Cir. 1977); Arrington v. Taylor, 380 F. Supp. 1348 (M.D.N.C. 1974), aff'd, 526 F.2d 587 (4th Cir. 1975); Veed v. Schwartkopf, 353 F. Supp. 149 (D. Neb. 1973), aff'd, 478 F.2d 1407 (8th Cir. 1973), cert. denied, 444 U.S. 1135 (1974).

201. Galda v. Rutgers, 589 F. Supp. 479 (1984).

202. Id., at 481 quoting from a prior opinion of Third Circuit Court of Appeals in this litigation. Galda v. Bloustein, 686 F.2d 159, 166-67 (3rd Cir. 1982). The Third Circuit also noted that even if the plaintiffs met this burden of proof, the university might prevail by "demonstrating a compelling state interest by establishing the importance of the challenged group's contribution to the university forum." Id.

203. Id., at 496-497, n. 12

204. Good v. Associated Students of U. of Wash., 542 P.2d 762 (1975).

205. Widmar v. Vincent, 454 U.S. 263, 267 n. 5 (1981).

206. Brooks v. Auburn University, 412 F.2d 1171 (5th Cir. 1969) (president's veto of choice of speaker Public Affairs Seminar Board violates right to hear of students and faculty); Vail v. Bd.

of Educ. of Portsmouth, 354 F. Supp. 592 (D. N.H. 1973) (striking down the veto by school officials of a request by students for permission for the vice-presidential candidate of the Socialist Workers party to speak in the school after Democratic and Republican candidates had spoken at Portsmouth High School). *See also,* Pickings v. Bruce, 430 F.2d 595 (8th Cir. 1970) (imposing sanctions on faculty advisors of student group because the organization invitation to a controversial speaker to campus violated free speech rights of advisors and students).

207. Stacy v. Williams, 306 F. Supp. 963 (N.D. Miss. 1969).

208. Solmitz v. Maine Sch. Administrative Dist., 495 A.2d 812 (1985). *Cf.,* Pickings v. Bruce, 430 F.2d 595 (8th Cir. 1970) (college administrators not justified in seeking cancellation of controversial speakers).

209. *See, e.g.,* Pratt v. Indep. School District 670 F.2d 771 (8th Cir. 1982) (holding that the board's decision to remove a film from classroom use was in response to the religiously based objections of parents); United States v. Yonkers Bd. of Educ., 624 F. Supp. 1276 (S.D. N.Y. 1985) (finding that public housing authority decisions were in response to the racially biased opposition of white constituents).

210. *See, e.g.,* People v. Deatherage, 81 N.E.2d 581 (Ill. 194); Carson v. State, 27 Ind. 465, 469 (1967). State statutes in some states specifically require that school facilities be made available to community groups. It is common for state statutes to require that school facilities be made available as polling places for state and local elections.

211. For an overview of cases in this area see Leroy J. Peterson, Richard A. Rossmiller, and Marlin M. Volz, *The Law and Public School Operation* (New York: Harper & Row, 1978), 208-15.

212. Goodman v. Bd. of Educ. of San Francisco, 120 P.2d 665 (Cal. 1941).

213. Perry v. Educ. Ass'n v. Perry Local Educators' Ass'n., 460 U.S. 37 (1983). Glover v. Cole, 762 F.2d 1197 (4th Cir. 1985) (upholding a prohibition against nonstudent groups engaging in sales and fund raising on campus). *Cf.,* Heffron v. Int'l Soc. for Krishna Consc., 452 U.S. 640 (1981).

214. Katz. v. McAulay, 438 F.2d 1058 (2d Cir. 1971), *cert. denied,* 405 U.S. 933 (1972) (prohibiting a state university from prohibiting the distribution of all handbills on a part of its campus that was open to the public). *Cf.,* Greer v. Spock, 424 U.S. 828 (1976) (upholding a bar against the distribution of political pamphlets and the making of political speeches even as to those streets on a military base unrestricted as to civilian traffic); United States v. Albertini, 710 F.2d 1410 (9th Cir. 1983) (Air Force had created a public forum).

215. Grayned v. Rockford, 408 U.S. 104 (1972).

216. 84 N.J. 535, 423 A.2d 615 (1980), *appeal dismissed,* 455 U.S. 100 (1982).

217. The state's constitution said, "Every person may freely speak, write and publish his sentiments on all subjects being responsible for the abuse of that right. No law shall be based to restrain or abridge the liberty of speech or of the press." N.J. Const., Art. 1, par. 6.

218. Mathew W. Finkin, "On 'Institutional' Academic Freedom," *Texas Law Review* 61 (1983): 817-57.

219. National Socialist White People's Party v. Ringers, 473 F.2d 1010 (4th Cir. 1973).

220. American Civil Liberties Union of Southern California v. Bd. of Educ. of City of Los Angeles, 55 Cal.2d 167, 10 Cal. Rptr. 647, 359 P.2d 45 (1961).

221. Lawrence University Bicentennial Commission v. City of Appleton, 409 F. Supp. 1319 (E.D. Wis. 1976); Goodman v. Bd. of Educ. of San Francisco, 120 P.2d 665 (Cal. 1941).

222. *Cf.,* Widmar v. Vincent, 454 U.S. 263 (1981) (striking the university's policy of not permitting student religious groups to use university facilities when those facilities had been made available to other groups). For a further discussion of this case, see §5.4.

223. American Civil Liberties Union of Southern California v. Bd. of Educ. of City of Los Angeles, 55 Cal.2d 167, 10 Cal. Rptr. 647, 359 P.2d 45 (1961).

224. Jarmen v. Williams, 753 F.2d 76 (8th Cir. 1985).

225. 618 F.2d 252 (3d Cir. 1980) (*American Futures 1*); 752 F.2d 854 (3d Cir. 1984) (*American Futures 3*). *American Futures 2* appears at 688 F.2d 907 (3d Cir. 1982).

226. Id., at 863, 865. The court relied on the tests developed by the Supreme Court in Central Hudson Gas v. Public Service Comm'n, 447 U.S. 557 (1980).

227. There is some evidence that a majority of the Supreme Court today interprets the "least restrictive means" requirement rather leniently, thereby permitting regulations to stand that serve purposes that could in fact be met by other less-sweeping prohibitions. *See* Clark v. Community for Creative Non-Violence, 104 S.Ct. 3065 (1984).

228. Id., at 866.

229. The university permitted group political speech activities in these common rooms; the Third Circuit held that the university's distinction between group political speech and group commercial speech was not "arbitrary." *American Future Systems 1*, 618 F.2d at 258-9.

230. 454 U.S. 263 (1981) (striking the university's policy of not permitting student religious groups to use university facilities when those facilities had been made available to other student groups).

231. *See, e.g.,* Southside Estate Baptist Church v. Trustees, 115 So.2d 697, 79 A.L.R.2d 1142 (1959); Baer v. Kolmorgen, 181 N.Y.S.2d 230 (1958).

7

Mandating the Minimally Adequate Program

7.1. INTRODUCTION

Chapters 3 and 4 dealt with two important aspects of the concept of equal educational opportunity. In chapter 3 we examined the judiciary's response to the exclusion of certain students from the public schools; in chapter 4 we examined the judiciary's response to racially based pupil assignment policies. We return now to the theme of equal educational opportunity as it arises in connection with the financing of education, the placement and tracking of pupils, competency testing, and the education of special pupil populations—the handicapped and non-English-speaking pupils. As we shall see, the courts have frequently been asked to settle disputes over whether or not a particular group of students has been denied equal educational opportunity (this difficult concept will be discussed more fully below). The courts, finding the question to be a particularly complex problem, have often, but not always, sought ways to avoid wrestling with it. The central strategy used by the courts to limit their involvement, yet at the same time to protect students, has been to deny the claims for equal treatment while hinting that its reaction might be different if it were established that the claimant were receiving a minimally inadequate education. Thus, most courts have avoided declaring that the state has a constitutional duty to educate effectively.[1] This point is further underscored by the unwillingness of most courts to permit the schools to be sued for educational malpractice. The major exceptions to the judiciary's avoidance of deep involvement in shaping the school program are the school desegregation cases in which the courts have been willing to order the adoption of specific educational programs as a required remedy to restore victims of racial segregation to the level of educational competence they would have attained but for the unconstitutional conduct of the school officials.[2]

Though the judiciary has been reluctant to use its power to shape the educational program, Congress has passed a variety of pieces of legislation that specifically seek to protect the handicapped, language minority students, women, and racial minorities against educational programs that may have been discriminatory merely because of their impact. Thus, with some few limited exceptions, the most important body of law today working to assure the adequacy of the school program is federal statutory law. We shall examine that body of law in §§7.7 and 7.4.

A crucial difficulty any legislative body, court, school official, or parent confronts when dealing with the notion of "equal educational opportunity" is defining the term. Many definitions are possible; and varying definitions have been used by different litigants, courts, legislatures, other policy-makers, and advocates.

To explore the concept, we can begin with the question, equality for whom?[3] Two important answers suggest themselves: "individual-regarding" equality, and "bloc-regarding" equality.[4] Under the concept of individual-regarding equality, we must define a class of individuals, e.g., all public school students. Each person within the class is then viewed as the equal of all the rest, with a pair-by-pair comparison of individuals to each other used as the basis for determining if inequality exists. Under the notion of bloc-equality, the subjects of comparison are "blocs" of people, e.g., white pupils compared to black pupils. With this approach equality is required between these blocs rather than within them. The implications of the distinction between individual- and bloc-regarding concepts of equality will become more evident momentarily.

Another distinction important for our purposes is the distinction between "prospect-regarding" and "means-regarding" equality of opportunity.[5] The various versions of prospect-regarding equality of educational opportunity focus on the possible outcomes of educational programs, i.e., the chances of pupils achieving a certain level of competence in reading. The means-regarding notions of equal educational opportunity emphasize equality in the provision of the means to help students to achieve whatever outcomes they may be capable of achieving. Assuring students of means-regarding equality of opportunity does not assure them of prospect-regarding equal opportunity when students come to school differentially prepared by their parents, have different talents, and are differently motivated. Thus, under a means-regarding concept of equality a district's policy of treating all students the same way—each gets a desk, book, and the same instruction—would be acceptable even if some pupils because of their backgrounds could not make use of the services and facilities provided. It would be like serving soup to students, some of whom come to school with a spoon, but others of whom come to school equipped with only a fork.[6] Prospect-regarding notions of equality might require that the school provide spoons to those only with forks so that they could make effective use of what was provided. Each of these two basic versions of equal educational opportunity may be further subdivided and refined.

The means-regarding or input conception of equal opportunity can be stated in different negative and positive versions. A generalized version of the negative formulation goes like this:

The pattern of distribution of inputs (whether it be expenditures per pupil, books per pupil, pupil-teacher ratios) within a state (or school district, building, or even classroom) must not be a function of (be determined by, caused by, correlated with)_____ [7]

Depending on the kind of problem with which one is wrestling, the blank could be filled with such phrases as these: the race, religion, or ethnic origin of the pupils; the wealth of the pupils' own families; the per-pupil property wealth of the school district in which the student resides. This category of standard does not require equality in the allocation of resources; it only says that, if there are inequalities, they may not be determined by a particular variable. In contrast to this "negative" means-regarding standard, a "positive" means-regarding standard more directly controls the allocation of resources. Examples of such standards would include such requirements as the following: that equal resources must be spent per pupil, and that compensatory expenditures must be made for pupils with learning difficulties.

Prospect-regarding or output standards also come in negative and positive versions. An example of a negative prospect-regarding standard would state that academic achievement must not be function of, or dependent upon the social-class background of a student. A version of a positive prospect-regarding standard might be that all children of normal or above normal ability shall learn to read at a ninth-grade reading level as measured by a standardized test. [8]

We now can combine these distinctions to arrive at illustrative examples of new principles of equal educational opportunity.

1. Individual-regarding principles
   a. Negative means-regarding principles:
      Differences in per pupil expenditures must not be a function of race.
   b. Positive means-regarding principles:
      Equal dollars must be spent per pupil.
   c. Negative prospect-regarding principles:
      The academic achievement of a student must not be a function of the student's social class.
   d. Positive prospect-regarding principles:
      Each student upon graduation will be able to read at a ninth-grade level.
2. Bloc-regarding principles
   a. Negative means-regarding principles:
      The amount of money spent on black and white students will not be a function of the average income of the groups.
   b. Positive means-regarding principles:
      The group with the lower average reading scores will receive compensatory services.

   c. Negative prospect-regarding principles:
      The average educational achievement of black and white pupils shall
      not be a function of the average family income of the groups.
   d. Positive prospect-regarding principles:
      The average reading achievement scores of black students will equal
      that of white students.

Many important ideological and philosophical debates rage over the choice of the appropriate category of standard and the particular version of that category. Some may prefer prospect-regarding standards because they are truly educationally meaningful; while the means-regarding standards may be educationally trivial, i.e., requiring that equal dollars be spent per pupil may provide formal equality but may not lead to improved achievement of students from disadvantaged backgrounds. Equality in the provision of means does not translate into equality of achievement. On the other hand, the prospect-regarding standards are difficult to administer and may be both very costly and politically controversial because they may require spending more money on poorly performing students than on above-average and gifted students. Furthermore, the causal link between inputs purchased for use in schools and student achievement is not well understood; thus, the technological and scientific base for implementing prospect-regarding standards is weak.[9]

Other issues arise in trying to select between individual- and block-regarding principles. For example, equalizing the average achievement of black and white pupils still leaves untouched the inequalities in achievement within these blocs; yet this bloc-regarding standard is attractive because it addresses a crucial widely recognized, politically salient problem. But, efforts to equalize the average achievement of black students may result in more money being spent per pupil on black students than on white students. As a result, white students with learning difficulties as severe as any black student may feel they have been discriminated against solely on the basis of their race.

The existence of these different versions of equal educational opportunity point to an important difficulty facing lawmakers and courts: the absence of an unambiguous American Creed with which to approach the interpretation of the broad and general phrases of the Constitution and state and federal statutes. To date the Supreme Court has not embraced the prospect-regarding notions of equality. Whether the Court might in the future adopt some limited prospect-regarding principle can only be a matter of speculation. As for the means-regarding notions of equality, it also seems safe to say the Court would at least accept the notion that differences in educational programs may not be purposefully a function of race or one's status as an illegal alien. (See §3.3; chapter 4; §§7.4, 7.5.) As we shall see in §7.2, the Court does not accept principles that require that equal dollars be spent per pupil or that expenditures may not be a function of where a student lives. On the other hand, the Court arguably seems to have embraced a principle that requires pupils be provided a "minimally adequate program," e.g., the provision of a minimally adequate program may not be depend on where a student lives. In short, constitutional doctrine regarding equality of educational opportunity is inchoate and open to further changes and refinements. Similarly, the concept of equal educational opportunity behind the various federal statutes to be discussed in this chapter remains fuzzy. At least this much seems clear: these statutes do not embrace any pure version of a prospect-regarding principle. At most they require the adoption of policies that have a reasonable chance of improving a student's prospects. Furthermore, only certain groups of pupils have been the beneficiaries of this body of legislation, thus suggesting that Congress may also be operating on the basis of a loosely defined bloc-regarding policy. State educational policies are no more grounded in a clear and coherent concept of equal educational opportunity.

7.2. SCHOOL FINANCE AND THE MINIMALLY ADEQUATE EDUCATION

If nothing else, variations among school districts in the amount of money spent per pupil can mean differences among school districts in the pupil-teacher ratio; the range of services, courses, and extracurricular activities made available; and the quality of the equipment and other facilities provided. Whether, or under what circumstances, variations in the amount of money spent per pupil affects student achievement is a matter of some scientific controversy.[10] Nevertheless, many states and school districts operate on the assumption that spending more money is causally related to student achievement in such basic subjects as reading and math; and, in the minds of many parents, spending less money per pupil in their district compared with other districts is a sign that their children are being provided with a lower quality education.

Inequalities in the amount of money spent per pupil among school districts within a state have arisen because of the way most states have chosen to finance their schools. Thus, we find that in most states the local school district budget comprises money raised by a locally determined property tax on real property in the district, state financial assistance, and federal aid. Looking at the local property tax first, we find that differences among the districts in the value of the property per pupil is closely correlated with differences in the amount of money avai' ble from the local tax. A district with $100,000 in real property per pupil will raise considerably more money at a given tax rate (expressed in mills, i.e., one-tenth of one cent or one-thousandth of a dollar) than a district with $50,000 in real property per pupil. Though the "property-poor" district could raise the same amount of money as the property-rich district by imposing a higher tax rate, political and economic constraints may not make the imposition of the higher rate feasible. It is also important to note that the "effort" a district makes—as measured by the size of its tax rate—may also be a result of the "taste" of the electorate in that district for education and related to the other spending priorities of the district, e.g., police, fire, and health care services.[11]

Even if differences in real property values per pupil do result in differences in the amount of money locally raised per pupil, the within-state inequalities might still be eliminated or drastically reduced if sufficient state and federal assistance were to be distributed in inverse relationship to the ability of districts to raise money. Historically the amount of federal assistance available has been too low to overcome these inequalities. In recent years federal assistance has amounted to no more than approximately 8 percent of the average local school district budget. This leaves state aid as the principal method for reducing inter-district inequalities. State aid, however, has historically been distributed according to formulas that at best have had only a mild equalizing effect.[12] Though all the formulas for distributing state aid have in theory at least some modest equalizing effect, as actually designed and implemented, these formulas have not served to eliminate the inequalities arising from the differences in local district property wealth per pupil. For political reasons state legislatures have modified these formulas with special provisions, such as "save harmless" clauses, which guarantee districts the same amount of money they received the prior year, even though the formulas themselves would indicate they should receive less aid, in effect continuing the disparities among districts in the amount of money spent per pupil.

These interdistrict inequalities in the amount of money spent per pupil attracted the attention of a number of legal scholars, who argued that existing Supreme Court precedent as of about 1970 could be interpreted to support the claim that most state systems for financing public education violated the equal protection clause of the fourteenth amendment.[13] More specifically, John Coons and his associates argued that constitutional precedent required states to adhere to the following proposition that they called the principle of fiscal neutrality: The quality of public education may not be a function of wealth other than the total wealth of the state. Fully implemented, the principle would require an end to the correlation between local district property wealth per pupil and the amount of money spent per pupil. Hence, if the state system for financing education were to continue to rely on the local property tax to raise money, the system would have to be changed to assure that equal tax rates produced equal amounts of money per pupil. Districts would not be required to choose the same tax rates; thus an important degree of local control would be maintained. Districts might still end up spending varying amounts of money per pupil, but the differences would be related to effort or taste rather than to wealth. Coons and his colleagues assumed that once the capacity to raise money had been equalized, districts would equalize their efforts, thus providing similar educational offerings across the state. However, the equalization of educational offerings is not a necessary consequence of their principle; thus, it may best be understood as a taxpayer equity principle and not inherently a principle of educational equity.

Before turning to the constitutional argument in support of this principle, it might be useful to illustrate how, as a practical matter, the principle of fiscal neutrality could be implemented. One method of compliance would be to move toward total state financing of education. Under this approach the state would raise all education revenues and distribute them according to a formula that, for example, would provide equal dollars per pupil or provide for the varying educational needs of pupils. Because this method would end local control of educational finance, Coons, Clune, and Sugarman suggested an alternative system that they dubbed "district power equalizing" (DPE). Under this approach the state would establish a schedule of tax rates and guaranteed yields. For instance, all districts choosing a tax rate of 4 percent would be guaranteed by the state that they would "raise" $500 per pupil. If a district were property poor and could only raise $300 at this rate, the state would make up the difference; if the district were property rich and raised $800, the state would take $300 from that district and distribute it to the property poor districts. The schedule might require a minimum tax rate of, for example, 3 percent and impose a cap of, perhaps, 15 percent; districts would be free to choose any tax rate between these extremes. So long as a given tax rate produced the same revenues for the different districts, the fiscal neutrality principle would be satisfied. Beyond DPE are other remedies such as redrawing school district lines to equalize the property wealth per pupil in school districts. In short, the fiscal neutrality principle could be implemented in a variety of ways, each with differing consequences for the allocation of power between state and local officials, the quality of the educational programs of the various districts, and the extent to which inqualities in expenditures could still continue as a result of factors other than the wealth of the district.

We turn now to the constitutional argument Coons, Clune, and Sugarman made on behalf of their principle. Supreme Court precedent then, recognized that equal protection challenges were to be resolved by the use of either of two tests. In the absence of special circumstances, the rational-basis test was to be used. The complaining party had to establish that the unequal treatment resulting from a state policy was not rationally related to a legitimate purpose. Differences in treatment could exist to help the state reach a legitimate goal, as would be the case in denying the blind a driver's license, an opportunity afforded the well sighted. Historically, this had proven to be a test that worked to the advantage of government, since few governmental policies are in fact irrational (don't serve to some extent the purposes for which they were intended), and the number of occasions on which the purposes of these policies are not legitimate is limited.

If the state policy involved, however, a difference in treatment based on a "suspect" criterion for distinguishing people or classes of people (e.g., a racial criterion), or if the policy infringed upon a "fundamental interest" (e.g., the right to vote), then a different test was used. Under this test it was the government that had to establish that its policy of treating classes of people differently was necessary to achieve a compelling purpose. This standard was very difficult to satisfy; in fact, its use in a case almost guaranteed that the complaining party would win the suit, that the government would lose.

Coons, Clune, and Sugarman argued that precedent supported the use of the later test—the so-called strict-scrutiny test—when examining the constitutionality of state systems for financing eduction. Precedent, they argued, indicated that differential treatment of people on the basis of their wealth triggered the use of the strict-scrutiny test. When the amount of money spent per pupil differed depending on the property wealth of the district where the pupils resided, this was a form of discrimination on the basis of wealth analogous to treating a rich man differently from a poor man. Furthermore, education was a "fundamental" interest as that term had been understood by the Court; and for this additional reason the strict-scrutiny test should apply. In applying that test, they argued that existing systems of educational finance were not constitutional. The existing systems were not necessary to serve a compelling state purpose. Even if the purpose of the existing system were local control of education, and even if local control were a compelling and exceedingly important purpose, the existing systems were not "necessary" to maintain local control. Other systems, such as DPE, could preserve local control yet not make the quality of a child's educational program dependent upon the wealth of the district where the child resided. Of course, under DPE the amount of money spent in a district could remain a function of the desire of the electorate in that district to support education; thus some children, even under DPE, might be provided a less expensive program than other children. Coons, Clune, and Sugarman, however, did not believe inequalities that had their root in the taste of the electorate for education were unconstitutional, even if from the child's perspective a wealth-based and taste-based inequality were educationally the same thing.

Since Coons, Clune, and Sugarman published their book, a spate of challenges to state systems of finance have been brought. Many of these challenges, if not actually repeating their line of argument almost verbatim, were at least influenced by it.[14] Thus today in six states (Arkansas, California, Connecticut, New Jersey, Washington, and Wyoming) the highest courts have declared the state's system for financing education to be unconstitutional.[15] In West Virginia the highest court overturned and remanded for further consideration a lower court decision upholding the system of finance; on remand the lower court ruled the system to be unconstitutional.[16] The United States Supreme Court, in reviewing the Texas system for financing education, and the highest courts in nine other states (Arizona, Colorado, Georgia, Idaho, Maryland, Michigan, New York, Ohio, and Oregon) could find no constitutional infirmity with those states' educational finance systems.[17] Twenty-five states have not been faced with suits seeking a declaration that the state's system of financing education violates either the equal protection clauses or education clauses of state constitutions.[18] In several other states litigation challenging the state system is underway, but there has as yet been no final resolution by the state's highest court.[19]

We look next at the judicial response to these constitutional challenges. The Supreme Court's decision in the Texas educational finance case rejected Coon's argument, the principle of fiscal neutrality, and made clear that, insofar as the equal protection clause of the fourteenth amendment was concerned, the mere existence of even substantial interdistrict inequalities in the amount of money spent per pupil did not violate the U.S. Constitution. The Court arrived at this position by first rejecting the use of the strict-scrutiny test on the grounds that neither a suspect classification nor a fundamental interest was implicated in the case. As for the suspect classification problem, the Court said that discriminating against those children who happen to live in relatively poor school districts was not the kind of discrimination on the basis of wealth the Court had in the past said triggered the use of the strict-scrutiny test. The special protection of the Court manifested in the use of the strict-scrutiny test extended only to people who were personally poor and who had been absolutely deprived of some benefit. Here the children in the relatively property-poor school districts were not themselves as a group personally poor, nor were these children absolutely deprived of an education; there was no evidence in this case that any child was receiving less than a minimally adequate education.

As for the claim that the finance system interfered with a fundamental right precipitating the use of strict scrutiny, the Court said that though education was of grave importance to the individual and society, it was not a fundamental interest or right under the U.S. Constitution. Not every socially important interest was a right under the U.S. Constitution. However, the Court did acknowledge the connection between education and the effective use of the constitutionally recognized rights to free speech and to the vote, which suggested that education should be a constitutionally recognized fundamental interest after all. The Court responded by saying:

> The Court has long afforded zealous protection against unjustifiable governmental interference with the individual's rights to speak and to vote. Yet we have never presumed to possess either the ability or the authority to guarantee to the citizenry the most *effective* speech or the most *informed* electoral choice. That these may be desirable goals of a system of freedom of expression and of a representative form of government is not to be doubted. These are indeed goals to be pursued by a people whose thoughts and beliefs are freed from governmental interference. But they are not values to be implemented by judicial intrusion into otherwise legitimate state activities.
>
> Even if it were conceded that some identifiable quantum of education is a constitutionally protected prerequisite to the meaningful exercise of either right, we have no indication that the present levels of educational expenditure in Texas provide an education that falls short. . . . [N]o charge fairly could be made that the system fails to provide each child with an opportunity to acquire the basic

skills necessary for the enjoyment of the rights of speech and of full participation in the political process.[20]

More broadly, the Court expressed its concern that if education were declared a fundamental interest, so might food and shelter, leading to an expansive use of the strict-scrutiny test. It was generally preferable for the Court to employ the rational-basis test so as to limit judicial involvement in complex matters such as taxation and education—areas where the courts lack specialized knowledge and experience. In this connection the Court stressed that even scholarly and educational experts were divided on the question of whether there was a demonstrable correlation between educational expenditures and the quality of education. Furthermore, overturning the system of finance could have widespread and perverse consequences. The poor and racial minorities may not live in relatively property-poor school districts; the principle of fiscal neutrality could hurt them most.

Thus the Court turned to the rational-basis test and concluded that Texas's system was rationally related to the purpose of promoting local control of education. The fact that some property-poor districts had less flexibility and less control in raising money than others did not make the system irrational and unconstitutional.

The Court's decision in *Rodriguez* has been subjected to a variety of criticisms, including the claims that the majority misinterpreted precedent, selected the wrong standard of review, relied upon a flawed conception of a minimally adequate education, failed to consider that children per se may be a "suspect" class requiring special judicial solicitude, and improperly elevated a rather narrow conception of local control to too great an importance. It is possible that these arguable faults in the opinion were the product of a desire on the part of the majority to find some way to reach a result that kept the Court out of the business of regulating the adequacy of the public school programs in the some 17,000 school districts of the nation. There is much language in the opinion that the majority felt insecure in this task both because a scientific base for such an undertaking was missing, and because, historically, the control of the school program was a matter that had been left to the states. To rule other than the Court did might have marked a dramatic change in federal-state relations.

Although the Supreme Court said inequalities in the financing of education do not violate the U.S. Constitution, the possibility remained that those inequalities might violate the equal protection and/or educaton clauses of the state constitutions. As noted earlier, the state courts have divided on this question. We consider first those courts that did conclude that their state's system for financing education violated their state constitution. Courts in California, Connecticut, and Wyoming embraced the claim that the Coons, Clune, and Sugarman argument was a correct interpretation of their state's constitution.[21] They agreed that education was a fundamental interest under their state constitution and that conditioning the educational spending on the wealth of the district where students lived was a form of wealth discrimination. These differences in expenditures, the courts agreed, did affect the breadth and quality of the education available. "It is nothing more than an illusion to believe that the extensive disparity in financial resources does not relate directly to the quality of education."[22] Then, relying on the strict-scrutiny test, these courts concluded that the existing systems were unconstitutional: the present method of financing the schools simply was not "necessary" to the preservation of local control. The remedies these courts ordered differed. In California the court ordered the state to reduce inequalities in interdistrict expenditures per pupil to less than one hundred dollars per pupil.[23] The courts in Connecticut and Wyoming merely ordered their legislatures to revamp the system of finance to bring it into compliance with the principle of fiscal neutrality.[24]

The three other state supreme courts that struck down their state's system for financing education based their decisions on the education clauses in their state's constitutions and on lines of analysis different from that of Coons, Clune, and Sugarman. In New Jersey the court relied on the constitutional clause requiring the state legislature to provide "a thorough and efficient system" of public schools to conclude that the system was unconstitutional.[25] Adopting a balancing test, the court weighed the "denial" against the public justification of the system and concluded this system did not provide students with an equal educational opportunity. The court offered no definition of its conception of equal educational opportunity except to say, "The constitutional mandate could not be said to be satisfied unless we were to suppose the unlikely proposition that the lowest level of dollar performance happens to coincide with the constitutional mandate and that all efforts beyond the lowest level are attributable to local decision to do more than the state was obliged to do." The lack of guidance from the court may have contributed to the long legal and political process that followed the issuance of this decision and that only ended after the New Jersey Supreme Court closed the entire public school system in the state as a way of putting pressure on the legislature to comply with the original ruling.[26]

In Arkansas the court relied on both the state's equal protection clause and the educational clause, clauses that required provision of a general, suitable, and efficient system of education.[27] The court found the system served no legitimate state purpose when some districts could provide the "bare rudiments of educational opportunities" and other districts had generously endowed programs. "Bare and minimal sufficiency does not translate into equal educational opportunity." The basic principle the court apparently adopted was that "the educational opportunity of the children in this state should not be controlled by the fortuitous circumstances of residence." It is not clear whether the court meant this principle to be a restatement of the fiscal neutrality principle or whether it meant something more drastic, i.e., significant inequalities in expenditures per pupil are unconstitutional regardless of the cause.

The highest court in Washington State attempted to provide its legislature with somewhat more guidance.[28] It interpreted the state constitutional provision, which required the legislature to "make ample provision" for education, to mean the legislature had a duty itself to fund a "basic education" as distinguished from "total education" by means of dependable and regular tax sources.[29] As for defining a basic education, the court seemed to offer two different conceptions. On the one hand, it arguably adopted a means-regarding conception when it spoke of the state having a duty to provide "broad educational opportunities needed in the contemporary setting to equip our children for their role as citizens and as potential competitors in today's market as well as the marketplace of ideas." On the other hand, the court seemed to adopt a prospect-regarding conception of equal educational opportunity when it stressed that the right to have the state make ample provision would be hollow "if the possessor of the right could not compete adequately in our open political system, labor market, and marketplace of ideas." This ambiguity was resolved later in the opinion in favor of a means-regarding conception when the court seemed to say that any of three measures of "ample provision" would be constitutionally acceptable: (1) the definition adopted by the State Board of Education and Superintendent of Public Instruction that spoke in terms of inputs, i.e., staff ratios, etc.; (2) the State Board of Education's accreditation standards that also spoke in terms of inputs; and (3) the "collective wisdom" standard. This later standard involved assessing the adequacy of a particular program in terms of the "statewide aggregate average per pupil deployment of certificated and classified staff and nonsalary related costs for the maintenance and operation of a school program for the normal range of student."

In West Virginia the state's highest court reversed the trial court's dismissal of the complaint, remanded the case for trial, and at the same time provided a definition of the "thorough and efficient" clause in the state's constitution.[30] A "thorough and efficient" system, said the court, "develops . . . the minds, bodies and social morality of its charges to prepare them for useful and happy occupations, recreation and citizenship, and does so economically." The court then included the following elements in this definition:

> development in every child to his or her capacity of (1) literacy; (2) ability to add, subtract, multiply and divide numbers; (3) knowledge of government to the extent that the child will be equipped as a citizen to make informed choices among persons and issues that affect his own governance; (4) self-knowledge and knowledge of his or her total environment to allow the child to intelligently choose life work—to know his or her options; (5) work-training and advanced academic training as the child may intelligently choose; (6) recreational pursuits; (7) interests in all creative arts, such as music, theatre, literature, and the visual arts; (8) social ethics, both behavioral and abstract, to facilitate compatibility with others in this society.
>
> Implicit are supportive services: (1) good physical facilities, instructional materials and personnel; (2) careful state and local supervision to prevent waste and to monitor pupil, teacher and administrative competency.[31]

We turn now to those state courts that have refused to declare their state system for financing education to be unconstitutional despite the existence of severe interdistrict inequalities in money spent per pupil. The contrast between the opinions these courts issued in response to a Coons, Clune, and Sugarman type of argument and the opinions reviewed above is instructive.[32] In many respects these courts echoed the Supreme Court's opinion in *Rodriguez,* taking the position that judicial involvement in such a complex field as tax and educational policy was ill-advised, that the cost-quality debate was one the courts could not resolve, that the existing programs were not shown to be minimally inadequate, that the strict-scrutiny test should not be used,[33] and that the existing system served the purpose of ensuring local control of education.

The technical legal arguments in these opinions aside, the clear message of these courts was that their state constitutions struck the balance between strong local control of education and equality in the provision of educational services in such a way that local control was the preferred value; unless it was very clear that the educational program in the poorer districts was manifestly inadequate, the legislatures should be free to choose how to encourage local control. Thus, equality in expenditures was not a constitutional requirement, and wealth-determined inequalities were constitutionally acceptable. The Court of Appeals in New York put it most bluntly: "If what is made available by this system (which is what is to be maintained and supported) may properly be said to constitute an education, the [state] constitutional mandate is satisfied."[34] In another case the Court of Appeals said the state constitution's education clause "was never intended to impose a duty flowing directly from a school district to individual pupils to ensure that each pupil receives a minimum level of education, the breach of which duty would entitle a pupil to compensatory damages."[35]

The variety of judicial responses to the claim that interdistrict inequalities in the expenditures of funds are unconstitutional is striking. The courts that refused to accept this argument tended to stress that the only constitutional obligation of the state was to assure all students of a minimally adequate education—that some students had a better than minimally adequate education was not a constitutional problem. A central difficulty with this analysis is that what constitutes a minimally adequate education in a competitive situation, e.g., the job market, may be a function of the quality of education other students are getting.[36] Can a program of instruction be deemed minimally adequate if someone else gets a better educational program and thereby consistently wins in the competition for money and status? The harm is comparable whether one is absolutely deprived of a minimally adequate education or whether one is only provided a relatively unequal education when in competition with others for scarce resources. As for the courts that did strike down their system of financing education, many fell into the same difficulty. They may have eliminated disparities based on property wealth, but not disparities that were the product of differences in the average income of district voters or differences in the taste for education. Thus, even in most of the judicially reformed states (whether the state legislatures have in fact complied with the judicial orders is a separate empirical question), under this analysis many students will still be receiving a "minimally inadequate education." Only in California have the courts and legislature gone the extra step virtually to eliminate inequalities in expenditures regardless of cause.

The decisions reviewed here do not address three additional forms of inequalities: intradistrict inequalities, intraschool inequalities, and interfamily inequalities. It is arguable that these forms of inequalities are educationally far more significant than the interdistrict inequalities that have drawn most of the judicial and political attention.[37] Nevertheless, there has been little litigation touching on these forms of inequality.[38] If education is a fundamental interest, one wonders why there have been so few suits addressing intradistrict and intraschool disparities. The failure to obtain judicial attention to interfamily inequalities is more understandable. Clearly any effort to deal with this problem could require a reform of how we publicly support educational services that goes far beyond any of the reforms contemplated in the litigation to date, and/or could risk severe intrusions on the autonomy of the family.[39]

7.3. AN APPROPRIATE EDUCATION FOR THE HANDICAPPED

Although the effort to protect all children in the public schools against inequalities in expenditures has met with decidedly mixed results, efforts to protect handicapped children both through judicial and legislative channels have been markedly successful in recent years. The story may be said to begin with *Pennsylvania Association for Retarded Children (PARC) v. Pennsylvania*[40] and *Mills v. Board of Education*,[41] which recognized that handicapped children must be admitted to the public schools and must be provided educational services appropriate to their needs.[42] Two pieces of federal legislation followed in the wake of these decisions. The first to be adopted was the Rehabilitation Act of 1973, a civil rights-style act that prohibits discrimination in federally assisted programs against any otherwise qualified handicapped person solely on the basis of the handicapping condition.[43] The second to be adopted was the Education For All Handicapped Children Act of 1975 (EAHCA),[44] a funding statute that mandates, as a condition to receiving funds, that the states comply with certain requirements. As discussed below, only New Mexico has chosen not to participate in the EAHCA; but because its educational programs receive other federal funds, the state has been required to comply with the Rehabilitation Act.[45] Many of the regulations issued under the Rehabilitation Act are similar to those under EAHCA and dovetail with EAHCA.[46] While the definition of a handicapped person under the Rehabilitation Act is broader than the definition used in EAHCA, the differences will have only modest practical significance with regard to children in the public schools.[47] Furthermore, the Supreme Court has determined that suit under the Rehabilitation Act will not be allowed if a remedy is available under EAHCA.[48] Thus, the analysis to follow will concentrate on EAHCA following a brief mention of the significance of the Rehabilitation Act.

The Rehabilitation Act becomes most significant when a state, as New Mexico did, refuses to participate in the EAHCA funding program and, therefore, is not subject to the requirements of EAHCA. In these circumstances the Tenth Circuit Court of Appeals held that the Rehabilitation Act must nevertheless be followed because New Mexico is a recipient of other federal funds.[49] The court interpreted the Rehabilitation Act as requiring a similar response by school districts to the handicapped as Title VI requires with regard to non-English-speaking pupils. (See §7.4.) Thus, to be in compliance with the act, public schools must adjust their programs for the handicapped to accommodate their needs so that they may enjoy the program's benefits. The accommodation would not be required if the financial burden would be excessive or would not enable the handicapped to realize the benefits of the educational program. Failure to make these adjustments constitutes discrimination within the meaning of the law. Among the practices that arguably violate the law are failure to identify and diagnose the handicapped children needing special education; failure to accommodate and integrate those children into physical education, counseling, learning, and personal guidance programs; and permitting great disparity in how local districts treat their handicapped pupils.

Section 504 was also used to prohibit the New York City Board of Education from excluding from the regular school classes mentally retarded children who were carriers of serum hepatitis when the board failed to establish that the presence of these children in the regular classrooms posed a health risk for the other students.[50] The implications of this decision for policies excluding children with AIDS (Acquired Immune Deficiency Syndrome) are obvious. Another court ruled that §504 was not available to challenge the misclassification of normal children as children in need of special education.[51] However, §504 does afford relief for policies that unintentionally have a disparate impact upon the handicapped,[52] but in order to recover damages under this section, several courts have held that the plaintiff must prove bad faith or the intent to discriminate on the basis of handicap.[53]

We turn now to EAHCA. That act requires that handicapped school-aged children between the ages of six and eighteen and in need of special education be identified, located, and evaluated.[54] As to these children, EAHCA requires that recipients of federal aid under the act provide them a "free appropriate public education" (FAPE), which includes "special education,"[55] and "related services."[56] The FAPE must be "provided in conformity with [an] individualized education program" [IEP].[57] The IEP is defined as a "written statement for each handicapped child" that describes the child's present level of performance, the short-term goals and longer-term objectives of the education program, the services to be provided, the extent to which the child will be able to participate in regular education programs, and the objective criteria and evaluation procedures for assessing the success of the program at least on an annual basis.[58] The IEP, which specifies the specially designed instruction program to meet the unique needs of the handicapped child, must be jointly developed at a meeting attended by the child's parents, the teacher, a school representative, and, when appropriate, the child.[59] The assessment of handicapped children must be done in the child's native language and by tests and criteria that are not culturally or racially biased; and no single criterion, such as an IQ test, may be the sole criterion for determining the appropriate program for the child.[60] To the "maximum extent appropriate," handicapped children must be educated with non-handicapped children.[61] Nevertheless, when the severity or nature of the handicapping condition is such that "education in regular classes with the use of supplementary aids and services cannot be achieved satisfactorily," then the child can be placed in special classes, or even separate schools, whether they are publicly or privately operated.[62]

Because disagreements may arise between parents and school officials over the IEP, the evaluation of the child, the programs to be offered that child, and the child's placement, EAHCA establishes a complex set of procedures for handling these disputes. These safeguards include a right on the part of parents to inspect all relevant records; prior notice if the school proposes to initiate or change or refuses to initiate or change the identification, evaluation, or placement of the child; a right to a hearing before a hearing officer who is not involved in the education or care of the child;[63] a right to be accompanied at the hearing by counsel and other experts; a right to cross-examine witnesses and present evidence at the hearing; a right to a record of the hearing; and a right to written findings of fact and decision.[64] Any party, parent, or school district aggrieved by the decision of the hearing officer may appeal to the state educational agency,[65] and/or to a court.[66] The EAHCA also stipulates that "[d]uring the pendency of any proceedings conducted pursuant to this section, unless State or local educational agency and the parents or guardian otherwise agree, the child shall remain in the then current educational placement of such child, or, if applying for initial admission to a public school, shall with the consent of the parents or guardian, be placed in the public school program until all such proceedings have been completed."[67]

We turn now to a more detailed discussion of the central requirement that handicapped children be provided a FAPE. The discussion will be divided as follows: (a) the basic standard, (b) year-around schooling and residential placement, (c) related services, and (d) change of placement.

The Basic Standard

The definition of a FAPE in EAHCA is phrased in very general language, and, as might be expected, the differences of opinion as to its meaning were taken to the Supreme Court for resolution.[68] The case on which today's operative interpretation of FAPE is based arose when the parents of Amy Rowley, who suffered from a significant hearing impairment, and the school district disagreed over the refusal of the school to provide Amy with a sign-language interpreter to accompany her to the regular classrooms to which she was assigned.[69] The school district believed that Amy, who was an intelligent and highly motivated youngster, would achieve adequately in the regular classroom if she were simply provided a special hearing aid, a tutor for the deaf who would meet with her on a daily basis, and three hours per week of speech therapy. The district based its decision not to include the interpreter in the IEP on several considerations. An interpreter had been placed in Amy's kindergarten class for a two-week experimental period at the end of which the interpreter said Amy did not require his services. Furthermore, Amy had demonstrated good social adjustment and was performing without an interpreter at a better-than-average level. Amy was capable of lip reading and had some residual hearing. Amy's parents, however, believed Amy was still missing an important portion of the class discussion and would perform even better academically with an interpreter.

The school district's position was upheld by the impartial hearing officer and on appeal by the state commissioner of education. The Rowleys appealed to the federal district court that concluded that Amy had not been provided with a FAPE. The court concluded that EAHCA meant that a handicapped child should receive something more than an "adequate" program, yet something less than a program that would enable her to achieve her "full potential." Instead, EAHCA required that a handicapped child "be given an opportunity to achieve his full potential commensurate with the opportunity provided to other children."[70] In a per curiam opinion the Second Circuit affirmed.

By a five-to-four vote the Supreme Court reversed. Justice Rehnquist, writing for the majority, began his analysis by noting that Congress adopted EAHCA primarily to end the exclusion of handicapped children from the public schools; thus "Congress did not impose upon the States any greater substantive educational standard than would be necessary to make such access meaningful." As to the nature of that substantive standard, he rejected the district court's emphasis upon providing an opportunity to the handicapped to develop full potential that was equal to the opportunity provided the nonhandicapped.

> The educational opportunities provided by our public school systems undoubtedly differ from student to student, depending upon a myriad of factors that might affect a particular student's ability to assimiliate information presented in the classroom. The requirement that States provide "equal" educational opportunities would thus seem to present an entirely unworkable standard requiring impossible measurements and comparisons.[71]

Continuing, Justice Rehnquist also noted that providing the handicapped only the services available to nonhandicapped children would violate the FAPE requirement, and that requiring services necessary for a handicapped child to maximize her potential would be to require more than Congress intended. Thus, Justice Rehnquist adopted what he undoubtedly hoped would be accepted as a middle or compromise position. "We therefore conclude that the 'basic floor of opportunity' provided by [EAHCA] consists of access to specialized instruction and related services which are individually designed to provide educational benefit to the handicapped child." If the child were being educated in a regular classroom, Justice Rehnquist noted, the educational program outlined in the IEP "should be reasonably calculated to enable the child to achieve passing marks and advance from grade to grade."

As to determining if a handicapped child is receiving, or will receive, "sufficient educational benefits" from the program defined in the IEP to satisfy EAHCA, the Court refused to establish any one test to cover all the types of children covered by the EAHCA. In examining IEPs that have not yet been fully implemented, the Court said that reviewing courts should merely determine (1) if the procedures in the act have been complied with, and (2) if the program is "reasonably calculated to enable the child to receive educational benefits." In that connection Justice Rehnquist stressed courts should be "careful to avoid imposing their view of preferable educational methods upon the States."[72] As to a case like Amy Rowley's where the IEP was being implemented and the child was in a regular classroom, Justice Rehnquist was a bit more specific. As to children being educated in the regular classrooms, the Court suggested that the handicapped child who advances from grade to grade according to the usual requirements for the nonhandicapped would be deemed to have received sufficient educational benefits. "Children who graduate from our public school systems are considered by our society to have been 'educated' at least to the grade level they have completed, and access to an 'education' for handicapped children is precisely what Congress sought to provide in the Act."

Applying these principles, Justice Rehnquist concluded that the school district had provided Amy with a FAPE. Amy, after all, was receiving personalized instruction; and the evidence showed she performed better than average and was advancing easily from grade to grade. The decision of the lower courts to provide provision of an interpreter was reversed.

Just as EAHCA was subject to different interpretations, so is the *Rowley* opinion.[73] Professor Wegner argues the opinion should not be read as contemplating that each handicapped child "receive some net educational benefit, without attempting to measure that benefit against the child's individual goals and objectives."[74] She argues that *Rowley* "requires both careful examination of the child's abilities, needs, and objectives, and an assessment of whether he is receiving some educational benefit as measured against those objectives." The EAHCA itself requires that a child's educational program be designed to meet his or her unique needs.[75] As Professor Wegner stresses, both the assessment of needs and of benefits are difficult steps that have produced and will continue to produce considerable disagreement.

An important implication of the *Rowley* decision is that handicapped students will not necessarily receive the same services as the nonhandicapped if they cannot benefit from those services. For example, a handicapped pupil under *Rowley* would not be eligible for extracurricular activities if it were established that the child could not benefit from those activities.[76]

Before turning to the examination of several recurring problems in the defining of a FAPE, the question of the relevance of the costs of proposed programs should be discussed. The *Mills* decision noted earlier made clear that as a matter of constitutional law, insufficiency of funds was not an adequate justification for excluding the handicapped from public schooling. As for EAHCA, though *Rowley* places on schools only the modest duty of assuring handicapped children of a program that will provide some educational benefits, the decision can be interpreted "to make that duty absolute, unqualified by any defense based on cost."[77] Given *Rowley*, perhaps the approach for taking costs into consideration is best expressed by the Sixth District Court of Appeals when it wrote that "[C]ost considerations are only relevant when choosing between several options, all of which offer an appropriate education."[78] Thus, if choosing between two options, both of which meet the standards as specified in *Rowley*, the less expensive program may be chosen, even if the more expensive option might provide an even better education.[79]

When a state has adopted legislation that imposes a standard higher than EAHCA, it is that standard that governs the assessment of the appropriateness of the educational program under EAHCA.[80] That is, EAHCA has been interpreted as incorporating these higher state standards as the standards to be enforced in the name of EAHCA itself.

It is the party attacking an IEP, which has been upheld in an administrative hearing, who bears the burden of persuasion.[81] Similarly, the party advocating a change in an existing placement carries the burden of persuasion.[81]

School District Limits on the Amount of Education; Residential Placement

Not surprisingly, when parents have sought year-around educational services for their children, states and school districts have resisted having to take on the expenses of these programs.[82] The courts have said with apparent unanimity that the a priori refusal to provide services for more than 180 days violates EAHCA and the requirement to provide a FAPE. Refusing to consider offering an extended school year violates the requirement that the EPI be designed to meet the unique needs of each handicapped child.[84]

In one case the school district sought to limit to twelve the number of years of schooling provided a handicapped child, while other children who failed a grade were entitled to thirteen, fourteen, or more years of education.[85] An appropriate education under EAHCA, said the court, requires more than the passage of time for its successful completion. The EAHCA requires school districts to establish educational objectives in the IEP that satisfy the requirements of the EAHCA as interpreted by *Rowley*, and that the district must attempt to satisfy even if the effort takes more than the conventional twelve years of schooling. What the court did not say, but what is required by EAHCA, is that whatever the content of the program provided the handicapped, the handicapped may not be offered fewer years of free instruction than the nonhandicapped.

An inherently more difficult problem arises in using the *Rowley* principles to determine if residential placement of a child is required by EAHCA as a matter of law.[86] (Similar issues can arise regarding the placement of a child either by his or her parents or by the school district in a private day school.) One point seems clear: EAHCA does not require the state or local school district to support residential placements required for noneducationally related reasons. For example, the placement of the child outside the home because a parent sexually abuses or neglects the child would not be covered by EAHCA.[87] The EAHCA becomes relevant, however, (1) if the parties disagree over the type of educational program required, with the residential school offering one type of program and the public school offering a different program; (2) if a particular service is arguably educational and could only be adequately provided in a residential setting; or (3) if other arguably noneducational services need to be provided in order for the child to benefit from services that are directed to learning skills and acquiring knowledge, and these arguably noneducational services cannot be provided except in a residential placement. The legal issues that have been raised in connection with these three situations are different.

Turning to the first situation, the central question is whether the public school placement provides the level of benefit *Rowley* says is required. The parties to the case, in other words, are in disagreement over the likely benefits of two available programs. These difficult issues can only be resolved by the judge evaluating the conflicting evidence presented in the case.[88] Courts have, however, refused to consider residential placement if the public education service is appropriate.[88]

The issue in the second situation is whether a broad range of services often called "treatments" should be deemed to be educational services, hence for that reason alone governed by EAHCA. The courts have adopted a broad conception of education. Thus, training students in such basic life skills as using a fork, toilet training, and dressing has been viewed as forms of education that are most appropriately provided in a residential setting.[90]

We confront the third situation when a child is emotionally handicapped and, arguably, residential placement is required merely to treat that problem, and not in order to provide the child with educational services. Though the courts have split in their approaches in handling this problem, the trend seems to be toward ordering residential placement if providing treatment for the emotional need is a predicate for making academic gains.[91] The Third Circuit Court of Appeals stated the issue this way: "The relevant question in the present case is whether residential placement is part and parcel of a 'specially designed instruction . . . to meet the unique needs of the handicapped child.'"[92] We get a different perspective on the problem from *Parks v. Pavkovic*.[93] In that case the state refused to pay $100 of the living expenses of Lester Parks, a nineteen year old, living in a private institution, who was afflicted with autism and mental retardation. The state defended the deduction on the ground that Parks was in the institution not because he had special educational needs, but because he had a "developmental disability" attributable to mental retardation. The court rejected the state's argument saying that, "To assign a person to a residential facility because his mind is backward is, except perhaps in the severest cases, to assert a need for special education."[94] The court went even further in supporting a broad reading of EACHA when it wrote, "[T]he courts which have considered the question have rejected the argument that a state can avoid its obligations under the Act by showing the child would have had to be institutionalized quite apart from educational needs that also required institutionalization."[95]

It might be recalled at this point that EAHCA requires that handicapped children be educated with the nonhandicapped to the maximum extent appropriate. How this requirement is to be taken into consideration in choosing an educational placement for the child has not been clearly settled by the courts. Perhaps as a practical matter this so-called "least restrictive environment" requirement has served as a rebuttable presumption.[96] Thus, the courts have presumed that residential placement is more restrictive than providing special educational services in the public school, but have been willing to order residential placement when it is clear that it is necessary to provide the child with any educational benefits. The First Circuit Court of Appeals put it this way: "The placement is not to be made mechanically choosing the least restrictive environment; rather, the decision must consider the child's own needs, the location of the programs available."[97]

Related Services

EAHCA requires the provision of related services that include medical and counseling services for diagnostic and evaluation purposes only.[98] Thus the question has frequently arisen whether such services as clean, intermittent catherization (CIC), a tracheotomy, and psychotherapy are required to be provided to enable the child to achieve some educational benefits. In *Irving Independent School District v. Tatro* the Supreme Court established important principles for answering these questions.[99] The Court ruled that CIC was a related service because it was like other services listed in EAHCA. "A service that enables a handicapped child to remain at school during the day," thus, "is an important means of providing the child with meaningful access to education that Congress envisioned." The Court also agreed that CIC was not a "medical service" that the school would not, according to EAHCA, have to provide. The Court said that all services that were like those traditionally offered by a school nurse or other qualified personnel, and were like those routinely provided to the non-handicapped could not be deemed to be excluded medical services and must be viewed as related services. However, the Court did stress that these services need only be provided if "necessary" to help the handicapped child to benefit from special education, and if they can be performed by a nurse or other qualified person.

In other words, the Court's analysis of EAHCA went something like this: EAHCA excludes the provision of medical services because it was a service "that might well prove unduly expensive and beyond the range of [the school's] competence." On the other hand, services that could be provided and have traditionally been provided by a nurse or other qualified personnel are valuable services; EAHCA does not seek to prevent the traditional service from continuing. At the same time, EAHCA requires, in the name of equal educational opportunity, that similar services—similar in terms of expense and expertise needed to carry them out—be made available to the handicapped so that they too could benefit from an educational program.

Although decided before *Tatro,* the decision of the Ninth Circuit Court of Appeals in *Department of Education, State of Hawaii v. Katherine D.*[100] can now be explained using the *Tatro* approach. Seven-year-old Katherine suffered from cystic fibrosis and tracheomalacia, which caused her windpipes to be floppy instead of rigid. She wore a tracheostomy tube, which allowed her to breathe and to expel mucous secretions from her lungs two or three times a day. The state department of education proposed an IEP that involved homebound instruction because it determined the medical services Katherine might need could not be provided in a public school. Katherine's parents rejected the IEP. The impartial hearing officer concluded that Katherine had not been provided a FAPE and ordered that she be admitted to the public school. The newly revised IEP required the training of the staff to dispense Katherine's medication, to suction her lungs, and to reinsert the tube if it were to become dislodged. The state appealed to the federal district court, which affirmed the decision of the hearing officer, as did the court of appeals. The courts concluded that Katherine was capable of participating in the regular classes with nonhandicapped pupils, that the services would enable her to attend these regular classes, that the services Katherine might need had in fact been provided by her mother when Katherine was attending a private school, and that these services could now be provided by a school nurse or other qualified person. In terms of the *Tatro* principles, we can see that these services were comparable to other, more traditional services provided the nonhandicapped in terms of the expense and skill needed to implement them, and were necessary to afford Katherine a comparable equal opportunity to benefit from school. The result in the case also assured that the "least restrictive environment" requirement was satisfied.

The question of whether psychotherapy is a related service or a medical service that need not be provided at public expense raises a more difficult problem. An important part of the difficulty in this area arises because psychotherapeutic services can be offered by both trained social workers and psychologists and by psychiatrists who are licensed physicians, or by social workers and psychologists working under the direction of a physician.[101] The EAHCA, in the definition of related services, merely refers to psychological and counseling services. The regulations implementing EAHCA define counseling services as "services provided by qualified social workers, psychologists, guidance counselors, or other qualified personnel."[102] Psychological services include the performance of several specific diagnostic, interpretive, and counseling functions.[103] The exclusion of any reference to psychiatrists suggests that psychotherapy is not a related service.

The trend in the decisions seems to be in favor of (1) finding that psychotherapy is a related service, but (2) only requiring its provision if it is necessary for the student to receive educational benefits. The court in *Max M. v. Thompson* perhaps stated the analysis most clearly.[104] The court noted that many services that are clearly "related services" could be provided by a physician, thus the mere fact a service could be provided and is in fact being provided by a physician does not dictate its removal from the list of required services. The court implied, however, that if the service in question could only have been provided by a licensed physician, it would not be a related service but an excluded medical service. Other courts have denied the state payment for psychotherapy when they viewed the service as not necessary for primarily educational reasons.[105]

Change of Placement

Under EAHCA a school district must provide notice and a full hearing before it can change the educational placement of a handicapped child.[106] Thus, the question arises as to what constitutes a change in the child's "educational placement." Different courts have adopted different definitions of a change of placement. The Second Circuit has said a change in placement occurs when there is a change in the "general educational program in which the child is enrolled, rather than mere variations in the program itself."[107] The Sixth District has said a chance of placement occurs when a modified educational program is "not comparable to the plan set forth in the original IEP."[108] The Third Circuit approached the issue by saying that the touchstone "has to be whether the decision [change in the program] is likely to affect in some significant way the child's learning experience."[109] Expulsion of a handicapped pupil is considered a change in placement invoking the procedural protections of EAHCA.[110] The statute specifically authorizes individuals to seek redress in the courts for alleged violations of EAHCA.[111] (For a further discussion of the disciplining of handicapped pupils see §8.8.)

Finally, brief mention should be made of the remedies available to parents under EAHCA. As noted above, the Supreme Court has said the Rehabilitation Act may not be used if a remedy is available under EAHCA.[112] The Court has also said that §1983 may not be used for equal protection claims, given the existence of EAHCA, but it might be available to raise procedural due process claims.[113]

While it is clear that EAHCA permits parents to seek injunctive relief,[114] it has been unclear what monetary reimbursements and damages could be awarded under EAHCA. In a recent case the Supreme Court has said that (1) "parents who unilaterally change their child's placement [e.g., to a private tuition-charging school] during the pendency of review proceedings, without consent of state or local school officials, do so at their own financial risk";[115] (2) "If the courts ultimately determine that the IEP proposed by the school official was appropriate, the parents would be barred from obtaining reimbursement for any interim period in which their child's placement violated [EAHCA]";[116] but that (3) if the court ultimately determines that the private school placement was the appropriate placement, the court may order school authorities to reimburse the parents for their expenditures.[117] The lower courts are in agreement that general damages, e.g., for mental anguish, are not available under EAHCA;[118] but because §1983 appears to be available to challenge procedural violations under EAHCA and damages are available under §1983, parents may be able to obtain damages for procedural violations.[119] Assuming the Rehabilitation Act of 1973 is available as a basis for suit because EAHCA does not provide the exclusive remedy, the prevailing view appears to be that recovery of damages is only available upon proof of an intent to discriminate on the basis of handicap.[120] Finally, as for attorneys' fees, the "American Rule" is that attorneys' fees are only available if there is statutory authority to award them.[121] Since EAHCA does not include a provision for attorneys' fees, claimants have sought to combine EAHCA claims with a claim under §1983 and §504, both of which permit the collection of attorneys' fees.[122] But, in *Smith v. Robinson*[123] the Supreme Court held that a claimant under EAHCA could not raise §1983 and §504 claims, consequently their attorneys' fees provisions were not available.

7.4. MINORITY LANGUAGE STUDENTS

Children who present themselves at the schoolhouse door whose native tongue is a language other than English and who are of limited English proficiency are in an obviously difficult position to gain benefits from a program of instruction conducted solely in English. Several equal protection arguments can be offered on their behalf. First, it could be argued that the school has discriminated against these pupils by offering a program of instruction to them from which they cannot benefit, while offering other students a program of instruction from which they could benefit. If the purpose of schooling is to teach students to read, write, and do arithmetic, the provision of education solely in the medium of English is not rationally related to the purpose and should be struck down. An all-English program of instruction does not afford an equal educational opportunity, especially if special assistance is not provided to overcome the language barrier. Two responses can be made that most courts would probably accept: (1) The school has not discriminated. It simply has offered the same program to all students, and if some students are not able to take advantage of the program in the way other student can, this is not the fault of the school district. All students come to school with different inherent abilities and at different levels of achievement (e.g., some students come to kindergarten already having learned to read), and those differences are not caused by anything the school has done. (2) In any event, the purpose of schooling is to instruct students to improve their ability to read, write, and do other work in English. The existing program is rationally related to its purpose.

A second closely related argument, offered in *Lau v. Nichols* (1979), has been developed in order to seek constitutional protection for limited English speaking students who also happen to belong to a racial minority.[124] This argument was similar to the first except that it claimed that the disadvantaged students constitute a "suspect class"; that is, the apparently neutral policy of offering all students, regardless of language background, the same program has the effect of denying an equal opportunity to learn to an identifiable racial minority, e.g., Chinese pupils who don't speak English. Because the discrimination in this case was based on a characteristic interwined with their nationality and their language, it was in practice a form of racial discrimination. The combination of an absolute denial of an educational opportunity plus the use of a suspect classification triggers the use of the strict-scrutiny test. Applying such a test, it cannot be maintained that the all-English program is constitutional. There is no compelling state justification for providing educational instruction that some students can make use of but not to others.

The court of appeals rejected this constitutional argument and accepted the school district's claim that they could not be held responsible for disabilities they did not cause. The mere fact, said the court, that these disabilities could be overcome if the school district paid attention to them, did not amount to a "denial" of equal protection if the school district fails to give them special attention.[125]

On appeal the Supreme Court reversed.[126] The Court, avoiding ruling on the constitutional argument of the plaintiffs, instead ruled that the district's failure to try to overcome the plaintiffs' language difficulties discriminated on the basis of national origin and therefore violated Title VI.[127] This failure denied "the Chinese-speaking minority . . . a meaningful opportunity to participate in the [district's] educational program." Because of the discriminatory effect of the district's policies, regardless of any intent to discriminate, Title VI had been violated.[128]

Legal developments since the *Lau* decision have proceeded on three fronts:

(1) the issuance of new guidelines, (2) the interpretation of Title VI and the passage of new legislation, and (3) recent judicial orders dealing with instructional programs to assist in the learning of English. We turn first to the issuance of new guidelines. Following *Lau* it was unclear exactly what districts were expected to do to overcome the language deficiencies of their students, because the Court did not deal with this problem. In 1975 the Office for Civil Rights in the Department of Health, Education and Welfare issued the Lau guidelines, which specified the remedies for Title VI violations.[129] These guidelines required that school officials identify the "primary language" of their students.[130] These students were in turn divided into five categories: (1) monolingual primary language speakers, (2) primary language dominant, (3) bilingual (no dominant language), (4) English dominant, and (5) monolingual English speakers. Depending on a student's grade level and language category, the guidelines either required the provision of bilingual instruction or permitted the provision of either bilingual instruction or the use of English-as-a-second language (ESL).[131] These guidelines were going to be withdrawn by the Carter administration, which planned to issue a new set of regulations placing even more stress on the provision of bilingual instruction. When the Reagan administration came to office, the proposed Carter regulations were withdrawn, and the Lau guidelines remained basic policy. More recently the Reagan administration has moved away from the Lau guidelines by stressing through proposed new regulations that local school districts have substantial discretion to decide the extent and duration of native-language instruction needed and the manner in which it will be used in projects. Stated more directly, school districts are not bound to use bilingual instruction in order to satisfy their legal responsibilities.

We turn now to the further interpretation of Title VI. In *Lau* the Court accepted the view that Title VI could be violated by policies that had an adverse impact that was not intended. In a later opinion, however, five members of the Court adopted the view that Title VI prohibited only those forms of discrimination that would violate the equal protection clause of the fourteenth amendment, i.e., it would only prohibit intentional racial discrimination.[132] If this interpretation of Title VI were to remain standing,[132] the Lau decision would be undermined and the protection of non-English-speaking students severely hampered. But two developments have placed the *Lau* opinion back on a secure footing. In several recent opinions the Court concluded though Title VI itself directly reached only instances of intentional discrimination, actions having an unjustifiable disparate impact on minorities could be redressed if an agency of the federal government has issued regulations designed to implement the purpose of Title VI by prohibiting the disparate impact.[133] In 1974 Congress adopted the Equal Educational Opportunity Act of 1974 [EEOA], which in effect adopted the interpretation in *Lau* of Title VI as an express legislative requirement.[134] The judiciary has interpreted this provision to not require proof of discriminatory intent.[135]

We look next at recent judicial orders dealing with the question of the sort of instructional program schools must offer to meet the requirements of Title VI and EEOA.

Many educators argue that the favoring of bilingual methods of instruction over ESL is sound educational policy because evidence suggests that bilingual education ultimately does a better job in helping the students learn English and in preventing them from falling behind in their studies while doing so.[136] Nevertheless, bilingual education remains controversial. It is viewed as a method for maintaining the non-English-language skills of students, with the possible consequence that the United States would become a bilingual nation with serious cultural, economic, and, most important, political consequences. Supporters, in addition to pointing to its educational value, argue bilingual-bicultural instruction is a right that must be provided to help minorities maintain their cultural heritage and ethnic identity.

With this as background, it is not surprising the courts are split as to whether Title VI and EEOA require the use of bilingual programs. Two opinions may be interpreted as saying that bilingual education is the legally required method for overcoming language barriers.[137] Other courts have stressed that while these statutes require that effective measures be taken to overcome language barriers, those effective methods need not as a matter of law be bilingual education. Failure to implement an adequate nonbilingual program, however, has resulted in an order requiring the provision of bilingual education.[138] The Fifth Circuit's approach is particularly instructive. To determine if a particular language remediation program is adequate, the court said three points must be examined: a court must examine the soundness of the educational theory upon which the program is based; it must see if the actual program adopted is reasonably calculated to implement effectively the educational theory adopted by the school; and a court must determine if the program, after a sufficient trial, is actually producing results in overcoming the language barriers faced by students.[139] Applying this approach, the court concluded that it was permissible under EEOA for a district to offer a program of instruction that emphasized, in the early grades, the learning of English even if this means there is an interim sacrifice in the learning of such subjects as math, science, and social studies. Though EEOA requires that the district provide limited English speaking students with assistance in other areas where their equal participation may be impaired during the time the students participate in the language remediation program, EEOA leaves the school district with the choice of discharging this obligation simultaneously with the provision of language remediation or in sequence, by first addressing the language deficiency and then later providing compensatory and supplementary services to remedy the deficiencies in the other areas. In sum, the policy of the Reagan administration, as discussed above, appears to be consistent with this opinion.

EEOA has been extended to protect black children who speak a dialect called "black English." Finding that black English was a dialect that impeded equal participation of students in the school program, the court ordered the district to develop a plan to teach standard English to speakers of black English.[140] The court's conclusion that Congress intended EEOA to protect speakers of black English is arguable, as is the conclusion that speakers of black English suffer a similar form of exclusion from participation in the school program as do speakers of languages other than English.

7.5. MATCHING STUDENT AND PROGRAM: TRACKING AND ABILITY GROUPING

Public schools have developed ways of matching programs and students in ways that roughly take into account the students' abilities and backgrounds. The grade structure and ability grouping and tracking systems are examples of such an effort. Having established these systems for differentially educating students, what happens if parents and schools disagree on the assignment of a student to a particular class? That is, what happens if parents believe a student was improperly excluded from a class or program? The rough answer is that having decided to treat students differently, the schools are constrained by the equal protection clause of the fourteenth amendment.

Thus, courts relying on the equal protection clause have struck down tracking systems, even in the absence of proof of an intent to discriminate, when used in former dual-school systems that have not been found to be "fully unitary," and when the use of the tracking system had the effect of producing segregation within the newly desegregated school buildings.[141] In Washington, D.C., having found the school district to be segregated, federal courts, relying on constitutional equal protection doctrines not accepted today by the Supreme Court, struck down aspects of the district's tracking system because it resulted in the permanent disproportionate placement of poor and minority students in the lower tracks, where they received a watered-down education and inadequate remedial and compensatory assistance to aid them in getting out of the lower tracks.[142] Today the same results could be reached under Title VI of the Civil Rights Act of 1964 if an agency of the federal government has issued regulations implementing the purpose of Title VI and that deal with programs that have a disparate impact upon minorities.[143]

Indeed, Title VI may be available to attack ability grouping systems (including systems for assigning pupils to special education classes) that have a disproportionate impact on minority students even in districts without a prior history of purposeful racial segregation. To make out a case of a disparate impact, the plaintiff must first show by a preponderance of the evidence that a policy neutral on its face has a disproportionate impact.[144] If the plaintiff succeeds, the burden shifts to the defendant to prove a substantial legitimate justification for the system. That is, the defendant school district can prevail if it establishes an "educational necessity" for the grouping practices it follows. The plaintiff may ultimately prevail by proffering an equally effective alternative practice that has a less disproportionate impact, or proof that the legitimate practice is a pretext for discrimination.

As discussed in chapter 4, racial discrimination charges brought against tracking systems in districts that have not been found to have engaged in inter-school segregation must, to be successful, establish that the pattern of segregation within the school buildings themselves was intentionally caused. (The issue of racial bias in tests used to sort pupils will be taken up in §7.6.) As the Fifth Circuit has said, "school systems are free to employ ability grouping, even when such a policy has a segregative effect, so long, of course, as such a practice is genuinely motivated by educational concerns and not discriminatory motives."[145]

In chapter 5 we saw that excluding students from programs on the basis of gender raises problems under the equal protection clause and Title IX.[146] Note also might be made that an equally divided Supreme Court (one justice did not participate in the decision) upheld, under the fourteenth amendment, a federal circuit court's decision that it was permissible for Philadelphia to exclude a female student from an all-male academic high school because the city also offered an equally good academic all-female high school, as well as a number of non-academic coeducational schools.[147] However, in a later decision the Supreme Court struck down a policy of excluding males from admittance to an all-female college of nursing.[148] In yet another lower court case, the Boston School Committee's admissions policies to two academic high schools were challenged.[149] Because the seating capacity at Boston Latin School was 3,000, the cut-off score on an admissions test was 120 out of a possible 200 points; but the seating capacity for Girls Latin was 1,500, hence the cut-off point was set at 133. The Court concluded that the use of separate and different standards was unconstitutional discrimination against female students solely on the basis of their sex. As noted earlier, in a number of instances the lower courts have also overturned the exclusion of female students from all-male athletic teams, and Title IX regulations prohibit the exclusion from courses of students on the basis of gender.[150]

Challenges to the placement of students not based on claims of racial or gender discrimination have been unsuccessful. Courts have refused to order the early admission of students to the public schools, even if the student appeared to be ready for school.[151] The courts have generally refused to order the placement of pupils in academically advanced programs or to order the grade promotion of a child who did not meet the school's reading requirements.[152] The Supreme Court itself, in a case in which a university student alleged that the university had acted arbitrarily in dropping him from a program without permitting him to retake an examination, said the Court may not override an academic decision "unless it is such a substantial departure from accepted academic norms as to demonstrate that the person or committee responsible did not actually exercise professional judgment."[153] In addition to a concern for a lack of standards by which to judge these problems, the Court noted it was reluctant to "trench upon the prerogatives of state and local educational institutions and our responsibility to safeguard their academic freedom, 'a special concern of the First Amendment.'"

It is unlikely the courts would be sympathetic to claims that students have a right to an impartial hearing prior to or after they have been denied admission to a particular track or course. Even if a court were to agree that a student in this situation had the kind of interests at stake that would warrant the provision of procedural due process,[154] the courts are likely to say that these issues of the academic ability and achievement of students and their assignment to particular tracks and classes are best left to informal decision-making processes. The decision assigning a pupil to a program is arguably like the decision of a teacher in assigning a grade to a pupil: it requires the "expert evaluation of cumulative information and is not readily adapted to the procedural tools of judicial or administrative decision-making."[155] In other words, it is unlikely the Supreme Court today would constitutionally require the sort of procedural safeguards for other students that EAHCA provides for the handicapped.[156]

The success of a general equal protection attack on tracking and ability grouping systems would probably depend on where the suit was brought—in federal court or in a state court that has recognized education as a fundamental interest.[157] Such a suit might be based on research that tends to show that ability grouping and tracking systems result in placements of a disproportionate number of poor and minority students in the low tracks, reduced educational quality in the low groupings, limited access to higher education and some occupations for students in low groups, the stigmatization of low-tracked students; tend to be permanent; and are often the result of an inappropriate or haphazard classification process.[158] Furthermore, "the considerable amount of existing research on the relationship between tracking and academic achievement has not demonstrated that this type of grouping and, presumably, the differential treatment that accompanies it have led to gains in student achievement for students at all ability levels [footnote omitted]. In addition, a number of these and other studies have shown that tracking has had negative effects on students in average and lower groups with the most adverse effects on those students at the bottom levels."[159] Despite evidence of this sort, if the rational-basis equal protection test were used to examine a tracking or ability grouping system (recall that under that test the plaintiff must establish that the classification system is not rationally related to a legitimate purpose of government), it is unlikely the suit would be successful. If nothing else, tracking and ability grouping systems serve the purpose of making classroom instruction easier and more efficient. Thus, if a general equal protection attack on a tracking system were to have a reasonable chance of success, the strict-scrutiny test would have to be brought to bear. That test would only be available, however, if the classification system used a "suspect" criterion, i.e., race, or if it affected a fundamental interest. Since we are assuming at this point that intentional racial discrimination is not at issue, the question is whether education is a fundamental interest triggering use of the strict-scrutiny test. As we have seen in §7.2, the Supreme Court has said education is not a fundamental interest (except perhaps the denial of a minimally adequate education) under the U.S. Constitution. Several state courts have said education is a fundamental interest under the state constitutions, and, at least in these states, tracking systems may be reviewed with the strict-scrutiny test. Given the evidence that has mounted against tracking systems, it is unlikely states and schools could establish that the tracking system is "necessary" to achieve a compelling purpose of government. Homogeneous grouping of pupils, coupled with the preparation of individualized educational programs, is available as an alternative, albeit a more expensive and administratively complex alternative.

7.6. ADMISSION, IQ, AND COMPETENCY TESTING

Formal standardized testing programs are prominent features of the modern school. Besides their use in program evaluation, the tests are used to evaluate students for purposes of assigning them to programs, to decide whether students will be promoted from grade to grade, to decide whether they will be given a high school diploma, and to decide if they will be admitted to college and university programs. Recently these mechanisms for sorting and awarding have come under legal attack, especially on the grounds that they discriminate on the basis of race. A review of the cases follows.

An interesting problem was raised in *Bester v. Tuscaloosa City Board of Education*[160] Between 1970 and 1981, Tuscaloosa had been subject to litigation to desegregate its schools. A consent decree was entered in July 1981 that permitted three of the five formerly all-black elementary schools to remain all black. Prior to March 1982, the promotion policies in these schools differed. The racially mixed but primarily white schools did not promote students who could not read at minimum levels, but the all-black schools did not hold such students back. When the policy was changed in March 1982 so that students who were reading below grade level were not promoted, the effect in grades one through five was that 23.6 percent of black children were retained while only 5.8 percent of white children were held back. The court stated the constitutional claim in the case this way: "[P]laintiff's position is that a school system that has been accepting unsatisfactory work as a basis for promotion may not shift to a promotion standard requiring satisfactory work if the shift, measured statistically, impacts more heavily on black students than on white students, since presumably the heavier impact on black students is a consequence of their having been previously in a segregated school system." The court rejected the argument on two counts. First, the court said, "Students have no legitimate expectation that the meaning of 'satisfactory work' done in the classroom will remain constantly fixed at a level that in truth is academically unsatisfactory." Second, the new promotion policy did not promote resegregation of schools, hence could not be struck down on that ground.

If it had been established and proven in *Bester* that the tests used had a disproportionate impact on black students and were not valid predictors of reading ability, the plaintiffs could have succeeded in eliminating the use of those tests as a violation of Title VI's prohibition against policies that have the effect of discriminating on the basis of race.[161] Even under the more demanding "intent to discriminate" standard the Court uses in applying the equal protection clause of the fourteenth amendment, plaintiffs have been successful in challenging the use of tests for the assignment of pupils to special education classes. The litigation in *Larry P. v. Riles*[162] resulted in an order forbidding, unless the court gave prior approval, all California schools from using IQ tests to determine if students should be placed in classes for the educable mentally retarded. The court concluded that the disproportionate number of minority students in these classes could be explained by the cultural bias of the test, which, in turn, the court concluded was used because of, and not in spite of, this bias.[163] The district court also concluded that the placement mechanisms for the educable mentally retarded (EMR) classes operated with a discriminatory effect in violation of Title VI.[164] On appeal the Ninth Circuit reversed the lower court's finding that the state had engaged in intentional discrimination on the basis of race thereby violating the equal protection clause of the fourteenth amendment, but upheld the district court's conclusion that Title VI had been violated.[165] A similar finding of an intent to discriminate was found in *Lora v. Board of Education of New York*,[166] where the procedure for placement of students in special schools for the emotionally disturbed involved both testing and subjective criteria. In short, the courts have concluded that students assigned to special classes in these cases had been excluded from the regular school program where they belonged, and were instead placed in special classes not suited to their educational needs merely because they were black or Hispanic. Most recently in a case claiming racial and handicap discrimination in the assignment of students to classrooms and programs for the educable mentally retarded [EMR], a federal district court has said that if the overrepresentation of black students in lower-level classrooms and in EMR classes is an effect of prior de jure segregation, no proof of an intent to discriminate would be needed to establish a constitutional violation.[167] The court did stress that "[p]roof of constitutionally impermissible conduct predicated on the past necessarily becomes more difficult as the causal link becomes more attenuated." If the present assignment of pupils is not the product of past de jure discrimination, it must be established that the pattern is a product of intentional discrimination today.

Competency tests used for determining if a student has achieved enough academically to be eligible for a high school diploma have also come under legal attack. In Florida plaintiffs complained that the state's competency test violated both the due process and equal protection clauses of the fourteenth amendment. The federal district court concluded and the appeals court affirmed that approximately one year's notice that passing the test was a prerequisite to graduation from high school was insufficient and violated the student's right to due process of law, and the phenomenon of the disproportionate number of black students who failed the test as of spring 1979 resulted from the inferior education they received when Florida's schools were still purposefully segregated; hence, immediate use of the diploma sanction for not passing the test punished black pupils for deficiencies created by the former dual-school system. However, they determined that the test did have construct validity, i.e., it did test functional literacy as defined by the state.[168] The appeals court remanded the case on two issues: first, the issue of curricular validity (if the test were found on remand *not* to test pupils on materials they actually were taught, then imposition of the test would violate the equal protection clause); and second, the continuing role and effect of past discrimination on black students. Following a trial, the federal district court found that the state had proven that the test had both curricular validity and instructional validity, that is, the official curriculum did cover what was included on the test, and a majority of the teachers in the state recognized those skills as something they should teach.[169] The court also concluded that as of 1983 any causal link between the disproportionate failure rate of black students and the effects of past segregation had been broken; hence, starting with the class of 1983 Florida could deny diplomas to those who failed to pass the test.[170]

The significance of the Florida litigation lies not merely in the fact that the courts are requiring states to adhere to basic principles of fairness when they impose upon students a new requirement for graduation and/or grade promotion, but also that when a state does adopt a system of competency tests, the Constitution requires that each teacher in fact teach to the test, for failure to do so by the teacher makes the test instructionally invalid for his or her pupils. It follows that state-imposed competency tests both dramatically reduce the teacher's discretion and centralize control of the school program in the hands of the state. It should go without saying that the principles established in the Florida litigation also apply to competency tests imposed by the individual school district, perhaps even to teacher-prepared tests.[171] As significant as the adequate notice and validity requirements are, it should be stressed that the courts have consistently supported the authority of the state and school board to make successful completion of the tests a requirement for a diploma, even in the face of challenges brought by mentally impaired students claiming that such a requirement discriminates against them.[172]

Finally, in 1981 the Texas state legislature enacted a requirement that applicants for admission to approved teacher-education programs must achieve satisfactory performance on a competency examination as a condition for admission.[173] The test chosen by the state board of education was the Pre-Professional

Skills Test (PPST) that tested skills in math, reading, and writing. A student who fell below the preclusionary scores set by the state board on any of the three parts of the test could not take more than six hours of courses in education until such time as he or she passed all sections of the test. As administered, the test had a heavy disproportionate impact on minority candidates, and suit was brought claiming the test had been adopted as a form of purposeful racial discrimination. Relying heavily on the foreseeability test (see §4.4) the district court concluded, on a motion for a preliminary injunction, that it was likely plaintiffs would in a full trial be able to establish that the adoption of PPST was motivated by an intent to discriminate.[174] The court also concluded that plaintiffs were also likely to succeed in establishing that the due process clause had been violated because the state failed to provide reasonable notice of the new requirement and because the test had not been properly validated.

7.7. EDUCATION MALPRACTICE: AN INCENTIVE FOR ADEQUATE PROGRAMS

Constitutional and statutory law—the forms of law that we have been dealing with throughout this chapter—are not the only kinds of law that have been used for challenging the mechanisms for placing students in programs, as well as challenging the adequacy of the programs themselves. The common-law body of doctrine dealing with medical malpractice offered litigants an inviting analogy on which to base legal arguments for awarding monetary damages for both the misdiagnosis of student learning difficulties and for negligence in the provision of programs. In addition, common-law doctrines of misrepresentation and fraud suggested an alternative route to obtaining redress for schools that promoted from grade to grade and awarded diplomas to students who could not read.

In the first of the educational malpractice suits, the complaint combined all three elements: charges of misdiagnosis, negligence in the operation of the educational program, and fraudulent representation.[175] Peter W. sued the school from which he was graduated, alleging (1) that the district failed to "apprehend" his reading disabilities; and, somewhat inconsistently, (2) that he had been promoted from grade to grade, even though it was known he had not achieved the necessary skills to benefit from subsequent courses; (3) that he was graduated, although he could not read at the eighth-grade level as required by California law; and (4) that he had been assigned to classes in which the instructors were unqualified or not "geared" to his reading level. Based on these alleged facts, Peter W. said the district's negligent acts and omissions breached a duty of care owed to him and were the proximate cause of his loss of earning capacity and his inability to qualify for more than laboring jobs. Peter W. also alleged the schools had both intentionally and negligently misrepresented that he had been performing at or near grade level; and, as a consequence, he suffered damages.

The court dismissed the suit, saying California law did not permit suits for either negligence or negligent misrepresentation against public school districts.[176] First, the court refused to recognize as a matter of common law that school districts even owed a legal duty of care to their students. There simply were no "readily acceptable standards of care" in education against which to measure the quality of the performance of school teachers and other school officials. Second, the reasons a student may not be able to read may be the result of so many factors beyond the control of the schools—physical, neurological, emotional, cultural, environmental—that proving that school acts of omission or commission were the cause was not possible. Third, opening schools to this kind of suit would burden the already fiscally strained schools beyond calculation. For the same reasons the court also disallowed the claim of negligent misrepresentation.

The opinion can be criticized on a number of points. The court neglected to note that courts are frequently asked to make judgments based on an educational standard of care when they review the dismissal of teachers for incompetence or unprofessional conduct. (See chapter 9.) Further, the mere probability that many factors may contribute to the student's injury should not immunize the school from liability regardless of how substantial the school's own contribution to the injury was.[177] The court improperly discounts the importance of damage remedies as a deterrence to bureaucratic neglect and abuse, especially in large urban districts.[178] The court may also have exaggerated the extent to which frivolous or malicious suits would be brought.[179] Finally, the court paid insufficient separate attention to the first point raised in the complaint: the school district "failed to apprehend his reading abilities." This particular claim stresses the failure of the district to test and diagnose Peter W.'s problem adequately. It is not a claim that the method of instruction was negligent, but that the district through negligence did not even come to understand that he had a reading problem, a necessary premise for any proper judgments as to what should be done next. Requiring districts to take due care in ascertaining the facts would not impose a unique requirement on schools. The EAHCA imposes precisely this requirement for the handicapped. "The determination of the professional's exercise of due care in the manner in which he makes his judgments" does not impose an extraordinary burden on the professional, since it only "requires the trier fact [the court] to draw upon his understanding of the commonly experienced and appreciated human attribute of diligence, carefulness, and attentiveness to one's duties, whatever those duties may be."[180]

The complaint in the second major malpractice suit was significantly different in that it more clearly focused on the problem of misdiagnosis. In *Donahue v. Copiague Union Free School District*,[181] a student was also graduated from high school, even though allegedly he lacked the reading ability even to fill out applications for employment. At the heart of the complaint was the claim that the district failed to evaluate his mental ability and capacity properly, failed to ascertain his ability to comprehend and understand, and failed to test and evaluate his intelligence and "intellectual absorption." The New York Court of Appeals, New York's highest court, agreed that the forging of a clear standard for duty of care for educators was possible and even that the causation problem could be dealt with. However, even though an intelligible malpractice suit could be forged, the court said educational malpractice suits should not be entertained as a matter of public policy.

> To entertain a cause of action for "educational malpractice" would require the courts not merely to make judgments as to the validity of broad educational policies—but, more importantly, to sit in review of the day-to-day implementation of these policies. . . . [This] would constitute blatant interference with the responsibility for the administration of the public school system lodged by Constitution and statute in school administrative agencies.[182]

It is important to note that the court's comments were directed toward all forms of "educational malpractice" and were not specifically tailored to the claim of misdiagnosis made in this suit.[183] The court's reasons for not entertaining educational malpractice cases in general are not convincing as to the more narrowly specified claim in this case. The next suit to arise focused even more clearly on the problem of misdiagnosis. When Daniel Hoffman entered kindergarten in 1956, a school psychologist determined he had an IQ of 74, but the psychologist was not certain of his findings because Daniel suffered from a severe speech defect. Accordingly, Dr. Gottsegen recommended that Daniel's intelligence level be reevaluated within a two-year period "so that a more accurate estimation of his abilities can be made."[184] Daniel was assigned to classes for the mentally retarded for the next twelve years. He was never retested despite indications based on standardized achievement tests given in 1959 and 1960 that he was not mentally retarded. Daniel sued, claiming negligence in how he was classified. On appeal from a $750,000 verdict in Daniel's favor the New York Court of Appeals reversed. The court wrote in *Hoffman v. Board of Education*:

> [T]he decision of school officials and educators who classified plaintiff as retarded and continued his enrollment in [special] classes was based upon the results of a recognized intelligence test administered by a qualified psychologist and the daily observation of plaintiff's teachers. In order to affirm a finding of liability in these circumstances, this court would be required to allow the finder of fact to substitute its judgment for the professional judgment of the board of education as to the type of psychometric devices to be used and the frequency with which such tests are to be given. Such a decision would also allow a court or a jury to second-guess the determinations of each of plaintiff's teachers. To do so would open the door to an examination of the propriety of each of the procedures used in the education of every student in our school system. Clearly, each and every time a student fails to progress academically, it can be argued that he or she would have done better and received a greater benefit if another educational approach or diagnostic tool had been utilized. Similarly, whenever there was a

failure to implement a recommendation made by any person in the school system with respect to the evaluation of a pupil or his or her educational program, it could be said as here, that liability could be predicated on misfeasance. However, the court system is not the proper forum to test the validity of the educational decision to place a particular student in one of the many educational programs offered by the schools of this State. In our view, any dispute concerning the proper placement of a child in a particular program can best be resolved by seeking review of such professional educational judgment through the administrative processes provided by statute.[185]

The Court of Appeals' opinion clearly suggested that it was not the school so much as the parents who had the responsibility for making sure students were not misclassified. If parents believed that a student was misclassified, their only recourse was to appeal the misclassification to the state commissioner of education. But what of the child whose parents or guardians are themselves trusting, ignorant, indifferent, or negligent in this respect? Does a child have any legal recourse against these "protectors"?

The issue arose in *Torres v. Little Flower Children's Services.*[186] When Frank Torres was abandoned by his mother in 1964, the Department of Social Services (DSS) assumed responsibility for his care. The department in turn placed him with Little Flower Children's Services, an authorized child care agency that was contractually obliged to provide him with basic care, religious training, education, and vocational training. Frank was fluent in Spanish but spoke and understood little English. In 1967 the city school district submitted a report to DSS and Little Flower, based on tests administered in English, saying Frank suffered from borderline retardation. As a consequence of the report, though Frank was retained in the regular classes, he was assigned a lesser workload than other students. He began to learn English in about the third grade and did work in math at a normal level; but he continued to have reading problems. Frank's reading problems were regularly discussed by Little Flower staff members and school officials. In 1976 a Little Flower social worker took Frank to a reading specialist, who tested him with a view toward developing an education plan to be initiated after he completed the eighth grade. This specialist concluded that Frank was not retarded but suffered from a complex reading disability. The plan was never executed, but tutoring was arranged for Frank after he finished eighth grade. He stopped attending the tutoring because no transportation was available, and the walk to the sessions took forty-five minutes each way. In October 1972 Frank was enrolled in another school for the educable retarded but was expelled in 1973 after various difficulties. He was discharged from Little Flower's care in 1976. Frank subsequently initiated a suit against Little Flower, DSS, and the school district, charging negligence and a breach of contract leading to his being functionally illiterate. For the reasons expressed in *Hoffman* and *Donohue* the court dismissed the suit. The policies expressed in those cases, said the court, were equally applicable "whether the student challenges educational decisions made by the Board of Education or by his guardians in response to actions taken by school officials, for in either situation the court would be thrust into the position of reviewing the wisdom of educators' choices and evaluations."

The decisions in *Torres* and *Hoffman* need to be compared with another decision rendered at the same time as *Torres*. In *Snow v. State of New York*,[187] Donald Snow, a deaf child, was misdiagnosed as mentally retarded and placed in a class for the retarded. An intelligence test inappropriate for use with deaf children was used. The Court of Appeals affirmed the lower court's ruling that the claim was a medical and not an educational malpractice claim. Accordingly, the court upheld the $1.5 million awarded Donald for the original misdiagnosis and the subsequent failure to reevaluate him. The majority in *Torres* said *Snow* presented a different case, saying that, "While mistaken evaluations are central to both *Snow* and *Torres,* such factors as age of the child upon entry [Donald Snow was three years old when first misdiagnosed], nature of the institution [Donald was in a state institution where "patients" received medical and psychological treatment], and kind of care administered mark the difference between medical and educational malpractice claims."[188] Judge Meyer, dissenting in *Torres,* responded by saying:

> Educational policy is no more involved in Frank Torres' illiteracy than it was in Donald Snow's stunted intellectual growth. In Snow's case those in charge of his custody breached their duty by failing to ascertain that he was totally deaf; in Torres', what defendants failed to ascertain, though obliged to do so, was that he had no understanding of, or ability to speak in, any language but Spanish while he was being raised in an almost entirely English speaking environment. In Snow's case the action has been held maintainable because predicated on medical, rather than educational, malpractice; in like manner Torres' claim should be held maintainable because based on custodial, rather than educational, breach of duty.[189]

New York courts have been consistent. They have also rejected suits against private schools, thus rejecting the claim that suits for breach of contract as to the quality of the educational service provided was distinguishable from a mere claim of deficient services due to negligence.[190]

The notable lack of success claimants have had in bringing educational malpractice suits has been balanced by only one successful suit. In *B. M. v. State,*[191] the court remanded for trial a suit involving the misclassification of a child as mentally retarded who was then placed in a resource room for the educable mentally retarded for 40 percent of the school day without her foster parents' knowledge.[192] That the one case in which the claimant won even a partial victory involved the mislabeling of a child is not surprising. It would seem that as to the diagnosis of pupils, the usual arguments for avoiding liability, e.g., the fear that the courts will take over the daily operation of the schools, do not cut deeply. That is, if courts are going to get over their trepidations about the educational malpractice suits, it would seem that cases like *Hoffman* and *B. M. v. State* provide the best opportunity for a change of heart. In these cases students have suffered major and avoidable harm; the cause of the harm is easily traceable to the actions (or inactions) of school officials; the standards for determining the level of care are easily ascertained; and judicial involvement is held to a minimum. It might even be argued that this kind of case is closer to being a medical malpractice as opposed to an educational malpractice case. For example, the personnel involved may be psychologists and not educators, who rely on a basis of knowledge and expertise that is as much medical as it is educational.[193]

7.8. EQUAL EDUCATIONAL OPPORTUNITY IN PERSPECTIVE: A RIGHT TO AN EFFECTIVE EDUCATION?

The concept and practice of educational opportunity in the United States is confused. The law has hit upon no single definition of equal educational opportunity and permits simultaneously a variety of forms of unequal treatment. In most states, even those in which the state's highest court has struck down the system of finance (with the exception perhaps of California), significant inter-district inequalities in the amount of money spent per pupil are constitutionally acceptable. At the same time, federal and state laws have pushed districts into spending considerably more per pupil on their handicapped and non-English-speaking pupils than on other students. Tracking is a further way differential treatment is legally permissible.

The misclassification and mismatching of student and program present another area of curious confusion and contradiction. Take the example of a language-minority student whom the district fails to identify as having a language problem and, in turn, fails to provide with special assistance to learn English. The school district's failures would violate both Title VI and the Equal Educational Opportunity Act of 1974. (See §7.4.) The student might even be able to sue in federal court for damages for his mistreatment under Title VI, the Equal Educational Opportunity Act of 1974, and/or §1983, if the misclassification were a form of intentional discrimination. However in state court, the student would not have a damage remedy for educational malpractice. The situation is reversed if a student were severely beaten in school. In that case state courts would be open to the student to sue for money damages for the battery, but federal courts would in all likelihood be closed. (See chapter 8.) Even in a state like California in which the highest court has said in *Serrano* that education is a fundamental interest under the state constitution, that same court in *Peter W.* has said students may not seek legal redress for educational malpractice.

The ironies go further. The legal reforms taken on behalf of the handicapped and language-minority students were taken in the name of providing them with a comparable opportunity to that provided other students. The result has been that handicapped and language-minority students enjoy more protection than other students. While the handicapped are provided procedural safeguards and the right to an individually planned program to suit their special needs, the nonhandicapped have no such rights and are vulnerable to misclassification and assignment to inappropriate courses and programs. The law today, as a practical matter, does more to help assure that the handicapped and non-English-speaking student will achieve to their fullest ability than it does for the other students. The misclassified nonhandicapped English-speaking student has no legal recourse.

A greater degree of protection for students not labeled handicapped or as limited English speaking would be provided if the courts were to accept the suggestion of Gershon Ratner that federal and state constitutional law, as well as the state common law of negligence, were interpreted to impose upon schools a legal duty to require public schools "to educate successfully in basic skills the vast majority of its students, regardless of the proportions of poor and minority students."[194] He argues that it is established that public schools can meet such a standard because evidence from schools in New York, Houston, and Philadelphia show that those schools were successful in meeting the standard by adopting certain practices and procedures.[195] Professor Elson argues in response that the research on "effective schools" on which Ratner relies is unpersuasive, inadmissible in a court, and too imprecise to provide judicially manageable standards. Professor Yudof makes many of the same points in a satirical, hypothetical majority opinion embracing Ratner's position.[196] Yudof's Judge Greenwood, in an opinion relying on the effective schools research, orders the Norden Independent School District to hire principals with "leadership" capabilities (perhaps selected with a leadership test?) and/or institute an in-service training program to turn principals into leaders. Students and faculty are to be reminded "of the instructional focus [of the school] through daily announcements on the public address system, appropriate assemblies, and billboard displays." Judge Greenwood also orders the defendant to offer in-service training programs so that teachers will be taught to "take responsibility for all students, all the time, everywhere in the school." Norden is also expected to teach teachers to deal with disciplinary problems "decisively, rapidly, fairly, and firmly." Teachers must be taught not merely to "believe in their charges," but also to "act as though they have confidence in the learning abilities of their students, irrespective of the prejudices that may lurk in their minds."

Yudof's mock opinion accurately reflects the basic finding of the effective schools research and at the same time points to the difficulties of judicial efforts to develop orders based on that research. We thus have another illustration of why courts have been so cautious in seeking to assure students of a minimally adequate program.[197] It may be, however, that while Ratner's approach is flawed, other approaches may be practicable and useful. For example, educational malpractice suits claiming that a pupil was improperly diagnosed would not raise the same kinds of problems as Ratner's approach. And if public school teachers are correct in their claim that theirs is a "profession," might it not also be the case that there are accepted professional practices that, if not carried out, have a high probability of causing harm, and to which the profession can and should be held accountable? But this is another topic requiring more extensive research at a later time.

NOTES

1. Section 7.8 further discusses the notion of a child's constitutional right to an adequate or effective education.

2. Milliken v. Bradley, 433 U.S. 267, 274-75, 280, 287 (1977).

3. Douglas Rae, *Equalities* (Cambridge, Mass.: Harvard University Press, 1981), 20.

4. Id.

5. Id., at 65.

6. Frederick Mosteller, as quoted in David L. Kirp, "The Poor, The Schools, and Equal Protection," *Harvard Educational Review* 38 (1968): 652.

7. Mark G. Yudof, David L. Kirp, Tyll van Geel, and Betsy Levin, *Educational Policy and the Law*, 2d ed. (Berkeley, Calif.: McCutchan Publishing Corporation, 1982), 569. For another interesting discussion of the different concepts of equal educational opportunity see Arthur Wise, *Rich Schools, Poor Schools* (Chicago: University of Chicago Press, 1967), 143-59.

8. Id., at 569-70.

9. Erick Hanushek, "Economics of Schooling: Production and Efficiency in Public School," *Journal of Economic Literature* 24 (1986): 1141; Erick Hanushek, "Throwing Money at Schools," *Journal of Policy Analysis and Management* 1 (1981): 19.

10. Id.

11. For a more detailed discussion of the property tax see Walter I. Garms, James W. Guthrie, and Lawrence C. Pierce, *School Finance* (Englewood Cliffs, N.J.: Prentice-Hall and Company, 1978).

12. Three basic state formulas have been used by most states. The "flat grant" distributes an equal amount of money per pupil to all districts. The "foundation program" is designed to assure each district a minimum level of revenue per pupil, provided the district makes a minimum effort of its own by imposing a state-determined minimum property tax rate. The entitlement of the district to state aid is the difference (if greater than zero) between the guaranteed minimum level of revenue per pupil and the amount actually raised by the district at the required tax rate. The third traditional formula is called "percentage equalizing." The idea here is that the lower the property values per pupil of a district, the higher the percentage of that school district's budget provided by the state. This formula has the advantage of encouraging the property-poor district to make a significant effort to support its educational program because, no matter the total amount of money raised by district, the state will provide the percent of the budget determined by the formula. It is to be stressed that this percentage varies inversely with the amount of property available per pupil—the poorer the district in these terms, the higher the percentage picked up by the district. For a review of these formulas see Garms, Guthrie, and Pierce, *School Finance, supra,* note 11.

13. Wise, *Rich Schools, Poor Schools: The Promise of Equal Educational Opportunity, supra,* note 7; John Coons, William Clune, Stephen Sugarman, *Private Wealth and Public Education* (Cambridge, Mass.: Harvard University Press, 1970).

14. Two cases were decided prior to the publication of *Private Wealth and Public Education*. In McInnis v. Shapiro, 293 F. Supp. 327 (N.D. Ill. 1968), *aff'd sub nom.*, McInnis v. Ogilvie, 394 U.S. 322 (1969) the court turned the challenge away saying the Constitution did not require either the allocation of school funds on the basis of need or on the basis of equal dollars per pupil. The court also stressed that the need standard was not judicially manageable, that the financing of education was a matter best left to the legislature, and that the present system promoted local control. *Accord*, Burruss v. Wilkerson, 310 F. Supp. 572 (W.D. Va. 1969), *aff'd mem.*, 397 U.S. 44 (1970).

15. Dupree v. Alma Sch. Dist., No. 30, 279 Ark. 340, 651 S.W.2d 90 (Ark. 1983); Serrano v. Priest, 5 Cal. 3d 584, 487 P.2d 1241, 96 Cal. Rptr. 601 (1971); Horton v. Meskill, 172 Conn. 615, 376 A.2d 359 (1977), *affirming*, 31 Conn. Supp. 377, 332 A.2d 113 (Hartford County Superior Court, 1974); Robinson v. Cahill, 62 N.J. 473, 303 A.2d 273 (1973), *cert. denied sub nom.*, Dickey v. Robinson, 414 U.S. 976 (1973); Seattle Sch. Dist. v. State of Washington, 90 Wash. 2d 476, 585 P.2d 71 (1978) (en banc); Washakie Cty. Sch. Dist. No. 1 v. Herschler, 606 P. 2d 310 (1980), *ren'g denied*, 606 P.2d 340 (1980), *cert. denied*, 449 U.S. 824 (1980).

16. Pauley v. Bailey, C.A. no. 75-126 (Circuit Court of Kanawha Cty.) (1982), on remand from Pauley v. Kelly, 255 S.E.2d 859 (1979).

17. San Antonio Indep. Sch. Dist. v. Rodriguez, 411 U.S. 1 (1973); Hollins v. Schofstall, 110 Ariz. 88, 515 P.2d 590 (1973) (en banc); Lujan v. Colorado State Bd. of Educ., 649 P.2d 1005 (1982); McDaniel v. Thomas, 248 Ga. 632, 285 S.E.2d 156 (1981); Thomas v. Engelking, 96 Ida. 793, 537 P.2d 635 (1975); Hornbeck v. Somerset Cty. Bd. of Educ., 295 Md. 597, 458 A.2d 758 (1983); Milliken v. Green 389 Mich. 1, 203 N.W.2d 457 (1972), *vacated*, 390 Mich. 389, 212 N.W.2d 711 (1973) (en banc); Bd. of Educ., Levittown Union Free Sch. Dist. v. Nyquist, 57 N.Y.2d 27, 439 N.E.2d 359, 453 N.Y.S.2d 643 (1982); Bd. of Educ. of the City Sch. Dist. of Cincinnati v. Walter, 58 Ohio St.2d 368, 390 N.E.2d 813 (1979), *cert. denied*, 444 U.S. 1015 (1980); Olsen v. Oregon, 276 Or. 9, 554 P.2d 139 (1976).

18. Michael W. LaMorte and Jeffrey D. Williams, "Court Decisions and School Finance Reform," *Educational Administration Quarterly* 21 (1985): 59, table 1, 67.

19. Id.

20. San Antonio Indep. Sch. Dist. v. Rodriguez, 411 U.S., at 36-37.

21. See citations in footnote 15, *supra*. The California litigation had a tangled history. In *Serrano I* the Court adopted the principle of fiscal neutrality and remanded the case for trial to determine if the state system of finance complied with that principle. The lower court concluded that it did not and ordered the state to reduce per pupil expenditure disparities to less than one hundred dollars per pupil and to make insubstantial within six years variations in tax rates. Serrano v. Priest, No. 938, 254 (Super. Ct., County of Los Angeles, Calif., April 10, 1974). On appeal the California Supreme Court affirmed. Serrano v. Priest, 18 Cal. 3d 728, 557 P.2d 929, 135 Cal. Rptr. 345 (1977). Several years later the plaintiffs were back in court claiming the state had not complied with the order to equalize expenditures, but the court concluded that the state had achieved substantial compliance. Serrano v. Priest, Superior Court of State of California, statement of decision, No. 1554, January 14, 1984. This decision was affirmed by the Court of Appeals, 180 Cal. App. 3d 1187 (1986). That decision has been appealed once again to the California Supreme Court. The requirement that actual expenditures be equalized does not logically follow from the fiscal neutrality principle.

22. Washakie Cty. Sch. Dist. No. 1 v. Herschler, 606 P.2d 310, 334 (1980), *reh'g denied*, 606 P.2d 340 (1980), *cert. denied*, 449 U.S. 824 (1980).

23. See materials in note 15, *supra*.

24. In Connecticut the legislative response to the court's order was itself constitutionally challenged. On appeal the court concluded the reform legislation of 1979 was constitutional as originally enacted, but it remanded for further consideration post-1979 legislation that affected the implementation of the 1979 reform legislation. Horton v. Meskill, 195 Conn. 24, 486 A.2d 1099 (Conn. 1985).

25. Robinson v. Cahill, 62 N.J. 473, 303 A.2d 273 (1973), *cert. denied sub nom.*, Dickey v. Robinson, 414 U.S. 976 (1973).

26. For a brief summary of the aftermath to *Robinson I* see Yudof, Kirp, van Geel, and Levin, *Educational Policy and the Law, supra* note 7, at 611-12.

27. Dupree v. Alma Sch. Dist. Crawford Cty., 279 Ark. 340, 651 S.W.2d 90 (1983).

28. Seattle Sch. Dist. v. State of Washington, 90 Wash.2d 476, 585 P.2d 71 (1978).

29. Thus the court prohibited the system of authorizing local school districts to supplement insufficent state funding for the basic education program by means of special excess-levy elections. The special levy system was not a sufficiently reliable and dependable method of funding the basic education program; it could be used for funding an "enrichment program" that went beyond that required by the constitution.

30. Pauley v. Kelly, 255 S.E.2d 859 (1979).

31. Id., at 877.

32. This discussion will not refer to specific opinions but will offer some generalizations in the hope that they are accurate as to all the opinions. The opinions upon which this discussion is based are listed in note 13, *supra*.

33. It is interesting to see how these opinions dealt with the claim that under the *state* constitution the strict-scrutiny test was required because, as far as the state constitution was concerned (with its specific mention of a legislative duty to provide for a thorough and efficient system of public education), education was a fundamental interest. One response was to say that to declare education a fundamental interest could lead to the declaration of such other services as police protection to be fundamental with too far-reaching consequences. Another response was in effect to short-circuit the analysis by saying that the educational provision in the constitution did not require more than provision of a minimally adequate education, and did not require equality in expenditures. (The analysis was short-circuited because, taking this approach, the court does not even bother to select a test—strict scrutiny or rational basis—and then to apply it to the system to determine its constitutionality.) A third response was to say that mentioning education in the state constitution differs from mentioning education in the federal constitution. State constitutions are from a theoretical perspective a different kind of document. They make reference to many specific things that are not of fundamental import; thus, whether or not a right is fundamental cannot be determined by its explicit mention in the state constitution. State constitutions frequently contain matters that might well have been left to statutory articulation.

34. Bd. of Educ., Levittown v. Nyquist, 57 N.Y.2d 27, 439 N.E.2d 359, 369, 453 N.Y.S.2d 643 (1982). The New York case included several additional claims, not usually found in these cases, that were raised by the four major cities of the state, New York, Rochester, Buffalo, and Syracuse. They argued that big cities faced two forms of "municipal overburden," and the failure of the finance system to take municipal overburden into account meant that the system violated the state equal protection clause. First, education in big cities had to compete for tax dollars with an extensive and expensive range of other municipal services—police, fire, and hospital care. Second, big city schools were populated with students with special educational needs, e.g., socially disadvantaged students and a higher percentage of handicapped pupils. The Court of Appeals responded by saying that the competition for tax dollars only meant the cities had to determine their priorities, and that it was beyond the power of the court to intervene in the setting of such priorities. Further, that the big city schools faced difficult educational problems could not be attributed to the legislature.

35. Donohue v. Copiague Union Free Sch. Dist., 47 N.Y.2d 440, 443, 391 N.E.2d 352, 418 N.Y.S.2d 375 (1979). This educational malpractice suit will be discussed in §7.7

36. *See* Frank I. Michelman, "The Supreme Court 1968 Term—Foreword: On Protecting the Poor Through the Fourteenth Amendment," *Harvard Law Review* 83 (1969): 7, 38, 58.

37. *See* Christopher Jencks *et al., Inequality* (New York: Basic Books, Inc., 1972); Frederick Mosteller and Daniel P. Moynihan, eds., *On Equality of Educational Opportunity* (New York: Vintage Books, 1972); Anita A. Summers and Barbara L. Wolfe, "Do Schools Make a Difference?" *American Economic Review* 67 (1977): 639.

38. Intradistrict inequalities in expenditures per pupil were addressed in a series of cases dealing with the District of Columbia School system. Relying on an interpretation of the equal protection clause not accepted today by the Supreme Court, the courts declared unconstitutional inequities in teacher expenditures that worked to the disadvantage of black students. Hobson v. Hansen, 269 F. Supp. 401 (D.C.C. 1967), *aff'd en banc. sub nom.* Smuck v. Hobson, 408 F.2d 175 (D.C. Cir. 1969); Hobson v. Hansen, 327 F. Supp. 844 (D.D.C. 1971). *See also* Brown v. Bd. of Educ., Chicago, 386 F. Supp. 110 (N.D. Ill. 1974).

39. John Coons and Stephen D. Sugarman, "Family Choice in Education: A Model State System for Vouchers," *California Law Review* 59 (1971): 321; James S. Fishkin, *Justice, Equal Opportunity and the Family* (New Haven, Conn: Yale University Press, 1983).

40. 343 F. Supp. 279 (E.D. Pa. 1972); *see also* 334 F. Supp. 1257 (E.D. Pa. 1971) (earlier consent decree).

41. 348 F. Supp. 866 (D.D.C. 1972).

42. Besides the decisions in *Mills* and *PARC* there are a number of other cases dealing with the constitutional rights of handicapped children. Cuyahoga Cty. Ass'n for Retarded Children and Adults v. Essex, 411 F. Supp. 46 (N.D. Ohio 1976) (upholding a statute similar to the one struck down in *PARC*); Fialkowski v. Shapp, 405 F. Supp. 946 (E.D. Pa. 1975) (holding that placement of severely mentally retarded brothers in a program emphasizing reading and writing skills was a denial of equal access to a minimally adequate education for them); Panitch v. Wisconsin, 444 F. Supp. 320 (E.D. Wis. 1977) (handicapped child constitutionally entitled to an education commensurate with needs). *But see* New York State Ass'n for Retarded Children v. Rockefeller, 357 F. Supp. 752 (E.D. N.Y. 1973); Sherer v. Waier, 457 F. Supp. 1039 (W.D. Mo. 1977).

43. Rehabilitation Acts of 1973 (§504), 29 U.S.C. §794 (1982).

44. 20 U.S.C. §§1400-61 (1982).

45. New Mexico Ass'n for Retarded Citizens v. New Mexico, 495 F. Supp. 391 (D. N.M. 1980), *rev'd on other grounds,* 678 F.2d 847 (10th Cir. 1982).

46. The regulations of the Rehabilitation Act require recipients of federal funds to provide a free appropriate education designed to meet the individual needs of handicapped children in the least restrictive environment. 34 C.F.R. §§104.33, 104.34 (1985). As will be discussed later, EAHCA imposes the same requirements. The regulations of the Rehabilitation Act also called for implementation of an individualized education program as developed under EAHCA. 34 C.F.R. §§84.33(b) (2) (1985). The regulations enforcing the Rehabilitation Act specifically state that provision of an individual education program in accordance with the EAHCA is one means of complying with The Rehabilitation Act. 34 C.F.R. §104.33 (b) (2) (1985). *See also* 34 C.F.R. 104.36 (1985).

47. "Handicapped children" under EAHCA are defined as those who are: "mentally retarded, hard of hearing, deaf, speech impaired, visually handicapped, seriously emotionally disturbed, orthopedically impaired, or other health impaired children, or children with specific learning disabilities, *who by reasons thereof require special education and related services."* 20 U.S.C. §1401(1) (1982). However the definition of a handicapped individual under the Rehabilitation Act includes "any person who (i) has a physical or mental impairment which substantially limits one or more of such person's major life activities, (ii) has a record of such an impairment, or (iii) is regarded as having such an impairment." 29 U.S.C. §706(7)(B)(Supp. 3 1979). This provision makes no reference to the handicapping conditions bearing on the need for special education. Thus a child with epilepsy may be protected by the Rehabilitation Act but not by EAHCA.

48. Smith v. Robinson, 104 S. Ct. 3457 (1984). The Court acknowledged two exceptions to the rule. Section 504 may be used where EAHCA is not available or where §504 guarantees substantive rights greater than those under EAHCA. Second, if a state provided services beyond those required under EAHCA and discriminated against the handicap in the provision of those services, §504 would be available for relief. *Id.,* at 3474, 3473 n.22.

The Eleventh Circuit has interpreted Robinson narrowly. That circuit court said the exclusive avenue doctrine of Robinson only applies when the plaintiff sues under both EAHCA and §504; if the plaintiff sues only under §504 the plaintiff may not be precluded from all relief even when EAHCA provides equivalent substantive rights. Ga. State Conf. of Br. of NAACP v. State of Ga., 775 F.2d 1403, 1425 (11th Cir. 1985).

49. New Mexico Ass'n for Retarded Citizens v. State of New Mexico, 678 F.2d 847 (10th Cir. 1982).

50. New York State Ass'n for Retarded Children, Inc. v. Carey, 612 F.2d 644 (2d Cir. 1979).

51. Ga. State Conf. of Br. of NAACP v. State of Ga., 775 F.2d 1403, 1428 (11th Cir. 1985).

52. *See* Stutts v. Freeman, 694 F.2d 666 (11th Cir. 1983); Prewitt v. United States Postal Service, 662 F.2d 292 (5th Cir. Unit B. 1981).

53. *See* Ga. State Conf. of Br. of NAACP v. State of Ga., 775 F.2d 1403, 1428 (11th Cir. 1985); Scokin v. State of Texas, 723 F.2d 432, 441 (5th Cir. 1984).

54. 20 U.S.C. §1412(b) §1412(2)(c) (1982). Children younger than six and older than eighteen may have to be provided services under certain circumstances. 34 C.F.R. §300.300(b) (1985). Educators are not in agreement on the nature and definition of certain educational handicaps. There is disagreement, for example, over the criteria for determining if a child has a "specific learning disability." See the statutory definition of handicapped children in note 47, *supra*. New York State attempted to distinguish between the slow learner and the child with a specific learning disability by requiring that the learning disabled child exhibit a 50 percent or more discrepancy between expected and actual achievement as measured by standardized tests. A federal district court struck down this requirement. Riley v. Ambach, 508 F. Supp. 1222 (E.D. N.Y. 1980), *rev'd on other grounds,* 668 F.2d 635 (2nd Cir. 1981).

55. Special education is defined as "specially designed instruction, at no cost to parents or guardians, to meet the unique needs of a handicapped child, including classroom instruction, instruction in physical education, home instruction, and instruction in hospitals and institutions." 20 U.S.C.§1401(6) (1982). The regulations specifically add that nonacademic services and physical education should be made available as part of a handicapped child's education program. 34 C.F.R. §§300.306, 300.307 (1985). Nonacademic services and extracurricular activities include counseling services, athletics, clubs, and employment assistance. Incorporating handicapped students into these activities may require school districts to make special efforts to assure provision. See text at note 76, *infra.*

56. Related services include "transportation, and such developmental corrective and other supportive services (including speech pathology and audiology, psychological services, physical and occupational therapy, recreation, and medical and counseling services, except that such medical services shall be for diagnostic and evaluative purposes only) as may be required to assist a handicapped child to benefit from special education, and includes the early identification and assessment of handicapping conditions in children." 20 U.S.C.§1401(17), (1982). The regulations further define the term "related services." 34 C.F.R. §300. 13(a)(1985).

57. 20 U.S.C. §1401(18)(D)(1982).

58. 20 U.S.C. §1401(19)(1982).

59. Id.

60. 20 U.S.C.§1412(5)(c) (1982).

61. 20 U.S.C.§1412(5)(b) (1982).

62. Id.

63. 34 C.F.R. §300.57 (1985). In a surprising decision in Mayson v. Teague, 749 F.2d 652 (11th Cir. 1984) the court held that even officers and employees of local boards employed in systems in which the child in question is not enrolled could not serve as impartial hearing officers.

64. 20 U.S.C.§1415 (1982).

65. Id. Several courts have held that employees of the state board of education may not serve as impartial hearing officers in appeals to the state. Mayson v. Teague, 749 F.2d 652 (11th Cir. 1984); Robert M. v. Benton, 634 F.2d 1139 (8th Cir. 1980); Vogel v. Sch. Bd. of Montrose, 491 F. Supp. 989 (W.D. Mo. 1980).

66. In Adler v. Educ. Dept. of State of N.Y., 760 F.2d 454 (2d Cir. 1985) the court held that the state's four-month statute of limitations applied to appeals under EAHCA. *See also* Scokin v. Texas, 723 F.2d 432 (5th Cir. 1984); Dept. of Educ. v. Carl D., 695 F.2d 1154 (9th Cir. 1983).

The courts are not fully in agreement on if and when claimants need not exhaust their administrative remedies before appealing to the court. *See* Mountain View-Los Altos High Sch. Dist. v. Sharron B.H., 709 F.2d 28 (9th Cir. 1983); Marvin H. v. Austin Indep. Sch. Dist., 714 F.2d 1348 (5th Cir. 1983); Quackenbush v. Johnson City Sch. Dist., 716 F.2d 141 (2d Cir. 1983), *cert. denied*, 104 S. Ct. 1426 (1984).

67. 20 U.S.C.§1415(e)(4) (1982).

68. *See supra*, text accompanying notes 55-57.

69. Bd. of Educ. v. Rowley, 458 U.S. 176 (1982), *reversing*, 632 F.2d 945 (2d Cir. 1980), *which had affirmed*, 483 F. Supp. 528 (S.D. N.Y.).

70. 483 F. Supp. at 534.

71. Bd. of Educ. v. Rowley, 458 U.S., at 198.

72. Lower courts have begun to wrestle with the question of how much weight to give to the findings and conclusions of the local and state administrative proceedings. *See* Roncker ex. rel. Roncker v. Walter, 700 F.2d 1058 (6th Cir.), *cert. denied*, 104 S. Ct. 196 (1983); Quackenbush v. Johnson City Sch. Dist., 716 F.2d 141 (2d Cir. 1983), *cert. denied*, 104 S. Ct. 1426 (1984).

73. The effect of *Rowley* seems to have been one of restraining the lower courts in overturning the IEPs proposed by local school districts. Rettig v. Kent City Sch. Dist., 720 F.2d 463 (6th Cir. 1983), *cert. denied*, 104 S. Ct. 2379 (1984); Colin v. Schmidt, 714 F.2d 1 (1st Cir. 1983); Springdale Sch. Dist. No. 50 of Wash. v. Grace, 693 F.2d 41 (8th Cir. 1982), *cert. denied*, 461 U.S. 927 (1983).

74. Judith Welch Wegner, "Variations on a Theme—The Concept of Equal Educational Opportunity and Programming Decisions Under the Education for All Handicapped Children Act of 1975," *Law and Contemporary Problems* 48 (1985): 169, 186.

75. 20 U.S.C.§1401(16) (1982).

76. Rettig v. Kent City Sch. Dist., 720 F.2d 463 (6th Cir. 1986). The Sixth Circuit held that Thomas Rettig would not benefit from extracurricular activities, hence was not entitled to extracurricular activities. The court also concluded that strict "equality of opportunity" in the provision of extracurricular activities was not required. Thus, to the extent 34 C.F.R. §300.306 (1985), which states that handicapped pupils be provided an "equal opportunity for participation" in extracurricular activities, requires strict equality of opportunity, it is inconsistent with EAHCA, hence invalid.

77. Katharine T. Bartlett, "The Role of Cost in Education Decision-making for the Handicapped Child," *Law and Contemporary Problems* 48 (1985): 7, 15.

78. Clevenger v. Oak Ridge Sch. Bd., 744 F.2d 514, 517 (6th Cir. 1984).

79. Abrahamson v. Hershman, 701 F.2d 223, 227 (1st Cir. 1983).

80. David D. v. Dartmouth Sch. Comm., 775 F.2d 411 (1st Cir. 1985).

81. Tracey v. McDaniel, 610 F. Supp. 947 (D.C.Ga. 1985). The district court notes that other courts have come to a contrary conclusion.

82. Tatro v. State of Texas, 703 F.2d 823, 830 (5th Cir. 1983); Burger v. Murray Cty. Sch. Dist., 612 F. Supp. 434 (N.D. Ga. 1984).

83. In New York City the average cost of special education was $5897 per pupil as compared with $2294 for the regular program. Leigh S. Marriner, "The Cost of Educating Handicapped Pupils in New York City," *Journal of Educational Finance* 3 (1977): 82, 86-88.

84. Yaris v. Special Sch. Dist. of St. Louis Cty., 728 F.2d 1055 (8th Cir. 1984); Crawford v. Pittman, 708 F.2d 1028 (5th Cir. 1983); Battle v. Commonwealth of Pennsylvania, 629 F.2d 269 (3d Cir. 1980), *cert. denied sub nom.*, Scanlon v. Battle, 452 U.S. 968 (1981).

85. Helms v. Indep. Sch. Dist. No. 3, 750 F.2d 820 (10th Cir. 1984).

86. In Clevenger v. Oak Ridge Sch. Dist., 744 F.2d 514 (6th Cir. 1984) the court ordered a residential placement costing $88,000 per year.

87. Abrahamson v. Hershman, 701 F.2d 223, 227 (1st Cir. 1983) (dictum); Thomas B. Mooney and Lorraine M. Aronson, "Solomon Revisited: Separating Educational and Other Than Educational Needs in Special Education Residential Placements," *Connecticut Law Review* 14 (1982): 531, 540.

88. *See, e.g.,* Diamond v. McKenzie, 602 F. Supp. 632 (D.D.C. 1985); Geis v. Bd. of Educ. of Parsipany-Troy Hills, Morris Cty., 589 F. Supp. 269 (D. N.J. 1984).

89. Heasler v. State Bd. of Educ. of Maryland, 700 F.2d 134, 138 (4th Cir. 1983). Courts will order residential placement if appropriate despite the enormous cost. *See* Clevenger v. Oak Ridge Sch. Bd., 744 F.2d 514 (6th Cir. 1984) (cost of residential placement of emotionally disturbed child was $88,000 per year). State statutory ceilings on the amount that will be paid to a private school may be unconstitutional. Kruse v. Campbell, 431 F. Supp. 180, 187 (E.D.Va. 1977), *vacated,* 434 U.S. 808 (1977); Halderman v. Pittenger, 391 F. Supp. 872, 876 (E.D. Pa. 1975). *See also* Fallis v. Ambach, 710 F.2d 49 (2d Cir. 1983).

90. *See, e.g.,* Abrahamson v. Hershman, 701 F.2d 223 (1st Cir. 1983); Battle v. Commonwealth of Pennsylvania, 629 F.2d 269, 275 (3rd Cir. 1980). For a review of cases of this sort see Lauren A. Larson, "Comment—Beyond Conventional Education: A Definition of Education Under the Education for All Handicapped Children Act of 1975," *Law and Contemporary Problems* 48 (1985): 63, 73-76.

91. In McKenzie v. Jefferson, 566 F. Supp. 404 (D.D.C. 1983) the court said hospitalization for emotional needs was like being hospitalized for an operation: the treatment provided was not instruction related to education.

92. Kruelle v. New Castle Cty. Sch. Dist., 642 F.2d 687 (3d Cir. 1981) (ordering residential placement for the child). *See also* McKenzie v. Smith, 771 F.2d 1527 (D.C. Cir. 1985) (upholding residential placement because educational and emotional needs could not be separated); North v. District of Columbia Bd. of Educ., 471 F. Supp. 136 (D.D.C. 1979); Papacoda v. Connecticut, 528 F. Supp. 68 (D. Conn. 1981). For a discussion of these and other cases see Larson, "Comment—Beyond Conventional Education: A Definition of Education Under the Education for All Handicapped Children Act of 1975," *supra,* note 90; Wegner, "Variations on a Theme, . . ." *supra,* note 74. Wegner writes "that the critical issue in determining whether a child's needs are educational in character is whether they relate to his ability to master pertinent skills." *Id.,* at 203.

93. 753 F.2d 1397 (7th Cir. 1985), *cert. denied sub nom.,* Belletire v. Parks, 105 S.Ct. 3529 (1985).

94. 753 F.2d at 1406.

95. Id., at 1405-1406.

96. H. Rutherford Turnbull, III, Esq., and Craig R. Fiedler, Esq., *Judicial Interpretation of the Eduction for All Handicapped Children Act* (Eric Clearinghouse on Handicapped and Gifted Children, 1984), 11.

97. Abrahamson v. Hershman, 701 F.2d 223, 230 (1st Cir. 1983).

98. The statutory definition of "related services" is provided in note 56, *supra.*

99. 104 S. Ct. 3371 (1984). In this case if the public were to provide eight-year-old Amber Tatro with CIC, a treatment that could be taught a layperson in less than an hour's training, she could remain in the public school where she would receive her special educational program.

100. 727 F.2d 809 (9th Cir. 1984).

101. Wegner, "Variations on a Theme, . . ." *supra* note 74, at 215.

102. 34 C.F.R. §300.13(b)(2) (1985).

103. Id., at §300. 13(b)(8).

104. 592 F. Supp. 1437 (N.D. Ill. 1984). *See also* Papacoda v. State of Connecticut, 528 F. Supp. 68 (D. Conn. 1981); Gary B. v. Cronin, 542 F. Supp. 102 (N.D. Ill. 1980); In the Matter of "A" Family, 184 Mont. 145, 602 P.2d 157 (1979).

105. McKenzie v. Jefferson, 566 F. Supp. 404 (D.D.C. 1983); Darlene L. v. Illinois State Bd. of Educ., 568 F. Supp. 1340 (N.D. Ill. 1983).

106. 20 U.S.C. §§1415(b)(1)(C), 1415(b)(2), 1415(b)(1)(E) (1982). While the hearing takes place, the child must remain in his or her current educational placement unless the parent agrees to a change. *Id.*, §1415(e)(3).

107. Concerned Parents v. New York City Bd. of Educ., 629 F.2d 751, 754 (2d Cir. 1980), *cert. denied*, 449 U.S. 1078 (1981) (when one school closed, the transfer of student to a similar but less innovative program not a change in placement). *See also* Lunceford v. Dist. of Columbia Bd. of Educ., 745 F.2d 1577 (D.C. Cir. 1984) (transfer leading to a change in feeding program not a change in educational placement).

108. Tilton v. Jefferson Cty. Bd. of Educ., 705 F.2d 800, 804 (6th Cir. 1983) (holding the new program was not comparable to the old program).

109. DeLeon v. Susquehanna Comm. Sch. Dist., 747 F.2d 149 (3d Cir. 1984) (change in how student was transported to school not a change in placement). *See also* Brookline Sch. Comm. v. Golden, 628 F. Supp. 113 (D. Mass. 1986).

110. Sch. Bd. of Cty. of Prince William, Va. v. Malone, 762 F.2d 1210 (4th Cir. 1985); Kaelin v. Grubbs, 682 F.2d 595 (6th Cir. 1982); S-1 v. Turlington, 635 F.2d 342 (5th Cir. 1981), *cert. denied*, 454 U.S. 1030 (1981).

111. 20. U.S.C. §1416(e)(2) (1982).

112. Smith v. Robinson, 104 S. Ct. 3457 (1984).

113. Id., at 3468, 3470-71 n. 17.

114. 20 U.S.C. §1416(e)(2) (1982).

115. Burlington Sch. Comm. of the Town of Burlington, Mass. v. Dept. of Educ. of Comm'w. of Mass., 105 S. Ct. 1996, 2005 (1985).

116. Id.

117. Id., at 2003.

118. *See* Miener v. State of Mo., 673 F.2d 969 (8th Cir. 1982), *cert. denied*, 459 U.S. 909 (1982); Anderson v. Thompson, 658 F.2d 1205 (7th Cir. 1981); Austin v. Brown Local Sch. Dist., 746 F.2d 1161 (6th Cir. 1984), *cert. denied*, S. Ct. (1985); Hymes v. Harnett Cty. Bd. of Educ., 664 F.2d 410 (4th Cir. 1981).

119. Manecke v. Sch. Bd. of Pinellas Cty., 762 F.2d 912 (11th Cir. 1985).

120. Georgia State Conf. of Br. of NAACP v. State of Georgia, 775 F.2d 1403 (11th Cir. 1985); Scokin v. State of Texas, 723 F.2d 432 (5th Cir. 1984). *Cf.*, Miener v. State of Mo., 673 F.2d 969 (8th Cir. 1982), *cert. denied*, 459 U.S. 909 (1982) (private damage remedy available).

121. Alyeska Pipeline Serv. Co. v. Wilderness Soc'y, 421 U.S. 240 (1975).

122. 42 U.S.C. §1983, §1988 (1982); 29 U.S.C. §794, §794a(b) (1982).

123. 104 S. Ct. 3457 (1984).

124. 483 F.2d 791 (9th Cir. 1973), *rev'd.*, 414 U.S. 563 (1974). The petitioners in the case were among the 2,856 non-English-speaking Chinese pupils in the San Francisco schools who were not receiving special instruction to learn English. They did not challenge the use of English as the medium of instruction or the requirement that mastery of English was a requirement for graduation.

125. 483 F.2d at 797-8. Similar constitutional arguments have failed in other cases. *See, e.g.*, Otero v. Mesa Cty. Valley Sch. Dist. No. 51, 408 F. Supp. 162 (D. Colo. 1975), *vacated on other grounds*, 568 F.2d 1312 (10th Cir. 1977)

126. 414 U.S. 563 (1974).

127. Title VI reads: "No person in the United States shall, on the ground of race, color, or national origin, be excluded from participation in, be denied the benefits of, or be subjected to discrimination under any program or activity receiving Federal financial assistance." Civil Rights Act of 1964, Title VI §601, 42 U.S.C. §2000(d) (1976 & Supp. V 1981).

128. In interpreting Title VI the Court relied heavily upon the interpretation developed by the then Department of Health, Education and Welfare and the Office for Civil Rights, as embodied in regulations and clarifying guidelines. Most important were the guidelines issued by

the Office for Civil Rights that stated Title VI required schools to take "affirmative steps to rectify the language deficiency in order to open its instructional program to" non-English-speaking national-origin minority group children. 35 Fed. Reg. 11, 595 (1970).

129. Office for Civil Rights, Dep't of Health, Education & Welfare, "Task Force Findings Specifying Remedies Available to Eliminate Past Educational Practices Declared Unlawful Under Lau v. Nichols 2" [hereinafter cited as Lau Guidelines].

130. The primary language was said to be other than English if the student's first language was other than English, or if the language most often spoken by the student was other than English, or if the language most often spoken in the home was other than English, regardless of the language spoken by the student. *Id.*, at 1.

131. Bilingual instruction typically involves use of the student's primary language as the medium of instruction in substantive subjects (math, science, reading), combined with intensive instruction in English. Under ESL the basic medium of instruction continues to be English, but the non-English-speaking child is periodically in the week pulled from the regular classes for instruction in English, often by teachers who do not speak the student's primary language.

The Lau guidelines require the following forms of instruction: as to elementary school students, those in the first two categories must receive bilingual instruction; ESL is specifically ruled out; intermediate school students in the first category must receive bilingual instruction those in the second category may be given ESL or bilingual instruction; secondary students in the first category may be provided a form of bilingual instruction, ESL, or an total immersion program designed to teach a new language; those in the second category could be provided bilingual or ESL.

132. Regents of the University of California v. Bakke, 438 U.S. 265 (1978).

133. Alexander v. Choate, 105 S. Ct. 712, 717 (1985); Guardian Assn. v. Civil Service Commission, 463 U.S. 582 (1983).

134. 20 U.S.C. §§1701-1758 (1982). Section 1703 states: "No State shall deny equal educational opportunity to an individual on account of his or her race, color, sex, or national origin, by . . . (f) the failure by an educational agency to take appropriate action to overcome language barriers that impede equal participation by its students in its instructional programs."

135. *See, e.g.*, Castaneda v. Pickard, 648 F.2d 989 (5th Cir. 1981); Morales v. Shannon, 516 F.2d 411 (5th Cir. 1975), *cert. denied*, 423 U.S. 1034 (1975); Cintron v. Brentwood Union Free Sch. Dist., 455 F. Supp. 57 (E.D. N.Y. 1978). *See also* Jonathan D. Haft, "Assuring Equal Educational Opportunity for Language Minority Students: Bilingual Education and Equal Educational Opportunity Act of 1974," *Columbia Journal of Law and Social Problems* 18 (1983):209.

136. For a review of the evidence in support of bilingual as opposed to ESL *see* Haft, "Assuring Equal Educational Opportunity for Language-Minority Students: Bilingual Education and Equal Educational Opportunity Act of 1974," at 250-258. *See also* Ann C. Willig, "A Meta-Analysis of Selected Studies on the Effectiveness of Bilingual Education," *Review of Educational Research* 55 (1985): 269; Russell Gersten, "Structured Immersion for Language Minority Students: Results of a Longitudinal Evaluation," *Educational Evaluation and Policy Analysis* 7 (1985): 187.

137. Cintron v. Brentwood Union Free Sch. Dist., 455 F. Supp. 57 (E.D. N.Y. 1978); Rios v. Reed, 480 F. Supp. 14 (E.D. N.Y. 1978). Serna v. Portales Mun. Sch. Dist., 499 F.2d 1147 (10th Cir. 1974) was decided on the basis of Title VI alone and ordered the provision of bilingual education.

138. Castaneda v. Pickard, 648 F.2d 989 (5th Cir. 1981); Guadalupe Organization, Inc. v. Tempe Elementary Sch. Dist., 587 F.2d 1022 (9th Cir. 1978); United States v. Texas, 506 F. Supp. 405 (E.D. Tex. 1981), *rev'd*, 680 F.2d 356 (5th Cir. 1982).

139. Castaneda v. Pickard, 648 F.2d 989, 1009-1010 (5th Cir. 1981).

140. Martin Luther King Jr. Elementary Sch. Children v. Michigan Bd. of Educ., 451 F. Supp. 1324 (E.D. Mich. 1978), and 473 F. Supp. 1371 (E.D. Mich. 1979). *See* Tyll van Geel, "The

Right to Be Taught Standard English: Exploring the Implications of Lau v. Nichols for Black Americans," *Syracuse Law Review* 25 (1974): 863.

141. See, e.g., McNeal v. Tate Cty. Sch. Dist., 508 F.2d 1017 (5th Cir. 1975); Lemon v. Bossier Parish Sch. Bd., 444 F.2d 1400 (5th Cir. 1971); Anderson v. Banks, 520 F. Supp. 472 (S.D. Ga. 1981). Typically the segregation arises because black students are disproportionately assigned to the lower tracks. The courts have viewed the within-building segregation produced by these tracking systems as a vestigial effect of the prior practice of de jure segregation on the academic achievement of black students. *See also* Ga. State Conf. of Br. of NAACP v. State of Ga., 775 F.2d 1403, 1412-1416 (11th Cir. 1985) (upholding ability grouping systems in several school districts that had not been *judicially* declared to be "fully unitary" systems). In that case the court concluded that the district court had not erroneously concluded that the ability grouping schemes will remedy the consequences of prior segregation.

142. Hobson v. Hansen, 269 F. Supp. 401 (D.D.C. 1967), *aff'd nom.*, Smuck v. Hobson, 408 F.2d 175 (D.C. 1969) (en banc).

143. *See supra*, 127 for the text of Title VI. Alexander v. Choate, 105 S. Ct. 712 (1985); Guardians Ass'n v. Civil Service Commission, 463 U.S. 582 (1983).

144. Ga. State Conf. of Br. of NAACP v. State of Ga., 775 F.2d 1403, 1417 (11th Cir. 1985). In this case the defendants were able to establish that their grouping practices bore a manifest demonstrable relationship to classroom education. *Id.*, at 1418.

145. Castaneda v. Pickard, 648 F.2d 989, 996 (5th Cir. 1981). *See also* Ga. State Conf. of Br. of NAACP v. State of Ga., 775 F.2d 1403 (11th Cir. 1985). *Cf.*, Bond v. Keck, 616 F. Supp. 581 (D.C. Mo. 1985) (denying claim that assignment of a student to a particular math class was based on race).

146. Education Amendments of 1972, Title IX, 20 U.S.C.§1681 (1982).

147. Vorcheimer v. Sch. Dist. of Philadelphia, 532 F.2d 880 (3rd Cir. 1976), *aff'd by an equally divided Court,* 430 U.S. 703 (1977).

148. Mississippi University for Women v. Hogan, 458 U.S. 718 (1982).

149. Bray v. Lee, 337 F. Supp. 934 (D. Mass. 1972).

150. 45 C.F.R. §106.34 (1985).

151. Hammond v. Marx, 406 F. Supp. 853 (D. Me. 1975); Isquith v. Levitt, 285 A.D. 833, 137 N.Y.S.2d 497 (A.D.2d 1955).

152. Sandlin v. Johnson, 643 F.2d 1027 (4th Cir. 1981). *See* Johnpoll v. Elias, 513 F. Supp. 430 (E.D. N.Y. 1980) (no denial of a right to education to attend high school of his choice).

153. Regents of the University of Michigan v. Ewing, 106 S. Ct. 507, (1985) (holding the decision to dismiss Ewing was not a substantial departure from accepted academic norms).

154. To trigger a right to procedural due process, the plaintiffs would have to establish that they have either a "property" interest or a "liberty" interest at stake. Goss v. Lopez, 419 U.S. 565 (1975).

155. Bd. of Curators of the University of Missouri v. Horowitz, 435 U.S. 78 (1978) (denying a request for a formal hearing prior to dismissal from medical school).

156. *See supra*, text accompanying notes 63 and 67.

157. For an excellent, but now somewhat out of date, analysis of the constitutionality of ability and tracking systems *see* David L. Kirp, "The Schools as Sorters: The Constitutional and Policy Implications of Student Classification," *University of Pennsylvania Law Review* 121 (1973): 705.

158. Jeannie Oaks, "Tracking and Ability Grouping in American Schools: Some Constitutional Questions," *Teachers College Record* 84 (1983): 801, 802-6.

159. Id., at 803.

160. 722 F.2d 1514 (11th Cir. 1984).

161. For the text of Title VI see note 127, *supra*. Alexander v. Choate, 105 S. Ct. 712 (1985). Under the disparate impact analysis the plaintiffs would be required to prove the tests had a

disproportionate impact upon minorities, but the district could still prevail if it could show substantial educational justification for the test. The plaintiff may still rebut by proffering an equally effective alternative practice, or by providing proof that the test was a pretext for discrimination. Ga. State Conf. of Br. of NAACP v. State of Ga., 775 F.2d 1403, 1417 (11th Cir. 1985).

162. 495 F. Supp. 926 (N.D. Cal. 1967).

163. *But see* Parents in Action on Special Education v. Hannon, 506 F. Supp. 831 (N.D. Ill. 1980). The court in this case also agreed that there were test items used in the IQ test that were culturally biased. Nevertheless, he concluded that those items would not cause inappropriate placement because of the way the tests were administered and scored, and the fact that other considerations entered into an EMR placement decision, e.g., teacher referral, a multidisciplinary professional assessment, and the recommendation of a psychologist.

164. Larry P. v. Riles, 495 F. Supp. at 965.

165. Larry P. by Lucille P. v. Riles, 793 F.2d 969, 983, 984 (9th Cir. 1984).

166. 456 F. Supp. 1211 (E.D. N.Y. 1978), *vacated and remanded,* 623 F.2d 248 (2d Cir. 1980).

167. Georgia State Conference v. State of Georgia, 570 F. Supp. 314 (1983).

168. Debra P. v. Turlington, 474 F. Supp. 244 (M.D. Fla. 1979), *aff'd in part, vacated in part and remanded,* 644 F.2d. 397 (5th Cir. 1981). *See* Anderson v. Banks, 520 F. Supp. 472 (S.D. Ga. 1981).

169. *Cf.,* Anderson v. Banks, 520 F. Supp. 472 (S.D. Ga. 1981).

170. Debra P. v. Turlington, 564 F. Supp. 177 (M.D. Fla. 1983), *aff'd,* 730 F.2d 1405 (11th Cir. 1984).

171. Brookhart v. Ill. State Bd. of Educ., 534 F. Supp. 725 (C.D. Ill. 1982), *rev'd,* 697 F.2d 179 (7th Cir. 1983).

172. Id.; *See also* Bd. of Educ. Northport-East Northport Union Free Sch. Dist. v. Ambach, 458 N.Y.S.2d 680 (App. Div. 1982), *aff'd mem.,* 469 N.Y.S.2d 669 (1983), *cert. denied,* 52 U.S.L.W. 3575 (1984).

173. United States v. State of Texas, 628 F. Supp. 304, 305 (E.D. Tex. 1985).

174. The impact of the test, the lack of a coordinated attempt to institute an organized program of remediation, and the fact the state board of education was composed of twenty-seven members of which only one was black and one was Hispanic were considered by the court in reaching its conclusion. The court also placed great weight on the fact that in the face of a teacher shortage the legislature waived other requirements (dealing with teacher education courses and student teaching) but held firm to the PPST requirement. The court's mention that the case came up against a historical background of racial discrimination in Texas was also significant. *Id.,* at 315-18.

175. Peter W. v. San Francisco Unified Sch. Dist., 60 Cal. App. 3d 814, 131 Cal. Rptr. 854 (1976). In Bogust v. Iverson, 102 N.W.2d 228 (Wis. 1960) a college counselor was sued for negligence in connection with the counseling of a student who committed suicide five weeks after the counseling sessions had terminated. The counselor had consulted Jane with regard to personal, vocational, educational, scholastic, and other problems. The parents claimed the counselor should have recognized Jane needed emergency psychiatric treatment and informed them of Jane's problems. The Wisconsin Supreme Court refused to allow the suit on the grounds that this "teacher" could not be expected to recognize and diagnose in a specialized and technical medical field. Besides, weeks passed between the end of the sessions and the suicide, and it was mere speculation to assume Jane would not have committed suicide if the parents had been advised or even if psychiatric help had been secured.

176. The court seemed to acknowledge a suit for intentional misrepresentation might be recognized in California law, but in this case the plaintiff had not alleged facts showing he had relied upon the misrepresentation.

177. John Elson, "A Common Law Remedy for the Educational Harms Caused by Incompetent or Careless Teaching," *Northwestern University Law Review* 73 (1978): 641, 696, 747-54.

178. Id., at 657-59, 665-67.

179. Id., at 652.

180. Id., at 736.

181. 47 N.Y.2d 440, 391 N.E.2d 352, 418 N.Y.S.2d 375 (1979).

182. Id., at 445.

183. The court's reasons for dismissal of the suit evokes the notions of sovereign immunity from suit. *See* Myers v. Medford Lakes Bd. of Educ., 199 N.J. Super. 511, 516, 489 A.2d 1240, 1242 (1985) (dismissal of educational malpractice claim on grounds, among other things, that there was immunity from liability for exercises of judgment or discretion). Other courts have discussed the possibility of governmental immunity as a possible defense. *See* Peter W. v. San Francisco Unified Sch. Dist., 60 Cal. App. 3d 814, 819, 131 Cal. Reptr. 854, 857 (1976); Tubell v. Cty. Pub. Schools, 419 So.2d 388, 389 (Fla. Dist. Ct. App. 1982) (improper testing of pupil led to misclassification of pupil for a number of years). The notion of sovereign immunity has been abolished in most states, see §8.2, but immunity for discretionary actions has been retained in some states. *See, e.g.,* Cal. Gov. Code §820.2 (West 1980 & Supp. 1985).

184. Hoffman v. Bd. of Educ., 49 N.Y.2d 121, 124, 400 N.E. 2d 317, 424 N.Y.S.2d 376 (1979). *See also* Doe v. Bd. of Educ., 295 Md. 67, 453 A.2d 814 (1982). In this case the school psychiatrist in 1967 recommended placement of the child in a brain-damaged class and reevaluation in ten months. Neither was done. In 1968 a private physician diagnosed dyslexia, not brain damage. Another examination by a school psychologist led to more testing in 1975; again, no brain damage was found. Ultimately the student's only problem was determined to be dyslexia. Meanwhile the student had been placed in programs for the mentally retarded for seven years. The suit was disallowed on the grounds that such negligence claims would make the courts overseers of the day-to-day operations of the public schools. *Id.,* at 488, 439 A.2d at 585.

185. Id., at 127.

186. 64 N.Y.2d 119, 485 N.Y.S.2d 15 (1984), *U.S. cert. denied,* 106 U.S. 181 (1985).

187. 64 N.Y.2d.745 (1984), *affirming,* 98 A.D.2d 442, 469 N.Y.S.2d 959 (A.D. 2d Dept. 1983).

188. 485 N.Y.S.2d at 18 n. 2.

189. 485 N.Y.S.2d at 20.

190. Paladino v. Adelphi University, 89 A.2d 85, 454 N.Y.S.2d 868 (1982). *Cf.,* Village Community Sch. v. Adler, 124 Misc. 2d 817, 478 N.Y.S.2d 546 (N.Y. Civ. Ct. 1984) (recognition of breach of contract and fraudulent misrepresentation suit based on representations by school that it would detect and treat any learning disability).

191. 649 P.2d 425 (Mont. 1982).

192. The child's IQ score was 76, whereas the educably mentally retarded are usually considered those with scores between 50 and 75.

193. *See* Doe v. Bd. of Educ., 295 Md. 67, 80, 453 A.2d 814, 820 (Eldridge, J., dissenting) (arguing that the claim should not have been dismissed because the plaintiff had alleged negligence by a health professional—a psychologist—hired by the district).

194. Gershon M. Ratner, "A New Legal Duty for Urban Public Schools: Effective Education in Basic Skills," *Texas Law Revew* 63 (1985): 777, 781. Ratner suggests that a successful school be measured against the following standard: no more than 20 percent of the students in any grade two through six be one year or more below grade level in reading, mathematics, or composite basic skills, and that no more than 10 percent be more than two or more years below grade level. *Id.,* 799. Ratner's development of the legal duty is too complex fully to state here. Roughly speaking, he argues that inadequate schools effect a fundamental interest and/or discriminate in urban school districts against a suspect class. Thus, a strict-scrutiny test should apply to determine the constitutionality of the school program. He argues that the district will be able to establish that its present program is necessary to achieve a compelling state interest. The effective schools research establishes that more effective schools can be established at reasonable costs even in

schools heavily populated by low income and racial minority students. Ratner is especially persuasive in mounting his legal argument in his reliance on those state school finance cases that interpret the state constitution as imposing on the state a duty to assure that the public school program must, for example, assure students are effectively educated in basic skills. (For a review of these cases see §7.2.)

195. John S. Elson, "Suing to Make Schools Effective, or How to Make a Bad Situation Worse: A Response to Ratner," *Texas Law Revew* 63 (1985): 889.

196. Mark G. Yudof, "Effective Schools and Federal and State Constitutions: A Variety of Opinions," *Texas Law Revew* 63 (1985): 865.

197. *See* Valdez v. Graham, 474 F. Supp. 149 (M.D. Fla. 1979) (refusing to intervene on behalf of migrant children who claim that the educational program offered them does satisfy the federal statutory requirements that migrant children be provided with programs designed to meet their special educational needs).

8

The Safe and Orderly School

8.1. INTRODUCTION

Few topics have attracted the attention of parents, students, teachers, school administrators, politicians, and the media more than the topic of discipline, disorder, and drugs in the public schools. This chapter will review the legal basis for a school duty to establish a safe and orderly environment. But, assuring that the school is safe and orderly must be accomplished within constraints imposed by the U.S. Constitution. For example, though school officials may feel legally obliged to see to it that the school is kept free of drugs, the fourth amendment imposes limits as to when and how students may be searched.[1] This chapter will explore those important constitutional rights of students that may have the unintended effect of making more difficult the provision of a safe and orderly school.

Just as U.S. constitutional doctrine limits state law and policy, the Supreme Court has itself limited the development of constitutional doctrine in deference to state law. The Court's concern with federal-state relations discussed in chapter 2 reveals itself in the way the Court has refused to define expansively U.S. constitutional rights and to impose duties on states and localities to provide a safe school environment. Plaintiffs frustrated by the Court's resistance to broadening federal rights to be free from physical harm in the public schools have no recourse but to rely on what state law is available.[2] Thus, students who themselves seek compensation for harm done to them in the public schools must rely primarily on state law for their remedy, while the schools that seek to avoid having to face such suits must try to fulfill their duty to provide safe schools without violating the rights of those who may be the source of the trouble.

8.2. TORTS

A legal duty to provide a safe school can arise from a number of sources. It may be imposed by a constitution,[3] by statute,[4] and it may arise by contract.[5] The oldest source of the duty of the public schools for providing a safe environment is to be found in that branch of the common law known as torts.[6] Though this is a basically well settled body of law, it has undergone changes during the last thirty years, changes that have served to increase the opportunity of students to receive legal redress, usually in the form of monetary compensation, for injuries they have sustained in school.[7] By providing students with the opportunity to obtain through the courts substantial compensation for injuries they have sustained in school, tort law creates an incentive for the schools to take prospective steps to assure their students remain safe from a variety of harms. Of course, the easier it is for a plaintiff to win substantial damages in court, the more risk-averse and cautious will school officials become, perhaps so cautious as to damage the quality of the school program they offer. In developing this body of tort law the courts, thus, have had to balance a number of considerations, e.g., the goal that students not be harmed as they pursue their education, and the need not to make the operation of schools excessively expensive (through steps taken to insure student safety). It is the effort at balancing these and other considerations that helps to account for many of the technical rules that have emerged in this area.

To explore this general theme we might consider, first, the torts of assault and battery.[8] It is desirable that people, including students, not be subjected to either assaults or batteries, hence the law imposes a duty on others not to do either on pain of having to pay monetary compensation to the victim. The threat and some use of physical force is also thought to be desirable for the control and education of children; hence the law recognizes a "privilege" in parents and teachers to do to children what would, absent this privilege, be a tortious act. Thus, a teacher or parent may use force, including corporal punishment,[9] for the discipline and control of the child to maintain order and decorum in the school. Because excessive force would on balance do more harm than good, the law permits only reasonable force to be used. The reasonableness of the force is determined by considering the age, sex, physical and mental condition of the child, the nature of the offense, the influence of the child's example on the other children, the extent of the harm inflicted, whether the force was disproportionate to the offense, or was unnecessarily degrading.[10] In addition to the teacher's special privilege to use force, the teacher shares with everyone else the privilege to use reasonable force in self-defense. Again, the legal doctrines spelling out the scope and limits of the privilege of self-defense are chosen in light of the balance that needs to be struck.[11] The aim is to permit the *optimal* amount of deterrence, i.e, deterrence that prevents the potential cost of the assault without imposing a cost that exceeds the costs that would have occurred if the attack were to be successful.

The use of the principles can be illustrated. In a suit for damages for an assault in *Hogenson v. Williams,*[12] the court rejected a football coach's claim of privilege because the court said force may only be used by a teacher to enforce compliance with a proper command or to punish a child for prohibited conduct. Here, the coach hit the boy's helmet with enough force to knock him to the ground and then grabbed his face mask after the coach had become unhappy with the student's performance of a blocking assignment; he used the force to "fire him up," "to instill spirit in him."[13] The court wrote that "we do not accept the proposition that a teacher may use physical violence against a child merely because the child is unable or fails to perform, either academically or athletically, at a desired level of ability, even though the teacher considers such violence to be 'instruction and encouragement.'"[14] The use of force by the coach can profitably be compared to the force used by an eighth grade teacher in forcibly ejecting a disruptive student from class.[15] The student's disruption of the class led to the teacher's ordering him to leave, to which the student responded by saying to his friends, "I don't have to do what this mother-fucker says." Again, the student was ordered out of the class but remained sitting at the desk. At this point the teacher approached the student and started physically to lead him from the class, but the student resisted and started to swing his arm. The teacher now clamped the boy's arm to his side and headed him toward the shut door. At the door the teacher shoved the boy forward and reached to grab the knob in an effort to get the door open and the boy through it in one motion. When he released the boy's arm, it swung up and through the window resulting in cuts to the arm. The boy sued for assault and battery claiming he had been wantonly shoved into a door and window. The jury returned a ruling in favor of the teacher, and the court of appeals affirmed.

From time to time in encounters with students, teachers may have to resort to self-defense. The scope of this privilege is illustrated by two other cases. In one case the teacher, having forcibly escorted a student from class, stopped to talk privately with him, away from the other pupils. At this point the student clenched his fist and uttered a vulgar remark. Believing he was about to be hit, the teacher slapped the student across the face with the back of his hand. The court agreed that the teacher's use of force was reasonably necessary to restrain the threatened violence and to maintain discipline in the school. Stated more generally, a person may use reasonable force to prevent any threatened bodily contact.[16] One may act not just when there is real danger, but also when there is a reasonable belief of the existence of danger. The teacher need not wait until he or she has been struck. The privilege permits only the use of that amount of force that is reasonably necessary for protection. For example, in another case a boy, five feet tall and 101 pounds, who was being forcibly escorted from the basketball court by a coach, five feet eight inches and 230 pounds, resisted and attempted to strike the coach. The coach responded by lifting, shaking, and dropping the boy to the ground resulting in a fracture of the boy's arm. The court in ruling for the pupil said the coach had used force in excess of that required to either protect himself or to discipline the pupil.[17] Finally, it should be noted that once the initial student-teacher confrontation is over, the privilege of self-defense is no longer available and may not be used by a teacher who violently reinitiates the conflict ten or fifteen minutes later.[18]

It is not just the amount of force used by teachers in maintaining discipline that has proven to be important in these cases, but also the kind of force used. In *McKinney v. Greene* the court agreed with the student that, when an elementary school teacher had lightly kicked him with the side of his foot to get his attention and to get him to stop pushing in a lunch line, the force used was not "reasonable and appropriate."[19] In another case the court upheld the dismissal of a sixth-grade teacher who used a cattle prod to discipline the pupils in his class.[20] The court wrote:

> That the plaintiff had a disciplinary problem in his classroom is well established by the evidence, however, we harbor the gravest of doubts as to the wisdom of the methods used by the plaintiff in his effort to cope with this problem. . . . [W]e cannot equate the use of the cattle prod with the use of a hickory switch or the sharp crack of a rule across one's knuckles. It is apparent from the record that the recipients of the electric shocks from the prod were actually cowed into submission. They would plead for amnesty which was on occasion promised but not granted. They were embarrassed by the laughing and hilarity of other students when the prod was applied and equally as cruel as the electric charge received by the victim was the humiliation suffered by one who was publicly classified by the plaintiff as a coward when one's name was posted on the blackboard as a member of the coward's list.[21]

We turn now from the so-called intentional torts of assault and battery to the area of negligence. The legal award of money damages to victims of negligence serves not only to compensate the victim for his or her injuries but also to create an incentive for the school district and its employees to take steps to avoid these accidents in the future. Thus, tort law encourages districts to incur a cost to avoid accidents when the potential cost of the accident is larger than the cost of avoiding it. It is socially better to encourage the spending of a $1000 now to avoid an accident than to run the risk of incurring a later injury with a cost of $2000.[22] On the other hand, if it is estimated that potential victims could avoid this kind of accident themselves at a cost less than the school district's, the law does not impose a duty on the district to take steps to avoid the accident, and the cost of the accident is left to fall on the victim. In this way it is the potential victim who has the incentive to take steps to avoid this kind of accident, and society is better off because the incentive to avoid the accident is placed on the person who can avoid the accident at the least total social cost.

The many technical doctrines that have evolved in this area may be interpreted as the law's way of carrying out this policy.[23] Rather than go into these often legally crucial technicalities, it might be more profitable simply to indicate the kinds of accidents the law has said school districts and teachers can be expected to spend time, effort, and money on to avoid. Surely few would disagree that injuries to students related to the physical condition of the school plant are in most instances most easily avoided at least cost by the district itself taking precautions. Hence, it should not be surprising that students who are on school grounds during school hours are considered to be "invitees" toward whom the district owes a duty of care that entails not negligently creating hazards (i.e., providing defective shop or athletic equipment, leaving floors slippery, allowing missing light bulbs or inadequate handrails, using unstable heavy equipment such as lockers and pianos) and correcting those hazards that could have been discovered after due diligence.[24] Thus one court held that a student who pays a parking fee is an invitee and can obtain damages from the college for an attack by an individual hiding in foliage that had been used by previous attackers.[25] In another case the court imposed a duty on the state to keep the dormitory safe from intruders who may rape.[26] The courts may be particularly willing to find liability when the school provides equipment that violates safety standards.[27] One may anticipate in this regard that there may be lawsuits brought in the future against school boards for failure to remove asbestos from the district's buildings.[28] The law takes a different attitude toward children and adults who are not "invitees," but who may be using school facilities at their own request by permission of the district. The law only requires that these "licensees" be warned of concealed hazards and to avoid affirmative action that unreasonably imperils them.[29] By lowering the duty on the school district, the law makes it more difficult for the licensee to win the lawsuit; thus the law creates an incentive for licensees to be themselves cautious. The law imposes no duty to make premises safe or to warn unknown trespassers of hazards. Only limited duties are imposed as regards discovered trespassers: to warn them of concealed hazards and to avoid affirmatively injuring them.[30] The assumption here is that the accidents can most easily be avoided by the trespasser by simply not trespassing.[31]

Turning now to the duty to provide adequate supervision of students, the accidents that can arise involve those resulting from failure to issue instructions and warnings, the issuance of improper instructions and commands, action taken by an individual student that results in the student injuring himself (as in using a piece of shop machinery), and by one student harming another. The law is especially complex because of the difficulties involved in sorting out who in a particular situation was in the best position to have taken steps to avoid the accident at least cost—teacher or student—a question sometimes phrased in the law in terms of whether the incident was foreseeable by the teacher or in terms of whether the teacher's inaction was the "proximate cause" of the injury.[32] Since violence in schools is today a topic of considerable concern, it might be most interesting to illustate how the law operates to impose an incentive on schools to protect students from the violent acts of other students. One court stated the duty of the school board in the following terms:

The duty of reasonable supervision does not require the [board] to provide personnel to supervise every portion of the school buildings and campus area. However, if certain specific areas are known to the [board] as dangerous, or the [board] knew or should have known that certain students would or may conduct themselves in a manner dangerous to the welfare of others, duty of reasonable supervision would require specific supervision of those situations.[33]

In another case the court sustained a jury verdict that the district had been negligent in not protecting one student from another student who had openly threatened to harm the plaintiff when school officials were aware of the threat and depth of anger of the student who committed the assault.[34] In another case a New York court held that a school district could be held liable for the emotional distress suffered by a girl because of a year's worth of harassment suffered at the hands of another student.[35] School districts may be held liable for injuries sustained by students through "hazing" at initiation ceremonies of school clubs.[36] In another case the district was held liable for injuries of a white student when her wrist was slashed by a black student while attending a school-sponsored film, and the school was aware that the film depicted racial violence and there was racial tension in the school, and no supervision of students was provided at the theater.[37]

A California court held the Fall River school district liable when a student from another district was injured in a car driven by a Fall River student who was chosen to act as a host for the visiting student. The Fall River district had a duty of care in the selection of host families, and members of the host families could be viewed as employees of the host district.[38]

As for the duty of the individual teacher, typical situations that have reached the courts include the cases in which one student hurts another after the teacher has stepped out of the classroom, or a fight breaks out on the playground and one student hurts another. In these situations the teacher is held to have acted negligently if a reasonable person would have foreseen the occurrence of an accident of the sort that did occur and would have taken steps to avoid it.[39] Liability is more likely to be found if a teacher leaves a classroom and there were students with known assaultive propensities in the class, there were dangerous instrumentalities in the class, the students were young and immature, the teacher's departure was for more than a moment, and there was history of disruptions in this class. Factors that tend to suggest the teacher could not have avoided the accident and, accordingly, lower the risk of a finding of liability include: the teacher's appointment of a monitor on leaving the classroom; the teacher's specific instructions given to the pupils and designed to avert such an incident; the impulsiveness of the student's action in harming another student; the sequence of events leading to the injury were sufficiently unusual they could not have been reasonably foreseen, and the shortness of the departure.[40] In brief, two central issues tend to dominate these cases: whether an incident of this sort could have been foreseen by school officials, and whether the act of the student causing the injury could have been prevented even if supervision had been better.[41] Thus, one court held that a teacher was not liable for negligent supervision when during her brief absence a student's eye was injured by a pencil that had been propelled from the hand of a classmate who tripped.[42] The teacher could not have anticipated this incident regarding students who were not known as hellions, and, indeed, said the court, the students involved had been instructed to remain in their seats. Even when a pencil was deliberately thrown, the court ruled in favor of the teacher who was only briefly absent from the classroom.[43] In another case two boys had been slap boxing for five to ten minutes in front of a crowd of some thirty students when one boy, after being slapped, fell backwards on the asphalt pavement sustaining a mortal fracture of his skull.[44] The physical education department, which was responsible for supervising this section of the campus, had an informal arrangement for supervision—the task was simply left to the person in the gym office. The teacher in the office at the time of the incident was sitting at a desk facing away from the windows, and a wall obscured his view of the area where the slap boxing took place. Furthermore, he was concentrating on preparing for afternoon classes and eating his lunch. The California Supreme Court concluded there was sufficient evidence from which a jury could find negligence. Teachers were also held to have breached their duty of care in failing to anticipate that a mentally retarded seventeen-year-old with a mental age of about seven or eight, who possessed poor auditory ability and a short attention span and who had difficulty following instructions, would impulsively run across a street into the path of an oncoming automobile when walking to practice with a Special Olympics basketball team.[45] Inadequate supervision was provided and the safest route to the gymnasium had not been selected. The court stressed that the duty of care become more onerous when the student body consists of mentally retarded students.

School personnel probably open themselves up to the greatest risk of liability in connection with faulty instruction and teaching that directly leads to an injury. This most frequently occurs in connection with physical education, shop, and laboratory classes in which the teacher fails adequately to instruct the pupils in the use of equipment, mismatches contestants in an athletic event, fails to properly instruct pupils in the execution of an athletic exercise or in the use of chemicals.[46] Generally speaking, the duty of school personnel is that of a reasonable or prudent person under the circumstances; hence the level of care required of a teacher must vary with the degree of danger inherent in the situation.[47] For example, failure to enforce wearing of safety goggles, in violation of a statute, can be deemed negligence per se.[48] As might be expected, the outcome of these cases can be affected by the contributory negligence of the student.[49] The younger the child and the more mentally incompetent the child, the less likely a defense of contributory negligence will be effective.[50]

The reach of tort liability is well illustrated by a New York case in which two fifteen-year-old summer employees improperly took chemicals from an unlocked school laboratory and left them sequestered behind bushes on the school grounds.[51] Injury occurred when an eight-year-old who found the chemicals played with them with matches causing an explosion. The district was held liable because the presence of the eight-year-old on school grounds was foreseeable, and because the district failed to supervise its student employees and failed in adequately securing dangerous chemicals in violation of its own safety regulations. While normally the intervening intentional criminal act will sever the liability of the defendant in a tort suit, in this case the intervening act of the student employees was a danger that could be reasonably foreseen.

As for off-campus activities, since school officials are typically not in the best position to prevent accidents in these locations, the law has imposed no general duty to supervise these activities unless the school assumes responsibility and has knowledge of the specific danger involved.[52] There are, however, several important exceptions to this proposition. First, school districts and/or school officials may be held liable for the injuries of a student sustained off school grounds even if the student left the premises without permission if his leaving was the result of inadequate supervision.[53] Schools do, however, owe a duty of care regarding field trips and other school sponsored activities.[54] If schools do provide transportation to and from school, liability may be found for unsafe equipment, negligent operation of the bus, and negligent supervision of students at bus stops.[55]

The state law assuring students a safe and orderly schooling is undergoing change in several respects. Legislation in some states establishes safety requirements, say, for safe school bus operations. Perhaps the most striking development is the adoption in California of an amendment to the state constitution that says, "All students and staff of primary, elementary, junior high and senior high schools have an inalienable right to attend campuses which are safe, secure, and peaceful."[56] This provision may without further legislation impose an affirmative duty, enforceable in the courts through injunctions and damage remedies, on schools to take steps to assure the schools are safe.[57] Various doctrines that in the past have served to limit the possibility of an individual obtaining a damage award, therefore reducing the incentive on school districts and their employees to take precautions to protect the pupils, are changing. First, certain officials, such as the individual school board member, not mere employees, may enjoy a qualified official immunity from suit as regards their policymaking decisions, as opposed to mere "ministerial acts" and malicious or intentional wrongdoing.[58] To protect students the courts seem to be willing to define a wider range of activities as ministerial activities.[59] Second, while the board itself may be vicariously liable under the principle of "respondeat superior" for the actions of its employees, it will only be held liable if the employee's action fell within the scope of his or her authority or employment. But even if the employee's action were within the scope of employment and were not an intentional tort (in some states the doctrine of respondeat superior does not apply to intentional torts), the district itself may not be liable if (1) the state legislature or courts have not limited or abolished the doctrine that says the government itself is immune for tort liability, or (2) the activity did not fall within one of the standard exceptions to the governmental immunity doctrine.[60] Significantly, the clear trend in the law has been for state legislatures and courts to limit or even abolish the governmental immunity doctrine.[61]

8.3. A CONSTITUTIONAL RIGHT TO SAFE SCHOOLS AND SECTION 1983

Despite the fact state tort law has been available to protect people, the Supreme Court has moved cautiously toward recognizing a constitutional right to physical safety in certain governmentally run institutions.[62] Thus, today prisoners and those involuntarily committed to mental institutions are protected in modest ways by the eighth and fourteenth amendments against confinement in institutions in which their physical safety is in danger as a result of the general conditions of the institutions in which they are confined.[63] Yet in a more recent decision the Court has ruled that the due process clause of the fourteenth amendment is not implicated by the *negligent* acts of officials that cause the unintended loss of or injury to life, liberty, or property.[64] The Court noted that the guarantee of due process has historically been applied to *deliberate* decisions of officials to deprive a person of life, liberty, or property.[65] Based on this principle, the Court in a companion decision said that a claim that prison officials were negligent in protecting the plaintiff from an assault by another prisoner did not raise a constitutional issue.[66] The Court did, however, pointedly note that this case was different from one involving injuries by an unjustified attack by prison guards, or a case where officials stand by and permit an attack to proceed. Even those who have not become dependent upon the government for care enjoy a constitutional right not to be subjected unnecessarily to serious physical harm by governmental officials.[67] One federal district court held that police officials could be held liable for a second rape of a women by the same man who raped her in the first place when the police were aware of the rapist's identity after the first rape, and were aware the rapist might attempt a second rape.[68]

While the development of a constitutional right to a safe environment has progressed quickly outside the school context, the courts have to date been reluctant to extend this line of thought to the schools. Turning first to the use of violence by school officials themselves, the Supreme Court has addressed the question only once. In that case the Court said that the eighth amendment's protections against "cruel and unusual punishment" is not applicable to students in public schools.[69] Thus, litigants have turned to the fourteenth amendment, leading one court in *Hall v. Tawney* to say a student's right to bodily security would only be constitutionally violated if the force applied to the student by school officials was "so disproportionate to the need presented, and was so inspired by malice or sadism" that it amounted to a "brutal and inhumane abuse of official power literally shocking to the conscience."[70] Other courts have taken a different approach. Relying on the lower court opinion in *Daniels*[71] that the Supreme Court affirmed, one court dismissed a claim that the student's constitutional rights had been violated when a teacher pierced her upper left arm with a straight pin.[72] The court dismissed the suit for two reasons: (1) even assuming the *Hall* case stated the law, there was nothing alleged which amounted to conscience-shocking behavior by the teacher; but that, (2) in any event, said the court, the proper approach was not to be based on the amount of force used or the justification for it. Rather, in order to make out a constitutional violation, the court said, it had to be proven that the battery was intended to violate a constitutional right, and proof of such intent was missing here.

Turning now to a right to protection from violence by other students, in *Williams v. City of Boston*[73] plaintiffs sought damages for the death of a black high school student who was a victim of an attack while attending a football game held at a predominantly white high school. The plaintiffs alleged the city knew or should have known that violent attacks on black athletes would occur in this section of town and that it failed to implement adequate security measures. The court in dismissing the suit said that, among other things, there was no constitutional right to basic services such as adequate police protection and that mere inaction by the government did not provide a basis for a civil rights remedy. Cases protecting the right of the mentally ill to a safe institutional environment, the court said, were distinguishable from this case. In this case the state had not placed the victim in peril by taking control of him—the victim here was a voluntary participant in the extracurricular activity. The resistance of the court to these claims was importantly based on a desire to avoid having every state tort suit literally becoming a "federal case."

Though suits against school districts implicating a nascent constitutional right to physical safety have not been successful, it is clear the door has not been closed to all such suits. Students compelled by the compulsory education law to attend school are on a footing not unlike prisoners and the mentally ill. Thus, if a school district were grievously negligent in providing supervision and this led to the severe beating of a student by another student, by intruders into the school, or even a teacher, the courts would be more willing to entertain the suit. It is important to stress, however, that for the school district itself to be liable under §1983 a number of important hurdles have to be overcome by the plaintiffs.[74] Though the Supreme Court has opened the door to §1983 suits that might also be dealt with under state tort law, it has only opened the door a bit in order not to expand federal authority by turning every potential tort suit into a constitutional claim.

8.4. LIMITS ON THE SCHOOL'S AUTHORITY TO SET STANDARDS OF CONDUCT

In §§8.2-8.3 we examined the legal duty of schools to provide a safe environment. We now turn to the limits the law imposes in fulfilling that duty. Although those limits may appear to frustrate the effort to assure that schools are safe, each limit exists for reasons, i.e., the law does not adopt the position that safety is to be promoted regardless of any other considerations or values. Whether the courts have gone too far in imposing these limits, thereby contributing to what is perceived as a spate of violence and crime in the schools, is a matter of considerable debate.

As discussed in chapter 2, school districts as creatures of the state legislature only have that express or implied authority delegated to them by the state legislature. It thus follows that a particular school rule directed toward assuring a safe environment may be *ultra vires,* i.e., beyond the power of the school board. For example, it has been held in most states that in the absence of smallpox in the community or indications of a clear and imminent danger of a smallpox outbreak, a school board without explicit statutory authority to do so may not exclude an unvaccinated child from school.[75] The most difficult issues arise when a school board acts pursuant to a general grant of power to maintain order in the schools and it is claimed that this general grant does not, even implicitly, give the board authority to impose its specific action, e.g., excluding a mother from school when her child was conceived out of wedlock but born after her marriage, or regulating the off-school ground activities of students.[76] To resolve these cases the courts must "interpret" the statutory grant of authority, an activity that in reality may amount to a judicial determination as to whether permitting the school rule to stand makes good sense when one considers the educational needs of the excluded student and the well-being of the other pupils in the school.[77] Though it may seem logical for the courts simply to permit local districts to do what the district deems necessary and wise to promote order and discipline, the fact remains it is the state legislature that is the constitutionally designated, preeminent policymaking body in the state, and if its authority is not to be usurped, the courts must somehow consider what is or seems to be the legislative policy on school discipline. Thus, the Supreme Court of Oklahoma began its inquiry as to whether a school board had the statutory authority to regulate hairstyles by noting that the scope of the board's authority was limited to rules that have a reasonable connection with the educational function entrusted to it.[78] The court concluded the district lacked the authority to regulate hairstyles. Since students spend more time out of school than in school, hairstyle regulations had a greater effect on the life of students out of school than in school, and boards did not have the authority to regulate out-of-school activities.

Even if a local board may enjoy the statutory authority to issue a particular school rule, it may be constrained in issuing the rule by other external limits.

Because of the supremacy clause of the U.S. Constitution, school disciplinary rules that conflict with federal statutes must give way.[79] Thus, the courts have overturned the disciplinary suspension of handicapped pupils when accomplished in a way that conflicts with federal laws regulating the education of the handicapped.[80] Relying on federal law, the Second Circuit barred the exclusion from regular classes of mentally retarded children who were carriers of serum hepatitis when school officials were unable to establish that the presence of these children in the classes posed a health risk to the other students.[81]

During the last thirty years the most significant efforts to impose external limits on the authority of school boards have been based on arguments rooted in the U.S. Constitution. For example, it has been argued that school boards should only be permitted to discipline students (and teachers) on the basis of a preexisting written rule, because this failure to give fair notice of what is impermissible conduct violates the due process clause of the fourteenth amendment. Only in this way can it be assured that schools do not make impermissible after the event what had been permissible before the event. "The formality is grounded in the supposition that the values of fairness, liberty, dignity, and participation require the promulgation of general rules applied in a uniform fashion. Critics of legalization, however, have focused on the need to maintain authority relationships and a sense of shared community purpose in public schools, and they perceive legalization as a threat to those values. Ultimately the question is one of balance between rule and discretion, formality and informality, trusting and adversarial relationships."[82]

The balance struck by the courts, however, has favored informality. "[T]he prevailing law, at least for students, appears to be that school officials may discipline students for conduct disruptive of the educational process or conduct that endangers the health and safety of students and school personnel without having adopted a prior rule forbidding the behavior and specifying the penalties."[83] The basis of this policy is that school officials need flexibility to meet unexpected events in the school, and that, in any event, most students know, without the benefit of written rules, what is and is not permissible conduct. But, at least one state has legislatively required all school rules to be in writing.[84]

When school districts do promulgate written rules they are frequently stated in broad and general language in order to retain flexibility in dealing with students. Rules with a broad, open texture are open to being challenged for violating the constitutional principle that a law is void if it is so vague that persons "of common intelligence must necessarily guess at its meaning and differ as to its application."[85] The judicial response to these challenges has been mixed. Thus, one court upheld a school rule that stated "students should behave in a manner that will be a credit upon themselves"; whereas another court struck down as impermissibly vague a school rule which prohibited "misconduct."[86]

The most frequently brought constitutional challenges to school disciplinary action have not been based on the vagueness of the rules, but on the basis that the disciplinary action and/or the rule on which it is based violates, for example, the right of freedom of speech, the free exercise of religion, liberty and privacy, and/or the right to the equal protection of the laws. Thus, as has been discussed in chapter 6, school disciplinary rules that infringe on the free speech rights of students may not serve as a basis for suspending or otherwise punishing pupils unless that speech activity "materially and substantially" disrupts the school program.[87] School regulation of hairstyles in order to prevent "extreme" styles from disrupting the schools has split the courts, with some saying the choice of hairstyle is a personal liberty that must be protected in the absence of clear evidence a hairstyle does in fact disrupt the schools, and others saying the choice is a trivial liberty not protected by the due process clause of the fourteenth amendment.[88] Policies that infringe on the free exercise of religion may also fail.[89] Disciplinary practices that purposefully discriminate on the basis of race will be struck down under the fourteenth amendment, and may even fail under Title VI or IX merely because they have the effect of discriminating on the basis of race or gender, respectively.[90] The concern with the possibility that a school disciplinary code might be used in a racially discriminatory way led one court to require the district to revise its disciplinary code by removing reliance on subjective criteria and by substituting objective guidelines.[91]

8.5. SEARCHING STUDENTS TO OBTAIN EVIDENCE OF A RULE INFRACTION

The enforcement of permissible school rules by the disciplining of students who violate those rules may only be constitutionally accomplished if there is evidence to support the conclusion the student has violated the rule.[92] The gathering of this evidence sometimes entails the search of students and their lockers, thus the question is raised as to what the limits are on the power of school officials to search. Again the question is inevitably one of balance: Should school officials remain free of the restraints of the fourth amendment in order to maximize their ability to maintain the order and safety of the school, or should they be restrained to some degree in order to protect the students' interests in privacy?[93]

The Supreme Court addressed this question for the first time in January of 1985 in a case entitled *New Jersey v. T.L.O.*[94] It all started when a teacher, who found two girls including the 14-year-old T.L.O smoking in a school lavatory, brought them down to the principal's office. Under questioning by Assistant Vice Principal Choplick one girl admitted she had been smoking, but T.L.O. denied she had been smoking, and claimed she did not smoke at all. Mr. Choplick asked T.L.O. into his private office and demanded to see her purse. On opening the purse he found a package of cigarettes and he removed them from the purse revealing a package of cigarette rolling papers. Because such rolling papers were associated with the use of marijuana, Mr. Choplick suspected a closer examination of the purse would yield additional evidence of drug use. A further thorough search of the purse, including the opening of zippered compartments, revealed a small amount of marijuana, a pipe, a number of empty plastic bags, $40.98 in single dollar bills and change, an index card that appeared to be a list of students who owed money to T.L.O., and two letters further implicating T.L.O. in marijuana dealing. On the basis of this evidence, which had been turned over to the police, and a confession by T.L.O., the state brought delinquency charges against T.L.O. Arguing that the search of her purse violated the fourth amendment, T.L.O. moved to suppress the evidence found in her purse as well as the confession that it was claimed was tainted by the allegedly unlawful search. The case ultimately reached the New Jersey Supreme Court. The court ruled: (1) the fourth amendment did apply to searches conducted by school officials; (2) a search warrant was not needed for a school official to search; (3) the warrantless search would be permissible if the official "has reasonable grounds to believe that a student possess evidence of illegal activity or activity that would interfere with school discipline and order"; (4) the search of T.L.O. was impermissible under this standard because mere possession of cigarettes did not violate school rules and had no bearing on the accusation against her. In addition, the court ruled that Mr. Choplick could not have had a reasonable suspicion T.L.O. had cigarettes in the purse as no one had furnished him with information there were cigarettes to be found in the purse, and that the evidence he found when he removed the cigarettes did not justify the extensive "rummaging" through the purse. Therefore, (4) the evidence of drug dealing was not admissable in the criminal proceeding brought against T.L.O.

On appeal the Supreme Court agreed with the New Jersey Supreme Court that the fourth amendment did apply in the context of public schooling, that school officials did not need to obtain a warrant to search students, and that "the legality of a search of a student should depend simply on the reasonableness, under all the circumstances, of the search."[95]

Determining the reasonableness of any search involves a twofold inquiry: first, one must consider "whether the . . . action was justified at its inception" . . . second, one must determine whether the search as actually conducted "was reasonably related in scope to the circumstances which justified the interference in the first place.". . . Under ordinary circumstances, a search of a student by a teacher or other school official [footnote omitted] will be "justified at its inception" when there are reasonable grounds for suspecting that the search will turn up evidence that the student has violated or is violating either the law or the rules of the school [footnote omitted]. Such a search will be permissible in its scope when the measures adopted are reasonably related to the objectives of the search and not excessively intrusive in light of the age and sex of the student and the nature of the infraction [footnote omitted].[96]

Based on this standard the Court reversed the New Jersey Supreme Court's conclusion that the search of T.L.O.'s purse was unreasonable. The Court first noted that there were two separate searches involved in the case, the search for the cigarettes and the second search for marijuana. "Although it is the fruits of the second search that are at issue here, the validity of the search for marijuana must depend on the reasonableness of the initial search for cigarettes, as there would have been no reason to suspect that T.L.O. possessed marijuana had the first search not taken place." The first search was reasonable, concluded the Court, because (1) possession of cigarettes was relevant in the sense it helped to make more probable that she did violate the no smoking rule, and (2) because the teacher's accusation made reasonable the hypothesis T.L.O. was carrying cigarettes.[97] The Court also concluded the second search was reasonable because (1) the picking up of the package of cigarettes was a natural reaction and not a constitutional violation; (2) the finding of the rolling papers in turn gave rise to a reasonable suspicion T.L.O. was carrying marijuana in her purse, justifying the search that turned up with pipe, plastic bags, and money; and (3) this finding in turn further justified the extension of the search to a separate zippered compartment, which revealed the index cards the contents of which further justified the examination of the letters that were also found in the compartment. Because the Court concluded the search was reasonable under all the circumstances, it did not decide the question of whether evidence seized by a school in violation of the fourth amendment had to be excluded from a criminal proceeding or a school disciplinary proceeding.[98]

As important as the *T.L.O.* opinion is, it leaves a number of significant questions without an answer from the Supreme Court: (1) Are there certain efforts to gather evidence in schools to which the fourth amendment does not apply because it is not a "search" within the meaning of the fourth amendment? (2) What does the *T.L.O* "reasonable grounds" standard mean? (3) Are there circumstances when *T.L.O.* is not to be used and either a more lenient or tougher standard is to be substituted, or even when the search may proceed without the need to meet any standard? Finally, (4) there are a number of important related problems the opinion did not and could not have been expected to address, e.g., the applicability of the exclusionary rule, the question of a student's consenting to a search, the search of college dormitory rooms, warnings of a right to remain silent in the face of questioning, and the effect of police involvement in the search of a student. We shall turn now to a brief examination of the three questions and the related problems.

The Scope of the Fourth

The *T.L.O.* standard does not apply if the effort to collect evidence does not amount to a search within the meaning of the fourth amendment. Thus, contraband seen in "plain or open" view would not have been discovered by a "search," as might occur when a school official sees evidence through the window of a car parked on the school parking lot, or discovers contraband in a lost purse being examined to discover the name of the owner.[99]

When we turn to the inspection of lockers, the inspection may not be a "search" depending on "whether a schoolchild has a legitimate expectation of privacy in lockers, desks or other school property provided for the storage of school supplies."[100] A majority of the lower courts have adopted the view that since lockers are jointly controlled by the student and school, the student does not have a reasonable expection of privacy as to them; hence the examination of the locker is not a search.[101] It is difficult to see why a purse carried by a student in a building owned by the school board may not be searched unless the *T.L.O.* standards are met, but a purse in a locker in that building may be searched.[102] In any event, the central question is whether school officials should have a free hand unrestrained by the fourth amendment to search lockers and all purses, briefcases, and other packages in them.

The Supreme Court has held that the use of dogs to sniff luggage is not a search.[103] Thus, it would seem to follow that the dog sniffing of other inanimate containers like student lockers and automobiles is also not a search.[104] As for the use of sniffer dogs on students themselves, the Supreme Court has not reached this issue, and the lower courts are split as to whether the use of the dogs to detect drugs on students themselves is a search.[105] The better reasoning would seem to be that young children and adolescents expect that their body odors are a private matter not available for examination by animals whenever school officials decide that some people in the school may be carrying contraband.

The Meaning of the *T.L.O.* Standard—Part One

Assuming for the moment the *T.L.O.* standard does govern the legitimacy of a particular search, the very difficult question arises as to the meaning of that standard. Recall that the *T.L.O.* standard is a two-part test, and the first part of the standard says a search is justified if there are "reasonable grounds for suspecting that the search will turn up evidence that the student has violated or is violating either the law or the rules of the school." Thus, for the search to be justified it must be a search for *evidence*. Accordingly, if a student were caught cutting classes, this by itself would not provide a basis for a search since a search in this case would not yield evidence that could be used to prove the student was cutting classes.[106] Note also that the Court said that the evidence to be searched for must be *relevant*. Relevant evidence need only have "any tendency to make the existence of any fact that is of consequence to the determination of the action more probable or less probable than it would be without the evidence."[107] Evidence would be irrelevant if one could not justify any reasonble inference from it as to the fact at issue.[108] Hence, a search for cigarettes would not be justified in a case in which the student was accused of triggering the school's fire alarm.

Next, the standard requires that there be *reasonable grounds* to believe evidence will be found. The "reasonable grounds" requirement is probably an objective test. In other words, a search would not be permissible merely because the school official subjectively believed that he or she had grounds for the search. The question to be asked is whether a (hypothetical) reasonable school official would conclude there were reasonable grounds for conducting the search. We may also assume that this hypothetical school official has a certain amount of expertise with regard to, for example, detecting the signs of drug use. Hence, our hypothetical school official could have reasonable grounds to suspect drugs when a lay-person would not, e.g., upon seeing a certain kind of colored pill known by drug experts to be an illegal substance.

We turn now to a closer examination of the notion of "reasonable grounds." Given the Court's concern with maintaining swift and informal disciplinary procedures, one plausible interpretation of the *T.L.O.* standard is that it is merely designed to prohibit those searches undertaken without any evidence whatsoever supportive of a suspicion that the search will turn up evidence of a violation.[109] Thus, under this interpretation, only the totally baseless search, based on perhaps whim or malice, is prohibited. A search would be warranted under this interpretation if any *one* of the following factors were observed: a furtive gesture to the pocket as the teacher approached; flight as the teacher approached; evasive or false answers to questions; many quick visits to a toilet facility; presence in an area of the school where drug dealing is known to occur; being found in the presence of a known drug dealer; possession of an item associated with the use of drugs or marijuana; being observed placing something in a sock or shoe; being found in a place where the presence of the smell of marijuana smoke is detectable, and the odor of alcohol on a student's breath.[110]

The difficulty, of course, with this interpretation of *T.L.O.* is that it will inevitably lead to the searching of many innocent pupils who just happen to make what appears to be a furtive gesture, or who just happen to be in the toilet facilities where the marijuana smoke of other students is hanging in the air. The possibility of so many "false positives" suggests that the *T.L.O.* standard should be interpreted to require greater discrimination.

The illumination of the meaning of the *T.L.O.* standard can be carried a step further by looking more closely at some of the common forms of evidence school officials might have available when deciding whether they may constitutionally proceed with a search. Reliance on the "citizen informer" is likely to be an accepted basis for a search.[111] Overheard student conversations may be ambiguous and might only provide a basis for searching in conjunction with other indications of a school violation.[112] The furtive gesture of a student when seen against a background of known drug use by the student in question can provide a basis for a search.[113] Suspicious behavior in a location known to be a place where drugs are used or exchanged provides a basis for searching.[114] However, a student who was legitimately near lockers from which an item was stolen at about the time he was near the lockers is not a strong candidate for searching.[115] Whether all students found in a toilet facility filled with marijuana smoke may be searched is not a question yet resolved by the courts.[116] Students seen with objects closely associated with drug use probably may be searched.[117] Seeing students exchange packages for money can be the basis for a search especially when the students engaged in the exchange are known to the observer to have in the past been involved with drugs.[118]

The Meaning of the *T.L.O.* Standard—Part Two

The second prong of the *T.L.O.* test deals with the scope of a search which was justified at its inception. The Court wrote that a "search will be permissible in its scope when the measures adopted are reasonably related to the objectives of the search and not excessively intrusive in light of the age and sex of the student and the nature of the infraction."[119] The requirement that the search be reasonably related to its objectives suggests, for example, that a strip search for cigarettes would be impermissible since it is unlikely students would sequester cigarettes in their undergarments. Similarly, a strip search for a gun would seem to be unnecessary since such a weapon could be detected by other less-intrusive means, i.e., a pat-down of the outer clothing, and/or an examination of purse and backpack. The requirement that the search be related to the nature of the infraction suggests that the more intrusive searches should only be used in connection with violations of those school rules that threaten the order and safety of the school.[120] The Court also seems to suggest that the younger the student, the more cautious must school officials be in undertaking such intrusive searches as a strip search. The Court's reference to the sex of the student is less easily understood. Presumably the Court means at least this much—the strip searching of males and females may only be accomplished by male and female school officials, respectively. Whether the Court also means to suggest, for example, that female students may not be subjected to the same intensive searches as male students is less clear. An interesting question raised by the *T.L.O.* case is whether *T.L.O.* herself could have been strip searched after the discovery of evidence of drug dealing in her purse.

Modification of the *T.L.O.* Standard

Given the danger of weapons in the public schools we might speculate that the Court would agree to a non-intrusive frisk (a patting down of the clothing of the student) by a school official detaining a student for questioning if the official has the slightest suspicion that the student may be carrying a weapon.[121] The problem here is, of course, that the detention of the student may itself be but a pretext in order to be able to engage in a search for other kinds of contraband, thus careful attention must be paid to when the detention itself is legitimate.

The airport-style search of all students might also be justified on the grounds that (1) in certain schools a special problem exists that needs to be combated; (2) acceptable results cannot be achieved any other way; (3) the degree of the invasion is slight; (4) there is no detention; (5) the search does not impose a stigma; (6) the search does not annoy, frighten, or humiliate; and (7) it does not single out some individuals for special embarrassing treatment.[122] The difference between using metal detectors in schools and airports is that in the case of the airline passenger the search may be avoided by merely deciding not to fly. However, students subjected to the compulsory education law have no such practicable choice; hence their right to attend public schools would be conditioned on waiver of their fourth amendment rights. Furthermore, it is not clear that the airport-style search is the only way to obtain acceptable results in reducing violence in the public schools. Nevertheless, given a sufficiently strong showing of a weapons problem by school officials, it seems likely courts would approve the airport-style search at the schoolhouse door. But, note that the Supreme Court of the State of Washington has rejected a search of the luggage of all members of a band as a precondition for going on a trip. The court said that before the luggage of a student may be searched, there must be a reasonable belief that drugs or alcohol would be found in the luggage of that particular student.[123]

As the searching becomes more intrusive, the chances increase that the courts will disapprove of the search in the absence of individualized suspicion.[124] For example, it is doubtful that involuntary drug testing of pupils without individualized suspicion would survive judicial challenge. First, the testing procedure itself can be an embarrassing and humiliating experience. Second, if those tested are selected at random, the risk is run that the reputations of those students singled out for testing will suffer severe damage. Even if an effort is made to maintain the confidentiality of the testing, there is a reasonable probability that word of the testing would leak out, not to speak of the results of the test itself. Third, given the fact that these tests are not 100 percent accurate, the leaking of test results runs the further real danger that some students will be falsely labeled as drug users.[125] For these reasons drug testing should not proceed without individualized suspicion.

It is less clear how those courts that agree that dog sniffing is a "search" would respond to universal sniffing of all students. Chances are that if a court agrees that a dog sniff is a search, the court would also agree that the sniff is intrusive and potentially embarrassing, hence may not be executed in the absence of individualized suspicion. The central question is whether school officials should be free of fourth amendment restraints when they believe some unidentified individual in a particular group may have contraband or evidence of a school violation.

Finally, it might be argued that for the search of a dormitory room by university and college officials to be permissible, it must meet a *tougher* standard than the *T.L.O.* standard. Most college and university students are not minors; the dormitory room is for all practical purposes their home; and students have a strong subjective expectation of privacy regarding the place where they live, keep their most personal belongings and live out their most intimate relationships there.[126] It follows that those courts that say a student waives his right to privacy by signing a lease on the dorm room in a public university that permits the search of their rooms are incorrect in recognizing the waiver.[127] Public universities may not condition access to public benefits on the waiver of constitutional rights.

Additional Problems

Though it is clear adults may consent to a search and make permissible what would otherwise be an impermissible search, there is a serious question whether consent by a minor should be recognized, and if so, when and under what circumstances.[128] Given the inherently coercive atmosphere of the school, at a minimum it would seem that for the consent to be valid it must be voluntary in fact: the student should be informed he or she may withhold consent; there should be no evidence of coercion, or whatever evidence of coercion that exists is effectively rebutted and the consent has been specifically and unequivocally expressed.[129] Some lower courts, however, have upheld the validity of a search based on the student's consent even when the student had been pressured with threats to give his consent.[130] One point may be inferred from the *T.L.O.* facts. Since the Court did not conclude T.L.O. had consented to the search merely because she complied with a demand that her purse be turned over to the school official for inspection, compliance with such an order may not be deemed to be consent. An important question now arises as to whether the refusal to consent to the search may itself be evidence supporting the conclusion that there are reasonable grounds to search.[131] Allowing a refusal to consent to be relevant evidence for supporting a search would clearly weaken the notion of a right not to consent.

The lower courts have agreed that students are not entitled to a "Miranda" warning prior to being questioned by school officials, and are not entitled to notification that he/she has a right to have his or her parents present during questioning.[132] Other commentators have, however, urged that these rights be recognized as necessary to protect the student's interest in liberty and to preserve the schools as educational institutions, as opposed to instruments for law enforcement.[133]

The involvement of the police in a school search raises another set of complex questions that the Supreme Court noted were not raised in *T.L.O.*[134] Assuming a police search is to be governed by the usual probable-cause standard and a search by school officials is governed by the *T.L.O.* standard,[135] the question to be answered is when is a search that involves both the police and school officials to be deemed a police search? Establishing guidelines for making this determination requires balancing several considerations. On the one hand, if we are too quick in saying that any police-school collaboration is a police search triggering the use of the stiffer probable-cause standard, then such collaboration will be discouraged or at least made covert. On the other hand, if we permit extensive police-school collaboration, then the police will be encouraged to involve school officials as a way of circumventing the probable-cause standard. One balanced solution might be to say that if the police initiate the search and actually arrive at the school to oversee and participate in the search for evidence relevant to a criminal prosecution, then we should call it a police search. We can say the police "caused" this search since it is their purposes and incentives that are behind the search. In other words, if school officials have little independence of action, little discretion as to whether the search will be conducted or not, then it is a police search. Several courts seem to have adopted a rule of this sort.[136] Other courts have reached a different conclusion. In a case involving a police-initiated search of a high school student's locker, the court refused to require adherence to the usual fourth amendment requirements even though the opening of the locker was jointly carried out by the police and a school official. The court said the school officials had a duty and the right to search lockers; accordingly, despite the fact the fourth amendment had not been complied with, the evidence found could be used against the student in a youthful offender proceeding.[137] However, in a college case a court held that a search warrant was required when it was the police who initiated and conducted a successful room search for drugs, without the participation of school officials.[138]

But, whose search is it, what set of incentives and purposes are driving the search when (1) the police provide a tip to school officials; (2) a school official conducts the search; and (3) the evidence found is turned over to the police? The answer probably lies in determining how much independence of action and how much discretion the school official had in the situation, and in whether the school official had his or her own reasons for executing the search.[139] If the school official was basically free to ignore the tip, was not operating under an agreement—either explicit or implicit—that all tips from the police would produce a search, and had his or her own reasons for conducting the search, then the decision to search would be an autonomous decision of the school official. The courts have reached decisions consistent with this line of analysis.[140]

Neither would the search be a police search if the school official merely called the police in to conduct the search because he or she felt incapable of handling the search. Several courts seem to have reached the same conclusion.[141]

The lower courts have split on the question of whether the fruits of an illegal search by school officials may be used in *school disciplinary* proceedings.[142] Those that uphold its use say it will serve as an incentive to discourage illegal searches; whereas the other courts take the view this remedy for an illegal search is too extreme and infringes too greatly on the duty of school officials to enforce school rules. A similar split appears in the lower courts regarding the use of the exclusionary rule to exclude evidence illegally seized by school officials from a *criminal proceeding*.[143]

It should be stressed that the exclusion of illegally seized evidence is not the only remedy students have available. In addition, suits for damages for privacy violations are available under state law; §1983 also may be used to sue for damages for violations of the student's fourth amendment rights. As discussed earlier, §1983 has been read to include a qualified immunity, which means school officials are shielded from liability if their conduct did not violate "clearly established statutory or constitutional rights of which a reasonable person would have known."[144] Given the unsettled state of constitutional doctrine in this area, it is no surprise that students have achieved only mixed results in overcoming the qualified immunity of school officials in damage suits for fourth amendment violations.[145]

8.6. PROCEDURAL DUE PROCESS

The fourteenth amendment prohibits states from depriving "any person of life, liberty, or property without due process of law." This clause has been a source for two branches of constitutional law, substantive due process (doctrine that recognizes and defines rights belonging to citizens as citizens, including personal liberty and private property, and that impose an external check on the policies government may adopt), and procedural due process. Procedural due process doctrine specifies the characteristics of proceedings instituted with a view toward depriving a person of life, liberty, or property. If a student enjoys a right to procedural due process he or she may require officials to conduct some sort of quasi-judicial, trial-type hearing before taking action that disadvantages them, e.g., suspending them from school. (The right to procedural due process in private education institutions is governed by the contract between student and school.)[146]

The judicial recognition that students had a right to procedural due process in connection with suspensions and expulsions began in the late 1960s in the face of the student activism of the period.[147] While the circuit courts agreed that some form of procedural due process was due in connection with longer suspensions,[148] other circuit courts said the due process clause did not apply to short-term suspensions.[149] The federal district courts during this period reached widely conflicting results.[150]

The arguments in favor of recognizing such a right were multiple. By affording students a chance to participate in some sort of hearing prior to being disciplined, mistaken judgments might be avoided—the student, if given a chance to contest the charges, might prove them to be in error. The hearing process might help to assure that school discipline would be impartially implemented, free of the taint of conclusions based on self-interest, personal malice, bias, and racial prejudice. Furthermore, a hearing process afforded the student some modicum of dignity and respect: he or she would be heard and would not merely be treated as an object. The arguments against the introduction of procedural due process rights into the school disciplinary context were also multiple. Cumbersome hearing procedures would be time consuming, expensive, and interfere with the ability of school officials to deal swiftly with disruptions of the school order and the educational process. Imposing these requirements would undermine the authority of teachers and other officials; students would be encouraged to challenge official decisions, thereby making even more difficult the task of maintaining discipline in the schools. Procedural requirements could undercut the ability of the school to inculcate pupils in the necessity of authority, rules, and obedience.

In 1975 in *Goss v. Lopez*[151] the Supreme Court positioned itself in this debate. Two issues had to be resolved: (1) May school officials suspend pupils by any procedure the school chooses? (2) If not, what procedure must school officials follow, in what circumstances, when disciplining students? The answer to the first question turned on whether the threat of suspension infringed interests of students that the Constitution protected them from losing without some sort of prior hearing. The Court concluded that even a short suspension of up to ten days would deprive a student of two protected interests: the state-created entitlement to an education (a species of property under the fourteenth amendment), and the student's interest in his or her good name and reputation, damage to which would harm later opportunities for higher education and employment (a species of liberty). The Court, therefore, concluded that school officials could not choose any suspension procedure they preferred.

After weighing and balancing several considerations in the second issue— the student's interest in an accurate determination of guilt, and the school's interest in avoiding procedures that were either prohibitively expensive or cumbersome—the Court concluded that in connection with a suspension of ten days or less the student must be given an "oral or written notice of the charges against him and, if he denies them, an explanation of the evidence the authorities have and an opportunity to present his side of the story." The Court added that there need be no delay between the "giving of the notice and the time of the hearing." In the great majority of cases the disciplinarian may informally discuss the alleged misconduct with the student "minutes after it has occurred." As a general rule, notice and hearing should proceed the suspension; but if a student's presence "poses a continuing danger to persons or property or an ongoing threat of disrupting the academic process," he or she may be immediately removed with the necessary hearing following as soon as practicable. The Court concluded by noting that for suspensions exceeding ten days or in "unusual situations" more formal procedures than the rudimentary procedures outlined above would be required.

The questions that remain open after *Goss* are several: (1) Is a right to procedural due process triggered every time school officials take an action that disadvantages a student? (2) What constitutes a sufficient emergency to warrant excluding a student first and providing a hearing afterwards? (3) As to suspensions of more than ten days, what are the elements of a more formal procedure to which a student has a right? (4) If a district departs from its own voluntarily adopted set of procedures, is that a constitutional violation?

Perhaps out of a desire to keep the legalization of school dispute resolution to a minimum, the Supreme Court and lower courts have sharply limited the occasions when school actions require the provision of even an informal hearing. In *Ingraham v. Wright*[152] the Court concluded that though corporal punishment did trigger a right to procedural due process, the only process that was constitutionally due were the post-paddling remedies available in state courts, e.g., tort suits for the excessive use of force.[153] Besides believing these tort remedies would adequately protect a child, the Court said that to impose a right to even an informal hearing prior to paddling would so burden the use of corporal punishment that its use might be abandoned and other less effective disciplinary measures turned to. The openness of the school and the presence of other teachers and students would also serve to reduce the risk of erroneous and excessive implementation of the paddle.[154] One year later in *Board of Curators of the University of Missouri v. Horowitz*[155] the Court assumed without deciding that the dismissal of a student from medical schools did deprive her of a liberty interest in pursuing a medical career, but concluded that the procedures afforded her provided her with at least as much due process as the fourteenth amendment required. Over a two-year period Horowitz's performance as a medical student was reviewed by a council composed of students and teachers, faculty members, practicing physicians, a committee composed solely of faculty members, and the dean. At no point did she personally appear before these committees to discuss her case. The Court concluded that when it came to academic dismissals this nonadversarial and flexible procedure was appropriate, given the subjective and evaluative nature of the judgment that needed to be reached. "Like the decision of an individual professor as to the proper grade for a student in his course, the determination whether to dismiss a student for academic reasons requires an expert evaluation of cumulative information and is not readily adapted to the procedural tools of judicial or administrative decisionmaking." The Court's reluctance to get involved in academic judgments is also reflected in *Regents of the University of Michigan v. Ewing*[156] in which the Court rejected the claim of a student that the university had acted arbitrarily—had substantially departed from accepted academic norms—in dropping him from a six-year undergraduate and medical school program after he failed a crucial two-day written test. The Court expressed its reluctance to trench on the prerogatives of educational institutions in holding that the decision to drop Ewing "rested on an academic judgment that is not beyond the pale of reasoned academic decision-making." The lower courts have expressed a similar reluctance to get involved in academic decisions. The Eighth Circuit stated the rule this way: "An actional deprivation [of a property interest] in an academic dismissal case is proved only if there was no rational basis for the university's decision, or if the decision was motivated by bad faith or ill will unrelated to academic performance."[157] It is important to realize that the line between academic and disciplinary sanctions is blurry, and districts may be able to avoid the procedural due process requirements by classifying their policy as academic rather than disciplinary.[158]

An important unresolved question is whether a suspension of ten days or less that is accompanied by a reduction of grades and/or a denial of an opportunity to make up missed work and tests triggers a right to a more formal set of procedures than would be required for the ten-day suspension itself.[159] Courts have held that the disciplinary transfer of a student from a school to another school implicates interests which trigger a right of due process.[160] The rescinding of a degree on grounds it was obtained through fraudulent work implicates a property and liberty interest and triggers a right to procedural due process.[161] Finally, the lower courts have uniformly agreed that the exclusion of a student from an extracurricular activity does not implicate the kind of liberty or property interest that would trigger a due process requirement.[162]

A federal district court in *White v. Salisbury Township School District*[163] addressed the question of when a student may be suspended prior to providing a hearing. The court concluded that a police accusation of smoking marijuana on school grounds raised the "possibility of danger to persons and property as well as the threat of disruption of the academic process," justifying a suspension prior to the hearing. The school officials, however, could not have been too worried about these dangers, since after they learned of the infraction from the police on Monday, they told the student he could remain in school for the rest of the day but was simply not to report to classes on Tuesday, with the hearing to follow. The school district's nonchalance in the matter should have suggested to the court that no harm would have been done by holding the hearing prior to suspension.

We turn now to the question of the constitutionally required elements of a formal hearing that could lead to a suspension of ten or more days. As will be seen, the courts have been cautious in the development of these requirements in an effort to balance the interests of the student in a fair proceeding that avoids reaching an erroneous conclusion, and the interest of the school in avoiding the educationally disruptive fiscal and administrative burdens that a full trial-type hearing could impose.[164]

Notice

Adequate notice of the charges delivered a reasonable time before the hearing is important to permit the student to prepare adequately for the hearing. What constitutes an adequate notice and sufficient time to prepare for the hearing is not uniformly settled.[165] What seems clear though is that the notice should include a reasonably specific statement of the charges, including reference to the school rule or policy the accused is said to have violated, to permit the student to prepare a defense.[166] In addition, the date, time, place, and nature of the proceeding should be clearly stated. Presumably, the notice must be in a language the student and parents understand.[167]

Impartial Tribunal

Few would argue that students have a right to have their case heard and decided by an impartial decision-maker. A tribunal may not be impartial because of conflict of interests, personal animosity of the decision-maker, and/or because the decision-maker has prejudged the case. Despite the importance of impartiality, courts have not been troubled when school officials have combined the functions of prosecutor and decision-maker.[168] The courts have upheld the presumed impartiality of the superintendent,[169] and disagreed on the question of whether impartiality is lost when the school board's regular attorney acts as prosecutor.[170] To succeed in establishing bias, the courts ask for specific evidence of personal bias on the part of the decision-maker accused of bias.[171] The mere appearance or possibility of bias is insufficient to disqualify a decision-maker.[172] (Compare the law as it bears on the right of teachers to an impartial tribunal. See §9.18.)

Right to a List of Witnesses

A majority of courts have held that the accused student does not have a right to a list of witnesses and a summary of their testimony.[173] It is unclear why students must enter the hearing ignorant of the nature of the evidence to be presented against them. The point of the hearing should be to arrive at the truth, and this is better achieved if both sides have an equal chance to prepare in advance. The technique of the surprise witness may be good drama, but not a trustworthy method of arriving at the truth.

Right to Confront and Cross-Examine Witnesses

The risks of error are reduced if the accused can confront and question the witnesses against him or her. If testimony is presented wholly through written affidavits, the opportunity to uncover mistakes and deceptions is made more difficult. Nevertheless, a number of courts have permitted the use of the affidavit or recorded statement as a way of protecting the anonymity of accusing students who might otherwise be subjected to reprisals.[174] Other courts have, however, stressed the importance of cross-examination if the outcome of the case turned on the credibility of conflicting witnesses.[175] These later rulings are undoubtedly correct.

Right to Present Evidence

Clearly essential to a fair hearing, to assuring that an erroneous decision will not be rendered, is the right of the accused to present his or her own evidence.[176] Some courts have denied the student a right to summary process—a right to compel witnesses to come to testify.[177] Not to permit students to compel witnesses to testify appears to be a flagrant violation of principle that the hearing is intended to arrive at the truth.

Substantial Evidence

Due process requires that students only be suspended on the basis of substantial evidence.[178] The question whether hearsay evidence, which normally may not be used in judicial trials because it is unreliable, may be used in school disciplinary proceedings has arisen in several cases. The courts are split on this question.[179] The middle position, which may in fact be the position embraced by most courts, is that hearsay may be used to supplement other evidence, but that hearsay alone is insufficient to support expulsion.[180] Note that the question of the use of hearsay evidence is closely related to the question of the student's right to question witnesess: an affidavit is a form of hearsay evidence.

Right to Be Represented

The courts are split on the question of whether a student has a right to be represented by an attorney at a suspension hearing.[181] If the board is represented by an attorney, the right of the student to representation seems more assured.[182] Similarly, the more severe the penalty the student faces, arguably the greater the chances the courts will recognize a right to counsel.[183] If the hearing is classified as a counseling or advisory session, the courts have refused the request of parents to have an attorney present.[184] The appropriate rule would most clearly seem to be that students should be permitted to be represented by an attorney. Not to permit them to have experienced representation would place them at a severe disadvantage, regardless of whether the school administration is represented by an attorney or a sophisticated school official familiar with the techniques of the hearing process.

Right to a Recording or Transcript

The prevailing view seems to be that students have no right to a transcript or recording of their hearing.[185] The better rule is that students should be provided with a transcript as an important safeguard assuring the decision was based solely on evidence admitted at the hearing, and to provide a basis for appeal.

Right to a Written Statement of Reasons

Again, the courts are split on this issue, but the prevailing opinion appears to be that students do not have a right to a detailed statement of reasons explaining the decision to suspend.[186] The better rule would seem to be that students should be provided with such a written statement to assure that the decision was indeed based on the record, and to provide a sound basis for appeal. The statement of reasons may also have an important educative value.

We turn now to a different problem. Suppose a school district establishes a formal procedure for suspending students but then violates its own procedures in a particular case. Claims that the violation of the school's own procedures constitutes a constitutional violation have been rejected by the courts. The irregularity itself is not per se a consitutional violation; for there to be a constitutional violation the procedure in fact followed would itself have to be constitutionally insufficient.[187] The source of procedural guarantees is in the Constitution itself and not in the specific procedures adopted by the school.[188]

State statutes, however, are another important source for procedural guarantees. Though the statutory guarantees may not afford less protection than that provided by the due process clause of the Constitution, states are free to develop procedural guarantees that are more demanding. New York, for example, requires the opportunity for a formal hearing prior to any suspension that exceeds five days.[189]

8.7. LEGAL LIMITS ON THE PUNISHMENT ITSELF

Though a student may have been found to have violated a legitimate school rule on the basis of evidence legally collected and assessed in a constitutionally adequate hearing, the punishment itself must not exceed certain legal limits. We turn first to corporal punishment.

Today, the most significant controls on corporal punishment are to be found in state law. This is true because the efforts to obtain from the federal courts U.S. constitutional limitations on corporal punishment have been notably unsuccessful. In *Ingraham v. Wright*[190] the Court held that regardless of the severity and brutality of disciplinary corporal punishment, the eighth amendment's prohibition against cruel and unusual punishments did not apply outside the criminal field to protect public school students. The Court based its conclusion on the eighth amendment's history, the Court's own prior decisions, and on a policy argument that contrasted the open school setting with the closed prison environment. It is this last point that deserves further elaboration. The Court wrote:

The openness of the public school and its supervision by the community afford significant safeguards against the kinds of abuses from which the Eighth Amendment protects the prisoner. In virtually every community where corporal punishment is permitted in the schools, these safeguards are reinforced by the legal constraints of the common law. Public school teachers and administrators are privileged at common law to inflict only such corporal punishment as is reasonably necessary for the proper education and discipline of the child; any punishment going beyond the privilege may result in both civil and criminal liability. . . . As long as the schools are open to public scrutiny, there is no reason to believe that the common-law constraints will not effectively remedy and deter excesses such as those alleged in this case.[191]

In addition to denying the eighth amendment argument the Court refused to review the conclusion of the Fifth Circuit Court of Appeals that the punishment involved in this case was so severe and oppressive that it violated the due process clause of the fourteenth amendment.[192] Thus, today only one Circuit Court of Appeals seems to have agreed that corporal punishment can be so severe as to violate the student's interest in bodily integrity.[193] Even when parents object to the use of corporal punishment the Constitution provides no obstacle to its use.[194]

We, thus, must turn to state law to determine the limits, if any, on the use of corporal punishment. Two states by legislation, Massachusetts and New Jersey, and one state by regulation have banned the use of corporal punishment.[195] According to the Supreme Court twenty-one states have by legislation authorized the moderate use of corporal punishment. "Of these only a few have elaborated on the common-law test of reasonableness, typically providing for approval or notification of the child's parents [California, Florida, Montana], or for the infliction of punishment only by the principal [Maryland], or in the presence of an adult witness [Florida, Hawaii, Montana]."[196] In the remaining states the common-law rule that teachers enjoy a privilege to use reasonable force in disciplining children prevails.[197]

A teacher who uses excessive force may be subject to a tort suit for assault, may be dismissed or otherwise sanctioned by the school district for, say, unprofessional conduct, and may be subject to criminal penalties if the force is especially excessive. The highest court in New York has made clear that a teacher may be dismissed for the excessive use of force even if that force was not so excessive as to violate the criminal law.[198] If a local school board adopts its own policy prohibiting corporal punishment, teachers who disobey this policy may be disciplined for insubordination.[199]

When we turn from corporal punishments to expulsions and suspensions we find fewer legal restrictions. Thus, courts have said that lengthy suspensions (forty days and more) for drug-related violations did not violate the due process clause of the fourteenth amendment.[200] Automatic penalties for school violations have also been upheld.[201]

The reduction of grades as a form of discipline for nonacademic violations, such as unauthorized absences, and in conjunction with suspensions has met with a mixed judicial response. As for grade reductions in association with a disciplinary suspension from school (grades might be affected because the student is not permitted to make up work, including tests, missed during the suspension or because of a requirement of a fixed reduction in the student's average for each day absent), the courts are badly split.[202] Using grades to punish truancy has also produced a split in the decisions.[203] At issue in these cases are both the question of whether the school board had the statutory authority to lower grades in connection with a suspension or truancy, and whether the lowering of grades was an abuse of discretion.

A New York court concluded it was an abuse of discretion for school officials to impose as a sanction for fighting denial of permission to attend the school's graduation ceremony even though the student had satisfactorily completed her studies.[204]

8.8. DISCIPLINE OF THE HANDICAPPED

As discussed in chapter 7 the Education for All Handicapped Children Act of 1975 was enacted to assure handicapped children the right to a free appropriate education.[205] Under the act each handicapped child must receive an Individualized Education Program (IEP) designed specially for that child's educational needs. The act also provides these children with procedural protections that are to be followed both in connection with the initial educational placement of the child and in connection with any subsequent change in placement.[206]

In several cases the question has arisen as to the bearing of these provisions upon the discipline of the handicapped child. The Sixth Circuit Court of Appeals has summarized the results of these cases as follows. First, a handicapped child may be suspended temporarily without first resorting to the procedures in the Act.[207] (This action is warranted as an emergency measure to assure either the safety of the school and/or of the handicapped child.) Second, if the procedural protections of the act are followed (e.g., a hearing), a handicapped child may actually be expelled from school in appropriate circumstances.[208] (In other words, expulsion is a change of placement within the meaning of the Act, therefore, handicapped students may not be suspended from school without following the change of placement procedures in the Act.) However, if the handicapped child's disruptive behavior is a manifestation of his handicap, the child may not be expelled.[209] To hold otherwise would be to expel a child for behavior over which he or she may not have control. Furthermore, a finding that the child's behavior was caused by his or her handicap suggests that consideration should be given to a change in the child's placement or a less harsh form of discipline than expulsion.[210] Third, even during the period of explusion there may not be a complete cessation of educational services.[211]

8.9. PRIVACY AND CONFIDENTIALITY: STUDENT RECORDS, COUNSELORS, AND PSYCHIATRIC TESTING

In 1974 Congress passed what is commonly known as the Buckley Amendment, more properly called the Family Educational Rights and Privacy Act (FERPA), to deal basically with two alleged abuses in the handling of student records.[212] The first was the release of these records to law enforcement agencies, prospective employers, and others without first obtaining the permission of the student or his or her parents. The second was the inclusion in the records of erroneous, highly prejudicial, and derogatory facts and comments. The little case law that existed at the time did provide some relief for parents and students as regards gaining access to these records and excising from them erroneous materials,[213] but the reports of abuses were so widespread that Congress acted.

The FERPA and its implementing regulations[214] provide students and their parents with a right of access to the "education records" of the student; provide for a formal and informal system whereby challenges may be brought to amend the records to remove inaccurate or misleading information; and establish a set of limitations and procedures regarding the release of these records to third parties. Upon reaching age eighteen students may exercise the rights guaranteed to the parents under the law.

The FERPA does not cover the personal records of teachers and administrators that are in the sole possession of that person and not revealed to other people except a substitute.[215] Nor does it cover the admission-application forms of a person who has applied for admission to a post-secondary institution but has not yet been admitted.[216] The usual restrictions on disclosure are not applicable to such matters as a student's name, address, telephone number, date and place of birth, field of study, participation in official activities, weight and height of members of athletic teams, degrees, awards, and the more recent educational institution attended.[217]

Requests for files must be complied with within forty-five days and the right to review the records includes a right to obtain copies, at the expense of the person making the request, if the making of copies is necessary to effectively exercise the right of access.[218] Access may not be gained to letters and statements that were solicited with a written assurance of confidentiality.[219] If a student or parents challenge the content of a record and the school refuses to change the record, the student or parent may demand a hearing that may be conducted by any party, including an employee of the district, who does not have a direct interest in the outcome of the hearing. Any appeal from this decision must be administrative in nature since no private right of action to seek review in the courts is available.[220] Before any personally identifiable information may be disclosed, permission must be obtained from the parent or eligible student, except as regards the disclosure to certain specifically listed agencies and officials.[221] The law also imposes limits on the redisclosure of information without further written consent of the student or parent.[222]

Beyond FERPA is the Education for All Handicapped Children Act of 1975 that contains its own separate set of requirements regarding the records of handicapped pupils.[223] The requirements are similar in important respects except that interpreters must be provided if necessary to read the contents of the records for parents.

A number of states have also enacted legislation dealing with student records.[224]

We turn now to the privilege of confidentiality. This privilege "refers to the right of a person in a 'special relationship' to prevent the disclosure in legal proceedings of information given in confidence" in the course of that relationship.[225] State law in most states does not create such a student privilege to bar the disclosure of information given to the counselor or teacher in confidence.[226] States that do grant varying degrees of protection are Delaware, Idaho, Indiana, Maine, Maryland, Michigan, Montana, Nevada, North Carolina, Oklahoma, Oregon, Pennyslvania, South Carolina, South Dakota, and Washington.[227] When counselors in the course of their duties do testify or make comments that may reflect badly on the student and/or parents, they are protected against libel suits by the notion of a qualified privilege.[228]

A federal law purportedly seeks to protect student's interests in privacy in yet a different way. The statute reads as follows:[229]

(a) All instructional materials, including teacher's manuals, films, tapes, or other supplementary instructional material which will be used in connection with any research or experimentation program or project shall be available for inspection by the parents or guardians of the children engaged in such program or project. For the purpose of this section "research or experimentation program or project" means any program or project in any applicable program designed to explore or develop new or unproven teaching methods or techniques.

(b) No student shall be required, as part of any applicable program, to submit to psychiatric examination, testing or treatment, or psychological examination, testing, or treatment, in which the primary purpose is to reveal information concerning:

(1) political affiliations;

(2) mental and psychological problems potentially embarrassing to the student or his family;

(3) sex behavior or attitudes;

(4) illegal, anti-social, self-incriminating and demeaning behavior;

(5) critical appraisals of other individuals with whom respondents have close family relationships;

(6) legally recognized privileged and analogous relationships, such as those of lawyers, physicians, and ministers; or

(7) income (other than that required by law to determine eligibility for participation in a program for receiving financial assistance under such program) without the prior consent of the student (if the student is an adult or emancipated minor), or in the case of unemancipated minor, without the prior written consent of the parent.

The many ambiguities in this statute make its application very difficult. For example, parents must be permitted to inspect materials used in exploring "new or unproven teaching methods or techniques." School officials and parents seeking to apply this provision must puzzle over whether the term "new" means "new on the face of the earth" or, more narrowly, new to this particular teacher, this school building, or this school district. The term "unproven" is even more difficult to interpret. For example, the term could be used as a synonym for "new," or it could refer to materials that, though widely used and familiar, have not been shown through rigorous evaluations to have "positive effects" (whatever those effects might be), or, alternatively, have not been shown to have any "negative effects" (whatever those effects might be). These thoughts, unfortunately, represent only the beginning of speculation regarding the meaning of this term.

Section (b) of the statute is filled with equally perplexing difficulties. The terms psychiatric and psychological are undefined, as are the terms these words qualify, i.e., examination, testing, and treatment. The introductory section of subpart (b) also speaks of "the primary purpose" of these tests, but we need to ask whether "the" means "a" and how the (or, "a") primary purpose is to be proven. Is it a matter of the subjective intent of the test givers, or is the purpose to be established by the effects of the exam or test? These ambiguities, when coupled with the ambiguities of the terms used in subparts (1)-(7), raise a number of interesting problems. To take one example only, subsection (b)(4) could serve to prevent school districts from inquiring of a student regarding substance abuse. In short, this statute is fraught with difficult issues generated in part by the use of ambiguous, even vague, terms. These problems are confounded by other forms of poor drafting. For example, section (b)(7) prohibits a student from being examined regarding "income." Once again, the term is undefined and those familiar with the difficulties with this word in the context of tax law will recognize the complexities opened by the lack of any definition. Furthermore, the section makes no reference to whether the "income" that may not be asked about is the "income" of the student him- or herself, the "income" of his or her parents, or both.

NOTES

1. The fourth amendment states: "The Right of the people to be secure in their persons, houses, papers, and effects, against unreasonable searches and seizures, shall not be violated, and no Warrants shall issue, but upon probable cause, supported by Oath or affirmation, and particularly describing the place to be searched, and the persons or things to be seized." U.S. Constitution, Amendment 4. See §8.5.

2. See §§8.3 and 8.7 in this volume.

3. See §8.3.

4. See §8.4.

5. Students contracting with a private school for educational services may contract for the provision of a safe school environment. The law of private contracts is a branch of the common law.

6. Tort law is a vast body of law that encompasses harms done to individuals and to their property. Defamation, false imprisonment, medical malpractice, trespass, nuisance, assault and battery, and negligence are among the areas touched on by tort law. For a review of this body of law see W. P. Keeton, *et al., Prosser and Keeton on Torts,* 5th Ed. (St. Paul, Minn.: West Publishing Co., 1984).

7. A tort suit is different from a criminal suit. A tort suit is a civil action initiated and pursued by the injured party against another party (individual or government) for the purpose of obtaining monetary compensation for the injury. A criminal proceeding is brought by the state against an individual for the purpose of seeking a criminal conviction leading to the punishment of the criminal by the state. Because tort law and criminal law sometimes address the same wrongdoing and use the same terms, the two bodies of law are sometimes confused. For example, one may sue someone else for committing an "assault" and "battery," and at the same time government may criminally prosecute the individual for having violated the criminal law against assault and battery. If the person loses both cases, he or she faces having to pay a monetary compensation to the victim as required by tort law, and a fine and/or jail sentence as required by the criminal law.

8. An assault involves an overt act such as a display of force of such a nature as to cause reasonable apprehension of immediate bodily harm. The battery involves the actual unwanted (unconsented) touching of another, whether in anger, or as a joke, or even out of affection, as in a kiss. Excessive use of force on a student may be the basis for a suit that relies on a claim of battery and a claim for negligent injury. Sansone v. Bechtel, 180 Conn. 96, 429 Atl. 2d 820 (1980)(teacher held liable for battery and negligent injury because he grabbed student's arm and swung him against a wall causing a fracture of the clavicle).

9. Corporal punishment will be discussed at great length in §8.7.

10. American Law Institute, "Intentional Harms to Persons, Land and Chattels," in *Restatement of the Law of Torts Second* (St. Paul, Minn: American Law Institute Publishers), §150.

11. The privilege arises where a person has a reasonable, even if mistaken, belief that he or she is threatened with harm, whether intended or negligent. The force used must be that which appears reasonably necessary for protection; if force in excess of what is necessary is used it is tortious. After the threat is past the privilege ends; self-defense cannot be used as a defense for an action taken merely in revenge. To invoke the privilege of self-defense, the law in a majority of states does not require one to retreat first to avoid the oncoming harm.

12. 542 S.W.2d 456 (Ct. Civil Appeals, 1976).

13. The coach was twenty-eight years old, 5'11", and weighed 195 pounds. The boy was twelve and weighed 115 pounds. He suffered a cervical sprain and a bruised brachial plexus that kept him in the hospital eight days; complete recovery followed several months later.

14. Id., at 460.

15. Simms v. Sch. Dist. No. 1, Multnomah Cty., 13 Or. A. 119, 508 P.2d 236 (Ct. App. 1973).

16. Keeton, *Prosser and Keeton on Torts, supra* note 6, at 124.

17. Frank v. Orleans Parish Sch. Bd., 195 So. 2d 451 (La. App. 1967).

18. 389 So.2d 405 (Ct. App. 1980)

19. 379 So.2d 69 (Ct. App.1980). The school board's rules permitted teachers to use only "reasonable and appropriate" physical force. But compare Thompson v. Iberville Parish Sch. Bd., 372 So.2d 642 (Ct. App. 1979) in which a teacher kicked a twelve-year-old boy, in order to get his attention; the boy had turned in his seat facing away from the blackboard and was talking to other pupils while the teacher was lecturing and writing on the blackboard. There were no objective symptoms of an injury. The court wrote: "We do not believe that a teacher's use of his foot to make contact with a student automatically places him outside the scope of his limited immunity. Significantly, we can conceive of very few situations in which a kick, no matter how

gentle, would meet the test of reasonableness. However, the situation present in the instant case is one such incident."

20. Rolando v. Sch. Directors of Dist. No. 25, Cty. of LaSalle, 44 Ill. App.3d 658, 3 Ill. Dec. 402, 358 N.E.2d 945 (App. Ct. 1976). The cattle prod was a cylinder two feet long with electrodes on one end that provided a shock supplied by five size-C, high-amperage heavy-duty stock-prod batteries. The students said the shock stung and made them shaky. Two students cried when the shock was used on them. Students could choose to avoid the shock by having their name written on the blackboard under the caption "Coward's List."

21. Id., at 947.

22. Richard A. Posner, *Economic Analysis of Law*, 2d ed. (Boston: Little, Brown and Company, 1977), 122.

23. If it is decided a certain class of accident is avoidable at the least cost by the school district or teacher, the law establishes (1) a duty on the district to conform to a certain standard of care. To win a negligence case the plaintiff must establish that (2) the district's or teacher's behavior fell below that standard of care, that (3) the breach of the duty was the "proximate cause" of a (4) proven injury. Failure on the part of the plaintiff to establish any of these four points defeats the claim. Similarly the defendant can either defeat the claim or at least reduce the amount of damages he may have to pay by establishing either that the plaintiff (a) contributed to the injury by his own negligence (failure to meet a standard of care the law imposes on him), (b) engaged in comparative negligence, (c) voluntarily assumed the risk of injury, and/or (d) voluntarily released the district of liability. Surrounding each of these points (1-4, a-d) is a vast technical body of law that further defines and refines doctrines. For example, the doctrines of contributory negligence and assumption of risk require careful interpretation and use when applied to children. For further details on these points see William D. Valente, *Law in the Schools* (Columbus, Ohio: Charles E. Merrill Pub. Co., 1980), chap. 8; Leroy J. Peterson, Richard A. Rossmiller, and Marlin M. Volz, *The Law and Public School Operation*, 2d ed. (New York: Harper & Row, Publishers Inc., 1978), chap. 11; Kern Alexander and M. David Alexander, *American Public School Law*, 2d ed. (St. Paul, Minn.: West Publishing Company, 1985), chap. 11.

The way in which these legal doctrines can be interpreted to serve the policy outlined in the text can be illustrated. The duty of care (1) is often phrased in terms of that degree of care a reasonable person of ordinary prudence would exercise for the safety of others in like circumstances. The test (2) used in all states except Illinois to determine whether the duty was breached is phrased in terms of whether the teacher or school district should have reasonably foreseen the type of accident that did occur, and therefore taken steps to avoid it. If the court concludes this general kind of accident would have been foreseeable by the average prudent person, it is saying the average person could have avoided it at a cost less than the cost of the accident. Now if the defendant succeeds in claiming the plaintiff was contributorily negligent, that may be understood to mean that the plaintiff himself in this particular circumstance could have avoided the accident as well at a cost less than the defendant. Thus the plaintiff must suffer the loss as an incentive to people in the future to take steps to avoid this kind of injury to themselves. Posner, *Economic Analysis of Law, supra* note 22, at 123-25.

24. Annot., 34 A.L.R.3d 1166 (1970); Valente, *The Law in the Schools, supra* note 23, at 356-57. Liability may be reduced if the student were him or herself negligent and thereby contributed to his or her own injuries. Annot., 34 A.L.R.3d at 1173.

25. Peterson v. San Francisco Community College Dist.,36 Cal. 3d 799, 685 P.2d 1193, 205 Cal. Rptr. 842 (Cal. 1984)(en banc).

26. Miller v. State, 62 N.Y.2d 506, 467 N.E.2d 493, 478 N.Y.S.2d 829 (N.Y. App. Div. 1984).

27. Lehman v. Los Angeles Bd. of Educ.,154 Ca.2d 256, 316 P.2d 55 (Dist. Ct. App. 1957).

28. To date the litigation has involved school districts bringing suits against asbestos manufacturers to recover the costs of asbestos detection and clean up, as well as suits for fraud,

negligence, and strict product liability, breach of warranty, and nuisance.

29. The classic example of this problem is the child who enters the school grounds after school hours to play. Goldstein v. Bd. of Educ. of Union Free Sch. Dist. No. 23, 266 N.Y.S.2d 1 (1965). This child must take the school grounds as he or she finds them.

30. Special rules apply to trespassing children. A property owner or possessor may be liable to trespassing children if there is an "artificial condition" upon the land; the possessor is aware or has reason to know of this condition, which he realizes or should realize involves unreasonable risk of death or serious bodily harm to children; children because of their youth do not discover the condition or realize the risk in becoming involved with it; the utility to the possessor of maintaining the condition and the burden of eliminating is slight compared to the risk; and the possessor failed to exercise reasonable care to eliminate the risk or otherwise protect the children. Keeton, *Prosser and Keeton on Torts, supra* note 6, at 402ff. This is a reformulation of the "attractive nuisance doctrine," which has been used to hold, for example, property owners liable for children who drown in swimming pools.

31. Posner, *Economic Analysis of Law, supra* note 22, at 128.

32. The problem of adequate supervision arises in a variety of contexts: the use of athletic equipment and the engaging in sport activities; the use of equipment in laboratories and shop; the playground; buses; bus stops; and the ordinary classroom. For a synopsis of many opinions touching on problems arising in these areas see Valente, *The Law in the Schools, supra* note 23, at 357-64; Annot. 36 A.L.R.3d 330 (1971).

33. Miller v. Yoshimoto, 56 Hawaii 333, 536 P.2d 1195 (Hawaii, 1975). Similarly in another case the school board was not liable for injury to a child's eye because of an object thrown by another student. The teacher was not present at the start of the class when the incident occurred because he had been assigned to duty as a hall or cafeteria supervisor. The court recognized the district had to choose between supervising hundreds of students in the corridors and cafeteria and fourteen students in a classroom. Butler v. District of Columbia, 417 F.2d 1150 (D.C. Cir. 1969). In McLeod v. Grant County Sch. Dist. No. 128, 42 Wash.2d 316, 255 P.2d 360 (1953)(en banc) the district was held liable for damages to a girl attacked in an unlighted room adjacent to the school's gymnasium. In Sly v. Bd. of Educ., 213 Kan. 415, 516 P.2d 895 (1973) the district was not held liable for an assault on one student by other students before school hours on school grounds because the assault could not have been foreseen—there had been no prior fighting between students and there was no knowledge of prior conflict between students.

34. Gammon v. Edwardsville Community Unit. Sch., 82 Ill.App. 3d 586, 38 Ill. Dec. 28, 403 N.E.2d 43 (1980).

35. Cavello v. Sherburne-Earleville Central Sch. Dist., 494 N.Y.S.2d 466 (App.Div.1985).

36. Bryant v. Sch. Bd. of Duval Cty., Fla., 399 So.2d 417 (App. Div. 1 1981).

37. Raleigh v. Indep. Sch. Dist., 275 N.W.2d 572 (1978). The standard of negligence is particularly stiff in Illinois where a district may only be liable for willful and wanton conduct. Broker v. Chicago Bd. of Educ., 75 Ill. App.3d 381, 31 Ill. Dec. 250, 394 N.E.2d (1979)(no liability for when student was physically assaulted in bathroom even though monitor appointed for bathroom was the alleged leader of the classmates who threatened student). In Collins v. Sch. Bd. of Broward Cty., 471 So. 2d 560 (Dist. Ct. App. 1985) the board was held liable for a homosexual assault during shop class.

38. Swearinger v. Fall River Joint Unified Sch. Dist., 212 Cal. Rptr. 400 (Ct. App. 1985).

39. Teachers who must supervise thirty and forty students cannot be expected to give constant and undeviating supervision to each child. Ferguson v. DeSoto Parish Sch. Bd., 467 So.2d 1257 (La. App. 2 Cir. 1985)(no liability when boy who crawls in back of a swinging batter to retrieve his glove gets hit with a mortal blow to the skull).

40. For one analytical review of the cases see Annot., 38 A.L.R. 2d 830 (1938). In Illinois, liability attaches only if the teacher's failure to anticipate the violent behavior of a student was willful and wanton. Clay v. Chicago Bd. of Educ., 22 Ill. App. 3d 437, 318 N.E.2d 153 (1974).

41. For an overview of many of these cases see Annot., 36 A.L.R.3d 330 (1971).

42. Simonetti v. Sch. Dist. of Philadelphia, 308 Pa. Super. 555, 454 A.2d 1038 (1982).

43. Ohman v. Bd. of Educ., 275 A.D. 840, 88 N.Y.S.2d 273 (1949), *aff'd,* 301 N.Y. 662, 93 N.E.2d 927 (1950).

44. Dailey v. Los Angeles Unified Sch. Dist., 2 Cal. 3d 741, 87 Cal. Rptr. 376, 470 P.2d 360 (Cal. 1970)(en banc).

45. Foster v. Houston General Ins. Co., 407 So.2d 759 (La. App. 1982), *cert. denied,* 409 So.2d 660 (1982).

46. Roberts v. Robertson Cty. Bd. of Educ., 692 S.W.2d 863, 872 (Ct. App. 1985)(inadequate instructions and supervision to shop students proximate cause of injury); Bush v. Oscoda Area Schools, 405 Mich. 216, 275 N.W.2d 268 (1979)(science equipment explodes); Brooks v. Bd. of Educ. of City of New York, 12 N.Y.2d 971, 189 N.E.2d 497 (N.Y. 1963)(contestants in a game mismatched in size); LaValley v. Stanford, 272 A.D. 183, 70 N.Y.S.2d 460 (1947)(students not properly instructed in boxing and not properly supervised); Simmons v. Beauregard Parish. Sch. Bd., 315 So.2d 883 (La. 1975)(work with explosives not properly supervised).

47. *See generally,* Annot., 35 A.L.R.3d 758, 763 (1971).

48. Scott v. Indep. Sch. Dist., 256 N.W.2d 485 (1977).

49. Id., at 765.

50. Foster v. Houston General Ins. Co., 407 So.2d 759 (La. App. 1982), *cert. denied,* 409 So.2d 660 (1982).

51. Kush v. Buffalo, 59 N.Y.2d 26, 449 N.E.2d 725, 462 N.Y.S.2d 831 (1983).

52. Hoyem v. Manhattan Beach City Sch. Dist., 22 Cal.3d 508, 150 Cal. Rptr. 1, 585 P.2d 851 (1978).

53. Id.

54. Morris v. Douglas Cty. Sch. Dist., No. 9, 241 Or. 23, 403 P.2d 775 (Ore. 1965); Swearinger v. Fall River Joint Unified Sch. Dist., 212 Cal. Rptr. 400 (Ct. App. 1985); *compare* Mancha v. Field Museum of Natural History, 5 Ill. App. 3d 699, 283 N.E.2d 899 (1972).

55. An extensive review of transportation-related cases may be found in Annot., 34 A.L.R.3d 1210 (1970).

56. California Constitution, Article 1, section 28(c).

57. Kimberly A. Sawyer, "The Right to Safe Schools: A Newly Recognized Inalienable Right," *Pacific Law Journal* 14 (1983): 1309.

58. Stein v. Highland Park Ind. Sch. Dist., 540 S.W.2d 551 (Tex. 1976).

59. The distinction between policymaking or discretionary conduct and ministerial conduct is fuzzy. The failure to maintain safe premises has been termed a ministerial act. Elgin v. District of Columbia, 337 F.2d 152 (D.C. Cir. 1964). The Michigan Supreme Court has ruled that instruction and supervision of pupils are ministerial-operational activities for which there is not immunity. Regulski v. Murphy and Trezzi, 363 N.W.2d 641 (Mich. 1984).

60. Annot. 33 A.L.R.3d 703 (1970); Valente, *Law in the Schools, supra* note 23, at 366-71; Alexander and Alexander, *American Public School Law, supra* note 23, at 484-86. The exceptions are that school districts may be liable for the maintenance of "nuisances" and in the conduct of their "proprietary" activities, or the execution of "ministerial" as opposed to "discretionary" activities. The case law is confused as to the definition of these terms.

61. Annot., 33 A.L.R.3d 703 (1970). The Georgia Supreme Court ruled that a school board that purchased liability insurance waived its governmental immunity pro tanto with regard to an action brought by parents of a child who was injured from a fall off a slide on the school playground. Thigpen v. McDuffie Cty. Bd. of Educ., 335 S.E.2d 112 (Ga. 1985).

62. Outside these institutions the courts have refused to recognize a constitutional right to provision of services designed to protect the safety of citizens. *See* Bradberry v. Pinellas Cty., 789 F.2d 1513 (11th Cir. 1986)(no constituional duty to provide lifeguards); Jackson v. Byrne, 738 F.2d 1443 (7th Cir. 1984)(no constitutional obligation to provide firemen).

63. Youngberg v. Romeo, 457 U.S. 307 (1982)(finding a constitutional right to safety on part of involuntarily committed mentally retarded person); Bell v. Wolfish, 441 U.S. 520 (1978);

Estelle v. Gamble, 429 U.S. 97 (1976)(holding that medical malpractice does not become a constitutional violation merely because the victim is a prisoner, but suggesting that intentional deprivation of medical care could rise to a constitutional violation). A single isolated incident of harm done to a prisoner or asylum inmate by another prisoner, patient, or staff member is insufficient to raise a constitutional claim against the institution itself and its governing officials. For the institution to be held liable, there must be proof of a pattern, practice, or policy that provides a link between the harm done and the institution and its officers. City of Oklahoma v. Tuttle, 85 105 S.Ct. 2427 (1985); Rizzo v. Goode, 423 U.S. 362 (1976).

64. Daniels v. Williams, 106 S.Ct. 662 (1986)(dismissal of claim of prisoner injured when he slipped on a newspaper and pillows left on stairway in a Virginia prison). The Court specifically left open the question whether §1983 liability can be predicated upon gross negligence. The Supreme Court has placed limits on the use of §1983 to vindicate the loss of property rights. Parratt v. Taylor, 451 U.S. 527 (1981); Hudson v. Palmer, 104 S. Ct. 3194 (1984).

65. In another case the Court held that jail officials have a constitutional duty not to be deliberately indifferent to a prisoner's serious medical needs. Estelle v. Gamble, 429 U.S. 97 (1976). See, e.g., Slakan v. Porter, 737 F.2d 368 (4th Cir. 1984)(use of force by prison guards violated eighth amendment); Simons v. City of Columbus, 593 F.Supp. 876 (N.D. Miss., E.D. 1984)(denying motion to dismiss complaint against police officer).

66. Davidson v. Cannon, 106 S.Ct. 688 (1986). See also Webster v. Foltz, 582 F. Supp. 28 (W.D. Mich, S.D. 1983)(failure to prevent one isolated assault does not amount to a constitutional violation—something like gross negligence or deliberate indifference is needed to establish such a violation).

67. Tennesee v. Garner, 105 S.Ct. 1694 (1985)(holding the fourth amendment is violated when the police use deadly force to prevent the escape of a suspect who appears to be unarmed and not dangerous).

68. Lowers v. City of Streator, 627 F. Supp. 244 (N.D. Ill. 1985).

69. Ingraham v. Wright, 430 U.S. 651 (1977). For further discussion of this opinion see §8.7.

70. 621 F.2d 607, 613 (4th Cir. 1980). The court held that a complaint alleging a beating did raise an issue as to whether the beating was unconstitutional and ought to be sent to trial. It was alleged that a teacher without provocation struck the minor across her hip and thigh with a paddle made of hard rubber about five inches thick, twisted the minors arm in the course of a struggle, and again repeatedly hit her with the paddle. The student alleged traumatic injury to the soft tissue on her hip, thigh, and buttock and possible permanent damage to her lower back and spine.

71. See supra note 64.

72. Brooks v. Sch. Bd. of City of Richmond, Va., 569 F. Supp. 1534 (E.D. Vir. 1983).

73. 599 F. Supp. 363 (D.C. Mass. 1984), aff'd, 784 F.2d 430 (1st Cir. 1986). In affirming the district court opinion the First Circuit stressed that the plaintiff alleged nothing more than "simple negligence" and that under decision in Daniels. See supra note 64, such an allegation does not state a claim for deprivation of liberty without due process of law.

74. City of Oklahoma v. Tuttle, 105 S.Ct. 2427 (1985)(One single incident of use of excessive force is not per se enough to establish existence of a policy or practice of insufficient training by municipality and hence municipal responsibility for the incident); Monell v. Department of Social Services, 435 U.S. 658 (1978)(doctrine of respondeat superior not applicable in a §1983 proceeding); Rizzo v. Good, 423 U.S. 362 (1976)(must establish a link between individual act of employee and policy of employer for employer to be liable).

75. Stephen R. Goldstein, "The Scope of School Board Authority to Regulate Student Conduct and Status: A Nonconstitutional Analysis," University of Pennsylvania Law Review 117 (1969): 403-4. If school districts have statutory authority to exclude unvaccinated students, the courts have been unanimous in upholding the validity of such exclusions. Id., at 404 n. 101.

76. Nutt v. Bd. of Educ., 128 Kan. 507, 278 P. 1065 (1929); Annot., 53 A.L.R.3d 1124 (1973). In the *Nutt* case the court ruled the district did not have the authority to exclude the student. As to off school ground activities, the courts have agreed that the power of school authorities over pupils does not simply cease when pupils leave school premises. Students may be disciplined for off school ground activites that may have a direct and immediate effect on discipline or the general welfare of the school. *See, e.g.,* Smith v. Little Rock Sch. Dist., 582 F. Supp. 159 (E.D. Ark., W.D. 1984)(student suspended after killing someone off school grounds who had a brother and sister attending his school).

77. Goldstein, "The Scope and Sources of School Board Authority to Regulate Student Conduct and Status: A Nonconstitutional Analysis," *supra* note 75. *See, e.g.,* Board of Directors of the Indep. Sch. Dist. of Waterloo v. Green, 147 N.W.2d 854 (1976) in which the Supreme Court of Iowa upheld the school rule prohibiting participation in extracurricular activities by married pupils. The court accepted the district's arguments that married students needed to concentrate on their marriages and the basic education program; that teenage marriage needed to be discouraged; and that the presence of married students in extracurricular programs created moral and disciplinary problems.

78. Indep. Sch. Dist. No. 8 v. Swanson, 553 P.2d 496 (1976). *Cf.,* Johnson v. Joint School Dist. No. 60, 95 Idaho 317, 508 P.2d 547 (1973)(holding a school lacked authority to proscribe female students from wearing slacks, pantsuits, and culottes to school). The constitutionality of hair and dress codes is taken up in §5.10.

79. The U.S. Constitution, federal laws, and treaties are the supreme law of the land according to Article 6, section 2 of the U.S. Constitution.

80. S-1 v. Turlington, 635 F.2d 342 (5th Cir. 1981), *cert. denied,* 454 U.S. 1030 (1981); Kaelin v. Grubbs, 682 F.2d 595 (6th Cir. 1982). For a further discussion of these cases see §8.8.

81. New York State Ass'n for Retarded Children v. Carey, 612 F.2d 644 (2d Cir. 1979).

82. Mark G. Yudof, David L. Kirp, Tyll van Geel, and Betsy Levin, *Educational Policy and the Law,* 2d. ed. (Berkeley, Calif.: McCutchan Publishing Company, 1982), 227.

83. Id., at 229, citing Richards v. Thurston, 424 F.2d 1281 (1st Cir. 1970); Hasson v. Boothby, 318 F. Supp. 1183 (D. Mass. 1970). *See also* Shanley v. Northeast Indep. Sch. Dist., 462 F.2d 960 (5th Cir. 1972)(when conduct is patently wrongful prior notice not necessary). *But see* Nitzberg v. Parks, 525 F.2d 378 (4th Cir. 1975) and Leibner v. Sharbaugh, 429 F. Supp. 744 (E.D. Va. 1977)(published rules required where speech-related activities are involved or where penalties are severe).

84. Ind. Code §20-8.1-5-3 (1985).

85. Connally v. General Construction Co., 269 U.S. 385 (1926). Vague rules fail to provide fair notice of what is permissible and what is not permissible, open the door to ex post facto interpretations making impermissible after the fact what had not been permissible before, and invite discriminatory enforcement by officials who are left with enormous discretion to interpret the rule differently from case to case.

86. Alex v. Allen 409 F. Supp. 379 (W.D. Pa. 1976); Soglin v. Kaufman, 418 F.2d 163 (7th Cir. 1969). *See also* Shamloo v. Mississippi State Bd. of Trustees, 620 F.2d 516, 523 (5th Cir. 1980); Sullivan v. Houston Indep. Sch. Dist., 307 F. Supp. 1328, 1343-46 (S.D. Tex. 1969).

87. Chapter 6.

88. *See* §5.11. *See also* Dillon v. Pulaski Cty. Special Sch. Dist., 468 F. Supp. 54 (E.D. Ark. 1978)(upholding enforcement of school rule against public displays of affection).

89. In Keller v. Gardner Com. Consol. Grade Sch. Dist., 552 F. Supp.512 (N.D. Ill. 1982) the court upheld the rule of a school basketball coach requiring players to attend practice except in case of illness or a death in the family. The student claimed the rule conflicted with his free exercise of religion because he faced being dropped from the team if he attended catechism class that was scheduled at the same time as basketball practice. The court said the school had a significant interest in the attendance rule, and that the student could easily attend catechism class by taking the class in a different church where the class schedule was different.

90. *Cf.*, Hawkins v. Coleman, 376 F. Supp. 1330 (N.D. Tex. 1974); Rhyne v. Childs, 359 F. Supp. 1085 (N.D. Fla. 1973), *aff'd,* 507 F.2d 675 (5th Cir. 1975). See also chap. 4.

91. Sherpell v. Humnoke Sch. Dist. No. 5 of Lonoke, 619 F. Supp. 670 (D.C. Ark. 1985). The school rules prohibited, for example. "cruel teasing, rude jestures, or put downs," and "rude or disrespectful behavior toward staff members." One broad catch-all rule also stated that "If a student causes unusual circumstances to occur which is not covered above, he or she may be severed."

92. *See* §8.6.

93. For text of fourth amendment see *supra* note 1.

94. 105 S. Ct. 733 (1984).

95. Id., at 743–44. The Court concluded that since school officials acted as representatives of the state and "not merely as surrogates for the parents," the protections of the fourth amendment were available to students. Then, after balancing the student's interest in privacy and the school's "equally legitimate need to maintain an environment in which learning can take place," the Court concluded that to impose a warrant requirement "would unduly interfere with the maintenance of swift and informal disciplinary procedures needed in the schools." Balancing the same considerations the Court concluded that the usual requirement that a search be based only on "probable cause" a violation of law has occurred needed to be modified.

96. Id., at 744.

97. It was irrelevant that other hypotheses, e.g., T.L.O. borrowed a cigarette from someone else to smoke, were also consistent with the teacher's accusation. The requirement of reasonable suspicion "is not a requirement of absolute certainty." *Id.,* at 745.

98. Justices Powell and Blackmun wrote two separate concurring opinions. Justice Brennan, joined by Justice Marshall, concurred that the fourth amendment did apply in the public school context but dissented on the majority's rejection of the use of the probable-cause standard—the usual fourth amendment test. Justice Stevens dissented, arguing for yet a different standard. He urged the adoption of a standard that would permit searches when teachers and administrators "have reason to believe that the search will uncover evidence that the student is violating the law or engaging in conduct that is seriously disruptive of school order, or the educational process." *Id.,* at 763. He was concerned that the majority opinion would permit searches to obtain evidence of violation of even trivial school rules.

99. State v. D.T.W., 425 So.2d 1383 (Fla. App. 1983)(inspection of cars); Speake v. Grantham, 317 F. Supp. 1253 (S.D. Miss. 1970), *aff'd,* 440 F.2d 1351 (5th Cir. 1971)(car inspection); Arizona v. Johnson, 23 Ariz. App. 64 (1975)(purse inspection); Arizona v. Kappes, 26 Ariz. 567, 550 P.2d 121 (Ct. App. 1976)(contraband spotted during room safety inspection).

100. New Jersey v. T.L.O., 105 S. Ct., at 741 n. 5.

101. Zamora v. Pomery, 639 F.2d 662 (10th Cir. 1981); People v. Overton, 24 N.Y.2d 522, 301 N.Y.S.2d 479 (N.Y. 1969); State v. Stein, 203 Kan. 638, 456 P.2d 1 (1969); *contra,* State v. Engerud, 94 N.J. 331, 348 A.2d 934, 943 (N.J. 1983), *rev'd on other grounds,* 105 S. Ct. 733 (1985). In Horton v. Goose Creek Indep. Sch. Dist., 690 F.2d 470 (5th Cir. 1982)(en banc), *cert. denied,* 103 S. Ct. 3536 (1983) the issue arose whether the use of dogs to detect illegal contraband in lockers and on persons was a search. The court concluded that the sniffing of lockers was not a search but sniffing a student was. The court reasoned that sniffing lockers would not cause students the kind of embarrassment that sniffing their bodies would.

102. Ownership of a location has never been crucial in determining whether fourth amendment protections extended to an individual. Katz v. United States, 389 U.S. 347 (1967). In any event, since the school board owns both the building and the locker, it is not clear why shifting the purse from one part of the building to another should make a difference.

103. United States v. Place, 462 U.S. 696 (1983).

104. Horton v. Goose Creek Indep. Sch. Dist., 690 F.2d 470 (5th Cir. 1982). *(en banc.), cert denied,* 103 S.Ct. 3536 (1953). *Cf.,* Jones v. Latexo Ind. Sch. Dist., 499 F. Supp. 223 (E.D. Tex. 1980)(holding that sniffing of students and their automobiles was a search.)

105. *Concluding it is not a search subject to the fourth amendment:* Zamora v. Pomery, 639 F.2d 662 (10th Cir. 1981); Doe v. Renfrow, 475 F. Supp. 1012 (N.D. Ind. 1979), *aff'd in part*, 631 F.2d 91 (7th Cir. 1980), *cert. denied*, 451 U.S.1022 (1981). *Concluding it is a search:* Horton v. Goose Creek Indep. Sch. Dist., 690 F.2d 470 (5th Cir. 1982) *(en banc), cert. denied*, 103 S.Ct. 3536 (1953); Jones v. Latexo Indep. Sch. Dist., 499 F. Supp. 223 (E.D. Tex. 1980).

106. In Cales v. Howell Pub. Schools, 635 F. Supp. 454 (E.D. Mich. 1985) Ruth Cales had been seen, at a time when she should have been in school, in the parking lot attempting to avoid detection by ducking behind a parked car. After being apprehended she was taken to an assistant principal's office where she was made to dump out the contents of her purse revealing that she had "readmittance" slips which she should not have had. Ruth was then instructed to empty her jean pockets and subsequently ordered, under supervision of a Mary Steinhelper, to remove her outer clothing and to bend over so Steinhelper could visually examine the contents of her brassiere. The illegal drugs Ruth was suspected of carrying were not found. Ruth sued for a violation of her constitutional rights to privacy. The district court ruled that the search violated the *T.L.O.* guidelines and that the assistant principal, Daniel McCarthy, who had ordered the search, was liable. "It is clear that plaintiff's conduct created reasonable grounds for suspecting that some school rule or law had been violated. However, it does not create a reasonable suspicion that a search would turn up evidence of drug usage. Plaintiff's conduct was clearly ambiguous. . . . In short, it could have signified that plaintiff had violated any of an infinite number of laws or school rules. The Court does not read *T.L.O.* so broadly as to allow a school administrator the right to search a student because that student acts in such a way so as to create a reasonable suspicion that the student has violated *some* rule or law. Rather, the burden is on the administrator to establish that the student's conduct is such that it creates a reasonable suspicion that a specific rule or law has been violated and that a search could reasonably expect to produce evidence of that violation." *Id.*, at 457.

107. New Jersey v. T.L.O., 105 S. Ct. at 746 (quoting Fed. Rule. Evid. 401).

108. Edward W. Cleary, *McCormick on Evidence* (St. Paul, Minn.: West Publishing Co., 1984), §185, p. 544.

109. The question of whether individualized suspicion is an essential element of the *T.L.O.* standard will be taken up below.

110. There are numerous student-search cases with facts similar to those listed in the text. *See, e.g.,* Bilbrey v. Brown, 738 F.2d 1462 (9th Cir. 1984); Tartar v. Raybuck, 742 F.2d 977 (6th Cir. 1984); M. V. Bd. of Educ. of Ball-Chatham C.U.S.D. No. 5, 429 F. Supp. 288 (S.D. Ill. S.D. 1977); State v. Joseph T., 336 S.E.2d 728 (W. Va. 1985); In re Bobby B., 218 Cal. Rptr. 253 (Cal. Ct. App. 1985); State v. Young, 234 Ga. 488, 216 S.E.2d 586 (1975), *cert. denied;* 423 U.S. 1039 (1975); Interest of L.L., 90 Wis. 2d 585, 280 N.W.2d 343 (Ct. App. 1979); Commonwealth v. Dingfelt, 277 Pa. Super. 380, 323 A.2d 145 (1974); People v. Scott D., 34 N.Y. 2d 483, 315 N.E.2d 466, 358 N.Y.S.2d 403 (N.Y. 1974).

111. A number of cases have upheld searches undertaken after the school officials had received an anonymous tip. State v. Brooks, 718 P.2d 837 (Wash. App. 1986); Interest J.A., 85 Ill. App.3d 567, 40 Ill. Dec. 755, 406 N.E.2d 958 (Ill. App. 1980); M. v. Bd. of Educ. of Ball-Chatham C.U.S.D. No. 5, 429 F. Supp.288 (S.D. Ill. 1977); In re C., 26 Cal. App.3d 320, 120 Cal. Rptr. 682 (1972); In re G., 11 Cal. App. 3d 1195, 90 Cal. Rptr. 361 (App. 1970); In re Donaldson, 269 Cal. App.2d 509, 75 Cal. Rptr. 220 (App. 1969); In re Boykin, 39 Ill.2d 617, 237 N.E.2d 460 (Ill. 1968). The search was determined to be reasonable in all these cases. *Cf.,* State of West Virginia v. Joseph T., 336 S.E.2d 728 (W. Va. 1985). In that case the assistant principal, after smelling alcohol on Warren M., questioned him and learned that Warren had consumed beer at the home of Joseph T., an eighth grade student, prior to coming to school. The assistant principal then undertook to search the locker of Joseph T. on the theory that Joseph might have brought beer to the school. No evidence of beer was found, but the principal also searched the pockets of a jacket in the locker finding rolling papers, wooden pipes, and a plastic box containing handmade cigarettes that appeared to be made of marijuana. The court upheld the search under the *T.L.O.*

standard. A strong dissent said that the mere fact that Warren had consumed beer with Joseph at his home hardly provided a basis for assuming that Joseph brought beer to the school, hence the search of the locker was not constitutional. *Id.,* at 741.

112. *Cf.* A.B. v. State, 440 So.2d 500 (Fla. App. 2 Dist.1983) and State v. F.W.E., 360 So.2d 148 (Fla. App. 1 Dist. 1978). In one case the principal noted that William was carrying a small black vinyl bag, later identified as a calculator case, which the assistant principal thought had an odd looking bulge. When William was confronted as to why he was late for class he palmed the bag and moved it to his side and back. When asked what he had in the bag, William said, "Nothing." When the assistant principal attmepted to seek the bag, William resisted saying "You can't search me," and then "You need a warrant for this." Ultimately the assistant principal forceably searched the bag finding marijuana, a gram scale and cigarette papers. The court concluded the search was illegal. The court said that the furtive gesture alone, even combined with the fact that William was late for class, was an insufficient basis under *T.L.O.* to conduct a search. William's furtive gesture and resistance to being searched could not by itself trigger reasonable suspicion, if the right to privacy is to have any meaning. In Re William G., 221 Cal. Rptr. 118 (Cal. 1985).

113. State v. Young, 234 Ga. 488, 216 S.E.2d 586 (1975), *cert. denied,* 423 U.S. 1039 (1975); State v. Baccino, 282 A.2d 869 (1971).

114. Tarter v. Raybuck, 742 F.2d 977 (6th Cir. 1984), *cert. denied,* 105 S. Ct. 1749 (1985); In re Bobby B., 218 Cal. Rptr. 253 (Cal. App. 2 Dist. 1985). Under the *T.L.O.* standard it seems likely that the Supreme Court would have decided People v. Scott D., 34 N.Y.2d 483, 315 N.E.2d 466, 358 N.Y.S.2d 403 (1974) differently from the decision of the New York Court of Appeals. The court of appeals ruled there was no reasonable basis for searching even though the student in question was suspected of drug dealing and had been seen entering a toilet facility with fellow students and leaving quickly several times. *See also* In re Robert B., 218 Cal. Rptr. 337 (Cal. Ct. App. 1985)(student seen exchanging money and shifting cigarette package from pocket to inside sleeve of jacket).

115. In re Dominic W., 48 Md. App. 236, 426 A.2d 432 (1981).

116. In Nelson v. State, 319 So.2d 154 (Fla. App. 2 Dist. 1975) two boys were found near a tractor shed on school grounds where the odor of marijuana was detected. The search yielded marijuana and a pipe. The court upheld the search on the basis of the "reasonable suspicion" standard. For a review of cases dealing with similar problems as to adults see Wayne P. La Fave, *Search and Seizure* (St. Paul, Minn.: West Publishing Co., 1978), §3.6 at 648.

117. In *T.L.O.* the Court said that the discovery of the rolling papers "gave rise to the reasonable suspicion that T.L.O. was carrying marijuana as well as cigarettes in her purse." New Jersey v. T.L.O., 105 S. Ct. at 747.

118. In re Robert B., 218 Cal. Rptr. 337 (Cal. App. 2 Dist. 1985). *Cf.,* Bilbrey v. Brown, 738 F.2d 1462 (9th Cir. 1984) (bus driver's report of student's exchanging something insufficient basis for strip search that turned up no contraband).

119. New Jersey v. T.L.O., 105 S.Ct. at 744. *See* Cales v. Howell Pub. Schools, 635 F. Supp. 454 (E.D. Mich. 1985).

120. Note that the majority specifically rejected the notion that the nature of the infraction has a bearing on whether the search is justified at its inception. The nature of the infraction only has a bearing on the scope of the search itself.

121. *Cf.,* Terry v. Ohio, 392 U.S. 1 (1968). As to the police stopping and frisking citizens on the streets, the stop itself must meet fourth amendment requirements, and the frisk may only take place if the policeman has evidence that leads him reasonably to conclude that persons with whom he is dealing may be armed and dangerous. In some cases the right to frisk may follow automatically from the right to stop, e.g., when the suspect is stopped upon suspicion of involvement with a crime that would entail the use of weapons.

The Supreme Court in *T.L.O.* specifically left open the question of whether and when individualized suspicion is needed to conduct a search. New Jersey v. T.L.O., 105 S.Ct. at 735 n. 8.

122. United States v. Albarado, 495 F.2d 799 (2d Cir. 1974); United States v. Davis, 482 F.2d 893 (9th Cir. 1973). *Cf.*, Camara v. Municipal Court, 387 U.S. 523 (1967).

123. Kuehn v. Renton Sch. Dist. No. 403, 694 P.2d 1078 (Wash. 1985)(en banc). In Collier v. Miller, 414 F.Supp. 1357 (S.D. Tex. 1976) the court said the random searching of people for alcohol by guards stationed at the entrance of a stadium was improper.

124. Bellnier v. Lund, 438 F. Supp. 47 (N.D. N.Y. 1977)(holding impermissible the strip searching of a fifth-grade class for allegedly stolen money).

125. *Cf.*, Jones v. McKenzie, 628 F. Supp. 1500 (D. D. C. 1986)(termination of school bus attendant on basis of single, unconfirmed positive urinanalysis drug test was arbitrary and capricious).

126. In Smyth v. Lubbers, 398 F. Supp. 777 (W.D. Mich. S.D. 1975) the court went so far as to hold that a dormitory room could not be searched by school officials without a warrant. *Contra*, Moore v. Student Affairs Committee, 284 F. Supp. 725 (M.D. Ala. 1968). *See also* Piazolla v. Watkins, 316 F. Supp. 624 (M.D. Ala. 1970), *aff'd*, 442 F.2d 284 (5th Cir. 1971). One court has held that health and safety inspections of dorm rooms are permissible without a warrant, and evidence found in plain view in the course of such an inspection may be used in a criminal prosecution. Arizona v. Kappes, 26 Ariz. App. 567, 550 P.2d 121 (1976).

127. Moore v. Student Affairs Committee, 284 F. Supp. 725 (M.D. Ala. 1968). The court in this case said that the student did not and could not be forced to waive his constitutional rights as a condition precedent to admission to the school. The court did say that the school could properly reserve the right to inspect rooms despite the fact this reserved authority may infringe the outer bounds of the fourth amendment rights of students. At another point in the opinion the court also said that when a student rents a room from the school, he waives objections to any reasonable search conducted pursuant to the school regulation in the case. *Contra*, Smyth v. Lubbers, 398 F. Supp. 777 (W.D. Mich., S.D. 1975); Morale v. Grigel, 422 F. Supp. 988, 999 (D. N.H. 1976)(both rejecting the view that the room contract may be used to waive a constitutional right).

128. Whether an adult has voluntarily consented to a search is "a question of fact to be determined from the totality of all the circumstances" in the case. Schneckloth v. Bustamonte, 412 U.S. 218 (1973).

129. *Cf.*, Institute of Judicial Administration-American Bar Association Joint Commission on Juvenile Justice Standards, *Standards Relating to Schools and Education* (Cambridge, Mass.: Ballinger Publishing Company, 1982), 57.

130. *See, e.g.*, State v. Feazell, 360 So. 2d 907 (La. Ct. App. 1978). *Contra*, Tarter v. Raybuck, 742 F.2d 977 (6th Cir. 1984). *Cf.*, State v. Wingerd, 40 Ohio App. 2d 236, 318 N.E.2d 866 (Ct. Apps. Ohio 1974)(college student consented to search; no evidence of coercion).

131. The court in In re Fred C., 26 Cal. App.3d 320, 102 Cal. Rptr. 682 (1972) said the refusal to consent to a search was one permissible factor on which to infer guilt and conduct a search.

132. *See, e.g.*, Boyton v. Casey, 543 F.Supp. 995 (D. Me. 1982). The "Miranda" warning must be given before a criminal suspect is questioned by the police. The suspect must be told he has a right to remain silent, that any statement he does make may be used as evidence against him, and that he has a right to the presence of an attorney, either retained or appointed. Miranda v. Arizona, 384 U.S. 436 (1966).

133. IJA-ABA Joint Commission on Juvenile Justice Standards, *Standards Relating to Schools and Education, supra* note 127, at 145.

134. New Jersey v. T.L.O., 105 S. Ct. at 744 n. 7.

135. An important reason for holding the police and school officials to different standards is that they are working from different purposes and incentives. The police are driven, more than school officials, by a set of concerns and have a degree of power that suggests the need for a strong check on the use of their authority.

136. Tarter v. Raybuck, 742 F.2d 977 (6th Cir. 1984), *cert. denied,* 105 S. Ct. 1749 (1985); Martens v. Dist. No. 220, Bd. of Educ., 620 F.Supp. 29 (D.C. Ill. 1985); State v. McKinnon, 88 Wash.2d 75, 558 P.2d 781 (1977)(en banc).

137. People v. Overton, 24 N.Y.2d 522, 249 N.E.2d 366, 301 N.Y.S.2d 479 (1969).

138. Piazolla v. Watkins, 316 F. Supp. 624 (M.D. Ala. 1970), *aff'd*, 442 F.2d 284 (5th Cir. 1971).

139. *Cf.,* Gold v. U.S., 378 F.2d 588 (9th Cir. 1967).

140. State v. McKinnon, 88 Wash. 2d 75, 558 P.2d 781 (1977)*(en banc);* Martens v. District No. 220, Bd. of Educ., 620 F. Supp. 29, 32 (D.C. Ill. 1985).

141. Tarter v. Raybuck, 742 F.2d 977 (6th Cir. 1984), *cert. denied;* 105 S. Ct. 1749 (1985); In re Boykin, 39 Ill.2d 617, 237 N.E.2d 460 (Ill. 1968). *Cf.,* Potts v. Wright, 357 F. Supp. 215 (E.D. Pa. 1973); Picha v. Wieglos, 410 F. Supp. 1214 (N.D. Ill. 1976).

142. *Applying the exclusionary rule:* Jones v. Latexo Ind. Sch. Dist., 499 F. Supp. 223 (E.D. Tex. 1980); Smyth v. Lubbers, 398 F. Supp. 777 (W.D. Mich. 1975). *Rejecting use of exclusionary rule:* Morale v. Grigel, 422 F. Supp. 988, 999-1001 (D. N.H. 1976). *See also* Speake v. Grantham, 317 F. Supp. 1253 (S.D. Miss. 1970), *aff'd,* 440 F.2d 1351 (5th Cir. 1971); Keene v. Rogers, 316 F. Supp. 217 (D. Me. 1970); Gordon J. v. Santa Ana Unified Sch. Dist., 162 Cal. App.3d 530, 208 Cal. Rptr. 657 (Cal. App. 1984).

143. State v. Engerud, 94 N.J. 331, 463 A.2d 934 (1983), *rev'd on other grounds,* 105 S. Ct. 733 (1985); People v. Scott D., 34 N.Y.2d 483, 315 N.E.2d 466, 358 N.Y.S.2d 403 (N.Y. 1974); Gordon J. v. Santa Ana Unified Sch. Dist., 162 Cal. App.3d 530, 208 Cal. Rptr. 657 (Cal. App. 1984) (all applying the exclusionary rule); *contra,* State v. Young, 234 Ga. 488, 216 S.E.2d 586, *cert. denied,* 423 U.S. 1039 (1975)(dictum).

144. Harlow v. Fitzgerald, 457 U.S. 800, 818 (1982).

145. In Cales v. Howell Pub. Schools, 635 F. Supp. 454 (E.D. Mich. 1985) the court held that an assistant principal did not enjoy qualified immunity from suit. (The facts of the case are discussed, *supra,* note 106.) Despite the fact that the events which served as the basis for the suit for damages against the assistant principal arose prior to the decision in *T.L.O.* the court held that there was sufficient legal precedent to place the assistant principal on notice that "at a minimum reasonable cause or reasonable suspicion was necessary to justify a search by school administrators." *Id.,* at 458. Another school employee who acted under orders issued by the assistant principal in conducting the strip search, however, was granted qualified immunity. It is not clear from the court's opinion, however, whether immunity was granted because this employee was merely acting under orders, and/or because the way in which she conducted the strip search comported with the second branch of the *T.L.O.* standard. Bilbrey v. Brown, 738 F.2d 1462 (9th Cir. 1984)(no immunity from suit); Doe v. Renfrow, 631 F.2d 91 (7th Cir.), *rehearing and rehearing en banc denied,* 635 F.2d 582 (7th Cir. 1980)(school officials not immune from liability); *contra,* Bellnier v. Lund, 438 F. Supp. 47 (N.D. N.Y. 1977).

146. *See* Cloud v. Trustees of Boston University, 720 F.2d 721 (1st Cir. 1983).

147. *See, e.g.,* Dixon v. Alabama State Bd. of Educ., 294 F.2d 150 (5th Cir. 1961), *cert. denied,* 368 U.S. 930 (1961); Hagopian v. Knowlton, 470 F.2d 201 (2d Cir. 1972); Wasson v. Trowbridge, 382 F.2d 807 (2d Cir. 1967); Esteban v. Central Mo. State College, 415 F.2d 1077 (8th Cir. 1969), *cert. denied,* 398 U.S. 965 (1970).

148. *See, e.g.,* Pervis v. Lamarque Indep. Sch. Dist., 466 F.2d 1054 (5th Cir. 1972).

149. *See, e.g.,* Dunn v. Tyler Indep. Sch. Dist., 460 F.2d 137 (5th Cir. 1972)(three-day suspension).

150. *Cf., e.g.,* Mills v. Bd. of Educ. of the District of Columbia, 348 F. Supp. 866 (D.D.C. 1972)(due process applies to all suspensions), with Hernandez v. Sch. Dist. No. 1, Denver Cty., 315 F. Supp. 289 (D. Colo. 1970)(due process does not apply to suspensions of twenty-five days).

151. 419 U.S. 565 (1975).

152. 430 U.S. 651 (1977).

153. *See* §8.7.

154. The conclusions and reasoning of the opinion have been strongly and effectively criticized. Irene Merker Rosenberg, "*Ingraham v. Wright:* The Supreme Court's Whipping Boy," *Columbia Law Review* 78 (1978):75.

155. 435 U.S. 78 (1978).

156. 106 S. Ct. 507 (1985).

157. Ikpeazu v. University of Nebraska, 775 F.2d 250, 253 (8th Cir. 1985). *See also,* Hines v. Rinker, 667 F.2d 699 (8th Cir. 1981); Green v. Bailey, 519 F.2d (8th Cir. 1975); Gaspar v. Bruton, 513 F.2d 843 (10th Cir. 1975).

158. In Campell v. Bd. of Educ. of New Milford, 475 A.2d 289 (Conn. 1984) the court agreed with the district that a grade reduction of five points for each unexcused absence was an academic penalty because there was a connection between classroom attendance and academic performance.

159. *See* Keough v. Tate Cty. Bd. of Educ., 748 F.2d 1077, 1080-81 (5th Cir. 1984). In that case the court in dictum said, "*Goss* makes no distinction between ten-day suspensions that occur during examination period and those that do not, and it seems to us, for obvious reasons . . . [T]o hold that the *Goss* guidelines do not apply to suspension periods that include scheduled examinations would significantly undermine, if not nullify, its definitive holding." In response it may be argued that this comment is inconsistent with the Supreme Court's concern in *Goss* that procedures become more formal as the penalty becomes more severe.

160. Betts v. Bd. of Educ. of City of Chicago, 466 F.2d 629 (7th Cir. 1972); Everett v. Marcase, 426 F. Supp. 397 (E.D. Pa. 1977).

161. Crook v. Baker, 584 F. Supp. 1531 (E.D. Mich. 1984).

162. Herbert v. Ventetuolo, 638 F.2d 5 (1st Cir. 1981)(no property right to play interscholastic sports); Bernstein v. Menard, 557 F. Supp. 90 (E.D. Va. 1982)(no constitutional right to play in the band); Karnstein v. Pewaukee Sch. Bd., 557 F. Supp. 565 (E.D. Wis. 1983)(no liberty or property interest in joining National Honor Society).

163. 588 F. Supp. 608 (E.D. Pa.1984). A second issue in the case was whether the hearing was held sufficiently promptly after the suspension. The court concluded the one-day delay had been agreed to by the student himself.

164. *Cf.,* Mathews v. Eldridge, 424 U.S. 319 (1976).

165. *See, e.g.,* Strickland v. Inlow, 519 F.2d 744 (8th Cir. 1975); Jenkins v. La. State. Bd. of Educ., 506 F.2d 992 (5th Cir. 1975)(en banc); Dixon v. Alabama State Bd. of Educ., 294 F.2d 150 (5th Cir. 1961), *cert denied,* 368 U.S. 930 (1961); Davis v. Ann Arbor Pub. Sch., 313 F. Supp. 1217 (E.D. Mich. 1970)(telephone notice sufficient); Vought v. Van Buren Pub. Sch., 306 F. Supp. 1388 (E.D. Mich. 1969)(five-day notice required).

166. Dixon v. Alabama State Bd. of Educ., 294 F.2d 150 (5th Cir.) *cert. denied,* 368 U.S. 930 (1961); Gonzales v. McEuen, 435 F. Supp. 460 (C.D. Cal.1977); De Jesus v. Penberthy, 344 F. Supp. 70 (D.C. Conn. 1972).

167. *Cf.,* Montoya v. Sanger Unified Sch. Dist., 502 F. Supp. 209 (E.D. Cal. 1980)(holding that a state statute required notice to be given in the primary language of the accused).

168. Hillman v. Elliott, 436 F. Supp. 812 (W.D. Va., 1977). In Jones v. State Bd. of Educ. of and for the State of Tenn., 279 F. Supp. 190, 200 (M.D. Tenn., 1968), *aff'd,* 407 F.2d 836 (6th Cir. 1969), *cert. denied,* 397 U.S. 31 (1970) the court permitted a member of the Faculty Advisory Committee to both provide the F.A.C. with information concerning the case and to sit on the F.A.C. In De Jesus v. Penberthy, 344 F. Supp. 70, 77 (D. Conn. 1972) the court appears to have ruled that there was no constitutional violation when members of the school administration joined the board in executive session to decide a disciplinary case. The court did advise the board that they may wish to change the practice in order to maintain the appearance of impartiality.

169. Murray v. W. Baton Rouge Parish Sch. Bd., 472 F.2d 438 (5th Cir. 1973).

170. Id. (impartiality lost). *See also* Gonzales v. McEuen, 435 F. Supp. 460 (C.D. Cal.1977). *Contra,* Tasby v. Estes, 643 F.2d 1103 (5th Cir. 1981); Alex v. Allen, 409 F. Supp. 379 (W.D. Pa. 1976).

171. Winnick v. Manning 460 F.2d 545 (2d Cir. 1972).

172. *Cf.,* Pierce v. Sch. Comm. of New Bedford, 322 F. Supp. 957 (D. Mass. 1971)(rejection of claim that board members were biased because they knew the accused student had repeatedly referred to them and the administration as "fascist pigs"). The court was concerned that a student could simply disqualify a decision-maker by hurling epithets. *Cf.,* Gonzales v. McEuen, 435 F. Supp. 460 (C.D. Cal.1977); Sullivan v. Houston Indep. Sch. Dist., 475 F.2d 1071 (5th Cir.), *cert. denied,* 414 U.S. 1032 (1973). In *Sullivan* the incidents leading to the suspension of the pupil involved a personal confrontation between pupil and principal; the court found that the principal's primary aim in conducting the hearing was not to hear the student's side of the story but to obtain an apology.

173. Keough v. Tate Cty. Bd. of Educ., 748 F.2d 1077 (5th Cir. 1984)(no prejudice in this case in not being provided a list of witnesses and summary of testimony); Linwood v. Bd. of Educ., City of Peoria, Sch. Dist. No. 150, 463 F.2d 763 (7th Cir. 1972), *cert. denied,* 409 U.S. 1027 (1972); Whiteside v. Kay, 446 F. Supp. 716 (W.D. La. 1978); *contra,* Williams v. Dade Cty. Sch. Bd., 441 F.2d 299 (5th Cir. 1971)(list must be provided); Dixon v. Alabama State Bd. of Educ., 294 F.2d 150 (5th Cir. 1961), *cert. denied,* 368 U.S. 930 (1961).

174. *See, e.g.,* Jaksa v. Regents of the University of Michigan, 597 F.Supp. 1245 (E.D. Mich., S.D. 1984), and cases cited therein; McClain v. Lafayette Cty. Bd. of Educ., 673 F.2d 106 (5th Cir. 1982), *rehearing denied,* 687 F.2d 121 (5th Cir. 1982); Whiteside v. Kay, 446 F. Supp. 716 (W.D. La., 1978). In a seminal case, Dixon v. Alabama State Bd. of Educ., 294 F.2d 150, 159 (5th Cir. 1961), *cert. denied,* 368 U.S. 930 (1961), the court indicated that students did not have a right to a full-dress judicial hearing with a right to cross-examine.

175. De Jesus v. Penberthy, 334 F. Supp. 70, 75 (D. Conn. 1972); Fielder v. Bd. of Educ., 346 F. Supp. 722 (D. Neb. 1972); Tibbs v. Bd. of Educ. of the Township of Franklin, 284 A.2d 179 (1971). *Cf.,* Winnick v. Manning, 460 F.2d 545, 549 (2d Cir. 1972)(holding no right of cross-examination required in this case).

176. Dixon v. Alabama State Bd. of Educ., 294 F.2d 150 (5th Cir. 1961), *cert. denied* 368 U.S. 930 (1961); Dillon v. Pulaski Cty. Special Sch. Dist., 468 F. Supp. 54 (E.D. Ark., 1978).

177. Whiteside v. Kay, 446 F. Supp. 716 (W.D. La. 1978); Ring v. Reorganized Sch. Dist. No. 3, 609 S.W.2d 241 (W.D. Mo. 1980).

178. Jackson v. Hayakawa, 761 F.2d 525 (9th Cir. 1985); Jones v. State Bd. of Educ. of and for the State of Tenn., 279 F. Supp. 190 (M.D. Tenn., 1968), *aff'd,* 407 F.2d 836 (6th Cir. 1969), *cert. denied,* 397 U.S. 31 (1970).

179. *Hearsay may be used:* Tasby v. Estes, 643 F.2d 1103 (5th Cir. 1981); Boykins v. Fairfield Bd. of Educ., 492 F.2d 697 (5th Cir. 1974), *cert. denied,* 420 U.S. 962 (1975); Linwood v. Bd. of Educ., City of Peoria Sch. Dist. No. 150, 463 F.2d 763 (7th Cir.), *cert. denied,* 409 U.S. 1027 (1972); Racine Unified Sch. Dist. v. Thompson, 321 N.W.2d 334 (Wis. 1982). *Hearsay may not be used:* Gonzales v. McEuen, 435 F. Supp. 460 (C.D. Cal., 1977); Fiedler v. Bd. of Educ., 346 F. Supp. 722 (D. Neb. 1972); De Jesus v. Penberthy, 344 F. Supp. 70 (Conn. 1972).

180. Franklin v. Dist. Sch. Bd., 356 So. 2d 931 (App. Ct. 1978).

181. *No right to legal representation:* Jaksa v. Regents of the University of Michigan, 597 F.Supp. 1245 (E.D. Mich., S.D. 1984)(no right of representation); Everett v. Marcase, 426 F. Supp. 397 (E.D. Penn. 1977). *Right to legal representation:* Givens v. Poe, 346 F. Supp. 202 (W.D. N.C. 1972); Esteban v. Central Missouri State College, 277 F. Supp. 649 (W.D. Mo. 1967), *aff'd,* 415 F.2d 1077 (8th Cir. 1969), *cert. denied,* 398 U.S. 965 (1970).

182. Wasson v. Trowbridge, 382 F.2d 807, 812 (2d Cir. 1967).

183. Gonzales v. McEuen, 435 F. Supp. 460 (1977).

184. Madera v. Bd. of Educ., 386 F.2d 778 (2d Cir. 1967), *cert. denied,* 390 U.S. 1028 (1968); Cosme v. Bd. of Educ. of City of New York, 270 N.Y.S.2d 231 (Sup. Ct. 1966).

185. Jaksa v. Regents of the University of Michigan, 597 F. Supp. 1245 (E.D. Mich., S.D. 1984); Wasson v. Trowbridge, 382 F.2d 807 (2d Cir. 1967); Whitefield v. Simpson, 312 F. Supp. 889 (E.D. Ill. 1970). *Contra,* Mills v. Bd. of Educ. of Dist. of Columbia, 348 F. Supp. 866 (D.D.C. 1972).

186. *See* Jaksa v. Regents of the University of Michigan, 597 F. Supp. 1245 (E.D. Mich., S.D. 1984) and cases cited therein. Contra, Morale v. Grigel, 422 F. Supp. 988, 1004 (D. N.H. 1976); Graham v. Knutzen, 362 F. Supp. 881 (D. Neb. 1973).

187. Jones v. Board of Governors of University of North Carolina, 704 F.2d 713 (4th Cir. 1983); Jaksa v. Regents of the University of Michigan, 597 F. Supp. 1245 (E.D. Mich., S.D. 1984).

188. It is important to recognize that students in private schools may have a right to procedural due process based on contract. In that case the source of procedural guarantees would be in the specific procedures adopted by the school and incorporated into the contract between student and school. Tedeschi v. Wagner College, 49 N.Y.2d 652, 404 N.E.2d 1302, 427 N.Y.S.2d 760 (N.Y. 1980); *cf.,* Clayton v. Trustees of Princeton University, 608 F. Supp. 413 (D.C. N.J. 1985); Corso v. Creighton University, 731 F.2d 529 (8th Cir. 1984).

189. New York Education Law, §3213 (McKinney, 1981).

190. 430 U.S. 651 (1977).

191. Id., at 670.

192. The *Ingraham* case came to the Supreme Court on appeal from a decision on the Fifth Circuit Court of Appeals that neither the eighth nor the fourteenth amendment served to provide limits on the use of corporal punishment.

193. Hall v. Tawney, 621 F.2d 607 (4th Cir. 1980). *Contra,* Hale v. Pringle, 562 F. Supp. 58 (M.D. Ala. 1983); Paul v. McGhee, 577 F. Sup. 460 (E.D. Tenn. 1983). A three-member panel of the Fifth Circuit in the *Ingraham* case originally concluded that both the eighth and fourteenth amendment were violated by severe and oppressive corporal punishment. 498 F.2d 248 (5th Cir. 1974). Upon rehearing en banc, the fifteen-judge Fifth Circuit reversed on both points, and it was this decision that was appealed to the Supreme Court. 525 F.2d 909 (5th Cir. 1976 (en banc).

194. Baker v. Owen, 395 F. Supp. 294 (M.D. N.C. 1975), *aff'd mem.,* 423 U.S. 907 (1975).

195. Mass. Gen. Laws Ann., c. 71 §37G. (Supp. 1985); N.J. Stat. Ann. †18A:6-1(1968). N.Y.C.R.R. Title 8, §19.5 (1985).

196. Ingraham v. Wright, 430 U.S. 651, 662-63 (1977).

197. The burden of proving the corporal punishment was excessive rests with the parent or child. The cases frequently turn on disputed facts that have to be resolved by a jury. What is "reasonable" or "excessive" remains a difficult issue. The factors typically considered include the age, sex, physical and mental condition of the child, the nature of the offense, and the degrading nature of the punishment. American Law Institute, "Intentional Harms to Persons, Land and Chattels," in *Restatement of the Law of Torts Second,* (St. Paul, Minn.: American Law Institute Publishers, 1965), §150. Thus, courts have upheld hitting pupils two or three blows, but have concluded that ten blows were excessive. LeBlanc v. Tyler, 381 So.2d 908 (Ct. App. La. 1980); People v. Ball, 58 Ill. 36, 317 N.E.2d 54 (Ill. 1974). The use of rubber straps to hit students on the hand three or four times was upheld. LeBoyd v. Jenkins, 381 So.2d 1290 (La. App. 1980). Another Louisiana court upheld hitting a student on the buttocks sufficiently hard and frequently to produce a bruise and black marks. "The bruises sustained on the posterior of the plaintiff's son are clearly indicative of what this Court would expect from being struck with the aforementioned 'paddle.'" Roy v. Continental Insurance Company, 313 So. 2d 349, 355 (La. App. 1975). When students are permanently damaged, however, liability is likely to be found. Thus, when a teacher hit an eight-year-old boy with sufficient force to break an eardrum, liability was found. Calway v. Williamson, 130 Conn. 575, 36 A.2d 377 (Conn. 1944).

198. Bott v. Bd. of Educ., Deposit Cent. Sch. Dist., 41 N.Y.2d 265, 392 N.Y.S.2d 274 (N.Y. 1977).

199. *Cf.,* Belasco v. Bd. of Pub. Educ. of the Sch. Dist. of Pittsburgh, 486 A.2d 538 (Pa. Commw. 1985) (hitting student once with wooden paddle did not amount to willful and persistent violation of the board's prohibition against corporal punishment).

200. Petrey v. Flaugher, 505 F. Supp. 1087 (E.D. Ky. 1981); Fisher v. Buckburnett Indep. Sch. Dist., 419 F. Supp. 1200 (N.D. Tex. 1976), Abremski v. Southeastern Sch. Dist. 421 A.2d 485 (Pa. Commonw. 1980).

201. Dunn v. Tyler Indep. Sch. Dist., 460 F.2d 137 (5th Cir. 1972).

202. *Upholding grade reductions:* Fisher v. Buckburnett, 419 F. Supp. 1200 (N.D. Tex. 1976); New Braunfels Indep. Sch. Dist. v. Armke, 658 S.W.2d 330 (Tex. Civ. App. 1983); Donaldson v. Bd. of Educ. for Danville Sch. Dist., 424 N.E.2d 737 (Ill. App. Ct. 1981). *Disallowing grade reductions:* Katzman v. Cumberland Valley Sch. Dist., 84 PaC. 474, 479 A.2d 671 (Pa. Commonw. 1984); Gutierrez v. Sch. Dist. 4–1, 585 P.2d 935 (Colo. Ct. App. 1978).

203. *Upholding grade reductions:* Raymon v. Alvord Indep. Sch. Dist. 639 F.2d 257 (5th Cir. 1981); Campbell v. Bd. of Educ. of the Town of New Milford, 193 Conn. 93, 475 A.2d 289 (1984); Johnson v. Shineman, 658 S.W.2d 910 (Mo. Ct. App. 1983); Knight v. Bd. of Educ. of Tri-Point Sch. Dist., 38 Ill. App.3d 603, 348 N.E.2d 299 (1976). *Disallowing grade reductions:* Hamer v. Bd. of Educ., 66 Ill. App.3d 7, 22 Ill. D. 755, 383 N.E. 2d 231 (1978); Dorsey v. Bale, 521 S.W.2d 76 (Ky. 1975).

204. Ladson v. Bd. of Educ., Union Free Sch. Dist. No. 9, 323 N.Y.S.2d 545 (Sup. Ct. 1971).

205. 20 U.S.C. §§ 1400-61 (1982).

206. 20 U.S.C. § 1415(b) (1982).

207. Kaelin v. Grubbs, 682 F.2d 595, 602 (6th Cir. 1982), citing Stuart v. Nappi, 443 F. Supp. 1235, 1242 (D. Conn. 1978); Sherry v. New York State Educ. Dept., 479 F. Supp. 1328, 1337 (W.D. N.Y. 1979); and Doe v. Koger, 480 F. Supp. 225,229 (N.D. Ind. 1979).

In Jackson v. Franklin Cty. Sch. Bd., 606 F. Supp. 152 (S.D. Miss. 1985), *aff'd.,* 767 F.2d 535 (5th Cir. 1985) the court agreed with the school district that a student who had been suspended in January for sexual misconduct and spent the intervening months under treatment did not have to be readmitted in the fall under the old individualized educational program when it appeared the student would continue to pose a safety threat.

208. Id., citing S-1 v. Turlington, 635 F.2d 342 (5th Cir.), *cert. denied,* 454 U.S. 1030 (1981); Sch. Bd. of Prince Cty., William, Va. v. Malone, 762 F.2d 1210 (4th Cir. 1985); H.R. v. Hornbeck, 524 F. Supp. 215, 219 (D. Md. 1981); and Doe v. Koger, 480 F.Supp. 225, 229 (N.D. Ind. 1979).

209. Id., citing S-1 v. Turlington, 635 F.2d at 348; and Doe v. Koger, 480 F. Supp. at 229.

210. Sch. Bd. of Prince Cty., William, Va. v. Malone, 762 F.2d 1210, 1217 (4th Cir. 1985).

211. Id., citing S-1 v. Turlington, 635 F.2d at 348.

212. 20 U.S.C. §1232g (1982).

213. Van Allen v. McCleary, 27 Misc.2d 81, 211 N.Y.S.2d 501 (1961); Dawkins v. Billingsley, 172 P. 69 (Okla. 1918).

214. 34 C.F.R. Part 99 (1985).

215. 34 C.F.R. §99.3, "Education Records."

216. Id., "Student."

217. Id., "Director Information;" §99.37.

218. 34 C.F.R. §99.11 (1985).

219. 34 C.F.R. §99.12 (1985).

220. Girardier v. Webster College, 563 F.2d 1267 (8th Cir. 1977).

221. 34 C.F.R. §§99.30-99.36.

222. 34 C.F.R. §99.33.

223. 20 U.S.C. §§1400-61 (1982).

224. See, *e.g.,* Ind. Code Ann. Title 4, Chap. 6 §§4-1-6-2 to 4-1-6-5 (1982).

225. Louis Fischer and Gail Paulus Sorenson, *School Law for Counselors, Psychologists, and Social Workers* (New York: Longman, 1985), 14.

226. Id., at 18.

227. Id., 18-19.

228. Dick v. Watowan Cty., 551 F. Supp. 983 (D. Minn. 1982)

229. 20 U.S.C.A. §1232h (Cum. Sup. 1985).

9

The New Law of Teacher Rights

9.1. INTRODUCTION

Developments in federal constitutional and statutory law have over the last two decades worked a revolution in teacher rights. Although prior to this time state law provided teachers with some important protections, it was Congress in conjunction with the federal courts that reformed the relationship between teacher and school board by expanding the list of prohibited grounds upon which personnel decisions may be made. Thus, today teachers are protected by constitutional doctrine and federal statute against decisions based, for example, merely on disagreement with what the teacher has publicly advocated, on distaste for the teacher's personal life style, on racial prejudice, on stereotypical views of women, and/or on handicapping condition. Even the decision-making procedures to be used in dismissing a teacher have been left untouched by the courts.

Besides limiting the grounds upon which personnel actions may be taken, this new body of law works to protect teachers through the allocation of the burden of proof. That is, an important device for protecting teachers from improperly grounded decisions is to, once the plaintiff has made out a prima facie case, place on school officials the burden of persuading the judiciary that their decision was made for legitimate and not prohibited reasons. This is not to say that a teacher may merely "cry foul" without any basis in fact, thereby placing on the school the risk of nonpersuasion, the risk of failing to persuade a court that its actions were properly grounded. If the law were to operate in this fashion, teachers would be encouraged too much to allege wrongdoing, and school districts would become timorous in making personnel decisions. As will be seen, the law structures the allocation of the burden of producing evidence and the burden of persuasion in a more balanced way. Even so, complaints have been raised that the law has gone too far in protecting teachers. For example, it has been argued that it has become too easy for teachers to get a court to make a prima facie case of discrimination thereby forcing a court to consider the claims of improper decision-making, and that the burden of persuasion imposed on the employer has been made too heavy. The consequence, it has further been argued, is that inefficient teachers are too well protected by the law to the detriment of the quality of the educational program. Whether or not these allegations are correct, they do point to an important lesson: in shaping the law there are inevitable trade-offs that must be considered, and in this area that trade-off can be extremely painful, namely, teacher rights versus student interests.

It should be stressed, however, that the tenor of these comments may misrepresent the true picture. With equal force one may claim that the recent strong protection of teacher rights has served to protect the interests of students. Thus, the excellent black teacher is now protected from dismissal merely because he or she is black. The inspirational teacher with the unconventional life style has a better chance of not being removed from the classroom. The school remains more of a marketplace of ideas, more stimulating and less deadening, when the academic freedom rights of teachers are protected.

In brief, whether the new law of teacher rights has, on balance, helped or harmed students is a complex topic that has yet to receive any sort of adequate treatment. What we do know, however, is that the law today is very different from what it was twenty or twenty-five years ago. This chapter will concentrate on highlighting these developments, but it begins with a very brief sketch in the first two sections of the older legal background to which the more recent developments were added.

9.2. CERTIFICATION

As noted in chapter 2, basic control of the public school system resides in the state, and among the most important areas in which states have exerted control is in establishing the terms and conditions of the employment of teachers in the public schools. State legislatures in all states have both prohibited the employment of public school teachers who are not certified in the area of subjects to which they are assigned,[1] with certain exceptions, and established the requirements that teachers must meet in order to obtain certification. The kinds of certificates and the qualifications for them vary from state to state, and basic administration of the certification program is delegated to the state boards and departments of education.[2]

The requirements for a certificate typically involve the obtaining of a college degree, a certain minimum number of credit hours or courses in the area of specialization, perhaps the passing of a teachers' examination—a requirement that has spread to many states in recent years—and possession of such other personal characteristics as a good moral character.[3] The signing of a loyalty oath and U.S. citizenship may be additional requirements.[4] States may and do change the certification requirements from time to time.

The denial of a certificate can be the basis for a variety of legal challenges. If the teacher has met all the legal requirements for the certificate, it must be issued and the courts will overturn the capricious or unauthorized denial of a certificate.[5] The denial of a certification must not be based on reasons that violate the state or federal constitutions or federal statutory law. For example, the denial of a certificate solely on the basis of race would clearly violate the equal protection clause of the fourteenth amendment. More difficult is the question of whether a teachers' examination that disproportionately disqualifies black applicants may be used. A federal district court upheld the use of the National Teacher Examination for certification and salary purposes in South Carolina.[6] Under the test 83 percent of the black applicants and 17.5 of the white applicants did not achieve the required score. Despite the disproportionate impact the federal court ruled that the test was not unconstitutional because the plaintiffs failed to establish it had been adopted for the purpose of discriminating on the basis of race.[7] However, teacher competency tests that have a racially disproportionate impact may be challengeable under Title VI.[8]

The revocation of certificates is also controlled by state law subject to important constitutional limitations. Common statutory bases for the revocation of certificates include immorality, incompetence, neglect of duty, and contract violations. Today it is common for courts to provide a limiting interpretation to these statutory provisions by specifying that revocation is only permissible if there is a showing that, for example, the immoral conduct had an adverse effect on the teacher's fitness to teach, i.e., on his or her performance in the classroom. Conduct that might arguably be deemed immoral, the courts have said, does not automatically and invariably make a person unfit to teach. To rule otherwise would vest the state with authority to interfere with private, personal conduct regardless of its effect on his or her teaching.[9] Furthermore, for the revocation of certificates hearings on the charges are usually required either by state statute or constitutional law.[10]

9.3. EMPLOYMENT AND JOB ASSIGNMENT

As noted earlier, it is in connection with the hiring, assignment, suspension, and termination of teachers that the developments in the new law of teacher rights have been most important. Of course, prior to these recent developments state law provided, as it still does today, basic control and guidance. Thus, the law of teacher rights today comprises the older basic state-law provisions—to be reviewed in this section—as well as the newer federal statutory and constitutional law, to be reviewed in the remaining sections of this chapter. As a consequence, a given incident, such as the dismissal of a tenured teacher, may therefore involve both state statutory law and federal constitutional and statutory law.

It is the local board of education, acting as a board, that enjoys the delegated authority in local school districts to hire and appoint teachers. In this capacity the board may require even the certified teacher to meet additional standards beyond those required for certification. For example, boards may require prospective employees to live in the district[11] and to satisfy continuing education requirements.[12] The principles of contract law apply to the formation, invalidation, and enforcement of board-teacher contracts.[13] Both the individual contract between teacher and board and the collective bargaining contract must conform to state and federal law, thus those contract provisions inconsistent with law are not enforceable.[14] It is important to recognize that in bargaining over a contract, boards may not insist that teachers waive their constitutional and statutory rights.

Subject to state certification requirements, it is the local board that has the authority to assign teachers to schools, grades, and subjects, and teachers who refuse lawful assignment may be discharged for insubordination.[15] Assignments made in bad faith or in violation of constitutional and federal statutory requirements may be challenged.[16] Of course, once the assignment has been incorporated into a contract, the board may not reassign the teacher in violation of the contract.

The transfer of teachers may be used as a disciplinary measure as a way of enforcing lawful school rules.[17] Transferring teachers who have merely exercised a constitutional right is, of course, not permissible. Another important limitation on the transfer and reassignment of teachers is that in most states, if the transfer involves a demotion, it may be unlawful if not done for disciplinary purposes or the more efficient management of the school.[18] The particular laws of the state should be examined to determine the limits on transfers, and the extent to which notice and hearing must be afforded to teachers on a transfer deemed to be a "demotion." The constitutional due process requirements will be taken up in §§ 9.17 and 9.18.

In addition to assigning teachers to particular positions, boards have the authority to assign teachers to nonteaching duties when those assignments are distributed impartially, are reasonable in number and the hours required, are equitably distributed, and are consistent with the teacher's professional status and related to his or her employment duties.[19]

9.4. GRANTING TENURE, DISMISSAL FOR CAUSE, AND REDUCTION IN FORCE

Most states permit the grant of tenure by the school board to teachers (as well as administrators and supervisors in some states) upon having served a probationary period, usually three years.[20] Tenure might also be achieved in some states if the board by oversight simply fails to terminate a probationary teacher and the teacher in fact serves beyond the probationary period.[21]

Tenure is a contractual right that ensures that employment will only be terminated for adequate cause (e.g., immorality, incompetence, incapacity, insubordination, neglect of duty, unprofessional conduct) or because economic exigencies dictate a reduction in force.[22] Tenure most importantly protects teachers by placing on the district the burden to prove that just cause exists for dismissal, and by assuring that certain procedures will be followed in the dismissal process. Tenure serves to provide teachers with an important degree of employment security in that a tenured teacher can expect to continue in employment from year to year unless charges are brought and proven justifying termination, or unless a reduction in force is warranted. Tenure is thus a "continuing contract," as opposed to a "term contract" pursuant to which the teacher can expect employment only for the fixed term of the contract. It is important to recognize that the scope of tenure rights varies from state to state. In some states teachers may obtain tenure in an area defined by the scope of his or her certificate, but in other states the tenure area is more limited, e.g., elementary grades, driver education, high school English.

At the end of the probationary period, boards may refuse to grant tenure. Some states permit a board to refuse to renew for any reason other than a constitutionally impermissible one. In other states the board's statutory authority is somewhat more limited, but the burden of proving the board acted improperly rests with the complaining teacher.[23] Courts have permitted nonrenewal of a teacher whose performance was satisfactory when the board believed it could find an even better teacher.[24] The question of whether a probationary teacher has a constitutional right to hearing prior to or after nonrenewal will be taken up in § 9.17.

As noted earlier, having been granted tenure, teachers may only be dismissed for cause and in accordance with the procedures established by statute. The cases interpreting what constitutes immorality, incompetence, incapacity, insubordination, neglect of duty, and unprofessional conduct are numerous and will not be thoroughly reviewed here.[25] The following listing provides an indication of how the courts have interpreted these statutory terms:

Immorality:
    Criminal activity.
    Unconventional sexual activity.
    Sexual involvement with students.
    Homosexuality.
    Pregnancy out of wedlock.
    Unconventional life style.
    Use of abusive, stigmatizing language with pupils.

Incapacity:
    Physical, mental, or emotional illness or disability that is incurable and incapacitates the employee from performing his or her job.
    Undergoing a sex-transformation operation.

Incompetence:
 Lack of classroom management and control.
 Lack of knowledge.
 Failure to adopt new teaching methods.
 Deficiencies in teaching methods.
 Mistreatment of pupils.
 Negligence.
 Sexual harassment.

Insubordination:
 Inflicting corporal punishment in violation of school rules.
 Taking time off without permission.
 Encouraging student disobedience of school rules.
 Refusal to follow grooming regulations.
 Refusal to carry out assigned duties.

Neglect of Duty:
 Failure to meet classes.
 Failure to control classes.
 Failure to meet with parents.
 Failure to comply with continuing education requirements.

Unprofessional Conduct:
 Excessive corporal punishment of pupils.
 Various forms of conduct defined as immoral (see above).
 Various forms of insubordination (see above).
 Neglect of duty (see above).

Several points need to be made about this body of law. First, the grounds for dismissal are broadly phrased and overlap in coverage, hence the same conduct may be subject to multiple charges or treated as a different offense in different states. Second, the generality of the bases for discharge is such as to permit evolving interpretations as social mores and culture change. The courts will also seek to limit the sweeping terms of the statutes by, for example, interpreting them to prevent dismissal for minor deviations from appropriate study.[26] Third, it is not uncommon today for courts to insist that the charges be linked to the teacher's fitness to teach.[27] That is, as a way of narrowing the meaning of the statute to avoid the constitutional vice of vagueness, and as a way of assuring that the basis of the dismissal is rationally related to the legitimate school purposes, the courts have insisted that there be a nexus between the teacher's behavior and an effect upon the school.[28] Proof of an impact on the school stemming from the teacher's behavior is not, however, insisted upon in cases in which it has been established a teacher sexually touched or had intercourse with a student.[29] The proof of a nexus may also not be required in insubordination cases.[30] Fourth, it is the district that carries the burden of proving the charges with substantial evidence.[31] Fifth, in connection with dismissals based on incompetence, the law in some states requires the district to establish that the teacher was notified of his or her deficiencies, and then dismissal is only permitted if these deficiencies are irremediable.[32] Sixth, generally the courts are reluctant to second-guess school officials, especially as regards judgments that teachers are incompetent, but occasionally the courts will act to prevent dismissals.[33] Seventh, many of these statutory bases of dismissal touch upon constitutional rights, and, as we shall see, the federal courts have been active in preventing the violation of those rights.[34]

Tenured and nontenured teachers may lose their jobs not just for cause, but also when school districts, faced with fiscal shortfalls and/or declining enrollments, decide to reduce their staffs.[35] Statutes impose important limits on the authority of the board to dismiss teachers to achieve a reduction in force. First, the abolition of the position must not be subterfuge merely to get rid of one teacher in order to hire another,[36] or to take retaliatory action against a teacher for an exercise of a constitutionally protected right.[37] Second, state statutes often control the order in which teachers are to be released; thus, for example, a state statute might require that layoffs take place in terms of seniority within the affected tenure area. This may mean the entire teaching staff within that tenure area may have to be reassigned to new teaching duties in order to assure that the more senior teachers retain jobs and the essential courses are still taught.[38] This reassignment may prove to be difficult if the teachers retained lack the requisite certification to teach the courses to which they may be assigned because of the reduction in force.[39] Many other important problems can arise in connection with these reassignments, and the law of the particular states should be consulted for their treatment of these problems.

The order of recall after layoffs is also governed by state law. Typically, seniority in the system guides the order of recall,[40] but teachers need not be recalled to positions for which they are not certified.[41]

9.5. FREEDOM OF EXPRESSION

With this section we begin our exploration of the newer law of teacher rights, a body of constitutional and federal statutory laws that has done much to reduce the discretion of school boards in dealing with their personnel. As has been discussed at various points throughout the book, teachers do not shed their right of freedom of expression upon signing an employment contract with the public schools. However, because this topic has been taken up at various points in this volume, there is no need now to repeat those discussions. For convenience, a listing of various topics and the sections where they might be found is provided:

Most of these topics deal with the question of what constitutes a constitutionally protected free speech activity. A teacher who hopes to succeed in a suit claiming a deprivation of the right of freedom of expression must first convince the court that he or she had been engaged in a constitutionally protected form of free speech. Establishing this point is only a necessary and not a sufficient condition for winning a suit claiming that the dismissal, suspension, loss of pay, transfer, demotion, or other form of discipline was constitutionally impermissible. In addition, the teacher must establish that his or her conduct—his engaging in this constitutionally protected activity—was a "substantial factor," a "motivating factor" in the board's decision.[42] Crucial for the plaintiff in meeting this initial burden is establishing that the board knew of the plaintiff's involvement in the protected activity when it imposed the disciplinary sanction. Once the plaintiff has met this burden, the board must be given the opportunity to establish by a preponderance of the evidence that it would have reached the "same decision" in the absence of the protected conduct.[43] That is, the board is given the opportunity to establish that it would have, for example, dismissed the plaintiff for other reasons even if it had not considered the plaintiff's involvement in the protected activity. Obviously, if the board is to succeed in making this case, it must establish the existence of reasons for acting that are not trivial. Arguing, for example, that the same decision to dismiss would have been reached because the teacher had been late for class once would not convince the court that there were ample, sound reasons for the board's decision that were or could have been relied upon by themselves. The ultimate burden of persuasion that it acted, or could have acted, for legitimate reasons thus rests with the board, and in this way the teacher's right of freedom of speech is given strong protection. At the same time, the board's flexibility to act for legitimate reasons is not eliminated. The *Mt. Healthy* allocation of the burden of producing evidence and the risk of nonpersuasion attempts to strike a careful balance between the interests of the teacher and the board.

9.6. RIGHT TO PRIVACY: FREEDOM
TO PURSUE ONE'S PERSONAL LIFE STYLE

Teachers historically have been held to standards of personal conduct that embodied the conventional ideal of admirable behavior of the moment.[44] Failure to conform to these standards opened the teacher to dismissal under state law for "immoral" and "unprofessional" behavior. The effort on the part of school officials to assure that their teachers are the ideal role models for their children continues today, but against a very changed constitutional-law background. The lower federal courts especially have interpreted several Supreme Court opinions as extending to public school teachers a presumptive constitutional right of privacy—a right to be free from regulations that intrude upon a variety of personal choices and behaviors. Whether this protection will be further extended, or, in fact, reduced in the wake of a more conservative mood in the country, remains to be seen.

We begin our review of the case law in this area with several nonschool Supreme Court opinions that started the movement toward protection of the personal freedom and life style of teachers. In 1965, relying on the due process clause of the fourteenth amendment, the Supreme Court struck down a Connecticut state law that made it a crime to use any drug or instrument to prevent contraception.[45] The Court reached this conclusion despite the fact there is no provision in the Constitution expressly protecting a right of privacy in matters of reproduction. Nevertheless, the majority concluded that the due process clause, as well as other amendments to the Constitution, implicitly embodied a right of privacy that was "fundamental" and could not be invaded by government by means that sweep unnecessarily broadly. In subsequent cases the Court expanded its protection of matters of personal choice. Thus, in 1969 the Court struck down a statute that punished the possession of obscene films in the privacy of one's home.[46] In 1973 the Court expanded the notion of the right of privacy to include a woman's decision whether or not to terminate her pregnancy by means of an abortion.[47]

One year later the Court invalidated school regulations that required pregnant teachers to take a leave of absence at least four months before the expected birth, and to remain on leave for several months after giving birth.[48] The decision, said the Court, whether to bear or beget a child was a fundamental right that had to be left free of unwarranted restrictions. The Court rejected the district's argument that all teachers five months pregnant could be presumed to be unfit to teach, that the mandatory leave requirement helped to assure continuity in the teaching staff (the Court concluded the rule produced incontinuity), and the rule was necessary to protect the health of the teacher and the fetus. (The Court left the door open to a board-required individualized determination by the teacher's doctor of whether the teacher was able to continue at her job). The requirement that a teacher remain away from teaching until the child was three months old was also struck down as an unnecessary penalty of the teacher's right to bear children. The Court did uphold a rule making a teacher eligible for reemployment upon submission of a medical certificate from her physician and guaranteeing return to work no later than the beginning of the next school year following the termination of eligibility.

In 1977 and 1978 the Court further defined the right to privacy to include choices concerning family living relationships and the decision to marry.[49]

Two related points have emerged from these cases. First, the Court has recognized a new right to privacy, but has not specifically defined that right, has not sketched its scope or what behaviors it protects. Of course, we do know that the use of contraception, the decision whether or not to have an abortion, etc., fall within the notion of a right to privacy. Second, the Court developed an approach, a way of dealing with constitutional claims that assert a right of privacy for which there is no clearly settled precedent. This approach requires the court, first, to decide if the regulated behavior should be viewed as falling within the protections of the notion of the right to privacy—no easy task for the lower courts given the paucity of precedent from the Supreme Court and the absence of a specified technique for resolving this problem. Deciding an issue of this sort is much easier if the regulated behavior is the same as, or very similar to, the behavior already declared by the Supreme Court to be properly classified as falling within right of privacy. Assuming the court concludes the regulated behavior is a "fundamental" interest, is part of the notion of a right to privacy, then the state law or policy affecting that interest is presumed unconstitutional and will only be upheld if the state or school board can establish that its rule is "necessary" in order to achieve the realization of a "compelling state interest."[50]

To better understand the use of this test, let's take what would be an unrealistic example today. A board issues a rule prohibiting teachers from marrying. Let's assume Mr. Smith goes to work claiming that the right to marry is a fundamental interest, part of the notion of the right to privacy, and the board's rule improperly infringes on his right. Mr. Smith would have some Supreme Court precedent supporting his claim.[51] If a court agrees, then the burden of persuasion would be placed on the school district to justify its rule by convincing the court the policy was "necessary" to achieve a "compelling state interest." Most likely the school would argue it had a compelling state interest to assure itself a corps of dedicated teachers, that marriage distracted a teacher from his or her devotion to teaching, and that the rule was necessary to assure this dedication. The court *might* agree that dedication to the job was a compelling school interest but conclude that forbidding teachers from marrying was not the only means available to assure the proper degree of dedication, i.e., the rule was not "necessary." Hence, the court would conclude that this rule was unconstitutional.

We now turn to a review of lower court opinions. The discussion will divide the cases into two main categories: (1) sexually related behavior; and (2) other personal life style choices.

Sexually Related Behavior

The lower courts have developed a doctrine that provides some degree of protection for a teacher's decision to live with a person not his or her spouse.[52] However, the teacher will only be protected if the board fails to establish that his or her behavior adversely affects his or her teaching effectiveness. (Such a showing may be possible if the board can establish that sufficient publicity was given to the case to make the teacher's behavior notorious.) Note also that one court has said that the mere appearance of sexual impropriety is not enough to warrant dismissal—the board must establish that in fact the teacher engaged in "sexual misconduct."[53] It should go without saying that teachers can expect no protection from the courts if their even consensual sexual activity involved a student in the school.[54]

Most lower courts that have dealt with the issue have protected unwed pregnant teachers from dismissal.[55] The prevailing line of analysis stresses both the right of the teacher to privacy in sexual matters and the inability of the board to establish that the teacher's mere continued presence in the school would in fact encourage unwed parenthood. The Fifth Circuit has also rejected the proposition that unwed parenthood is prima facie proof of immorality.[56] The Eighth Circuit has hinted that boards might be allowed to remove unwed mothers from the classroom by asking them to take a leave of absence for the remainder of the school term, or by transferring them to a nonteaching position.[57]

As the sexual activity of the teachers becomes more public and more unconventional, the courts offer less protection. Thus, the First Circuit rejected the claim of a teacher that his constitutional right of privacy had been violated when the board dismissed him because he was seen by neighbors undressing and caressing a mannequin in his own backyard.[58] In New Jersey two courts upheld the dismissal of a tenured music teacher who, after fourteen years of satisfactory service as a man, had a sex change operation.[59] In Florida a state court upheld the dismissal of a teacher who had in his own home performed cunnilingus on his nine-year-old step-daughter; the court found this behavior was indirect but sufficient evidence that he was a danger to school children.[60] In another case a court concluded that a teacher who was editor and part-owner of a sexually explicit magazine in which the teacher himself appeared with a partially nude woman was not constitutionally protected from dismissal.[61]

A major unresolved issue is whether homosexuals constitutionally may be prohibited from teaching and/or be dismissed from their teaching positions. The current trend in the decisions suggests that neither the Supreme Court nor the lower federal courts will soon recognize a constitutional right not to be dismissed because of sexual preference. In *Bowers v. Hardwick* the Supreme Court held that homosexuals did not have a fundamental constitutional right to engage in consensual sodomy.[62] Several federal circuit courts of appeal have upheld the authority of the armed forces to discharge servicemen for homosexual conduct.[63]

Most significant is the refusal of the courts to interpret the Supreme Court's contraception and abortion decisions as embracing principles broad enough to encompass a right to engage in homosexual conduct. In 1984 the Tenth Circuit upheld a statute that permitted a teacher to be dismissed for engaging in "*public* homosexual activity*," while striking down that portion of the statute that permitted punishment for "advocating . . . public or private homosexual activity in a manner that creates a substantial risk that such conduct will come to the attention of school children or school employees."[64] The Sixth Circuit has upheld the dismissal of a teacher who had informed a school secretary, the assistant principal and several teachers that she was bisexual and had a female lover.[65] The central issue of whether a teacher could be dismissed for her sexual preferences was sidestepped since the case was litigated on the narrower question of whether a teacher could be dismissed on the basis of discussing her personal sex life with other employees. On this point the court concluded that the teacher had no first amendment claim because her sex life was not a matter of public concern,[66] and that there was no proof she had been treated differently from the way heterosexual teachers would have been treated if they had made their personal sexual preferences the topic of comment and discussion in the school. Thus, the central constitutional issue of whether, merely because of sexual preference, the mere nondisruptive expression of sexual preference, or private homosexual activity, a teacher may be dismissed remains unresolved.[67] In another case a court upheld the dismissal of a teacher who lied on his application form about his sexual preference.[68]

As for state statutory law and the dismissal of teachers for their sexual preferences, the Supreme Court of Washington has held that a homosexual teacher may be dismissed for immorality under state law.[69] The California Supreme Court concluded that a single homosexual experience did not establish that a teacher was unfit to teach, therefore it overturned the revocation of the teacher's teaching certificate.[70]

Other Personal Life Style Choices

In addition to choices relating to sex and procreation, shaping one's personal life style includes a multitude of other decisions touching on a wide range of matters, such as the use of drugs, where one lives, and how one dresses. As might be expected, school boards have had definite views on these matters and have attempted to impose those views on their employees. As also might be expected, teachers have gone to court claiming the boards' policies violate teacher rights to privacy and liberty. Teachers have been most successful challenging board policies based simply on disapproval of a teacher's personal out-of-school life style. Thus, failure to rehire a teacher because she was involved in a divorce was held to violate the teacher's freedom of personal choice in matters of marriage and family life.[71] The Tenth Circuit protected a teacher living in a predominantly Mormon community in Wyoming from dismissal merely because she was obese, failed to attend church, played cards, and was rumored to be having an affair.[72]

Among the more difficult cases courts have had to face are those in which school personnel have been dismissed for sending their children to private schools. The right of a parent to send his or her child to private school has been given constitutional protection by the Supreme Court,[73] yet a plausible case can be made that in certain circumstances when teachers send their children to private schools their choice has a unique impact upon the public school, different from that which occurs when other parents choose the private education alternative. The Fifth Circuit confronted the issue twice. In *Cook v. Hudson*[74] the court upheld the nonrenewal of the plaintiff's teaching contract because she sent her children to an all-white private school in face of court orders to desegregate the public schools. One judge simply held that those seeking employment in public schools have no right to do so on their own terms. The other judge in the majority stressed that the decision not to rehire was justified by the desire of the public schools to strengthen local support for the court-ordered requirement to desegregate. Eight years later the Fifth Circuit arrived at a more coherent position when it ruled that a cafeteria worker could only be dismissed for sending her child to a private school if the school district could establish that the enrollment of the child in the private school materially and substantially interfered with the operation or effectiveness of the public school program.[75]

The Fifth Circuit also concluded that a teacher's decision to arrange to breast-feed her child in school enjoyed constitutional protection.[76] The court recognized the district had important interests in avoiding distraction and disruption, and avoiding potential liability for accidents, but the court said the regulation forbidding teachers from bringing their children to school had to be examined to determine whether it was sufficiently narrowly drawn to avoid unnecessary infringement of the teacher's right. The possibilities of the problems the district feared arising in this case were minimal since prior to adoption of the rule the teacher had arranged to have her child delivered to her in school during her duty-free hour, at which time in a private, locked room she breast-fed her baby.

Other matters of personal life style have not met with such favorable treatment, even from the Fifth Circuit. That same circuit concluded that a school policy against moonlighting had been applied only to bar substantial outside employment; hence the policy was constitutional as reasonably related to the legitimate state interest in ensuring that teachers devoted their professional energies to the education of children.[77] It is also clear that school districts infringe no constitutional right of teachers by requiring them to live in the district after employment.[78] A requirement of residency of a given duration prior to employment would, however, infringe the right to interstate travel.[79]

Few decisions are more visibly and intimately connected with a person's choice of life style than one's decision as to how to dress and groom oneself. Nevertheless, the trend in the opinions has been to permit public employers to regulate the dress and hairstyles of their employees. In *Kelley v. Johnson,*[80] a case involving police department hair-grooming regulations, the Court made clear that one's hairstyle preference was not a fundamental interest deserving of strong judicial protection. Thus, the appropriate test to be applied in these cases is one that states that the regulation will only be declared to be unconstitutional if the complaining teacher can establish it is so irrational as to be arbitrary. Most lower court decisions rendered before and after the decision in *Kelley* are consistent with this approach and have concluded that school dress and grooming regulations are rationally related to the school board's purpose of encouraging respect for authority, traditional values, discipline in the classroom, and good grooming.[81] A different result might hold with regard to the hair regulations of institutions of higher education,[82] or with regard to school employees that are not perceived as occupying positions in which they are expected to be role models for pupils.[83]

The judicial response to the dismissal of teachers involved in criminal activities has varied. In one case a teacher's dismissal was upheld after the teacher, in legal papers filed in a court proceeding on behalf of a friend, attacked antimarijuana laws and admitted using marijuana daily for twenty years.[84] According to the court, the open admission of a continuing violation of law with which he personally disagreed carried a message to the students that law breaking was permissible; this was evidence of the teacher's lack of competence to teach. In another case, a teacher actually convicted of cultivating a marijuana plant kept his job because it appeared the teacher would not repeat his crime, and that his return to the classroom would not have a negative effect on the classroom.[85] Thus, it appears that today's decisions determining whether commission of a crime is grounds for dismissal under state law makes schools focus on the question whether the crime will affect the teacher's performance in the classroom.[86] Whether this interpretation of state statutes is constitutionally required is a matter of debate. At least this much is certain: the courts have rejected the bald claim that the private use of marijuana is a constitutionally protected right.[87]

An important unresolved issue in the area of privacy rights of teachers is the question whether it is the teacher who has the burden of proof that he or she remains a valuable teacher (is fit to teach) despite the out-of-school behavior, or whether it is the district that must prove disruption and an impairment of the teacher's effectiveness.[88]

9.7. EMPLOYMENT DISCRIMINATION: AN INTRODUCTION

The extensive and intensive effort by the federal judiciary, Congress, and the executive branch of the federal government to end discrimination against students has been matched by an equal effort to end discrimination in employment. The resulting body of law is complex, involving constitutional doctrine and numerous statutes touching on discrimination on the basis of race, gender, handicap, age, and religion. Adding to the complexity are numerous state laws modeled after the federal laws and, in some instances, providing more protection against employment discrimination than the federal laws.[89]

Several points about this body of law are worth noting at the outset. First, constitutional doctrine has taken, in some important respects, a direction different from statutory doctrine dealing with the same problems. Second, though there is considerable similarity in the doctrines dealing with the different forms of discrimination, there are important differences. Most particularly, the allocation and nature of the burden of proof vary from area to area. Third, in applying these statutes to educational institutions, the courts have been sensitive to the fact that educational institutions are different in relevant aspects from other employers and, accordingly, the courts have modified generally applicable doctrines to take these differences into account. Last, employment discrimination law has been among the most sensitive political issues, as different groups argue that the law either insufficiently protects or overprotects the employee to the detriment of the efficiency of the employer. The crucial issue in this debate is the law's allocation of the burden of proof between employer and employee. Thus, describing how the law allocates the burden of production of the evidence and the burden of persuasion is a central purpose of the following sections.

It should be noted that the materials to follow are highly selective in two important respects: No analysis is provided of the many state laws dealing with employment discrimination; and, many employment discrimination issues that do not commonly arise in the field of education are not discussed, e.g., assignment of "light" work to women and "heavy" work to men.

9.8. GENDER DISCRIMINATION AND THE CONSTITUTION

Constitutional doctrine deals with two forms of gender discrimination: (1) policies that expressly treat males and females differently for reasons the employer claims are legitimate, and (2) policies that affect males and females differently and that are based on illegitimate discriminatory attitudes toward males or females and that are kept secret and denied. The Constitution does not make illegal policies that simply have a discriminatory impact on males and females. We turn first to cases of express gender discrimination.

During the course of the twentieth century, the Supreme Court's application of the fourteenth amendment to expressly stated gender classifications has varied. (What constitutes an expressly stated gender discrimination is a subject that itself has generated considerable controversy.)[90] Until the 1970s the Court relied on the supposed dependence and physical weakness of women to uphold legislation that would have been struck down as unconstitutional if it had been directed toward men.[91] In upholding this legislation the Court used the most lenient of the tests—the rational-basis test (see §3.1). Thus, the Court imposed upon the plaintiff the task of persuading the judiciary that the differences in treatment were not rationally related to any legitimate purpose. Then, beginning in the 1970s, the Court made a dramatic shift that culminated in the holding that classifications based on gender, like those based on race, are "inherently suspect" and therefore must be subject to the closest judicial scrutiny.[92] The use of that test in gender discrimination cases (under that test it is government that has the burden of establishing that the difference in treatment based on the gender of the person is necessary to achieve a compelling state interest) was short-lived. In 1976 the Court backed away from equating racial and gender discrimination and adopted an intermediate test for use in gender discrimination cases. This latest test imposes on government the burden of persuading a court that a classification is substantially related to an important governmental objective.[93] Thus, in order for a policy of assigning only males and females to teach, respectively, the boys' and girls' physical education classes to be upheld, the government must establish that its job assignment policy is substantially related to an important governmental purpose. Perhaps because plaintiffs know the courts are reluctant to make constitutional decisions when a case can be resolved on the basis of a statute, litigants have not pressed constitutional challenges to gender discrimination in employment.[94]

We turn now to the second kind of case. For there to be a constitutional claim the plaintiff must establish that, although the employer has not openly acknowledged treating male and female differently, it has in fact based policy on considerations of gender. That is, the plaintiff must prove that the difference in treatment was a form of purposeful gender discrimination, and not merely an accidental by-product of a policy based on other considerations.[95] Stated differently, the plaintiff must establish that the school board adopted the policy because of its adverse impact upon one gender and not in spite of that impact. If the plaintiff is able to make out the prima facie case, then the burden shifts to the employer to establish that the "same decision" would have been reached even if the impermissible purpose had not been considered.[96] Perhaps because the initial burden on the plaintiff is arguably more difficult to meet than the burden imposed upon plaintiffs making a "disparate treatment" claim under Title VII of the Civil Rights Act of 1964, most gender discrimination suits in employment have been brought under the statute.[97] Thus, it is to an examination of the statutory law that we now turn.

9.9. TITLE VII AND GENDER DISCRIMINATION IN EMPLOYMENT

Title VII of the Civil Rights Act of 1964[98] forbids discrimination in public and private employment on the basis of sex as well as race, color, religion, or origin. The act also specifically forbids discrimination against employees opposed to practices made unlawful by Title VII or because the employee filed a suit charging the employer with discrimination, or because the employee otherwise participated in an investigation or proceeding dealing with employer discrimination.[99] The statute permits an employer to defend gender discrimination in *hiring* if gender is a bona fide occupational qualification (BFOQ). (The BFOQ defense is not available as a defense in cases charging discrimination in employment based on race.) The statute also permits employers to use ability tests and to discriminate on the basis of a bona fide seniority system if neither is intended to be used to discriminate on the basis of gender. The statute specifically says the employer will not be required to grant preferential treatment on the basis of sex (or race) because of any imbalance in the work force. However, affirmative action may be ordered by the courts as a remedy for illegal discrimination.

The federal agency charged with enforcing Title VII is the Equal Employment Opportunity Commission (EEOC), and it is to this commission and the relevant state fair-employment agency that an employee must first turn to file a complaint. Once a charge has been filed with the EEOC, the commission has exclusive jurisdiction of the case for up to 180 days. During that time the EEOC may investigate the charges to determine if there is reasonable cause to believe that the statute has been violated. If it appears Title VII has been violated, the EEOC must try to eliminate the practice by "conference, conciliation and persuasion." If after 30 days from filing of the charge conciliation has not worked, the EEOC may file a complaint in federal court; or if the employer is a state or local government the matter is referred to the attorney general for possible judicial action. If the EEOC chooses not to sue, the claimant will be notified of his or her right to bring private legal action in court. Also, if the EEOC proceedings are not completed within 180 days, the charging party may seek a letter to sue from the EEOC; this letter is granted as a matter of course and the claimant may go to federal court with a private suit. Appeals are possible from the federal district court opinion, but the reviewing court may only overturn the decision of the district court if the decision was "clearly erroneous."[100]

To better understand Title VII it is important to divide the gender discrimination cases into several categories: disparate treatment cases; pattern and practice cases; and disparate impact cases. Each kind of case will be briefly discussed.

In disparate treatment cases the employer is charged with treating some people less favorably than others because of their gender (or race, color, religion, or national origin).[101] Now these disparate treatment cases can themselves be subdivided into several categories. In some cases the difference in treatment is expressly and openly acknowledged by the employer, e.g., the employer insists on hiring a female guidance counselor to assure that a woman is available for female students who would be embarrassed to confide in a male counselor.[102] Naturally, there is no issue in these cases of whether gender is being used to discriminate; the real issue is whether the employer has an adequate defense for the difference in treatment, i.e., whether gender is a BFOQ. The more frequent occurrence in education is that the employer denies making a gender-based decision; thus, the crucial issue becomes whether the employer did in fact act on the basis of a discriminatory motive. There are two ways for the plaintiff to establish this point: either by direct evidence or by a complex method of indirect proof.

With regard to the disparate treatment-overt discrimination cases, the Supreme Court has said the BFOQ defense is "a narrow exception to the general prohibition of discrimination on the basis of sex."[103] As the Eleventh Circuit has put it, the BFOQ defense is "available only when the employer can show that the excluded class is unable to perform the duties that Title VII defines as 'necessary to the normal operation of the particular business or enterprises.'"[104] Thus, the Third Circuit ruled that the University of Pennsylvania should be permitted to attempt to establish that being female was a BFOQ for a job as night-time security officer.[105] The court was convinced by the university's argument that the requirement for a female officer was prompted by the needs of rape victims to have a female participate in the investigation of the rape charge. Recall that the BFOQ defense is not available for nonhiring decisions.

The Supreme Court has said that employers are not permitted to defend express discrimination on the basis of gender in nonhiring policies on the grounds of cost savings. Thus, the Court has said it is a violation of Title VII to require female employees to make larger contributions to pension funds than male employees on the grounds that women as a group tend to live longer than men, i.e., there is a difference in cost in providing pension benefits to males and females.[106]

We move now from the overt to the covert use of gender as a basis for decisions. As noted, covert reliance upon an improper discriminatory purpose by an employer can be established by direct evidence. That is, the plaintiff can meet his or her initial burden and win the case by persuading a court with direct evidence that a discriminatory reason motivated the employer.[107] Direct evidence consists of statements from school officials indicating they based their decisions on considerations of gender. For example, a strong inference of an improper motive was raised when Carmen Rodriguez, an art teacher, was transferred from a junior high school to an elementary school despite the fact two male junior high teachers had fewer credentials, and one was less senior than Rodriguez. The direct evidence supporting the inference of gender discrimination was a comment from a female school principal that, "They wouldn't have a male grade school teacher."[108] The Eleventh Circuit has issued its own, apparently unique ruling. That court has held that where a prima facie case for discrimination is proved by direct evidence, and the trier of fact is convinced that the ultimate issue of improper motivation has been proven, then the only rebuttal allowed to the employer is proof by a preponderance of the evidence that the "same decision" would have been reached even absent the improper factor.[109]

In the absence of direct evidence of an improper motive, the plaintiff, in order to win, must persuade the court by using an indirect method of proof. The First Circuit characterized the indirect method as follows: "[T]he best way of proving a bad reason being to show the incorrectness of the claimed good one."[110] The Supreme Court stated it this way: The plaintiff may succeed by "showing the employer's proffered explanation is unworthy of credence."[111] Thus, by merely showing that the employer's explanation of his or her actions is not credible, the plaintiff establishes that an improper motive was at work.

The Supreme Court has developed a method by which the plaintiff can discredit the employer's explanation.[112] First, with a preponderance of the evidence the plaintiff must make out a prima facie case of discrimination. For example, in a hiring case the plaintiff needs to establish that (1) she applied for an available position; (2) she met the qualifications for the position; (3) that despite the qualifications she was rejected; (4) that after the rejection the job remained open and the employer continued to seek applicants from persons of complainant's background; and (5) that a male was hired with the same qualifications. The burden of establishing a prima facie case "is not onerous." If the plaintiff has made out a prima facie case an inference of discrimination is raised, i.e., it is presumed the employer unlawfully discriminated. If the employer is silent in the face of this presumption, the court must enter a judgment for the plaintiff. The employer must be given an opportunity to rebut the inference of improper conduct. Thus, second, the burden shifts to the employer to articulate a legitimate, nondiscriminatory reason for the employment decision. The employer need not persuade the court that it was in fact motivated by the proffered reason—the employer need produce admissible evidence that would allow the trier of fact to conclude the employment decision was not motivated by an improper purpose. In addition, the employer must present its case with sufficient clarity so that the plaintiff has a full and fair opportunity to demonstrate the employer's argument is pretextual. In this way an issue of fact is raised, and because the ultimate burden of persuasion rests with the plaintiff, the plaintiff must now prove by a preponderance of the evidence that the legitimate reasons offered by defendant was not the true reason, but was a pretext for discrimination.

Several comments on the use of this basic framework are in order. First, a variety of pieces of evidence can be used by the plaintiff to make out her prima facie case. Proof of the use of vague and subjective criteria in hiring and promotions is suggestive of a discriminatory motive.[113] The use of a double standard is another especially strong piece of evidence of discrimination.[114] The weakness of the reasons offered by the employer for not promoting an employee may also be argued.[115] The fact that primarily men are involved in making employment decisions is also supportive of an improper motive.[116] The Ninth Circuit, in a higher education case involving the denial of a merit increase and tenure, said that, "A disdain for women's issues, and a diminished opinion of those who concentrate on those issues, is evidence of a discriminatory attitude towards women."[117] Statistical evidence tending to establish a pattern of discrimination can be used to bolster the case of individual disparate treatment.[118] Second, in individual disparate treatment cases the qualifications of the plaintiff compared to the person who got the job or who was promoted is frequently an important issue. The courts have been reluctant to discount the judgments of school officials that the plaintiff was less qualified than the applicant who got the job.[119] In particular, the courts have been willing to let educational institutions determine whether a particular credential is or is not a necessary requirement for a job.[120]

Third, most courts have proven to be particularly reluctant to intrude on tenure decisions. As the Tenth Circuit Court of Appeals wrote, "School districts are given wide latitude in discretion concerning whom to award tenure."[121] "We are mindful that tenure decisions in an academic setting involve a combination of factors which tend to set them apart from employment decisions in general."[122] The Second Circuit has noted that, "Where the tenure file contains the conflicting views of specialized scholars, triers of fact cannot hope to master the academic field sufficiently to review the merits of such views and resolve the differences of scholarly opinion. . . . Finally, statements of peer judgments as to departmental needs, collegial relationships and individual merit may not be disregarded absent evidence that they are a facade for discrimination."[123] The court continued, "Given the elusive nature of tenure decisions, we believe that a prima facie case that a member of a protected class is qualified for tenure is made out by a showing that some significant portion of the departmental faculty, referrants, or other scholars in the particular field hold a favorable view on the question."[124] The court added that for the plaintiff to succeed, "more [was needed] than a denial of tenure in the context of disagreement about the scholarly merits of the candidate's academic work, the candidate's teaching ability, or the academic needs of the department or university."[125] Absent such evidence of an improper motive, "universities are free to establish departmental priorities, to set their own required levels of academic potential and achievement and to act upon the good faith judgments of their departmental faculties or reviewing authorities." The Seventh Circuit was especially frank. While stressing that it was permissible to compare the decision made in the claimant's case against a tenure decision made as regards the promotion of a male professor to determine pretextuality, it was not the judiciary's job to decide the tenure decision *de novo*.[126] Further, the court stressed that it could not question the validity of the conclusion of an experienced faculty committee that a particular candidate lacked sufficient academic potential. "[W]inning the esteem of one's colleagues is just an essential part of securing tenure. And that seems to mean that in a case of this sort, where it is a matter of comparing qualification against qualification, the plaintiff is bound to lose."[127]

Claims of retaliatory discharge are a type of disparate treatment case, but the framework for analyzing these cases is somewhat different. The Fifth Circuit has held that the claimant must "'establish a prima facie case of retaliation by showing (1) that she had engaged in an activity protected by Title VII; (2) that an adverse employment action occurred; and (3) that there was a causal connection between the participation in the protected activity and the adverse employment decision.'"[128] The employer then has the burden of producing evidence of legitimate nondiscriminatory reasons for the adverse employment decision. If the employer satisfies this burden, the claimant must prove that the proffered reason was a pretext for retaliation, i.e., the plaintiff must establish that the "but for" cause of the adverse employment decision was a motive to take retaliatory action.

We turn now from the individual disparate treatment case to the pattern and practice type of disparate treatment case. As with the case of individual discrimination, the plaintiff (who may be a class of individuals or the Attorney General of the United States who is authorized by statute to bring suit when he or she has reasonable cause to believe an employer is engaged in a pattern or practice of resistance to Title VII)[129] must establish an intent to discriminate, but now the plaintiffs are a class of people who must establish by a preponderance of the evidence that the employer engaged in a pattern or practice of unlawful discrimination, that "discrimination was the [employer's] standard operating procedure—the regular rather than the unusual practice."[130] The basic method of proof in these cases is through the mounting of statistical evidence that seeks to establish that it is not a matter of chance that, for example, women are paid less than males, are underrepresented in the tenure ranks.[131] The statistical evidence may also be supplemented with nonstatistical evidence, e.g., the testimony of individuals who claim they were discriminated against. The plaintiff need not establish that each person for whom it will ultimately receive relief was a victim of the discriminatory policy.[132] Given that this is the method of proof, the Supreme Court has observed that it is possible that a plaintiff will be unable to prove that a pattern or practice of discrimination exists "even though discrimination against one or two individuals has been proved."[133] It also follows that the employer's basic response to the plaintiff's claim must be to attack the statistical case made by the plaintiff, i.e., the employer can argue the data base used was flawed in some way, that it made too few employment decisions to justify an inference of a regular practice of discrimination, and/or the statistical methodology used was flawed, that the assumptions relied on in compiling and analyzing the data were wrong, and present its own statistical counterargument.[134] Employers may also seek to rebut the plaintiff's statistical case with nonstatistical evidence, e.g., evidence of an employer affirmative action plan. In one interesting case Sears Roebuck & Company successfully rebutted the statistical case made by the EEOC by attacking the assumption used by the EEOC that men and women were equally interested in the kinds of positions with regard to which EEOC charged Sears was discriminating.[135] Sears relied on the testimony of its own store employees, national survey evidence, and the testimony of an expert witness, Dr. Rosalind Rosenberg, who testified that men and women did have different job preferences.[136]

Failure to rebut the plaintiff's statistical case means the trial court can conclude a violation has occurred.[137] This battle of statistical presentations is best carried out, several courts have noted, without reliance on the complex burden-switching approach used in the individual disparate treatment cases.[138] But note: additional proceedings are ordinarily required to determine what relief individual members of the class will receive.

It is also the case that the statistically proven case can have a bearing on an individual disparate treatment claim also made as part of the same case. Proof of classwide discrimination can raise a presumption that specific employment decisions were the product of an unlawful reason.[139] "The finding of a prohibited pattern or practice transmogrifies the employer from a presumptively innocent litigant whose liability, though alleged, is not yet established to be a 'proved wrongdoer.'"[140] At the same time, failure to prove a discriminatory company-wide policy does not preclude proving that there was discrimination against one or two individuals. In fact, the conclusion of a court that the employer did not engage in a pattern or practice of discrimination does not bar individual employees from raising disparate treatment suits.[141]

Again, it is interesting to note how some courts have modified their usual approach to pattern and practice cases when it is a university that has been charged with discrimination. The Second Circuit has written that "generalized statistical data may be less persuasive evidence of discrimination where an employer hires 'highly educated, specially qualified people' . . . on a decentralized basis than where the positions in question involve general skills and a central office does the hiring. . . . Where uncoordinated and independent decisions are made by different persons, statistics as to hiring by the overall entity may be less significant in demonstrating bias than where a single office makes all employment decisions."[142]

From the disparate treatment cases, we turn to the disparate impact case. The Supreme Court has distinguished the disparate treatment case from the disparate impact case in the following way: "The latter involve employment practices that are facially neutral in their treatment of different groups but that in fact fall more harshly on one group than another and cannot be justified by business necessity. Proof of discriminatory motive, we have held, is not required under a disparate impact theory."[143] One month after the Court wrote these words it elaborated further upon the disparate impact case.[144] The plaintiff, said the Court, to make out a prima facie case of discrimination need only show that the facially neutral standards selected applicants in a significantly discriminatory pattern. Once this discriminatory effect has been established, the employer must show that the requirement has a manifest relationship to the employment in question. If the employer meets this burden, then the plaintiff may show that other selection devices or criteria that do not have a similar discriminatory effect would also serve the employer's legitimate purpose.[145] In the case in which the Court provided this elaboration, a female plaintiff challenged the state's height and weight requirements for all law enforcement officers. The Court agreed with the plaintiff that these blanket requirements had a discriminatory impact on women, and that the state failed to provide any evidence substantiating that these requirements were essential to effective job performance as a correctional counselor in a state prison.

The significance of this line of attack is that it may be used to challenge any number of employment requirements—degree requirements, job hiring and promotion procedures generally,[146] employment tests and systems for determining the pay of employees.[147] The nature of this kind of challenge can be illustrated by the claim made in one case that the requirement of a master's degree in library science from an accredited school had a discriminatory impact on women and was not justified as a business necessity.[148] The court disagreed, saying that even if the plaintiff could make out a prima facie case of disparate impact, the degree requirement was a justified business necessity. The degree was a useful, objective way to screen potential employees to insure they have appropriate knowledge. There was also testimony that accredited degree holders exhibited superior reliability and dependability. Any other approach to screening applicants would impose an unreasonable burden on the university. The court also noted that about 80 percent of all other colleges and universities established this as a requirement. In another case a court ruled that the coupling of two jobs— biology teacher and assistant football coach—as one job had a discriminatory impact upon women applicants that was not justified by business necessity.[149]

The disparate impact theory may only apply to specific neutral policies of employers and not to, for example, hiring and promotion processes that are subjective in nature.[150] Claims of bias in the operation of such hiring and promotion systems must be addressed with a different theory, e.g., disparate treatment.

9.10. EQUAL PAY AND COMPARABLE WORTH; PREGNANCY; SEXUAL HARASSMENT; TITLE IX

Title VII is a broad statute that covers discrimination with regard to a wide range of employment practices, e.g., hiring, promotions, sexual harassment, and it shares with the Equal Pay Act[151] the job of prohibiting discrimination in pay. The relationship between Title VII an the Equal Pay Act is, however, complex.

The Equal Pay Act is violated when unequal wages are paid for "equal work on jobs the performance of which requires equal skill, effort, and responsibility and which are performed under similar work conditions."[152] Note that the stress here is on the fact that the *jobs* have a comparable content, involve a comparable kind of set of activities.[153] A difference in pay, however, can be justified in terms of four defenses: a seniority system, a merit system, a system that measures pay by quality and quantity of production, or any other factor not based on sex.[154] In determining what is "equal work," the Supreme

Court has accepted the view that differences in pay for work that is "substantially equal"—as opposed to work that is identical—violates the act.[155] Thus, in each Equal Pay Act case the central question is whether the jobs are substantially equal in terms of skill, effort, and responsibility and in terms of the working conditions under which the job is performed. The burden of proving substantial equality rests with the plaintiff.[156] Actual job performance and content, rather than job descriptions, titles, or classifications, are determinative; hence jobs from different academic disciplines can be established to be substantially equal.[157] For example, in comparing the jobs of female and male coaches, the courts look into such matters as the length of the work year, responsibility for recruiting, and responsibility for producing revenue for the school in the forms of scholarship contributions and season-ticket purchases.[158] Under the Equal Pay Act the plaintiff need not directly prove an intent to discriminate. The burden of persuasion shifts to the defendant after the plaintiff has shown that the employer pays workers of one sex more than workers of the other sex for equal work. The employer then bears the burden of persuading a court that the difference in pay is justified under one of the four exceptions specified in the act.[159]

A plaintiff suing under Title VII need not meet the substantially equal standard of the Equal Pay Act.[160] (However, the four defenses available under the Equal Pay Act are also available under Title VII.)[161] Before discussing the significance of this difference between Title VII and the Equal Pay Act, it should be noted that Title VII will support, as discussed above, both disparate treatment (both the individual and pattern and practice types) and disparate impact challenges to wage differentials.[162] As might be expected, statistical evidence typically plays a crucial evidentiary role in these cases.[163]

The fact that the plaintiff bringing a Title VII suit need not meet the "substantially equal" standard opens the door to the comparable worth suit. In essence, the "comparable worth theory" holds that men, women, and minorities must be paid equally for jobs that are of comparable value to the employer. Thus, it does not matter if the jobs require different tasks, so long as the jobs are of comparable value to the employer. Although the content of the jobs, their tasks, may be different, e.g., school secretary versus school janitor, they may be of comparable worth to the employer as measured by such criteria as required knowledge and skills, mental demands, accountability, and working conditions.[164] The major social significance of this approach is that wage differences between classifications of jobs traditionally held by females and males may be attacked even if the employer simply set the wages paid the two groups of workers according to market prices. The theory is obviously controversial insofar as it rejects the market as the basis for determining wages and instead places wage determination in the hands of whomever is given the task of determining whether two classifications of jobs are of equal worth to the employer. Those who accept the theory argue that it is necessary to eliminate wage discrimination because the market has improperly undervalued the work women have traditionally done. Whether Title VII requires an employer to ignore the wage, for example, secretaries or nurses or truck drivers command in the market has not been settled by the Supreme Court,[165] but the Ninth Circuit has held that reliance by the employer upon the competitive market for setting wages does not violate Title VII.[166]

Turning now to employer policies that distinguish between pregnancy-related and other disabilities, Title VII specifically prohibits discrimination based on pregnancy, childbirth, or related medical conditions.[167] In other words, pregnancy-related disabilities must be treated the same way as any other disability under any health or disability insurance or sick leave plan.[168] Other fringe benefits, such as retirement plans, must also be provided on a gender-neutral basis; thus women cannot be asked to contribute more to a retirement plan or receive less by way of payments merely because as a group they live longer than men.[169]

Harassment on the basis of sex also violates Title VII. The regulations implementing Title VII define sexual harassment as follows:

> Unwelcome sexual advances, requests for sexual favors, and other verbal or physical conduct of a sexual nature constitutes sexual harassment when (1) submission to such conduct is made either explicitly or implicitly a term or condition of an individual's employment, (2) submission to or rejection of such conduct by an individual is used as the basis for employment decisions affecting such individual, or (3) such conduct has the purpose or effect of unreasonably interfering with an individual's work performance or creating an intimidating, hostile, or offensive working environment.[170]

According to the regulations, an employer is responsible for sexual harassment by supervisors "regardless of whether the specific acts complained of were authorized or even forbidden by the employer,"[171] As for sexual harassment between employees, according to the EEOC the employer is responsible if it "knows or should have known of the conduct, unless it can show that it took immediate and appropriate corrective action."[172] Not surprisingly, school districts have the authority to dismiss for incompetence administrators who themselves sexually harass teachers and, perhaps, even for their failure to stop sexual harassment by others.[173]

There are two different forms of sexual harassment. One category, quid pro quo harassment, is harassment in which an employee is forced to choose between providing sexual favors in exchange for job benefits, continued employment, or promotion.[174] Proving this form of harassment can be accomplished following the disparate treatment framework (see §9.9).[175] The second category involves claims that the female employees are subjected to a sexually intimidating, hostile, or offensive working environment.[176] At the heart of this category of case is the claim that as a woman she should not have to tolerate a sexually abusive environment in order to earn a living. The prevailing view among the courts is that the disparate treatment framework is not applicable to this kind of case.[177] But proof of the existence of a sexually abusive environment can be established by proof of sexually stereotypical insults, demeaning propositions, or unwanted touching that poison the psychological and work environment. To help support her case, the claimant may also elicit from other women testimony that they also were subjected to similar treatment.[178] Proof of the existence of such an environment can be rebutted by proof that the incidents complained about were isolated or trivial.[179] Thus, while the courts have protected women from sustained and systematic efforts by male employees to humiliate female employees with sexual requests and comments,[180] they also have said that an environment characterized by vulgar language and the occasional display of posters of naked women did not amount to the kind of environment that interferes with work performance, or that creates an intimidating, hostile, or offensive working environment.[181] The courts have said that homosexual advances are covered by Title VII.[182] Although some courts have followed the guidelines as to when the employer is liable for offensive conduct by supervisors and employees,[183] other courts have taken a different approach. The Ninth Circuit seems to take the position the employer is strictly liable for all sexual harassment by its employees,[184] but the Eleventh Circuit has said employers are strictly liable for quid pro quo harassment but only directly liable for other forms of harassment.[185]

Employees in education programs might also turn to Title IX,[186] which prohibits discrimination in programs receiving federal financial assistance, to obtain relief from employment discrimination.[187] The courts have placed a variety of obstacles in the way of using this statute. First, the Supreme Court said that Title IX only applies to the particular program in an educational institution receiving federal funds,[188] thus lower courts have, for example, refused to let a physical education instructor use Title IX because the physical education division in the school received no federal funds.[189] Another court said that Title IX should not be used to seek money damages when Title VII was available.[190]

9.11. RACIAL DISCRIMINATION IN EMPLOYMENT AND THE CONSTITUTION

As discussed in §4.4, a successful racial discrimination suit under the equal protection clause of the fourteenth amendment requires that the plaintiff establish the school purposefully discriminated on the basis of race. (Typically, the plaintiff will be a teacher or class of teachers, but students and their parents may also complain that racial discrimination in employment infringes their rights under the Constitution and the Equal Education Opportunity Act.)[191] One approach for dealing with this problem would be to require the plaintiff to make out a prima facie case of unlawful discrimination and then to permit the defendant to establish that the "same decision" would have been made even had the impermissible purpose not been considered.[192] The Fifth Circuit has said that a constitutionally based claim of purposeful racial discrimination in employment can be established by the indirect method of proof used in Title VII disparate treatment cases.[193] Though the plaintiff was successful in this case, the difficulties in proving intentional racial discrimination are illustrated by *United States v. State of South Carolina*[194] in which it was alleged that the use by South Carolina of the National Teacher Examination violated the equal protection clause because of the disproportionate number of black candidates who failed the exam. (In 1969-70, 41 percent of the graduates of predominantly black colleges and 1 percent of the graduates of predominantly white colleges failed to achieve the required score.) The court ruled that intentional discrimination was not proved in the face of the fact that an independent, nonprofit organization of recognized professional reputation (Educational Testing Service) had developed and administered the exam, and there was no proof that the exam itself discriminated on the basis of race. Thus, the mere fact that an employer's policy has a disproportionate adverse impact on one race does not violate the equal protection clause.[195] (A disproportionate impact may, however, violate Titles VI and VII.)[196]

Staff reductions because of the elimination of a number of positions in school districts under court orders to desegregate can lead to the layoff and demotion of minority teachers. To assure court-orderd desegregation (as opposed to voluntary desegregation) is done in a nondiscriminatory manner, the Fifth Circuit Court of Appeals laid down criteria—now generally accepted—to guide the movement from a dual to a unitary school system.[197] The *Singleton* criteria require that (1) race must not be a factor in hiring, assignment, promotion, demotion, salary, or dismissal; (2) a reduction in the professional staff must be based on objective and reasonable nondiscriminatory standards; and (3) nonracial objective criteria are to be developed by the school board prior to any reductions. The court also specifically defined a demotion as a reassignment involving less pay, responsibility, or skill than the position previously held, or a transfer to a teaching position for which the teacher is not certified in regard to which he or she does not have substantial experience.[198] If there is a dismissal or demotion, no vacancy may be filled by a person of a different race from that of the individual dismissed or demoted until each displaced and qualified employee has had an opportunity to fill the vacancy and failed to accept such an offer.[199] In working with objective criteria the district should not simply attempt to maintain the same ratio of black-to-white teachers at the time the district was segregated.[200] The need to follow the *Singleton* criteria ends once the district has operated a unitary system for a number of years.[201]

The desegregation of school districts may also involve the reassignment of teachers, and schools may be ordered to assign black and white teachers to schools in a particular ratio in order to achieve a particular degree of faculty desegregation.[202] The use of such ratios is constitutional even if the requirement affects lawful seniority systems.[203]

9.12. TITLE VII AND RACIAL DISCRIMINATION IN EMPLOYMENT

Title VII suits alleging racial discrimination in employment may be grouped into the same disparate treatment and disparate impact categories discussed in §9.9. The discussion of that section will not be repeated here, but instead we shall highlight some of the important differences between gender and racial discrimination cases.

Disparate treatment expressly based on a racial criterion cannot be defended by the employer, unlike the express use of a gender criterion, by reliance on the claim that the race is a BFOQ because Title VII does not recognize the BFOQ defense in cases of an express classification based on race. Thus, whether all-black institutions of higher education may expressly prefer black faculty members remains an interesting question.[204]

As was true in gender cases, an alleged case of individual disparate treatment based on race may be established by either the indirect or direct method of proof. We turn to the most important of these types, the cases involving the indirect method of proof. The application of the four-part test used for dealing with circumstantial evidence in race discrimination cases is the same as in gender discrimination cases.[205] The ultimate burden of persuasion remains on the plaintiff to establish that the employer's proffered reasons for the decision were pretextual. The lower courts have suggested an important modification of this approach. Roughly speaking, in a Title VII suit brought against a district with a recent history of maintaining a segregated school system, the ultimate burden of persuasion lies with the district.[206]

> Although [the usual approach] places only the burden of production on the defendant once a prima facie case is stated, this Court believes that [this approach] was not intended to diminish the burden placed on school systems defending Title VII cases arising in the context of school desegregation where proof of recent racial discrimination is clear. . . . In a Title VII case arising in the context of a school system with a proven record of discrimination, the defendant must rebut the plaintiff's prima facie case with clear and convincing evidence that the challenged employment decisions were motivated by legitimate, nondiscriminatory reasons.[207]

Employers may defend themselves against disparate treatment charges on the ground that their decisions were based on the operation of a bona fide seniority system. Thus, in one case unsuccessful job applicants lost the case when the court ruled that the giving of preference to current employees over external candidates was a seniority system.[208]

Racial pattern and practice cases raise the same problems of statistical proof as posed in the gender cases.[209] Again, if the pattern or practice is established, the ultimate burden of persuasion shifts to the defendant to show, with regard to individual complainants, that the hiring decision was not due to the discriminatory policy but to another legitimate consideration.[210] It is also not uncommon for claimants to charge that the employer's recruitment practices were discriminatory with the result that the ethnic composition of the applicant pool itself was skewed. Defining the relevant labor market, the ethnic composition of which is to be compared to the ethnic composition of the employer's workforce and applicant pool, is a frequently contested issue.[211]

Another common complaint is that the facially neutral policy of the employer has a disproportionate impact on minority applicants or employees. For example, the Supreme Court has said that Title VII is violated by the use of tests that have a disproportionate impact upon minority applicants or employees and that have not been proven, by the employer, to be demonstrably a reasonable measure of job performance.[212] The Supreme Court has not itself established criteria for test validation,[213] but the Court has said that validation does not require a comparison between test performance and job performance—an entry level test could be validated by pointing to success in the training program.[214] Important guidance on the validation of tests, as well as educational requirements, may be found in guidelines—not regulations that would have carried more weight—issued by the Equal Employment Opportunity Commission.[215]

The most significant disparate impact attacks in the field of education have been brought against the use of the National Teacher Examination (NTE) in determining certification, pay levels, and retention of teachers. In North Carolina the State was unable to establish that a score of 950 indicated a certification candidate would be a competent teacher.[216] In another case, however, the court ruled that the use of NTE to certify teachers was permissible since the test had content validity (the test did test the content of the teacher-training programs in South Carolina) and because it was justified as a business necessity. That is, the test was an important method of measuring whether individual students mastered the course content to which they had been exposed, course content that was directly relevant (but not sufficient in itself) to assure competency.[217] Another court granted a preliminary injunction stopping the use of NTE for determining which nontenured teachers would be retained from year to year.[218] A federal district court ruled that the Pre-Professional Skills Test, which was used by Texas as a screening device for entrance into teacher education programs, might not have been adequately validated.[219]

It should also be noted that a majority of the Court has concluded that although Title VI of the Civil Rights Act of 1964[220] does itself reach only instances of intentional racial discrimination, actions that have an unjustifiable disparate impact on minorities might be redressed through federal agency regulations designed to implement Title VI.[221]

Finally, note should be made that racial harassment is also a violation of Title VII.[222]

9.13. AFFIRMATIVE ACTION ON THE BASIS OF RACE AND GENDER

There are few areas of law where the division between the "liberals" and "conservatives" is clearer than as regards affirmative action. Whether one speaks of the law of affirmative action under the fourteenth amendment or Title VII, whether this law is to be applied to judicial orders (including consent decrees) or voluntary affirmative action policies by employers, and whether those judicial orders or voluntary policies deal with hiring, layoffs, promotions, or the grant of retroactive seniority, a sharp division has emerged on the Court. We explore this division by describing in general terms the conservative and liberal approach to affirmative action.[223]

The conservatives on the Court have accepted affirmative action only insofar as needed to rectify discrimination by a particular employer. (Affirmative action can take the form of hiring goals, hiring quotas, the grant of retroactive credit, promotion goals, and promotion quotas. That is, for the conservatives affirmative action in employment may not be used as a form of reparations for past "societal discrimination," as a cure for the unequal social condition blacks or women may find themselves in today, or as a means of serving any other goal (such as assuring that black students will be provided with black role models) except the goal of rectifying specific instances of racial discrimination in employment. The conservatives reject the view that the principle of equality behind either Title VII or the fourteenth amendment is to be interpreted as directed toward rectifying inequalities among racial *groups*. To the conservatives the principle of equality is concerned with the unequal treatment of individuals. From this perspective they insist that affirmative action plans may not provide relief to individuals who were not themselves victims of specific instances of discrimination, i.e., racial preferences may only assist identified victims of racial discrimination at the hands of a particular employer. This restriction in effect requires that courts and employers may only adopt "make-whole" affirmative plans; broad remedial plans intended to break up a past pattern or practice of discrimination, or send a message that the past policies of racial discrimination are over, are not acceptable. Even narrowly designed affirmative action plans must respect the settled expectations of existing employees. Thus, the conservatives strongly resist affirmative action plans that violate legitimate seniority plans (plans not adopted with an intent to discriminate). Innocent individual employees should not be injured by limited remedial affirmative action plans until after careful consideration of the equities, after a concerted effort has been made to reconcile the competing interests.[224] In short, the conservative justices will closely examine any affirmative action plan whether ordered by a court or voluntarily adopted by an employer to assure it serves only the compelling purpose of rectifying past injustice by the employer, and that the plan itself is narrowly tailored to this limited end.

The liberal approach to affirmative action plans is strikingly different. The liberal justices believe that Title VII and the equal protection clause of the fourteenth amendment were intended to serve the purpose of ending the unequal status of racial and other *groups*. Hence, the liberal justices accept affirmative action plans that are designed to rectify "societal discrimination," which provide relief to people who may not have themselves been actual victims of discrimination so long as they are members of a *group* that remains in an unequal social-economic position. Indeed, the liberal justices approve of affirmative action plans that invade the settled and legitimate expectations of innocent white employees since they belong to a *group* that is in a superior economic and social position. The liberal justice is, however, aware of the drastic implications these plans can have, and hence stresses that such plans should be only a temporary measure and not unnecessarily trammel the interests of white and/or male employees. Nevertheless, the liberal justices approve of broad remedial powers in the courts because the existence of such powers not only serves the purpose of correcting specific employment policies of particular employers, but also the purposes of dissipating lingering effects of pervasive discrimination and of discouraging employers in general from engaging in discrimination, i.e., the prospect of broad retroactive relief can serve as a spur or catalyst causing employers and unions to self-evaluate their employment practices. The strength of the commitment to social and economic reform of the liberal justices is seen in their willingness to uphold the use of quotas, as opposed to mere hiring goals; indeed, voluntarily adopted affirmative action plans and those agreed to as part of a consent decree may use hiring quotas and layoffs even in the absence of any evidence that the employer has engaged in discrimination in the past. In sum, affirmative action plans with sweeping components that may assist nonvictims and hurt innocent employees may be adopted to serve the broad social goals of ending inequalities among racial groups in the society.

The sharp differences of approach between the conservative and liberal wings of the Court were dramatically on display in *Wyngant v. Jackson Board of Education*.[225] In that case in settlement of a complaint claiming the school board had engaged in various discriminatory practices, the board agreed to several measures including a promise to take affirmative steps to recruit, hire, and promote minority teachers and counselors. The percentage of minority teachers and counselors to be hired was keyed to the percent of minority students enrolled in the school district. As a result of these efforts the board increased the percent of minority teachers from 3.9 percent to 8.8 percent. Subsequently, the board and teachers' union reached agreement on a new provision to the collective bargaining contract that required that teachers with the most seniority be retained "except that at no time will there be a greater percentage of minority personnel laid off than the current percentage of minority personnel employed at the time of the layoff." When layoffs become necessary, the board resisted complying with the contract provision but were ordered to do so by a court. As a result nonminority teachers were laid off while minority teachers with less seniority kept their jobs. The displaced nonminority teachers challenged the implementation of the contract provision as a violation of the equal protection clause of the fourteenth amendment and Title VII.

A conservative plurality of the Court said the layoff plan had to be searchingly examined, i.e., to be constitutional the plan must serve a compelling governmental interest, and the plan must be narrowly tailored to the achievement of that goal.[226] Addressing the purposes of the layoff plan first, the plurality said "societal discrimination, without more, is too amorphous a basis for a racially classified remedy."[227] Neither could the desire to provide black students with role models justify the policy. "[B]ecause the role model theory does not necessarily bear a relationship to the harm caused by prior discriminatory hiring practices, it actually could be used to escape the obligation to remedy such practices by justifying the small percentage of black teachers by reference to the small percentage of black students."[228] The plurality added that for this plan to be justified as remedial action for past discriminatory policies of this employer, it would have been necessary for the trial court to have first concluded that "the employer had a strong basis in evidence for its conclusion that remedial action was necessary."[229] Having said this, the plurality went on to say that even if this plan had been intended to remedy past discrimination by the board, it was not a legally appropriate means because it was not sufficiently narrowly framed to accomplish that purpose.[230] A layoff plan such as this one "imposes the entire burden of achieving racial equality on particular individuals, often resulting in serious disruption of their lives. That burden is too intrusive."[231] The plurality stressed that seniority rights make up the most valuable capital asset that a worker owns. Other less intrusive means—such as the adoption of hiring goals—could accomplish the same purpose, but in that case "the burden to be born by innocent individuals is diffused to a considerable extent among society generally. Though hiring goals may burden some innocent individuals, they simply do not impose the same kind of injury that layoffs impose."[232]

In her concurring opinion Justice O'Connor commented, among other things, that the layoff provision here failed because it was keyed to the percentage of minority students in the school, hence it served to "maintain levels of minority hiring that have no relation to remedying employment discrimination."[233] But Justice O'Connor was also careful to suggest that an affirmative action plan that was designed to remedy past or present discrimination would be upheld even if, when the plan was adopted, there was no contemporaneous or antecedent finding of past discrimination by a court, other competent body, or the employer itself. She rejected the assumption that in the absence of such a contemporaneous finding any discrimination addressed by an affirmative action plan must be termed "societal." However, once the plan is challenged, the employer must then be able to demonstrate that it had a firm basis for establishing the plan. She suggested that the kind of statistical case adequate to make a prima facie case of pattern or practice discrimination under Title VII (see, §9.9) would provide such a base. In turn she said it was the nonminority plaintiffs who bear the burden of persuading the court that the school board's evidence did not support an inference of prior discrimination against minorities.

Dissenting, Justice Marshall said the layoff plan could survive even the strict-scrutiny test since it served as a "means of preserving the effects of an affirmative hiring policy, the constitutionality of which is unchallenged."[234] The hiring policy itself was justified, said Justice Marshall, because it "sought to achieve diversity and stability for the benefit of *all* students."[235] "As a matter of logic as well as fact, a hiring policy achieves no purpose at all if it is eviscerated by layoffs."[236] Continuing, Justice Marshall said any per se protection against layoffs rested on a flawed premise that "seniority is so fundamental that its modification can never be permitted."[237] He also stressed that this layoff provision was narrow because it was not used to increase minority representation, was better than a random system that would have placed all teachers in equal jeopardy, was less burdensome than a freeze on layoffs of minority teachers, and "because it allocates the impact of unavoidable burden proportionately between two racial groups."[238]

Justice Stevens's dissent raised an interesting point that echoed Justice Powell's decision in *Bakke*. (See §4.7.) He wrote that the affirmative action plan could be justified as serving the purpose of assuring that students were provided with a multi-ethnic teaching faculty. Given the diversity of the student population in the public schools, it was sound educational practice, he said, to present the students with a diverse faculty so that the truth taught in schools that beauty is only skin-deep could be conveyed in the most convincing way.

The struggle within the Court over affirmative action continued in several subsequent opinions. Two months after the decision in *Wyngant* it was the liberal coalition that prevailed.[239] Then about a year later the liberals prevailed again in a case in which they upheld a lower court's order that required, as a remedy for past illegal discrimination, the Alabama Department of Public Safety to implement a one-white-for-one-black promotion requirement.[240] This important decision spelled out in greater detail the authority of the courts to fashion affirmative action remedies in cases in which the employer had a proven history of discrimination, but it was the Court's decision in *Johnson v. Transportation Agency, Santa Clara County, California* that drew the most attention.[241]

The story begins in December, 1978, with the adoption by the County Transportation Agency (hereafter, Agency) of an affirmative action employment plan intended to achieve an "equitable representation of minorities, women and handicapped persons." The Agency's plan found that women comprised about

36 percent of the area labor market but only about 22 percent of the Agency employees were women. Furthermore, the women working for the agency were concentrated in certain job categories traditionally held by women, i.e., office and clerical workers, and none of the 238 Skilled Craft Workers were women. (Ethnic minorities were also underrepresented in certain job categories.) Accordingly, the plan established a long-term goal of a work force whose composition mirrored the proportion of minorities and women in the area work force. Thus for the skilled craft worker category, including the position of road dispatcher, the goal was to have 36 percent of the jobs occupied by women. But the plan also concluded that it was unreasonable to rely on this long-term goal to evaluate the Agency's progress in expanding job opportunities for women and minorities because certain factors made it unrealistic to expect immediate results, i.e., the limited number of women in the area labor pool qualified for positions in the skilled craft classification. Hence the plan required that short-range goals be established and annually adjusted to serve as realistic guides. The plan specifically said that these goals were not to be construed as "quotas." (Dissenting Justice Scalia, however, claimed that the goals in fact were implemented as quotas.) The actual selection of the short-term goal for the skilled craft worker category was not made until 1982, two years after the occurrence of the specific incident that gave rise to this case.

On December 12, 1979, the Agency announced a vacancy for the position of road dispatcher. Nine of twelve applicants were deemed qualified for the job, and seven of these scored above 70 on an interview, including Paul Johnson (with 75 points he tied for second place) and Diane Joyce (with 73 points she was in fourth place). A second interview led to the recommendation that Johnson be promoted, but the Affirmative Action Coordinator of the Agency recommended to the agency director that Joyce get the job. The director testified that after considering a combination of factors—test scores, expertise, experience, background, and affirmative action—he decided in mid-1980 to promote Joyce. (Johnson retained employment at the Agency and in fact was promoted to road dispatcher in 1983.) The majority and dissenting justices' analysis of the director's decision-making calculus conflict. The majority, including concurring Justice O'Connor, said that the director only considered gender as one factor among many in deciding whether to promote Joyce.[242] However, dissenting Justice Scalia pointed out that the federal district court had concluded that gender was the determining factor, and that, in fact, the director had not even inspected the examination records of either Johnson or Joyce before making his decision, thus the "whole picture" had not been considered in making the promotion decision.[243] In any event, Johnson filed suit claiming he had been denied promotion on the basis of sex in violation of Title VII. The federal district court agreed, the Ninth Circuit reversed, and the Supreme Court affirmed upholding the decision to promote Joyce.

It is important to recognize that since Johnson did not raise a constitutional challenge, the majority decision of Justice Brennan did not directly address the constitutional issues that could have been raised. However, it seems safe to assume that the majority's understanding of Title VII was developed with an eye on the equal protection clause. That is, the majority did not write an opinion saying Title VII was not violated in this case while at the same time keeping the door open to negating the Agency's policy pursuant to the fourteenth amendment in a substantial case.[244]

Justice Brennan approached the case using the basic framework for analyzing disparate treatment claims under Title VII. (See §9.9.) He gave Johnson the ultimate burden of persuading the Court that the affirmative action plan and decision to promote Joyce violated Title VII, and he concluded that Johnson had failed to establish that the plan did not satisfy Title VII's requirements for a valid affirmative action plan.[245]

Justice Brennan began by indicating that an affirmative action plan would be permissible (as this one was) if designed to eliminate a "manifest imbalance" in a "traditionally segregated job category." He said this requirement provided assurance that sex or race would be taken in account "in a manner consistent with Title VII's purpose of eliminating the effects of employment discrimination."[246] Brennan's conception of "employment discrimination" is broad indeed since no one attributed the gender imbalance in the work force to employer discrimination. And in fact, Justice Brennan rejected the suggestion of Justice O'Connor that the manifest imbalance be such as to support a prime facie case of *employer* discrimination—Title VII as interpreted by *Weber,* he said, was concerned with statistical imbalances as such.[247] At the same time, Justice Brennan wrote that "had the Plan simply calculated imbalances in all categories according to the proportion of women in the area's *general* labor pool, and then directed that hiring be governed solely by these figures, its validity could be called into question. This is because analysis of a more *specialized* labor pool normally is necessary in determining underrepresentation in some [i.e., skilled] positions."[248] "Blind hiring" by the numbers would not be permissible. (But recall that "short-range" goals designed to take this factor into account had not yet been developed when Joyce was promoted over Johnson.) In addition, Justice Brennan implied that any plan (including this one) was especially acceptable if it established "goals" and not "quotas," and if it people were not hired solely by reference to statistics but that numerous factors be taken into account, including gender and/or race.[249] (Yet he also hinted that quotas might be permissible when he wrote that "Express assurance that a program is only temporary may be necessary if that program actually sets aside positions according to specific numbers."[250] This plan had no time limits as to its duration.) Finally, Justice Brennan said that an acceptable plan such as this one may not unnecessarily trammel the rights of employees adversely affected by the plan. Not setting aside positions for women, not relying on quotas, the consideration of many factors in deciding whether or not to promote, and not seeking to "maintain" a balance as opposed to merely seeking to "attain" balance were factors to be considered in approving such plans.[251] In finding that the plan in this case reflected all these characteristics, Justice Brennan also noted that Johnson still retained his job at the same salary, and remained eligible for other promotions, and that, in any event, Johnson had no "absolute entitlement" to the road dispatcher position.[252]

In his concurring opinion Justice Stevens emphasized a central point in Justice Brennan's opinion and then went beyond. He made clear that an employer had no obligation when establishing an affirmative action plan to tie the plan to an arguable violation by it of Title VII or even to tie the plan to past societal discrimination. He said that "in many instances the employer will find it more appropriate to consider other legitimate reasons to give preferences to members of under-represented groups."[253] At this point Justice Stevens quoted from a law review article supporting affirmative action to serve a broad range of purposes, i.e., to improve the educational achievement of black students, and to avert racial tension.[254] In short, Justice Stevens stressed that the majority opinion did not establish the outer limits of what constituted a permissible affirmative action plan.[255]

Justice O'Connor rejected Justice Stevens's willingness to embrace affirmative action programs intended to serve a wide range of purposes, and insisted that these programs could only be valid if the employer could point to a "statistical disparity sufficient to support a prima facie claim under Title VII" that it had in fact violated Title VII.[256] Such a requirement, she said, was a way of establishing that the employer was in fact addressing its own past improper activities as opposed to merely seeking to redress "general societal discrimination."[257] She also complained that the majority rejected this approach and offered "little guidance for what statistical imbalance is sufficient to support an affirmative action plan."[258] As for the employer's remedial goal, she said this goal must only be one that takes into account the number of women and minorities qualified for the relevant position—only in this way can we be sure the program is truly remedial. Having laid down a set of stricter guidelines than favored by the majority, Justice O'Connor nevertheless agreed that this plan satisfied those requirements. In her view the statistical disparity here did make out a prima facie case that Title VII had been violated and the plan itself was properly tied to remedying only an imbalance measured in terms of the *qualified* women in the area work force.[259]

Justice Scalia, joined by Chief Justice Rehnquist and Justice White, issued a scathing dissent which concluded that a statute which had been intended to guarantee that race and sex would not be considered in employment determinations, had been turned into a "powerful engine of racism and sexism," which in practical effect compelled race- and sex-based discrimination and replaced the goal of a discrimination-free society with the "quite incompatible goal of proportionate representation by race and sex in the workplace."[260] He based these conclusions on several observations and arguments. First, he noted that the plan's objective was, to achieve a state of affairs that this Court has dubiously assumed would result from an absence of discrimination—an overall work force "more or less representative of the racial and ethnic composition of the population in the community." . . . Rather, the oft-stated goal was to mirror the racial and sexual composition of the entire county labor force, not merely in the Agency work force as a whole, but in each and every individual job category at the Agency. In a discrimination-free world, it would obviously be a statistical oddity for every job category to match the racial and sexual composition of even that portion of the county work force *qualified* for that job; it would be utterly miraculous for each of them to match, as the plan expected, the composition of the *entire* work force. Quite obviously, the plan did not seek to replicate what a lack of discrimination would produce, but rather imposed racial and sexual tailoring that would, in defiance of normal expectations and laws of probability, give each protected racial and sexual group a governmentally determined "proper" proportion of each job category.[261]

Thus, he said the majority approved a plan designed not merely to end "societal discrimination" but also to rectify social attitudes, including the attitudes of women themselves, as to what counts as desirable work.[262]

Second, Justice Scalia argued that under the Agency's plan the job performance of supervisors was to be assessed in terms of the affirmative action numbers they produced.[263] Three, as noted earlier, the plan in operation made gender the determining factor in decisions to promote. Four, the plan approved by the majority consisted in no more than eliminating "from the applicant pool those who are not even *minimally qualified* for the job. Once that has been done, once the promoting officer assures himself that all the candidates before him are "M.Q.s" (minimally qualifieds), he can ignore, as the Agency Director did here, how much better than minimally qualified some of the candidates may be, and can proceed to appoint from the pool solely on the basis of race or sex. . . ."[264]

Finally, Justice Scalia observed that employers, faced with the possible expense and bad publicity attending even groundless Title VII suits women and minorities might bring, may now choose to engage in affirmative action as the legally safer and less costly alternative. "Thus, after today's decision the *failure* to engage in reverse discrimination is economic folly, and arguably a breach of duty to shareholders or taxpayers where the cost of anticipated Title VII litigation exceeds the cost of hiring less capable (though still minimally capable) workers.[265] And since this situation, he argued, is more likely to arise in connection with the least skilled jobs, the decision today created an incentive to "discriminate against precisely those members of nonfavored groups [i.e., lower class white males] *least* likely to have profited from societal discrimination in the past. . . . The irony is that these individuals—predominantly unknown, unaffluent, unorganized—suffer this injustice at the hands of a Court fond of thinking of itself the champion of the politically impotent."[266]

The key to the *Johnson* case would seem to be the "manifest imbalance" in a job category that had been traditionally gender segregated as well as the fact that the remedial steps in this case were merely designed to end the imbalance, not maintain a balance, and that the plan imposed relatively modest harms on innocent employees like Johnson. Contrary to Justice Scalia's view, the data here did seem to suggest a pattern of employer discrimination. The position of road dispatcher was not such that one would expect that it was the attitude of women themselves which lead to their under-representation. (Road dispatchers assigned crews, equipment, and material to road maintenance job sites. They had to keep accurate records on the availability of workers, materials, and equipment and need a working knowledge of those things as well as of the various roads maintained by the county.[267]) Thus under the facts of this case it would seem that the affirmative action plan was tied, albeit loosely, to rectifying past wrong-doing by the employer. Hence a narrow interpretation of the majority opinion would limit it to those cases in which there was at least a reasonable inference of employer discrimination. Assuming, however, that Justice Scalia's characterization of the majority's opinion is correct, that the majority did intend to move toward a society in which employers are expected to seek and maintain a work force that in all respects replicates the proportions of women and minorities in the labor pool, then the majority has embraced a principle of equality that is extremely controversial and difficult to defend. It appears Justice O'Connor is closest to the mark in her efforts to narrow the scope of the majority opinion while at the same time rejecting the extreme conservative position that affirmative action may only be undertaken to rectify specific judicially proven acts of discrimination.

The six-to-three liberal victory in *Johnson* is significant. Sweeping approval of voluntary affirmative action plans was given by such a strong majority that even if President Reagan were to have the opportunity to appoint another justice to the Court, the outcome in a case like *Johnson* would not be changed. Employers, including school districts and universities, have been given a green light to adopt affirmative action plans without having to confess to any past employment improprieties. But several important ambiguities remain, including the question of what kind of "manifest imbalance" must exist to warrant an affirmative action plan: Must those imbalances exist only in "traditionally segregated" job categories? And what counts as a "traditionally segregated" job category? By not defining these terms the majority has invited further litigation and a case-by-case fleshing out of the meaning of these terms. The possibility also remains that the liberal coalition established in *Johnson* will break down in future cases. For example, if an affirmative action plan were challenged that sought to correct a statistical imbalance less extreme than the one in the skilled craft workers category in this case, it is probable that not only Justice O'Connor would rule differently but also Justice Powell, a man more moderate in his views than the extreme liberal wing of the Court. Finally, reemergence of the conservative coalition seems more likely in those cases in which, as in *Wyngant*, the affirmative action plan entails the loss of a job or a setback to seniority rights.

9.14. DISCRIMINATION ON THE BASIS OF HANDICAP

It is common for states and local school districts to adopt health and physical standards for teachers, and for the courts to uphold the dismissal of teachers who have become so physically, mentally, or emotionally disabled that they are not able to perform their jobs.[268] Today, new federal and state laws prohibit discrimination on the basis of handicap.[269] The Rehabilitation Act of 1973, §504, is the most significant of these laws and provides in part that "no otherwise qualified handicapped individual" shall be excluded from participation in a program receiving federal financial assistance "solely by reason of his handicap."[270] It should be noted that §504 only applies to programs receiving federal funds.[271]

The coverage of the Rehabilitation Act raises several questions. First, do its requirements apply to all the employer's programs or only to those that are direct recipients of federal financial assistance? This issue has not yet been authoritatively answered by the Supreme Court.[272] The second question, whether the Act applies when the financial assistance provided is for a purpose other than employment, has been answered in the affirmative by the Supreme Court.[273] Third is the question of what counts as a handicapping condition. The statute provides that a handicapped person is one who "has a physical or mental impairment which substantially limits one or more such person's major life activities."[274] This provision has been interpreted to mean that the handicapping condition must affect their employability in general and not merely affect their ability to do the specific job they are seeking.[275] The statute specifically states that alcoholism and drug addition are not handicapping conditions within the meaning of the law,[276] but the Supreme Court has ruled that a person afflicted with tuberculosis is a handicapped individual within the meaning of §504.[277] Of course the mere fact that a person with a contagious disease falls within the protections of §504 does not automatically mean he or she must be employed, or at least employed in his or her current position. The Court noted that such a person must still be "otherwise qualified" to teach and this required an individualized inquiry. The purpose of the inquiry would be to protect the handicapped individual from prejudice, stereotypic thinking, and unfounded fear, while giving the appropriate weight to the interest of the employer to avoid exposing others to significant health and safety risks. In making this determination the Supreme Court said lower courts should normally defer to the reasonable medical judgments of public health officials. The courts must then consider whether the employer could reasonably accommodate the employee, i.e., continue to employ the handicapped person while protecting the students and other employees. In an important footnote the Court noted that it did not reach the question of whether a person who was simply a carrier of disease but did not him or herself suffer physical disabilities from it was a handicapped person within the meaning of §504. Thus the Court did not decide if a person who was only a carrier of the Acquired Immune Deficiency Syndrome (AIDS) virus was protected by §504.

For these purposes there are two important categories of cases: those in which the employer establishes as a job requirement the ability to carry out a certain task or possession of a certain physical capacity, e.g., acuity of hearing; and those cases in which the plaintiff alleges that a particular adverse employment decision was based on an improper discriminatory motive, a bias against the handicapped. In cases falling into the first category, different courts have adopted somewhat different approaches. Under one approach, the plaintiff, in order to win the suit, must ultimately persuade the court that: (1) he is a handicapped individual under §504; (2) he is "otherwise qualified" for the position sought; (3) he was excluded from the position solely by reason of his handicap; and that (4) the program or activity in question receives federal financial assistance.[278] Point one was discussed above. Point three is not a serious issue because, by definition, the plaintiff was excluded because he did not meet certain expressly stated job qualifications. Point four can become a significant issue if the employer contends that the program in which the plaintiff works is not federally funded.[279] It is point three that is usually the central issue in these cases, and it is a point on which the plaintiff retains the ultimate burden of persuasion.[280] The Supreme Court has said that an "otherwise qualified" handicapped individual is one who can meet all of a program's (job's) requirements in spite of the handicap, and that a person may be "otherwise qualified" in some cases even though he cannot meet all the requirements if the defendant's refusal to modify an existing program (job)—to accommodate the handicapped individual—is unreasonable.[281] Two considerations enter into a determination of the reasonableness of a refusal to accommodate: (a) requiring accommodation would be unreasonable if it would necessitate modification of the essential nature of the program, the essential nature of the job;[282] and (b) requiring the accommodation would be unreasonable if it would place undue burdens, such as high costs, on the defendant.[283] Applying these guidelines the Third Circuit required the Department of Transportation in Pennsylvania to permit a hearing-impaired individual to qualify as a school bus driver despite his inability to meet the state's minimum hearing requirements—requirements that according to the state regulations had to be met without assistance of a hearing aid.[284] The court said the state would be required to make a reasonable accommodation by permitting Strathie to meet its requirements with a hearing aid of a certain design. Thus, the court ruled that the state failed to meet its burden of persuasion by failing to show the necessity of an individual meeting that state's hearing requirements without the assistance of a hearing aid. In another case a court said a school could not simply refuse to consider the hiring of a handicapped teacher merely because some features of the job might have to be changed to accommodate the individual.[285] Thus, in order to accommodate the handicapped applicant, the school in this case might have to eliminate the (arguably nonessential) job requirement that the holder of this particular teaching position drive a school bus.

We turn now to the case in which the employer denies having relied on the plaintiff's handicap in reaching an employment decision. One court has described the approach to be taken in these cases this way:

> [T]he plaintiff has the ultimate burden of proving by a fair prepondernace of the evidence that the defendant discriminated against him on the basis of an impermissible factor. [H]e may establish a prima facie case by proving that he applied for a position for which he was qualified and was rejected, under circumstances indicating discrimination on the basis of an impermissible factor. The burden then shifts to the defendant to rebut the presumption of discrimination by coming forward with evidence that the plaintiff was rejected for a legitimate reason, whereupon the plaintiff must prove the reason was not true but a pretext for impermissible discrimination.[286]

Using this framework the Eighth Circuit upheld a lower court decision that a legally blind applicant for position of librarian in a public school had not been rejected solely on the basis of handicap.[287] If the plaintiff had managed to establish that she was rejected because she was blind, the defendant would raise the issue that she was not an "otherwise qualified" handicapped individual.

The Tenth Circuit has adopted a different approach.[288] Under this approach the plaintiff must establish a prima facie case by showing he was an otherwise qualified handicapped person "apart from" his handicap (he was qualified in spite of his handicap) and was rejected under circumstances that gave rise to the inference he was rejected solely on the basis of handicap. Now the ultimate burden of persuasion switches to the defendant to establish either that the plaintiff was not an otherwise qualified person who was able to meet all job requirements in spite of the handicap or that rejection was based on a reason other than handicap. The plaintiff may now establish that the defendant acted based on misconceptions or unfounded factual conclusions, and that the reasons articulated for the rejection other than the handicap encompass unjustified consideration of the handicap itself.

9.15. RELIGIOUS FREEDOM: DISCRIMINATION ON THE BASIS OF RELIGION

As discussed in chapter 5, the establishment clause of the first amendment has been interpreted by the courts as imposing sharp limits on the authority of public schools to bring religion into the classroom. At the same time the free exercise clause of that same amendment arguably protects the religious liberty of teachers, even in the classroom. Hence arises the possibility of a conflict between these two clauses of the first amendment. The conflict would be presented in its starkest form if a teacher insisted on the right to proselytize or conduct a prayer session in the classroom: must the school board permit the teacher to proselytize or must the school forbid the teacher? There is little doubt the courts would view such teacher-led activities as a violation of the establishment clause despite claims of religious freedom.[289] A federal court has held that schools may prohibit its employees from gathering before the start of the work day to hold meetings for prayer, religious devotions, and religous speech.[290] On the other hand, a school district violates the establishment clause if it dismisses a teacher because the teacher answered a student's question on scientific and theological matters in a way that conflicts with the religious beliefs of the parents; to require teachers to answer only in accordance with the beliefs of most parents establishes a religious orthodoxy.[291] A conflict between the two religion clauses of the first amendment can also arise if a teacher seeks to wear religious garb in the classroom. The Supreme Court has not settled this issue; the lower courts have reached conflicting conclusions.[292] It is unlikely, however, that any court would uphold a school rule, or itself order that a teacher not wear a small religious symbol such as a cross or Star of David, or an unobtrusive article of clothing like the yarmulka.[293]

A different kind of conflict arises when teachers seek to be exempted from facially neutral school requirements on the grounds that those requirements infringe their religious freedom. Thus, a teacher claimed a religious right not to lead her class in the flag salute and in the singing of patrotic songs; she also refused to teach about the flag, love of country, and other matters related to patriotic holidays such as Lincoln's birthday. The Seventh Circuit said, however, the school board's authority to make sure the school's curriculum was taught should prevail.[294] In another case a Quaker teacher refused to participate in the flag salute as a matter of conscience, and the court upheld her refusal and protected her from dismissal.[295] These two cases are distinguishable in that in the second case there was another teacher in the classroom who continued to lead the students in the flag salute; the teacher's refusal to participate did not disrupt the class; and the students in the class were high school students who were capable of understanding the situation. In the first case there was only one teacher in the elementary-grade classroom.

The taking of religious holidays by teachers has produced another set of conflicts. One conflict has been over the dismissal of teachers for being absent without permission in order to observe a religious holiday. The California Supreme Court ruled in such a case that the dismissal violated a prohibition in the California State Constitution against discrimination on the basis of religion.[296] The court said that the district was required to accommodate the teacher's religious needs by allowing a reasonable amount of unpaid leave (five to ten days per year). The court brushed aside objections from the district that such a requirement would be disruptive of the school program; the court also noted that since the leave would be unpaid, finding a substitute could be done at no additional cost to the district. A different problem arose when Gerald Pinsker claimed the district's schedule and leave policy discriminated against him and other Jewish teachers on the basis of religion.[297] His claim was based on the policy of the district to close the schools on several Christian holidays, thus enabling Christian teachers to celebrate their holidays without using a personal leave day or taking unpaid leave, while he and the other Jewish teachers who did not work on the Jewish holidays had to use personal leave or take unpaid leave. The court rejected the claim saying that loss of a day's pay for time not worked did not constitute substantial pressure to modify his behavior, hence was not an infringement of his religious liberty.

In addition to the free exercise clause, teachers are protected by Title VII of the Civil Rights Act of 1964 that prohibits, among other things, discrimination in hiring, firing, compensation, terms, conditions, or privileges of employment on the basis of religion.[298] Title VII specifically notes that "religion includes all aspects of religious observances and practice as well as belief, unless an employer demonstrates that he is unable to accommodate to an employee's or prospective employee's religious observance or practice without undue hardship on the conduct of the employer's business."[299]

The terms "religion" and "religious" are not defined in the statute, hence the courts have adopted the definition of religion used by the Supreme Court in other contexts,[300] e.g., all that is required is a "sincere and meaningful belief occupying in the life of its possessors a place parallel to that filled by God of those admittedly qualified for the exception."[301] The courts have also extended the protection of the statute to atheists.[302] From the broad language of the quoted provision in the previous paragraph, it is clear the statute prohibits a refusal to hire because of the clothing or hairstyle required by the religion of the applicant. The statute also permits the employer to defend rules that infringe religious "observances and practices" by demonstrating that he is unable reasonably to accommodate to the employee's religious observances or practices without undue hardship.

The application of Title VII to education is illustrated by the Supreme Court's decision in *Ansonia Board of Education v. Philbrook*.[303] Ronald Philbrook was a member of the Worldwide Church of God the tenets of which required members to refrain from secular employment during designated holy days, a requirement that caused Philbrook to miss approximately six school days each year. The collective bargaining contract with the district permitted employees to take three days annual leave for observation of mandatory religious holidays. For a number of years Philbrook satisfied his religious requirement by using the three days granted in the contract and by taking an additional three days of unauthorized and unpaid leave. Dissatisfied with this arrangement Philbrook repeatedly suggested that he either be allowed to use "personal business leave" for his religious observance (this would give him three additional days of paid leave), or that he receive full pay for the additional three days he missed but that he pay the cost of a substitute. The school district rejected both proposals.[304]

Philbrook filed a complaint in federal court alleging that he had been discriminated against on the basis of religion in violation of Title VII. The federal district court concluded that he failed to establish a case of religious discrimination, but the Second Circuit reversed. It ruled that a plaintiff in this kind of case was required to make out a prima facie case of religious discrimination by proving that (1) he had a bona fide religious belief that conflicted with an employment requirement; (2) he informed the school board of his belief; and that (3) he was disciplined for failure to comply with the conflicting employment requirement.[305] The Second Circuit agreed that the plaintiff had satisfied this burden, thus the remaining issue was whether the district could make a reasonable accommodation without undue hardship. Taking account of the fact that in an important case the Supreme Court itself had said that to require an employer to bear more than a *de minimis* cost to accommodate an employee would be undue hardship, the Second Circuit ruled that where employer and employee both propose an accommodation, Title VII requires adoption of the employee's suggestion unless it causes undue hardshiop, i.e., leads to greater than de minimis expenditure by the employer.[306]

The Supreme Court affirmed the Second Circuit's decision to remand the case for trial but disagreed with the Second Circuit's interpretation of Title VII. Chief Justice Rehnquist (see, chapter 10) said Title VII did not require an employer to choose any particular reasonable accommodation.[307] Where an employer has reasonably accommodated an employee's religious needs, the inquiry is at an end. The employer need not demonstrate that the suggestion of the employee of an alternative to that offered by the employer would result in undue hardship. The Court then remanded the case to determine whether the school board's policy constituted a reasonable accommodation of Philbrook's religious beliefs.

Religious harassment, which can take forms analogous to sexual harassment, is unlawful under Title VII.[308]

9.16. DISCRIMINATION ON THE BASIS OF AGE

In a case dealing with a Massachusetts law requiring uniformed state police officers to retire at age fifty, the Supreme Court upheld the law saying that it was rationally related to the need to assure police officers were physically able to conduct police work.[309] Subsequently in *Gault v. Garrison*,[310] the Seventh Circuit, in reversing an order dismissing a complaint attacking the constitutionality of a mandatory retirement law for teachers, held that in the absence of evidence there was no reason to assume there was any relationship between age and fitness to teach. In fact, the court suggested that the knowledge and experience necessary for teaching increased with age.

A different result was reached in *Palmer v. Ticcione*.[311] The Second Circuit said that contrary to the assumption of *Gault*, mandatory retirement laws serve not only to weed out the physically unfit, but they also opened the system for younger employees with new ideas and techniques and made the management of pension plans easier. Given these purposes the mandatory retirement system was rationally related to the state's objectives.

It is not only the Constitution that can serve as a basis for attacking employment policies based on age. The Age Discrimination in Employment Act of 1978 (ADEA) also protects people between the ages of forty and seventy from discrimination on the basis of age with regard to hiring, firing, and the terms and conditions of employment.[312] However, an employer may defend itself by showing that age is a bona fide occupational qualification; by showing that the adverse employment decision was based on reasonable factors other than age; by establishing that it was observing a bona fide seniority system or a bona fide employment benefit plan that are not subterfuges to evade the law; or by showing that a discharge was for good cause.[313] But, no seniority system or employment benefit plan can require a person to retire because of age.[314]

For resolving cases involving express discrimination on the basis of age, the Supreme Court has adopted the following framework:[315] (1) sometimes an age criteria is so tangentially related to the essence of a business that no age discrimination can be justified; (2) age qualifications must be "reasonably necessary" to the particular business, and this could only be so when the employer is compelled to rely on age as a proxy for safety-related job qualifications.[316] In a case pre-dating the Supreme Court's decision, the Second Circuit upheld a lower court opinion rejecting New York's sixty-five-year age limit for school bus drivers.[317]

In both the individual disparate treatment[318] and disparate impact[319] types of cases the courts have adopted the frameworks used in connection with gender and race discrimination. The Second Circuit has held that a policy of not hiring teachers with more than five years experience violated the act because it had a disparate impact on older teachers.[320] A federal district court has extended the disparate impact framework for analysis to school district compensation policies, but in doing so rejected the claim that the ADEA is violated by a compensation scheme that provided lower salary increases to those older teachers at the top of salary scale.[321]

Several courts have held that the ADEA does not preclude an employer from adopting a bona fide benefit plan that provides an incentive for early voluntary retirement.[322] It is important, however, that these plans not be adopted as a subterfuge to evade the purposes of ADEA.

9.17. PROCEDURAL DUE PROCESS: ESTABLISHING THE RIGHT

Roughly speaking, if someone has a right to procedural due process they have the right to a trial-type hearing before being condemned to suffer a serious loss.[323] The fourteenth amendment provides that no state shall "deprive any person of life, liberty or property without due process of law."[324] In two cases the Supreme Court, in reliance on this language, held that a teacher is entitled to procedural due process if the school deprives him or her of "liberty" or "property."[325] Consequently, in order to trigger the right to procedural due process, the employer must first deprive, or be about to deprive, the employee of either his or her "liberty" or "property." (As discussed below, damage to the employee's liberty interest must also be accompanied by a significant change in employment status, a notion that can be referred to as "liberty-plus.") Thus, the first issue that needs to be addressed in a case in which an employee claims a right to procedural due process is the question whether the employer did deprive the employee of either his or her interest in "liberty-plus" or "property."

Once the court has agreed the employee has been deprived of "liberty-plus" or "property," the next question is "what process is due?" i.e., precisely what procedural due process protections must be provided. This question will be taken up following the discussion in §9.18 of what constitutes a loss of "property" or "liberty-plus." It should be noted at this point that state statutes may also guarantee a teacher a right to procedural safeguards before, for example, dismissal, safeguards that may be more extensive than those constitutionally required.[326] The constitutional difficulty only arises if a state or school board provides a lower level of procedural protection than required by the Constitution. Several courts have held that even if an employer violates its own procedural rules, the due process clause of the Constitution is not necessarily violated. So long as the procedures afforded the employer meet constitutional requirements, the mere fact that those procedures do not conform to the employer's own rules does not mean the employee's due process rights were violated.[327] Note, however, that other courts have suggested that an employer's violation of its own rules may constitute a substantive due process violation.[328]

We turn first to the question of when does an employee suffer a "property" loss in connection with an adverse employment decision. This question can be further resolved into two questions: What sorts of employment decisions might deprive a teacher of a property interest; and what precisely is a property interest, and how does a teacher get to have such an interest? There is no dispute that a decision to terminate an employee, either for cause or simply as part of an effort to reduce the employee force for economic reasons,[329] *may* result in a loss of a property interest *if the employee has a property interest in the job.* One court has held that placement of a teacher on a health leave for psychological problems did involve a deprivation of a property interest.[330] Similarly an employee may have a property interest in a particular position, hence a transfer or demotion may involve a deprivation of property.[331] A suspension might also involve loss of a property interest. Failure to promote or to provide a salary increase might also involve deprivation of a property interest, if, for example, by seniority the employee has a right to the salary increase or promotion.[332]

How does a teacher obtain a property interest in a job, in a position, in a promotion, and/or in a salary increase? This is a complex matter, but at least this much is clear: the mere fact the employee unilaterally needs, hopes, desires, or expects to retain his or her job or position or to obtain a salary increase or promotion does not create a property interest.[333] The teacher must have a "legitimate claim of entitlement" that state law has created.[334] To establish whether a teacher has a "legitimate claim of entitlement," a court examines the law of the state and evidence presented by the teacher (the kind of evidence that needs to be presented will be discussed in a moment) to determine if the teacher has been given by the state a property interest, i.e., whether the interest obtained by the teacher from the school rises to the level of a legitimate claim entitled to protection by procedural due process.[335]

What evidence should a teacher produce to establish that he or she has a legitimate claim of entitlement in the job, position, promotion, or salary increase? (Note that a teacher may claim a property interest in a job, but not in a particular position; hence the relevant evidence for each claimed interest can and may have to be different.) There is no dispute that a tenured teacher enjoys an interest in continued employment protected by due process.[336] The interesting question is how can a teacher establish he or she has tenure when the question is in doubt, e.g., when the teacher cannot point to any formal action by the school board granting tenure. Proof of tenure can be accomplished in the absence of a formal action by establishing that de facto tenure was obtained,[337] or that tenure by estoppel was achieved.[338] But, the most common problem to arise is not in connection with teachers who have tenure or claim tenure, but with regard to the dismissal of teachers without tenure who nevertheless claim that they have a legitimate expectancy of continued employment, i.e., a property right safeguarded by due process. The easiest of these cases to resolve is the case of the teacher who is dismissed in the middle of a contract of a specified term—the contract itself creates a recognized property interest in continued employment.[339] In the absence of such a clear basis for expecting continued employment, teachers who have not had their contracts renewed have argued, sometimes with success, that the teacher's handbook,[340] school custom and practice,[341] a school rule, state statute,[342] a record of having had a long series of one-year contracts,[343] or the university's own *procedures* for nonrenewal created a property interest in the job,[344] and that a promise of contract renewal provided a basis for a legitimate claim of continued expected employment.[345] The mere fact that one faculty committee has recommended a candidate for tenure does not create a property interest unless, at least, it is shown that such recommendations routinely lead to a grant of tenure.[346] Failure to establish an objective basis for expecting continued employment means the teacher has only a subjective expectation that is not given protection.[347]

Some school personnel who have been transferred or demoted have claimed due process protections by arguing they had a legitimate claim to the particular position from which they were removed. They have relied on arguments similar to those listed above, usually without success, because the evidence proffered did not support the existence of a legitimate claim.[348] Nevertheless, a number of courts have determined that a property interest was infringed by a suspension,[349] and that denial of an annual salary increment was a loss of a protected interest because by contract the increment could not be denied unless the teacher performed unsatisfactorily.[350] The Third Circuit found a property interest to a place on an eligibility list.[351] The Second Circuit concluded New York public school teachers had an interest in their pension rights protectable by procedural safeguards.[352]

Regardless of whether a teacher can demonstrate a "property" interest, procedural safeguards may nevertheless be due if the school board's employment decision adversely affects his or her interest in "liberty," *plus* the teacher suffers some significant change in his or her employment status.[353] The "plus" may be job termination, suspension without pay,[354] or transfer with loss of status.[355] Thus despite the absence of a property interest, the probationary teacher whose contract is not renewed may be entitled to a hearing if his or her interest in "liberty" has been adversely affected in the course of the nonrenewal.

How is proof of infringement of the interest in liberty established? Nonrenewal per se does not adversely affect the teachers' liberty interest. Rather, the Supreme Court has said deprivation of liberty occurs if (1) the adverse decision was based on a charge "that might seriously damage his standing and associations in his community," or (2) the board in making its decision imposed on a teacher "a stigma or other disability that foreclosed his freedom to take advantage of other employment opportunities."[356] Since the point of the hearing is to provide the teacher an opportunity to clear his or her name, it follows that if the teacher does not contest the charges,[357] or if the damaging comments are made after a hearing has validated the charges,[358] then there is no right to the procedural safeguards. In sum, the Supreme Court's "stigma-plus" test requires the claimant to establish the reasons for the adverse employment decisions imposed a stigma, the reasons were "publicized," that he or she challenged the validity of the employer's assertions, and the imposition of the stigma was accompanied by a concurrent loss in a state-created right or status.

We turn now to the first way in which a liberty interest might be harmed, damage to the teacher's reputation in the community. Two basic issues arise here: (1) what kinds of charges are sufficiently damaging as to harm the liberty interest, and (2) what kind of publicity must those charges have been given in order for the potential of a reputational harm to occur. As for the kind of charges, the Seventh Circuit has said the charges must be so critical that people in the community would no longer want to associate with the persons so charged.[359] Thus, one court held the liberty interest of a coach was not implicated by criticism that he used profanity, had problems with discipline, and that good athletes did not want to go out for sports because of the coach.[360] However, when the allegations charge immoral behavior, a drinking problem, emotional instability, or a lack of veracity, then the liberty interest is implicated.[361]

For these allegations to become damaging, they must be made public,[362] but the charges need not be formally lodged, i.e., knowledge of the charges may become public simply because of the circumstances surrounding the case.[363]

We turn now to the second way the liberty interest might be affected: employment opportunities are foreclosed. The types of reasons recognized as having a potential for foreclosing employment opportunities are broader than the types that might harm community reputation. Thus, charges of insubordination, intoxication on the job, and serious delinquency have been accepted as possibly foreclosing job opportunities.[364] The mere fact that an employee's work was not of the quality the board wanted is not a sufficient charge to implicate the liberty interest.[365] Disclosure of such charges to prospective employers, or placement of the charges in files that are available to prospective employers produces the foreclosure necessary to trigger a right to procedural safeguards.[366] One court has said that the eventual reemployment of the teachers does not itself establish that his opportunities had not been foreclosed by imposition of a stigma.[367]

9.18. PROCEDURAL DUE PROCESS: WHAT PROCESS IS DUE AND WHEN?

Once it is decided that the due process clause applies to an adverse employment decision, the only question is what process is due and when. This question has to be settled by a practical balancing of the interests of the employee and the employer.[368] Adopting this approach the Supreme Court has concluded that a teacher who has a right to procedural due process because he or she has a property right in continued employment has a right to the hearing prior to termination.[369] Such a pretermination hearing need not "definitely resolve the propriety of the discharge," but should be an "initial check agianst mistaken decisions—essentially, a determination of whether there are reasonable grounds to believe that the charges against the employee are true and support the proposed action."[370] (If keeping the employee on the job poses a significant hazard, the employer can suspend him or her with pay.[371] The pretermination procedures need not be elaborate: the employee is to be given oral or written notice of the charges, an explanation of the evidence against him or her, and an opportunity to present his or her side of the story either in person or *in writ-*

ing.[372] In short, the Court seems to contemplate the possibility of a comparatively informal pretermination hearing, suspension/dismissal without pay if probable cause has been established, and then a full-evidentiary hearing to definitely resolve the case.

This opinion has several important limitations. It did not address the case of termination of an employee who did not have a property right, but instead had a liberty interest that was affected by his or her termination.[373] Neither did the Court address the right to a pretermination hearing in connection with a suspension, transfer, or demotion, regardless of whether procedural safeguards are due because of an adversely affected property interest or liberty interest.[374]

Over the years the lower courts have elaborated upon the kind of process that is due in order definitively to resolve the charges against a teacher. The safeguards elaborated upon by the courts include: right to adequate and timely notice; right to an impartial hearing; right to be made aware of the evidence in advance of the hearing; right to counsel; right to confront and cross-examine witnesses; right of access to documents used in the hearing; right to a decision on the record; a right to a written statement of reasons; and a right to a transcript. Note that in a number of respects the law as to teacher due process rights is different from that as to students. For a comparison see §8.6.

Notice

An accused teacher must be provided written[375] notice of when the hearing will be and of the charges made[376] sufficiently in advance of the hearing to allow adequate time to prepare a defense.[377] To further assist in the mounting of a defense, the courts have also required the provision to the teacher of a list of the names of witnesses and nature of the testimony against him or her.[378]

Impartial Hearing

A basic requirement of due process, at least outside the field of public employment, is provision of an impartial tribunal.[379] Impartiality can be compromised in several ways: (1) the decision-maker may have a conflict of interest; (2) the decision-maker may have personal animosity toward the accused teacher; (3) the decision-maker may have prejudged the case; (4) participants, such as the decision-maker or "prosecuting attorney," may serve dual roles in the proceeding.

The necessary starting point for understanding the law in this area as it bears on public employment is *Hortonville District v. Hortonville Education Association*[380] in which the Supreme Court concluded that it was not a violation of the due process clause for a school board to be the decision-maker in deciding whether to dismiss teachers engaged in an illegal strike against the board. The opinion in the case has been extended to the dismissal of a teacher for incompetence.[381] The *Hortonville* opinion itself has confused the issue regarding conflict of interest. Generally speaking, decision-makers who have something to gain—either personally or in their official capacity—from the outcome of a case may not sit as decision-makers,[382] but in dictum in *Hortonville* the Court left open the question whether the cases elaborating this principle govern a public employer dealing with public employees.[383] Nevertheless, it is difficult to believe the Court would permit a teacher to be judged by decision-makers who have an immediate personal stake in his or her dismissal.[384]

The *Hortonville* opinion also muddied the waters regarding the applicable principles for dealing with claims that a decisionmaker holds personal animosity toward a teacher.[385] Lower courts, in decisions prior to the decision in *Hortonville,* have, however, refused to disqualify decisionmakers unless there is a showing of actual bias or prejudice.[386] The mere fact that the teacher had heated exchanges or had publicly attacked the decision-maker is not enough to establish actual personal bias—proof of the possibility of bias has insufficient.[387]

When the school board's regular attorney acts as the "prosecuting" attorney in a teacher-termination case, the possibility arises that the board will not assess both sides of the case with impartiality. This possibility seems not to have troubled the courts.[388] When the board's counsel not only prosecutes, but also joins the board in its deliberations of the case, the problem is compounded. (The "prosecution" gets a second chance to influence the board without the defense being given the opportunity to offer rebuttal evidence and arguments.) Nevertheless, the courts are split as to whether this practice is constitutionally permissible in teacher-termination cases.[389]

Prejudgment

The body of law in this area consists of many finely drawn distinctions. The Court in *Hortonville* has said that a decision-maker is not disqualified "simply because he has taken a position, even in public, on a policy related to the dispute, in the absence of a showing that he is not 'capable of judging a particular controversy fairly on the basis of its own circumstances.'"[390] Thus, prejudgment on matters of policy is permissible (i.e., any teacher who engaged in an illegal strike must be dismissed), whereas prejudgment of the merits of a particular case can be a form of bias that is not constitutionally permissible.[391] Prejudgment of the merits must be distinguished from mere prior familiarity with the facts of the case. In *Hortonville* the mere fact the board was familiar with the facts of the illegal strike did not disqualify the board from acting as decision-maker in discharge proceedings against individual teachers.[392] The Court has even said that a board may engage in a preliminary investigation of a case, make a preliminary determination that the proceeding ought to be held, and then later sit as the decision-maker in an adversary hearing.[393] The test to be used to determine if a combination of investigative and adjudicative functions creates bias is whether the combination of functions creates a risk of actual bias or prejudgment.[394]

Hence, the combination of functions itself does not violate due process, but additional facts may be presented to show that in this case the risk of bias is unacceptably high.[395] In the wake of such pronouncements by the Supreme Court, it is not surprising that the lower courts have generally rejected claims of prejudgment either because of a combination of functions or because the board in other ways became familiar with a case prior to its final decision.[396] Some courts seem to be more willing to find a due process violation when an administrator associated with the prosecution of the case joins in the board's private deliberations to decide the case.[397] Finally, providing the teacher with the opportunity to voir dire individual board members to determine their personal bias is not constitutionally required.[398]

Right to Counsel

While several circuit courts have held that public employees do not have a right to be represented by legal counsel in a termination hearing, several federal district courts have held otherwise.[399] The better rule would seem to be that teachers should be allowed to be represented by legal counsel, especially when they are being prosecuted by a lawyer and/or a school official experienced in handling proceedings of this sort.

Right to Confront and Cross-examine Witnesses and
Have Access to Documentary Evidence

Basically, when the case involves disputed issues of fact, but not when it does not, a teacher has a right to confront and cross-examine the adverse witnesses.[400] It may be that when the issues involved are not factual but a matter of professional judgment and evaluation of a teacher's performance, the right to confront and cross-examine may be modified.[401] Just as it is important for the teacher to gain access to witnesses, so is it important for the teacher to gain access to documents being used in the hearing.[402] The right to cross-examine is violated when evidence is presented by witnesses to the decision-makers in ex parte communications.[403]

Decision Based Only on the Record

The formal hearing would become a meaningless exercise if decision-makers could rely on information and facts not formally introduced and open to challenge at a hearing. Thus, the courts have protected the right of the employee to a decision based "on the record."[404] It follows that a board acts improperly if it acts on the basis of a report from an impartial hearing officer that does not contain a statement of reasons and evidence for the recommendation of the hearing officer.[405] Implied in this is the further point that the ultimate decision-maker need not him- or herself personally read and review all the evidence.[406]

Decision Backed by Evidence

Due process bars educational institutions from making adverse employment decisions affecting a liberty or property interest not supported by evidence.[407] Because hearsay evidence is not reliable, basing a case against a teacher on hearsay evidence is constitutionally suspect, and courts have, in fact, not permitted the use of hearsay evidence in dismissal proceedings.[408]

Right to Statement of Reasons and Transcript

To help to assure that the decision is based "on the record" (a requirement that itself serves to assure that the right to confront and cross-examine witnesses is protected) the courts have said the teacher has a right to a decision accompanied by a statement of reasons and the evidence relied on.[409] A right that a transcript be made of the proceedings would further assure that the decision was based "on the record."[410] It is not clear whether the teacher has a right to a copy of the transcript at public expense.

In sum, the specific elements of procedural due process discussed above are the basic standard against which to evaluate state statutes and school practices. The mere fact that an educational institution departs from its announced procedures does not entail a constitutional violation so long as the procedures followed in fact meet the minimum standards required by the Constitution.[411]

9.19. THE RIGHT TO WITHHOLD INFORMATION

The first strand of the concept of privacy—autonomy in the making of personal decisions relating to sex, procreation, marriage and life style—was discussed in §9.6. We turn now to the second strand of the notion of privacy—the right to withhold information about oneself that may be embarrassing or otherwise cause legal or political difficulties. We begin with the constitutional limits on school boards to ask questions of their employees. In *Shelton v. Tucker*[412] the Supreme Court struck down as a violation of the teacher's first amendment rights of freedom of association and speech a state law that required each teacher, as a condition of employment in the public schools, annually to file an affidavit listing every organization to which he or she belonged or regularly contributed in the preceding five years. The Court acknowledged the right of the state to investigate the competence and fitness of its teachers, but a law such as this also impaired the teacher's right of freedom of association since disclosure of membership in organizations such as the National Association for the Advancement of Colored People could expose the teacher to harassment and worse. Balancing the interests of the school against the fundamental interest of the teachers in freedom of association, the Court said this particular law was unnecessarily sweeping in light of its purpose. The law did not promise confidentiality, and the unlimited scope of its inquiry clearly led to an investigation of relationships that had no bearing on occupational competence or fitness. The Court also pointedly noted that, even if the information collected were not disclosed to the general public, it placed pressure on the teachers to avoid ties that might displease those who have control over his or her professional destiny. The stress on the fact that the law was too sweeping, however, left open the possibility that a more limited inquiry might be constitutional.

The fifth amendment's prohibition against compelling a person to be a witness against himself plays a modest role in protecting teachers. Thus a teacher may not be discharged because he or she refuses to answer questions put by the employer regarding criminal misconduct relating to his or her employment if the teacher is not given immunity from criminal prosecution.[413] However, the Supreme Court has said that a teacher may be dismissed for incompetency for refusing to answer, on the grounds of self-incrimination, school officials' questions regarding subversive associations.[414] It is important to realize, however, that the first amendment provides an important degree of protection against being required to answer questions regarding suspected subversive activities.[415]

Public employees have not only successfully found protection by invoking specific constitutional amendments, but also by claiming that the existence of an implicit constitutional right to privacy protects them from being required to answer questions about their private sexual activities.[416] One teacher failed in making the claim that her constitutional rights to privacy protected her from an order to turn over to her principal a term paper she wrote for a college course—a case study of a student—when the principal wanted the paper to assist in evaluating the student.[417] The court concluded that the teacher did not have a reasonable expectancy of privacy in the paper since she had given the paper to her college professor without restrictions and to a fellow panel member on the team (which included the principal) set up to evaluate pupils with special needs. On the other hand, financial disclosure requirements have been upheld when narrowly drawn to serve legitimate purposes and when privacy interests are protected by guarding against disclosure of the information.[418] Disclosure requirements that require information relating to the employee's spouse, children, and other dependents are also vulnerable as not having a substantial relationship between the information sought and a subject of compelling state interest.[419]

We turn now to the question of what protection, if any, the fourth amendment's prohibition against unreasonable searches affords teachers from searches by their employer of their persons, belongings, desks, file cabinets, and the like. The Supreme Court addressed this question in *O'Connor v. Ortega*[420] in which Dr. Magno Ortega sued his employer under §1983 for searching his office including his desk and file cabinet. All the justices, the four who signed the plurality opinion, concurring Justice Scalia, and the four dissenters, agreed on the rather general proposition that public employees do not lose their fourth amendment protection merely because they work for the government.[421] There was, however, a major and peculiar split within the Court on the narrower issue as to when the fourth amendment rights of an employee are implicated by an employer search. On this issue Justice Scalia, who otherwise concurred in the judgment of the plurality, joined the four dissenting justices. These five justices held that the offices, desks, and files within those offices are always covered by the fourth amendment.[422] The plurality opinion's position was more complex.

> The operational realities of the workplace, however, make *some* employees' expectations of privacy unreasonable when an intrusion is by a supervisor rather than a law enforcement official. Public employees' expectations of privacy in their offices, desks, and file cabinets, like similar expectations of employees in the private sector, may be reduced by virtue of actual office practices and procedures, or by legitimate regulations.[423]

Following this line of thought the plurality suggested that some governmental offices may be so open to other employees or the public that the "owner" of the office could have no reasonable expectation of privacy. Whether an expectation of privacy should be recognized must be determined, said the plurality, case-by-case.[424] Regardless of the approach used, however, the justices unanimously agreed that in this case Dr. Ortega had a reasonable expectation of privacy as to his office, desk, and file cabinet.[425]

A different combination of five justices, the plurality joined by Justice Scalia, agreed that employers did not need to obtain a warrant in order to search an employee's office, desk, or file cabinet.[426] But there was no majority on the crucial question of the standard for determining when an employer's search was permissible and not a violation of the employee's fourth amendment rights. The four justices who signed the plurality opinion adopted a modified version of the standard the Court promulgated in *New Jersey v. T.L.O.*, the student search case (see §8.5). Thus, as to either "noninvestigatory work-related intrusions," e.g., an inventory search, or an "investigatory search for evidence of suspected work-related employee misfeasance" the plurality wrote that,

> Ordinarily, a search of an employee's office by a supervisor will be "justified at its inception" when there are reasonable grounds for suspecting that the search will turn up evidence that the employee is guilty of work-related misconduct, or that the search is necessary for noninvestigatory work-related purpose such as to retrieve a needed file. . . . The search will be permissible in its scope when "the measures adopted are reasonably related to the objectives of the search and not excessively intrusive in light of . . . the nature of the [misconduct]."[427]

(For an exploration of the meaning of this standard see §8.5.) Justice Scalia seemed to argue for an even more lenient standard when he said "I would hold that government searches to retrieve work-related materials or to investigate violations of workplace rules—searches of the sort that are regarded as reasonable and normal in the private-employer context—do not violate the Fourth Amendment."[428] Based on this standard, Justice Scalia agreed with the plurality that the case needed to be remanded for trial—a trial at which the standard adopted by the plurality would be used to determine if the search of Dr. Ortega's office was reasonable.

As was the case with the Court's decision in the student search case of *New Jersey v. T.L.O.,* this opinion raises as many questions as it answers. Although a majority of the Court has rejected the probable cause standard, we still do not have a majority in support of an alternative standard. The Court did not examine the question of whether or not individualized suspicion would be needed to search, nor the question of the standard to be used if an employer seeks to search the employee him or herself, or her personal belongings such as a purse or briefcase.[429] One lower court has held that the fourth amendment protected a school bus attendant from being required to be subjected to drug testing without particularized suspicion that she was a drug user.[430] In dictum the court noted, however, that mandatory testing may be permissible with regard to school bus drivers and mechanics directly responsible for the operation and maintenance of school buses. In addition, the court also reached a conclusion that would be applicable not only to school bus attendants but also to school bus drivers and mechanics: dismissal on the basis of a single, unconfirmed urinalysis test is arbitrary, capricious, and a violation of the law of the District of Columbia. The court did not reach the question whether dismissal on the basis of a single, unconfirmed test would violate substantive due process protections, but its holding under the law of the District of Columbia suggests that it would have.[431]

The plurality opinion left open the question of what criteria were to be used for deciding if employer practices, procedures, or policies have reduced employee expectations of privacy. For example, does a teacher or guidance counselor lose fourth amendment protections when he or she uses his or her office, desk, and/or files for the storage of official school files? The plurality seemed to place great stress on the fact that in this case Dr. Ortega had kept only personal items in his office. Similarly, the plurality intimated that fourth amendment protections might be unavailable if Dr. Ortega has shared an office. Nor did the opinion address the standard to be used if the employer engages in a search to uncover evidence of criminal behavior. Neither did the Court comment upon such other issues as the criteria to determine when an employee has voluntarily consented to a search, the criteria for determining when a search with police involvement is a police search subject to the warrant requirement and a probable cause standard. Nor did the Court discuss the applicability of the exclusionary rule to employee disciplinary cases.[432]

Finally, it should be noted that two courts have held that a professor has no constitutionally based privilege to withhold information regarding his or her vote on a promotion case that is now before the courts for review to determine if the promotion was unlawfully denied.[433] To recognize such a privilege, say the courts, could frustrate the efforts of plaintiffs to vindicate their constitutional and statutory rights. Other courts have approached the problem by balancing a qualified privilege against the need for the information.[434]

9.20. REMEDIES IN EMPLOYMENT CASES

Section 1983, also known as the Civil Rights Act of 1871, gives to federal courts the authority to provide a person deprived of his or her federal constitutional or statutory rights a variety of remedies including monetary damages.[435] Important details regarding the liability of the school board and the "limited liability" of school officials are taken up in §2.3.

We concentrate here on the question of the remedies courts will order pursuant to a suit based on §1983 in which the teacher has successfully established that his or her rights under the Constitution and/or a federal statute were violated. (Note that it is not uncommon for the courts to say that §1983 is not available as a remedy in conjunction with a suit based on another federal statute, e.g., Title VII, because the more specific statute was intended by Congress to be the sole and exclusive source of remedies.)

The range of remedies that the courts have ordered pursuant to §1983 include: reinstatement and back pay;[436] the granting of tenure;[437] actual damages;[438] damages for emotional and mental distress;[439] expungement of the employment file;[440] and the granting of a hearing.[441] Punitive damages—a monetary award intended not to compensate the teacher for harm done but to punish the employer—are not available under §1983 against governmental entities (school boards) or officials sued in their official capacities; however, school officials may be sued when acting in their "individual" capacities.[442] However, punitive damages are available against individual defendants when "the defendant's conduct is shown to be motivated by evil motive or intent, or when it invokes reckless or callous indifference to the federally protected rights of others."[443] Under the Civil Rights Attorneys' Fees Awards Act of 1976 reasonable attorney's fees may be awarded to the prevailing party in a §1983 action.[444]

Title VII expressly provides that the courts may order reinstatement, back pay, or other equitable relief the court deems appropriate.[445] Additional remedies the courts have ordered include the granting of tenure,[446] granting a promotion,[447] the establishment of a search for job applicants who might have been discouraged by the discriminatory hiring policies of the employer,[448] the establishment of complaint procedures and other steps to prevent sexual harassment,[449] and the retroactive grant of seniority.[450] Punitive and other damages are available under Title VII.[451] Title VII also provides for the award of attorney's fees.[452] Plaintiffs in sexual harassment cases have been allowed to bring tort claims pendant to their claims under Title VII.[453] Compensatory damages for sexual harassment may also be available under state civil rights statutes.[454] It has been held that the Rehabilitation Act[455] permits the awarding of damages for intentional discrimination on the basis of handicap.[456] The Age Discrimination in Employment Act[457] permits the grant of equitable and legal (damages) relief. It has been held that Title IX[458] does not provide a private remedy in employment discrimination cases when Title VII and §1983 are available.[459] As for Title VI,[460] at least one circuit has held that relief under this act is limited to cessation of discriminatory activity; back pay and other losses are not recoverable.[461]

NOTES

1. Chapman v. Bd. of Educ., 57 A.D. 2d 835, 394 N.Y.S.2d 52 (App. Div. 1977) (dismissal of teacher who lacked certification).
2. In New York the legislature has delegated certification authority to the New York City School District. Chavich v. Bd. of Examiners, Bd. of Educ. of City of N.Y., 23 A.D.2d 57, 258 N.Y.S.2d 677 (App. Div. 1965) (city-certifying board may set higher certification requirements than those set by the state).
3. Bay v. State Bd. of Educ., 233 Or. 601, 378 P.2d 558 (1963) (en banc) (evidence of having committed a burglary eight years prior to the application for a certificate was relevant in assessing moral character). Courts are generally reluctant to second-guess the wisdom of the certifying agencies assessment of character.
4. For a discussion of these requirements *see* §6.2.
5. *See* Commonwealth Dept. of Educ. v. Great Valley Sch. Dist., 23 Pa. Commonw. 423, 352 A.2d 252 (Pa. 1976).
6. United States and South Carolina, National Educ. Ass'n v. South Carolina, 445 F. Supp. 1094 (D.S.C. 1977), *aff'd*, 434 U.S. 1026 (1978).
7. *Cf.*, United States v. State of Texas, 628 F. Supp. 304 (E. D. Tex. 1985) (holding that adoption of the requirement that applicants for teacher education programs achieve a satisfactory score on the Pre-Professional Skills Test was racially motivated). For a further discussion of this case *see* §7.6.
8. Title VI prohibits discrimination on the basis of race in programs receiving federal financial assistance. 42 U.S.C. §2000d (1982). Whether the tests may be challenged depends on whether the testing program is part of a program that receives federal assistance and whether a federal agency has issued regulations bearing on testing that prohibits policies that have a discriminatory impact. Alexander v. Choate, 105 S. Ct. 712, 717 (1985).
9. Erb v. Iowa State Bd. of Pub. Inst., 216 N.W.2d 339 (Iowa, 1974) (overturning revocation of certificate for an act of adultery); Morrison v. State Bd. of Educ., 461 P.2d 375 (Cal. 1969) *(en banc)* (overturning revocation of certification for a single homosexual act); Comings v. State Bd. of Educ., 23 Cal. App. 3d 94, 100 Cal. Rptr., 73 (Cal. App. 1972) (overturning revocation of teacher who had been convicted of possession of marijuana). *Cf.*, Pettit v. State Bd. of Educ., 109 Cal. Rptr. 665, 513 P.2d 889 (Cal., 1973) *(en banc)* (upholding revocation of certificate of teacher who participated in a "swingers" club and appeared in disguise on television to discuss non-

conventional sexual behavior). *See* Annot., 47 A.L.R.3d 1973).

10. For a discussion of procedural due process requirements see §§ 9.17 and 9.18.

11. McCarthy v. Philadelphia Civil Service Comm., 424 U.S. 645 (1976) (no constitutional bar to requiring firefighters to live in city); Wardwell v. Bd. of Educ., 529 F.2d 625 (6th Cir. 1976) (teachers).

12. Harrah Indep. Sch. Dist. v. Martin, 440 U.S. 194 (constitutionally permissible to dismiss teachers who did not meet continuing education requirement).

13. Kirk v. Miller, 83 Wash. 2d 77, 522 P.2d 843 (1974) *(en banc)*. *See* Linn v. Andover-Newton Theological School, 638 F. Supp. 1114 (D. Mass. 1986).

14. *See, e.g.,* Halsey v. Bd. of Educ., 273 Md. 566, 331 A.2d 306 (1975); DeLong v. Bd. of Educ. of Southwest Sch. Dist., 37 Ohio App. 2d 69, 306 N.E.2d 774 (Ohio App. 1973) (refusal to rehire nontenured teacher without giving reasons is a denial neither of substantive due process nor procedural due process).

15. Harrisburg R-VIII Sch. Dist. v. O'Brian, 540 S.W.2d 945 (Miss. 1976). *Cf.,* Coe v. Bogart, 519 F.2d 10 (6th Cir. 1975).

16. *Cf.,* State *ex rel.* State Bd. of Educ. v. Montoya, 73 N.M. 162, 386 P.2d 252 (1963).

17. Brough v. Bd. of Educ., 23 Utah 2d 353, 463 P.2d 567 (1970).

18. *See, e.g.,* Smith v. Sch. Dist. No. 18, Pondera Cty., 115 Mont., 102, 139 P.2d 518 (Mont. 1943) (transfer disallowed).

19. Dist. 300 Educ. Ass'n v. Bd. of Educ., 31 Ill. App. 3d 550, 334 N.E.2d 165 (App. Ct. 1975); McGrath v. Burkhard, 280 P.2d 865 (Cal. 1955). *Cf.,* Pease v. Millcreek Twp. Sch. Dist., 412 Pa. 378, 195 A.2d 104 (1963) (cannot discharge teacher for refusing to sponsor nonschool-sponsored bowling club).

20. What counts as probtionary service toward tenure varies from state to state. For example, continuous part-time teaching counts as probationary service in some states but not others. Indep. Sch. Dist. No. 10 v. Lollar, 547 P.2d 1324 (Okla. 1976) (yes); Thompson v. E. Baton Rouge Parish Sch. Bd., 303 So.2d 855 (La. 1974) (no); Oak Harbor Sch. Dist. v. Oak Harbor Educ. Ass'n, 86 Wash. 2d 497, 545 P.2d 1197 (1976) (en banc) (allowed). Nagy v. Bd. of Educ., 31 Colo. App. 45, 500 P.2d 987 (1972) (service in administrative post does not count as tenure as teacher).

21. Mathews v. Nyquist, 67 A.D.2d 790, 412 N.Y.S.2d 501 (App. Div. 1979). *Cf.,* Morse v. Wozniak, 398 F. Supp. 597 (E.D. Mich. 1975), *rev'd on other grounds,* 565 F.2d 959 (6th Cir. 1977).

22. When the state law granting tenure is interpreted as having created a contractual right, the legislature may not subsequently remove the right since this would be a violation of Article 1, §10 of the Constitution providing that the obligations of contract may not be impaired. Indiana *ex rel.* Anderson v. Brand, 303 U.S. 95 (1938). *See also,* Linn v. Andover-Newton Theological School, 638 F. Supp. 1114 (D. Mass. 1986).

23. Robert E. Phay, "Arbitrary and Capricious Nonrenewal Decisions," in *School Law Update 1985,* ed. T. Jones and D. P. Semler (Topeka, Kans.: National Organization on Legal Problems of Education, 1985), 177-79. *See, e.g.,* Donaldson v. Bd. of Educ., 65 N.J. 236, 320 A.2d 857, 859 (1974) ("The board's determination not to grant tenure need not be grounded on unsatisfactory classroom or professional performance, for there are many unrelated but nonetheless equally valid reasons why a board, having had the benefits of observation during the probationary period, may conclude that tenure should not be granted").

24. Branch v. Sch. Dist., 432 F. Supp. 608 (D. Mont. 1977); Tilton v. Southwest Sch. Corp., 281 N.E.2d 117 (Ind. Ct. App. 1972).

25. For an extensive list of cases see Annot., 4 A.L.R. 3d 1090 (1965); Annot., 78 A.L.R.3d 83 (1977); Annot., 78 A.L.R.3d 19 (1977); Annot., 47 A.L.R.3d 754 (1973); W. Valente, *Law in the Schools* (Columbus, Ohio: Charles E. Merrill Publishing Co., 1980), 180-88.

26. Hale v. Bd. of Educ., City of Lancaster, 13 Ohio St. 2d 92, 234 N.E.2d 583 (1968).

27. Thompson v. Southwest Sch. Dist., 483 F. Supp. 1170 (W.D. Mo. 1980); Bd. of Educ. of Long Beach Unified Sch. Dist. of Los Angeles Cty. v. Jack M., 139 Cal. Rptr. 700, 566 P.2d 602 (Cal. 1977) (en banc).

28. Thompson v. Southwest Sch. Dist., 483 F. Supp. 1170 (W.D. Mo. 1980).

29. Denton v. South Kitsap Sch. Dist., 10 Wash. App. 69, 516 P.2d 1080 (App. Ct. 1973). See Floyd G. Delon, "A Teacher's Sexual Involvement with Pupils: 'Reasonable Cause for Dismissal,'", Educational Law Reporter 22 (1985): 1085.

30. Welch v. Bd. of Educ. of Chandler Unified Sch. Dist. No. 80, 136 Ariz. 552, 667 P.2d 746 (Ct. App. 1983).

31. See §9.18 discussing the constitutional requirement that the decision be made for reasons in fact and on evidence in the record.

32. Ill. Ann. State, ch. 122 §24-12 (Smith-Hurd Supp. 1985); Aulwurm v. Bd. of Educ. of Murphysboro Comm. Unity Sch. Dist. No. 186, 67 Ill.2d 434, 10 Ill. Dec. 571, 367 N.E.2d 1337 (Ill. 1977); Gilliland v. Bd. of Educ. of Pleasant View Consolidated Sch. Dist., 35 Ill. App. 3d 861, 343 N.E.2d 704 (Ill. App. 1976); Kroll v. Indep. Sch. Dist. No. 593, 304 N.W.2d 338 (1981).

33. Scheelhaase v. Woodbury Central Comm. Sch. Dist., 488 F.2d 237 (8th Cir. 1973) (dismissal did not raise substantive due process issue); Hollingsworth v. Bd. of Educ. of Sch. Dist. of Alliance, 208 Neb. 350, 303 N.W.2d 506 (1981) (allegations insufficient to establish that teacher was incompetent).

34. See §§9.6 and 9.7.

35. The law as regards dismissal of college and university professors for reasons of financial exigency is different. See Annette B. Johnson, "The Problems of Contraction: Legal Considerations in University Retrenchment," Journal of Law & Education 10 (1981): 269.

36. Baron v. Mackreth, 26 N.Y.2d 1039, 260 N.E.2d 554 (1970).

37. Zoll v. Eastern Allamakee Community Sch. Dist., 588 F.2d 246 (8th Cir. 1978).

38. Steele v. Bd. of Educ., 40 N.Y.2d 456 (1976); Amos v. Bd. of Educ., 54 A.D.2d 297, 388 N.Y.S.2d 435 (1976).

39. The New York Commissioner of Education has said school officials are not required to rearrange faculty schedules in order to avoid assigning teachers to subjects in which they are not certified when doing so would require payment of additional salaries to any of the teachers involved in the reassignment. McDonald v. Bellmore-Merrick Central High Sch. Dist., Dec. No. 9439, June 20, 1977.

40. New York Education Law, § 2510 (3) (McKinneys, 1981).

41. Chauvel v. Nyquist, 55 A.D. 2d 76, 389 N.Y.S.2d 636 (App. Div. 1976).

42. Mt. Healthy City Sch. Dist. Bd. of Educ. v. Doyle, 429 U.S. 274 (1977).

43. Id.

44. The West Virginia Board of Education in 1915 published the following Rules of Conduct for Teachers: "(1) You will not marry during the term of your contract. (2) You are not to keep company with men. (3) You must be home between the hours of 8:00 P.M. and 6:00 A.M. unless attending a school function. (4) You may not loiter downtown in ice cream stores. (5) You may not travel beyond the city limits unless you have the permission of the chairman of the board. (6) You may not ride in a carriage or automobile with any man unless he is your father or brother. (7) You may not smoke cigarettes. (8) You may not dress in bright colors. (9) You may under no circumstances dye your hair. (10) You must wear at least two petticoats. (11) Your dresses must not be any shorter than two inches above the ankle. (12) To keep the schoolroom neat and clean, you must sweep the floor at least once daily; scrub the floor at least once a week with hot, soapy water; clean the blackboards at least once a day, and start the fire at 7:00 A.M. so that room will be warm by 8:00 A.M." Quoted in M. LaMorte, School Law: Cases and Concepts (Englewood Cliffs, N.J.: Prentice-Hall, Inc., 1982), 216.

45. Griswold v. Connecticut, 381 U.S. 479 (1965). The Court has continued its protection of

the right of married and single people, and even minors, to obtain and use contraception. Carey v. Population Services International, 431 U.S. 678 (1977); Eisenstadt v. Baird, 405 U.S. 438 (1972).

46. Stanley v. Georgia, 394 U.S. 557 (1969).

47. Roe v. Wade, 410 U.S. 113 (1973).

48. Cleveland Bd. of Educ. v. LaFleur, 414 U.S. 632 (1974). *See also* §9.10.

49. Moore v. East Cleveland, 431 U.S. 494 (1977); Zablocki v. Redhail, 434 U.S. 374 (1978).

50. The elaboration of this approach is perhaps most fully developed in Roe v. Wade, 410 U.S. 113 (1973).

51. Zablocki v. Rehail, 434 U.S. 374 (1978).

52. Sullivan v. Meade Indep. Sch. Dist. No. 101, 530 F.2d 799 (8th Cir. 1976) (dismissal upheld); Sedule v. Capitol Sch. Dist., 425 F. Supp. 552 (D.D.C. 1976), *aff'd mem.* 565 F.2d 153 (3d 1977), *cert. denied,* 434 U.S. 1039 (1978) (dismissal upheld—amorous affair led to neglect of duties; teacher also mailed nude photos to husband of woman with whom she was involved in order to induce a separation); Hollenbaugh and Philburn v. Carnegie Free Library, 578 F.2d 1374 (3d Cir. 1978), *cert. denied,* 439 U.S. 1052 (1979) (upholding dismissal of two employees living in "open adultery"). *But see* Fisher v. Snyder, 476 F.2d 375 (8th Cir. 1973) (dismissal barred); Thompson v. Southwest Sch. Dist., 483 F. Supp. 1170 (W.D. Mo. 1980) (dismissal barred—nexus not established). *Cf.,* Erb. v. Iowa State Bd. of Pub. Inst., 216 N.W.2d 339 (1974); Carter v. United States, 407 F.2d 1238 (D.C. Cir. 1968). In Sherburne v. Sch. Bd. of Suwannee Cty., 455 So.2d 1057 (Fla. App. 1984) the state court said that under state law a teacher could not be refused reemployment for off-campus consensual sexual conduct with an adult of the opposite sex.

53. Fisher v. Snyder, 476 F.2d 375 (8th Cir. 1973) (dismissal barred). In this Nebraska case Mrs. Fisher, a middle-aged divorcee who lived in a one-bedroom apartment, had entertained overnight visitors—young ladies, married couples, and young men who were friends of her son. One man, aged twenty-six, was a particularly frequent visitor. His parents lived in California and he regularly visited Mrs. Fisher during his school vacations and other times. The court said that this evidence at most raised a question of improper behavior, provided no inkling of improper behavior beyond subtle implication and innuendo. Nor was there evidence of community reaction against her, nor evidence that she was incapable of maintaining discipline in the classroom. Her openness about her association with the young man and the age differential also convinced the court no inference of impropriety could be drawn.

54. Bd. of Trustees v. Stubblefield, 16 Cal. App.3rd 820, 94 Cal. Rptr. 318 (1971). *Cf.,* Jerry v. Bd. of Educ., 35 N.Y.2d 534, 364 N.Y.S.2d 440, 324 N.E.2d 106 (N.Y. 1974); Goldin v. Bd. of Central Sch. Dist. No. 1, 78 Misc.2d 972 359 N.Y.S.2d 384 (1973) (teacher may not be dismissed for having sex with former student in absence of proof the activity was a continuation of conduct that had started before the student graduated).

55. Avery v. Homewood City. Bd. of Educ., 674 F.2d 337 (5th Cir. 1982), *cert. denied,* 461 U.S. 943 (1983); Andrews v. Drew Municipal Separate Sch. Dist., 507 F.2d 611 (5th Cir. 1975), *cert. granted,* 423 U.S. 820 (1975), *cert. dismissed,* 425 U.S. 559 (1976); Eckman v. Bd. of Hawthorn Sch. Dist. No. 17, 636 F. Supp. 1214 (N.D. Ill. 1986). Lewis v. Delaware State College, 455 F. Supp. 239 (D. Del. 1978); Drake v. Covington City Bd. of Educ., 371 F. Supp. 974; (M.D. Ala. 1974); New Mexico State Bd. of Educ. v. Stoudt, 91 N.M. 183, 571 P.2d 1186 (1977). *Contra,* Brown v. Bathke, 416 F. Supp. 1194 (D. Neb. 1976), *rev'd on other grounds,* 566 F.2d 588 (8th Cir. 1977); Wardlaw v. Austin Sch. Dist., 10 FEP Cases 982 (W.D. Tex. 1975).

56. Avery v. Homewood City Bd. of Educ., 674 F.2d 337 (5th Cir. 1982), *cert. denied,* 461 U.S. 943 (1983); Andrews v. Drew Municipal Separate Sch. Dist., 507 F.2d 611 (5th Cir. 1975), *cert. granted,* 423 U.S. 820 (1975), *cert. dismissed,* 425 U.S. 559 (1976).

57. Brown v. Bathke, 566 F.2d 588, 592 (8th Cir. 1977).

58. Wishart v. McDonald, 500 F.2d 1110 (1st cir. 1974). *Cf.,* Pettit v. State Bd. of Education, 10 Cal. 3d 29, 513 P.2d 889, 109 Cal. Rptr. 665 (1973) (upholding revocation of teaching certificate of teacher who had been discovered by police working undercover engaging in fellatio with men other than her husband in a private "swingers" club).

59. In re Grossman, 127 N.J. Super.13, 316 A.2d 39 (App. Div. 1974); Grossman v. Bernards Township Bd. of Educ., 538 F.2d 319 (3d Cir.), *cert. denied,* 429 U.S. 897 (1976).

60. Tomerlin v. Dade Cty. Sch. Bd., 318 So.2d 159, 160 (Fla. Dist. Ct. App. 1975).

61. Weissbaum v. Hannon, 439 F. Supp. 873 (N.D. Ill. 1977).

62. 106 S.Ct. 2841 (1986). *See also* Doe v. Commonwealth's Attorney, 403 F. Supp. 1199 (E.D. Va. 1975), aff'd, 425 U.S. 901 (1976).

63. Dronenburg v. Zech, 714 F.2d 1388 (D.C.C. 1984); Rich v. Sec. of the Army, 735 F.2d 1220 (10th Cir. 1984).

64. Nat. Gay Task Force v. Bd. of Educ. of City of Oklahoma, 729 F.2d 1270 (10th Cir. 1984), *aff'd by an equally divided Court,* 105 S.Ct. 1858 (1985). The Court concluded the advocacy section of the statute was overbroad and accordingly had a deterrent effect on legitimate expression. *Cf.,* Acanfora v. Bd. of Educ., 491 F.2d 498 (4th Cir. 1974), *cert. denied,* 419 U.S. 836 (1974) (holding, inter alia, homosexual teacher could not be dismissed for discussing homosexuality on television).

65. Rowland v. Mad River Local Sch. Dist., Montgomery Cty., 730 F.2d 444 (6th Cir. 1984), *cert. denied,* 105 S.Ct. 1373 (1985).

66. *See* §§2.6, 6.4.

67. In dissenting from the denial of certiorari, Justice Brennan argued, *inter alia,* that discrimination against homosexuals or bisexuals raised significant equal protection questions, and that he had serious doubts that the lower court opinion sustaining the dismissal could be upheld under any equal protection test. He could see little justification for dismissing someone for having a particular sexual preference and for the nondisruptive expression of that preference. 105 S. Ct. at 1376-79.

68. Acanfora v. Bd. of Educ., 491 F.2d 498 (4th Cir. 1974), *cert. denied,* 419 U.S. 836 (1974). *See also* Burton v. Cascade Sch. Dist., 353 F. Supp. 254 (D. Or. 1973), *aff'd,* 512 F.2d 850 (9th Cir. 1975), *cert. denied,* 423 U.S. 839 (1975).

69. Gaylord v. Tacoma Sch. Dist., 85 Wash.2d 348, 535 P.2d 804 (1975), *cert. denied,* 434 U.S. 879 (1977), *aff'd,* 88 Wash.2d. 286, 559 P.2d 1340 (1977). The main opinion is a poorly drafted and confused opinion.

70. Morrison v. State Bd. of Educ., 1 Cal. 3d 214, 461 P.2d 375, 82 Cal. Rptr. 175 (1969).

71. Littlejohn v. Rose, 768 F.2d 765 (6th Cir. 1985).

72. Stoddard v. Sch. Dist. No. 1, 590 F.2d 829 (10th Cir. 1979). The board had claimed she was dismssed because she inadequately disciplined her students, kept an untidy classroom, and was generally unsatisfactory as a teacher. The court concluded these were not the real reasons for the dismissal.

73. *See* §1.4.

74. 511 F.2d 744 (5th Cir. 1975), *rehearing denied,* 515 F.2d 762 (5th Cir. 1975), *cert. dismissed as improvidently granted,* 429 U.S. 165 (1976).

75. Brantley v. Surles, 718 F.2d 1354 (5th Cir. 1983). On remand the trial judge found that Brantley had not materially and substantially disrupted the school by enrolling her son in the private school. 765 F.2d 478 (5th Cir. 1985). *See also* Stough v. Crenshaw Cty. Bd. of Educ., 579 F. Supp. 1091 (M.D. Ala. 1983), *aff'd,* 744 F.2d 1479 (11th Cir. 1984).

76. Dike v. Sch. Bd. of Orange City, Fla., 650 F.2d 783 (5th Cir. 1981).

77. Goseny v. Sonora Indep. Sch. Dist., 603 F.2d 522 (5th Cir. 1979). The plaintiff, however, won this case on equal protection grounds because the policy had been discriminatorily applied to him, and not to other similarly situated teachers. *Cf.,* LaBuhn v. White, 257 Iowa 606, 133 N.W.2d 903 (1965) (prohibiting a person from serving on both the local board and the county board concurrently).

78. McCarthy v. Philadelphia Civil Service Comm'n, 424 U.S. 645 (1976); Wardwell v. Bd. of Educ. of the City Sch. Dist. of Cincinnati, 529 F.2d 625 (6th Cir. 1976). Such rules are said to encourage commitment to the district, encourage greater involvement with parents and children

in the district, encourage greater understanding of the children in the district and the problems they may face.

79. McCarthy v. Philadelphia Civil Service Comm'n, 424 U.S. 645 (1976).

80. 425 U.S. 238 (1976).

81. Ball v. Bd. of Trustees of the Kerrville Indep. Sch. Dist., 584 F.2d 684 (5th Cir. 1978), *cert. denied*, 440 U.S. 972 (1979); East Hartford Educ. Ass'n v. Bd. of Educ., 562 F.2d 838 (2nd Cir. 1977) (en banc); Miller v. Sch. Dist. No. 167, 495 F.2d 658 (7th Cir. 1974); Tardif v. Quinn, 545 F.2d 761 (1st Cir. 1976). *Contra*, Conard v. Goolsby, 350 F. Supp. 713 (N.D. Miss. 1972); Finot v. Pasadena City Bd. of Educ., 250 Cal. App. 2d 189, 58 Cal. Rptr. 520 (Ct. App. 1967).

82. *See* Hander v. San Jacinto Junior College, 519 F.2d 273, 277 (5th Cir. 1975).

83. Pence v. Rosenquist, 573 F.2d 395 (7th Cir. 1978) (grooming regulation applied to school bus drivers struck down).

84. Governing Board v. Brennan, 18 Cal. App. 3d 396, 95 Cal. Rptr., 712 (App. Ct. 1973). *See also* Annot., 47 A.L.R.3d 754 (1973).

85. Bd. of Trustees of Santa Maria Joint Union High Sch. Dist. v. Judge, 50 Cal. App. 920, 123 Cal. Rptr. 830 (1975).

86. Comings v. State Bd. of Educ., 23 Cal. App. 3d 94, 100 Cal. Rptr. 73 (App. Ct. 1972). *But see* Logan v. Warren Cty. Bd. of Educ., 549 F. Supp. 145 (S.D. Ga. 1982) (upholding dismissal after conviction for submitting false documents to the Internal Revenue Service); Adams v. State Professional Practices Council, 406 So.2d 1170 (Fla. Dist. Ct. App. 1981) (possession of fifty-two marijuana plants sufficient to establish moral turpitude); Lesley v. Oxford Area Sch. Dist., 54 Pa. Commw. 120, 420 A.2d 764 (Commw Ct. 1980) (dismissal after admitting to shoplifting); Skripchuck v. Austin, 379 A.2d 1142 (Del. 1977) (dismissal after pleading guilty to charges of theft and aggravated assault); Watson v. State Bd. of Educ., 22 Cal. App.3d 559, 99 Cal. Rptr. 468 (1971) (dismissal of a teacher convicted six times of driving while intoxicated).

87. *See* Louisiana Affiliate of National Organization for Reform of Marijuana Laws v. Guste, 380 F. Supp. 404 (E.D. La. 1974), *aff'd*, 511 F.2d 1400 (5th Cir.), *cert. denied*, 423 U.S. 867 (1974).

88. S. Rubin and S. Greenhouse, *The Rights of Teachers* (New York: Bantam Books, 1983), 154.

89. For one listing of such laws, see S. D. Ross and A. Barcher, *The Rights of Women* (New York: Bantam Books, 1983), 303-55.

90. In Geduldig v. Aiello, 417 U.S. 484 (1974) the Court held that the exclusion of pregnancy from disability insurance coverage did not constitute discrimination on the basis of gender. The Court also interpreted Title VII of the Civil Rights Act of 1964 the same way. General Electric Co. v. Gilbert, 429 U.S. 125 (1976). In 1976 Congress overturned the Gilbert ruling when it amended Title VII by specifically prohibiting employers from excluding pregnancy benefits from comprehensive medical and disability insurance plans. This change requires employers to treat a pregnancy-related disability the same way as any other disability for purposes of insurance and sick leave.

91. Goesaert v. Cleary, 335 U.S. 464 (1948) (upholding a law that provided that no woman could obtain a bartender's license unless she was "the wife or daughter of the male owner" of a licensed liquor establishment). *See also* Muller v. Oregon, 208 U.S. 412 (1908). In this case the Court upheld a law that prohibited women from being employed in a factory or laundry more than ten hours a day. In that same period the Court struck down similar laws as they applied to men. Lochner v. New York, 198 U.S. 45 (1905).

92. Frontiero v. Richardson, 411 U.S. 677 (1973).

93. Craig v. Boren, 429 U.S. 190 (1976). *See also* Mississippi University for Women v. Hogan, 458 U.S. 718 (1982).

94. For a discussion of Title VII and employment discrimination see, § 9.9.

95. Personnel Administrator of Mass. v. Feeney, 442 U.S. 256 (1979) (upholding a Massachusetts law granting an "absolute lifetime" preference to veterans for state civil service positions

even though the preference operated overwhelmingly to the advantage of males).

96. *See* Village of Arlington Heights v. Metropolitan Housing Development Corporation, 429 U.S. 252, 270 n. 21 (1977).

97. The differences in the initial burden placed upon the plaintiff in a constitutional and Title VII case will be discussed below.

98. 42 U.S.C. § 2000(e) (1982).

99. 42 U.S.C. § 2000e-3(a) (1982).

100. Anderson v. City of Bessemer City, 105 S. Ct. 1504 (1985).

101. International Brotherhood of Teamsters v. United States, 431 U.S. 324, 355 n. 15 (1977).

102. *See* Stone v. Belgrade Sch. Dist., 703 P.2d 136 (1984) (holding that evidence supported finding that female students' interests in privacy warranted conclusion that gender was a BFOQ for the hiring of a guidance counselor when there were no female guidance counselors).

103. Dothard v. Rawlinson, 433 U.S. 321, 334 (1977) (holding, among other things, that being male is a BFOQ for the job of correctional counselor in a "contact" position in a male maximum-security penitentiary). The Court has also accepted the proposition that some job qualifications may be so peripheral to the mission of the business that no age discrimination can be viewed as reasonably necessary to the operation of the business. Western Airlines Inc. v. Criswell, 105 S.Ct. 2743, 2751 (1985).

104. Hayes v. Shelby Memorial Hospital, 726 F.2d 1543, 1549 (11th Cir. 1984).

105. Moteles v. University of Pennsylvania, 730 F.2d 913 (3d Cir. 1984), *cert. denied*, 105 S. Ct. 179 (1984).

106. City of Los Angeles v. Manhart, 435 U.S. 702 (1978). In Arizona Governing Committee for Tax Deferral Annuity Plans v. Norris, 463 U.S.1073 (1983) the Court held that paying women lower monthly retirement benefits than men because women tend to live longer than men violates Title VII.

107. McDonnell Douglas Corp. v. Green 411 U.S. 792, 804-5 (1973); Texas Dept. of Community Affairs v. Burdine, 450 U.S. 248 (1981).

108. Rodriguez v. Bd. of Educ. of Eastchester U. Free Sch. Dist., 620 F.2d 362, 364. (2nd Cir. 1980).

109. Thompkins v. Morris Brown College, 752 F.2d 558 (11th Cir. 1985); Lee v. Russell Cty. Bd. of Educ., 684 F.2d 769 (11th Cir. 1982).

110. Banerjee v. Bd. of Trustees of Smith College, 648 F.2d 61, 64 (1st Cir. 1981), *cert. denied*, 454 U.S. 1098 (1981).

111. Texas Department of Community Affairs v. Burdine, 450 U.S. 248, 256 (1981).

Employees may also attempt to establish that their resignation from a job was in fact a discriminatory "constructive discharge." The federal circuit courts of appeal have adopted two standards for determining whether constructive discharge has taken place. The First, Second, Third, Fifth, Sixth, Ninth, Eleventh, and District of Columbia Circuit Courts of Appeal have held that a constructive discharge has been established when the plaintiff has shown that his or her conditions of employment were sufficiently intolerable that a reasonable employee would have resigned. Alicea Orsado v. Garcia Santiago, 562 F.2d 114 (1st cir. 1977); Pena v. Brattleboro Retreat, 702 F.2d 322 (2d 1983); Goss v. Exxon Office Sys. Co., 747 F.2d 885 (3d Cir. 1984); Bourque v. Powell Elec. Mfg. Co., 617 F.2d 61 (5th Cir. 1980); Held v. Gulf Oil Co., 684 F.2d 427 (6th Cir. 1982); Heagney v. University of Wash., 652 F.2d 1157 (9th Cir. 1981); Wardwell v. Sch. Bd. of Palm Beach City, Fla., 786 F.2d 1554 (11th Cir. 1986); Clark v. Marsh, 665 F.2d 1168 (D.C. Cir. 1981). The Fourth, Eighth, and Tenth Circuit Courts of Appeal hold that not only must the plaintiff establish the existence of intolerable conditions, but also that the employer had the specific intent of coercing her resignation. E.E.O.C. v. Federal Reserve Bank, 698 F.2d 633 (4th Cir. 1983, *rev'd on other grounds sub nom.*, Cooper v. Federal Reserve Bank, 467 U.S. 876 (1984); Johnson v. Bunny Bread Co., 646 F.2d 1250 (8th Cir. 1981); Muller v. United States Steel Corp., 409 F.2d 923 (10th Cir. 1975).

112. Texas Department of Community Affairs v. Burdine, 450 U.S. 248 (1981).

113. Nagel v. Avon Bd. of Educ., 575 F. Supp. 105 (D. Conn. 1983). *See also* Harris v. Birmingham Bd. of Educ., 712 F.2d 1377, 1383 (11th Cir. 1983).

114. Coble v. Hot Springs Sch. Dist. No. 6, 682 F.2d 721 (8th Cir. 1982) (Finding disparate treatment in a case in which the employer expressed concern that the plaintiff had family responsibilities that would distract her from performance of the job but did not stress the same concern with the male applicant.

115. Sweeney v. Bd. of Trustees of Keene State College, 604 F.2d 106, 113 (1st Cir. 1979).

116. Id.

117. Lynn v. Regents of the University of California, 656 F.2d 1337, 1343 (9th Cir. 1981). *cert. denied,* 459 U.S. 823 (1982).

118. Lynn v. Regents of the University of California, 656 F.2d 1337, 1342-43 (9th Cir. 1981), *cert. denied,* 459 U.S. 823 (1982); Chang v. University of Rhode Island, 606 F. Supp. 1161 (D. R.I. 1985); Furnco Constr. Corp. v. Waters, 438 U.S. 567, 580 (1978). Obviously, the employer may seek to challenge this evidence. Chang v. University of Rhode Island, 606 F. Supp. at 1188; Lamphere v. Brown University, 685 F.2d 743 (1st Cir. 1982).

119. *See, e.g.,* Nagel v. Avon Bd. of Educ., 575 F. Supp. 105 (D. Conn. 1983).

120. Danzl v. North St. Paul-Maplewood-Oakdale Indep. Sch. Dist. No. 622, 706 F.2d 813 (8th Cir. 1983) (agreeing with the school district that seven years of administrative experience was a more important job qualification than a Ph.D.); Merwine v. Board of Trustees for State Institutions of Higher Learning, 754 F.2d 631 (5th Cir. 1985) (holding that a requirement of a master's of library science degree from an accredited school was not pretextual).

121. Carlile v. South Routt Sch. Dist. Re-3J, 739 F.2d 1496, 1501 (10th Cir. 1984).

122. Id., at 1500; Lieberman v. Gant, 630 F.2d 60, 64 (2d Cir. 1980). The Second Circuit listed five factors that set this decision apart from other employment decisions: (1) tenure entails commitments as to length of time and collegial relationships; (2) tenure decisions are often noncompetitive—denial of tenure to one person does not necessarily lead to tenure for another; (3) tenure decisions are usually highly decentralized; (4) the number of factors to be considered is quite extensive; (5) tenure decisions are a source of great disagreement.

123. Zahorik v. Cornell University, 729 F.2d 85, 93 (2d Cir. 1984).

124. Id., at 93-94.

125. Id., at 94.

126. Namenwirth v. Bd. of Regents of U. of Wis. System, 769 F.2d 1235, 1242 (7th Cir. 1985).

127. Id., at 1243. The First Circuit stated that it was understandable that "the clarity of articulation of reasons for refusing tenure by" a collegial decision-making process "may differ from that given by a business employer." Banerjee v. Bd. of Trustees of Smith College, 648 F.2d 61, 64 (1st Cir. 1981). The First Circuit stressed that a university could insist that a professor teach the average student excellently and not just the advanced or particularly good students. Kumar v. Bd. of Trustees, U. of Mass., 774 F.2d 1 (1st Cir. 1985).

128. McDaniel v. Temple Indep. Sch. Dist., 770 F.2d 1340, 1346 (5th Cir. 1985).

129. 42 U.S.C. §2000e-6(a) (1982).

130. International Brotherhood of Teamsters v. United States, 431 U.S. 324, 336 (1977); Cooper v. Federal Reserve Bank of Richmond, 104 S. Ct. 2794, 2800 (1984). The stress is on proving the employer's general policies and practices are motivated by a discriminatory purpose. General Telephone Co. of Southwest v. Falcon, 457 U.S. 147, 157-58 (1982).

131. Usually, the statistical method of the plaintiffs will "control" for those nondiscriminatory reasons that could explain and justify the differences in treatment and attempt to prove the pattern can best be explained by the employee's use of an improper motive in making personnel decisions.

132. International Brotherhood of Teamsters v. United States, 431 U.S. 324, 360 (1977).

133. Id., at 2801. In other words, proof of isolated or sporadic discriminatory acts is insufficient to establish a prima facie case of a pattern or practice of discrimination. Cooper v. Federal Reserve Bank of Richmond, 104 S. Ct. 2794 (1984).

134. A classic issue in pattern or practice suits is the proper basis of comparison when it is alleged that the employer has discriminated in the hiring of women or blacks. The percentage of women in the employer's workforce is to be compared against what other relevant pool? The Supreme Court has said the proper comparison is between the gender or racial composition of the employer's workforce and the gender or racial composition of the "qualified school teacher population in the relevant labor market." Hazelwood Sch. Dist. v. United States, 433 U.S. 299, 308 (1977). The Court has approved of a statistical method for determining if the disparity between the percentage of women on the employer's workforce and in the relevant comparison population raises an inference of discrimination. This method involves calculating the expected number of women in the workforce if there were no discrimination, and determining how many standard deviations from that expected number is the actual number. The Court has said a standard deviation of more than two or three undercuts the hypothesis that decisions were being made randomly. *Id.*, at 311 n. 17.

135. E.E.O.C. v. Sears, Roebuck & Co., 628 F. Supp. 1264 (N.D. Ill. 1986). The jobs in question were sales jobs that operated on the basis of a commission.

136. Id., at 1306-15.

137. International Brotherhood of Teamsters v. United States, 431 U.S. 324, 361 (1977).

138. Craik v. Minnesota State University Bd., 731 F.2d 465, 470 n. 7 (8th Cir. 1984); Chang v. University of Rhode Island, 606 F. Supp. 1161, 1186 (D. R.I. 1985).

139. Chang. v. University of Rhode Island, 606 F. Supp. at 1186-87. The Supreme Court stated the point this way: "By 'demonstrating the existence of a discriminatory hiring pattern and practice,' the plaintiffs had made out a prima facie case of discrimination against the individual class members; . . . upon proof of that allegation there were reasonable grounds to infer that individual hiring decisions were made in pursuit of the discriminatory policy and to require the employer to come forth with evidence dispelling that inference." International Brotherhood of Teamsters v. United States, 431 U.S. 324, 359 (1977).

140. Id., at 1187.

141. Cooper v. Federal Reserve Bank of Richmond, 104 S. Ct. 2794 (1984). A finding of no discrimination on the pattern and practice suit does (1) bar class members from bringing another class action for the relevant time period, and (2) precludes the class members in other litigation from relitigating the question of discrimination against the class.

142. Coser v. Moore, 739 F.2d 746, 750 (2d Cir. 1984).

143. International Brotherhood of Teamsters v. United States, 431 U.S. 324, 335 n. 15 (1977).

144. Dothard v. Rawlinson, 433 U.S. 321, 329 (1977).

145. As stated by the Supreme Court, the plaintiff may attempt to show that less discriminatory alternatives would also "serve the employer's legitimate interest in 'efficient and trustworthy workmanship.'" Albermarle Paper Co. v. Moody, 422 U.S. 405 (1975). Such a showing would be evidence that the employer had not adopted the policy as a pretext for discrimination.

146. Zahorik v. Cornell University, 729 F.2d 85 (2d Cir. 1983).

147. The most frequent complaint about employment tests is that they have a discriminatory racial impact. Griggs v. Duke Power Co., 401 U.S. 424 (1971). *See* §9.11. The question of discrimination in pay will be taken up in §9.10.

148. Merwine v. Bd. of Trustees for State Institutions of Higher Learning, 754 F.2d 631, 639 (5th Cir. 1985).

149. Civil Rights Div. of Arizona Dept. of Law v. Amphitheater Unified Sch. Dist., 693 P.2d 342 (Ct. App. Ariz. 1983).

150. To date, all the Supreme Court decisions using the disparate impact theory have applied to specific, neutral policies, e.g., a degree requirement. *See, e.g.,* Griggs v. Duke Power Co., 401 U.S. 424 (1971). Several lower courts have refused to extend the Griggs disparate impact theory to subjective hiring decisions. *See, e.g.,* Pouncy v. Prudential Insurance Company of America, 668 F.2d 795 (5th Cir. 1982); E.E.O.C. v. Sears, Roebuck & Company, 628 F. Supp. 1264 (N.D. Ill. 1986).

151. 29 U.S.C. §206(d) (1982).

152. 29 U.S.C. §206(d)(1) (1982).

153. That the job holders themselves have similar skills and training is irrelevant: the question is whether the jobs demand similar skills. Hein v. Oregon College of Educ., 718 F.2d 910, 914 (9th Cir. 1983).

154. 29 U.S.C. §206(d) (1982).

155. Corning Glass v. Brennan, 417 U.S. 188, 203-4 n. 24 (1974); Gunther v. Cty. of Washington, 623 F.2d 1303, 1309 (9th Cir. 1979), *aff'd on other grounds*, 452 U.S. 161 (1981).

156. Id., at 195.

157. Spaulding v. University of Washington, 740 F.2d 686, 697 (9th Cir. 1984).

158. Brock v. Georgia Southwestern College, 765 F.2d 1026 (11th Cir. 1985); Hein v. Oregon College of Educ., 718 F.2d 910 (9th Cir. 1983); Jacobs v. College of William and Mary, 517 F. Supp. 791 (E.D. Va. 1980), *aff'd mem.*, 661 F.2d 922 (4th Cir.), *cert. denied*, 454 U.S. 1033 (1981).

159. Corning Glass Works v. Brennan, 417 U.S. 188, 196 (1974).

160. County of Washington v. Gunther, 452 U.S. 161 (1981).

161. Id. One lower court has held that when Congress incorporated the four defenses of the Equal Pay Act into Title VII, Congress did not also intend to incorporate the Equal Pay Act's system for allocating the burden of proof. E.E.O.C. v. Sears, Roebuck & Co., 628 F. Supp. 1264, 1331-32 (N.D. Ill. 1986).

162. *See* §9.9 for a discussion of these different types of discrimination suits.

163. Coser v. Moore, 739 F.2d 746 (2d Cir. 1984); Craik v. Minnesota State University Bd., 731 F.2d 465 (8th Cir. 1984); Chang v. University of Rhode Island, 606 F. Supp. 1161 (D. R. I. 1985); Melani v. Bd. of Higher Educ. of City of New York, 561 F. Supp. 769 (S.D. N.Y. 1983).

164. American Federation of State, Cty., and Municipal Employees v. State of Washington, 578 F. Supp. 846, 862 (D. Wash. 1983), *rev'd*, 770 F.2d 1401 (9th Cir. 1985). Under this theory, obviously, someone other than the employer or employee will have to determine if the two sets of jobs are of equal worth to the employer. The mere fact that in the market a university truck driver commands a higher wage than a university secretary would be irrelevant to the determination of the worth of the two jobs to the university.

165. Spaulding v. University of Washington, 740 F.2d 686 (9th Cir. 1984) (rejecting the comparable worth theory); American Federation of State, Cty., and Municipal Employees v. State of Washington, 578 F. Supp. 846 (W.D. Wash. 1983) (accepting the comparable worth theory). This decision was reversed in 770 F.2d 1401 (9th Cir. 1985).

166. American Federation of State, Cty., and Municipal Employees v. State of Washington, 770 F.2d 1401 (9th Cir. 1985).

167. 42 U.S.C. §2000(e)(k) (1982). Connen v. University of Tenn. Press, 558 F. Supp. 38 (E.D. Tenn. 1982).

168. 29 C.F.R. §1604.10 (1985).

169. Arizona Governing Committee for Tax Deferral Annuity Plans v. Norris, 463 U.S. 1073 (1983); City of Los Angeles v. Manhart, 435 U.S. 702 (1978).

170. 29 C.F.R. §1604.11(a) (1985) (emphasis added). *See* Meritor Savings Bank v. Vinson, 106 S. Ct. 2399 (1986) (upholding the EEOC's interpretation of Title VII as prohibiting both quid pro quo sexual harassment and sexual harassment creating a hostile work environment.

171. Id., at §1604.11(c). In Meritor Savings Bank v. Vinson, 106 S.Ct. at 2408, the Court declined to rule on the question of whether Title VII is correctly interpreted to make an employer strictly liable for a hostile environment created by a superior's sexual advances regardless of whether the employer knew or should have known of the misconduct.

172. Id., at §1604.11(d).

173. Phillips v. Plaqueminus Parish Sch. Bd., 465 So.2d 53 (La. Ct. App. 1985).

174. *See, e.g.*, Henson v. City of Dundee, 682 F.2d 897 (11th Cir. 1982).

175. "Sexual Harassment Claims of Abusive Work Environment Under Title VII," *Harvard Law Review* 97 (1984): 1499, 1454.

176. Vinson v. Taylor, 753 F.2d 141 (D.C. Cir. 1985), *aff'd and remanded,* 106 S. Ct. 2399 (1986); Bundy v. Jackson, 641 F.2d 934, 943-47 (D.C. Cir. 1981).

177. Katz v. Dole, 709 F.2d 251 (4th Cir. 1983); Bundy v. Jackson, 641 F.2d 934 (D.C. Cir. 1981); *contra,* Henson v. City of Dundee, 682 F.2d 897 (11th Cir. 1982).

178. Vinson v. Taylor, 753 F.2d 141 (D.C. Cir. 1985), *aff'd and remanded,* 106 S. Ct. 2399 (1986); Bundy v. Jackson, 641 F.2d 934, (D.C. Cir. 1981).

179. Katz v. Dole, 709 F.2d 251 (4th Cir. 1983).

180. *See, e.g.,* Zabkowicz v. West Bend Co., 589 F. Supp. 780 (E.D. Wis. 1984); Mays v. Williamson and Sons, Janitorial Services, Inc., 591 F. Supp. 1518 (E.D. Ark. 1984), *aff'd,* 775 F.2d 258 (8th Cir. 1985).

181. Rabidue Osceola Refining Co., 584 F. Supp. 419 (E.D. Mich. 1984).

182. *See, e.g.,* Joyner v. A.A.A. Cooper Transportation, 597 F. Supp. 537 (M.D. Ala. 1983), *aff'd,* 749 F.2d 732 (11th Cir. 1984).

183. Vinson v. Taylor, 753 F.2d 141 (D.C. Cir. 1985), *aff'd* and remanded 106 S.Ct. 2399 (1986). Bundy v. Jackson, 641 F.2d 934 (D.C. Cir. 1981). *See supra,* note 171.

184. Miller v. Bank of Am., 600 F.2d 211 (9th Cir. 1979); "Sexual Harassment Claims of Abusive Work Environment Under Title VII," *Harvard Law Review, supra,* note 175, at 1460-61.

185. Henson v. City of Dundee, 682 F.2d 897, 910 (11th Cir. 1982).

186. Education Amendments of 1972, Title IX, 20 U.S.C. §1681 (1982).

187. North Haven v. Bell, 456 U.S. 512 (1982) (holding that Title IX is applicable to employment discrimination in education programs on the basis of gender). The regulations enforcing Title IX make it clear that Title IX's prohibitions against discrimination on the basis of gender apply to recruitment, advertising, the process of application for employment, hiring, promotion, award of tenure, marital status, transfer, layoffs, nepotism policies, rehiring, pay, job assignments, seniority, collective-bargaining agreements, leaves of absence, leave for pregnancy, fringe benefits, selection and financial support for training, sabbaticals, social and recreational programs, and any other term, condition, or privilege of employment. 34 C.F.R. §106.1 (1985). These regulations detail prohibitions regarding all these areas. The regulations also state that the employer "may take action otherwise prohibited by this subpart provided it is shown that sex is a bona-fide occupational qualification for that action, such that consideration of sex with regard to such action is essential to successful operation of the employment function concerned. A recipient shall take no action pursuant to this section which is based upon alleged comparative employment characteristics or stereotyped characterizations of one or the other sex, or upon preference based on sex of the recipient [i.e., employer], employees, students or other persons, but nothing contained in this section shall prevent a recipient from considering an employee's sex in relation to employment in a locker room or toilet facility used only by members of one sex." 34 C.F.R. § 106.61 (1985).

188. Grove City College v. Bell, 104 S. Ct. 1211 (1984).

189. O'Connor v. Peru State College, 605 F. Supp. 753 (D. Neb. 1985); Mabry v. State Bd. for Community Colleges and Occupational Educ., 597 F. Supp. 1235 (D. Colo. 1984). In Walters v. President and Fellows of Harvard College, 601 F. Supp. 867 (D. Mass. 1985) suit under Title IX was not allowed because the plaintiff worked for the building and grounds department, and the court ruled Title IX covered only "education" programs and activities.

190. Storey v. Bd. of Regents of the University of Wisconsin System, 604 F. Supp. 1200 (W.D. Wis. 1985).

191. Castaneda v. Pickard, 648 F.2d 989 (5th Cir. 1981). The Equal Opportunities Act provides in §1703(d) that "discrimination by an educational agency on the basis of race, color or national origin in the employment . . . of faculty or staff" is a denial of equal educational opportunity. 20 U.S.C. §1701 et seq. (1982). Title VI prohibits discrimination on the basis of race in federal assistance programs. 42 U.S.C. §2000(d) (1982).

192. Village of Arlington Heights v. Metropolitan Housing Development Corp., 429 U.S. 252, 270 n. 21 (1977); Lee v. Russell Cty. Bd. of Educ., 684 F.2d 769 (11th Cir. 1982).

193. Lee v. Conecuh Cty. Bd. of Educ., 634 F.2d 959 (5th Cir. 1981). For a discussion of the,

indirect method of proof used in Title VII disparate treatment cases see §9.9.

To prove an intent to discriminate, the plaintiff may point to the impact of the challenged action, the sequence of events leading up to the adoption of the policy, departures from normal procedural sequences, inconsistent departures from policy, and direct statements evidencing racial bias. Village of Arlington Heights v. Metropolitan Housing Development Corp., 429 U.S. 252, 266-68 (1977).

194. 445 F. Supp. 1094 (D. S.C. 1977), *aff'd,* 434 U.S. 1026 (1978). In Baker v. Columbus Mun. Sep. Sch. Dist., 462 F.2d 1112 (5th Cir. 1972) an intent to discriminate was found in the use of the National Teacher Examination. *See also* Georgia Ass'n of Educators Inc. v. Nix, 407 F. Supp. 1102 (N.D. Ga. 1976).

195. Washington v. Davis, 426 U.S. 229 (1976). *Cf.,* United States v. State of Texas, 628 F. Supp. 304 (E.D. Tex. 1985) (finding that adoption of a requirement that applicants for teacher education programs achieve a satisfactory score on the Pre-Professional Skills Test was motivated by an intent to discriminate on the basis of race).

196. *See* § 9.12.

197. Singleton v. Jackson Municipal Separate Sch. Dist., 419 F.2d 1211 (5th Cir. 1970), *cert. denied,* 402 U.S. 944 (1971). These rights are not available to somebody simply claiming a Title VII violation. Lujan v. Franklin Cty. Bd. of Educ., 766 F.2d 917, 923 (6th Cir. 1985).

198. For opinions dealing with this problem see Lee v. Russell Cty. Bd. of Educ., 563 F.2d 1159 (5th Cir. 1977); Lee v. Macon Cty. Bd. of Educ., 453 F.2d 1104 (5th Cir. 1971).

199. Singleton v. Jackson Municipal Separate Sch. Dist., 419 F.2d at 1218.

200. Carter v. West Feliciana Parish Sch. Bd., 432 F.2d 875 (5th Cir. 1970). Hence a decrease in the number of black teachers does not per se prove discrimination in layoffs when objective criteria have been used. Lee v. Walker Cty. Sch. System, 594 F.2d 156, 159 (5th Cir. 1979).

201. *See* Lee v. Walker Cty. Sch. System, 594 F.2d 156, 158 (5th Cir. 1979); Barnes v. Jones Cty. Sch. Dist., 544 F.2d 804, 806 (5th Cir. 1977).

202. Swann v. Charlotte-Mecklenburg Bd. of Educ., 402 U.S. 1, 19 (1971). It is not uncommon for the integration plan to require the same ratio of black and white teachers in each school as exists in the district as a whole. Singleton v. Jackson Municipal Separate Sch. Dist., 419 F.2d 1211, 1217-18 (5th Cir. 1969), *cert. denied,* 396 U.S. 1032 (1970).

203. Bradley v. Milliken, 460 F. Supp. 299 (E.D. Mich. 1978), *remanded,* 620 F.2d 1143 (6th Cir.), *cert. denied,* 449 U.S. 870 (1980).

204. *Cf.,* Dybczak v. Tuskegee Institute, 737 F.2d 1524 (11th Cir. 1984); Turner v. Barber-Scotia College, 604 F. Supp. 1450 (M.D. N.C. 1985).

205. *See, e.g.,* Lujan v. Franklin Cty. Bd. of Educ., 766 F.2d 917 (6th Cir. 1985); Harris v. Birmingham Bd. of Educ., 712 F.2d 1377 (1983); Love v. Special Sch. Dist. of St. Louis Cty., 606 F. Supp. 1320 (E.D. Mo. 1985); Patterson v. Masem, 594 F. Supp. 386 (E.D. Ark. 1984); Hammond v. Rapides Parish Sch. Bd., 590 F. Supp. 988 (W.D. La. 1984); Love v. Alamance Cty. Bd. of Educ., 581 F. Supp. 1079 (M.D. N.C. 1984).

The Eleventh Circuit suggested one modification in the usual four-part test when applied to discharge cases. The plaintiff must make out a prima facie case by proving with a preponderance of the evidence that she is a member of a protected class, was qualified for the position, was discharged and replaced by a person *outside the protected class or was discharged while a person outside of the class with equal or lesser qualification was retained.* Lee v. Russell Cty. Bd. of Educ., 684 F.2d 769, 773 (11th Cir. 1982). This modification may also apply to gender discrimination cases.

206. Lujan v. Franklin Cty. Bd. of Educ., 766 F.2d 917, 925 (6th Cir. 1985); Cooper v. Williamson Cty. Bd. of Educ., 587 F. Supp. 1082 (M.D. Tenn. 1983). In a carefully drafted opinion the Sixth District discusses alternative notions as to precisely what circumstances the burden should shift to the employer.

207. Id., at 1092.

208. Allen v. Prince George's Cty., Md., 737 F.2d 1299 (4th Cir. 1984).

209. Hazelwood Sch. Dist. v. United States, 433 U.S. 299 (1977). In this case the United States Attorney General brought suit alleging the school district was engaged in a pattern or practice of discrimination in employment on the basis of race. For a brief discussion of the case see §9.9.

210. International Brotherhood of Teamsters v. United States, 431 U.S. 324, 359 (1977).

211. *See, e.g.,* Castaneda v. Pickard, 648 F.2d 989, 1002-3 (5th Cir. 1981).

212. Griggs v. Duke Power Co., 401 U.S. 424 (1971).

213. In Albermarle Paper Co. v. Moody, 422 U.S. 405 (1975) the Court, in commenting on certain tests that had not been properly validated, provided indirect guidance on this question. Thus, the Court noted the tests in the case were validated for some jobs and not others; were validated using vague, ambiguous rankings of employees' performance; that the validation referred to higher job categories and it was not clear employees were regularly promoted to these jobs; and that the validation study used more experienced workers whereas the applicants were largly inexperienced.

214. Washington v. Davis, 426 U.S. 229 (1976).

215. 29 C.F.R. Part 1607 (1985).

216. United States v. North Carolina, 400 F. Supp. 343 (E.D. N.C. 1975), *vacated,* 425 F. Supp. 789 (E.D. N.C. 1977). *Cf.,* Allen v. Alabama State Bd. of Educ., 612 F. Supp. 1046 (M.D. Ala. 1985).

217. United States v. South Carolina, 445 F. Supp. 1094 (Columbia D. S.C. 1977), *aff'd mem.,* 434 U.S. 1026 (1978). The court also upheld the use of NTE for purpose of setting teacher pay scales—a kind of merit pay system.

218. York v. Alabama State Bd. of Educ., 581 F. Supp. 799 (M.D. Ala. 1983). The judge stressed that the Educational Testing Service, whose test NTE is, discouraged the use of arbitrary cutoff scores, that the NTE was not intended to be used for this purpose, and that the school board had not validated the test for this purpose.

219. United States v. State of Texas, 628 F. Supp. 304, 320 (E.D. Tex. 1985). The court issued a preliminary injunction against continuing use of the test also on the grounds that its use appeared to have been motivated by a purpose to discriminate on the basis of race.

220. 42 U.S.C. §2000(c) (1982). Title VI prohibits discrimination on the basis of race in programs receiving federal financial assistance.

221. Alexander v. Choate, 105 S. Ct. 712 (1985).

222. The regulations dealing with sexual harassment carry a footnote stating that "The principles involved here apply to race, color, religion or national origin." 29 C.F.R. §1604.11 (1985).

223. This analysis is drawn from a number of cases. United States v. Paradise, 55 U.S.L.W. 4211 (February 24, 1987); Wyngant v. Jackson Bd. of Educ., 90 L. Ed.2d 260 (1986); Sheetmetal Workers v. E.E.O.C., 106 S.Ct. 3019 (1986); Firefighters v. Cleveland, 92 L. Ed.2d 405 (1986); Firefighters v. Stotts, 467 U.S. 561 (1985); Steelworkers v. Weber, 443 U.S. 193 (1979); International Brotherhood of Teamsters v. United States, 431 U.S. 324 (1977); Franks v. Bowman Transportation Co., 424 U.S. 747 (1976). *See also* Fullilove v. Klutznick, 448 U.S. 448 (1980); Regents of the University of California v. Bakke, 438 U.S. 265 (1978).

224. In United States v. Paradise, 55 U.S.L.W. 4211 (February 24, 1987) the Supreme Court affirmed a lower court's order that the Alabama Department of Public Safety adopt a one-black-for-one-white promotion requirement as an interim measure subject to certain conditions, e.g., the order was to remain in effect until 25 percent of those in the rank of corporal were black. The order was imposed as a remedy for a long history of racial discrimination by the department. The central issue in the case was whether this order was sufficiently narrowly tailored. Dissenting Justice O'Connor, Chief Justice Rehnquist, and Justice Scalia argued that there was no evidence in the case that the one-for-one promotion quota was necessary to eradicate the past effects of racial discrimination. They stressed that the promotion quota must be more closely related to the percentage of blacks eligible for promotion in the relevant labor pool. They also stressed that it was encumbent upon the courts in fashioning affirmative action remedies to consider alternative

means, and in this case there were alternative remedies available that could have achieved compliance with the consent decrees, which had been issued in the course of the litigation in this case, without trammeling on the rights of nonminority troopers. The majority disagreed saying the alternative suggested, e.g., imposing heavy fines on the department, would not have worked and would not have compensted the *plaintiffs* for the long delays in implementing acceptable promotion procedures. *Id.,* at 4218.

225. 106 S. Ct. 1842 (1986).

226. Id., at 1846. The plurality opinion written by Justice Powell was joined by Chief Justice Burger and Justice Rehnquist. Justice O'Connor joined this opinion in part and concurred in the judgment in a separate concurring opinion. Justice White made up the fifth member of the majority in an opinion concurring in the judgment. Justice White simply said that the discharge of white teachers to make room for blacks who had not been shown to be victims of discriminations violated the equal protection clause. Justice Marshall dissented in an opinion joined by Justices Brennan and Blackmun. Justice Stevens dissented in a separate opinion.

227. Id., at 1848.

228. Id.

229. Id. All members of the Court agreed that "a contemporaneous or antecedent finding of past discrimination by a court or other competent body is not a constitutional prerequisite to a public employer's voluntary agreement to an affirmative action plan." *Id.,* at 1855 (O'Connor, J., concurring). As the majority stated it, "In particular, a public employer like the Board must ensure that, before it embarks on an affirmative action program, it has convincing evidence that remedial action is warranted. That is, it must have sufficient evidence to justify the conclusion that there has been prior discrimination." *Id.,* at 1848. Then in a puzzling statement the plurality added, "The ultimate burden remains with the employees to demonstrate the unconstitutionality of an affirmative action plan." *Id.* This statement is puzzling because the strict-scrutiny test adopted by the plurality for testing affirmative action plans presumes that it is government, the employer, that has the ultimate burden of proof in the case. Has the plurality in affirmative action cases switched the normal burden of proof associated with use of the strict-scrutiny test? Or does this comment of the Court intend to directed to the narrow issue of whether an adequate predicate exists for undering an affirmative action plan? Even this narrower interpretation represents a modification, albeit a less drastic modification, of the usual rule regarding which party has the burden of proof.

230. Id., at 1849 et. seq.

231. Id., at 1851-52.

232. Id., at 1851.

233. Id., at 1857.

234. Id., at 1858.

235. Id., at 1863.

236. Id., at 1864.

237. Id.

238. Id., at 1865.

239. Sheet Metal Workers v. E.E.O.C., 106 S. Ct. 3019 (1986) (holding that in a case of proven prior racial discrimination a court may order preferential remedies benefitting individuals who are not the actual victims of discrimination); Firefighters v. Cleveland, 106 S. Ct. 3063 (1986) (holding that Title VII does not bar a court from approving a consent agreement that provides benefits to individuals who were not actual victims of a particular employer's discriminatory practices).

240. United States v. Paradise, 55 U.S.L.W. 4211 (February 24, 1987).

241. 47 S. Ct. Bull. (CCH), p. B1677 (March 25, 1987).

242. Justice Brennan writing for the majority said the plan and decision process resembled the "Harvard Plan," approvingly noted in Justice Powell's opinion in *Bakke.* (See §4.7) Id., at 1699. Justice O'Connor noted that the director had testified that if Joyce's experience had been less than Johnson's by a larger margin, then Johnson might have received the promotion. Id., at 1718.

243. Id., at 1726-1727.

244. That is not to say that a different affirmative action plan from the one involved in this case, which might be permissible under Title VII, would not be impermissible under the equal protection clause. Id., at 1688, n.6.

245. Justice Brennan drew upon the decision in Steelworkers v. Weber, 443 U.S. 193 (1979) for developing the criteria of an acceptable plan. Id., at 1688. Justice Scalia, with whom Chief Justice Rehnquist joined, argued that Weber should not be extended to public employers (the decision involved a private employer); that Weber was originally wrongly decided insofar as it permitted any employment policies premised on racial distinctions and that Weber should be overruled as a violation of the express language of Title VII and as inconsistent with the fourteenth amendment. Id., at 1732-1734. The majority responded saying that Weber could not have misconstrued the meaning of Title VII since Congress had made no effort to amend the statute so as to reject the Court's interpretation of it. Id., at 1690, n.7. Justice Scalia in turn responded that the failure of Congress to amend the statute, could not, for a variety of reasons be a basis for inferring that Congress approved of the interpretation of the statute in Weber: failure to enact legislation, given the difficulties of adopting legislation, does not establish approval of Weber. Id., p. 1735. For its part the majority noted that Congress in the past has in fact amended Title VII to override judicial interpretations of that act. Id., at 1690, n.7. Finally, Justice Scalia noted that, if inaction to overrule the court's interpretation of a statute indicates Congressional approval of the interpretation, then the court was itself wrong in overruling one of its own cases on the grounds it incorrectly interpreted a statute when for seventeen years after that "erroneous" decision Congress had made no move to amend the statute in question. Congress must have approved of the "erroneous" decision by not acting to amend the statute. Id., at 1736.

246. Id., at 1693.

247. Id., at 293, 1711 (O'Connor, J., concurring).

248. Id., at 1697.

249. Id., at 1696-97.

250. Id., at 1700.

251. Id., at 1698-1700.

252. Id., at 1699.

253. Id., at 1708-09.

254. Id., at 1709.

255. Id., at 1704.

256. Id., at 1711. In making out such a statistical justification the employer could not rely on the mere imbalance between the percentage of women in the work force generally and the percentage of women in the particular specialized job classification. Id., at 1714. Such a statistical presentation was not acceptable because it would rest on the unrealistic assumption that individuals of each sex would gravitate with mathematical exactitude to each employer and employment category. Id., at 1716. Justice O'Connor argued that the decision in Wyngant required this approach. Id., at 1713.

257. Id., at 1715.

258. Id., at 1714.

259. Id., at 1717, 1719.

260. Id., at 1721-22, 1740. Justice White only joined in parts I and II of Justice Scalia's dissent, but he agreed with the conclusion of part III of Scalia's opinion, that Weber be overruled.

261. Id., at 1723.

262. Id., at 1728, 1731-32.

263. Id., at 1725.

264. Id., at 1738.

265. Id., at 1740.

266. Id., at 1740, 1741.

267. 748 F.2d. 1308, 1315 (9th Cir. 1984), *aff'd*, 47 S. Ct. Bull. (CCH), p. B1677 (March 25, 1987) (Wallace, J., concurring and dissenting in part).

268. *See* Newman v. Bd. of Educ. of the City Sch. Dist. of New York, 594 F.2d 299 (2nd Cir. 1979); Anonymous v. Bd. of Examiners, 318 N.Y.S.2d 163 (1970). These standards, however, must not be arbitrary. A New York court ruled, for example, that obesity per se, was not a basis for dismissal since it was not reasonably related to the ability to teach or to maintain discipline. Parolisi v. Bd. of Examiners of City of New York, 55 Misc. 2d 546, 285 N.Y.S.2d 936 (1973).

269. Constitutional challenges to discrimination on the basis of handicap have been infrequent. Gurmankin v. Costanzo, 556 F.2d 184 (3d Cir. 1977) and 626 F.2d 1132 (3d Cir. 1980) (holding that refusing even to consider a blind teacher for a teaching position violated the teacher's due process rights because she was not given the opportunity to demonstrate her competence).

270. 29 U.S.C. §701 (1982). The requirements of §504 applied to all phases of recruitment, applications, hiring, promotions, award of tenure, transfers, layoffs, terminations, rehiring, pay, job assignments, leaves of absence, sick leave, fringe benefits, selection and financial support for employer-sponsored activities, and any other term, condition, or privilege of employment. 34 C.F.R. §104.11 (1985). One detail of these regulations is worth emphasizing. Applicants may not be asked whether they are handicapped or about the nature or severity of a handicap except when remedial action to overcome past discrimination is being pursued. 34 C.F.R. §104.14 (1985). However, inquiries into whether the applicant can perform job related functions are permissible. *Id.* Thus, it would be permissible to ask a job applicant whether he or she is capable of dealing with stress in the classroom, but the applicant may not be asked whether he or she has been treated for stress. Doe v. Syracuse Sch. Dist. 508 F. Supp. 333 (N.D. N.Y. 1981).

Other provisions of the regulations prohibit the employer from employing policies that have the effect of discriminating against the handicapped. 34 C.F.R. §§ 104.4(b)(4), 104.11(a)(4) (1985). Employers are required to establish a grievance procedure for the handicapped and to take positive steps to employ the handicapped. 34 C.F.R. §§ 104.7, 104.11(a)(2) (1985). The employer is required to operate each program or activity to which § 504 applies "so that the program of activity, when viewed in its entirety, is readily accessible to handicapped persons." 34 C.F.R. §104.22 (1985).

271. 29 U.S.C. §794 (1982).

272. *See, e.g.,* Doyle v. University of Ala., 680 F.2d 1323 (11th Cir. 1982) (university as a whole not subject to §504 merely because some of its programs receive federal financial assistance). *See also,* Consolidated Rail Corp. v. Darrone, 104 S. Ct. 1248 (1984); Grove City College v. Bell, 104 S. Ct. 1211 (1984).

273. Consolidated Rail Corp. v. Darrone, 104 S. Ct. 1248 (1984) (suit can be maintained even if primary objective of financial assistance was not to provide employment).

274. 29 U.S.C. §706(7)(B)(i) (1982).

275. Jasany v. United States Postal Service, 755 F.2d 1244 (6th Cir. 1985) (rejecting the claim that crossed eyes was a handicapping condition, a claim made by an individual who, because of the crossed eyes, was unable to operate a mail sorting machine for the Postal Service). The court noted that if a handicap was anything that prevented one from performing a specific job, then being of average height and weight would be a handicapping condition for purposes of playing certain professional sports.

276. 29 U.S.C. §706(7)(B) (1982).

277. School Bd. of Nassau Cty., Fla. v. Arline (No. 85-1277) 107 S. Ct. 1123 (1987) (March 11, 1987), at 20.

278. Strathie v. Dept. of Transportation, 716 F.2d 227, 230 (3d Cir. 1983). The ninth circuit has adopted a somewhat different approach. Under this approach the plaintiff must prove: (1) he applied for a job; (2) he was qualified for job in spite of the handicap under all but the physical criteria being challenged as discriminatory; (3) his handicap prevents meeting this requirement under the physical criteria for employment; (4) the standard has a disproportionate impact on

person with the plaintiff's handicap; (5) despite his qualifications his application was rejected; and (6) the position remained open and the employer sought applicants who did not have the handicap. If the plaintiff meets these requirements, then the employer has the burden of producing credible evidence to show: (1) the physical requirement is job related—i.e., people with the plaintiff's handicap cannot safely and efficiently perform the essential functions of the job; and (2) if the issue of reasonable accommodation is raised, the defendant must show that accommodation cannot reasonably be done that would enable the applicant to perform the essentials of the job safely. Sisson v. Helms, 751 F.2d 991, 993 (9th Cir. 1985), *cert. denied*, 106 S. Ct. 137 (1985). The Second Circuit's approach is different again. Under this approach the plaintiff must make out a prima facie case that must establish he is a handicapped person, and that, although qualified apart from the handicapping condition, was denied employment because of his handicap. The burden then shifts to the employer to rebut the inference of improper discrimination by going forward with evidence that the handicap is relevant to the qualifications for the position sought. Then the plaintiff must bear the ultimate burden of persuasion and with a preponderance of the evidence show that in spite of the handicap he is qualified; and where the employer has shown he is less qualified than other applicants, show that he is at least as well qualified as the other applicants who were accepted. Doe v. New York University, 666 F.2d 761 (2d Cir. 1981). *Cf.,* Prewitt Jr. v. United States Postal Service, 662 F.2d 292 (5th Cir. 1981).

279. Grove City College v. Bell, 104 S. Ct. 1211 (1984).

280. Doe v. New York University, 666 F.2d 761, 776-77 (2d Cir. 1981).

281. Southwestern Community College v. Davis, 442 U.S. 397, 406, 412-13 (1979). The statute should not be read literally. If read literally it could mean that persons who are qualified except for the handicap, rather than in spite of the handicap, are protected. Under a literal reading a blind person possessing all the qualifications for driving a bus except sight could be said to be otherwise qualified. 45 C.F.R. pt. 84, app. A, at 312 (1985).

282. The courts look to the position descriptions in determining the essential functions of a job. *See, e.g.,* Guinn v. Bolger, 598 F. Supp. 196 (D.C. D.C. 1984). The term "essential functions" is used to emphasize that the handicapped should not be disqualified merely because they have difficulty doing tasks that are only marginally related to a particular job. 45 C.F.R. pt. 84, app. A at 312 (1985).

283. 45 C.F.R. §84 (12(c); pt. 84, app. A at 315-16.

284. Strathie v. Department of Transportation, 716 F.2d 227 (3d Cir. 1983).

285. Fitzgerald v. Green Valley Area Educ. Agency, 589 F. Supp. 1130 (S.D. Iowa, 1984).

286. Doe v. New York University, 666 F.2d 761, 776 (2d Cir. 1981).

287. Norcross v. Sneed, 755 F.2d 113 (8th Cir. 1985).

288. Pushkin v. Regents of University of Colorado, 658 F.2d 1372 (10th Cir. 1981).

289. DeSpain v. DeKalb Co. Comm. Sch. Dist., 348 F.2d 836 (7th Cir. 1967), *cert. denied,* 390 U.S. 906 (1968) (prohibiting a kindergarten teacher from leading the class in a Thanksgiving recitation ["We thank you for the flowers so sweet; we thank you for the food we eat; we thank you for the birds that sing; we thank you for everything."]).

290. May v. Evansville-Vanderburgh Sch. Corp., 787 F.2d 1105 (7th Cir. 1986). *See* §§5.4, 6.11.

291. Moore v. Gaston Cty. Bd. of Educ., 357 F. Supp. 1037 (W.D. N.C. 1973).

292. Hysong v. Sch. Dist., 164 Pa. 629, 30 A.2d 482 (1894) (upholding right of nuns to teach in the public schools and to wear their distinctive dress); Rawlings v. Butler, 60 A.2d 285, 290 S.W.2d 801 (Ky. 1956) (upholding right of minister to wear his religious garb). *Contra,* Cooper v. Eugene Sch. Dist. No. 45, 708 P.2d 1161 (Or. Ct. App. 1985) (upholding authority of state to prohibit wearing of religious garb in the classroom but holding that the sanction of revocation of the teacher's certificate was unconstitutionally severe); Commonwealth v. Herr, 22 Pa. 1342, 78 A. 68 (Pa. 1910) (upholding state statute forbidding the wearing of religious garb); O'Connor v.

Hendrich, 77 N.E. 612 (N.Y. 1906) (upholding superintendent's order forbidding the wearing of religious garb). *See also,* Annot. 60 A.L.R.2d 300 (1958).

293. *Cf.,* Goldman v. Weinberger, 106 S. Ct. 1310 (1986) (holding that the free exercise clause does not prohibit the Air Force from enforcing a rule that as applied prohibited plaintiff from wearing a yarmulke). *See also* Cooper v. Eugene Sch. Dist. No. 45, 708 P.2d 1161 (Or. Ct. App. 1985) (upholding authority of state to prohibit a Sikh from wearing religious garb in the classroom but holding that the sanction of revocation of the teacher's certificate was unconstitutionally severe).

294. Palmer v. Bd. of Educ. City of Chicago, 603 F.2d 1271 (7th Cir. 1979), *cert. denied,* 444 U.S. 1026 (1980).

295. Russo v. Central Sch. Dist. No. 1, 469 F.2d 623 (2d Cir. 1972), *cert. denied,* 411 U.S. 932 (1973). *See* Opinions of the Justices to the Governor, 372 Mass. 874, 363 N.E.2d 251 (1971) (advising the governor that requiring teachers to salute the flag would violate their first amendment rights).

296. Rankins v. Commission on Professional Competence, 24 Cal. 3d 167, 593 P.2d 852, 154 Cal. Rptr. 907 (1979).

297. Pinsker v. Joint Dist. No. 28J of Adams and Arapahoe Counties, 735 F.2d 388 (10th Cir. 1984).

298. 42 U.S.C. §2000(3) (1982).

299. 42 U.S.C. §2000e(j) (1982).

300. Reid v. Memphis Pub. Co., 468 F.2d 346 (6th Cir. 1972).

301. United States v. Seeger, 380 U.S. 163 (1965).

302. Young v. Southwestern Savings & Loan Ass'n, 509 F.2d 140 (5th Cir. 1975).

303. 55 U.S.L.W. 4019 (November 17, 1986).

304. Id., at 4020.

305. Philbrook v. Ansonia Bd. of Educ., 757 F.2d 476 (2d Cir. 1985), *aff'd,* 55 U.S.L.W. 4019 (November 17, 1986). *See also* Pinsker v. Joint Dist. No. 28J of Adams and Arapahoe Counties, 735 F.2d 388 (10th Cir. 1984).

306. The Second Circuit relied on Transworld Airlines, Inc. v. Hardison, 432 U.S. 63 (1977). In that case the employee refused to work on Saturdays because that was his church's sabbath. The employer was faced with the choice of either leaving the position empty (but that would have impaired the functions of the shop where the employee worked) or paying premium wages to get someone to fill the slot. The Court said any accommodation in these circumstances would impose undue hardship on the employer.

307. 55 U.S.L.W., at 4021.

308. *Cf.,* Weiss v. United States, 595 F. Supp. 1050 (E.D. Vir. 1984).

309. Massachusetts Bd. of Retirement v. Murgia, 427 U.S. 158 (1976).

310. 569 F.2d 993 (7th Cir. 1977), *cert. denied,* 440 U.S. 945 (1979).

311. 576 F.2d 459 (2d Cir. 1978).

312. 29 U.S.C. §§621, 623, et seq. (1982).

313. 29 U.S.C. §623(f) (1982).

314. 29 U.S.C. §613(f)(2) (1982). E.E.O.C. v. Fox Point-Bayside Sch. Dist., 772 F.2d 1294 (7th Cir. 1985).

315. Western Airlines Inc. v. Criswell, 105 S. Ct. 2743, 2751-2753 (1985).

316. Id. The Court went on to state two ways in which the employer could make this showing. First, the employer could establish it had reasonable cause to believe that all or substantially all people over a certain age could be unable to perform the job safely and efficiently. In the alternative, the employer could establish the high impracticability of dealing with older employees on an individualized basis, i.e., prediction of unsafe and inefficient job performance cannot be made other than by knowledge of the employee's relationship in the class defined by the age qualification.

317. Maki v. Comm'n of Educ. of State of New York, 568 F. Supp. 252 (N.D. N.Y. 1983), aff'd without opinion, 742 F.2d 1437 (2d Cir. 1984).

318. For a discussion of the nature of this type of case see §9.9. See, e.g., Maxfield v. Sinclair International, 766 F.2d 788 (3d Cir. 1985); Sakellar v. Lockheed Missiles and Space Co., 765 F.2d 1453 (9th Cir. 1985).

319. Woodfield v. Heckler, 591 F. Supp. 1390 (E.D. Pa. 1984).

320. Geller v. Markham, 635 F.2d 1027 (2d Cir. 1980), cert. denied, 451 U.S. 945 (1981).

321. E.E.O.C. v. Governor Mifflin Sch. Dist. 623 F. Supp. 734 (E.D. Pa. 1985).

322. Cipriano v. Bd. of Educ. of City Sch. Dist., 785 F.2d 51 (2d Cir. 1986); Patterson v. Indep. Sch. Dist. No. 709, 742 F.2d 465 (8th Cir. 1984).

323. Joint Anti-Fascist Refugee Committee v. McGrath, 341 U.S. 123, 168 (1951) (Frankfurter, J., concurring).

324. United States Constitution, Amendment 14, §1.

325. Board of Regents v. Roth, 408 U.S. 564 (1972); Perry v. Sinderman, 408 U.S. 593 (1972).

326. See, e.g., Abell v. Nash Cty. Bd.of Educ., 71 N.C. App. 48, 321 S.E.2d 502 (N.C. App. 1984); Bridger Educ. Ass'n v. Bd. of Trustees, Carbon Cty. Sch. Dist. No. 2, 678 P.2d 659 (1984).

327. Levitt v. University of Texas at El Paso, 759 F.2d 1224, 1229 (5th Cir. 1985). In Brandywine Affiliate NCCEA/DSEA v. Brandywine Bd. of Educ., 555 F. Supp. 852 (D. Del. 1983) the court even said that violation of the procedures mandated by state statute did not violate the plaintiff's constitutional rights when the plaintiff received all the process that was due under the Constitution.

328. Brenna v. Southern Colorado State College, 589 F.2d 475, 477 (10th Cir. 1978); Bignall v. North Idaho College, 538 F.2d 243, 248-49 (9th Cir. 1976). A more recent Ninth Circuit opinion held that a university's own procedural requirements do not create a constitutionally protected interest unless those restrictions were intended to be a "significant substantive restriction" on a university's decision-making. Otherwise there is no constitutionally protected interest in the procedures. Goodisman v. Lytle, 724 F.2d 818, 820 (9th Cir. 1984).

329. DeSimone v. Bd. of Educ. S. Huntington U. Free Sch. Dist., 612 F. Supp. 1568 (E.D. N.Y. 1985) (requiring a hearing before reduction in force takes place). Cf., Lacy v. Dayton Bd. of Educ., 550 F. Supp. 835 (S.D. Ohio, 1982).

330. Doe v. Anker, 451 F. Supp. 242 (S.D. N.Y. 1978).

331. Thomas v. Bd. of Trustees, 515 F. Supp. 280 (S.D. Tex. 1981). If the employee has no property interest in that position, the transfer would not trigger a right to due process. Sullivan v. Brown, 544 F.2d 279 (6th Cir. 1976).

332. Needleman v. Bohlen, 602 F.2d 1 (1st Cir. 1977) (holding that a teacher had property interest in an annual salary increment because the contract said it would not be denied unless the teacher's performance was determined to be unsatisfactory).

333. Board of Regents v. Roth, 408 U.S. 564, 577 (1972); Perry v. Sinderman, 408 U.S. 593, 602 (1972).

334. Bishop v. Wood, 426 U.S. 341, 344-45 (1976); Board of Regents v. Roth, 408 U.S. 564, 577 (1972); Perry v. Sinderman, 408 U.S. 593, 602 (1972). The Court has also noted that "While the legislature may elect not to confer a property interest in [public] employment, it may not constitutionally authorize the deprivation of such an interest, once conferred, without appropriate safeguards." Cleveland Bd. of Educ. v. Loudermill, 105 S. Ct. 1487 (1985). Thus today a majority of the Court rejects the "bitter with the sweet" approach. Under this approach, although state law may create a constitutionally protected property interest, if the grant of this interest is conditioned with limitations on the procedures that are to be used in determining continued enjoyment of the interest, a litigant must take the bitter with the sweet. Arnett v. Kennedy, 416 U.S. 134 (1974).

335. Memphis Light, Gas & Water Division v. Craft, 436 U.S. 1, 9 (1978). It is federal constitutional law that determines if the claim of entitlement created by the state is sufficient to warrant constitutional protection.

336. Board of Regents v. Roth, 408 U.S. 564, 576 (1972).

337. The central problem here is whether a teacher can claim de facto tenure in an institution with a formal system for granting tenure. The circuits are split on this question. *Recognizing possibility of de facto tenure:* Soni v. Bd. of Trustees, 513 F.2d 347 (6th Cir. 1975), *cert. denied,* 426 U.S. 919 (1976); Steinberg v. Elkins, 470 F.Supp. 1024, 1029 (D. Md. 1979). *Not recognizing de facto tenure:* Neddleman v. Bohlen, 602 F.2d 1 (1st Cir. 1979); Haimowitz v. University of Nevada, 579 F.2d 526 (9th Cir. 1978). When permitted to show he or she obtained de facto tenure, the teacher can point to such things as a contract that promises that tenure will be given automatically in the third year of employment. Harris v. Arizona Bd. of Regents, 528 F.Supp. 987 (D. Arizona, 1981).

338. Orshan v. Anker, 550 F. Supp. 538 (E.D. N.Y. 1982). Tenure by estoppel can be achieved in New York by the board acquiescing in the probationary employee's continued service beyond the three-year probationary period.

339. Vanelli v. Reynolds Sch. Dist. No. 7, 667 F.2d 773, 777 (9th Cir. 1982).

340. Goodisman v. Lytle, 724 F.2d 818 (9th Cir. 1984) (procedures for making decisions on promotion in faculty code did not establish a property interest); Thomas v. Ward, 529 F.2d 916 (4th Cir. 1975) (passages in faculty handbook stating that after a three-year probationary period teachers would be employed on a continuing contract basis and only dismissed on basis of incompetence or immorality created expectancy of employment).

341. Roane v. Callisburg Indep. Sch. Dist., 511 F.2d 633 (5th Cir. 1975) (concluding a superintendent had the equivalent of tenure based on the past practice of the district and a written rule of the district).

342. Burris v. Willis Indep. Sch. Dist., 713 F.2d 1087 (5th Cir. 1983) (no protected right in a district that had not adopted the continuing contract law); Perkins v. Bd. of Directors, 686 F.2d 49 (1st Cir. 1982) (nonrenewal statute did not require there be a cause of nonrenewal, hence did not confer property right); Zimmerman v. Bd. of Educ. of Town of Branford, 597 F. Supp. 72 (D. Conn. 1984) (finding no protectable interest under state law).

343. Martin v. Unified Sch. Dist. No. 434, Osage Cty., 728 F.2d 453 (10th Cir. 1984) (series of eleven one-year contracts did not establish legitimate claim of reemployment); Grimes v. Eastern Ill. University, 710 F.2d 386 (7th Cir. 1983) (continuing contract that could be terminated at will did not create property interest).

344. Goodisman v. Lytle, 724 F.2d 818 (9th Cir. 1984) (rejecting the claim that the procedures in this university sufficiently constrained the discretion of decision-makers to create a property interest in the job).

345. Haimowitz v. University of Nevada, 579 F.2d 526 (9th Cir. 1978) (promise of renewal if work is good does not create property interest); Sherrod v. Palm Beach Cty. Sch. Bd., 620 F. Supp. 1275 (D.C. Fla. 1985) (being informed one would be recommended for tenure if high level of work is maintained does not create protected interest); Vail v. Bd. of Educ. of Paris Union Sch. Dist. No. 95, 706 F.2d 1435 (7th Cir. 1983), *aff'd per curiam by divided court,* 466 U.S. 377 (1984) (promise by board at time initial contract was given that a second one-year contract would be issued created property interest); Hadley v. City of Du Page, 715 F.2d 1238 (7th Cir. 1983), *cert. denied,* 104 S. Ct. 1000 (1984) (assurances of continued employment from individual county board members does not create property interest since individual members cannot bind the board).

346. Staheli v. University of Mississippi, 621 F. Supp. 449 (D.C. Miss. 1985).

347. Wells v. Doland, 711 F.2d 670 (5th Cir. 1983). An applicant for a position has no property interest in the position even if he or she is the only applicant and meets the hiring standards. McCowan v. Tucker, 558 F. Supp. 31 (E.D. Tenn. 1982).

348. Smith v. Bd. of Educ. of Urbana Sch. Dist. No. 116, 708 F.2d 258 (7th Cir. 1983) (statutes did not create tenure in coaching positions); Lyznicki v. Bd. of Educ., Sch. Dist. of 167, 707 F.2d 949 (7th Cir. 1983) (contract did not create property interest in position of principal); Sullivan v. Brown, 544 F.2d 279 (6th Cir. 1976) (transfer from one high school to another did not

deprive teacher of property interest); Coe v. Bogart, 519 F.2d 10 (6th Cir. 1975) (transfer of tenured teacher from principalship back to teaching with a loss in pay did not deprive teacher of property interest); Wiggins v. Stone, 570 F. Supp. 1451 (M.D. La., 1983) (removal from chairmanship of department was not a loss of protected interest). Contra, Acanfora v. Bd. of Educ., 359 F. Supp. 843 (D. Md. 1973), *aff'd on other grounds,* 491 F.2d 498 (4th Cir.), *cert. denied,* 419 U.S. 836 (1974) (contract gave teacher interest in continuing to be teacher, hence transfer to curriculum department violated property interest).

349. Wilkinson v. Sch. Bd. of Cty. of Henrico, 566 F. Supp. 766 (E.D. Vir. 1983).

350. Needleman v. Bohlen, 602 F.2d 1 (1st Cir. 1979). *Cf.,* New Castle Cty. Vocational Technical Educ. Ass'n. v. Bd. of Educ., 569 F. Supp. 1482 (D. Del. 1983).

351. Stana v. Sch. Dist. of the City of Pittsburgh, 775 F.2d 122 (3d Cir. 1985).

352. Winston v. City of New York, 759 F. 2d 242 (2d Cir. 1985).

353. Paul v. Davis, 424 U.S. 693 (1976).

354. Blank v. Swan, 487 F. Supp. 452 (N.D. Ill. 1980).

355. Moore v. Otero, 557 F.2d 435, 438 (5th Cir. 1977).

356. Board of Regents v. Roth, 408 U.S. 564, 573 (1972).

357. Codd v. Velger, 429 U.S. 624 (1977); Meyer v. Bd. of Educ., 572 F.2d 1229 (8th Cir. 1978).

358. Jones v. Los Angeles Community College Dist., 702 F.2d 203 (9th Cir. 1983). One court went further, saying there is no deprivation of liberty when school authorities make public the damaging basis for their decision after the discharge even if there was no hearing. Gentile v. Wallen, 562 F.2d 193 (2d Cir. 1977). In another case disclosure that a teacher had been terminated for a drinking problem a month after dismissal was held to deprive the teacher of liberty. Dennis v. S & S Consolidated Rural H.S. Dist., 577 F.2d 338 (5th Cir. 1978).

359. Smith v. Bd. of Educ. of Urbana Sch. Dist. No. 116, 708 F.2d 258, 265 (7th Cir. 1983). The Seventh Circuit ruled that the following statement was not stigmatizing: "'[K]neupfer stressed that his action [in dismissing Hadley] was not based on any pending criminal indictments, but rather on Hadley's record of management or mismanagement.'" Hadley v. Cty. of Du Page, 715 F.2d 1238, 1245-6 (7th Cir. 1983), *cert. denied,* 104 S. Ct. 1000 (1984).

360. Id. Similarly, discharge because the teacher was an easy grader, lacked structure in the classroom, and failed to complete paper work on time did not implicate a liberty interest. Krynicky v. University of Pittsburgh, 560 F. Supp. 803 (W.D. Pa. 1983). *See also* Willens v. University of Mass., 570 F.2d 403 (1st Cir. 1978); Harris v. Arizona Bd. of Regents, 528 F. Supp. 987 (1981).

361. Board of Regents v. Roth, 408 U.S. 564, 573 (1972); Dennis v. S & S Consolidated Rural H.S. Dist., 577 F.2d 338 (5th Cir. 1978) (drinking problem); McGhee v. Draper, 564 F.2d 902 (10th Cir. 1977) (immoral conduct); Hostrop v. Bd. of Junior College Dist., 523 F.2d 569 (7th Cir. 1975), *cert. denied,* 425 U.S. 963 (1976) (dishonesty); Bomhoff v. White, 526 F. Supp. 488 (D. Arizona, 1981) (emotional instability).

362. Bishop v. Wood, 426 U.S. 341 (1976).

363. Quinn v. Syracuse Model Neighborhood Corp., 613 F.2d 438 (2d Cir. 1980); McGhee v. Draper, 564 F.2d 902 (10th Cir. 1977). *Cf.,* Beitzell v. Jeffery, 643 F.2d 870 (1st Cir. 1981) (unauthorized leaks do not have same stigmatizing effect as official charges). If the teacher him-or herself is responsible for the charges becoming public, the teacher's claim of his or her liberty interest being damaged is denied. Sherrod v. Palm Beach Cty. Sch. Bd., 620 F. Supp. 1275 (S.D. Fla. 1985). When state law requires a board to make the charges public in a tenure hearing, then the liberty claim will also be denied. Kendall v. Bd. of Educ. of Memphis City, 627 F.2d 1 (6th Cir. 1980).

364. Morris v. Bd. of Educ. of Laural Sch. Dist., 401 F. Supp. 188 (D. Del. 1975) (insubordination); McKnight v. Southeastern Pennsylvania Transportation Authority, 583 F.2d 1229 (3d Cir. 1979) (intoxication); Francis v. Ota, 356 F. Supp. 1029 (D. Hawaii 1973) delin-

uency and deliberate violation of rules). *Cf.*, Burris v. Willis, Indep. Sch. Dist., 713 F.2d 1087 (5th Cir. 1983) (merely rating person's honesty as unsatisfactory did not impose stigma).

365. In Board of Regents v. Roth, 408 U.S. 564, 575 n. 13 (1972) the Court said "[m]ere proof . . . that [the professor's] record of nonretention in one job, taken alone, might make him somewhat less attractive to some other employers it would hardly establish the kind of foreclosure of opportunities amounting to deprivation of 'liberty.'" See, e.g., Beitzell v. Jeffrey, 643 F.2d 870, 878 (1st Cir. 1981). As to school administrators, a mere charge of mismanagement does not give rise to a liberty interest requiring a hearing. Hadley v. Cty. of Du Page, 715 F.2d 1238, 1245 (7th Cir. 1983), *cert. denied*, 104 S. Ct. 1000 (1984).

366. Cato v. Collins, 539 F.2d 656 (8th Cir. 1976); Buhr v. Buffalo Pub. Sch. Dist., 509 F.2d 1196 (8th Cir. 1974); Stevens v. Joint Sch. Dist. No. 1, 429 F. Supp. 477 (W.D. 1977).

367. Whitaker v. Bd. of Higher Educ., 461 F. Supp. 99, 106 n. 5 (E.D. N.Y. 1978).

368. In Mathews v. Eldridge, 424 U.S. 319 (1976) the Court said the factors to be considered were the interest of the employee that might be lost, the risk of an error being used, the possible value of a different set of procedures, and the fiscal and administrative burdens a different set of procedures would impose on government.

369. Cleveland Bd. of Educ. v. Loudermill, 105 S. Ct. 1487 (1985).

370. Id., at 1495.

371. Id.

372. Id.

373. The Second Circuit has held that a pretermination hearing should be held. Huntley v. Community Sch. Bd., 543 F.2d 979, 985 (2d Cir. 1976), *cert. denied*, 430 U.S. 929 (1977). *See also* Vanelli v. Reynolds Sch. Dist. No. 7, 667 F.2d 773 (9th Cir. 1981).

374. Suspension of those with a property interest requires a pretermination hearing according to the Seventh Circuit. Muscare v. Quinn, 520 F.2d 1212, 1215 (7th Cir.), *cert. dismissed as improvidently granted*, 425 U.S. 560 (1975). Whether a presuspension hearing is required when the teacher claims infringement of a liberty interest appears not to have been addressed by the courts.

375. Bates v. Hinds, 334 F. Supp. 528 (N.D. Tex. 1971).

376. General allegations such that the teacher is charged with immorality or incompetency are insufficiently precise to allow the teacher to prepare a defense. Stanton v. Mayes, 552 F.2d 908 (10th Cir.), *cert. denied*, 434 U.S. 907 (1977); Bignall v. North Idaho College, 538 F.2d 243 (9th Cir. 1976).

377. One day's notice is probably generally insufficient, especially if there are many charges and the task of marshaling evidence in defense is complex. *See* Hawkins v. Bd. of Pub. Educ. in Wilmington, 468 F. Supp. 201 (D. Del. 1979).

378. King v. University of Minnesota, 774 F.2d 224 (8th Cir. 1985); Brouillette v. Bd. of Directors Merged Area IX, 519 F.2d 126 (8th Cir. 1975); Ferguson v. Thomas, 430 F.2d 852 (5th Cir. 1970).

379. Withrow v. Larkin, 421 U.S. 35 (1975).

380. 426 U.S. 482 (1976).

381. Barndt v. Wissahickon Sch. Dist., 475 F. Supp. 503 (E.D. Pa. 1979).

382. Ward v. Village of Monroeville, 409 U.S. 57 (1972) (striking down a statute that permitted mayors to sit as judges in traffic cases when a major part of the income of the village derived from fines imposed in the mayor's court).

383. Hortonville Dist. v. Hortonville Educ. Ass'n, 426 U.S. 482, 491 (1976). The Court also said the board's pecuniary interest in the paying of a tenured teacher did not disqualify the board from making the policy decision as to the response to be made to teachers who had been on strike. *Id.*, at 497.

384. *Cf.*, Salisbury v. Housing Authority of City of Newport, 615 F. Supp. 1433 (E.D. Ky. 1985).

385. Hortonville Dist. v. Hortonville Educ. Ass'n., 426 U.S., at 491-92. Again the Court left open, without deciding, the question of whether the usual doctrines apply when the decision-

maker is a public employer dealing with public employees. Existing doctrine prohibits, for example, a judge who has been vilified by a defendant from sitting as a trial judge in a case involving the defendant. Taylor v. Hayes, 418 U.S. 488 (1974); Mayberry v. Pennsylvania, 400 U.S. 455 (1971).

386. The mere appearance of bias on the part of decision-makers is insufficient to deny due process. Levitt v. University of Texas at El Paso, 759 F.2d 1224 (5th Cir. 1985).

387. Simard v. Bd. of Educ. of Town of Groton, 473 F.2d 988 (2d Cir. 1973); Duke v. North Texas State University, 469 F.2d 829 (5th Cir. 1972), cert. denied, 412 U.S. 932 (1973). But, in Fuentes v. Roher, 519 F.2d 379 (2d Cir. 1975) the court did suggest in dictum it would have been a violation of due process to place the decision to dismiss in the hands of the same school board the superintendent had personally attacked.

388. Niemi v. Bd. of Educ., 103 Mich. App. 818, 303 N.W.2d 105 (Mich. App. 1981).

389. Kinsella v. Bd. of Educ., 378 F. Supp. 54, 60 (W.D. N.Y. 1974) (three-judge court), aff'd, 542 F.2d 1165 (2d Cir. 1976) (permissible); contra, Miller v. Bd. of Educ., 51 Ill. App. 2d 20, 200 N.E.2d 838 (1964).

390. Hortonville Dist. v. Hortonville Educ. Ass'n, 426 U.S. 482, 493 (1976).

391. Corstvet v. Boger, 757 F. 2d 223 (10th Cir. 1985) (regents did not have predetermined bias against professor merely because they had issued a statement, after the professor had been charged with homosexual solicitation, that acts of homosexual solicitation were not acceptable on the university campus).

392. The Court wrote, "Mere familiarity with the facts of a case gained by an agency in the performance of its statutory duty does not . . . disqualify a decision-maker." Hortonville Dist. v. Hortonville Educ. Ass'n., 426 U.S. 482, 493 (1976).

393. Withrow v. Larkin, 421 U.S. 35 (1975).

394. Id., at 47.

395. Id., at 48.

396. Holley v. Seminole Cty. Dist., 755 F.2d 1492 (11th Cir. 1985). In Vanelli v. Reynolds Sch. Dist. No. 7, 667 F.2d 773 (9th Cir. 1982) the board actually voted to terminate a teacher prior to holding the adversary hearing, yet the court found no prejudgment. In Welch v. Barham, 635 F.2d 1322 (8th Cir. 1980) the court found no prejudgment even though two board members testified in court that they did not think any evidence could have been presented at the hearing that would have changed their minds about dismissal. See Simard v. Bd. of Educ. of Town of Groton, 473 F.2d 988 (2d Cir. 1973).

But, in Staton v. Mayes, 552 F.2d 908 (10th Cir. 1977), cert. denied, 434 U.S. 907 (1977) the court concluded that due process had been denied when a superintendent of schools was dismissed on charges of willful neglect of duty and incompetence by a five-member school board on a vote of three to one. The court found that two members of the majority had campaigned for their offices on the basis that the problems of the district would not be solved until there was a new superintendent. The court noted that the hearing on the charges against the superintendent involved the possibility of erroneous and unfair factual conclusions (it was not a case where the facts were not in dispute), yet the tribunal itself did not meet the due process requirements of fairness.

397. White v. Bd. of Educ., 54 Hawaii 10, 501 P.2d 358 (Hawaii, 1972).

398. Holley v. Seminole Cty. Sch. Dist., 755 F.2d 1492, 1498 (11th Cir. 1985); Chamberlain v. Wichita Falls Indep. Sch. Dist., 539 F.2d 566 (5th Cir. 1976).

399. No right to counsel: Frumkin v. Bd. of Trustees Kent State University, 626 F.2d 19 (6th Cir. 1980); Downing v. LeBritton, 550 F.2d 689 (1st Cir. 1977); Toney v. Reagan, 467 F.2d 953 (9th Cir. 1972), cert. denied, 409 U.S. 1130 (1973). Right to counsel: Cochran v. Chidester Sch. Dist., 456 F. Supp. 390 (W.D. Ark. 1978); Doe v. Anker, 451 F. Supp. 241 (S.D. N.Y. 1978), remanded, 614 F.2d 1286 (2d Cir. 1979), cert. denied, 446 U.S. 986 (1980).

400. See, e.g., McGhee v. Draper, 564 F.2d 902 (10th Cir. 1977); Hostrop v. Bd. of Junior

College Dist. No. 515, 471 F.2d 488 (7th Cir. 1972), *cert. denied,* 411 U.S. 967 (1973).

401. *Cf.,* Cha-Tsu SIU v. Johnson, 748 F.2d 238 (4th Cir. 1984).

402. Lynn v. Regents of the University of California, 656 F.2d 1337 (9th Cir. 1981), *cert. denied,* 459 U.S. 823 (1982); Davis v. Alabama State University, 613 F. Supp. 134 (M.D. Ala. 1985).

403. Nevels v. Hanlon, 656 F.2d 372 (8th Cir. 1981). *But see* Koster v. United States, 685 F.2d 407 (Ct. Cl. 1982).

404. Kinsella v. Bd. of Educ. of Central Sch. Dist. No. 7, 378 F. Supp. 54 (W.D. N.Y. 1974), *aff'd,* 542 F.2d 1165 (2d Cir. 1976).

405. McGhee v. Draper, 564 F.2d 902, 912 (10th Cir. 1977), *appeal after remand,* 639 F.2d 639 (10th Cir. 1981).

406. Bates v. Sponberg, 547 F.2d 325, 329 (6th Cir. 1976).

407. Bogart v. Unified Sch. Dist., 432 F. Supp. 895, 905 (D. Kan. 1977); Chase v. Fall Mountain Regional Sch. Dist., 330 F. Supp. 388 (D. N.H. 1971). *See also* Schware v. Bd. of Bar Examiners, 353 U.S. 232 (1957); Konigsberg v. State Bar, 353 U.S. 262 (1957).

408. Doran v. Bd. of Educ. of Western Boone Cty. Community Schools, 285 N.E.2d. 825 (1972).

409. McGhee v. Draper, 564 F.2d 902 (10th Cir. 1977), *appeal after remand,* 639 F.2d 639 (10th Cir. 1981); Staton v. Mayes, 552 F.2d 908 (10th Cir. 1977), *cert. denied,* 434 U.S. 907 (1977).

410. Sinderman v. Perry, 430 F.2d 939, 944 (5th Cir. 1970), *aff'd on other grounds,* 408 U.S. 593 (1972).

411. Franceski v. Plaquemines Parish Sch. Bd., 772 F.2d 197 (5th Cir. 1985); Levitt v. University of Texas at El Paso, 759 F.2d 1224 (5th Cir. 1985). *But see* Brenna v. Southern Colorado State College, 589 F.2d 475 (10th Cir. 1978); Bignall v. North Idaho College, 538 F.2d 243 (9th Cir. 1976).

412. 364 U.S. 479 (1960).

413. Gardner v. Broderick, 392 U.S. 273 (1968); Garrity v. New Jersey, 385 U.S. 493 (1967); Spevack v. Klein, 385 U.S. 511 (1967).

414. Beilan v. Board of Pub. Educ., 357 U.S. 399 (1958). *Cf.,* Bd. of Public Educ. Sch. Dist. of Philadelphia v. Intille, 401 Pa. 1, 163 A.2d 420 (Pa. 1960) (holding that a plea of constitutional privilege against self-incrimination does not carry a presumption of unfitness under state law).

415. Shelton v. Tucker, 364 U.S. 479 (1960); Cramp v. Bd. of Pub. Inst., 368 U.S. 278 (1961); Keyishian v. Bd. of Regents, 385 U.S. 589 (1967). *See* § 6.2.

416. Shuman v. City of Philadelphia, 470 F. Supp. 449 (E.D. Pa. 1979) (Protecting a policeman from having to answer questions put by his employer about his personal relationship with an eighteen-year-old woman because the questions had no bearing on his on-the-job performance); Gayer v. Laird, 332 F. Supp. 169 (D.C.D.C. 1971) (protecting plaintiff from answering questions about his homosexual activities put in connection with a security clearance). *See also* Scott v. Macy, 402 F. Supp. 644, 648 (D.C.D.C. 1968).

417. Alinovi v. Worchester Sch. Comm., 766 F.2d 660 (1st Cir. 1985).

418. Slevin v. City of New York, 477 F. Supp. 1051 (S.D. N.Y. 1979).

419. American Federation of Government Employees Local No. 421 v. Schlesinger, 443 F. Supp. 431 (D.C.D.C. 1978).

420. 47 Sup. Ct. Bull. (CCH), p. B1757 (March 31, 1987). *See also* Gillard v. Schmidt, 579 F.2d 825 (3d Cir. 1978)(holding that a guidance counselor had a legitimate expectancy of privacy in his desk where he stored sensitive student records).

421. Id., at 1765, 1778, 1786. The plurality opinion was written by Justice O'Connor with whom Chief Justice Rehnquist, and Justices White and Powell joined. Justice Scalia concurred in the judgment, and Justice Blackmun wrote a dissenting opinion in which Justices Brennan, Marshall, and Stevens joined.

422. Id., at 1780 (Scalia, J., concurring), 1788 (Blackmun, J., dissenting).

423. Id., at 1765.

424. Id., at 1766.

425. Using this complex test the plurality found that Dr. Ortega did not share his office, had occupied the office for 17 years, and he kept only personal files and materials in the office.

426. Id., at 1770, 1780 (Scalia, J., concurring). The dissenters argued that employers should not be generally excused from obtaining warrants and that this case was an example in which no special circumstances justified dispensing with the need to obtain a warrant based on probable cause from an impartial judicial officer. *Id.*, 1790-95.

427. Id., at 1774-75. The dissenting opinion charged that the phrases "noninvestigatory work-related intrusion" and "investigatory search for evidence of suspected work-related employee misfeasance" were so broadly defined that "it is difficult to imagine a search that would *not* fit into one or the other of the categories." *Id.*, at 1796. Thus the dissenters concluded that the standard announced by the plurality was applicable to *all* employer searches.

428. Id., at 1781.

429. Justice O'Connor wrote, "The appropriate standard for a workplace search does not necessarily apply to a piece of closed personal luggage, a handbag or a briefcase that happens to be within the employer's business address." *Id.*, at 1764.

430. Jones v. McKenzie, 628 F. Supp. 1500 (D.D.C. 1986).

431. Id., at 1506-7.

432. Cf., §8.5.

433. E.E.O.C. v. Franklin & Marshall College, 775 F.2d 110 (3d Cir. 1985); Dinnan v. Bd. of Regents of the University System of Georgia, 661 F.2d 426 (5th Cir. 1981), *cert. denied,* 457 U.S. 1106 (1982).

434. E.E.O.C. v. University of Notre Dame Du Lac, 715 F.2d 331 (7th Cir. 1983); Gray v. Bd. of Higher Educ., City of New York, 692 F.2d 901 (2d Cir. 1982). In Keyes v. Lenoir Rhyne College, 552 F.2d 579 (4th Cir.), *cert. denied,* 434 U.S. 904 (1977) the court said disclosure would have been required if the college had defended itself by reliance on the peer evaluations. *Cf.,* McKillop v. Regents of University of California, 386 F. Supp. 1270 (N.D. Cal. 1975).

435. 42 U.S.C. §1983 (1982) states: "Every person who, under color of any statute, ordinance, regulation, custom or usage of any State or Territory, subjects or causes to be subjected any citizen of the United States or other person within the jurisdiction thereof to the deprivation of any rights, privileges or immunities secured by the Constitution and law shall be liable to the party injured in an action at law, suit in equity or other proper proceeding for redress."

436. *See, e.g.,* Sterzing v. Ford Bend Indep. Sch. Dist., 496 F.2d 92 (5th Cir. 1974); McFerren v. Cty. Bd. of Educ., 455 F.2d 199 (6th Cir.), *cert. denied,* 407 U.S. 934 (1972). The period for which back pay is owed is the period between wrongful termination and effective reinstatement. Kingsville Indep. Sch. Dist. v. Cooper, 611 F.2d 1109, 1114 (5th Cir. 1980).

437. Hickman v. Valley Local Sch. Dist. Bd. of Educ., 619 F.2d 606 (6th Cir. 1980). If the grant of tenure would place the plaintiff in a better position than he or she would have been in had the constitutional violation not occurred, then the courts will not order tenure be granted. Gurmankin v. Costanzo, 626 F.2d 1115, 1125-26 (3d Cir. 1980), *cert. denied,* 450 U.S. 923 (1981).

438. Actual damages are damages beyond the loss of pay and can include: all related moving expenses including expenses involved in selling and buying a house; loss of retirement benefits; costs associated with finding a new job; and medical expenses for illness brought on by the trauma of the dismissal. *See, e.g.,* Stoddard v. Sch. Dist. No. 1, 590 F.2d 829 (10 Cir. 1979); Wall v. Stanly Cty. Bd. of Educ., 378 F.2d 275 (4th Cir. 1967); Eckmann v. Bd. of Educ. of Hawthorn Sch. Dist., 636 F. Supp. 1214 (N.D. Ill. 1986); Lucia v. Duggan, 303 F. Supp. 112 (D. Mass. 1969).

439. Carey v. Piphus, 435 U.S. 247, 262-63 (1978). *See* Jones v. Los Angeles Community College District, 702 F.2d 203 (9th Cir. 1983).

440. Schreffler v. Bd. of Educ., 506 F. Supp. 1300 (D.Del. 1981).

441. Winston v. City of New York, 759 F.2d 242 (2d Cir. 1985).

442. City of Newport v. Fact Concerts, Inc., 453 U.S. 247 (1981). *See also* Kentucky v.

Graham, 105 S. Ct. 3099 (1985); Eckmann v. Bd. of Educ. of Hawthorn Sch. Dist., 636 F. Supp. 1214 (N.D. Ill. 1986).

443. Smith v. Wade, 103 S. Ct. 1625, 1637, 1640 (1983). *Cf.*, McKinley v. Trattles, 732 F.2d 1320 (7th Cir. 1984); Stokes v. Delcambre, 710 F.2d 1120, 1126 (5th Cir. 1983); Clark v. Taylor, 710 F.2d 4 (1st Cir. 1983); Grimm v. Leinart, 705 F.2d 179 (6th Cir. 1983), *cert. denied,* 465 U.S. 1066 (1984). Kelly Frels has observed that in these cases the federal circuits seem not to have followed the Supreme Court's lead and have adopted somewhat different standards for determining whether punitive damages are appropriate. Kelly Frels, "Punitive Damages in Civil Rights Actions," in *School Law Update 1985,* ed. T. N. Jones and D. P. Semler (Topeka, Kans.: National Organization on Legal Problems of Education, 1985), 54.

444. 42 U.S.C. §1988 (1982).

445. 20 U.S.C. §2000e-5(g) (1982). Phillips v. Smalley Maintenance Servs., 711 F.2d 1524 (11th Cir. 1983) (awarding backpay and attorney's fees).

446. Kunda v. Muhlenburg College, 621 F.2d 532 (3d Cir. 1980).

447. Bundy v. Jackson, 641 F.2d 934 (D.C. Cir. 1981).

448. Catlett v. Missouri Highway and Transportation Commission, 589 F. Supp. 929 and 589 F. Supp. 949 (W.D. Mo. 1983).

449. Bundy v. Jackson, 641 F.2d 934 (D.C. C. 1981); Arnold v. City of Seminole, Okla., 614 F. Supp. 853 (D.C. Okla. 1985).

450. International Brotherhood of Teamsters v. United States, 431 U.S. 324 (1977).

451. See, e.g., Henson v. City of Dundee, 682 F.2d 897 (11 Cir. 1982); Shah v. Mt. Zion Hosp. & Medical Center, 642 F.2d 268 (9th Cir. 1981); Richerson v. Jones, 551 F.2d 918, 926-28 (3d Cir. 1977).

452. 42 U.S.C. §2000e-5(k) (1982). *See* New York Gaslight Club. v. Carey, 447 U.S. 54 (1980).

453. *See, e.g.,* Phillips v. Smalley Maintenance Servs., 711 F.2d 1524 (11th Cir. 1983). *But see* Jong-Yul Kim v. International Inst. of Metropolitan Detroit Inc., 510 F. Supp. 722 (E.D. Mich. 1981). At least one court has concluded that front pay, an award for future earnings in lieu of reinstatement, is permissible under the act. Maxfield v. Sinclair International, 766 F.2d 788 (3d Cir. 1985).

454. *See, e.g.,* Coley v. Consolidated Rail Corp., 561 F. Supp. 645 (E.D. Mich. 1982); Continental Can Co. v. State, 297 N.W.2d 241 (Minn. 1980).

455. 29 U.S.C. §701 et seq. (1982).

456. Georgia State Conf. of Br. of NAACP v. State of Ga., 775 F.2d 1403, 1428 (11th Cir. 1985); Sokin v. State of Texas, 723 F.2d 432, 441 (5th Cir. 1984).

457. 29 U.S.C. §621 (1982).

458. Education Act Amendments of 1972, 20 U.S.C. §1681 et seq. (1982).

459. Storey v. Bd. of Regents of the University of Wisconsin System, 604 F. Supp. 1200 (W.D. Wis. 1985).

460. 42 U.S.C. §2000d (1982).

461. Drayden v. Needville Indep. Sch. Dist., 642 F.2d 129, 133 (5th Cir. 1981). The Supreme Court's decision in Guardians Ass'n v. Civil Service Commission, 463 U.S. 582, 591-97 (1983) implies that a private right of action does exist under Title VI when only injunctive rather than compensatory relief is sought.

10

Afterword: The Rehnquist Court

On September 26, 1986, at 11:05 A.M. William H. Rehnquist, a justice on the Supreme Court since his appointment by President Richard Nixon in 1972, was sworn in at a ceremony in the White House as the nation's sixteenth Chief Justice of the United States Supreme Court. Minutes later, Antonin Scalia, formerly a judge on the United States Circuit Court of Appeals for the District of Columbia, also took the oath of office and thereby filled the vacancy created by the retirement of Chief Justice Warren E. Burger. With this double swearing-in it was certain that the conservative tide that began to run with increasing strength in the later years of the Burger Court would continue and, perhaps, become more steady and sure. But, since Chief Justice Rehnquist already sat on the Court and Justice Scalia, a purported conservative, will replace a conservative, it is unlikely that there will be an immediate, dramatic change in the outcome of the Court's rulings.

A more decisive change would come if President Ronald Reagan has the opportunity to appoint another justice. To understand why, one needs to look at the numbers. Today, there are perhaps only four reasonably certain conservative votes on the Court (Chief Justice Rehnquist, and Justices White, O'Connor, and Scalia), with an additional fifth conservative vote coming intermittently from a justice such as Justice Powell. The addition of another more-consistent conservative vote would assure more-frequent conservative victories. Of course, if President Reagan were to have the opportunity to appoint two more conservatives to the Court, the slow transformation of the Court from a liberal to a conservative citadel that began with the Nixon presidency would be complete.

The range of constitutional doctrine that a Rehnquist-led court will seek to bend to conservative values and priorities is extensive. As discussed in chapter 1, there is little doubt that if Chief Justice Rehnquist were to have his way the establishment clause of the first amendment would be interpreted in such a manner as to clear the way for new forms of financial asistance to private religious schools. The Court under Chief Justice Burger already has moved in this direction, and we might expect that forms of aid once not given judicial approval, i.e., the loan of maps and audio-visual equipment, might be given

447

approval by a Court with a majority reflective of Chief Justice Rehnquist's views. One can also anticipate that such a Rehnquist Court will side with the private religious schools, arguing that their interests in the free exercise of religion are infringed by state civil rights regulations controlling hiring, promotion, and dismissal policies. It seems clear that in the pantheon of conservative values, religion enjoys a high position, whereas civil rights does not hold the same central position as it does in liberal ideology.

A central defining feature of Chief Justice Rehnquist's jurisprudence is his belief that state sovereignty should serve as an external check on the scope of authority of the federal government.[1] A consistent pursuit of this vision of the federal system by a Rehnquist court would have a number of important implications. For example, federal statutes adopted pursuant to Congress's authority to enforce the fourteenth amendment would only be interpreted as intended to abrogate a state's eleventh amendment protection against suit if it were unmistakeably clear from the express language of the statute that this is what Congress intended. (See §2.3.)

Rehnquist's sympathy with state's rights was also on display in *Plyler v. Doe*,[2] a case in which then Justice Rehnquist dissented from the majority's decision to strike down Texas's policy of excluding illegal-alien children from its public schools. Rehnquist agreed with then-Chief Justice Burger that it was simply not irrational for a state to conclude that it does not have the same responsibility to provide public schooling to children whose presence in the state is illegal as it does for those children legally present in the state. Whether or not illegal aliens are to be permitted in the public schools was a matter for the states to decide.

The conservative response of the dissenters in *Plyler* evoked not only the conservative value of states' rights, but also the relative lack of salience that social inequalities hold for conservatives such a Chief Justice Rehnquist. For example, we can anticipate that the Burger Court's unwillingness to involve itself in how states finance their public education systems will continue in a Rehnquist-led Court. (See §7.2.) This willingness to tolerate intrastate inequalities in the amount of money spent per pupil fits with Rehnquist's willingness to tolerate, more than the liberals do, extensive de facto segregation. For example, Rehnquist has repeatedly insisted that remedies adopted by the federal courts to end illegal de jure segregation should be carefully tailored to eliminate only that quantum of segregation actually caused by the unconstitutional policies of the school district.[3] His conservative approach to the remedying of racial discrimination is also on display in the employment affirmative action cases. (See §9.13.) It will be recalled that, roughly speaking, the conservative approach to affirmative action as a remedy for employer discrimination stresses that these policies be limited to making whole those individuals who were themselves victims of past discrimination by a particular employer. This contrasts with the liberal approach that allows the use of racial preferences even for those who may not have been victims of past discrimination. However to date the efforts of Chief

Justice Rehnquist and his ally Justice Scalia to swing the Court to a consistently conservative position on affirmative action has not been successful. But we can anticipate that they will continue their efforts by seeking to persuade other Justices, especially Justice Powell, to interpret the liberal victories in this area as narrowly as possible. We can also expect that Chief Justice Rehnquist will continue to seek to limit other forms of governmental intrusion in the labor market undertaken in the name of civil liberties.

Hence, it would seem to follow that a Rehnquist-led Court could be expected to resist interpreting federal statutes as embracing the notion of comparable worth. (See §9.10.) More generally, we can expect a conservative Court to avoid expansive interpretations of the various federal laws protecting employees from discrimination on the basis of race, gender, handicap. (See §§9.9-9.14, 9.16.) A conservative Court's favorable attitude toward religion might, however, lead it to be more protective of employees' interests in protecting their religion. But one should be cautious here. The religious discrimination cases bring into conflict two conservative values: religion and the value of a free market.

A Court more consistently conservative can be expected, given the opportunity, to favor strong school board authority to inculcate pupils in community values. (See chapter 5.) And given the conservatives' appreciation of religion, we might expect a Rehnquist court to permit school boards to bring voluntary prayer back into the schools, so long as the school board does not too overtly favor one religion over the other. We might also anticipate that the conservatives would, given proper safeguards, hold that student-initiated religious organizations may not be denied the use of school facilities if those facilities are made available to other student organizations. A conservative Court could even go further, i.e., permit parents to exempt their children from reading materials to which they object for religious reasons, and allow states to require that creation science be taught if the theory of evolution is also taught.

The conservatives on the court may, however, find themselves in a dilemma if asked to rule upon the decision in *Smith v. Board of School Commissioners of Mobile County, Alabama,*[4] a decision in which a federal district court judge ordered forty-four history, social-studies, and home-economics textbooks removed from use in the Alabama public schools.[5] The court's reasoning, according to the opinion as excerpted in a newspaper account, in support of this controversial decision rested, first, on the observation that the books in use "discriminated against the very concept of religion, and theistic religions in particular" because they omitted reference to the religious aspects of significant American events.[6]

> The religious significance of much of the history of the Puritans is ignored. The Great Awakenings are generally not mentioned. Colonial missionaries are either not mentioned or represented as oppressors of native Americans. The religious influence on the abolitionist, modern civil-rights and peace movements is ignored

or diminished to insignificance. The role of religion in the lives of immigrants and minorities, especially southern blacks, is rarely mentioned. After the Civil War, religion is given almost no play. . . .

The court went on to say that, "The student would reasonably assume, absent other information, that theistic religion is, at best, extraneous to an intelligent understanding of this country's history." Second, the court concluded that these omissions offended the free exercise rights of the plaintiffs because the omissions meant the books were not merely bad history but equalled ideological promotion of secular humanism—a promotion that conflicted with the religious viewpoint of the plaintiffs. The court stressed that sufficient omissions violated religious freedom because these omissions "affect a person's ability to develop religious beliefs and exercise that religious freedom guaranteed by the Constitution." In a statement frought with enormous implications, the court also said that "some religious beliefs are so fundamental that the act of denying [the court *sub silento* equated "denial" with "omission"] them will completely undermine the religion."[7] Third, the court concluded that the viewpoint promoted by the omission of materials, secular humanism, was itself a religion, hence the books also violated that establishment clause of the first amendment.[8] This point in turn rested on another principle with enormous implications, namely, that denial (again the court equated "omission" with "denial") of truly fundamental religious beliefs has the effect of establishing an opposing religion. The court also rested on the assumption that omission of discussion of religious influences was the same thing as teaching a specific faith-theory to the exclusion of others.[9] Fourth, the court intimated that the omissions were themselves religiously motivated and for this separate reason a violation of the establishment clause. (See §5.5).

The dilemma that this case may present for the conservatives has several faces. First, the decision limits the authority of the public schools to inculcate pupils, authority that the conservatives on the Court have strongly defended. (See §5.8.) Stated differently, the decision invites extensive judicial supervision of the public school curriculum to assure religious sensibilities are protected—a move conservatives have strongly favored (See §§5.3, 1.3.)—but at the same time conservative justices have stressed the importance of judicial restraint. Second, the lower court's notion of how a religion can be established points to a real difficulty the conservatives' own position. That is, if a religion can be established by omission, does it not also follow that religion is more likely to be established if it is in fact mentioned and promoted, say, in the form of a prayer to open the school day. Hence, it would seem to follow that the conservative claim that religion is not estalished by the saying of a prayer at the start of the school day is in error. Third, this decision seems to require that fundamental religious propositions must be taught in the public schools, since failure to do so, according to the opinion, means affirmation of the contrary belief. But then no matter what the public schools do they will be in violation of the establishment clause—omitting religion establishes the religion of secularism, including religion establishes theistic religion. But maybe the district court was thinking that there was a way out of this dilemma—if the books were more balanced then no form of religion would be established. But on the premises of this opinion this escape is not available. If not mentioning a religious proposition affirms the contrary, does not mentioning of a religious proposition deny the contrary? And if this is true, then mentioning multiple religious propositions results in presenting students with a set of mutually contradictory propositions with the effect each cancels the other out. What are then we left with? Perhaps nihilism. But nihilism would also seem to fit the lower court's definition of religion, and we have once again found a new way to violate the establishment clause.

Although it is not perfectly clear how the conservative wing of the Supreme Court would respond to these and other difficulties in the lower court's opinion, a reasonable guess would be that the conservative disinclination to interject the courts into the public schools will prevail in the name of permitting the public schools to decide themselves how students should be educated and inculcated. It seems unlikely that the conservatives would want to make the judiciary over into a nation-wide textbook commission or board of censors.

The conservative disposition to permit schools to shape the beliefs of students represents only one-half of their view of what the first amendment permits and requires. Just as the conservative vision does not place a high priority upon a student's interest in freedom of belief, a conservative Court can be expected to place important limits on the right of students, as well as teachers, to express themselves in the context of the school. Indeed, in this respect the conservative trends in the Court are already evident. Recall the discussion in chapter 6 of the Court's decision in *Bethel School District No. 403 v. Fraser,*[10] in which the Court upheld the discipline of a student who delivered at a student assembly a speech built upon an elaborate sexual metaphor. The Court's refusal to even review a decision upholding the dismissal of a teacher for privately communicating to a small number of other school personnel that she was bisexual is further evidence of a conservative mood that will continue under Chief Justice Rehnquist.[11] In this connection one might anticipate that a Rehnquist-led Court will generally be unsympathetic to the claim of homosexual teachers that dismissal for being a homosexual violates a constitutional right of privacy.[12]

Finally, we might consider the Rehnquist Court's attitude toward school safety and student discipline. Here we can anticipate no significant departure from the Burger Court. For example, we can anticipate that the Rehnquist Court will refuse to create a full-fledged constitutional right to a safe school. (See §8.3.) At the same time we can anticipate that the Rehnquist Court will allow school officials considerable leeway in dealing with school discipline. For example, we can expect that a conservative majority on the Court will permit school officials to search student lockers without having to first satisfy the criteria for a legal search established in *New Jersey v. T.L.O.*[13] (See §8.5.)

In sum, the appointment of Justice Scalia to replace Chief Justice Burger helps to assure there will be at least four reasonably certain votes for the conservative position on the Court. It remains to be seen how these justices will work together and the extent to which they will be able to persuade other members of the Court to take their positions. Beyond this, the move of Justice Rehnquist into the position of Chief Justice will have another separate but important effect. The person who sits as chief justice has the prerogative of assigning the writer of the majority opinion when he or she votes with the majority; thus Chief Justice Rehnquist will not merely be able to continue to cast a conservative vote, but also to seek to assure that the reasons given for that outcome comport with his version of conservatism. Thus, while we cannot expect a truly dramatic and consistent swing to the conservative position until President Reagan has the opportunity to appoint another justice to the Court, we can expect that in those cases in which the chief justice is in the majority the doctrine used to justify the result will reflect Rehnquist's values and the priorities he places on those values. The public will hear most about the Constitution and world as understood by Chief Justice Rehnquist, and this educative effect of Rehnquist's tenure as chief justice may have the most important and long-term effect upon the country.

NOTES

1. Jeff Powell, "The Complete Jeffersonian: Justice Rehnquist and Federalism," *Yale Law Journal* 91 (1982): 1317.

2. 457 U.S. 202 (1982).

3. Dayton Bd. of Educ. v. Brinkman, 443 U.S. 526 (1979); Dayton Bd. of Educ. v. Brinkman, 433 U.S. 406 (1977).

4. At the time of this writing an official copy of the lower court's opinion was not available. Excerpts from the opinion were reported in *Education Week* (March 11, 1987), at 18, 21.

5. Id., at 1.

6. Id., at 21.

7. Id.

8. The court concluded that "secular humanism" was a religion because it addressed such topics as whether there was a supernatural being, the nature of man, the purposes of life, because it erected a moral code, and because it addressed the nature of the universe. The court also stressed that there was an institutional dimension to secular humanism insofar as principles of secular humanism were set forth in three key documents: *Humanist Manifesto I, Humanist Manifesto II,* and the *Secular Humanist Declaration.* Additionally, the court said the movement had leaders, John Dewey, Sidney Hook, Paul Kurtz, and Corliss Lamont. And the court stressed that secular humanism must be considered a religion for first amendment purposes because "it makes statements based on faith-assumptions." *Id.,* at 18.

9. Id.

10. 106 S. Ct. 3159.

11. Rowland v. Mad River Local Sch. Dist., Montgomery Cty., Ohio, 730 F.2d 444 (6th Cir. 1984), *cert. denied,* 105 S. Ct. 1373 (1985).

12. *Cf.,* Bowers v. Hardwick, 106 S. Ct. 2841 (1986).

13. 105 S. Ct. 7333 (1985).

Epilogue

Recent Developments

As this book was going to press two important developments occurred. The Supreme Court wrapped up its current term by issuing a number of important opinions, most notably the decision in *Edwards v. Aguillard*[1] in which seven of the nine justices concluded that Louisiana's Balanced Treatment for Creation Science and Evolution Science Act violated the establishment of religion clause.[2] Approximately one week later, on June 26, 1987, Justice Lewis F. Powell, Jr., announced his retirement from the Court, thereby giving President Reagan the opportunity to tip the ideological balance on the Supreme Court firmly toward the conservatives.[3]

We begin our brief comment on these developments with the *Edwards* decision. Under the Louisiana statute no school was required to teach either evolution or creation science, but if either were taught, the other also had to be taught. Evolution and creationism were required to be taught as theory rather than as proven scientific fact, or as the statute read, "the scientific evidences for [creation or evolution] and inferences from those scientific evidences." In the majority opinion Justice Brennan concluded that "creation science" was defined by those responsible for adoption of the statute as embracing the religious doctrine that a supernatural being created humankind, and he found that the Louisiana legislature adopted the law to advance this religious viewpoint. He said the law was designed either to promote this religious viewpoint by requiring that creation science be taught whenever evolution is taught, or to prohibit the teaching of evolution—a theory disfavored by certain religious sects—by saying it could not be taught unless creation science was also taught. Justice Brennan also rejected the claim that the statute was intended, not to advance religion, but to promote academic freedom. He found that the law did not provide Louisiana teachers with any new authority or flexibility that they did not already possess to discuss any scientific theory. Furthermore, he rejected the claim that the law served the function of basic fairness in the curriculum. If fairness had been the goal, Justice Brennan said, the law would have encouraged the teaching of all scientific theories of humankind, but under this law teachers who were once free in this way are now unable to do so.

453

Justice Scalia's dissent attacked the majority's continued willingness to invalidate legislation under the establishment clause on the basis of the purpose or motivation behind the legislation.[4] But he also argued that, even assuming the validity of the "purpose test," the Louisiana law should be upheld because it served "a" secular purpose, namely, to protect students from indoctrination. As he read the legislative record, the proponents of the statute believed that creation science could be taught without religious content and that by presenting all the scientific evidence on evolution and scientific creationism students would be free to decide for themselves about the origin of life. Justice Scalia also stressed that on the basis of the record, as it was developed in this case, there was no basis to conclude that scientific creation had no scientific evidence to support it, thus the only way it could be taught would be as a presentation of the Book of Genesis.

Despite the fact that a strong majority of the Court seems prepared to conclude in future cases that creation science is a religious doctrine, the *Edwards* case did not put to rest the question of whether creation science could be made part of the public school's curriculum. For example, one can imagine a statute, unlike the Louisiana statute, which simply requires the objective teaching of all theories of the origin of humankind. Since objective instruction in religion has not been prohibited by the Court, a statute of this sort might pass judicial review even if the purpose test, as interpreted by Justice Brennan, remains in place. Justices Powell and O'Connor hammered a related point home, namely, that school children should be informed of all aspects of the nation's religious heritage, that to be familiar with our history requires familiarity with the nature of religious beliefs, and that the establishment clause only prohibits use of the Bible and other religious documents when the purpose is to advance a particular religious belief.

Religious issues aside, *Edwards* is also significant because a majority on the Court took an important step toward recognizing a right of academic freedom on the part of public school teachers. Concurring Justices Powell and O'Connor wrote that the " 'academic freedom' of teachers to present information in public schools, and students to receive it is broad." (That Justice O'Connor would subscribe to this statement after her dissent in *Board of Education v. Pico* is surprising. See §5.8.) And the majority opinion, while not going nearly this far, stressed that the Louisiana statute interfered with the flexibility of public school teachers. While there were other important aspects of the opinions in this case space does not permit elaboration of these points. Of particular importance were questions pertaining to the meaning of the "purpose" test itself, as well as the advantages and disadvantages of such a test; the relationship of the establishment and free exercise clauses of the first amendment; the proper methods and relevant evidence for interpreting a statute; the use of legislative history; and the scope and nature of judicial review under the establishment clause.

The retirement of Justice Lewis F. Powell, Jr., has enormous implications for the public and private schools of this country. It was Justice Powell who cast the deciding vote on such issues as affirmative action, the right of illegal alien children to a free public education, and federal aid to parochial schools to pay for remedial education. More generally, in the last six years Justice Powell has been in the majority in 134 of the 189 cases decided by five to four votes.[5] Thus it is clear that a strongly conservative successor would tip the Court's ideological balance to the right and open the door to a reversal of a wide range of constitutional decisions of special relevance to education as well as other cases less directly relevant but of great importance, e.g., abortion rights.

On July 1, 1987, President Reagan nominated federal Judge Robert Bork to succeed Justice Powell. Judge Bork is a man noted for expressing very specific views on matters of judicial interpretation and the proper role of the federal courts in society. He believes that constitutional decisions should follow the original intent of the framers where that is known, that the Court should refrain from venturing into fields not originally intended for it to enter, and that federal courts have generally been too available for adjudicating "trivial" matters. On specific constitutional issues Judge Bork is known for his narrow view of the free speech clause of the first amendment: that only speech directed to political, moral, or scientific matters is properly protected. He is opposed to the Supreme Court's conclusion that the Constitution protects an individual right of privacy, including such matters as the right to use contraception and the right to have an abortion. It is also expected that he would take a conservative position on affirmative action, busing, women's issues (e.g., sexual harassment), and reapportionment. Less clear is his view of the Constitution as it pertains to religion. While Judge Bork is clearly opposed to many of the Supreme Court's past decisions in these areas, it is uncertain whether he would, if confirmed, vote to overturn those decisions or place importance on stability in constitutional doctrine.

The effort to get Judge Bork confirmed by a Democratically controlled Senate is going to be a long and bitter affair. The senators understand that elevating Judge Bork to the Court would go a long way toward firming up a conservative majority. Ironically, his appointment could make Justice Sandra Day O'Connor the most powerful member of the Court on many issues critical to education. That is, if Judge Bork is confirmed by the Senate it appears that on many issues crucial to education we would have a Court split between Brennan, Marshall, Blackmun, and Stevens on the liberal side, and Rehnquist, White, Scalia, and Bork on the conservative side. Justice O'Connor would thus emerge as the new "swing" justice on such issues as religion, affirmative action, and gender discrimination.

NOTES

1. 47 Sup. Ct. Bull. (CCH) B3591 (June 19, 1987). Justice Brennan wrote the majority opinion. Justices Powell and O'Connor concurred in a separate opinion. Justice White also concurred but only in the judgment. Justice Scalia, with whom Chief Justice Rehnquist joined, dissented.

2. La. Rev. Stat. Ann. §17:286.1 *et seq.* (West 1982).

3. Stuart Taylor, Jr., "Powell Leaves High Court: Took Key Role on Abortion and On Affirmative Action," *The New York Times* CXXXVI (June 27, 1987): 1.

4. See text accompanying notes 148, 155 in chapter 1.

5. Stephen Wemiel and Ellen Hume, "Task for Reagan Is to Find Conservative Acceptable to Democrats for Powell Post," *The Wall Street Journal* CCIX (June 29, 1987): 3, 14.

Index of Cases

(NOTE: Cases appearing in bold type are of major importance; some are followed by page numbers in bold type, which indicates where extensive discussion occurs.)

Index